457
Answer Book

Fourth Edition

457
Answer Book

Fourth Edition

Edited by
Gary S. Lesser, Esq.
Peter J. Gulia, Esq.
David W. Powell, Esq.

ASPEN
PUBLISHERS

111 Eighth Avenue, New York, NY 10011
www.aspenpublishers.com

This publication is designed to provide accurate and authoritative information in regard to the subject matter covered. It is sold with the understanding that the publisher is not engaged in rendering legal, accounting, or other professional services. If legal advice or other professional assistance is required, the services of a competent professional person should be sought.

—From a *Declaration of Principles* jointly adopted by
a Committee of the American Bar Association and
a Committee of Publishers and Associations

© 2005 Aspen Publishers, Inc.
a Wolters Kluwer business
www.aspenpublishers.com

Printed in the United States of America

ISBN 0-7355-4811-0

2 3 4 5 6 7 8 9 0

About Aspen Publishers

Aspen Publishers, headquartered in New York City, is a leading information provider for attorneys, business professionals, and law students. Written by preeminent authorities, our products consist of analytical and practical information covering both U.S. and international topics. We publish in the full range of formats, including updated manuals, books, periodicals, CDs, and online products.

Our proprietary content is complemented by 2,500 legal databases, containing over 11 million documents, available through our Loislaw division. Aspen Publishers also offers a wide range of topical **legal and** business databases linked to Loislaw's primary material. Our mission is to provide accurate, timely, and authoritative content in easily accessible formats, supported by unmatched customer care.

To order any Aspen Publishers title, go to *www.aspenpublishers.com* or call 1-800-638-8437.

To reinstate your manual update service, call 1-800-638-8437.

For more information on Loislaw products, go to *www.loislaw.com* or call 1-800-364-2512.

For Customer Care issues, e-mail *CustomerCare@aspenpublishers.com*; call 1-800-234-1660; or fax 1-800-901-9075.

Aspen Publishers
a Wolters Kluwer business

To the contributing authors, in appreciation of their
expertise, hard work, and professionalism.

Preface

Aspen Publishers' *457 Answer Book* is the first in-depth resource that provides answers to the need-to-know questions asked by tax-exempt organizations, state and local governments, their accountants, tax and legal advisors, 457 administrators, product providers, and investment counselors. The Fourth Edition covers all aspects of eligible and ineligible 457 plans, including the dramatic changes made by the final regulations to Code Section 457. The regulations reflect the changes made to Code Section 457 by the Tax Reform Act of 1986 (TRA '86), the Small Business Job Protection Act of 1996 (SBJPA), the Taxpayer Relief Act of 1997 (TRA '97), the Economic Growth and Tax Relief Reconciliation Act of 2001 (EGTRRA), the Job Creation and Worker Assistance Act of 2002 (JCWAA), and other legislation. The final regulations under Code Section 457 made numerous technical changes and some clarifications to the rules regarding excess deferrals; self-correction for excess deferrals to eligible plans of tax-exempt employers; reporting distributions of excess deferrals; aggregation rules for plan eligibility purposes; the deferral of sick, vacation, and back pay; unforeseeable emergency distributions; plan terminations; plan-to-plan transfers; rollovers; the ordering of partial distribution from plans containing rolled-over assets; and the effect of deemed IRAs on plan qualification. An entire chapter (chapter 7) is devoted to the ways in which the new rules affect mergers and acquisitions.

457 Answer Book, Fourth Edition, is written by a team of practicing experts, preeminent in their fields, who take you step by step through the life cycle of a 457 plan. You will learn how to:

- Recognize which plans and which types of employers are subject to Code Section 457. Grandfathered plans, severance pay plans, and other coverage exceptions are also discussed.

- Apply eligibility requirements, contribution and deferral limits, and when to make unforeseeable emergency withdrawals and distributions.

- Design a plan so that it remains an eligible plan even if an excess contribution is made.

- Recognize whether investment education is investment advice and how to use trust law principles to shift some of the fiduciary responsibility to participants.

- Determine what happens when 457(b) plans are merged, assets are transferred, or employees with plans are acquired.
- Determine the effects of a 457(b) plan termination and when and how participants are taxed.
- Apply the rules that govern the timing, taxation, and rate of distribution application to an eligible 457 plan, as well as minimum distribution requirements, and in-service and unforeseeable emergency withdrawals.
- Recognize securities and insurance law issues and why being subject to ERISA is a potential problem.

457 Answer Book, Fourth Edition, is a decision-making tool. Its combination of theory and practice-based advice provides you with a clear course of action to help you understand:

- The principal federal securities law that could apply to a 457 plan.
- When the assets of a governmental plan have to be held in trust and alternative funding methods.
- What happens when another employer acquires an employer sponsoring a 457 plan or what happens in the case of a merger.
- The opportunities and limitations in making a beneficiary designation.
- Why exempt plans have to be bona fide and how nonexempt plans can avoid conflicts between the Internal Revenue Code and ERISA.
- When plan assets may be protected from or available to the creditors or participants or their employer.
- How ineligible plan types work, how benefit structures are designed, and how taxation can be delayed. The meanings of the terms *substantial risk of forfeiture* and *occurrence of a condition related to a purpose of the transfer* are fully explored.
- How to comply with the IRS reporting requirements that apply to employers, trustees, custodians, and other payors.
- Why some deferred compensation plans provide for plan-approved domestic relations orders (PADROs). The requirements of PADROs are discussed in detail.
- The conditions under which an employer maintaining a 457(b) plan may apply for a ruling from the IRS.

Highlights of the Fourth Edition

Chapter 11 on ineligible plans and bona fide exceptions was expanded and revised by David Pratt. Joseph Zavoda has substantially rewritten chapters 3 and 12 on distribution requirements and IRS form reporting and related issues, respectively. In chapter 14, Carol Calhoun expands on some of the unusual 457 issues affecting national organizations, bar associations, and Native American tribes. In addition to revisions reflecting recent tax law changes and interpretations, this new edition covers the following:

- The implications of not making any change to the definition of compensation; thus, no individual may contribute more than 50 percent of his or her unreduced compensation.
- The effects of the repeal of the special coordination requirement for elective deferrals of the taxable year.
- How the repeal of the "same desk rule," which currently prevents employees in certain cases from receiving their 457 plan distributions, would be repealed by replacing the "separation from service" requirement with "severance from employment."
- Why acquiring entities will no longer have to assume sponsorship and administration of a discontinued eligible 457 plan.
- What statutory and constitutional issues involve the investment of plan assets and restrictions that may apply, as well as other matters pertaining to matching contributions, the reduction of future benefits, the consequences of a failed 457(b) plan, and plan-type alternatives.
- The application of eligible 457 plans to agencies, Native American tribes, and international organizations.
- When amounts paid from an eligible nonchurch government 457 plan are no longer treated as wages, and how such amounts will be governed by the tax-reporting and withholding rules that apply generally to qualified retirement plans.
- The expansion of the rollover rules to eligible government 457 plans and portability between 457 plans.
- When distributions from a traditional IRA are permitted to be rolled over into an eligible government 457 plan.
- How to fix a failure to file a "top-hat" statement.
- Under what circumstances individuals may receive a nonrefundable tax credit for a percentage of their contributions.
- When a 457 plan (as well as qualified plans and 403(b) plans) is permitted to accept traditional IRA or Roth IRA contributions, or both (voluntary employee contributions).
- When an employee must obtain an ERISA fidelity bond covering individuals who "handle" plan assets.
- How a commonplace failure to promptly invest participant contributions may be a crime.
- An expanded discussion of whether a plan sponsor or employer should permit life insurance as a retirement plan option.
- The protections from liability that a retirement plan administrator enjoys if it has delivered a prospectus to participants.
- Whether a plan administrator should direct investments for a "lost" or "missing" participant.

- An overview of the Uniform Management of Public Employee Retirement Systems Act proposed for governmental retirement plans.

- The sovereign immunity that may preclude monetary relief from a state or local government employer even when it has breached fiduciary duties.

- A recent court decision that illustrates why a directed trustee has an incentive to avoid trying to assist a plan administrator.

- Whether a plan administrator or service provider may give a participant or alternate payee legal advice about a divorce-ordered division of deferred compensation.

- What happens when a nonparticipant spouse fails to obtain a PADRO.

- Why a lawyer handling a divorce matter may need an actuary's evaluation, even when all employee benefits are in defined contribution plans.

- How commonlaw marriage affects beneficiary designations and retirement plan distributions in each state.

- How community property laws affect beneficiary designations and retirement plan distributions.

- How to use a qualified domestic relations order (QDRO) or qualified domestic trust (QDOT) to preserve the marital deduction when the beneficiary spouse is an alien.

- Addition of unusual issues affecting Native American tribes and international organizations.

457 Answer Book, Fourth Edition, includes several appendixes to aid 457 plan practitioners, a number of which have been updated or are new. Among the key documents provided are the following:

- Extracts of pertinent section of the Internal Revenue Code
- The final 457 Treasury Regulations
- A model state statute and a specimen top-hat statement
- A model 457(f) plan for a church hospital
- Indexed employee benefit limits and estimates for 2005

With its clear, comprehensive explanations and examples of how the final regulations affect the administration of 457 plans and how to make them work for plan sponsors and participants, *457 Answer Book, Fourth Edition,* is the one reference tool you will use on a daily basis to gain additional insight on and answer all of your questions concerning 457 plans.

Gary S. Lesser
Peter J. Gulia
David W. Powell
May 2004

Contributors

Technical Editors

Gary S. Lesser, Esq., is the principal of GSL Galactic Consulting, located in Indianapolis, Indiana. Mr. Lesser maintains a telephone-based consulting practice providing services to other professionals and business owners. He is a nationally known author, educator, and speaker on retirement plans for individuals and smaller businesses. Mr. Lesser has broad technical and practical knowledge of both qualified and nonqualified retirement plans.

Mr. Lesser is the technical editor and co-author of Aspen Publishers' *SIMPLE, SEP, and SARSEP Answer Book, Life Insurance Answer Book, Roth IRA Answer Book,* and *Quick Reference to IRAs.* Mr. Lesser is also the principal author and technical editor of *The AICPA Guide to Retirement Plans for Small Business Owners* (in press), a publication of the American Institute of Certified Public Accountants (AICPA). He has developed several software programs that are used by financial planners, accountants, and other pension practitioners to design and market retirement plans for smaller businesses. His two software programs—*QP-SEP Illustrator*^{TM} and *SIMPLE Illustrator*^{SM}—are marketed and distributed nationally. He has also been published in the *EP/EO Digest, Journal of Taxation of Employee Benefits, Journal of Compensation and Benefits, Journal of Pension Benefits, Life Insurance Selling, Rough Notes,* and *NAPFA Advisor.* Mr. Lesser is a member of the Financial Planning Association (FPA) and is an associated professional member of the American Society of Pension Actuaries (ASPA).

In 1974, Mr. Lesser started his employee benefits career with the Internal Revenue Service as a Tax Law Specialist/Attorney in the Employee Plans/ Exempt Organizations (EP/EO) Division. He later managed and operated a pension administration and actuarial service organization, was an ERISA marketing attorney for a national brokerage firm, and was a senior vice president/ director of retirement plans for several nationally known families of mutual funds and variable annuity products. Mr. Lesser graduated from New York Law School and received his B.A. in accounting from Fairleigh Dickinson University. He is admitted to the bars of the state of New York and the United States Tax Court. Mr. Lesser can be reached at GSL Galactic Consulting, 944 Stockton

St., Indianapolis, IN 46260-4925; (317) 254-0385; *QPSEP@aol.com*; or *http://www.garylesser.com.*

Peter J. Gulia, Esq., is Senior Vice President of CitiStreet Retirement Services. CitiStreet LLC is a State Street and Citigroup company. Since 1984, Mr. Gulia has focused on the design, management, fiduciary investment procedures, and administration of retirement plans; the design of investment advisory programs; and lobbying on employee benefits legislation and regulations. He is a contributing author and editor of Aspen Publishers' *403(b) Answer Book, Governmental Plans Answer Book, Roth IRA Answer Book, SIMPLE, SEP and SARSEP Answer Book,* and *Life Insurance Answer Book.*

In addition to CitiStreet's many publications, Mr. Gulia has contributed to *401(k) Advisor; CPA Administrative Report; Municipal Law Review; Planning Matters,* the *Journal of the International Association of Financial Planning;* and other publications. Mr. Gulia is a frequent speaker to associations of employee benefits practitioners. His pro bono practices include estate planning and charitable organization management.

David W. Powell, Esq., is a partner in the law firm of the Groom Law Group, Chartered, Washington, D.C. Mr. Powell received his law degree from the University of Texas School of Law in 1982 and has practiced in the tax and employee benefits field in New Orleans, New York City, and Washington, D.C. He is a certified public accountant, and is a past president of the Washington Employee Benefits Forum. Mr. Powell works with tax and ERISA issues relating to all types of employee pension and welfare benefit plans, including qualified, nonqualified, 403(b), 457, church, governmental, health care, and flexible benefits plans. He is a member of the Employee Benefits Committee of the District of Columbia Bar and the Employee Benefits Committee of the Tax Section of the American Bar Association, and has authored a number of articles on employee benefits subjects. Recent publications include "Tax Aspects of Church Plans" and "Mergers and Acquisitions," *403(b) Answer Book* (Aspen Publishers); "Pensions and Deferred Compensation for Financial Officers of Nonprofit Organizations," *Nonprofit Controllers Manual* (Warren, Gorham & Lamont); "Design and Use of Section 457 Plans," *Journal of Deferred Compensation;* "Tax Management Portfolio 372," *Church and Governmental Plans* (BNA); and numerous others.

Contributing Authors

Carol V. Calhoun, Esq., is a shareholder in the law firm of Calhoun Law Group, P.C., Washington, D.C. Her practice includes a special emphasis on employee benefits for governmental and tax-exempt clients, including 457 plans. Ms. Calhoun is co-author of Aspen Publishers' *Governmental Plans Answer Book.* Ms. Calhoun is charter fellow of the American College of Employee Benefits Counsel and a member of the National Council on Teacher Retirement and the National Association of Public Pension Attorneys. She is the former chair of both the American Bar Association Section on Taxation Employee Benefits Committee Subcommittee on Section 403(b), 457, and Exempt Organization Issues and the Subcommittee on Governmental Plans.

Ms. Calhoun is the founder of the Employee Benefits Legal Resource website *http://www.benefitsattorney.com*, which provides legal research materials, articles, speeches, and other employee benefits-related materials. She also moderates three Internet message boards in conjunction with BenefitsLink (*http://www.benefitslink.com*) for attorneys and other professionals to discuss issues of common concern. One message board is geared toward individuals who represent 457 plans, one toward those who represent governmental plans, and one toward those who represent 403(b) plans. Ms. Calhoun graduated from The Johns Hopkins University in 1976, and obtained her J.D. degree from the Georgetown University Law Center (where she was an associate editor of *The Tax Lawyer*) in 1980. Additional information on Ms. Calhoun can be found in the current edition of *Who's Who in the World*. She may be reached at *cvcalhoun@benefitsattorney.com*.

David S. Goldstein, Esq., is a partner in the law firm of Sutherland Asbill & Brennan LLP, in Washington, D.C. Mr. Goldstein has been with Sutherland since May of 1989. Before joining Sutherland, he served for three and a half years on the staff of the Securities and Exchange Commission (SEC). At the SEC, Mr. Goldstein was attorney adviser and later special counsel in the Division of Investment Management. From 1981 to 1985, he was assistant vice president, assistant general counsel, and assistant secretary of the Variable Annuity Life Insurance Company. Mr. Goldstein co-authored *A Reorganization of Insurance Company Separate Accounts Under Federal Securities Laws*, *The Business Lawyer* (1991), and is author of *Federal Securities Law Exemptions for Certain Section 457 Plans*, *The Investment Lawyer* (1995). He is a member of the District of Columbia, Texas, and Massachusetts bars; the American Bar Association, Section of Business Law (Committee on Federal Regulation of Securities and Subcommittee on Securities Activities of Insurance Companies); and the District of Columbia Bar Section on Corporation, Finance and Securities Law. Mr. Goldstein received his B.A. in 1978 from Hampshire College and his J.D. in 1981 from Boston University. He may be reached at *dgoldstein@sablaw.com*.

David R. Levin, Esq., is a partner in the Washington, D.C., office of Wiley Rein & Fielding LLP, specializing in all aspects of employee benefits law, including Department of Labor enforcement, plan audits, withdrawal liability, IRS voluntary compliance programs, employee benefit plan rights in corporate reorganizations under the Bankruptcy Code, employee benefit plan mergers, and pension plan terminations. Before going into private practice, Mr. Levin served as staff attorney and special counsel in the Office of the General Counsel of the Pension Benefit Guaranty Corporation (PBGC). Since entering private practice in 1983, he has been actively involved in the counseling of single employer and multiemployer welfare and pension benefit plans and the litigation of numerous issues of first impression under ERISA. Mr. Levin is admitted to practice before the United States district courts in Washington, D.C., Connecticut, and Michigan; the United States Tax Court; numerous United States courts of appeals; and the United States Supreme Court. He has practiced before the Department of Labor, the IRS, and the PBGC. Mr. Levin is also a member of the Multiemployer Pension Plan Amendments Act Panel of the

American Arbitration Association, and was a member of the PBGC Reportable Events Negotiated Rule-making Advisory Committee.

Mr. Levin has written extensively in his field. He co-authored the Aspen Publishers' *ERISA Fiduciary Answer Book*, and he is a Senior Editor of *Employee Benefits Law*, a treatise published by the Bureau of National Affairs. Mr. Levin is a charter fellow of the American College of Employee Benefits Counsel, and he recently completed a three-year term as Co-chair of the Employee Benefits Committee of the ABA's Section of Labor and Employment Law. Mr. Levin received a B.A. from George Washington University and a J.D. from Catholic University of America, Columbus School of Law, where he was a member of the law review. He may be reached at *dlevin@wrf.com*.

Marjorie Martin, EA, MAAA, MSPA, is a Vice President at Aon Consulting, Inc., in its Somerset, New Jersey, office. She is an active participant of the Regulations Subcommittee of the American Society of Pension Actuaries (ASPA) Government Affairs Committee and a member of the Technical Review Board for ASPA's publication, *The ASPA Journal*. Ms. Martin is also an editorial board member for the *Journal of Pensions Management and Qualified Plan Alert*. She has contributed articles to many publications, including Aspen Publishers' *Journal of Pension Benefits*, and is a member of the annual Enrolled Actuaries Meeting *Gray and Blue Book* Committee.

David A. Pratt, Esq., is a professor of law at Albany Law School in Albany, New York, where he teaches courses in federal income taxation, retirement plans and employee benefits, and elderlaw. He is also of counsel to Hodgson, Russ LLP, in Albany, New York, and Downs, Rachlin & Martin PLLC in Burlington, Vermont. Mr. Pratt received his law degree from Oxford University and is admitted to practice law in England and in New York.

Since 1976, Mr. Pratt has specialized in the design and implementation of retirement plans and other employee benefit programs for a wide range of private and public sector clients. He has written numerous articles on benefits topics and is a senior editor of the *Journal of Pension Benefits*. He is co-author of Aspen Publishers' *Social Security and Medicare Answer Book* and of *Taxation of Distributions from Qualified Plans*. He is also a frequent lecturer for organizations, including ASPA, the American Institute of Certified Public Accountants, the Practicing Law Institute, the New York State Bar Association, and the New York Employee Benefits Conference. In 2001, Mr. Pratt was elected a fellow of the American College of Employee Benefits Counsel. He is also a director of the New York Employee Benefits Conference and co-chair of the Tax Exempt and Governmental Plans subcommittee of ASPA's Government Affairs Committee. He can be contacted at *dprat@mail.als.edu*.

Anthony L. Scialabba, Esq., is a managing partner with the law firm of Scialabba & Associates, P.C., in Marlton, New Jersey. Mr. Scialabba was formerly an attorney at law firms in Baltimore and Philadelphia. In addition, he was a Tax Law Specialist with the Internal Revenue Service (National Office), Employee Plans/Exempt Organizations Office, Employee Plans Technical and Actuarial Division.

Mr. Scialabba is admitted to practice law in Pennsylvania, New Jersey, Ohio, and the District of Columbia. Mr. Scialabba received a B.A. in history from Cornell University in 1981, a J.D. from the University of Toledo College of Law in 1985, and a Master of Laws in Taxation from the Georgetown University Law Center in 1987. He has written extensively and lectured before many employers and practitioners on employee benefit topics. Mr. Scialabba has extensive experience in all forms of deferred compensation (including retirement) and welfare plan documentation. This includes drafting, plan design, and government submission. He also has significant experience in handling employee benefit matters with the Internal Revenue Service and the Department of Labor. Mr. Scialabba is an Editorial Board Advisor for the *Journal of Pension Benefits* and a Reviewing Editor for the *CCH Pension Plan Guide*.

Sal L. Tripodi, Esq., maintains a national consulting practice, TRI Pension Services, in the employee benefits area. TRI Pension Services provides technical training in ERISA-related areas, presenting seminars around the country, and authors a four-volume reference guide, *The ERISA Outline Book* (published by ASPA), and two quarterly newsletters, *ERISA Views* and *eRISA Update*. He conducts ERISA-related seminars for major financial institutions, trade and professional associations, and consulting firms all over the United States. For more information about TRI Pension Services, visit the website at *www.cybERISA.com*.

In addition to his duties at TRI Pension Services, Mr. Tripodi is an Adjunct Professor at the University of Denver Graduate Tax Program, where he also conducts classes and occasionally presents seminars. He also is a Vice President of ASPA and is a Co-Chair of ASPA's Government Affairs Committee. Mr. Tripodi started his employee benefits career with the Internal Revenue Service, as a Tax Law Specialist with the IRS National Office (1979-1983). Since 1983, Mr. Tripodi has been in the private sector, consulting on employee benefit matters, writing reference materials concerning employee benefit plans, and conducting numerous seminars. In 2001, Mr. Tripodi was named ASPA's Educator of the Year. Mr. Tripodi received a J.D. at Catholic University of America Law School (1979) and an LL.M. at Georgetown University Law School (1983). Mr. Tripodi can be reached at TRI Pension Services, PMB 120, 9457 S. University Blvd., Highlands Ranch, CO 80126-4976; (303) 470-7964; or at *trips@cyberisa.com*.

Joseph A. Zavoda, Esq., is Vice President of CitiStreet Retirement Services LLC. CitiStreet is a State Street and Citigroup company. Since 1985, Mr. Zavoda has focused on the design, implementation, management, communication, and operation of retirement programs. His specialized areas of expertise include nondiscrimination testing and annual reporting requirements of retirement plans.

Prior to joining CitiStreet, Mr. Zavoda worked at a "Big Six" accounting firm where he was the lead benefits consultant and relationship manager for a number of large healthcare institutions, law firms, and corporations. Mr. Zavoda frequently speaks on 401(k) and other retirement plan topics. In addition to CitiStreet's many publications, he was a contributing author and editor to a number of publications with Prentice Hall including *Prentice Hall's Complete Guide to the Tax Law of 1987, How to Take Advantage of the Many Benefits of Cash or Deferred Arrangements,* and *Complying with the New DOL Regulations on Plan Loans.* Mr. Zavoda is an attorney and a member of both the New Jersey and Pennsylvania Bars. He is also a Certified Employee Benefits Specialist. Mr. Zavoda received his B.A. from Rutgers University, his J.D. from Rutgers School of Law–Camden, his M.B.A. from Temple University School of Business Administration, and his certification as an Employee Benefits Specialist from the Wharton School, University of Pennsylvania, and the International Foundation of Employee Benefit Plans.

Acknowledgments

457 Answer Book is the product of the hard work, insight, and dedication of many people, without whom this book would not be possible. I would like to thank the following professionals for their skill and assistance in the writing of this book: Carol V. Calhoun; David S. Goldstein; Peter J. Gulia; David R. Levin; Marjorie R. Martin; David W. Powell; David A. Pratt; Anthony L. Scialabba; Sal Tripodi; and Joseph A. Zavoda. They are all accomplished experts in their fields. Their depth of knowledge of the subject matter was always refreshing and their thoroughness greatly appreciated.

I wish to express my great appreciation and deep gratitude to Ellen Ros and James Orefice for their expertise in managing the editorial effort on this edition, and to the rest of the professional staff at Aspen Publishers for making this book a reality.

When I first wrote the principal chapter on Code Section 457 (chapter 2), most of my research led to articles and other publications authored by David Powell. I even had the audacity to have David review that chapter. I eventually managed to get David to co-author chapter 2 and to prepare the annual updates. In this edition of *457 Answer Book*, David expands the coverage and guidance resulting from the final 457 regulations and the final regulations regarding required minimum distributions. Many thanks go to him for his keen insight and hard work. Chapter 2 is an enormous chapter, but it is clear, concise, and well-written.

Special thanks also go to Peter Gulia for his assistance in reviewing manuscripts and for sharing (some of) his vast practical and technical experience with me. His depth of knowledge and keen understanding of both state and federal rules and exceptions make his chapters on deferred compensation plan investments (chapter 3), beneficiary designations (chapter 5), and plan-approved domestic relations orders (chapter 13) essential reading. Whenever I read Peter's chapters, I am amazed at what I don't know and never imagined was possible or even an issue!

Over the years, contributing authors have changed. I'd like to thank the former contributing authors for taking the time—when they could and for as long as they could—to share their expertise. Needless to say, some of their contributions remain intact and I thank them for it. Former authors include: Susan D. Diehl; Yvonne C. Kepler; John J. Koresko; Pamela Perdue; and Lynn B. Witte (deceased).

Thanks also go to Lady Lucy of Canterbury Tails, Amber the Twerp, Butch the Beastslayer, Simon the Magnificent, Abi-2, and Hi-Ho Silver Zorro, for their astute feline conversation, companionship, warmth, and, least of all, their occasional assistance in typing and editing. Special thanks to Gracie for her security services and for protecting the manuscript during its preparation.

Gary S. Lesser
May 2004

How to Use This Book

457 Answer Book, Fourth Edition, is designed for professionals who need quick and authoritative answers. This book uses simple, straightforward language and avoids technical jargon as much as possible. Citations of authority are provided as research aids for those who need to pursue particular items in greater detail.

Because *457 Answer Book*'s contributing authors include practitioners who are active in this field, we ask our readers to consider the following general cautions. Each contributing author speaks only for himself or herself. The views stated by any author are solely the views of that author and do not necessarily reflect the views of any firm, business, organization, or government agency with which the author is currently or was previously associated. Likewise, any views stated do not necessarily reflect the views of any client or customer of any contributing author or his or her firm or business. Although some contributing authors may have requested that others serve as peer reviewers or editors of their work, any such review or editing should not be construed as any indication of concurrence in any views, which are solely those of the contributing author. Some of the court decisions, rulings, and other legal authorities cited in this book may relate to matters in which one or more of the contributing authors acted on behalf of a client or as a lobbyist.

The question-and-answer format, with its breadth of coverage and its plain-language explanations (plus numerous real-world examples), offers a clear and useful guide to understanding the complex and extremely important area of 457 plans.

Numbering System. The questions are numbered consecutively within each chapter (e.g., 2:1, 2:2, 2:3).

List of Questions. The detailed List of Questions that follows the Contents in the front of this book helps the reader locate areas of immediate interest. This list is like a detailed table of contents that provides both the question number and the page on which it appears.

Appendices. Various sample documents designed to help in the actual administration of 457 plans follow the chapters.

Tables. To facilitate easy access to a particular section of the Internal Revenue Code, Treasury Regulations, or United States Code, to IRS documents (Revenue Rulings, Revenue Procedures, Letter Rulings, Notices, Announcements, etc.), and to pertinent cases, tables of all the sections, documents, and cases, referenced by question number, have been included.

Index. An index is provided as a further aid to locate specific information. All references in the index are to question numbers rather than page numbers.

Contents

CHAPTER **5**

Beneficiary Designations and Estate Planning   5-1

Contents

Contents

Contents

List of Questions

Chapter 1 The History of 457 Plans

Contribution Limitations

Distribution Changes

Rollover Rules and Portability Between Plans

Low-Income Taxpayer Credit

Purchase of Service Credit

Miscellaneous Items

Sunset Provisions

Job Creation and Worker Assistance Act

Final 457 Treasury Regulations

Chapter 2 Eligible 457 Plans

Employers Subject to Code Section 457

Church and Church-Related Employers

Rural Cooperatives

Plans Subject to Code Section 457

Qualified Governmental Excess Benefit Arrangements

Coordination of Deferrals with Other Plans or Other Employers

Withholding and Reporting

Chapter 3 Distribution Rules

Rollovers

Other Distribution Rules

Chapter 4 Investments

Permitted Investments for Deferred Compensation Plans

Types of Investments

Protecting the Safety of Investments

Rabbi Trusts

Trusts for Governmental Deferred Compensation Plans

Employer Responsibility for Plan Investments

Protection Against Liability

Participant-Directed Investment

Chapter 5   Beneficiary Designations and Estate Planning

Effect of Beneficiary Designation

Ceremonial Marriage

Common-Law Marriage

Community Property

Tenancy by the Entirety

Premarital Agreements

Marital Agreements

Qualified Domestic Trusts for Aliens

Seeking Advice About Making a Beneficiary Designation

Chapter 6 ERISA, Its Exemptions, and Other Non-Tax Considerations for 457 Plans

ERISA in General

Governmental Plans

Church Plans

Selected Securities and Insurance Law Issues for 457 Plans

ERISA and Tax Consequences of Funded 457(f) Plans

Chapter 7 Mergers and Acquisitions

457 Plan Considerations

403(b) Considerations

Severance Pay and 403(b) Plans

Section 415 Considerations

Chapter 8 Defining a Top-Hat Plan in Connection with 457 Plans

457 Plans and ERISA

Top-Hat Group

Advisory Opinions and Case Law

Other Definitional Issues

Future DOL Guidance

Applying the Rules

Chapter 9 Creditors' Rights

Shumate and ERISA Qualified Plans

Consequences of the Bankruptcy of the Plan Sponsor

Chapter 10 Application of Federal Securities Law to 457 Plans

Federal Securities Laws and 457 Plans Generally

Eligible Public Employer 457 Plans Under Code Sections 457(b) and 457(e)(1)(A)

General 457 Reporting Rules

ERISA Reporting Requirements

FICA and FUTA

IRS Form 940—Employer's Annual FUTA Tax Return

Reporting Distributions on Form 1099-R

IRS Form W-3—Transmittal of Wage and Tax Statements

Chapter 13 Plan-Approved Domestic Relations Orders

Chapter 1

The History of 457 Plans

Gary S. Lesser, Esq.
GSL Galactic Consulting

Sal L. Tripodi, Esq.
TRI Consulting, Inc.

Section 457 of the Internal Revenue Code (Code) provides limitations on nonqualified deferred compensation paid by state and local governments and tax-exempt organizations (frequently referred to as eligible employers). Unlike a taxable organization, an eligible employer under Code Section 457 is not concerned with the timing of income tax deductions for compensation paid to its employees. With the deduction incentive missing, the eligible employer is more likely to enter into arrangements with employees that will result in a significant delay in the payment of compensation and, thus, in the income taxation of such compensation. Congress and the Internal Revenue Service (IRS) were concerned that an employee of an eligible employer would be able to defer more of his or her compensation than an employee of a taxable employer. Code Section 457 addressed this concern, first in 1978 with respect to public sector employers and then in 1986 with respect to private sector tax-exempt employers. A plan that is subject to Code Section 457 is either an eligible deferred compensation plan, which means it satisfies the requirements of Code Sections 457(b) and 457(d), or an ineligible deferred compensation plan, which means it is subject to the tax rules set forth in Code Section 457(f).

On July 11, 2003, the IRS updated the proposed regulations issued under Code Section 457 on May 8, 2002. The original, or 1982, regulations were published when Code Section 457 applied only to governmental entities. [67 Fed. Reg. 30,826

(May 8, 2002)] Many issues have been raised and many changes in the law have occurred over the last 20 years. The final regulations comprehensively restate the 1982 regulations and are discussed in chapter 2 and elsewhere in this book. Ineligible deferred compensation plans and excluded plans are more fully discussed in chapter 11.

The authors acknowledge the assistance of David Powell, who provided assistance in updating prior versions of this chapter.

Q 1:1 What guidance did the public sector initially rely on to establish deferred compensation arrangements?

Early guidance from the Internal Revenue Service (IRS) focused on deferred compensation plans in the private sector. Revenue Ruling 60-31 [1960-1 C.B. 174], the primary ruling on the subject, discussed the application of the constructive receipt doctrine to specific deferred compensation arrangements. Revenue Ruling 71-19 [1971-1 C.B. 43] (which was subsequently amended by Revenue Procedure 92-65 [1992-2 C.B. 94]) set forth the conditions under which the IRS would issue an advance ruling on a deferred compensation arrangement. The public sector relied on this guidance to establish deferred compensation arrangements with public sector employees and independent contractors. The first public sector deferred compensation plan was established in 1968 by a governmental unit in Utah.

Q 1:2 How did the IRS control the design of nonqualified plans?

In mid-1977, the IRS issued a moratorium on the approval of new deferred compensation plans and placed limits on existing plans. This was followed by the release of Proposed Treasury Regulations Section 1.61-16 in 1978. Qualified deferred compensation plans were governed by different rules.

Q 1:3 How did the proposed regulation affect nonqualified deferred compensation plans?

Under Proposed Treasury Regulations Section 1.61-16, if an individual elected to defer compensation from one year to a later year, the compensation would be taxed in the year in which it would have been paid had the election not been made. In other words, the proposed regulation treated the individual as being in constructive receipt of the deferred compensation in the earlier year.

Q 1:4   What types of employers were affected by the proposed regulation?

Proposed Treasury Regulations Section 1.61-16 applied to all nonqualified deferred compensation plans, whether maintained by private sector or public sector employers. The regulation set off a heated public debate, and Congress responded promptly with the Revenue Act of 1978 (Rev. Act of 1978), which suspended application of the proposed regulation and enacted Section 457 of the Internal Revenue Code (Code). [Rev. Act of 1978 § 131(a)]

Q 1:5   What types of employers were subject to Code Section 457 in 1978?

In its original incarnation, Code Section 457 applied only to state or local governments that maintained nonqualified deferred compensation plans. Tax-exempt employers continued to maintain nonqualified arrangements without the constraints of Code Section 457 until 1986. As originally enacted, Code Section 457 was applicable to taxable years ending on or after February 1, 1978.

Q 1:6   How did the Technical Corrections Act of 1979 affect 457 plans?

The Technical Corrections Act of 1979 made minor changes to the definition of "rural electric cooperative."

Q 1:7   How did the Tax Equity and Fiscal Responsibility Act of 1982 affect 457 plans?

The Tax Equity and Fiscal Responsibility Act of 1982 (TEFRA) made Code Section 457 inapplicable to qualified state judicial plans, thereby ensuring that state judges will not forgo the benefit of their deferred compensation plans simply because there is no substantial risk of forfeiture (see Q 2:17). [TEFRA § 252, amending Rev. Act of 1978 § 131(c)]

Q 1:8   When was Section 457 coverage expanded to include private sector tax-exempt employers?

The Tax Reform Act of 1986 (TRA 1986) expanded Code Section 457 to include nonqualified plans maintained by private sector tax-exempt organizations.

Q 1:9 How did Code Section 457 affect private sector tax-exempt plan design?

For many private sector tax-exempt employers, rather than creating design opportunities, Code Section 457 took away some important flexibility in designing nonqualified deferred compensation arrangements.

Q 1:10 What other important changes did the Tax Reform Act of 1986 bring about?

The Tax Reform Act of 1986 (TRA 1986) also added Code Section 457(d) to expand the distribution rules for 457 plans. Before the addition of Code Section 457(d), Code Section 457(b) required that amounts payable from a 457 plan be made available no earlier than on separation from service or on the occurrence of an unforeseeable emergency. The TRA 1986 amendment also incorporated the minimum distribution rules under Code Section 401(a)(9) into Code Section 457.

TRA 1986 was effective for plan years beginning after 1988. Changes under TRA 1986 included the following provisions:

1. Amounts deferred from an individual's gross income under 401(k) qualified cash or deferred arrangements and tax-sheltered annuities under Code Section 403(b) must be taken into account when determining whether Section 457 deferrals exceed statutory maximums (see Q 2:90). [I.R.C. § 457(c)] (Note: This requirement was repealed, effective January 1, 2002, by the Economic Growth and Tax Relief Reconciliation Act of 2001 (EGTRRA). See Q 1:14.)

   Example. Betty is an employee of a public school system. She is eligible to participate in both a grandfathered 401(k) plan because it was adopted before May 6, 1986, and an eligible plan under Code Section 457. Deferred amounts are added together to determine whether Betty has exceeded the Section 457 deferral limits. [TRA 1986 § 1116(f)(2)–(7), amended by Technical and Miscellaneous Revenue Act of 1988 (TAMRA) § 1011(k)(8)]

2. Existing unfounded plans of tax-exempt employers are subject to special transitional rules (see Q 2:17). [TRA 1986 § 1107(c)(1)–(3), (5)]

3. Employees of nongovernmental tax-exempt organizations, churches, and rural electric cooperatives can defer compensation under an eligible deferred compensation plan established and maintained pursuant to the provisions of Code Section 457. The Employee Retirement Income Security Act of 1974 (ERISA) typically limits participation in plans of nongovernmental tax-exempt employers to a select group of management or highly compensated employees. Such a plan is frequently called a "top-hat" plan. (See chapters 6 and 8 regarding ERISA coverage exceptions for top-hat plans.)

4. Minimum distribution requirements apply in the event that a participant dies prior to the date on which the participant's entire interest would have been distributed or prior to commencement of distributions (see chapter 3). [I.R.C. § 457(d)]

5. Certain distribution option election amounts (up to $5,000 for plan years beginning after August 5, 1997) were not treated as made available (see Qs 2:196, 2:197). [I.R.C. § 457(e)(9)]

6. Transfers of amounts between eligible plans are permitted (see Qs 2:228, 2:229, 2:230). [I.R.C. § 457(e)(10)]

[TRA 1986 § 1107; IRS Notice 87-13, § G, 1987-1 C.B. 432]

Q 1:11   What important change did TAMRA make to 457 plans?

TAMRA made clarifications which were necessitated by the inclusion of private sector tax-exempt employers under the umbrella of Code Section 457 [TAMRA § 6064], as follows:

- Under Code Section 457(e)(11), which codifies IRS Notice 88-68 [1988-1 C.B. 556], the rules of Code Section 457(e) do not apply to bona fide vacation leave, sick leave, compensatory time, severance pay, disability pay, and death benefit plans. Code Section 457(e)(11) also confirms that Code Section 457 applies to other nonelective deferred compensation arrangements. [TAMRA § 6064(a)(1)]

- Under Code Section 457(e)(12), the rules of Code Section 457 do not apply to certain nonelective plans for independent contractors (see Q 2:13). This exception does not permit independent contractors to enter into elective nonqualified deferred compensation arrangements, which are far more popular vehicles, without being subject to the Section 457 constraints. [TAMRA § 6064(b)(1)]

Example 1. Mercy Hospital maintains a nonelective arrangement that covers all doctors who have independent contractor agreements with the hospital. Because the arrangement is not elective and covers only independent contractors, Code Section 457 is not applicable in determining whether benefits are tax deferred.

- Under Code Section 457(e)(13), a church or qualified church-controlled organization (see Q 2:1) is exempt from Code Section 457. These organizations can continue to maintain nonqualified deferred compensation arrangements under the principles applicable to taxable employers (thus, the dollar limits under Code Section 457(b) are not applicable). [TAMRA § 6064(b)(1)]

- Organizations are prevented from avoiding the Section 457 deferral limits by forming affiliated service groups or leasing arrangements (see Q 2:109). [I.R.C. § 414(o)]

- When maximum deferral limits are exceeded, income deferral inclusions do not apply to excess deferrals. [TAMRA § 1011(e)(4)]

Example 2. Charles deferred $8,700 to an eligible 457 plan that has experienced investment performance of $400. Because the maximum deferral is $8,500 (using 2001 limits), both the $200 excess deferral ($8,700 minus

$8,500) and a portion of the investment performance of $400 have to be refunded to the participant.

- Transitional rules are provided for certain nonelective deferred compensation plans in existence on December 31, 1987, and maintained pursuant to one or more collective bargaining agreements; however, the transitional rules do not apply to any plan as of the effective date of its first material modification (see Q 2:17). [TAMRA § 6064(d)(2)]

Q 1:12   How did the Small Business Job Protection Act of 1996 affect 457 plans?

The Small Business Job Protection Act of 1996 (SBJPA) made changes that are effective for years beginning after December 31, 1996, unless otherwise noted. These changes include:

- The pre-1998 $7,500 deferral limit under Code Section 457(b) was indexed (see Q 2:98). This was the first indexing of the dollar limit since the enactment of Code Section 457. The adjusted dollar limits are listed in appendix J on the CD-ROM.

- One additional election is permitted to further postpone payment of compensation already deferred, if the election is made before benefits actually commence (see Q 2:72). This clarifies the rules for postponement of benefits after the initial deferral election.

- A state or local government that maintains an eligible 457 plan is required to maintain a trust for the exclusive benefit of the plan participants. In other words, the plan may no longer be an "unfunded" arrangement, and set-asides are no longer subject to the claims of the government's creditors. This rule is in response to several municipal bankruptcies that have jeopardized participants' benefits under a 457 plan. The trust is tax-exempt and does not cause the funded amounts to become taxable to the participants (i.e., the income inclusion rules of Code Section 457 continue to apply). Normally, if a 457 plan is funded, it no longer is a plan described in Code Section 457 and taxation of the benefits is governed by Code Section 402(b). Various effective dates apply to new and existing plans, but most governmental 457 plans needed to have a trust in place by the end of 1999 (see Q 2:39). A custodial account or annuity contract can also be used to satisfy the trust requirement.

- Amounts placed in trust under an eligible governmental plan may be loaned to participants under Section 72(p) rules (see Q 2:40).

- Code Section 457(e)(11) is amended to provide that length of service awards to bona fide volunteers are not subject to Code Section 457 (see Q 2:13).

Q 1:13   Were any changes made to Code Section 457 under the Taxpayer Relief Act of 1997?

Yes. The Taxpayer Relief Act of 1997 (TRA 1997) increased the limit on involuntary cash-outs to $5,000 from $3,500 (see Q 2:215).

Q 1:14   How does EGTRRA affect 457 plans?

EGTRRA [H.R. 1836] substantially affects 457 plans after 2001. It incorporates numerous changes affecting eligible 457 plans; these are discussed below.

Contribution Limitations

Maximum permitted deferral. EGTRRA increases the dollar and percentage limits on deferrals under an eligible 457 plan to conform to the general elective deferral limitation applicable to most other plans (see Qs 2:90, 2:91, 2:92). For taxable years prior to 2001, in general, the maximum permitted annual deferral limit is the lesser of 33⅓ percent of includible compensation or $8,500. Under EGTRRA, the deferral limits increase for taxable years beginning on or after January 1, 2002, as follows:

- The 33⅓ percent of compensation limitation on deferrals increases to 100 percent of compensation. [EGTRRA § 632(c)(1); I.R.C. § 457(b)(2)(B)]
- The elective deferral limit increases from its current limit of $8,500 to $11,000 and will increase in $1,000 annual increments until it reaches $15,000 in 2006. Thereafter, the elective deferral limit will be indexed for inflation in $500 increments.

The limit is twice the otherwise applicable dollar limit in the three years before retirement. Catch-up contributions (see below) are not permitted to be made in those years. [EGTRRA § 611(e)(1)(B); I.R.C. §§ 414(v)(6)(C), 457(b)(2)(A), 457(b)(3)(A), 457(c)(1), 457(e)(15)]

Note. Some states permit local government employers to provide matching or nonelective contributions under a plan qualified under Code Section 401(a). These contributions do not count against the 100 percent of compensation or elective deferral limits.

Catch-up contributions. An individual participating in a governmental 457(b) plan who attains the age of 50 by the end of the taxable year may make additional elective deferrals up to an "applicable dollar limit." Although the increased limits (see above) are effective for taxable years beginning after 2001, the catch-up elective deferral applies only to plan years beginning after January 1, 2001. The maximum amount of the catch-up contributions is the lesser of the participant's compensation for the year or the applicable dollar limit. The applicable dollar limits are as follows:

Plan Year	Catch-up Amount
2002	$1,000
2003	2,000
2004	3,000
2005	4,000
2006 and thereafter	5,000

The catch-up amount is in addition to the normal deferral limit for the applicable year. [I.R.C. § 414(v)(6)(C)] It may not be used in the three years before retirement, since the limit during those years is twice the otherwise applicable dollar limit (see Q 2:99).

[EGTRRA § 611(e); I.R.C. §§ 414(v)(6)(C), 457(b)(2)(A), 457(b)(3)(A)]

Note. Code Section 457(b) does not require that a 457 plan state any plan year. A participant might have a good-faith tax return position if the age 50 catch-up is applied on either the calendar year or the participant's taxable year.

For taxable years beginning after December 31, 2006, the catch-up limit of $5,000 will be subject to a cost-of-living allowance (COLA) in increments of $500. This COLA adjustment is separate from the COLA adjustment applicable to the normal elective deferral limit. [EGTRRA § 631(a); I.R.C. § 414(v)(2)(C)]

Compensation. The definition of compensation (the Code refers to "includible compensation") was not changed by EGTRRA (see Q 2:52). A technical correction was made by the Job Creation and Workers Assistance Act (JCWAA) (see Q 1:16). Prior to JCWAA, the Code requires that includible compensation be determined after all wage reductions, including any wage reduction under the eligible 457 plan; thus, compensation does not include elective contributions. [I.R.C. § 457(e)(5)] Compensation now has the meaning given to the term participant's compensation by Code Section 415(c)(3). [I.R.C. § 457(e)(5)]

Repeal of coordination requirement. Effective in 2002, the special coordination requirement for elective deferrals when an individual participates in an eligible 457 plan and another salary reduction plan is repealed (see Qs 1:16, 2:12, 2:13, 2:95, 2:119). [EGTRRA § 615(a)] Therefore, the aggregate deferral limit with respect to any individual will apply regardless of the type of salary reduction plan. Under the law in effect for 2001, if an individual participates in an eligible 457 plan and any other salary reduction plan, the annual aggregate deferral among all such plans is limited to $8,500.

Example 1. Anthony, the county engineer, is an employee of Marlton County. Anthony is also an employee of Engineers Unlimited. For 2001, Anthony makes elective contributions of $10,500 under the Engineers' 401(k) plan. Anthony is precluded from making any contribution under an eligible 457 plan because the $8,500 limit is reduced by Anthony's 401(k) contributions.

Example 2. The facts are the same as those in Example 1, except that it is 2002 and Anthony makes an elective deferral of $11,000 under the Engineers' 401(k) plan. Anthony may also contribute $11,000 under the Marlton County 457 plan.

Example 3. Candy, a teacher, is an employee of the Marion County School District. She earns $26,000. Candy may make elective deferrals of $11,000 under the Marion County 457 plan and another $11,000 under her tax-sheltered annuity or mutual fund custodial account under Code Section 403(b). Marion

County will report only $4,000 of taxable wages on Form W-2. Candy will report that amount on line 7 of her Form 1040 for 2002.

Example 4. Manny participates in two 457 plans in 2002. Each plan is maintained by a separate municipality. Manny contributes $11,000 under each plan. Although neither employer is responsible for the excess deferral, Manny must notify either or both of the plans to make a corrective distribution so that his total elective deferrals do not exceed his Section 457(b) deferral limit of $11,000 ($12,000 if the catch-up contribution applies).

Distribution Changes

Minimum distribution requirement. EGTRRA provides that eligible 457 plans are subject to the required minimum distribution (RMD) rules of Code Section 401(a)(9). (See Q 2:21 and chapter 3.) Thus, the five distribution restrictions under current law no longer apply to distributions made after 2001. [EGTRRA § 649; I.R.C. § 457(d)(2)]

Inclusion requirement. After 2001, amounts deferred under an eligible governmental 457(b) plan will be includible in the recipient's income when the amounts are actually paid, rather than when the amounts are either paid or "otherwise made available to the participant." [EGTRRA § 649(b)(1); I.R.C. § 457(a)(1)(A)] However, for plans of both tax-exempt and governmental employers, the same desk rule, which prevents employees from receiving their 457(b) plan distributions in certain cases, will be repealed through replacement of the "separation from service" requirement with "severance from employment" (see Q 2:128). [EGTRRA § 646(a)(3); I.R.C. § 457(d)(1)(A)(ii)] (A *separation from service* occurs only upon a participant's death, retirement, discharge, or resignation, and not when the employee continues in the same job for a different employer as a result of a liquidation, merger, consolidation, or other similar corporate transaction. (See Q 2:213.) On the other hand, a *severance from employment* occurs when a participant ceases to be employed by the employer that maintains the plan. Under the same desk rule, a participant's severance from employment does not necessarily result in a separation from service. [See Rev. Rul. 79-336, 1979-2 C.B. 187]) Consequently, acquiring entities will no longer have to assume sponsorship and administration of a discontinued eligible 457 plan. [See, under prior law, P.L.R. 9314006 (Dec. 28, 1992)] (See Qs 2:22, 2:214, 2:218.)

Note. This provision is effective for distributions after 2001, regardless of when severance from employment occurs. Employers that have not made distributions from plans because of the same desk rule can choose whether to allow for distributions beginning in 2002.

Caution. Except for the new severance from employment rules, the current law continues for nongovernmental tax-exempt organizations; that is, deferred compensation is income when paid or made available. This means that a participant is taxed when he or she has the right to get deferred compensation, even if it is not received. (See Q 2:128.) The typical eligible deferred compensation plan provides for irrevocable elections, so amounts are taxable when received. A governmental 457 plan can be amended to remove unnecessary irrevocable election provisions.

QDRO distributions. Distributions from a 457(b) plan pursuant to a qualified domestic relations order may receive favorable tax treatment if the plan permits such distributions and the distribution and the court order follow rules similar (although not necessarily identical) to those in place for 403(b) plans and qualified plans (see Qs 2:221–2:227, chapter 14). EGTRRA clarifies that any such distribution is income to the nonparticipant spouse or former spouse. [EGTRRA § 635(a)(1)–(2); I.R.C. §§ 414(p)(10)–(12), 457(d)]

Payments reported on Form 1099-R. Amounts paid from an eligible governmental 457 plan on or after January 1, 2002, will no longer be treated as wages. Instead, the reporting of such amounts will be governed by the tax reporting and withholding rules that apply generally to qualified retirement plans (see Q 2:136). [EGTRRA § 641(a)(1)(D)(i); I.R.C. § 3401(a)(12)(E)]

Caution. The current wage tax reporting and withholding rules still apply to a church or other nongovernmental 457 plan. [See I.R.C. § 3405(e)(1)(B)(i); Temp. Treas. Reg. § 35.3405-1, Q&A 23]

Update of life expectancy tables. The IRS is required to modify the life expectancy tables to reflect current life expectancy. The new proposed regulations under Code Section 401(a)(9) regarding RMDs changed the RMD rules, but did not change the old life expectancy tables. [Prop. Treas. Reg. § 1.401(a)-9] Instead, the regulations established a uniform table that can be used to determine lifetime RMDs, which has the effect of lengthening payout and reducing minimum payouts. The tables used in the new proposed regulations on RMDs were updated in the final regulations issued on April 16, 2002.

Rollover Rules and Portability Between Plans

EGTRRA contains numerous provisions to expand portability between various types of retirement plans for the purpose of retaining tax-favored treatment of the amounts distributed (see Q 2:242). The incentives for individuals to retain benefits in tax-favored accounts include the following new rollover rules.

Eligible rollover distributions. After 2001, eligible rollover distributions are permitted between a qualified plan and 403(b) annuity and custodial account plans and eligible governmental 457 plans without restriction, including rollovers from an eligible governmental 457 plan to a traditional IRA, subject to the following conditions:

1. The employer's plan must agree to accept rollovers from unlike plans and agree to keep separate accounts for such rollover amounts.

2. The rollover notice (for all plans) must include a description of the provisions under which distributions from the plan to which the distribution is rolled over may be subject to restrictions and tax consequences different from those applicable to distributions from the distributing plan.

After 2001, the rollover notice requirement of Code Section 402(f) and the direct rollover requirements of Code Section 401(a)(31) apply to eligible governmental 457 plans. A distribution from an eligible governmental 457 plan that is rolled over will be reported on Form 1099-R, Distributions from Pensions, Annuities, Retirement or Profit-Sharing Plans, IRAs, Insurance Contracts, Etc., in the same manner as distributions from other plans. Furthermore, the 20 percent mandatory withholding rules applicable to eligible rollover distributions that are not directly rolled over in a trustee-to-trustee transfer will apply to eligible governmental 457 plans. [EGTRRA § 641(a); I.R.C. §§ 72(o)(4), 402(c)(8)(B)(vi), 403(b)(8)(A)(ii)]

> **Note.** EGTRRA did not make distributions prior to age 59½ subject to the 10 percent penalty tax. However, if a distribution from a qualified plan or a 403(b) plan is rolled over into an eligible governmental 457 plan, subsequent distributions from the 457(b) plan attributable to the qualified plan or 403(b) plan rollover will still be subject to the 10 percent additional tax for premature distributions under Code Section 72(t). (See Q 2:245.) The rollover notice required under Code Section 402(f) will be revised to contain provisions under which distributions from the plan receiving the rollover may be subject to restrictions and tax consequences that are different from those applicable to distributions from the plan making the rollover distribution.

Surviving spouse rollover rules liberalized. A surviving spouse beneficiary is permitted to roll over a distribution received after 2001 from any of the plans mentioned above to any plan in which the surviving spouse is a participant, rather than just to a traditional IRA (as is the case for distributions received prior to 2002) (see Q 2:247). [EGTRRA § 641(d); I.R.C. § 402(c)(9)]

Rollovers of after-tax contributions. After-tax employee contributions to a defined contribution plan that are distributed after 2001 are permitted to be rolled over to another defined contribution plan or to a traditional IRA. The receiving plan must accept rollovers of after-tax employee contributions and agree to account separately for such amounts and the earnings on those amounts. If the rollover from a qualified plan is going to another qualified plan, it must be a direct rollover. [EGTRRA § 643(a); I.R.C. §§ 402(c)(2), 408(d)(3)(H)] However, after-tax contributions may not be rolled over from an IRA to a qualified plan, a 403(b) annuity or custodial account plan, or an eligible 457 plan. (See Q 2:246.)

> **Note.** The IRS is directed to prescribe rules for rollover transactions, including the reporting requirements. Form 8606 is mentioned in the EGTRRA conference report as a possible means of reporting such transactions. [H.R. Conf. Rep. No. 107-51 (2001)] Unlike qualified plans, IRAs are not required to account separately for after-tax employee contributions. [I.R.C. § 402(c)(2)]

Rollovers of IRAs to employer plans. Distributions made after 2001 from a traditional IRA can be rolled over to the individual's qualified plan, a 403(b) annuity or custodial account plan, or an eligible governmental 457 plan (see Q 2:242). This rule applies to all amounts in traditional IRAs (except nondeductible contributions), including conduit IRAs, SEP IRAs, and SIMPLE IRAs (but only after the two-year period applicable to SIMPLE IRAs has expired).

The rule does not apply to any amounts in a Roth IRA or Coverdell Education Savings Account. [EGTRRA § 642(a)–(b); I.R.C. § 408(d)(3)(A), (d)(3)(D)(i)]

Practice Pointer. Certain individuals must keep qualified plan distributions that could qualify for capital gains treatment (with respect to pre-1974 participation) or 10-year averaging for lump-sum distributions (for taxpayers born before 1936) in a conduit IRA to qualify or requalify for favorable tax treatment by transferring that IRA back into a qualified plan.

Rollovers of hardship distributions not permitted. All hardship distributions made after 2001 from all qualified plans and 403(b) plans (not just those applicable to elective deferrals) are not eligible rollover distributions. [EGTRRA § 636(b); I.R.C. § 402(c)(4)(C)]

Extension of 60-day rollover period. EGTRRA grants the IRS the authority to extend a taxpayer's 60-day rollover period for any eligible rollover distribution made after 2001 in cases of casualty, disaster, or other events beyond the reasonable control of the individual subject to the rollover period. [EGTRRA § 644(a); I.R.C. § 402(c)(3)(B)]

Rollovers for purposes of cash-outs. In the case of transfers, distributions, or payments made after 2001, an employer may disregard rollovers for purposes of the $5,000 cash-out amount (see Qs 2:196, 2:197). Thus, an eligible 457 plan will be permitted to exclude rollover contributions (including earnings allocable thereto) in determining whether a participant's benefit exceeds $5,000 for purposes of the involuntary cash-out rules of Code Section 411(a)(11). [EGTRRA § 648(a)(1); I.R.C. §§ 411(a)(11)(D), 457(e)(9)(A)(i)]

Low-Income Taxpayer Credit

For the next five taxable years beginning after 2001 (i.e., 2002–2006), certain individuals may receive a nonrefundable tax credit of up to $1,000 for a percentage of their contributions (see Q 2:248). The credit is based on a sliding scale percentage of up to the first $2,000 in contributions to a traditional IRA or Roth IRA, elective deferrals made to a SIMPLE, SEP, 401(k), 403(b), or 457(b) plan, and voluntary after-tax contributions to a qualified plan. This credit also will apply to Roth-403(b) and Roth-401(k) plans when they become effective in taxable years beginning after 2005. The credit is in addition to any other tax benefit (i.e., the possible tax deduction) that the contribution gives the taxpayer. [I.R.C. § 25B(a)–(b)]

The eligibility requirements for the contribution tax credit are as follows:

1. The taxpayer must be 18 years of age or older.

2. The taxpayer may not be a full-time student or be claimed as a dependent on another taxpayer's tax return.

3. The amount of contributions available for the credit for any year is reduced by any distribution taken during the "testing period." The testing period is the two preceding tax years, the tax year, and the period of time after such tax year and before the due date of the federal income

tax return of the individual (and the spouse of the individual if a joint return is filed) for such year, including extensions.

4. [I.R.C. § 25B(c)]

Example 5. John gets an extension of time to file his year 2002 tax return until October 15, 2003. He will be ineligible for the credit for 2002 if he takes distributions totaling at least $2,000 at any time between January 1, 2000 and October 15, 2003.

Example 6. Sally takes a distribution of $2,000 on March 1, 2003. She is ineligible to claim this credit for 2002, 2003, 2004, and 2005.

5. Credit rates are based on adjusted gross income (AGI) levels, as outlined below.

Joint Filers		Heads of Household		All Other Filers*		Credit Rate
over	not over	over	not over	over	not over	
$0	$30,000	$0	$22,500	$0	$15,000	50%
$30,000	$32,500	$22,500	$24,375	$15,000	$16,250	20%
$32,500	$50,000	$24,375	$37,500	$16,250	$25,000	10%
$50,000		$37,500		$25,000		0%

*Includes single filers and married filers filing separately. Unless changed by a technical correction, this column will also apply to surviving spouses. As enacted, EGTRRA puts a surviving spouse in an adverse position compared to a head of household with regard to computing this credit.

Example 7. Joey is a married person and files a joint tax return. His AGI for 2002 is $31,000 and he contributes $2,000 to an IRA or as an elective deferral. Joey's tax credit for 2002 is $400 ($2,000 × 0.20). Assume that Joey's contribution for 2002 is only $1,500. In that case, his tax credit for 2002 is $300 ($1,500 × 0.20).

Example 8. Janice is a single person. Her AGI for 2002 is $24,000 and she contributes $1,000 to an IRA or as an elective deferral. Janice's tax credit for 2002 is $100 ($1,000 × 0.10).

Although the credit could be an incentive to contribute to a Roth IRA rather than a traditional IRA, particularly if the credit could eliminate any income tax, there are situations where the IRS may pay for a traditional IRA contribution, since the IRA deduction is included in the calculation of the AGI.

Example 9. Gary and Candace file a joint tax return. Their AGI for 2002 is $30,100. Each contributes $2,950 to a Roth IRA in 2002. Assume that both Gary and Candace are under age 50. Therefore, their individual contribution limit for 2002 is $3,000. They are entitled to a combined tax credit of $1,180 ($5,900 × 0.20). If either Gary or Candace were to contribute an additional $100 to a traditional IRA, their AGI would become $30,000 and the credit percentage would jump from 20 percent to 50 percent. Gary and

Candace's combined tax credit would therefore increase from $1,180 to $2,000 ($2,000 × 2 × .5), giving them an $820 reduction in tax for the additional IRA contribution.

Older taxpayers qualify for the credit, even if they are over 70½. However, distributions, including RMDs, may make taxpayers ineligible for the credit. In that case, a Roth IRA conversion or, if the taxpayer is not a 5 percent owner, a transfer to an employer's plan (and not retiring) might be an acceptable solution.

Caution. Amounts withdrawn for first-time home purchases and for either medical or educational expenses have the potential to reduce or eliminate the credit for contributions or deferrals to retirement savings plans for the current year or future years even though the amount withdrawn may avoid the 10 percent early withdrawal penalty.

Certain types of withdrawals, including the return of an excess contribution, a rollover, a loan from an annuity contract, and so on, are not treated as distributions for this purpose. [See I.R.C. § 25B(d)(2)(C)]

Practice Pointer. The fact that the credit is available to spouses who file separate returns means that a lower-income spouse can qualify for the credit even if the couple's joint income is too high. For example, if one spouse had an AGI of $27,000 and the other spouse had an AGI of $24,000, the spouse with the $24,000 AGI would qualify for a credit of 10 percent of any qualified contribution on a separate return, even though the couple could not get any credit on a joint return.

Purchase of Service Credit

Under EGTRRA, a qualified retirement plan maintained by a state or local government employer may provide that a participant may make after-tax employee contributions to purchase permissive service credit, subject to Section 415 limits (see Qs 2:228, 2:249). (Permissive service credit means credit for a period of service recognized by the governmental plan provided the employee voluntarily contributes to the plan an amount (as determined by the plan) that does not exceed the amount necessary to fund the benefit attributable to the period of service and that is in addition to the regular employee contributions, if any, under the plan.) Any repayment of contributions and earnings to a governmental plan regarding an amount previously refunded as a result of a forfeiture of service credit under the plan (or another plan maintained by a state or local government employer in the same state) is not taken into account for purposes of the Section 415 limits on contributions and benefits. In addition, service credit obtained as a result of such a repayment is not considered permissive service credit for purposes of the Section 415 limits. [EGTRRA § 647; I.R.C. §§ 403(b)(13), 457(e)(17)]

Under pre-EGTRRA rules, a participant may not use a rollover or direct transfer of benefits from a 457 plan or a 403(b) annuity to purchase permissive service credits or to repay contributions and earnings regarding a forfeiture of service credit. Under EGTRRA, a participant in a state or local government plan is not required to include in gross income a direct trustee-to-trustee transfer to a governmental defined benefit plan from a 457 plan or a 403(b) annuity if the transferred amount is used to purchase permissive service credits under the plan or to repay contributions and earnings regarding an amount previously refunded on a forfeiture of service credit under the plan (or another plan maintained by a state or local government employer in the same state). [Id.] (See Qs 2:228, 2:249.)

Miscellaneous Items

Active participation rules. EGTRRA did not amend Code Section 219(g)(5) to include 457 plans under Code Section 457(b). Therefore, 457 plan participants are able to contribute and deduct $3,000 (or $3,500 with catch-up for 2002) if a contribution is made to a traditional IRA, regardless of their AGI or participation in the 457 plan.

Example 10. Evelyn is a participant in an eligible governmental 457 plan. She is planning to retire in 2005. Evelyn has worked for her employer for over 15 years and is over age 50. For 2002, her catch-up 457(b) deferral amount is $22,000 (double the 2002 limit of $11,000). In addition to the $22,000 that she can defer into the 457(b) plan, Evelyn can defer $14,000 into a 403(b) plan ($11,000 limit plus the $3,000 catch-up for 403(b) plans). This brings the total deferral amount for 2002 to $36,000. Evelyn also can contribute $3,500 to a traditional or Roth IRA. As an alternative, she can defer the $22,000 into the 457(b) plan and make (and most likely deduct) a $3,500 contribution to a traditional IRA.

Deemed IRA contributions under employer plans. For plan years beginning after 2002, governmental 457(b) plans, as well as qualified plans and 403(b) plans, are permitted to accept traditional IRA or Roth IRA contributions ("voluntary employee contributions"), or both, if such contributions

1. Are separately accounted for or made into a separate account under the plan;
2. Meet the eligibility and other requirements applicable to either traditional or Roth IRAs; and
3. Are permitted under the employer's plan.

The deemed IRA contributions are not subject to the ERISA reporting and disclosure rules or to participation, vesting, funding, and enforcement requirements.

Deemed IRA contributions made to employer plans are treated in the same manner as IRA contributions made to a trust or custodial IRA (or IRA annuity) at a financial institution. Thus, the employer's plan is subject to the same information reporting as other IRAs (Form 5498). In addition, the amount contributed as a deemed IRA contribution is part of the individual's IRA limit for the year.

[I.R.C. § 408(q); ERISA § 4(b)]

Clarification of employer-provided retirement education. EGTRRA clarifies that retirement planning advice provided to employees (and their spouses) after 2001 on an individual basis is a nontaxable fringe benefit to the extent that such services are made available on substantially equivalent terms to all employees. [EGTRRA § 665(b); I.R.C. § 132(a)(7), (m)(1)]

Sunset Provisions

EGTRRA's provisions have various effective dates. Most are effective in 2002; some provisions, however, were effective immediately. Furthermore, most provisions are to be phased in over several years, and some are set to expire sooner than others. The entire law will sunset after December 31, 2010. If Congress does not act before then to extend these provisions, the rules will be the same as those in effect prior to the enactment of EGTRRA.

Those involved in all aspects of financial planning and retirement planning, therefore, will have to consider the possibility that the law may be scaled back, or not substantially extended or reenacted, for years after 2010. In that event, lower pension limitations, higher federal income tax rates, and an estate tax could once again become reality.

Q 1:15 Have the regulations under Code Section 457 been updated?

Yes. The Treasury issued regulations under Code Section 457 in 1982. [Treas. Reg. §§ 1.457-1 to -4] No amendments had been made to the regulations until 2002. The prior regulations, of course, did not reflect any of the amendments or transitional rules implemented since the regulations were adopted in 1982. [T.D. 7836 (Sept. 23, 1982)]

The IRS issued some limited guidance under the prior regulations, but only on a few issues, in Notice 98-8 [1998-4 I.R.B. 6]. The IRS also published model amendments that could be added to 457(b) plan documents (see Q 2:124) to reflect changes made by the SBJPA (see Q 1:12) and by TRA 1997 (see Q 1:13). [See Rev. Proc. 98-41, 1998-2 C.B. 135] In addition, Announcement 2000-1 [2000-2 I.R.B. 294] provided interim guidance on bona fide severance pay plans offered by state or local governments, and Revenue Ruling 2000-33 [2000-31 I.R.B. 142] confirms the acceptability of using an automatic enrollment procedure for deferring compensation under a 457(b) plan. (See Q 2:239.)

The IRS updated the regulations under Code Section 457, published in 1982 when Code Section 457 applied only to governmental entities, in 2002. [REG-105885-99, 67 Fed. Reg. 30,826–30,846 (May 8, 2002)] As discussed in this chapter and more fully in chapter 2, many issues have been raised and many changes in the law have occurred over the last 20 years. The proposed regulations comprehensively restated the 1982 regulations through EGTRRA (including recent technical corrections, see Q 1:16) and make numerous changes and additions to the current rules.

Note. The regulations under Code Section 457 were finalized on July 11, 2003 (see Q 1:17 and chapter 2).

Job Creation and Worker Assistance Act

Q 1:16   How did the Job Creation and Worker Assistance Act modify EGTRRA?

The Job Creation and Worker Assistance Act (JCWAA) made technical corrections to the EGTRRA rules. Two changes were made:

1. The definition of *includible compensation* was changed to conform to the qualified plan rules. Compensation now has the meaning given it under Code Section 415(c)(3) regarding a participant's compensation (see Q 2:53). [Treas. Reg. § 1.457-2]

2. Special coordination rules regarding catch-up contributions were added. Catch-up contributions are generally determined on a plan and on an individual basis (see Qs 2:115, 2:116, 2:117). [Treas. Reg. § 1.457-4(c)(2)]

Example. Happy is chief executive officer of Laughing Loud, a 501(c)(3) charitable organization that maintains a 403(b) plan as well as a 457(b) plan. Happy has includible compensation of $80,000 for 2002. Happy may contribute $11,000 to her 403(b) plan and another $11,000 to her 457(b) plan, for a total of $22,000. If Happy has attained age 50 in 2002, she may contribute another $1,000 to the 403(b) plan.

Final 457 Treasury Regulations

Q 1:17   Have Final Regulations under Code Section 457 been issued?

Yes, On July 11, 2003, final regulations that provide guidance on deferred compensation plans of state and local governments and tax-exempt entities were issued by the Treasury Department and IRS. [T.D. 9075; 68 Fed. Reg. 133, 41,230–41,250] The regulations reflect the changes made to Code Section 457 by TRA 1986, the Small Business Job Protection Act of 1996 (SBJPA), TRA 1997, EGTRRA, JCWAA, and other legislation. The regulations also make numerous technical changes and some clarifications.

The final regulations generally apply to taxable years beginning after December 31, 2001. However, for tax years beginning after 2001 and before 2004, a failure to comply with the final regulations will not be treated as a violation of Code Section 457 if the plan is otherwise operated "in accordance with a reasonable, good faith interpretation of EGTRRA." [Treas. Reg. § 1.457-12(b)] Prior to 2002, the 1982 final regulations applied in determining whether a plan operated reasonably and in good faith. [Preamble, Final Treas. Reg. § 1.457, T.D. 9075, 68 Fed. Reg. 133, 41,233 (July 11, 2003); T.D. 7836 (the 1982 regulations), 47 Fed. Reg. 42,335 (July 11, 2003)]

Chapter 2

Eligible 457 Plans

David W. Powell, Esq.
Groom Law Group, Chartered

There are two types of 457 plans: eligible plans and ineligible plans. Eligible plans have to meet special rules but receive additional tax benefits; they can also contain permissive features. Such plans frequently are designated by the subsection of the Internal Revenue Code (Code) that they must satisfy to receive special tax treatment—Code Section 457(b). Ineligible plans, also called 457(f) plans, receive less favorable tax treatment.

This chapter focuses on the statutory requirements of eligible plans (ineligible 457 plans are discussed more fully in chapters 11 and 12). Employer and employee eligibility requirements, contribution and deferral limits, unforeseeable emergency withdrawals, distributions, taxation, and other statutory requirements and nonstatutory rules are discussed. The rules associated with the receipt of distributions under an eligible 457(b) plan, as well as the taxability of these distributions to employees, are also covered.

For plans of tax-exempt employers and for plans of governmental employers for years before 2002, compensation deferred under an eligible plan and any income attributable to the amounts deferred are included in the participant's gross federal income for the taxable year in which such compensation or other income is paid or otherwise made available to the participant or other beneficiary. For years after 2001, compensation deferred under an eligible governmental plan is taxed when paid, rather than when it is paid or otherwise made available as in the case of a non-governmental 457(b) plan.

This chapter reflects changes made by the Economic Growth and Tax Relief Reconciliation Act of 2001 (EGTRRA), signed by the President on June 7, 2001, and final regulations published in the July 11, 2003, Federal Register. It should be cautioned, though, that undoubtedly, important additional information on 457 plans will be provided through further guidance.

Employers Subject to Code Section 457

Q 2:1   Which employers are subject to Section 457 of the Internal Revenue Code?

Section 457 of the Internal Revenue Code (Code) applies to any plan maintained by a state or local government or a tax-exempt organization (other than a governmental unit) unless an exception applies (see Q 2:13). States, local governments, and tax-exempt organizations (other than governmental units) are referred to as *eligible* employers (see Qs 14:1, 14:3, 14:4). Rural cooperatives are eligible employers if they are exempt from tax (see Q 2:9). Only an eligible employer is subject to the rules of Code Section 457. Only an *eligible* employer can maintain an eligible plan. [I.R.C. §§ 457(b), 457(e)(1), 457(f)(1)]

Churches and qualified church-controlled organizations are not eligible employers (see Qs 2:6–2:8). Certain church-related organizations, however, including many colleges, universities, hospitals, and nursing homes, typically do not qualify as qualified church-controlled organizations; thus, plans they establish are subject to the Section 457 rules (see Q 6:8). (Appendix G on the CD-ROM contains a model 457(f) plan for a church hospital.)

Thus, a 457(b) plan can be offered only to employees of a state or local government or a nonchurch, nongovernmental tax-exempt employer.

An eligible employer can have an *ineligible* plan—that is, a plan that does not satisfy the statutory requirements to be an eligible plan. In such a case, Code Section 457(f) applies to the plan. The tax treatment of eligible and ineligible plans differs significantly (see Q 2:127). Ineligible plans are more fully discussed in chapters 11 and 12.

If the employer is not an eligible employer, Code Section 457 does not apply to the plan. In such a case, other provisions of the Code govern the plan and the taxability of contributions (see Q 2:127 and chapter 11). In most cases, these rules are more liberal than the rules governing 457 plans.

A 457 plan, including a 457 plan maintained by a nongovernmental tax-exempt organization, other than a church plan, is not statutorily exempt from Title I of the Employee Retirement Income Security Act of 1974 (ERISA); therefore, in the absence of a specific ERISA exclusion, a 457 plan is an employee pension plan subject to the participation, vesting, funding, trust documentation, and fiduciary responsibility rules of Title I of ERISA (see Qs 6:22, 8:3). [ERISA § 4(b); DOL News Rel. 86-257 (Dec. 19, 1986); P.L.R. 8950057] ERISA implications for 457 plans, especially those of nongovernmental tax-exempt employers and non-qualified church-controlled entities, are more fully discussed in chapter 6. Most 457 plans, of course, are designed to fit within one of the exemptions from ERISA.

Q 2:2 Which tax-exempt organizations are affected by Code Section 457?

Code Section 457 applies to any tax-exempt organization (other than a church or governmental unit) that is exempt from tax under Subtitle A of the Code, relating to income taxes—that is, Code Sections 1 through 1564. Most of the organizations that are exempt from tax are listed in Code Section 501(c). (See Q 2:3.) [I.R.C. § 457(e)(1)(B), (e)(13)]

Example. A large nongovernmental hospital adopts a qualified plan for its employees. The plan's trust, whose trustees are appointed by the hospital, holds the assets of the hospital's plan. The *trust* hires 10 employees. The trust, as an employer, may establish a 457(b) plan because the trust is treated as an organization exempt from tax under Code Section 501(a), although it is not specifically listed as an organization exempt from tax under that section. Because the trust is not a governmental employer, participation would have to be limited to the top-hat group (see Qs 2:32, 2:169, 8:1). [I.R.C. §§ 414(d), 501(c)(25)(C)(ii)]

Q 2:3 What is a Section 501(c) tax-exempt employer?

To establish and maintain a 457 plan, an employer must be tax-exempt (or, alternatively, a "state"; see Q 2:4). The following types of organizations are listed as tax-exempt under Code Section 457:

1. Corporations organized for the exclusive purpose of holding title to property and collecting income there from (the organization must turn over all of its income, reduced by expenses, to a tax-exempt organization) [I.R.C. § 501(c)(2)];

2. Corporations and foundations organized and operated exclusively for religious, charitable, scientific, testing for public safety, literary, or educational purposes [I.R.C. § 501(c)(3)];

3. Civic leagues or organizations that are not organized for profit and are operated exclusively for the promotion of social welfare [I.R.C. § 501(c)(4)];

4. Local municipal associations of employees where the net earnings are devoted exclusively to charitable, educational, or recreational purposes [I.R.C. § 501(c)(4)];

5. Labor, agricultural, or horticultural organizations [I.R.C. § 501(c)(5)];

6. Business leagues, chambers of commerce, real estate boards, boards of trade, or professional football leagues where no part of the earnings is paid to the benefit of any private shareholder or individual [I.R.C. § 501(c)(6)];

7. Clubs organized for pleasure, recreation, and other nonprofitable purposes where no part of the earnings is paid to the benefit of any private shareholder or individual [I.R.C. § 501(c)(7)];

8. Fraternal beneficiary societies and orders or associations operating under the lodge system and providing for the payment of life, sick, accident, or other benefits to lodge members or their dependents [I.R.C. § 501(c)(8)];

9. Voluntary employee beneficiary associations providing for the payment of life, sick, accident, or other benefits to members or their dependents where no part of the earnings is paid to the benefit of any private shareholder or individual [I.R.C. § 501(c)(9)];

10. Domestic fraternal orders, associations, or societies operating under the lodge system, the net earnings of which are devoted exclusively to religious, charitable, scientific, literary, educational, and fraternal purposes, and not providing for the payment of life, sick, accident, or other benefits [I.R.C. § 501(c)(10)];

11. Teachers' retirement fund associations of a local character where no earnings are paid to the benefit of any private shareholder or individual and income consists solely of amounts received from public taxation, amounts received from assessments on the teaching salaries of members, and investment income thereon [I.R.C. § 501(c)(11)];

12. Benevolent life insurance associations of a purely local nature, mutual ditch or irrigation companies, mutual or cooperative telephone companies, or like organizations [I.R.C. § 501(c)(12)];

13. Cemetery companies owned and operated exclusively for their members where no part of the earnings is paid to the benefit of any private shareholder or individual [I.R.C. § 501(c)(13)];

14. Credit unions without capital stock operated for mutual purposes and without profit [I.R.C. § 501(c)(14)];

15. Corporations or associations without capital stock organized for mutual purposes and without profit for the purpose of providing reserve funds for, and insurance of, shares or deposits in certain types of banks and domestic building and loan associations [I.R.C. § 501(c)(14)];

16. Insurance companies or associations, if the net written premiums for the taxable year do not exceed $350,000 [I.R.C. § 501(c)(15)];

17. Certain corporations organized by farmer's cooperatives or associations for the purpose of financing ordinary crop operations of members or other producers [I.R.C. § 501(c)(16)];

18. Supplemental unemployment compensation benefit trusts [I.R.C. § 501(c)(17)];

19. Certain employee benefit trusts created before June 25, 1959, that provide pension benefits that are funded solely by employee contributions [I.R.C. § 501(c)(18)];

20. A post or organization of past or present members of the armed forces of the United States [I.R.C. § 501(c)(19)];

21. An organization that provides qualified group legal services [I.R.C. § 501(c)(20)];

22. A domestic black lung trust [I.R.C. § 501(c)(21)];

23. A multiemployer withdrawal payment liability fund [I.R.C. § 501(c)(22)];

24. An association organized before 1880 the principal purpose of which is to provide insurance and other benefits to veterans or their dependents [I.R.C. § 501(c)(23)];

25. Certain trusts used in connection with making payments to participants and beneficiaries under certain terminated plans [I.R.C. §§ 501(c)(24), 4049 (prior to repeal)];

26. Certain trusts and organizations holding title to real property that benefits:

    a. A qualified plan that meets the requirements of Code Section 401(a);

    b. A governmental plan under Code Section 414(d), which, in relevant part, defines a *governmental plan* as a plan established and maintained for its employees by the government of any state or political subdivision thereof;

    c. The United States, a state, or a political subdivision thereof, or any agency or instrumentality of any of the foregoing [I.R.C. § 501(c)(25)]; or

    d. A corporation or foundation organized and operated exclusively for religious, charitable, scientific, testing for public safety, literary, or educational purposes [I.R.C. § 501(c)(3)];

27. State-sponsored organizations insuring high-risk individuals [I.R.C. § 501(c)(26)]; and

28. State-sponsored workers' compensation reinsurance organizations [I.R.C. § 501(c)(27)].

Example 1. The Giant Pension Trust holds the assets of a qualified plan that covers over 30,000 participants. The trust hires 10 employees to administer the trust. Because the trust is a tax-exempt entity under Code Section 501(a)(1), it may establish a 457(b) plan; however, the employer will have to limit participation to a select group of management or highly compensated employees—the "top-hat group" (see chapter 8 and Qs 2:2, 2:17, 2:32, 2:169, 8:1, 8:3).

Example 2. The Moose Society has 1,500 members. To handle its clerical requirements, it hires 15 employees. There are no life, sick, accident, or other benefits. Moose is a society operating under the lodge system. All of its net earnings are devoted exclusively to literary and fraternal purposes. Moose may establish a 457(b) plan for the top-hat group because it is an organization exempt from tax under Code Section 501(c)(10).

Example 3. The County Water District is a governmental entity. It may establish a 457(b) plan covering *all* of its employees, without regard to the top-hat exemption.

Example 4. A rural electric cooperative establishes a 457(b) plan. Because the organization is not exempt from tax under Code Section 501(c)(3), it may not establish a plan under Code Section 403(b). It may establish a 457(b) plan because it is exempt from tax under Code Section 501(c)(4), (c)(6), or (c)(12).

Q 2:4   What is a state?

An eligible 457(b) plan can be established and maintained by a state. For this purpose, the term *state* includes

- The 50 states of the United States and the District of Columbia;
- A political subdivision of a state; and
- Any agency or instrumentality of a state or political subdivision of a state (other than a governmental unit).

Ineligible plans are rarely adopted by a state. In most states, state enabling statutes do not authorize the creation of an ineligible plan.

Q 2:5   What is a political subdivision; what is an agency?

For tax purposes, a political subdivision includes an instrumentality of

- A state;
- One or more political subdivisions of a state; or
- A state and one or more of its political subdivisions.

[I.R.C. § 3121(j)(4)(C)]

Agencies and instrumentalities are entities formed by a state or by a political subdivision thereof.

Several letter rulings by the IRS considered factors contained in revenue rulings to decide whether an entity was an instrumentality of a state or political subdivision. In Private Letter Ruling 9540057, the IRS used the factors contained in Revenue Ruling 65-196 [1965-2 C.B. 388] as the basis for determining whether an organization was an instrumentality of a state or a political subdivision:

1. Whether the organization is used for a governmental purpose and performs a governmental function;
2. Whether performance of the organization's function is on behalf of one or more states or political subdivisions;
3. Whether any private interests are involved or whether the states or the political subdivisions involved have the powers and interest of an owner;
4. Whether control and supervision of the organization are vested in one or more public authorities;
5. Whether express or implied statutory or other authority is necessary or exists for the creation and use of the organization; and
6. The degree of the organization's financial autonomy and the source of its operating funds.

In its ruling the IRS stated:

> The Corporation was established as a private corporation with full corporate powers and is operated under the direction of a board. New members are elected by members of the Board. The City provides only

one third of the funding of the Corporation. Although its performance in the operation of its contract is subject to review by the City, such review appears to be no more than what is typical with respect to an independent contract to perform services for another entity and such contract constitutes only a third of the work of the Corporation. The Corporation also provides extensive services other than public health nursing and receives private funds and other funds for the performance of those services.

The IRS ruled that the corporation was not a wholly owned instrumentality of the state or of any political subdivision of the state. Thus, the corporation would not be eligible to establish an eligible plan under Code Section 457(b), and any plan adopted by the corporation would not be subject to the rules of Code Section 457(f) because the employer was not an eligible employer.

In Private Letter Ruling 9046042, the IRS considered the factors in Revenue Ruling 89-49 [1989-1 C.B. 117] in determining whether an organization was an instrumentality of a state or a political subdivision. In that ruling the IRS stated: "One of the most important factors to be considered is the degree of governmental control over the organization's everyday operations." Other factors cited in Revenue Ruling 89-49 include the following:

1. Whether there is specific legislation creating the organization;
2. The source of funds of the organization;
3. The manner in which the organization's trustees or operating board is selected; and
4. Whether the applicable governmental unit considers the employees of the organization to be employees of the applicable governmental unit.

Revenue Ruling 89-49 warns that, although all of these factors are considered in determining whether an organization is an agency of the government, the mere satisfaction of one or all of the factors is not necessarily determinative. In this ruling the IRS stated:

> The Board was established and authorized under specific state legislation to create public corporations to provide mental health services in the public interest. The Board receives the bulk of its operating revenue from governmental sources. The board of directors of the Board consists solely of appointees from each of the members of Municipalities. The members of the Board directly govern the Board's day to day operations. Finally, the State treats employees of the Board similarly to governmental employees for several purposes that affect the employees' compensation and benefits. The Board's employees are permitted to participate in the state employees' retirement system. Certain of the Board's employees are also considered public officials for purposes of the State's code of ethics.

The IRS ruled that the board qualified as an instrumentality of a state or a political subdivision thereof for purposes of Code Section 457(b).

In Private Letter Ruling 8946019, a public school system was found to be an agency of a state. In that ruling, the IRS stated: "The Board is a public body, corporate politic, created and existing by virtue of an Act of the State Legislature for the purpose of providing higher education within the State. The government, control and management of the System are vested in the Board, which operates institutions of higher learning throughout the State."

Even though the organization in question may not, depending on the facts, be an agency or instrumentality of a state, if it is a tax-exempt organization, it will be subject to the limits of Code Section 457.

Church and Church-Related Employers

Q 2:6   What types of church and church-related employers are not subject to Code Section 457?

An eligible employer does not include a church or "qualified church-controlled organization"; however, many church-related hospitals, colleges, and universities are eligible to establish 457 plans (see Q 6:8).

Church plans and exceptions are more fully discussed in chapter 6. (See also appendix G.)

Q 2:7   What is a church?

The term *church* means a church, a convention or association of churches, or an elementary or secondary school that is controlled, operated, or principally supported by a church or by a convention or association of churches. [I.R.C. § 3121(w)(3)(A)]

Q 2:8   What is a qualified church-controlled organization?

The term *qualified church-controlled organization* means any church-controlled tax-exempt organization described in Code Section 501(c)(3), other than an organization that (1) offers goods, services, or facilities for sale, other than on an incidental basis, to the general public, other than goods, services, or facilities that are sold at a nominal charge that is substantially less than the cost of providing such goods, services, or facilities; and (2) normally receives more than 25 percent of its support from either governmental sources or receipts from admissions, sales of merchandise, performance of services, or furnishing of facilities, in activities that are not unrelated trades or businesses, or both. [I.R.C. § 3121(w)(3)(B)]

Thus, the church exemption from the rules of Code Section 457 does not extend to entities that generally provide goods, services, or facilities to the general public and do not rely on internal church support. Such entities typically include many church-related hospitals, colleges and universities, and nursing homes, as well as charities that may rely heavily on government grants.

Example. A nonqualified deferred compensation plan can be set up by a synagogue for its rabbi, or by a church for its minister, without the need for compliance with the requirements of Code Section 457. Instead, the tax rules applicable to nonqualified deferred compensation plans of for-profit employers will apply. The synagogue or church may find it more advantageous, however, to set up a 403(b)(9) church retirement income account rather than a traditional nonqualified plan.

Rural Cooperatives

Q 2:9 What is a rural cooperative?

In general, the term *rural cooperative* means any organization that is exempt from tax under the Code or is a state or local government or political subdivision thereof (or an agency or instrumentality thereof) and that is engaged primarily in providing electric service either to the public or on a mutual or cooperative basis. [I.R.C. § 401(k)(7)(B)]

Q 2:10 What types of plans can a rural cooperative establish?

Cooperatives may provide several types of deferred compensation or retirement benefits for their employees. These include qualified plans and eligible and ineligible deferred compensation plans under Code Section 457. [T.D. 8836 (Sept. 23, 1982); Treas. Reg. § 1.457-2(e), (m)]

Note. Because a cooperative is neither exempt from tax under Code Section 501(c)(3) nor an educational institution of a state or local government, it cannot maintain a 403(b) annuity plan. [I.R.C. § 403(b)(1)] Any plan of a cooperative purporting to be a 403(b) plan would probably consist of either nonqualified annuity contracts or taxable custodial accounts or trusts, and would be a funded, nonqualified plan. [Ann. 96-24, 1996-16 I.R.B. 30]

Plans Subject to Code Section 457

Q 2:11 What types of plans are subject to Code Section 457?

In general, Code Section 457 applies to any type of deferred compensation agreement, plan, or arrangement between an eligible employer and an individual who performs services for such an entity. When Code Section 457 was enacted in 1978, it contained grandfather protection for certain plans (see Q 2:17).

Q 2:12 Are elective and nonelective plans subject to Code Section 457?

Yes. It does not matter whether the deferred compensation program is elective or nonelective in nature [I.R.C. § 457(e); IRS Notice 87-13, 1987-1 C.B. 432]; however, nonelective deferred compensation plans are subject to the provisions of Code Section 457 only for taxable years of the employer beginning after 1987. [IRS Notice 88-8, 1988-1 C.B. 477; see also IRS Notice 88-68, 1988-1 C.B. 556]

Q 2:13   What types of plans are excluded from Code Section 457?

Code Section 457 does not apply to the following types of plans:

1. A qualified pension, profit sharing, or stock bonus plan that includes a trust that is exempt from tax. [I.R.C. §§ 401(a), 457(f)(2)(A), 501(a)]
2. A qualified annuity plan. [I.R.C. §§ 403(a), 457(f)(2)(B)]
3. A tax-sheltered mutual fund custodial account. [I.R.C. §§ 403(b)(7), 457(f)(2)(B)]
4. A plan that consists of a transfer of property (other than money) described in Code Section 83 in connection with the performance of service. [I.R.C. § 457(f)(2)(C); Treas. Reg. § 1.457-11(d)]
5. An individual retirement account or annuity (IRA). [I.R.C. § 408(d)]
6. A nonqualified employer trust where the participant is subject to tax under Code Section 402(b). In general, this is a funded trust or portion of a funded trust that is not exempt from tax under Code Section 501(a). Under Code Section 402(b), participants generally are subject to tax when there is no longer a substantial risk of forfeiture. [I.R.C. §§ 402(b)(1), 457(f)(2)(D)]
7. A qualified governmental excess benefit arrangement providing benefits in excess of the limitations of Code Section 415. [I.R.C. §§ 457(e)(14), 415(m)(3)]

Contributions under some of these plans may have an effect on, or be affected by, contributions to an eligible 457 plan (see Qs 2:114, 2:115).

Code Section 457 does not apply to the following types of arrangements, which, if bona fide, do not provide for deferred compensation:

1. Vacation leave plans.
2. Sabbatical leave plans.
3. Sick leave pay plans.
4. Compensatory time pay plans.
5. Severance pay plans (see chapter 12).
6. Disability pay plans.
7. Death benefit plans. (Split dollar plans, depending on how structured, have historically been viewed as providing a death benefit rather than deferred compensation. [Rev. Rul. 64-326, 1964-2 C.B. 11] The IRS, however, has for some time been scrutinizing such plans (see Q 11:16). [TAM 9604001; see also "IRS Eyes COLI Policies Along with Split Dollar Insurance Arrangements," 70 *Tax Notes* 250 (Jan. 15, 1996)] It has recently issued additional guidance on their taxation. [See IRS Notice 2002-59, 36 I.R.B. 481; Notice 2002-8, 2002-4 I.R.B. 1])
8. Length of service award plans to volunteers.
9. Nonelective deferred compensation plans for all nonemployees, but only if all individuals who have satisfied any initial service requirement with the same relationship to the eligible employer are covered under

the same plan with no individual variations or options under the plan. For example, a hospital could maintain a nonelective arrangement that covers the doctors who have independent contractor agreements with the hospital. [Treas. Reg. § 1.457-2(k)(1)] Note that this exception does not permit independent contractors to enter into elective nonqualified deferred compensation arrangements, which are far more popular vehicles, without being subject to the constraints of Code Section 457.

For the plan or arrangement to be bona fide, it must not be merely a device to provide deferred compensation. There are no court decisions that elaborate on the meaning of bona fide in this context.

The foregoing exceptions are more fully discussed in chapters 11 and 12. [I.R.C. § 457(e)(11), (12); see IRS Notice 88-8, 1988-1 C.B. 477]

Q 2:14   Can a SARSEP be established by a tax-exempt or governmental employer?

No. [I.R.C. § 408(k)(6)(E)]

Q 2:15   Can a SEP or SIMPLE be established by a tax-exempt organization or governmental employer?

Yes. Unlike SARSEPs (salary reduction simplified employee pension plans), SEPs (simplified employee pensions) and SIMPLEs (savings incentive match plans for employees) are not expressly prohibited from being established by governmental employers or tax-exempt organizations. [I.R.C. § 408(k)(6)(E); IRS Notice 97-6, Q&A B-4, 1997-2 I.R.B. 26; P.L.R. 8833047, 8824019] Code Section 457(f) applies only to a "plan of an eligible employer providing for a deferral of compensation, if such plan is not an eligible deferred compensation plan." Apparently, a SEP or SIMPLE (or associated IRA) is not considered to defer compensation for this purpose. In the case of a SEP or SIMPLE, fully vested contributions are made to an IRA that is exempt from tax under Code Section 501(a). An IRA participant has immediate access to the amounts contributed and can draw on the funds at any time. If taxation is not accelerated under Code Section 457(f), some other section of the Code has to apply to include the amount in the participant's gross income. Code Section 408 does not apply. Code Section 402(h) applies to *distributions* from IRAs. Code Section 83 applies to property, other than cash, received in connection with the performance of services. Code Section 402(b)(relating to a nonexempt trust) does not apply to a trust exempt from tax under Code Section 501(a). The definition of *compensation* under IRS Form 5305-SIMPLE states: "Compensation also includes the salary reduction contributions made under this plan and, if applicable, compensation deferred under a section 457 plan. In determining the employee's compensation for prior years, the employee's elective deferrals under a 401(k) plan, a SARSEP, or a section 403(b) annuity contract are also included in the employee's compensation." Form 5305-SIMPLE does not prohibit a tax-exempt organization or a governmental employer from establishing and maintaining a SIMPLE. [IRS Form 5305-SIMPLE, Instructions for the Employer; Which Employers May Establish and Maintain a SIMPLE Plan, at 4]

In Letter Ruling 8824019, the IRS stated:

> Company M, a tax exempt organization, entered into a collective bargaining agreement on July 1, 1984. In a revised addendum to this collective bargaining agreement, dated March 13, 1985, Company M agreed to contribute. On April 1, 1987, Company M adopted a Simplified Employee Pension–Individual Retirement Account Contribution Agreement (SEP-IRA Agreement), effective as of December 31, 1986.

The IRS concluded that the contribution formula (80 cents per hour) was not in and of itself discriminatory. No other issues were discussed.

Although this was not stated in the letter ruling, the IRS may have used one of the grandfather exceptions to permit the SEP arrangement for the unionized employees without the plan's being subject to Code Section 457(f). (See Q 2:17 for the types of plans that are grandfathered.) It is unlikely that any of the grandfather exceptions would have applied in Private Letter Ruling 8833047. In that ruling, a nonprofit, tax-exempt organization proposed to establish a custodial account program that satisfied the requirements of Code Section 403(b)(7). That plan was in addition to a model SEP plan that was being maintained for the benefit of the organization's employees. Thus, under this later ruling a SEP clearly can be established by a tax-exempt organization.

A SIMPLE can be established by a tax-exempt organization that does not maintain a "qualified plan." [IRS Notice 97-6, Q&A B-4, 1997-2 I.R.B. 26] The exclusive plan requirement (made applicable to SIMPLEs by Code Section 408(p)(2)(D)) would not apply to a SIMPLE that was maintained by an employer that also maintained a plan subject to Code Section 457. [I.R.C. § 408(p)(2)(D)(ii)] A 457 plan is not a program treated as a "qualified plan" for purposes of the exclusive plan requirement (Lesser 1997). [I.R.C. § 219(g)(5)]

Q 2:16 May a governmental employer adopt a SIMPLE IRA or SIMPLE 401(k)?

A governmental employer may not maintain a SIMPLE in the form of a 401(k) plan [I.R.C. § 401(k)(4)(B)(ii)] but may adopt a SIMPLE in the form of an IRA (see Q 2:15).

Q 2:17 What types of plans are grandfathered?

Grandfather protection was extended to several types of plans. A plan that is grandfathered is not subject to Code Section 457. Such plans are governed by other Code sections as long as they remain grandfathered. Grandfather rules apply only to individuals who were covered under the plan agreement on

August 16, 1986, and not to new employees or participants. The following types of plans or deferrals received grandfather protection:

Prior-year deferrals under plans in writing on August 16, 1986. These are amounts deferred under a deferred compensation plan of a nongovernmental tax-exempt organization in writing on August 16, 1986, that are attributable to compensation that would have been paid or made available in taxable years of an individual beginning before January 1, 1987.

Future deferrals under plans in writing on August 16, 1986. These are deferrals of compensation to plans in writing on August 16, 1986, that would have been paid or made available in the taxable year of an individual beginning after 1986, to the extent that such deferrals were fixed under a written plan on August 16, 1986, where the written agreement specified a fixed amount or fixed formula for determining the amount of deferral. Any modification of the agreement's fixed amount or formula will cause the plan to be ineligible for grandfather protection. [IRS Notice 87-13, Q&A 28, 1987-1 C.B. 432, 445; see also P.L.R. 9538021] The right to elect a joint and survivor annuity does not affect the fixed status of the agreement for purposes of the grandfather rule. [P.L.R. 9146031]

Grandfathered amounts are taken into account for applying Code Section 457 to other amounts deferred under any other deferred compensation plan (see Qs 2:114, 2:115). [See S. Rep. No. 100-445, at 148 (1988)]

Example. Five individuals joined a Section 501(c)(6) trade association prior to August 1986 under a written agreement constituting a top-hat plan that mandated that the association defer 10 percent of their compensation each year. This plan, and the resulting deferral rate, will remain in effect for the five individuals concurrently with the eligible plan adopted by the association for the other employees in 1988. If the pre-August 1986 plan is modified to eliminate the fixed deferral requirement, at that time deferrals under the plan will become subject to Code Section 457.

Nonelective plans in existence on July 14, 1988. Because of some initial confusion over the applicability of Code Section 457 to nonelective as opposed to elective contributions, a grandfather rule was created for nonelective deferred compensation plans in existence on July 14, 1988. Amounts deferred under such an agreement after July 13, 1988 (which was a written agreement on July 14, 1988), are not subject to Code Section 457. The agreement must provide either for deferral of a fixed amount for each taxable year covered by the agreement or for deferral of an amount determined under a fixed formula and must cover the individual for whom the agreement was made. Grandfathered amounts are taken into account in applying Code Section 457 to other amounts deferred under any eligible 457(b) plan (see Q 2:18). [TAMRA § 6064(b)(3)] Code Section 457 applies to any tax year that ends after the effective date of a written pre-1989 agreement that increases a benefit by modifying either the fixed amount or the formula. Thus, a reduction of a fixed amount or formula amount is permissible.

Nonelective collectively bargained plans in existence on December 31, 1987. Nonelective deferred compensation under a plan in existence on December 31, 1987, and maintained pursuant to one or more collective bargaining agreements is exempt from the limitations of Code Section 457 until the earlier of (1) the effective date of any material modification to the plan after December 31, 1987, or (2) January 1, 1991.

If such a plan is modified to reflect changes in the benefit formula or expands the class of participants included in the pre-1988 plan definition, Code Section 457 applies. Such modifications do not include arrangements under which qualified plans with offsetting nonelective plan benefits are modified and the nonelective deferred compensation plan is modified to provide benefits that the qualified plan would have provided before its modification. If on December 31, 1987, participation extended to a broad group of nonunion employees on the same terms as participation was permitted for union employees, the transitional rules will continue to apply as long as the union employees constitute at least 25 percent of total participants. [TAMRA § 6064(d)(2); IRS Notice 88-98, 1988-2 C.B. 421] To date, regulations providing for the cutoff date of January 1, 1991, have not been promulgated; however, Notice 88-98, which called for the cutoff date to be provided in the yet unissued regulations, was an administrative pronouncement and can be relied on to the same extent as a revenue ruling or revenue procedure. [See Treas. Reg. § 1.6661-3(b)(2); see also Treas. Reg. § 1.457-2(k)(4)]

Qualified state judicial plans. Qualified state judicial plans generally are not subject to Code Section 457. Such a plan is qualified if:

1. The plan has been continuously in existence since December 31, 1978;
2. All judges eligible to benefit under the plan are required to participate and to contribute the same fixed percentage of their basic or regular rate of compensation;
3. A judge's retirement benefit under the plan is a percentage of the compensation of judges of the state holding similar positions;
4. Benefits for any year do not exceed the benefit limitation for qualified defined benefit plans (generally, the lesser of $160,000 (for 2002; $140,000 for 2001) or 100 percent of the participant's average compensation over the three highest-paid years) [I.R.C. § 415(b), (d)]; and
5. No judge can have an option concerning contributions or benefits that, if exercised, would affect the amount of the participant's currently includible compensation.

[TEFRA § 252]

Q 2:18   How are grandfathered amounts taken into account in applying the Section 457(b) deferral limit?

In applying the deferral ceiling under Code Section 457(b) (increased by EGTRRA, but, generally, $8,500 in 2001, $8,000 in 1998–2000, and $7,500 before 1998) to a deferral that is not grandfathered (e.g., deferrals under a new 457 plan), the grandfathered amounts are taken into account by reducing the limit otherwise determined.

Q 2:19   What are the tax consequences under a grandfathered plan?

The federal income tax consequences of a plan that remains grandfathered are contained in Code Sections 402(b), 403(c), and 83, which require that a participant recognize income when amounts are paid to a trust or insurance company unless there is a substantial risk of forfeiture as defined in Code Section 83(c)(1) and the participant's interest is nontransferable.

Q 2:20   Does Code Section 457 apply to a state's regular retirement system?

Yes. Originally, the treatment provided for eligible and ineligible plans apparently extended only to plans that provided an option to defer compensation and was inapplicable to a state's regular retirement system (whether or not such a plan was a tax-qualified plan) because such systems generally do not provide an option to defer compensation. [Rev. Act of 1978 § 131, H.R. Rep.] However, Code Section 457 was extended to nonelective plans by the Tax Reform Act of 1986 (TRA 1986). [See IRS Notice 87-13, 1987-1 C.B. 432]

Eligible 457(b) Plans

Q 2:21   What is an eligible 457(b) plan?

An eligible 457(b) plan is a deferred compensation plan that is maintained by an eligible employer—a state or local government or a nonchurch, nongovernmental tax-exempt organization—and that meets statutory requirements. Additional features that are not inconsistent with the statutory requirements are permitted. Thus, in addition to mandatory features, an eligible 457(b) plan may (but is not required to) include permissive features (see Qs 2:22, 2:24).

If a plan of an eligible employer does not meet the statutory requirements, it is treated as an ineligible plan, and different rules may apply. [I.R.C. § 457(f)]

Q 2:22   What are the mandatory features of an eligible 457(b) plan?

Following are the mandatory features of an eligible 457(b) plan (in some cases, a mandatory feature can be modified by the use of a permissive feature):

1. The sponsor must be a state or a political subdivision or an agency or instrumentality of a state or a political subdivision, or a nonchurch, nongovernmental tax-exempt organization.
2. The plan must provide that, in general, compensation is to be deferred for any calendar month only if an agreement providing for that deferral has been entered into before the first day of the month; however, a plan can provide special rules for newly hired employees and current employees who become eligible to participate (see Qs 2:66, 2:67).

3. The plan document must specify a deferral ceiling. For 2001, this is the lesser of (1) $8,500 (as indexed; the limit was $8,000 in 1998–2000 and $7,500 before 1998) or (2) 33 percent of includible compensation. For 2002 and thereafter, the deferral ceiling is the lesser of (1) $11,000 (in 2002), increasing by $1,000 per year until the dollar limit is $15,000 in 2006, or (2) 100 percent of includible compensation. However, a catch-up provision can be included to increase the deferral ceiling during the three-year period preceding normal retirement age. In the case of participants who are age 50 or older in taxable years beginning after 2001, a separate catch-up (if provided for in the plan) may be used (but not if in the same years the last-three-years catch-up is higher) (see Qs 1:14, 2:92). [Treas. Reg. § 1.457-4(c)(2)(ii)] The deferral ceiling must be stated in the plan document. [I.R.C. § 457(b)(2); Treas. Reg. § 1.457-3(a)]

4. Except in the case of a 457(g) trust required or permitted to be adopted by a state or local government employer (see Q 2:38), plan assets must remain employer assets until distributed to the employee. The plan must provide that all amounts of compensation deferred under the plan, all property and rights purchased with such amounts, and all income attributable to such amounts, property, or rights shall remain (until made available to the participant or other beneficiary) solely the property and rights of the employer (without being restricted to the provision of benefits under the plan), subject only to the claims of the employer's general creditors. Eligible 457 plans created after August 20, 1996, that are sponsored by a governmental entity must be held "in trust for the exclusive benefit of participants and their beneficiaries." Existing eligible 457(b) plans sponsored by a governmental entity had to comply with this trust requirement by 1999 (see Qs 2:37–2:40).

5. For years before 2002, an eligible plan of either a governmental or a tax-exempt employer must specify a fixed or determinable time of payment by reference to the occurrence of an event (e.g., retirement) that triggers the individual's right to receive or commence receiving amounts deferred under the plan (see Qs 2:192, 2:206); however, the participant can be given the right to elect (determine) when payments commence and the form in which they are to be paid, as long as no distribution can become payable until after the election period expires. The participant's election is irrevocable; however, the Small Business Job Protection Act of 1996 (SBJPA) amended the Code to allow for one additional distribution election to be made without causing the amount subject to the election to be treated as made available (see Q 2:72). For years after 2001, in the case of eligible plans of governmental employers only, distributions will be taxable when paid, and these irrevocable election requirements (see Q 2:72) will no longer apply.

6. Deferred compensation (which includes investment earnings on contributions or deferrals) must be payable to the participant only on attainment of age 70½, separation from service (after 2001, severance of employment), and the occurrence of unforeseeable emergencies (see Qs 2:72,

2:196, 2:198). A plan can provide that no distribution will be made until after a participant separates from the service of the employer (after 2001, severance of employment). Special rules apply upon the termination of an eligible plan (see Q 2:250).

7. Payment to a participant of deferred compensation and earnings on it must commence by the later of (1) April 1 of the calendar year following the calendar year in which the participant attains age 70½ or (2) April 1 following the calendar year in which the employee retires, provided the employee is not a 5 percent owner (which does not occur often in the case of an eligible employer).

In addition:

1. Benefit payments must meet the requirements of Code Section 401(a)(9);
2. Benefit payments must be made at least once each calendar year and must not substantially increase; and
3. For years before 2002, in the case of distributions that commence prior to death, the entire amount payable with respect to a participant must be paid during a period not to exceed 15 years or the life expectancy of the surviving spouse if the spouse is the beneficiary.

Note. EGTRRA repealed the special minimum distribution rules that applied only to Code Section 457(b) plans (items 2 and 3 above). Therefore, after 2001, an eligible plan need only satisfy the minimum distribution rules applicable to qualified plans under Code Section 401(a)(9). [I.R.C. § 457(d)(2)]

Before 1997, only governmental and church plans were permitted to delay payout until actual retirement even if retirement occurred after age 70½. [I.R.C. § 401(a)(9)(C)(i)]

Distribution requirements are discussed more fully in chapter 3.

Q 2:23   Must a 457(b) plan be in writing?

Prior to the 2002 proposed regulations, it was unclear whether a 457(b) plan had to be in writing. The final regulations make clear that a 457(b) plan must be in writing and comply with the regulations in form and operation. [Treas. Reg. § 1.457-3(a)] However, there is still some uncertainty as to what provisions must be in a plan.

Q 2:24   What permissive features can be included in an eligible 457(b) plan?

Eligible 457 plans can include the following permissive features:

1. An exception to the rule that compensation is to be deferred for any calendar month only if an agreement providing for such deferral has been entered into before the first day of the month can be provided for

newly hired employees and current employees who become eligible to participate (see Qs 2:65–2:67).

2. Within limits, a participant can be given the right to elect (determine) when payments commence and the form in which they are to be paid. One additional distribution election can be allowed without causing the amount subject to the election to be treated as made available (see Q 2:72). In each case, a fixed or determinable time must be specified. For eligible plans of governmental employers, this fixed or determinable time rule will no longer apply after 2001.

3. A participant can be permitted to direct the investment of his or her compensation deferred under the plan. For many state and local government employer plans, participant-directed investment is required by state law (see Qs 2:70, 2:71).

4. Within limits, a participant can select his or her own normal retirement age.

5. A catch-up provision can be included to increase the deferral ceiling during the three-year period preceding normal retirement age (see Qs 2:100, 2:101) and in taxable years age 50 is attained (see Q 2:92). The deferral ceiling must be stated in the plan document.

6. A governmental employer may also permit special catch-up elections beginning with the year the participant attains age 50.

7. A plan-approved domestic relations order (PADRO) can be provided, to allow certain distributions to a spouse or former spouse (see Qs 2:221–2:227).

8. A plan can provide for payments to be made to participants on the occurrence of an unforeseeable emergency (see Q 2:198).

9. A plan can provide for benefits under $5,000 to be paid in a single sum (see Q 2:215).

10. If installment payments are made (or selected), the plan can provide for acceleration of payments (to the extent necessary) on the occurrence of an unforeseeable emergency (see Q 2:198).

11. A plan can permit the transfer of a participant's interest to another eligible plan (see Q 2:228).

12. A governmental plan that uses a 457(g) trust, custodial account, or annuity contract can provide for loans to participants (see Q 2:39).

13. A 457(g) plan trust can suspend loan repayments during any period in which the individual is performing service in the uniformed services (as defined in 38 U.S.C. Chapter 43), the Uniformed Services Employment and Reemployment Rights Act, known as USERRA) even if that individual's reemployment rights are not protected by law. [I.R.C. § 414(u)(4), (5)] Note that it is currently unclear whether, for those on military leave, the Soldiers and Sailors Civil Relief Act of 1940 may limit the interest rate on the loan to no more than 6 percent. [See Keller, Christine, "You've Heard of USERRA, But Have You Heard of SSCRA?," *RIA Pension and Benefits Week*, Dec. 17, 2001]

Inconsistent Administration

Q 2:25   Can an ineligible employer establish an eligible 457(b) plan?

No. Not only must an eligible plan meet special statutory requirements, but in addition the employer that maintains the plan must be an eligible employer (one of the statutory requirements).

Q 2:26   Can an ineligible employer establish an ineligible 457 plan?

No. Only an eligible employer can have an ineligible plan under Code Section 457. [I.R.C. § 457(f)(1)] The tax rules applicable to nonqualified deferred compensation plans of for-profit employers generally are more generous than those of Code Section 457.

Q 2:27   What if an eligible 457(b) plan is administered in a manner inconsistent with the requirements of Code Section 457(b)?

An eligible 457(b) plan that is consistent with Code Section 457(b) as to form but is administered in a manner inconsistent with the requirements of that section may lose its status as an eligible plan. [I.R.C. § 457(b); Treas. Reg. § 1.457-3(a)] When the plan loses its eligible status depends on whether the employer is a governmental employer.

Q 2:28   When does an eligible governmental 457(b) plan administered in a manner inconsistent with the requirements of Code Section 457(b) become an ineligible plan?

If the employer is a state or local government or an agency or instrumentality thereof, the plan does not become ineligible until the beginning of the first plan year beginning more than 180 days after notification by the Secretary of the Treasury of the inconsistent administration. This provision is referred to as the grace period. [Treas. Reg. § 1.457-9(a); TAM 199903032 (Oct. 2, 1998); P.L.R. 8946019, supplementing P.L.R. 8629012] In recent years, the IRS has issued favorable private letter rulings on governmental 457(b) plans that incorporate various correction mechanisms. If the plan does not correct the inconsistencies specified in the written notice before the end of that period, amounts subsequently deferred by participants will be includible in gross income when deferred, or if later, when no longer subject to a substantial risk of forfeiture. Amounts deferred before that date and earnings thereon continue to be treated as if the plan were an eligible plan. [Id.]

Q 2:29   What happens if the eligible governmental 457(b) plan corrects the inconsistency?

If the inconsistency is corrected before the first day of the first plan year beginning more than 180 days after notification by the Secretary of the Treasury of the inconsistent administration (see Q 2:28), the plan remains an eligible plan. [Treas. Reg. § 1.457-9(a)]

Q 2:30   When does an eligible nongovernmental 457(b) plan administered in a manner inconsistent with the requirements of Code Section 457(b) become an ineligible plan?

The grace period discussed in Q 2:28 does not apply to plans of nongovernmental tax-exempt entities. [Treas. Reg. § 1.457-9(a)] Thus, any failure appears to be immediate, absolute, and irrevocable. Thereafter, the plan is treated as an ineligible plan and is subject to the rules of Code Section 457(f). [See Treas. Reg. §§ 1.457-4(e)(3), 1.457-9(b), 1.457-11] Nearly all commentators agree that the statute and the legislative history of Code Section 457(b) provide no latitude for nongovernmental tax-exempt employers. [TRA 1986, H.R. Conf. Rep., at II-399 to -400] A carefully drafted plan, however, could avoid some of the problems associated with inconsistent administration (Brisendine 1996). More often than not, inconsistent administration is caused by excess contributions, especially when vesting schedules are used. Nonetheless, under EPCRS, 457(b) plans will be accepted for correction by the Employee Plans Division of the IRS on a provisional basis outside of that current correction program. [Rev. Proc. 2003-44, § 2.02, 2003-25 I.R.B. 1051]

The final regulations, however, have a more lenient rule and allow excess deferrals (with allocable net income) to be distributed not later than April 15 of the year following the year of the excess deferral. In such a case, the excess deferral is included in gross income in the year of the deferral, but the plan will continue to be treated as an eligible plan. [Treas. Reg. § 1.457-4(e)(3)]

Q 2:31   Can double taxation result when a plan becomes ineligible?

No. When an employee sets aside an amount under a plan and that amount is taxed to the employee under Code Section 83 (relating to the taxability of property received for services), the employee will not be taxed on that amount again if the plan becomes ineligible.

Example 1. Barbara formally assigns a portion of her vested eligible 457(b) plan account as security for a $500 loan. She must include the $500 in income because it is treated as being made available, even though the amount is not currently payable to her. [Rev. Act of 1978 § 131, H.R. Rep.]

Example 2. The facts are the same as those in Example 1, except that the plan becomes ineligible. The $500 is not subject to tax again.

Application of ERISA to 457 Plans

Q 2:32   Are 457 plans subject to ERISA?

Generally no. Governmental plans are not subject to ERISA. [ERISA § 4(b); P.L.R. 9145010]

Eligible and ineligible 457 plans of nongovernmental tax-exempt employers are nearly always established as top-hat plans to avoid having to comply with parts of ERISA. Establishing the top-hat plan exception and determining the top-hat group are discussed in chapter 8. (See Scialabba 1997; O'Meara and Anderson 1992.)

Who Can Participate in a 457(b) Plan?

Q 2:33   Who can participate in an eligible 457(b) plan?

Any individual who performs services for the employer may participate. Thus, an independent contractor may be covered. Special consideration may apply to a governmental employer (see Q 14:5). [P.L.R. 9809038] Eligible 457(b) plans should not permit participation by an independent contractor that is not a natural person because that person is not an individual. (For special rules that apply in determining when and if an independent contractor has separated from service, see Q 2:218.)

Q 2:34   Who is a participant?

The term *participant* means an individual who is eligible to defer compensation under the plan. [I.R.C. § 457(e)(3)] Plan provisions or employer policy may limit participation to certain employees. For example, the employer may impose an age and/or service condition or limit participation to a defined group of employees. Only those individuals who satisfy the plan's requirements for participation can be participants.

Q 2:35   Must an eligible 457(b) plan cover all employees?

No. Under the Code, the employer has complete discretion as to whom it will allow to participate.

Nongovernmental tax-exempt organizations and nonqualified church-controlled organizations (see Q 2:8) must limit participation to only a select group of management or highly compensated employees; otherwise, the plan will become subject to the ERISA requirement that the plan be formally funded. Code Section 457(b) requires that a 457 plan be unfunded. [I.R.C. § 457(b)(6), (g)] If there is broad-based participation, ERISA applies and the plan must be funded. In such a case, the funding requirements "will cause the plan to fail to satisfy section 457(b)(6)," which requires all nongovernmental and nonqualified church-controlled organization 457 plans to be unfunded. [IRS Notice 87-13, Q&A A-25, 1987-1 C.B. 432; see also Treas. Reg. § 1.457-8(b)]

Coverage requirements applicable to 457 plans are more fully discussed in chapters 6 and 8.

Q 2:36   May seasonal and part-time employees participate in an eligible 457(b) plan?

Yes; special rules apply to employees who are in a FICA alternative retirement system (see chapter 13).

Trust Requirements for Eligible Governmental Plans

Q 2:37   What were the 457(b) trust requirements prior to the Small Business Job Protection Act of 1996?

Before August 20, 1996, the use of a trust that protected plan assets from the claims of the employer's general creditors was prohibited. Until deferrals were made available to a plan participant, the amounts deferred, all property and rights purchased with such amounts, and all income attributable to such amounts, property, or rights had to remain solely the property and rights of the employer, subject only to the claims of the employer's general creditors. The SBJPA makes a substantial change to these rules, but the new trust rules affect only 457(b) plans of governmental employers.

Q 2:38   What is the trust requirement for eligible deferred compensation plans of state and local governments?

All amounts deferred under an eligible 457(b) plan maintained by a state or local government employer have to be held in trust for the exclusive benefit of employees. The trust is provided tax-exempt status. Amounts are not considered made available merely because they are held in a trust. (The use of a custodial account or annuity contract is discussed in Qs 2:43–2:50.)

Q 2:39   When does the trust requirement apply?

The new trust requirement is generally effective with respect to amounts held on or after August 20, 1996. For plans in existence on August 20, 1996, the trust requirement had to be satisfied by January 1, 1999.

Thus, deferrals prior to and after the date of enactment of the SBJPA (and earnings on them) had to be held in trust (or in a custodial account or annuity contract) by January 1, 1999. [I.R.C. § 457(g); SBJPA § 1448(a)]

Q 2:40   Can amounts held in trust (or in a custodial account or an annuity contract) be loaned to governmental plan participants or beneficiaries?

Yes. [Treas. Reg. §§ 1.457-6(f), -7(b)(3)] Although there was originally some question about this [IRS Continuing Professional Education Exempt Organizations Technical Instruction Program for FY 1998, § I, at 179], according to the SBJPA conference report, amounts held in a 457(g) trust (or in a custodial account or annuity contract) can be loaned to plan participants or beneficiaries pursuant to rules applicable to loans from qualified plans under Code Section 72(p). [H.R. Conf. Rep., SBJPA; Staff of Joint Comm. on Taxation, *General Explanation of Tax Legislation Enacted in the 104th Congress* 163 (the "Blue Book")]

Furthermore, Code Section 72(p)(4)(A)(ii) expressly authorizes such loans for governmental plans, using a definition of qualified employer plan that would include governmental 457(b) plans.

Q 2:41   Is a 457(g) plan trust required to permit loans?

No. Loan provisions are permissive. [H.R. Conf. Rep., SBJPA] A loan from a 457(g) plan trust is treated as a distribution unless the loan generally:

1. Does not exceed certain limits (generally, the lesser of $50,000 or half of the participant's vested plan account);
2. Must be repaid within five years, except for a loan used to acquire any dwelling unit that within a reasonable time is to be used (determined at the time the loan is made) as the principal residence of the participant;
3. Must be amortized on a substantially level basis with payments at least quarterly;
4. Is a bona fide loan that the borrower has a good-faith intention to repay; and
5. Must also satisfy the exclusive benefit requirement. Thus, a bona fide loan must bear a reasonable rate of interest. [See Treas. Reg. § 1.457-6(f)(2)]

The IRS issued regulations under Code Section 72(p) generally effective for loans made after December 31, 2001. Code Section 72(p) generally provides that amounts received as a loan from a qualified employer plan by a participant or beneficiary are treated as received as a distribution except to the extent that certain conditions relating to the loan terms, repayment schedule, and amount are satisfied.

The regulations require that the loan be evidenced by an enforceable agreement, set forth in writing or in another form approved by the IRS, that includes terms that satisfy the statutory requirements. The agreement can be set forth in more than one document.

If the loan fails to satisfy the repayment requirements or the enforceable agreement requirement when made or at a later date, the proposed regulations provide that the balance then due under the loan will be treated as a plan distribution. If the amount of the loan exceeds the statutory limit on the amount permitted to be loaned, the excess is a deemed distribution.

The loan must be repaid within five years unless it is used to acquire a dwelling that is used as the participant's principal residence within a reasonable time. The regulation provides that the term *principal residence* has the same meaning as it does under Code Section 1034 (relating to the rollover of gain on the sale of a principal residence). The tracing rules established under Code Section 163(h)(3)(B) are used to determine whether the exception to the five-year rule applies.

The regulations permit loan repayments to be suspended during a leave of absence of up to one year if the participant's pay from the employer is insufficient to service the debt, as long as the loan is repaid by the latest date permitted under Code Section 72(p)(2)(B).

Loan amounts treated as distributions are subject to the normal rules of Code Section 72 if the participant's interest in the plan includes after-tax contributions.

Q 2:42   Do loans from multiple 457(b) plans and other plans have to be aggregated for the loan limits?

If the plans are maintained by the same employer, yes. [I.R.C. § 72(p)(2)(D)(ii), (p)(4)(A)(ii)] The controlled group rules apply for this purpose. [I.R.C. § 72(p)(2)(B)(i)]

Q 2:43   Do the income inclusion rules of Code Sections 83 and 402(b) apply in the case of a 457(g) plan trust (or custodial account or annuity contract)?

No. The income inclusion rules found in Code Sections 83 and 402(b) do not apply to amounts deferred under a Section 457 plan (and the income thereon) merely because such amounts are contributed to the trust (or custodial account or annuity contract). [I.R.C. § 457(g)(2)(B)]

Q 2:44   Are all annuity contracts and custodial accounts treated as 457(g) trusts?

No. To be treated as a 457(g) trust, an annuity contract or custodial account must be held for the exclusive benefit of the participant (or, in the event of the participant's death, the participant's beneficiary). [IRS Notice 98-8, § VI, 1998-4 I.R.B. 6] In addition, the annuity contract or custodial account must be part of a plan that satisfies the statutory requirements of Code Section 457(b). Code Section 457(g)(3) applies rules "similar to the rules under section 401(f)" that relate to custodial accounts and annuity contracts held in qualified plans. The assets in a custodial account must be held by a bank or a qualified nonbank custodian (see Q 2:188). A life, health, accident, property, casualty, or liability insurance contract does not qualify as an annuity contract for this purpose. [IRS Notice 98-8, § VII; see also Treas. Reg. § 1.457-8(a)(3)(iii)]

Q 2:45 Who should be the owner of an annuity contract under a governmental 457(b) plan?

The IRS has not given guidance on the Section 457(g) annuity requirements. Generally, the employer (or a trust) should be the owner, but by analogy to the rules for 401(a) annuities, it may be permissible to have the participant as owner of a contract or certificate on distribution, provided the contract or certificate otherwise complies with the Section 457(b) requirements. [See Treas. Reg. § 1.402(a)-1(a)(2)]

Q 2:46 Does a custodial account or annuity contract offer the same protection as a trust?

Some practitioners have raised potential creditor protection issues concerning custodial accounts and annuity contracts not held in trust. Custodial accounts may be subject to the claims of an employer's general creditors under applicable state law. A 457(g) trust (or custodial account or annuity contract) is not subject to ERISA protections. [ERISA § 4(b)] The burden of any exemption would fall on the person who wishes to defend the plan from creditors. The use of a trust under state law may offer greater protection and more certainty that assets will be protected from creditors.

It is not known whether restrictions contained in the annuity contract or custodial account are legally enforceable.

If a judgment against a participant is exercised against a participant's interest in an annuity contract, such an order would, in effect, be executed against a third party that was not a party to the order of attachment. The employer may have to incur legal costs in protecting the plan assets.

Q 2:47 How are gains from the disposition of property treated in a 457(g) trust?

Gains from the disposition of property are treated as income attributable to that property. All income and gains on such property must remain solely the property and rights of the trust until made available to a participant, former participant, or beneficiary under the plan.

Q 2:48 Can 457 plan assets be combined in a group trust with the assets of a qualified plan?

Yes, but only for governmental 457 plans. The trust may not be able to claim an exemption from securities laws if 457 plan assets of a nongovernmental employer are combined in a group trust with qualified plan assets (see Qs 10:5, 10:10, 10:11).

Q 2:49   Are custodial accounts and annuity contracts treated as trusts for the purpose of the exclusive benefit requirement applicable to eligible governmental 457(b) plans?

Custodial accounts and contracts described in Code Section 401(f) are treated as 457(g) trusts under rules similar to the rules under Code Section 401(f). Under that section, a custodial account, an annuity contract, or a contract (other than a life, health or accident, property, casualty, or liability insurance contract) issued by an insurance company qualified to do business in a state is treated as a trust if (1) the custodial account or contract would, except for the fact that it is not a trust, constitute a trust, and (2) in the case of a custodial account, the assets are held by a bank (as defined in Code Section 408(n)) or other approved entity (see Q 2:188).

Any such arrangement must, by its terms, comply with the requirements of Code Section 457(b). In addition, any such account or contract must satisfy the exclusive benefit requirement, that is, be protected from the employers' creditors. [IRS Notice 98-8, § VI, 1998-4 I.R.B. 6] Creditor protection is more fully discussed in chapter 9.

[See also Treas. Reg. § 1.457-8(a)(3)]

When an annuity contract is purchased under a 457(g) trust, the insurer frequently will issue a certificate on which the participant is named the owner of the contract. Where the form and election of payout have met the requirements of Code Section 457(b) and the owner cannot do anything to modify or accelerate payment, the issuance of the certificate should not cause an amount to be considered "made available" (see Qs 2:72, 2:128, 2:192, 2:212).

Q 2:50   Who is treated as the trustee of such an account or contract?

For federal income tax purposes, the person holding the assets of such an account or holding such a contract will be treated as the trustee thereof. [I.R.C. §§ 401(f), 457(g)(3); see also Q 2:45] In the case of an insurance contract, this would seem to be the insurer.

Q 2:51   Are contributions to a 457(g) plan trust irrevocable?

Yes, if the rules applicable to 401(a) trusts are applied by analogy. There are three possible situations in which plan contributions may be returned to an employer:

1. *Contributions made by a mistake in fact.* If a contribution (or any portion of a contribution) is made by the employer by a good-faith mistake

of fact, it may be returned to the employer. The plan trust would have to provide for mistaken contributions to be returned to the employer. ERISA Section 403, regarding the establishment of trusts, does not apply to a 457(g) trust.

2. *Termination of the plan trust.* The plan's trustee should have the power to terminate the trust if every investment is closed or terminated or settled, there are no successor investments, and there is no other trust asset.

3. *Court order.* The plan may provide that it may be terminated at any time upon court order by any appropriate court of the state or of the United States. On such termination, the trust investments should be transferred or used as instructed by the court.

Notwithstanding the foregoing, the IRS has issued favorable private letter rulings on governmental 457(b) plan documents that incorporated various correction mechanisms providing for corrective distributions to employers and employees, but the rulings did not expressly discuss the point.

The new Treasury Regulations also require governmental 457(b) plans to distribute any excess deferrals as soon as administratively practicable after the plan determines that the amount is an excess deferral. [Treas. Reg. § 1.457-4(e)(2)]

Compensation Limits for 457(b) Plans

Q 2:52   On what are 457(b) plan contribution limits based?

The contribution limitations applicable to an eligible plan under Code Section 457(b) are based on "includible compensation." [I.R.C. § 457(e)(5); Treas. Reg. § 1.457-4(c)] Before 2002, in operation and as a practical matter, gross compensation was often used, and the statutory percentage was lowered to accommodate the use of a higher (but known) amount (see Q 2:54).

Q 2:53   What is includible compensation?

Before 2002, the term *includible compensation* meant the compensation for services performed for the employer that is currently includible in gross income. Thus, the following amounts that were excluded from gross income were not ordinarily treated as compensation:

1. Amounts deferred under a 457 plan;
2. Amounts deferred under a cafeteria plan [I.R.C. § 125];
3. Contributions to qualified plans that are "picked up" by an employer under Code Section 414(h);
4. Contributions to a 401(k) cash or deferred arrangement;
5. Contributions to tax-sheltered annuity contracts and mutual fund custodial accounts [I.R.C. § 403(b)(1), (7)];

6. Amounts excluded under certain wage continuation plans under Code Section 105(d); and

7. Amounts excluded under Code Section 911 (relating to citizens or residents of the United States living abroad). Code Section 911 is not parallel to Code Section 403(b)(2)(D)(iii), which has an add-back for certain foreign missionaries.

Beginning in 2002, the definition of *includible compensation* has been amended to mean the participant's compensation as defined in Code Section 415(c)(3). [See Job Creation and Worker Assistance Act of 2002, § 411] Code Section 415(c)(3) allows the add-back of amounts excluded under Code Sections 402(g), 125, 132(f)(4), and 457.

Q 2:54   What was gross compensation before 2002?

Prior to 2002, the percentage limit on deferrals was often expressed in terms of gross compensation rather than includible compensation. In most situations, *gross compensation* means the gross taxable income (or compensation) that would have been received but for the agreement to reduce salary. (See Qs 2:90, 2:93–2:95 for additional examples.)

The legislative history of Code Section 457(b) indicated that, in a typical arrangement, the 33 percent of includible compensation limitation is equal to 25 percent of the compensation that would have been received but for the agreement to reduce salary (gross compensation). Thus, in the absence of any deferrals or exclusions other than the Section 457(b) deferral, 25 percent of gross compensation equals 33 percent of includible compensation. After 2001, similarly, the 100 percent of includible compensation limitation under EGTRRA generally was to be equal to 50 percent of gross compensation, but the JCWAA made this issue moot by amending the definition of *includible compensation*.

Example. In both 2001 and 2002, after Sunny elects to reduce her salary by $5,000 for a 457(b) plan contribution, Sunny's employer reports $75,000 as wages subject to federal income tax. In 2001, her includible compensation was $75,000, while her gross compensation is $80,000 ($75,000 + $5,000). In 2002, her includible compensation and gross compensation are both $80,000.

Q 2:55   Does includible compensation include employer matching or nonelective contributions?

No. Before 2002, however, matching and nonelective contributions made by the employer were not currently taxable; therefore, they could not be treated as includible compensation. After 2002, such amounts are still not treated as compensation because they are nonelective contributions. [I.R.C. § 415(c)(3)]

Example 1. Joe earns $29,000 in 2001, and from this amount he elects to defer $5,000 into an eligible 457(b) plan. His employer makes a matching contribution of $2,500. Joe's includible compensation is $24,000. All limitations are based on this amount and therefore $8,000 does not exceed more than one-third of Joe's includible compensation.

Example 2. Harry earns $12,000 in 2002, and from this amount he elects to defer $3,000 into an eligible 457(b) plan. His employer makes a matching contribution of $2,000. Harry's deferral of $3,000 is permissible, computed as follows:

$$\$12,000 \text{ (gross compensation)} \times 100\%$$

Under the statute, the lesser of $11,000 or 100 percent of Harry's includible compensation can be deferred under the plan for 2002. Thus, a $3,000 elective deferral is permissible. Additionally, $3,000 plus the matching contribution of $2,000 does not exceed 100 percent of includible compensation.

If Harry is age 50 and participates in a governmental 457(b) plan, he may be able to contribute another $1,000 as well in 2002.

Q 2:56 Can sick pay, vacation pay, and back pay be deferred to an eligible plan?

Yes, provided that an agreement is entered into before the beginning of the month in which the amounts would otherwise be paid or made available, and the participant is an employee in that month. [Treas. Reg. § 1.457-4(d)(1)] In the case of accumulated sick pay, vacation pay, or back pay that is payable before the participant has a severance of employment, the agreement must be entered into before the amount is currently available (as defined under the regulations of Code Section 401(k)). [Id.] An example in the regulations indicates that the sick, vacation, or back pay must be paid while the individual is still an employee. [Treas. Reg. § 1.457-4(d)(2) ex. 2(ii)] Also note that the regulation does not address severance pay (see also chapter 7).

Q 2:57 What is the taxable year for computing compensation?

It is based on the employee's taxable year (generally the calendar year). [I.R.C. § 457(e)(5); Treas. Reg. § 1.457-2(g)]

Q 2:58 May a participant who receives compensation from another employer participate in that employer's plan?

Yes; however, for years prior to 2002, the participant's contributions to a 457(b) plan are limited to the 457(b) plan limits (generally $8,500 in 2001, $8,000 for 1998–2000, and $7,500 before 1998) (see Q 2:91).

Q 2:59 How are deferrals without readily ascertainable value taken into account?

If the amount of a deferral is not readily ascertainable, the compensation is taken into account at its present value. An amount deferred under an eligible

457(b) plan is taken into account at its value at the time deferred; however, if the compensation deferred is subject to a substantial risk of forfeiture, such compensation should be taken into account at its value in the plan year in which such compensation is no longer subject to a substantial risk of forfeiture. [I.R.C. § 457(e)(6); Treas. Reg. § 1.457-2(b)] This amount is then compared with the includible compensation to determine whether the limitations on deferrals have been satisfied. [Rev. Act of 1978, S. Rep., at 67; see Treas. Reg. § 31.3121(v)(2)-1(c)(2)(iii) (defining present value of nonqualified deferred compensation for FICA purposes)]

Q 2:60   When is compensation determined?

Compensation is determined as of the close of the taxable year. [Treas. Reg. § 1.457-2(e)(1)(ii)]

Q 2:61   What is the present value of a normal salary reduction deferral agreement?

The amount withheld will be considered the present value of the compensation deferred.

Q 2:62   How is compensation determined for an independent contractor who agrees to perform services for some compensation payable currently and additional compensation payable in a later taxable year?

The present value of the right to receive a future payment or payments is used and then compared with the includible compensation for the taxable year to determine whether the limitations on deferrals have been exceeded.

Q 2:63   What if future payments are forfeitable?

If future payments are subject to a substantial risk of forfeiture, they are not valued until there is no longer a substantial risk of forfeiture. Thus, at the close of the first taxable year in which the future payments are no longer subject to a substantial risk of forfeiture, the present value of such payments must be compared with the includible compensation for that year to determine whether the deferral limitations have been met.

Q 2:64   Do community property laws apply in determining includible compensation?

No. The amount of includible compensation is determined without regard to any community property laws. [I.R.C. § 457(e)(7); Treas. Reg. § 1.457-2(g)]

Agreements to Defer Compensation

Q 2:65   When can compensation be deferred?

In general, the plan must provide that compensation can be deferred for any calendar month only if an agreement providing for such a deferral has been entered into before the first day of the month. [I.R.C. § 457(b)(4); Treas. Reg. § 1.457-4(b)] Special rules apply to newly hired employees and current employees who become eligible to participate (see Qs 2:66, 2:67).

Q 2:66   Must newly hired employees make elections prior to the month in which amounts are deferred?

No. With respect to a new employee, a plan may provide that compensation is to be deferred for the calendar month during which the participant first becomes an employee if an agreement providing for such a deferral is entered into on or before the first day on which the participant performs services for the eligible employer. [Treas. Reg. § 1.457-4(b)]

Q 2:67   Must elections be made prior to the month in which amounts are deferred if the plan is newly implemented or amended?

No. Neither the Code nor the regulations specifically address these issues; however, the House report on the Revenue Act of 1978 [Pub. L. No. 95-600] states:

> In the case of (1) persons first performing services for the sponsoring entity, and (2) newly implemented deferred compensation plans, employees or independent contractors would have a reasonable period of time from the date participation in the plan is offered to them to effect an election to defer. In such case, the election to defer compensation would become effective for pay periods beginning after the date the participation agreement is filed with the sponsoring entity. If a plan is amended to provide for participation by a group of employees or independent contractors not previously permitted to participate, or in the case of individuals first meeting any eligibility requirements provided under the plan, it is intended that a reasonable period of time will be allowed for affected individuals to elect to participate as if this were a newly implemented plan or as if these were new employees.

[Rev. Act of 1978 § 131, H.R. Rep.]

Q 2:68   How will compensation deferred under the plan be distributed?

Generally, the participant or beneficiary can elect the manner in which the compensation deferred under the plan will be distributed; however, the election must satisfy certain requirements (see Qs 1:14, 2:72, 2:191).

Q 2:69   When are benefits payable from an eligible 457(b) plan?

Except in the case of an unforeseeable emergency, benefits cannot be paid, or in the case of a plan of a tax-exempt entity, made available earlier than death, separation from service (severance of employment after 2001), or attainment of age 70½ (see Q 2:191). [I.R.C. § 457(d)(1)]

See Q 2:205 if no retirement age is specified under the regulations, if the plan must state the normal retirement age, or if the participant works beyond the normal retirement age specified in the plan.

Q 2:70   Will amounts be considered made available if the participant chooses the form of distribution or when payments will begin?

No (see Qs 2:71, 2:72, 2:191). [Treas. Reg. § 1.457-7]

Example 1.

a. Chuck is a participant in an eligible deferred compensation plan of a tax-exempt entity that provides the following:

   A. The total of the amounts deferred under the plan is payable to the participant in 120 substantially equal monthly installments commencing 30 days after the participant attains normal retirement age under the plan (age 65), unless the participant elects, within the 90-day period ending on the date the participant attains normal retirement age, to receive a single-sum payment of the deferred amounts. The single-sum payment is payable to a participant on the date the first of the monthly payments would otherwise be payable to the participant.

   B. If a participant separates from the service of the exempt employer before attaining normal retirement age, the total of the amounts deferred under the plan is payable to the participant in a single-sum payment on the date 90 days after the date of the separation, unless, before the date 30 days after the separation, the participant elects not to receive the single-sum payment. The election is irrevocable. If the participant makes the election, the total of the amounts deferred under the plan is payable to the participant as described in (A), either in monthly installments or, at the election of the participant, in a single-sum payment.

b. On June 6, 1994, Chuck, a 59-year-old calendar-year taxpayer, separates from the service of the tax-exempt entity. On June 18, 1994, Chuck elects not to receive the single-sum payment payable on account of the separation. Because of his election, no amount deferred under the plan is considered made available in 1994 by reason of Chuck's right to receive the single-sum payment.

c. On February 6, 2000, Chuck attains age 65. Chuck did not, within the 90-day period, elect the single-sum payment that is payable in lieu of the monthly installments. Amounts deferred under the plan are includible in

Chuck's gross income as they are paid to Chuck in the monthly installments. No amount is considered made available by reason of Chuck's right to elect the single-sum payment.

Example 2. The facts are the same as those in Example 1, except that the plan provides that notwithstanding that monthly installments have commenced under the plan, as described in (a)(A), above, the participant can, without restriction, elect to receive all or any portion of the amount remaining payable to the participant. The total of the amounts deferred under the plan is considered made available in 2000.

Example 3. The facts are the same as those in Example 1, except that the plan provides that once monthly installment payments have commenced under the plan, as described in (a)(A), above, the participant can accelerate the payment of the amount remaining payable to the participant on the occurrence of an unforeseeable emergency, as described in Treasury Regulations Section 1.457-6(c), in an amount not exceeding that described in that regulation. No amount is considered made available to Chuck on account of his right to accelerate payments on the occurrence of an unforeseeable emergency.

Example 4. In 2003, under an eligible plan of a tax-exempt entity in which David is a participant, normal retirement age is 65, at which time payments must begin. Payments can begin earlier on a separation from service. Under the plan, a participant who separates from service before age 65, or the participant's beneficiary if the separation happens because of the participant's death, can elect to defer the distribution of the amounts deferred until the year in which the participant attains or would have attained age 65. This election can be made only before any payments commence and once made cannot be revoked. If such an election is made, the participant, former participant, or beneficiary need not elect the method of payment—or, if one is elected, the participant, former participant, or beneficiary can change the method elected—until the date 30 days preceding the date on which payments are to commence. No amount is considered made available by reason of David's right to defer the distribution of the amounts deferred until age 65, or on account of David's right to delay the election of the method of payout. Similarly, if David dies at age 60, no amount is considered made available to his beneficiary by reason of the beneficiary's right to defer the distribution of the amounts deferred until the year in which David would have attained age 65, or on account of the beneficiary's right to delay the election of the method of payout.

Example 5. In 2003, under an eligible plan of a tax-exempt entity which Eunice is a participant, the maximum that can be deferred in any taxable year is 100 percent of includible compensation, not to exceed $12,000. The plan does not provide for a catch-up deferral under Code Section 457(b)(3). Eunice is under age 50. In one taxable year, Eunice elects to have amounts deferred in excess of the limitation provided for under the plan. The amounts deferred in excess of the limitation will be considered to have been made available to Eunice in the taxable year in which deferred, and the plan will cease to be an eligible plan.

Example 6. Under an unfunded eligible plan of a tax-exempt entity in which Frank is a participant, amounts deferred have been invested in a money market investment fund. The plan then transfers the amounts deferred to a life insurance company for the purchase of life insurance contracts as an investment medium. The entity sponsoring the plan (1) retains all of the incidents of ownership of the contracts, (2) is the sole beneficiary under the contracts, and (3) is under no obligation to transfer the contracts or to pass through the proceeds of the contracts to any participant or beneficiary. The movement of the amounts deferred to the life insurance company (whether or not made at the request of any plan participant) will not be considered to make the amounts available to the plan's participants. The cost of current life insurance protection under the life insurance contracts will not be considered made available to the plan's participants.

For governmental 457(b) plans, after 2001, the requirement of irrevocable distribution elections and restrictions on changes to these elections will not apply. [I.R.C. § 457(d)(3)] Instead, for these plans, rules similar to those for 401(a) or 403(b) plan distribution elections (including the minimum required distribution rules of I.R.C. § 401(a)(9)) will apply.

Q 2:71   Can a participant change the investment mode?

Yes. If a participant is given the opportunity to choose how contributions will be invested under the plan (investment mode), the selection may be changed in accordance with plan provisions as often as is permitted under the terms of the plan.

Q 2:72   Can a participant accelerate or postpone an election to defer commencement of distributions?

In the case of an eligible plan of a tax-exempt entity, and before 2002, in the case of a government plan, the general rule is that if a participant is given the right to choose when benefit payments commence, the election must be irrevocable; otherwise, the deferred compensation is treated as made available. The SBJPA however, amended the Code to allow for one additional distribution election to be made without causing the amount subject to the election to be treated as made available. The one additional election must be made before the commencement of distributions but after the time such amounts could be made available to participants under Code Section 457(d)(1)(A)—that is, on death, after separation from service, or on attaining age 70½. Thus, under the SBJPA, once a payout commences, it would be irrevocable. The one additional election may not be used to accelerate any payment under the plan. [IRS Notice 98-8, § IV, 1998-4 I.R.B. 6; see also Treas. Reg. § 1.457-7(c)(2)(iii)] The IRS has informally indicated that the additional one-time election cannot be used to elect a new payout period or option, such as changing from 10 annual installments to a lump sum. [IRS Continuing Professional Education Exempt Organizations Technical Instruction Program for FY 1998, § I, at 179]

For governmental 457(b) plans, after 2001, the requirement of irrevocable distribution elections and restrictions on changes to these elections will not apply. [I.R.C. § 457(d)(3)] Instead, for these plans, rules similar to those for 401(a) or 403(b) plan distribution elections will apply. [Treas. Reg. § 1.457-7(b)]

The Section 457(e)(9)(B) additional deferral election provision, as effective for plans of tax-exempt employers, and as effective until 2002 for plans of governmental employers, is illustrated by the following examples.

Example 1. Employee A is a participant in an eligible 457(b) plan. The plan provides that the total amount deferred under the plan is payable to a participant who separates from service before age 65. Payment is made in a lump sum 90 days after separation from service, unless, during a 30-day "window period" immediately following the separation, the participant elects to receive the payment at a later date or in 10 annual installments to begin 90 days after separation from service or at a later date. The plan also permits eligible participants to make a Section 457(e)(9)(B) additional deferral election.

Employee A separates from service at age 50. The next day, during the 30-day window period provided in the plan, Employee A elects to receive the distribution in the form of 10 annual installment payments beginning at age 55. Two weeks later, within the 30-day window period, Employee A makes a new election permitted under the plan to receive 10 annual installment payments beginning at age 60 (instead of at age 55).

The two elections Employee A makes during the 30-day window period are not Section 457(e)(9)(B) additional deferral elections (because they are made before the first permissible payout date under the plan) and therefore do not preclude the plan from allowing Employee A to make a Section 457(e)(9)(B) additional deferral election after Employee A's election to receive 10 annual installment payments beginning at age 60.

Example 2. The facts are the same as those in Example 1. Employee A has made no other deferral elections after the 30-day window period and before age 59. While age 59, Employee A elects to defer commencement of the installment payments until she attains age 65.

Under Code Section 457(e)(9)(B), the total amount payable to Employee A will not be treated as made available merely because Employee A made this additional election at age 59 (after the first permissible payout date under the plan but before commencement of distributions). After making this election, Employee A may make no further elections to change the date on which distributions commence.

Q 2:73   Is an employee required to defer a minimum amount?

The Code does not require that a minimum amount be deferred; however, an employer may wish to impose a reasonable minimum deferral to lessen administrative requirements. For example, the employer may establish a minimum deferral amount per pay period, per month, or per year. A minimum that is too high may tend to discourage participation by lower-paid employees.

Contributions by Employers

Q 2:74   Can employers make contributions to an eligible 457(b) plan?

Yes, provided, in the case of governmental plans, that state and local law permits the employer to make contributions.

Q 2:75   May employer contributions be made subject to a vesting schedule?

Yes. The employer may specify the conditions required to become vested or partially vested in employer matching and/or nonelective contributions. Such conditions generally are based on length of service. In some cases, age and service are used. Because of the unique nature of a 457(b) plan, vesting schedules may cause administrative problems by bunching deferrals into one year for purposes of the contribution limits (see Qs 2:30, 2:82). State law may not allow employer contributions to be forfeitable (i.e., made subject to a vesting schedule). In addition, contributions will be treated as wages for FICA tax purposes when vested. [I.R.C. § 3121(v)]

Q 2:76   Is a minimum vesting schedule required?

The employer has full discretion to meet its own needs and objectives. For example, if a participant must have 25 years of service to become vested in an employer contribution, service can be measured from the date employment commenced, the date each contribution is made, the date the matching contribution program was implemented, or any other date desired. The minimum vesting standards under the Code and ERISA do not apply to 457 plans. [I.R.C. § 411(a); ERISA §§ 4(b)(1), 203(a)] State law may apply.

Q 2:77   Why might an employer make a matching contribution?

Matching contributions are a good way to encourage employees to participate and save more of their money for retirement. Most employees do not have too much saved for retirement or pay too little in taxes.

Q 2:78   How might an employer make a matching contribution?

Matching contributions to the extent provided in the plan may be expressed as a percentage of the amount deferred by an employee or as a fixed or discretionary dollar amount.

Example 1. A plan provides that the employer will make a fully vested matching contribution equal to the amount elected to be deferred by the participant multiplied by 50 percent. For years before 2002, under such an arrangement, an employee ordinarily will not elect to defer more than $5,667. The plan should provide for a cap on elective contributions so that the applicable limits are not exceeded. If $5,667 is contributed, the employee will receive a matching contribution of $2,833 and the plan limit ($8,500 in 2001) will have been reached.

Example 2. A plan provides that the employer will make a matching contribution equal to $500 to each participant who elects to defer $500 or more.

Example 3. To control costs, a governmental plan provides that the employer will make a matching contribution equal to 25 percent of the amount elected to be deferred by each participant not in excess of 5 percent of compensation. If 80 percent of the employees elect to contribute 5 percent or more of their compensation, the employer's cost will be contained at 1 percent of payroll $(0.80 \times 0.05 \times 0.25 = 0.01)$.

Q 2:79   Can the employer choose the employees who will receive matching contributions?

Yes.

Example. To encourage participation by lower-paid employees, a governmental plan provides that the employer will make a dollar-for-dollar matching contribution to each participant who has gross compensation of less than $25,000.

Q 2:80   Must the match be made to a 457(b) plan?

No. Because of the annual dollar limit ($12,000 for 2003) on vested contributions, some governmental employers make the matching contribution to a separate 401(a) qualified plan. In that case, plan administration in general and distribution elections in particular are complicated by having two different types of plans, but the arrangement does permit the dollar limit to be used solely for the Section 457(b) salary reduction portion.

Q 2:81   Do higher-paid employees benefit more from a deferral or from employer matching contributions?

Although employees receive a reduction in current taxes for making an elective deferral, a matching contribution is made with the employer's funds. If all things are equal and compensation is not negotiable, it is more effective to receive a matching contribution than to make an elective contribution.

Example. Jean has a 30 percent marginal income tax rate (federal and state). If Jean defers $8,500 (her maximum in 2001) and waives the 50 percent employer matching contribution, she will save $2,550 in taxes. If Jean defers just $5,667, she will save only $1,700 in taxes, but she will also have received $2,833 from her employer. In both cases, Jean has deferred $8,500, but receiving the matching contribution is more effective overall.

For years after 2001, this advantage still holds, though the dollar limit is higher.

Q 2:82 How do vesting schedules cause problems?

Vesting schedules can cause various administrative problems for an employer.

Contribution limitation problems. Because only fully vested contributions are included toward the deferral limit, the employer must determine the extent to which prior contributions become vested during the current year. If several contributions all vest at one time (or at different rates), the current year's contribution limit might be reduced or even exceeded. The problem can be mitigated by making fully vested contributions on a graduated basis.

> **Example.** For each year of service an employer makes a matching contribution equal to 3 percent of the amount elected to be deferred by the participant under the eligible 457(b) plan. An employee with 10 years of service makes an elective deferral of $3,000. The employee is entitled to receive an employer contribution of $900 ($3,000 × 0.03 × 10). Another employee with only 5 years of service would receive a 15 percent matching contribution.

FICA tax problems. If the employer is subject to FICA (including Medicare) taxes, amounts may become vested (i.e., no longer subject to a substantial risk of forfeiture) in a year in which the employee has little or no compensation that can be used to pay the employee's share of such taxes. The employer will have to remit the proper amount (see Q 2:146).

USERRA Applicability

Q 2:83 Does the Uniformed Services Employment and Reemployment Rights Act of 1994 apply to eligible 457(b) plans?

Yes. All types of employee pension benefit plans, as described in ERISA Sections 3(2) and 3(33), are covered, as are plans covering governmental employees. Thus, the Uniformed Services Employment and Reemployment Rights Act of 1994 (USERRA) [Pub. L. No. 103-353] extends to eligible 457(b) plans and nonchurch 403(b) tax-sheltered annuity plans. [I.R.C. § 414(u)(6); H.R. Rep. No. 103-995 (1994)]

The IRS has released model amendments to assist plan sponsors in complying with USERRA. [Rev. Proc. 96-49, 1996-2 C.B. 369]

Q 2:84   What rights are protected under USERRA?

In addition to protecting employees who enter military service against employment discrimination and termination and providing them with reemployment rights, USERRA substantially expands and attempts to clarify the rights of employees returning from uniformed service regarding retirement benefits provided by their employer (Scialabba 1996).

Q 2:85   What retirement benefit rights does USERRA protect?

With regard to any uniformed service leave of absence, USERRA requires an employer, including a governmental employer, to be liable to fund benefits that would have accrued during the leave period to a plan in which the returning individual is a participant. [38 U.S.C. § 4318(b)(1)] After the employee is reemployed, the employer must provide makeup contributions for plan service periods during which the employee was in uniformed service.

Uniformed leave of absence includes any National Guard or other reserve component duty, such as two-week annual training and regular active duty, whether voluntary or involuntary. [38 U.S.C. § 4303(13)]

Example 1. An employee volunteers to go with his National Guard unit to Bosnia for nine months. His employment and benefit rights are protected by USERRA.

Example 2. An employee volunteers for a 60-day assignment with the National Guard Bureau. Her employment and benefits rights are protected by USERRA.

Q 2:86   How are elective deferral rights protected under USERRA?

During the specified period, a participant can make elective deferrals. The maximum amount of the elective deferrals that the individual can make is the amount he or she would have been permitted to make under the plan during the period of qualified military service if the individual had continued to be employed by the employer during that period and had received compensation based on the rate of pay he or she would have received. Proper adjustment must be made for any elective deferrals actually made during the period of qualified military service. The term *elective deferral* has the meaning it is given in Code Section 402(g)(3), except that an elective deferral includes any deferral of compensation under an eligible 457(b) plan. [I.R.C. § 414(u)(2)(B), (u)(7)]

With respect to any plan that provides for elective deferrals, the employer sponsoring the plan is treated as meeting the requirements of Code Section 414(u) only if

1. The employer permits the employee to make additional elective deferrals under the plan during the period that begins on the date of reemployment and whose length is the lesser of (a) three times the period of qualified military service that resulted in such rights or (b) five years; and

2. Where an employer's liability to make contributions on an employee's behalf depends on employee contributions (such as matching contributions), the employer makes matching contributions "to the same extent as would have been made if the employees had been actively employed and had made contributions in the years when they were in uniformed service."

(Scialabba, Fowler, and Morrison 1996) [See I.R.C. § 414(u)(2)(A)]

Q 2:87 How are conflicts with the Code resolved?

In general, contributions required or permitted to be made under USERRA are not subject to any otherwise applicable limitation contained in Code Section 402(g), 403(b), 404(a), 404(h), 408, 415, or 457 and are not taken into account in applying such limitations to other contributions or benefits under any plan with respect to the year in which the contribution is made.

A plan will not be treated as failing to meet the requirements of Code Section 401(a)(4), 401(a)(26), 401(k)(3), 401(k)(11), 401(k)(12), 401(m), 403(b)(12), 408(k)(3), 408(k)(6), 408(p), 410(b), or 416 by reason of the making of (or the right to make) such a contribution.

Q 2:88 Are vesting schedules affected by USERRA?

Yes. On reemployment, the employee must be given credit for service during the period of qualified military service. In addition, an employee is treated as not incurring a break in service during the period of qualified military service on his or her reemployment. [I.R.C. § 414(u)(8)]

Q 2:89 How are plan loan repayment schedules affected?

A 457(g) plan trust may suspend the participant's obligation for loan repayments during any period in which the individual is performing service in the uniformed service, even if the individual's reemployment rights are not protected by law. [I.R.C. § 414(u)(4), (5)] Note, however, that interest charged on the plan loan may be affected by the Soldiers and Sailors Civil Relief Act (see Q 2:25).

Limitations on Contributions

Q 2:90 What are the maximum deferral limitations before 2002?

For years before 2002, each participant in an eligible 457(b) plan can defer up to the lesser of $8,500 (as indexed in 2001; the limit was $8,000 in 1998–2000 and $7,500 before 1998) or 33 percent of includible compensation (generally meaning taxable compensation) in a taxable year (see Q 2:52). This limitation applies to elective and nonelective deferred compensation and is indexed (see Q 2:98). Under a limited catch-up provision, a participant can defer up to $15,000 in each of the last three taxable years before he or she reaches normal retirement age, but the increase over the normal limitation is available only to the extent of unused portions of the limitations for previous years (see Q 2:100). [See also Treas. Reg. § 1.457-4(c)]

The legislative history of Code Section 457(b) indicates that in a typical arrangement the 33 percent of includible compensation limitation is equal to 25 percent of the compensation that would have been received but for the agreement to reduce salary (gross compensation). Thus, 25 percent of gross compensation equals 33 percent of includible compensation.

Example 1. Saundra earns $32,000. From this amount she elects to defer $8,500 under her employer's eligible plan. The minimum amount of gross compensation needed to defer $8,500 is $34,000, computed as follows:

25 percent limitation:

$$\$34,000 \times 0.25 = \$8,500$$

33 percent limitation:

$$\$25,500(\$34,000 - \$8,500) \times 0.333 = \$8,500$$

Thus, $25,500 is the minimum amount of includible compensation needed to support an $8,500 contribution (in 2001), and 25 percent of gross compensation (pre-plan) equals 33 percent of includible compensation.

Example 2. An individual with $10,000 of gross compensation could have only $2,500 deferred ($10,000 × 0.25, which is the same as ($10,000 − $2,500) ÷ 3).

Q 2:91   What was the dollar limit before 2002?

Except for the limited catch-up provision (see Q 2:100), $8,500 (as indexed for 2001) is the maximum amount of compensation that can be deferred under the plan for any taxable year. [I.R.C. § 457(b)(2)] This dollar limit (as well as the percentage limitation) applies both at the individual level and at the plan level. It also applies to individuals who are participants in more than one plan (see Qs 2:112–2:114). [P.L.R. 9152026]

The limit in 1998–2000 was $8,000 (indexed for inflation). The limit before 1998 was $7,500.

Q 2:92   What are the maximum deferral limitations after 2001?

For years after 2001, the percentage limitation increases to 100 percent of includible compensation. The dollar limit increases to $11,000 in 2002, and thereafter increases $1,000 each year until it reaches $15,000 in 2006; beginning in 2007 it is adjusted for the cost of living. After 2001, catch-up contributions can be made by some individuals that attain age 50.

Catch-up contributions. An individual participating in a governmental 457(b) plan who attains the age of 50 by the end of the taxable year, may make additional elective deferrals up to an "applicable dollar limit." Nongovernmental plans are not permitted to contain catch-up contribution features other than the three-year catch-up (see Qs 2:22, 2:24, 2:100, 2:101). [I.R.C. § 414(v)(6)(A)(iii); Treas. Reg. § 1.457-4(c)(2)] Code Section 414(v) permitting age 50 and older catch-up contributions are effective and apply to contributions in taxable years beginning on or after January 1, 2002. It would also appear that the new catch-up rules would apply, for example, to a calendar year taxpayer in a 457(b) plan having a plan year ending in 2002. [Treas. Reg. § 1.414(v)-1(i)]

An individual that is projected to attain age 50 before the end of a calendar year is deemed to be age 50 as of January 1 of such year. [Treas. Reg. § 1.414(v)-1(g)(3)]

This catch-up amount is in addition to the normal deferral limit for the applicable year [I.R.C. § 414(v)(6)(C)] but may not be used in the three years before retirement when the limit is twice the otherwise applicable dollar limit during those years if that limit is higher. [Treas. Reg. § 1.457-4(c)(2)(ii)] The overall contribution limits are shown below:

Taxable Year	Normal Limit	Catch-Up Amount	Total Deferral
2002	$11,000	$1,000	$12,000
2003	$12,000	$2,000	$14,000
2004	$13,000	$3,000	$16,000
2005	$14,000	$4,000	$18,000
2006	$15,000	$5,000	$20,000

For taxable years beginning after 2006, the catch-up limit of $5,000 will be subject to COLAs in increments of $500. This COLA adjustment is separate from the COLA adjustment applicable to the normal elective deferral limit. This means that the $15,000 normal deferral limit will increase to $15,500 before the catch-up amount of $5,000 will increase to $5,500. [I.R.C. §§ 414(v)(2)(C), 414(v)(6)(C), 457(b)(2)(A), 457(b)(3)(A)]

Note. Regulations state that the age 50 catch-up is applied on the taxable year. [Treas. Reg. § 1.457-4(c)(2)(i)]

Regulations clarify that a participant in a governmental 457(b) plan could make second catch-up contributions to a SIMPLE, SARSEP, 403(b), or 401(k) plan in which he or she participated because a 457 plan is not subject to Code Section 402(g) regarding the limit on exclusions for elective deferrals (see Q 2:118). [Treas. Reg. § 1.414(v)-1(f)]

Example. Patty has compensation of $30,000 for 2003 and is a participant in an eligible 457 plan. She contributes the maximum elective contribution of $14,000 ($12,000 plus a catch-up contribution of $2,000) to an eligible governmental 457 plan OR the maximum elective contribution to an eligible tax-exempt employer's 457 plan. Patty is also a participant in a plan of another employer. Her compensation from that entity is $60,000. If Patty is also a participant in another plan, she may make additional contributions to that plan as shown below.

Maximum Elective Contributions to Another Plan

	If Participant in an Eligible Governmental 457 Plan		If Participant in an Eligible Tax-Exempt 457 Plan	
	Under age 50	*Catch-Up eligible*	*Under age 50*	*Catch-Up eligible*
401(k)[1]	$12,000	$14,000	$12,000	$14,000
403(b)[2]	$12,000	$14,000	$12,000	$14,000
457 (Gov't)	$0	$0	$0	$0
457 (Tax-Exempt)	$0	n/a	$0	n/a
SARSEP[3]	$12,000	$14,000	$12,000	$14,000
SIMPLE[4]	$8,000	$9,000	$8,000	$9,000

Note: From the participant's point of view, it would make no difference if the employers are related, although plan choice may be affected. The age 50 catch-up limit cannot be used under an eligible 457 plan in any year in which the last-three-years catch-up rule provides a higher limit. An eligible tax-exempt employer's 457 plan may not provide catch-up contributions.

[1] A 401(k) plan may be adopted by a tax-exempt employer, but not a governmental employer.

[2] Special rules permit increased elective contributions under a 403(b) plan for participants that have at least 15 years of service with a public school system, hospital, home health services agency, home health and welfare service agency, church, or convention of churches (or associated organizations). Elective contributions to a 403(b) plan reduce compensation for 457(b) plan purposes.

[3] A SARSEP may not be adopted by a government or tax-exempt employer. Under a SARSEP, normal elective contributions reduce compensation upon which the 25 percent participant exclusion limit is based. Catch-up contributions are separately excludible. [I.R.C. § 402(h)] $60,000 less $12,000, multiplied by .25 equals $12,000. Patty's contribution of $12,000, or $14,000 with catch-up contributions is excludible from her gross income, in addition to her 457 contributions.

[4] A SIMPLE IRA plan may be adopted by a government or tax-exempt employer. Elective limits are lower than in other elective plan types.

Q 2:93   Which contributions are subject to the maximum deferral limitations?

Nonforfeitable employer contributions and employee salary reduction deferrals (deferred compensation) to eligible 457(b) plans are subject to the maximum deferral limitations. An exception applies in the case of qualified governmental excess benefit arrangements described in Code Section 415(m). Benefits under such arrangements, which must be nonelective, are not subject to the dollar limit nor taken into account in determining the limit for other plans (see Qs 2:110, 2:111).

Example. A tax-exempt employer makes a $500 employer contribution into an eligible 457 plan on behalf of a participant. The amount contributed will become fully vested after the participant performs service for three years. The participant also elects to defer $1,000 of his salary into the 457 plan for the current year. Only $1,000 is treated as contributed this year for purposes of the dollar and percentage limitations. The $500 will become subject to the limitations in the year in which it becomes nonforfeitable (vests).

Q 2:94 On what is the percentage limitation on contributions based?

The 33⅓ percent (for years before 2002) of compensation limitation specified in the statute is based on includible compensation. Generally, this is the equivalent of 25 percent of gross (pre-plan) compensation.

Example 1. William earns $10,000 in 2001. His employer makes the maximum contribution of $2,500. This amount does not increase the amount on which the deferral limitations are computed, that is, $7,500, William's includible compensation.

Example 2. The facts are the same as those in Example 1, except that William can elect to receive the $2,500 in cash during the year or to defer that amount under the plan. Here, William's gross compensation has increased to $12,500. William can elect to defer an additional $625 under the plan:

$$\$12,500 \times 0.25 = \$3,125; \$3,125 - \$2,500 = \$625$$

Under the statute, if the maximum amount, $3,125, is contributed, includible compensation would equal $9,375 ($12,500 − $3,125). Using the 33⅓ percent limitation stated in the statute results in the same limitation:

$$\$9,375 \times 0.333 = \$3,125$$

Note that for years after 2001 the 100 percent of includible compensation limitation is, similarly, effectively 50 percent of gross compensation.

Q 2:95 Can an employer make a contribution equal to the maximum deferral amount for each participant or selected participants?

Yes. Nonelective contributions do not increase the amount that could otherwise have been deferred by the employee.

Example. In 2001, Henry earns $24,000, of which $6,000 ($24,000 × 0.25) can be contributed by his employer to an eligible 457 plan. This can also be calculated as follows: [($24,000 − $6,000) × ⅓]. The $6,000 contribution (deferred compensation) cannot be added to Henry's $24,000 of compensation in calculating his annual limitation.

Q 2:96 Can an employer have more than one eligible 457(b) plan?

Yes; however, all eligible 457(b) plans of an employer are aggregated, and no individual may defer a total of more than the dollar limit (or catch-up amount if applicable) in a taxable year even under plans of more than one employer (see SQ 2:112). [I.R.C. § 457(c)]

Q 2:97 Are the contribution limits imposed on the employer or the employee?

Both. An employee cannot exceed the general limits by participating in more than one eligible 457(b) plan (including eligible 457(b) plans of unrelated employers). [I.R.C. § 457(c)] For plans of tax-exempt employers, and for plans of governmental employers for years before 2002, the amount deferred (including any excess) should be shown in box 12 of Form W-2. Any amount deferred in excess of the limits generally should be reported by the participant as wages on Form 1040, line 7. (Reporting requirements are more fully discussed in chapter 13.) An employer that fails to operate a plan properly may cause the plan to lose its eligible status (see Q 2:27).

Q 2:98 Is the dollar amount indexed for cost-of-living increases?

Yes. The dollar amount is increased by a cost-of-living adjustment factor in $500 increments for years before 2002. [I.R.C. § 457(e)(15) as in effect prior to EGTRRA] The limit before 1998 was $7,500 [I.R. 96-42 (Oct 24, 1996)]; for 1998, 1999, and 2000, the limit was $8,000; for 2001, it is $8,500. The dollar limit increases to $11,000 in 2002 and thereafter further increases by $1,000 a year until 2006, when it is $15,000. For years after 2006, the $15,000 dollar limit again becomes adjusted for the cost of living in $500 increments. [I.R.C. § 457(e)(15)(B), added by EGTRRA]

Q 2:99 Is the $15,000 maximum catch-up amount increased?

Not for years before 2002. In contrast to the indexing of the dollar limit (see Q 2:98), pre-EGTRRA law had no provision for the $15,000 amount to be increased or adjusted for inflation (cost of living). Under EGTRRA, for years after 2001, this amount is effectively adjusted for the cost of living by making it twice the otherwise applicable dollar amount (which, for example, is $11,000 in 2002).

Q 2:100 What is the last-three-years catch-up provision before 2002?

A plan may provide that the $8,500/33 percent ceiling on contributions can be increased for one or more of the participant's last three taxable years ending before he or she attains normal retirement age under the plan. The increased ceiling cannot exceed the lesser of:

1. $15,000; or
2. The sum of:
   a. The plan ceiling established under the plan (not in excess of $8,500/ 33 percent of compensation) for the taxable year (determined without regard to any catch-up provision), plus

    b. As much of the plan ceiling of $8,500 or 33 percent of includible compensation (whichever is less) established for taxable years before the taxable year as has not previously been used.

[Treas. Reg. § 1.457-4(c)(3)] Thus, under the limited catch-up provision, the increase over the normal limitation is available only to the extent of the unused portions of the limitations for previous years. For determining the amount previously unused in years before 2002, all elective deferrals under 457(b), 401(k), SARSEP, SIMPLE IRA, and 403(b) plans are taken into account in determining the unused portion; the amounts for 2002 and thereafter take into account only 457(b) deferrals. [Treas. Reg. § 1.457-4(c)(3)(iv)]

Example. Alice, born on June 1, 1940, is a new participant in an eligible 457(b) deferred compensation plan providing a normal retirement age of 65. Alice will not be eligible for regular retirement until 2005, when she is age 65. The plan provides the general and catch-up limitations on deferrals up to the maximum permitted under Code Section 457(b).

For 2001, Alice, who will be 61, is scheduled to receive a salary of $20,000 from the state. Alice wants to defer the maximum amount possible in 2001. The maximum amount that she can defer under the plan is the lesser of $8,500 or 33 percent of her includible compensation (generally, the equivalent of 25 percent of gross compensation). Accordingly, if there are no other deferrals or exclusions, the maximum that Alice can defer for 2001 is $5,000 ($20,000 × 0.25). Alice is not able to use the plan's catch-up provisions in 2001 because the three years before Alice's normal retirement age are 2002, 2003, and 2004.

Q 2:101   How are catch-up provisions changed after 2001?

For years after 2001, the dollar limit for the last-three-years catch-up rule is increased from $15,000 to double the otherwise applicable dollar limit—for example, $22,000 (2 × $11,000) in 2002 and $30,000 (2 × $15,000) in 2006.

In addition, governmental eligible 457(b) plans may offer the age 50 catch-up provision after 2001 (see Q 2:92), but the age 50 catch-up limit cannot be used in any year in which the last-three-years catch-up limit applies if that limit is higher. [I.R.C. § 414(v)(6)(C); Treas. Reg. § 1.457-4(c)(2)(ii)]

Q 2:102   Are there other restrictions on using a plan's last-three-years catch-up provisions?

Yes. A plan cannot provide for its last-three-years catch-up provisions to commence more than once, whether or not the provisions are used in fewer than all of the three taxable years ending before the participant attains normal retirement age and whether or not the participant or former participant rejoins the plan or participates in another eligible plan after retirement. [Treas. Reg. § 1.457-4(c)(3)]

Example. A participant in an eligible 457(b) plan elects to use the plan's last-three-years catch-up provisions only for the one taxable year ending before his normal retirement age under the plan. After retirement at that age, the participant renders services for the employer as an independent contractor (or otherwise). The plan cannot provide that the participant can use the plan's catch-up provisions for any of the taxable years after retirement.

Q 2:103   Can deferrals exceed the participant's compensation?

No (see Qs 2:90, 2:92).

Q 2:104   How are the limits determined in an eligible 457(b) plan that is structured as a defined benefit plan?

A defined benefit plan specifies the benefit that a participant is to receive in the future rather than the amount that will be added to his or her account each year. A defined benefit plan often fixes a benefit based on factors such as compensation and length of service and usually provides a benefit in the form of an annuity or payments over a number of years. Benefits under a defined benefit plan do not depend on the performance of any investments acquired by the employer or held in a 457(g) trust. Applying the limits to a nonqualified defined benefit plan is more difficult than applying them to a defined contribution plan. The benefit subject to the limit in any year is the present value of the increase in the participant's accrued benefit during that year based on reasonable actuarial assumptions and matters. [See Treas. Reg. § 1.457-2(b)(3)] This present value usually will be different for each participant and often will change from year to year. Consult an enrolled actuary for assistance in determining the present value of such a benefit.

Q 2:105   Could an eligible 457(b) plan that is structured as a defined benefit plan apply an aggregate limit to the total accrued benefit?

No. It is important to remember that the limit applies to an increase in the participant's accrued benefit on a year-by-year basis. A plan would not satisfy this requirement if it merely applied an aggregate limit (based on all of the participant's service) to the total accrued benefit.

Q 2:106   How is the annual limit determined if an employee participates in both an eligible 457(b) defined benefit pension plan and an eligible 457(b) defined contribution plan?

An eligible 457(b) plan can be structured as a defined contribution plan or as a defined benefit plan. If an employee participates in both an eligible defined benefit plan and an eligible defined contribution plan, the annual limit applies to the sum of the present value of the increase in the accrued benefit under the defined benefit plan and the amount deferred under the defined contribution plan.

Some practitioners believe that it is reasonable to apply the Section 403(b) rules for taking defined benefit plan accruals into account for the maximum exclusion allowances for purposes of determining the present value of Section 457(b) accruals for the dollar and percentage of includible compensation limitations as well. [See Treas. Reg. § 1.403(b)-1(d)(4)]

Q 2:107   Are contributions or benefits considered if they are forfeitable?

No. For purposes of determining contribution deferral limits, amounts are considered contributed when or as they become nonforfeitable (vested). The same principles apply to an eligible 457(b) plan structured as a defined benefit pension plan. In most cases, and to avoid problems, contributions made to eligible 457(b) plans generally are fully vested when made (see Qs 2:27–2:30).

Q 2:108   Are eligible defined benefit 457(b) plans subject to minimum funding requirements?

No. Before 1996 (and after 1996 for nongovernmental employers), these plans generally were unfunded arrangements by definition. Consequently, although specific benefits may be established based on the needs and objectives of the employer, such plans generally are not permitted to provide formal benefit funding. A governmental plan using a 457(g) trust could provide for actuarially determinable contributions; however, the minimum funding requirements of Code Section 412 and ERISA Section 301 do not apply to governmental plans (or to unfunded deferred compensation plans of nonchurch, nongovernmental tax-exempt employers that do not provide for broad-based participation; see chapters 6 and 8). The enforcement of any obligation to contribute would have to be based on state law.

Q 2:109   Can the Section 457(b) deferral limits be circumvented by forming an affiliated organization or through leasing arrangements?

No. Organizations are prevented from avoiding the Section 457(b) deferral limits by forming affiliated service groups or leasing arrangements. [I.R.C. § 414(o); TAMRA § 1011(e)(4)]

Qualified Governmental Excess Benefit Arrangements

Q 2:110   What is a qualified governmental excess benefit arrangement?

A qualified governmental excess benefit arrangement is a governmental plan maintained solely for the purpose of providing benefits in excess of the

Section 415 limitations, is nonelective (i.e., no salary deferral elections are permitted), and is unfunded other than by a trust that is maintained solely for the purpose of providing such benefits. [I.R.C. § 415(m)]

Q 2:111   What rules apply to qualified governmental excess benefit arrangements?

For such arrangements, the taxable year for which amounts are includible in gross income by the employee and the treatment of those amounts are determined as if the plan were a nonqualified plan of a taxable employer. [I.R.C. § 415(m)(2)] The benefits are not taken into account for Section 415 purposes, and income accruing to the plan is exempt from tax under Code Section 115. [I.R.C. § 415(m)(1)] Benefits under qualified governmental excess benefit arrangements are also not subject to the Section 457(b) dollar limit, nor are they counted in determining the limit for any other 457(b) plan. [I.R.C. § 457(e)(14); P.L.R. 199923056]

Coordination of Deferrals with Other Plans or Other Employers

Q 2:112   Do the dollar and the percentage of includible compensation limitations apply to an individual who is a participant in more than one eligible 457 plan, even if the plan sponsors are not related?

Yes. The dollar and the percentage of includible compensation limitations under Code Section 457(b) apply to an individual who is a participant in more than one eligible 457 plan, even if the employers are unrelated. [I.R.C. § 457(c); Treas. Reg. § 1.457-5]

Q 2:113   What should a participant do if he or she participates in more than one plan?

If an individual participates in more than one plan (whether or not the plans are maintained by the same sponsoring entity), he or she must designate how the Code Section 457(b) dollar limit (or percentage of includible compensation limitation, if less) will be allocated among the various plans in which he or she participates (see Q 2:112).

Q 2:114   How are deferrals coordinated with other plans for years before 2002?

In general, for years before 2002, Code Section 457(c) requires that certain amounts excluded from gross income be coordinated with deferrals into other plans. This means that contributions to other plans generally are subtracted from the dollar (or catch-up) limitation.

Coordination was required in the case of a participant in an eligible 457(b) plan in the following situations:

1. Any amount is excluded from gross income attributable to elective and vested nonelective or matching contributions to a tax-sheltered annuity or custodial account under Code Section 403(b) (see Q 2:116).
2. Elective deferrals excluded from income made under:
   a. A 401(k) cash or deferred arrangement;
   b. A SARSEP; or
   c. A SIMPLE retirement account under Code Section 408(p).
3. Deductible contributions are made to an employee trust under Code Section 501(c)(18).

All amounts excluded from tax under a 403(b) arrangement were coordinated, but only elective deferrals under a 401(k) plan, SIMPLE IRA, or SEP must be coordinated. Likewise, amounts deferred under an eligible 457(b) plan were coordinated with amounts deferred under a 401(k) plan, 403(b) plan, SIMPLE IRA, or SEP; however, coordination was not required with respect to a participant in a rural cooperative plan (as defined in Code Section 401(k)(7)). [I.R.C. § 457(c)(2)]

It is especially important for an employee who participates in more than one plan of different employers to monitor the applicable limitation or limitations. It is unlikely in a multiple-employer situation that an employer will be able to coordinate contributions made under its plan with contributions made to other plans.

Example 1. Eunice earns $60,000 and is a participant in her employer's 401(k) plan. The employer is not a rural cooperative. She elects to defer $5,000 under that arrangement for 1998. She is also a participant under her employer's eligible 457(b) plan. Eunice will be able to defer only $8,000 (in a non-catch-up year) under the combination of 401(k) and 457 plans, even though a higher limitation might be available under the 401(k) plan alone. [I.R.C. § 457(c)(1)] Code Section 457(c)(2) treats amounts excluded from gross income under a cash or deferred arrangement as an amount deferred under an eligible 457(b) plan subject to the maximum dollar limitations applicable to the 457 plan. The employee must monitor this limitation. [I.R.C. § 457(b)(2)(B)]

Example 2. The facts are the same as those in Example 1, except that the 401(k) plan is maintained by a rural cooperative. In this case, the 457 plan limitation is not reduced. Although coordination is not required at the employer level, Eunice is responsible for monitoring the relevant limitation on the exclusion of elective deferrals under each of the plans.

Example 3. Barry is an employee of T-Bird Motor Company, a taxable corporation, and in 2001 elects to defer $8,000 under its 401(k) plan. Barry is also a participant in a tax-exempt organization's eligible 457(b) plan and defers $8,000 under that plan in a non-catch-up year. The employers are not related. Barry has exceeded the $8,500 limitation and must include $7,500 in income. The 457(b) plan contribution ($7,500) must be a mistaken contribution and (unless treated as forfeitable under the plan) should be returned and treated as never having been made. Barry will report this amount on Form 1040, line 7. Barry is also responsible for any taxes and penalties that may result from the excess deferral.

Thus, even though an individual can otherwise defer under the 401(k) plan a greater amount of gross income than he or she defers under the 457 plan, if the same individual also participates in an eligible 457(b) plan, he or she generally will be subject to the $8,500 or $15,000 limitation. To the extent that the employee contributes beyond that amount, his or her 457 plan deferrals have exceeded the limitations specified in Code Section 457(b).

Code Section 457(c)(2), as added by TRA 1986 Section 1107(a), provides that in applying Code Section 457(c)(1) any amount (1) excluded from gross income under Code Section 402(a)(8) (relating to 401(k) cash or deferred arrangements), Code Section 402(h)(1)(B) (relating to SEPs and SIMPLE retirement accounts), or Code Section 403(b) (relating to 403(b) tax-sheltered annuities) for the taxable year, or (2) with respect to which a deduction is allowable by reason of a contribution to an organization described in Code Section 501(c)(18) for the taxable year, must be treated as an amount deferred under Code Section 457(a). Code Section 402(a)(8) does not contain a corresponding provision. Thus, amounts deferred under Code Section 457(a) are not treated as amounts deferred under Code Section 402(a)(8). [I.R.C. § 457(c)(2)(A), (c)(2)(B); P.L.R. 9152026]

Q 2:115   How are 457(b) plan deferrals coordinated with contributions to other plans after 2001?

For years after 2001, EGTRRA has amended Code Section 457(c) so that 457(b) plan deferrals are no longer reduced for contributions to plans other than other 457(b) arrangements. This will allow an individual who participates in both a 457(b) plan and another type of plan, such as a 403(b) or 401(k) plan, to contribute to both up to the limit for each plan. [Treas. Reg. § 1.457-4]

Example. Margaret is chief executive officer of Laughter Is the Best Medicine, a Code Section 501(c)(3) charitable organization that maintains a 403(b) plan as well as a 457(b) plan. In 2002, Margaret has includible compensation of $80,000. Margaret may contribute $11,000 to her 403(b) plan and another $11,000 to her 457(b) plan, for a total of $22,000. If Margaret has attained age 50 in 2002, she may contribute another $1,000 to the 403(b) plan.

Q 2:116   Is the maximum amount that can be deferred under the eligible plan reduced if a participant has amounts contributed by a different employer for the purchase of a tax-sheltered annuity under Code Section 403(b)?

For years both before and after 2002, if the employer contributing amounts for the purchase of the annuity contract and the employer maintaining the eligible plan are different employers, the maximum deferral permitted under the eligible plan is not reduced by the amount contributed for the purchase of the annuity contract (see Q 2:112). [I.R.C. § 457(c)]

Q 2:117 How are amounts that exceed the dollar limit or percentage of includible compensation limitation treated?

Such amounts presumably are subject to the rules of Code Section 457(f), relating to ineligible plans. If the excess amounts are subject to a substantial risk of forfeiture, they are included in the participant's or beneficiary's gross income in the first taxable year in which there is no substantial risk of forfeiture or the benefits are assigned or alienated by the participant (see Q 2:132). They will be reported by the participant on line 7 of Form 1040. They should also be reported by the participant's employer on Form W-2 at that time.

Q 2:118 Can an employee who participates in an eligible 457 plan defer more than the dollar limit if he or she also participates in a 403(b) tax-sheltered annuity plan?

For years before 2002, the amount that a participant can defer under an eligible 457(b) plan is reduced, dollar for dollar, from the applicable dollar limit ($8,500 as adjusted in 2001, or up to $15,000 in a catch-up year) by any contributions made under a 403(b) tax-sheltered annuity that are excluded from the participant's gross income (see Qs 2:95, 2:114). [Prior Treas. Reg. § 1.457-2(e)(1)] This reduction is not made for years after 2001.

Example 1. Sheila is an employee of a public school and in 2000 has a contract salary of $30,000. She participates in the school's eligible 457(b) plan and in a tax-sheltered annuity under Code Section 403(b). All contributions are assumed to be made from her contract salary and are fully vested. This is Sheila's first year of service with the employer. Assume that Sheila does not elect to use any of the alternate 403(b) limitations and that the employer's limitation on contributions under Code Section 415 (computed below) has not been exceeded. For 2000, Sheila can elect to defer $6,000 under the 403(b) plan and $2,000 ($8,000 − $6,000) under the eligible 457(b) plan, calculated as follows:

403(b) plan limitation. Includible compensation for 403(b) purposes is $30,000 (for 2000, for 403(b) purposes, includible compensation is not reduced by salary reduction amounts contributed under 403(b) and 457(b) plans). Therefore, the 403(b) plan limitation is $6,000, computed as follows:

$$\$30,000 \times 20\% \times 1 \text{ (year of service)} - \$0 \text{ (prior contributions)}$$

The 20 percent factor is a statutory amount. There is no reduction for amounts previously excludable because this is Sheila's first year of service with the employer.

457(b) plan limitation. The 457(b) plan limitation is $2,000, which is the lesser of $8,000 reduced by the exclusion of $6,000 under Code Section 403(b), or

33 percent of $22,000 (includible compensation after reduction of contract salary by deferral under the 457(b) plan and after the reduction for the exclusion under Code Section 403(b)).

Although Code Section 457(e)(5), defining the term *includible compensation*, was amended by TRA 1986, the examples contained in the history of this section are inconsistent with the statute. The text and an example in a footnote to the committee reports on the Revenue Act of 1978 state that contributions excludable under Code Section 403(b) reduce both the $7,500 ($8,500 in 2001) and the 33 percent of includible compensation limitations even though the percentage of includible compensation is computed without regard to such exclusion. [Rev. Act of 1978, § 131, H.R. Rep., nn. 1, 2] The example contained in the footnote using $27,000 rather than $22,500 as includible compensation conflicts with the law as enacted (and as amended). For years after 2001, this issue has been made moot by the amendment to Code Section 457(e)(5) to refer to the definition of *compensation* under Code Section 415(c)(3).

The limitation under Code Section 415 can be computed as follows: $30,000 × 0.25 = $7,500, which is not less than the $6,000 403(b) contribution.

Example 2. The facts are the same as those in Example 1, except that it is Sheila's second year of service (2001) and she elects to defer the maximum amount possible under the 403(b) plan and to defer nothing under the eligible 457(b) plan. Sheila's maximum exclusion allowance is $4,000, computed as follows:

$$\$30,000 \text{ (403(b) plan includible compensation)} \times .20$$
$$\times \text{ 2 years of service} = \$12,000$$

$12,000 − $8,000 ($6,000 excluded under the 403 (b) plan in the prior taxable year (2000) plus $2,000 deferred under the eligible 457 (b) plan in the prior taxable year) = $4,000

In neither case (Example 1 or Example 2), is the employer's limitation under Code Section 415 (which is applicable to 403(b) plans) exceeded. The amount that can be deferred under the general rules of Code Section 403(b) cannot exceed the lesser of the exclusion allowance or the limitations on employer contributions under Code Section 415. This amount can be computed as follows:

Year 1.

$$\$30,000 \times .25 = \$7,500, \text{ which is not less than the 403(b)}$$
$$\text{plan contribution of } \$6,000$$

Year 2.

$$\$30,000 \times .25 = \$7,500, \text{ which is not less than the 403(b)}$$
$$\text{plan contribution of } \$4,000$$

Example 3. The facts are the same as those in Example 1, except that Sheila is in her second year of service (2001), receives a $10,000 bonus during that year, and elects to defer the maximum amount possible under the eligible 457 plan and to defer nothing under the 403(b) plan. Sheila can defer $8,000, computed as follows:

Lesser of $80,000 or $10,000 ($40,000 × 0.25)
based on her gross compensation

Using the 33⅓ percent limitation, the deferral limitation can be computed as follows:

Lesser of $80,000 or $10,667 ($40,000 − $80,000) ÷ 3
based on her includible compensation

For years after 2001, the dollar limit is not reduced for contributions to other types of plans. [I.R.C. § 457(b)(2), amended by EGTRRA § 615(a)]

Q 2:119 Does the Section 402(g) limit apply to an individual who participates only in a 457 plan?

No. The limit on elective deferrals ($12,000 for 2003) under Code Section 402(g) does not apply to a participant in a 457 plan. [I.R.C. § 402(g)(3)] Elective deferrals subject to Code Section 402(g) (e.g., 403(b) plan salary reduction amounts) will reduce the dollar limit on 457(b) plan contributions for years before 2002 (see Q 2:118).

Q 2:120 Can contributions be made after a participant attains age 70½?

Yes. There are no maximum age restrictions. Further, a plan cannot restrict the opportunity to make contributions by reason of age. This would violate federal age discrimination law.

Q 2:121 Can contributions be made by participants over age 70½ who are receiving distributions?

Yes. Note that the participant's distributions may have to be recalculated at the end of each year to consider the new contributions.

IRS Approval

Q 2:122 Does the IRS require that an eligible 457(b) plan be submitted to it for approval?

No, although some state and local laws may require that a 457 plan be submitted to and approved by the IRS. Employers can request a private letter ruling to obtain advance approval of such plans as to form. The request is submitted to the

National Office of the IRS. The IRS imposes a user fee ($6,000 for 2002), payable on submission of the request. [Rev. Proc. 2002-8, 2002-1 I.R.B. 152] Procedures for requesting a private letter ruling are contained in Revenue Procedure 2002-1 [2002-1 I.R.B. 1]. The IRS has opened a ruling process for SBJPA changes to 457 plans. [Rev. Proc. 98-40, 1998-2 C.B. 134] It is understood that the IRS will begin issuing rulings for 457(b) plans on EGTRRA issues, including, beginning in 2004, on plan loan provisions. [Rev. Proc. 2004-3, 2004-1 I.R.B. 114]

In addition to requesting assurances that the plan document satisfies Code Section 457(b) as to form, the letter ruling can request that the IRS determine that the contributions are excludable from gross income and not taxed until distributed or made available to participants under the plan.

Q 2:123   How is a 457(b) plan submitted to the IRS for a ruling?

In Revenue Procedure 98-40 [1998-2 C.B. 134], the IRS announced that it would begin to consider requests for private letter rulings on eligible 457(b) plans that take into account changes made by the SBJPA and the Taxpayer Relief Act of 1997 (TRA 1997). Prior to 2004, the IRS would not issue a ruling on a plan that had received a previous private letter ruling if the plan had been amended solely by adding one or more of the model amendments contained in Revenue Procedure 98-41 [1998-2 C.B. 135] (see Q 2:124), or by replacing obsolete terms or deleting provisions inconsistent with those model amendments, but this restriction was lifted in 2004. [Rev. Proc. 2004-3, 2004-1 I.R.B. 114] For a governmental 457(b) plan, the IRS will issue a private letter ruling only if the plan includes provisions relating to the funding requirement of Code Section 457(g). A copy (or, in some cases, representative samples) of the trust, custodial account, or annuity contract or agreement must be provided with the ruling request. The IRS will not issue a ruling for a 457 plan if the plan provides that a loan can be made from assets held by the plan to any plan participant or beneficiary. (With respect to funded governmental 457(b) plans, such loans may be available, but the IRS is still considering the matter. See Qs 2:40, 2:41.)

Q 2:124   Is there IRS model language for amending 457(b) plans to reflect changes in the law by the SBJPA and TRA 1997?

Yes. In Revenue Procedure 98-41 [1998-2 C.B. 135], the IRS provided model amendments that can be used by an eligible employer to amend its eligible 457(b) plan to reflect the revisions made to Code Section 457 by the SBJPA and TRA 1997. An employer that has received a previous IRS private letter ruling on its 457(b) plan can continue to rely on that letter ruling if it adopts one or more of the amendments set forth in that revenue procedure on a word-for-word basis. In adopting a model provision, the employer is also permitted to replace obsolete terms (such as replacing *bookkeeping accounts* or *hypothetical accounts* with *accounts*) or to delete prior provisions that are inconsistent with the model amendment. Although many employers may not technically be able to rely on the model language (e.g., because of a need to make wording changes to conform to other plan provisions or because they do not have a prior ruling), the model language is a useful guide for drafting purposes. Beginning in 2004, the IRS will issue rulings on plans using the SBJPA and TRA model language or offering plans. [Rev. Proc. 2004-3, 2004-1 I.R.B. 114] As this book goes to press, the IRS has not issued model language to reflect the changes made by EGTRRA.

Q 2:125   What do the model amendments of Revenue Procedure 98-41 include?

The model amendments of Revenue Procedure 98-41 [1998-2 C.B. 135] include the following:

1. An optional amendment to permit in-service distributions of $5,000 or less, in three versions: involuntary (mandatory) distributions; voluntary (at the election of the employee) distributions; and distributions that are involuntary up to one level, which is set between zero and $5,000 at the discretion of the employer, and voluntary between that level and $5,000;

2. An amendment to provide for the additional distribution election authorized by Code Section 457(e)(9)(B);

3. An amendment to provide for implementing the cost-of-living adjustments for the dollar limit; and

4. For governmental plans only, an amendment to reflect the Section 457(g) funding requirement, in three versions: one for trusts, one for custodial accounts, and one for annuity contracts.

After 2001, item 2 will not apply to governmental plans, and item 3 is modified for plans of both governmental and tax-exempt employers.

Federal Tax Consequences to Participants

Q 2:126   What is the primary tax benefit of an eligible 457(b) plan?

The primary tax benefit of a 457(b) plan is the pretax deferral of income to a subsequent taxable year.

Q 2:127   What are the tax consequences to participants in an unfunded 457 plan?

The tax consequences to participants in an unfunded 457 plan are contained in Code Section 457(f) and the regulations hereunder. An unfunded plan of a state or local government or an agency or instrumentality thereof, or of any other tax-exempt organization or rural cooperative, is either an eligible or an ineligible deferred compensation plan. The tax consequences differ significantly.

Eligible plans. Under Code Section 457(a), participants in an eligible plan are taxed on deferred amounts when those amounts are paid or made available to plan participants following separation from service, attainment of age 70½, or occurrence of an unforeseeable emergency. The same treatment applies to amounts held in a 457(g) trust of a governmental employer. [I.R.C. § 457(a), (g)(2)(B)]

Ineligible plans. If the plan is not an eligible plan under Code Section 457, plan participants are taxed when amounts are deferred unless there is a substantial risk of forfeiture (see Q 2:131). If amounts deferred are subject to a substantial risk of forfeiture, they are included in the participant's or beneficiary's gross income in the first taxable year in which there is no substantial risk of forfeiture or in which the benefits are assigned or alienated by the participant (see Q 2:132). Ineligible plans are discussed more fully in chapter 11.

Q 2:128 When is compensation deferred under an eligible 457(b) plan subject to federal income tax?

For plans of tax-exempt employers, and for plans of governmental employers for years before 2002, compensation deferred under an eligible plan and any income attributable to the amounts deferred (to the extent vested, see Q 2:129) are included in the participant's federal gross income for the taxable year in which such compensation or other income is paid or otherwise made available to the participant or other beneficiary. For years after 2001, compensation deferred (and any income thereon) under an eligible governmental plan is taxed when paid in a manner similar to 401(a) and 403(b) plan distributions. [I.R.C. § 457(a)(1)(A)] Nongovernmental plans continue to use the rule previously stated. [I.R.C. § 457(a)(1)(B)]

Q 2:129 When is deferred compensation under an ineligible 457 plan subject to federal income tax?

If the deferred compensation program is not eligible, the participant will be taxed on any compensation deferred under the plan in the first taxable year in which there is no substantial risk of forfeiture of the rights to such compensation. [I.R.C. § 457(f)(1)] Substantial risk of forfeiture is more fully discussed in chapter 11. Except as mentioned in Q 2:172, the employer is exempt from tax on investments made with compensation deferred under the plan.

Q 2:130 When are amounts held in a 457(g) trust includible in gross income?

Notwithstanding the plan's funding, amounts in a 457(g) trust are includible in the gross income of participants and beneficiaries only to the extent, and at the time, provided in Code Section 457. Thus, they are treated as either an eligible or an ineligible plan amount as the case may be, as described in Q 2:127. [I.R.C. § 457(a), (g)]

Q 2:131   What is a substantial risk of forfeiture?

The rights of a person to compensation are subject to a substantial risk of forfeiture if the person's rights to such compensation are conditioned on the future performance of substantial services by the individual. [I.R.C. § 457(f)(3)(B)] Other restrictions may, however, be treated as a substantial risk of forfeiture (see chapter 11).

Generally, when the period of risk lapses with respect to an employee arrangement, the deferred compensation will be includible in the gross income of that employee. The ability to extend the period of risk ("rolling risks of forfeiture") will permit the employee to further defer the receipt of compensation to a future date and avoid taxation on the amounts until that date. It is likely that the IRS will scrutinize these plans to determine whether the risk really exists and, in particular, whether the employee has the right to extend the risk period before the risk lapses (Brisendine 1996). [See also Exempt Organizations Technical Instruction Program for FY 1999, § I (IRS Training 4277-050 (July 1998)]

Q 2:132   What happens if a participant assigns or alienates
             457 plan benefits?

If a participant assigns or alienates his or her 457 plan benefits, the benefits are considered made available to the participant and therefore are included in his or her gross income. [Rev. Act of 1978 § 131, H.R. Rep., at 53]

Q 2:133   How are participants in a funded nonqualified plan treated
             for tax purposes?

Unless the plan is an eligible 457(b) plan of a governmental entity, taxation generally is based on forfeitability for a plan that is funded (e.g., through a trust, an annuity contract, or another vehicle insulating the assets from the employer's general creditors) but is not a qualified plan (governed by Code Section 401). The tax consequences of funded nonqualified plans (other than tax-sheltered annuities and custodial accounts under Code Section 403(b) or 403(b)(7)) are contained in Code Sections 402(b), 403(c), and 83, which require that a participant recognize income when amounts are paid to a trust or insurance company unless there is a substantial risk of forfeiture as defined in Code Section 83(c)(1) and the participant's interest is nontransferable.

Q 2:134   Will the IRS rule on the taxable year of inclusion in the case
             of an independent contractor?

The IRS will not rule on tax consequences to unidentified independent contractors in nonqualified unfunded deferred compensation plans of state and local governments and tax-exempt organizations under Code Section 451 or 457; however, a ruling with respect to a specific independent contractor's participation in such a plan may be issued. [Rev. Proc. 96-3, § 3(34), 1996-1 C.B. 456]

Q 2:135   Are deferrals made to eligible plans currently included in the gross income of a participant for state income tax purposes?

Nearly all states that have an income tax provide for a deferral of tax liability under an eligible 457(b) plan. Illinois exempts both elective deferrals and distributions from state income tax. New Jersey taxes 403(b) and 457(b) plan salary reduction contributions, but not 401(k) deferrals. Pennsylvania taxes all salary reduction contributions. Both New Jersey and Pennsylvania defer tax liability on all gain and employer nonelective or matching contributions (Harm 1993). Massachusetts used to tax 457(b) plan salary reduction contributions but no longer does. It should be noted that the Pension Source Act (see Q 2:151) does not prevent a state from denying exclusions for contributions made to a retirement or deferred compensation plan, or from including the amount contributed currently in the participant's income. Thus, with the back door closed to taxing nonresidents, states are still able to walk in the front door by not allowing exclusions from the employee's income.

In addition, it is important to verify applicable tax and nontax local law. A number of municipalities impose a local tax on and require income tax withholding on elective contributions. Furthermore, at the time this is written, not all states have conformed their laws to EGTRRA.

Withholding and Reporting

Q 2:136   What are the withholding and reporting requirements applicable to eligible 457 plans before 2004?

For eligible 457 plans of tax-exempt employers before 2004, and for eligible 457 plans of governmental employers for years before 2002, Notice 2000-38 [2000-33 I.R.B. 174] contains rules with respect to the following:

1. Income tax withholding and reporting for annual deferrals to and distributions from an eligible 457 plan;
2. FICA payment and reporting for annual deferrals;
3. Employer identification numbers used for trusts established under Code Section 457(g); and
4. The application of annual reporting requirements to eligible 457 plan administrators and trustees holding assets of an eligible 457 plan in accordance with Code Section 457(g).

Notice 2000-38 addresses only the reporting and withholding rules that apply to eligible 457 plan participants who are or were employees and does not cover special reporting rules that may apply to eligible 457 plan participants who are or were independent contractors.

For years after 2001, EGTRRA provides that eligible governmental plans will report in a manner similar to 401(a) plans. Such plans will use Form 1099-R.

Effective January 1, 2004, IRS Notice 2000-38 [2000-33 I.R.B. 174] has been superseded by Notice 2003-20 [2003-19 I.R.B. 894].

Q 2:137   When were the rules contained in Notice 2000-38 effective?

Notice 2000-38 applied to deferrals and distributions made after December 31, 2001. Plan sponsors, plan administrators, and taxpayers could rely on the notice for distributions and deferrals made before January 1, 2002. [IRS Notice 2000-38, § VIII, 2000-33 I.R.B. 174]

Notice 2000-38 did not apply to governmental 457(b) plans after 2001. The IRS has issued guidance on reporting by governmental plans, in Notice 2003-20. [2003-19 I.R.B. 894]

Q 2:138   What are the rules for withholding and reporting for 457(b) plans effective after 2003?

The IRS has issued Notice 2003-20 [2003-19 I.R.B. 894], which explains the withholding and reporting requirements for eligible deferred compensation plans described in Code Section 457(b). The Notice updates Notice 2000-38 [2000-33 I.R.B. 174] to reflect the changes made to the rules governing 457(b) plans by EGTRRA.

Notice 2003-20 applies to deferrals and distributions made after December 31, 2001, the general effective date of EGTRRA changes. However, compliance with the rules in Notice 2000-38 prior to January 1, 2004, will not be treated by the IRS as a failure to comply with the applicable reporting and withholding rules under the Notice. An effect of this transition rule is that benefits being paid as periodic payments that are currently being paid under the reporting and withholding rules of Notice 2000-38 must comply with the Notice's reporting and withholding rules with respect to any payments made on or after January 1, 2004, even if the stream of payments commenced before EGTRRA.

Significant distinctions between Notice 2003-20 and Notice 2000-38 are as follows:

1. *Plan distributions—governmental plans.* After EGTRRA, governmental 457(b) plans are subject to federal income tax withholding (FITW) under the same rules applicable to tax-favored retirement plans. Under these rules, eligible rollover distributions are subject to 20 percent mandatory withholding if they are not rolled over to an eligible retirement plan. Distributions that are not eligible rollover distributions are either subject to withholding as if these distributions were wages (if the distributions are periodic payments) or subject to 10 percent elective withholding (if the distributions are nonperiodic payments).

2. The plan administrator of a governmental 457(b) plan is responsible for compliance with the FITW obligation unless the payor of the distribution

has been directed to undertake these responsibilities pursuant to Code Section 3405(d)(2)(A). Distributions to participants and beneficiaries are reported on Form 1099-R instead of Form W-2.

The other provisions of Notice 2003-20 are as follows:

1. *Annual deferrals.* As under Notice 2000-38, annual deferrals are not subject to FITW, but are reported on Form W-2.

2. *Plan distributions—tax-exempt plans.* Payments from tax-exempt organization 457(b) plans remain subject to FITW under the rules applicable to wages, unless paid to beneficiaries. Distributions to participants are reported on Form W-2; distributions to beneficiaries, on Form 1099-R. The person having control of a distribution, as determined under Code section 3401(d)(1), is responsible for compliance with the FITW obligation.

3. *EINs for governmental plan trusts.* A plan administrator or payor may (1) use its own EIN, aggregate distributions for withholding purposes and file a single Form 945, (2) request an EIN solely for reporting the aggregate withholding from all 457(b) plans under its control and file a single Form 945 under this EIN, or (3) request separate EINs for each 457(g) trust (or custodial account or insurance contract) and file multiple Form 945s. The payor must use the same name and EIN number on Form 1099-R as used for Form 945. Prior to EGTRRA, this report was made on Form 941, Employer's Quarterly Federal Tax Return, but because Form 941 is used for wage payments only, Form 945, Annual Return of Withheld Federal Income Tax, is now the appropriate form.

4. *FICA and FUTA taxes.* State and local governments are always exempt from FUTA taxes and often are exempt from FICA taxes. Also, tax-exempt organizations described in 501(c)(3) are exempt from FUTA taxes. To the extent the employer is subject to FICA or FUTA taxes, the amount deferred under the 457 plan is taken into account as of the later of when the services are performed or when there is no longer a substantial risk of forfeiture (determined under the principles of section 83). Therefore, FICA and FUTA taxes generally apply either upon deferral (if 100 percent vested) or in accordance with the vesting schedule. If deferrals are not subjected to FICA at the required time, the investment earnings on the deferrals also may be subject to FICA when paid or made available. These rules are consistent with Notice 2000-38.

5. *Annual information returns:*

   a. *Governmental plan trusts.* Report on Form 990-T any unrelated business taxable income. Forms 990 (tax-exempt), 1041 (trust tax return), 1120 (corporate tax return), and 5500 (annual report) are not required. IRS has maintained its Notice 2000-38 position that these trusts may be subject to unrelated business income tax, but this may be a reference only to plans of state colleges and universities. [I.R.C. § 511(a)(2)(B)]

   b. *Tax-exempt organizations.* Consistent with Notice 2000-38, tax-exempt report annual deferrals and payments to certain participants on Form 990.

Q 2:139   What are the income tax withholding and reporting rules for annual deferrals made to an eligible 457 plan?

Code Section 457(a) provides that annual deferrals under an eligible 457 plan and any income attributable to the amounts so deferred will not be includible in a participant's gross income until those amounts are paid or made available to the participant or beneficiary. Therefore, annual deferrals under an eligible 457 plan are not subject to income tax withholding at the time of the deferral; however, a participant's annual deferrals under an eligible 457 plan during the taxable year are reported on Form W-2, Wage and Tax Statement, in the manner described in the instructions to that form. For this purpose, *annual deferrals* means the amount of compensation deferred under the plan in accordance with Code Section 457(b), whether by salary reduction or nonelective employer contribution, during a taxable year. [IRS Notice 2003-20, 2003-19 I.R.B. 894]

Q 2:140   What are the income tax withholding rules for distributions from eligible 457 plans?

Distributions from an eligible 457 plan to a participant or former participant include all amounts that are paid or made available under the plan. For plans of tax-exempt employers, and for plans of governmental employers for years prior to 2002, distributions to a participant or former participant from an eligible 457 plan are wages under Code Section 3401(a) that are subject to income tax withholding in accordance with the income tax withholding requirements of Code Section 3402(a). The pension withholding rules of Code Section 3405 do not apply. [IRS Notice 2003-20, § IV.A, 2003-19 I.R.B. 894; see Temp. Treas. Reg. § 35.3405-1T, Q&A A-23] Governmental 457(b) plans after 2001 are treated in a manner similar to 401(a) plans for withholding purposes. [I.R.C. § 3401(a)(12)(E), added by EGTRRA § 641(a)(1)(D)(i); IRS Notice 2003-20, 2003-19 I.R.B. 894]

Q 2:141   How is income tax withholding calculated under an eligible 457 plan?

For years after 2001, for plans other than governmental plans, income tax withholding on distributions to a participant or former participant under an eligible 457 plan is calculated in the same manner as withholding on other types of wage payments. Special rules apply to the use of the flat rate withholding method as a supplement to regular wage withholding in cases where the payor is paying wages to the participant in addition to the distribution from an eligible 457 plan. [See Treas. Reg. § 31.3402(g)-1(a); Rev. Rul. 82-46, 1982-1 C.B. 158] If an eligible payor uses the flat rate of withholding as an alternative to regular wage withholding on a lump-sum payment, Section 13273 of the Omnibus Budget Reconciliation Act of 1993 [Pub. L. No 103-66] provides that a 28 percent flat rate must be used. [IRS Notice 2003-20, § IV.A, 2003-19 I.R.B. 894]

Q 2:142   Who is the person responsible for income tax withholding on eligible 457 plan distributions?

Code Section 3402(a) requires every employer making wage payments to withhold income tax on those wages. Code Section 3401(d)(1), however, provides that if the person for whom an individual performed services as an employee does not have control of the payment of the wages for those services, the person having control of the payment of the wages is responsible for income tax withholding on those wages. [See Treas. Reg. § 31.3401(d)-1(f)] Thus, if distributions are made by a trustee of an eligible plan under Code Section 457(g) established by a state or local government, the trustee is responsible for income tax withholding and reporting on the distributions. Similarly, if distributions are made by a Section 457(g) custodian or insurance carrier treated as a trustee under Code Section 457(g), the custodian or insurance carrier is responsible for income tax withholding on the distributions (see Qs 2:143–2:150). When distributions are made under a 457(b) plan established by a tax-exempt organization, the tax-exempt organization or any other person having control of the payment of the distributions is responsible for income tax withholding on the distributions. [IRS Notice 2003-20, § IV.B, 2003-19 I.R.B. 894]

Q 2:143   How are distributions to a participant or former participant reported?

Distributions to a participant or former participant under an eligible 457 plan during a taxable year are reported on Form W-2, Wage and Tax Statement, in the manner described in the instructions to that form. [See Rev. Rul. 82-46, 1982-1 C.B. 158] Income tax withheld from distributions from an eligible 457(b) plan is reported quarterly on Form 941, Employer's Quarterly Federal Tax Return. [IRS Notice 2003-20, § IV.C, 2003-19 I.R.B. 894] This rule apparently supersedes the reference in the instructions to Form 1099-R, Distributions from Pensions, Annuities, Retirement or Profit-Sharing Plans, IRAs, Insurance Contracts, Etc., that distributions from commercial annuities under a nonqualified plan can be reported using Form 1099-R (except in the case of distributions to beneficiaries, as discussed in Q 2:144).

Q 2:144   How are distributions to a beneficiary of a deceased participant under an eligible 457 plan reported to the IRS?

Distributions to a beneficiary of a deceased participant under an eligible 457 plan are reported on Form 1099-R, Distributions from Pensions, Annuities, Retirement or Profit-Sharing Plans, IRAs, Insurance Contracts, Etc. [See Rev. Rul. 86-109, 1986-2 C.B. 196] No income tax withholding is required for distributions from an eligible 457 plan to beneficiaries. [Rev. Rul. 59-64, 1959-1 C.B. 31] The instructions for Form 1099-R describe how this form is completed for distributions made to a beneficiary. [IRS Notice 2003-20, § IV.D, 2003-19 I.R.B. 894]

Q 2:145 How are income tax deposits with respect to an eligible 457 plan trust reported?

Generally, the income tax withheld on distributions should be reported on Form 941 of the person responsible for withholding (see Q 2:142) and aggregated with other amounts reported by that person on Form 941 to determine the frequency of federal tax deposits under Treas. Reg. § 31.6302-1.

Note. This requirement is the same as the first alternative described in Announcement 84-40 [1984-17 I.R.B. 31]. Alternatively, the IRS will permit trustees of 457(g) trusts, or custodians or insurance carriers treated as trustees under Code Section 457(g)(3), to use the other two alternatives contained in Announcement 84-40 for the tax administration of such withholdings:

1. The trustee, custodian, or insurance carrier can request an employer identification number solely for the purpose of reporting the aggregated withholding from the distributions of every 457(g) trust, custodial account, or annuity contract under its control, making deposits and filing Form 941 accordingly.

2. The trustee, custodian, or insurance carrier can request and use a separate employer identification number for each 457(g) trust (or custodial account or insurance contract), making deposits and filing Form 941 accordingly. The trustee, custodian, or insurance carrier exercising any of the above alternatives for depositing and reporting the tax withheld from 457(g) trust distributions must follow the same option in filing the related information returns, such as Form W-2 (in the case of distributions to participants or former participants) or 1099-R (in the case of distributions to beneficiaries). That is, the trustee, custodian, or insurance carrier must use the same name and employer identification number on Form W-2 or 1099-R as those under which the tax was deposited and the quarterly return filed. The trustee, custodian, or insurance carrier must aggregate and deposit all taxes pursuant to Treasury Regulations Section 31.6302-1 under the employer identification number chosen. The above-described options relate only to trusts, annuity contracts, or custodial accounts established pursuant to Code Section 457(g) for amounts deferred under an eligible 457 plan. (See Qs 2:147, 2:148 relating to the remittance of Social Security, Medicare, and FUTA taxes by the employer.) [IRS Notice 2000-38, § IV.E, 2000-33 I.R.B. 174]

Q 2:146 To whom do the FICA and FUTA tax reporting rules apply?

The rules relating to FICA (Social Security and Medicare) tax apply to employees of state and local governments only if they are subject to Social Security or Medicare tax under Code Section 3121(u) (relating to Medicare), Code Section 3121(b)(7)(E) (relating to agreements entered into pursuant to Section 218 of the Social Security Act), or other provisions of the Code, such as Code Section 3121(b)(7)(F) (relating to state and local government employees who are not members of a state or local retirement system). The FICA rules generally apply to employees of tax-exempt organizations unless a specific exclusion is applicable. The FICA tax includes the employer's share of the FICA tax imposed under Code Section 3111 and the employee's share imposed under Code Sections 3101 and 3102.

The rules relating to the Federal Unemployment Tax Act (FUTA) do not apply to service for a state or local government entity because Code Section 3306(c)(7) provides a FUTA exemption for service performed in the employ of a state or any political subdivision thereof or any instrumentality of any one or more of the foregoing.

The rules relating to FUTA apply to service for a tax-exempt organization other than a tax-exempt organization described in Code Section 501(c)(3) [see I.R.C. § 3306(c)(8)]. [IRS Notice 2000-38, § V.A, 2000-33 I.R.B. 174]

Q 2:147   When are Social Security, Medicare, and FUTA taxes imposed?

Code Sections 3121(a) (relating to Social Security and Medicare) and 3306(b) (relating to FUTA) define *wages* as all remuneration for employment unless a specific exclusion applies (see Q 2:144). Code Sections 3121(v)(2) and 3306(r)(2) contain special timing rules that apply in determining when amounts deferred under a nonqualified deferred compensation plan are required to be taken into account for purposes of Social Security, Medicare, and FUTA. Under these sections, an amount deferred under a nonqualified deferred compensation plan, including an eligible 457 plan, is required to be taken into account for purposes of Social Security, Medicare, and FUTA taxes as of the later of when the services are performed or when there is no substantial risk of forfeiture of the rights to such amount. Thus, if an eligible 457 plan provides that annual deferrals are fully and immediately vested, annual deferrals are subject to Social Security, Medicare, and FUTA taxes at the time of deferral. If, however, the annual deferrals are not fully and immediately vested, but are subject to a substantial risk of forfeiture, the annual deferrals (and earnings thereon) generally are taken into account for purposes of Social Security, Medicare, and FUTA at the time such amounts are no longer subject to a substantial risk of forfeiture. For purposes of Social Security, Medicare, and FUTA taxes, the determination of whether a substantial risk of forfeiture exists is made in accordance with the principles of Code Section 83 and the regulations thereunder (see Qs 2:131, 11:7). [Treas. Reg. §§ 31.3121(v)(2)-1(e)(3), 31.3306(r)(2)-1]

If amounts deferred under an eligible 457 plan are properly taken into account as Social Security, Medicare, and FUTA wages when deferred (or, if later, when they cease to be subject to a substantial risk of forfeiture), the amounts subsequently paid or made available to a participant or beneficiary under the 457 plan are not subject to Social Security, Medicare, or FUTA taxes. [I.R.C. §§ 3121(v)(2)(B), 3306(r)(2)(B); Treas. Reg. § 31.3121(v)(2)-1(a)(2)(iii), -1(d)(2)] If an amount deferred for a period is not properly taken into account, distributions attributable to that amount, including income on the amounts deferred, may be wages for FICA purposes when paid or made available. [Treas. Reg. § 31.3121(v)(2)-1(d)(1)(ii)] Special rules apply to eligible 457 plans other than plans under which benefits are based on a participant's account balance. [Treas. Reg. § 31.3121(v)(2)-1(e)(4)]

Example 1. State R's eligible 457(b) plan provides for elective deferrals from current salary, as well as a 1 percent of salary nonelective contribution for each employee who participates in the plan and who is employed by State R during the plan year. All employees who participate in the plan are covered by an agreement under Section 218 of the Social Security Act. All deferrals and contributions, including the state's contribution, are fully and immediately vested. Because these contributions are not subject to a substantial risk of forfeiture (and the services to which they relate have already been performed), the elective deferrals are required to be taken into account as wages at the time of the deferral and State R's nonelective contribution is required to be taken into account as wages at the time of the contribution for purposes of the Social Security and Medicare tax.

Example 2. The facts are the same as those in Example 1, except that the plan has three-year vesting for State R's nonelective contribution. Therefore, an employee's rights to the nonelective contributions (and the associated earnings) are subject to a substantial risk of forfeiture until the employee has been employed by State R for three years. State R's nonelective contributions (and earnings thereon) are not wages for purposes of the Social Security and Medicare tax until the employee has completed three years of service. At that time, the aggregate amount of State R's nonelective contributions, plus earnings thereon, is required to be taken into account as wages for purposes of the Social Security and Medicare tax. Once an individual has met the vesting requirements, future nonelective contributions by State R are required to be taken into account as wages for purposes of the Social Security and Medicare tax at the time of the contribution.

[IRS Notice 2003-20, §§ VI.B, VI.C, 2003-19 I.R.B. 894]

Q 2:148 Must deposits relating to Social Security, Medicare, and FUTA taxes be aggregated?

Yes. The employer must aggregate and deposit Social Security and Medicare taxes associated with an eligible 457 plan (including the employer's share of Social Security and Medicare taxes under Code Section 3111) with all other Social Security and Medicare taxes and withheld income taxes paid on behalf of its employees in accordance with Treasury Regulations Section 31.6302-1 and must report these taxes on Form 941. Employers subject to FUTA must aggregate and deposit FUTA amounts associated with an eligible 457 plan with all other FUTA amounts paid on behalf of their employees in accordance with Treasury Regulations Section 31.6302(c)-3 and must report these payments on Form 940. [IRS Notice 2003-20, § VI.D, 2003-19 I.R.B. 894]

Q 2:149 How are annual deferrals to eligible 457 plans of tax-exempt organizations reported?

Annual deferrals to, and payments to certain participants in, an eligible 457 plan of a tax-exempt organization are reported on the organization's Form 990, Return of Organization Exempt From Income Tax, in the manner described in the instructions to that form. [IRS Notice 2003-20, § VII.A, 2003-19 I.R.B. 894] Different rules apply to 457(g) trusts (see Q 2:150).

Q 2:150 How are annual deferrals to 457(g) trusts reported, since 457(g) trusts do not have to file Form 990?

According to Notice 2000-38, a trust described in Code Section 457(g) is not required to file Form 990, Return of Organization Exempt From Income Tax; Form 1041, U.S. Income Tax Return for Estates and Trusts; Form 1120, U.S. Corporation Income Tax Return; or Form 5500, Annual Return/Report of Employee Benefit Plans. Revenue Procedure 95-48 [1995-2 C.B. 418] provides that governmental units and affiliates of governmental units that are exempt from federal income tax under Code Section 501(a) are not required to file annual information returns on Form 990.

A trust described in Code Section 457(g) may be required to file Form 990-T, Exempt Organization Business Income Tax Return. [See Treas. Reg. §§ 1.6012-2(e) and 1.6012-3(a)(5) for the requirements for filing Form 990-T]

Note. Further information regarding the reporting, payment, and depositing of employment taxes such as Social Security, Medicare, and FUTA taxes and withheld income tax can be found in Publication 15, Circular E, Employer's Tax Guide; Publication 15-A, Employer's Supplemental Tax Guide; and Publication 963, Federal-State Reference Guide: Social Security Coverage and FICA Reporting by State and Local Government Employers. These publications will be revised, as appropriate, to reflect the proper treatment of trusts under Code Section 457(g).

[IRS Notice 2003-20, § VII.B, 2003-19 I.R.B. 894]

State Taxation of Nonresidents

Q 2:151 Are nonresidents of a state subject to the state's income tax on distributions from an eligible 457(b) plan?

No. The Pension Source Act prohibits states (including political subdivisions of a state), the District of Columbia, and the possessions of the United States from imposing income tax on "retirement income" from an eligible 457(b) plan of an individual who is not a resident or domiciliary of the jurisdiction (as determined under the laws of that jurisdiction) (Lesser 1996; Mazawey 1996). [Pub. L. No. 104-95, amending 4 U.S.C. § 114] Making a nonresident pay tax on distributions of amounts deferred while he or she was a resident of a state is called source taxation.

Because the statute provides that domicile or residence is determined under the laws of the state seeking to tax the pension distributions, and not under the laws of the distributee's state of domicile or residence, it is possible for an individual's retirement income to be subject to state income tax in two or more states, and a state is not required to give credit for tax paid to any other state.

Q 2:152   What type of income is protected by the Pension Source Act?

"Retirement income" is protected. This includes any income from:

1. An eligible deferred compensation plan under Code Section 457 (protection from source taxation may also be available on distributions from an ineligible plan; see Q 2:155);
2. A governmental plan;
3. A qualified retirement plan under Code Section 401(a);
4. A qualified annuity plan under Code Section 403(a);
5. A SEP under Code Section 408(k);
6. A SIMPLE retirement account under Code Section 408(p);
7. A tax-sheltered annuity plan under Code Section 403(b);
8. An IRA under Code Section 408;
9. A trust created before June 25, 1959, that is part of a plan funded only by employee contributions; and
10. Certain retired or retainer pay of a member or former member of the uniformed services.

Payments to nonresidents from an ineligible mirror plan may also be protected from source taxation (see Q 2:156).

Q 2:153   What is retirement income under the Pension Source Act?

Retirement income means "any income" paid to nonresidents from the tax-favored plans listed in Q 2:152. Thus, death benefits, disability benefits, and any other payments from a tax-favored plan to a nonresident are protected from source taxation.

Q 2:154   How much income is protected from source taxation?

There is no dollar limit on the amount of income that can be treated as retirement income.

Q 2:155   Are distributions from an ineligible plan protected by the Pension Source Act?

Protection from source taxation may also be available on distributions from an ineligible plan. The term *retirement income* (see Q 2:152) also includes income from a nonqualified deferred compensation plan, provided such income is:

1. Part of a series of substantially equal periodic payments made over:
   a. The life or life expectancy of the recipient (or the joint lives or life expectancies of the recipient and the recipient's beneficiary); or
   b. A period not less than 10 years; or
2. A payment received after termination of employment from certain types of mirror plans.

Q 2:156   What is a mirror plan?

A mirror plan is a nonqualified retirement plan maintained by an employer for providing benefits in excess of certain limits on contributions and benefits contained in the Code that apply to qualified retirement plans. The benefits provided under a mirror plan are those that would have been provided under the terms of a qualified retirement plan (including certain designated tax-sanctioned retirement plans) but for the application of the following limits on contributions and benefits.

Code Section 403(b) limits the amount of annual contributions that can be made to a tax-sheltered annuity (maintained by certain tax-exempt entities and public educational organizations) for years prior to 2002 generally to the excess of the product of 20 percent of compensation and the participant's years of service over amounts contributed in prior years (the exclusion allowance). The exclusion allowance was repealed beginning in 2002. In addition to the Code Section 415 limit on employer and employee contributions, which applies to tax-sheltered annuities, there is an annual dollar limit on elective contributions. For 2001, this limit is $10,500, but it may be increased slightly (up to $3,000 to a $15,000 lifetime limit) if the employee has completed at least 15 years of service with a qualifying organization. For 2002 this limit is $11,000, and increases $1,000 per year until it is $15,000 in 2006, it is adjusted for cost-of-living thereafter.

Code Section 415 limits the amount of annual contributions that can be made to a participant in a defined contribution plan and the benefits that can be provided to a participant under a defined benefit pension plan. The annual defined contribution limit is $40,000 or 100 percent of compensation for 2002. For 2002, the maximum annual benefit that can be provided under a defined benefit plan is generally the lesser of 100 percent of highest three year's average compensation (this limit does not apply to governmental plans, see note in appendix J on the CD-ROM) or $160,000, payable in the form of a straight life annuity with no ancillary features. Depending on which of several elections are made by an employee, a tax-sheltered annuity arrangement under Code Section 403(b) could also be affected (until 2000) by Code Section 415(e)(5). Under that section, the participant's employer is considered to maintain the contract if the participant elects under Code Section 415(c)(4)(D) to have the provisions of Code Section 415(c)(4)(C) apply (the C election limitation or overall limit), or if the participant has more than 50 percent control of the employer within the meaning of subsection (b) or (c) of Code Section 414 (as modified by Code Section 415(h)). Under the overall limit, contributions to the tax-sheltered annuity program must be combined with all contributions made to qualified plans to determine whether the C election limitation has been exceeded.

Code Section 401(a)(17) limits the amount of annual compensation that can be taken into account under a qualified retirement plan for purposes of computing benefits and contributions to $170,000 for 2001 ($200,000 for 2002).

Code Section 401(k) limits the amount of elective deferrals (contributions at the election of the employee) that can be made by a highly compensated employee to a qualified cash or deferred arrangement (commonly called a 401(k) plan) according to a nondiscrimination test based on the amount of such contributions made on behalf of non-highly compensated employees.

Code Section 408(k) limits the amount of elective deferrals that can be made by a highly compensated employee to a SARSEP according to a nondiscrimination test based on the amount of such contributions made on behalf of non-highly compensated employees.

Code Section 401(m) limits the amounts of employer matching contributions and after-tax employee contributions that can be made to a 401(k) plan on behalf of highly compensated employees according to a nondiscrimination test based on the amount of such contributions made on behalf of non-highly compensated employees.

Code Section 402(g) limits the total annual amount of elective deferrals that can be made to a 401(k) plan (and similar arrangements) generally to $10,500 for 2001 ($11,000 plus catch-up contributions if age 50 for 2002).

Q 2:157   Will all mirror plans benefit from the Pension Source Act?

No. In the absence of regulations, determining when a plan is "maintained solely for the purpose of providing retirement benefits in excess of the limitations imposed by one or more of sections 401(a)(17), 401(k), 401(m), 402(g), 403(b), 408(k) or 415 of such Code or any other limitation on contribution or benefits in such Code on plans to which such sections apply" may be difficult to ascertain. Fortunately, the periodic payment rule (see Q 2:155) assumes that these amounts are not subjected to state income tax upon distribution. Commentators have suggested that employers may have to split their nonqualified plans into two or more arrangements to get the protection and benefit offered by the Pension Source Act (Shultz and Hall 1996). For example, a plan that contains a nonprotected benefit would not qualify under the "maintained solely" rule. As a consequence, distributions from such a plan could be subject to state source taxation. It also remains to be seen how aggressive states will be in determining when an individual is domiciled within a state and in subjecting unprotected benefits to taxation.

Q 2:158   Are in-service payments under a window plan protected from source taxation?

No. Only payments after termination of service from a plan that is maintained solely for the purpose of providing benefits in excess of limitations on contributions or benefits in the Code are protected by the Pension Source Act.

Excise Taxes

Q 2:159   Are distributions from an eligible 457(b) plan subject to the premature distribution penalty tax?

No, with one exception. Distributions generally are not subject to the 10 percent excise tax on distributions to individuals who have not attained age 59½. [I.R.C. § 72(t)(1)] However, amounts rolled over to a governmental 457(b) plan from an IRA, 401(a) plan, or 403(b) plan must be separately accounted for, and when distributed will be subject to the Section 72(t) excise tax. [I.R.C. § 72(t)(9), added by EGTRRA § 641(a)(2)(C)]

Q 2:160   Are distributions from an eligible 457(b) plan subject to the excess distribution penalty tax?

No. Distributions are not subject to the 15 percent excise tax on excess distributions. [I.R.C. § 4980A(e)] That tax has been repealed, effective January 1, 1997. [TRA 1997 § 1073(a)]

Q 2:161   Are excess 457(b) plan deferral amounts invested in mutual fund custodial accounts subject to the special 6 percent excess contribution penalty tax?

No. [I.R.C. § 4972(a)(2)]

Q 2:162   Are participants subject to the 50 percent excise tax on excess accumulations in a 457 plan?

Yes (see Q 3:54). [I.R.C. § 4974(a)]

Q 2:163   Are participants subject to the 10 percent excise tax on excess elective contributions?

No. [I.R.C. § 4979(e)]

Q 2:164   Are employers or employees subject to excise tax penalties if nondeductible contributions are made to a 457 plan?

Neither are subject to this excise tax. [I.R.C. §§ 501(a), 4972(d)(1)(A), 4972(d)(1)(B), 4973(a)]

Q 2:165   Are employers subject to the 10 percent or 15 percent prohibited transaction excise tax under the Code or ERISA?

The excise tax penalties under Code Section 4975 do not apply to 457 plans [I.R.C. § 4975(e)], and 457 plans generally are not subject to ERISA (see chapter 6).

If there is a prohibited transaction within the meaning of Code Section 503, that section would deny a tax exemption to the organization that engaged in the prohibited transaction. Only a few types of exempt organizations are subject to the prohibited transaction rule of Code Section 503. These generally include the following:

1. A supplemental unemployment compensation trust under Code Section 501(c)(17) after 1959;

2. After December 31, 1969, an employee benefit trust created before June 25, 1959, that provides pension benefits that are funded solely by employee contributions [I.R.C. § 501(c)(18)]; and

3. An organization described in Code Section 401(a), relating to a qualified plan that is a governmental plan within the meaning of Code Section 414(d) after March 1, 1954 (Code Section 414(d), in relevant part, defines *governmental plan* as a plan established and maintained for its employees by the government of any state or political subdivision of a state). It is not clear whether this applies to a 457(g) trust.

[See I.R.C. § 457(g)(2)(A)]

Thus, such organizations are not exempt from tax under Code Section 501(a) if they have engaged in a prohibited transaction; however, the exemption from taxation applies only for taxable years after the taxable year during which the organization is notified by the Secretary of the Treasury that it has engaged in a prohibited transaction, unless the organization entered into such a prohibited transaction with the purpose of diverting corpus or income of the organization from its exempt purposes and the transaction involved a substantial part of the organization's corpus or income. [I.R.C. § 503(a),(b)]

For tax-exemption purposes, under Code Section 503(b), the term *prohibited transaction* means any transaction in which an organization:

1. Lends any part of its income or corpus, without the receipt of adequate security and a reasonable rate of interest, to;

2. Pays any compensation, in excess of a reasonable allowance for salaries or other compensation for personal services actually rendered, to;

3. Makes any part of its services available on a preferential basis to;

4. Makes any substantial purchase of securities or any other property, for more than adequate consideration in money or money's worth, from;

5. Sells any substantial part of its securities or other property for less than an adequate consideration in money or money's worth to; or

6. Engages in any other transaction that results in a substantial diversion of its income or corpus to

the creator of the organization (if a trust); a person who has made a substantial contribution to the organization; a member of the family (as defined in Code Section 267(c)(4)) of an individual who is the creator of that trust or who has made a substantial contribution to the organization; or a corporation controlled by that creator or person through the ownership, directly or indirectly, of 50 percent or more of the total combined voting power of all classes of stock entitled to vote or 50 percent or more of the total value of shares of all classes of stock of the corporation.

Investment of 457 Plan Assets

Q 2:166   Will amounts deferred be considered made available if the participant may choose how deferrals are invested?

No. Furthermore, the plan may provide for the selection of investment modes for the investment of deferred amounts both before and after payments have begun. [Treas. Reg. § 1.457-1(b)(1)]

Q 2:167   Must the employee be given a choice as to investment modes?

No, participant direction is a permissive feature; however, for a state or local government employer's eligible plan, many state laws require participant-directed investment.

Q 2:168   Are fiduciaries of 457(g) trusts subject to ERISA?

No. Governmental plans are not subject to any of the provisions of Title I of ERISA. [ERISA § 4(b)(1)] The identity and conduct of any plan fiduciaries are governed solely by state law (including the trust document).

Q 2:169   Are fiduciaries of top-hat plans subject to the prohibited transaction rules and 15 percent excise taxes on prohibited transactions under ERISA and the Code?

No. A plan that is unfunded and maintained primarily for the purpose of providing deferred compensation for a select group of management or highly compensated employees is exempt from the fiduciary responsibility (and most other) provisions of ERISA. [ERISA § 401(a)(1); I.R.C. § 4975(e)(1)] (See chapters 6 and 8.)

Q 2:170   What kinds of investments can be used for a deferred compensation plan?

For a deferred compensation plan of a nongovernmental employer, any investment the employer permits can be used for the plan. For a deferred compensation plan of a state or local government employer, state law will regulate what investments may be held for the plan. Frequently, the types of permitted investments are specified by the state's enabling statute. Investments are more fully discussed in chapter 4.

Q 2:171 What is an enabling statute?

In local government law, political subdivisions of a state, such as cities and counties, do not have authority to take action until the state grants them legal power to do so. An enabling statute is a state statute that grants political subdivisions of a state the authority to take a particular action (see Q 4:2).

Q 2:172 Is income or gain generated on assets held in a 457(g) trust subject to tax?

No, but see Q 2:173 regarding the possible application of unrelated business income tax (UBIT). In the case of an eligible 457 governmental plan that has assets held in a 457(g) trust custodial account or annuity, the trust is exempt from tax. [I.R.C. § 457(g)(2)(A)]

In nearly all other cases (see Q 2:175), income on an informal set-aside that may be used to pay for the unfunded deferred compensation promise is not subject to tax because the employer is tax-exempt.

Q 2:173 Is a 457(g) trust subject to UBIT?

The answer is not currently clear. Prior to the enactment of the funding provision of Code Section 457(g), assets not held in trust by the governmental plan sponsor were not subject to UBIT, and governmental excess benefit arrangements are not subject to UBIT by application of Code Section 115. [I.R.C. § 415(m)(1)] Code Section 457(g)(2)(A) states, however, that such a trust "shall be treated as an organization exempt from taxation under section 501(a)." [See also Treas. Reg. § 1.457-8(a)(1)] Some practitioners believe that governmental 401(a) plans are subject to UBIT because they are 401(a) plans described in Code Section 511(a)(2)(A), and Form 990-T should be filed if necessary. Also, the IRS has stated that such filings may be required. [IRS Notice 2003-20, 2003-19 I.R.B. 894] However, this may be a reference only to plans of state colleges and universities. [I.R.C. § 511(a)(2)(B)]

Q 2:174 Can a tax-exempt organization purchase an annuity contract?

Yes, but a social club may have to pay a tax on the income on the annuity contract (see Q 2:175).

Q 2:175 Are social clubs subject to any special investment restrictions?

Yes. A social club (or other organization) that is exempt from tax under Code Section 501(c)(7) is subject to a special rule that could restrict its ability to invest funds needed to provide deferred compensation payments.

Although an organization exempt from tax is exempt from the application of Code Section 72(t), relating to growth inside an annuity contract not held by a natural person (as well as exempt from tax on other investment income, or gain), such an organization may have to pay tax on its unrelated business taxable income (UBTI). [I.R.C. §§ 501(b), 511(a)(2)(A)]

If an annuity contract is purchased by a social club or other organization exempt from tax under Code Section 501(c)(7), any growth inside the contract is treated as UBTI and may be subject to tax. Any income or gain realized on other investments of a Section 501(c)(7) organization is also UBTI.

Other types of exempt organizations are not adversely affected by the purchase of an annuity contract or other investments, because UBTI generally refers to business income, not investment income or gain. For Section 501(c)(7), (9), (17), and (20) organizations, UBTI means "the gross income (excluding any exempt function income), less the deductions allowed . . . which are directly connected with the production of the gross income. . . ." [I.R.C. § 512(a)(3)(A)] For this purpose, *exempt function income* means

> the gross income from dues, fees, charges, or similar amounts paid by members of the organization as consideration for providing such members or their dependents or guests goods, facilities, or services in furtherance of the purposes constituting the basis for the exemption of the organization to which such income is paid. [See GCM 39717 (Apr. 11, 1988)] Such term also means all income (other than an amount equal to the gross income derived from any unrelated trade or business regularly carried on by such organization . . .), which is set aside— . . . in the case of an organization described in paragraph (9), (17), or (20) of section 501(c), to provide for the payment of life, sick, accident, or other benefits.

[I.R.C. § 512(a)(3)(B)]

Because an organization described in Code Section 501(c)(7) is not listed, the *other benefits* (e.g., severance benefits or deferred compensation) are not treated as exempt function income. [See I.R.C. § 512(a)(3)(B)(ii)] As a result of not being considered exempt function income, any investment income or annuity growth is not excluded from the business's gross income, and becomes UBTI. These restrictions apply only to organizations exempt under Code Section 501(c)(7). [See I.R.C. § 512(a)(3)(A), (B)] If UBTI exceeds the specific deduction of $1,000, the organization must file Form 990-T (see chapter 13). [I.R.C. §§ 511(a), 512(b)(12), 6033(a)] Such an organization should consider investing in municipal securities or cash value life insurance. An unmanaged portfolio of non-dividend-paying securities may also be considered, provided the securities are distributed and not sold by the social club. A managed portfolio could generate UBTI as a result of trading gains. [Letter from Stanfield Hill, J.D., CLU MONY (Sept. 17, 1996)]

Q 2:176 Does federal securities law apply to 457 plans?

Possibly. The application of federal securities law to 457 plans is discussed more fully in chapter 10.

Life Insurance

Unfunded Eligible Plans

Q 2:177 Can premiums or mortality expense charges be based on gender-based rates?

No. The premium or mortality expense charges of a 457 life insurance or annuity contract must be based on gender-neutral rates. [Arizona Governing Committee for Tax Deferred Annuity & Deferred Compensation Plans v. Norris, 463 U.S. 1073 (1983)]

Q 2:178 Can life insurance protection be purchased in an unfunded, nongovernmental eligible 457(b) plan?

Yes. Purchasing life insurance contracts is a permissible investment option under an unfunded, nongovernmental eligible deferred compensation plan, provided the plan satisfies the following requirements:

1. The employer retains all incidents of ownership of the contracts;
2. The employer is the sole beneficiary of the contracts; and
3. The employer is under no obligation to transfer the contracts or to pass through the proceeds of such contracts to any participant or his or her beneficiary.

If the three requirements are not satisfied, the cost of the life insurance protection is considered to be made available and subject to income tax. [Rev. Act of 1978, H.R. Rep. at 53; Treas. Reg. § 1.457-1(b)(1), (b)(2), ex. 7; P.L.R. 9003021]

A 457 governmental trust is treated differently (see Qs 2:182–2:186).

Q 2:179 If life insurance is purchased in an unfunded eligible 457(b) plan, is the yearly renewable term cost or PS-58/Table 2001 cost included in the participant's gross income?

No. The investment of eligible plan assets in life insurance can be made at a plan participant's request. Even so, the yearly renewable term cost or

PS-58/Table 2001 costs representing the value of the current economic benefit (death protection) will not be considered made available to the plan participant provided the requirements specified in Q 2:178 are satisfied. [Treas. Reg. § 1.457-1(b)(2), ex. 7] The proceeds of such a policy are taxable to the recipient (see Q 2:178). The plan participant or beneficiary is taxed on the distribution from the plan, and the distribution does not get life insurance tax treatment. [Treas. Reg. §§ 1.101-1(b)(2)(ii), 1.457-1(c)] After 2001, PS-58 rates may no longer be used. New rates called Table 2001 rates must be used after 2001. [IRS Notice 2001-10, 2001-5 I.R.B. 459; see also IRS Notice 2002-59, 2002-36 I.R.B. 481] (See appendix J.)

Q 2:180   How are death benefits from an unfunded eligible plan treated for tax purposes?

Death benefits payable from a 457 plan did not qualify for the $5,000 death benefit exclusion under Code Section 101(b). [Treas. Reg. § 1.457-1(c)] (Code Section 101(b) was repealed by the SBJPA.)

Q 2:181   How are PS-58/Table 2001 costs reported in an unfunded eligible plan?

There are no PS-58/Table 2001 costs in an unfunded eligible plan.

Funded Eligible Governmental Plans

Q 2:182   Can a funded eligible governmental 457 plan purchase life insurance protection?

Yes. The three rules applicable to unfunded plans (see Q 2:178) would not apply to a funded governmental plan because all plan assets are required to be held in a trust under the exclusive benefit rule (see Qs 2:38, 2:39). Thus, the trust would be the owner and beneficiary of the contract if the 401(a) trust rules will apply by analogy. Note that a life insurance contract does not satisfy the requirements of a 457(g) annuity. It must be held in an express trust or custodial account (see Q 2:44). Upon a proper plan distribution, the trust would be obligated to transfer the contracts or to pass through the proceeds of such contracts to a participant or his or her beneficiary. [I.R.C. § 457(g)]

Q 2:183   Is the cost of the pure life insurance protection (PS-58/Table 2001 cost) currently taxable to the participant in a funded 457 plan?

Probably. [Rev. Act of 1978 § 131, H.R. Rep.] By analogy to the 401(a) trust rules, the life insurance protection provides a current economic benefit to the participant and should be treated as being made available. Thus, it should represent currently taxable income to the participant.

Q 2:184 Are death proceeds from life insurance contracts purchased in a funded 457 plan taxable to the recipient?

Although a life insurance contract is permitted as an investment in a 457(b) plan, it is not generally purchased because no amount paid or made available as a death benefit or life insurance proceeds from the plan is excludable under Code Section 101. [Treas. Reg. § 1.457-10(d)] For governmental 457(b) plans, life insurance must be held in a trust or custodial account. [Treas. Reg. § 1.457-8(a)(3)(iii)]

Q 2:185 How much of the proceeds are excludable from the recipient's gross income when received from an eligible funded governmental 457 plan?

Final regulations provide that all amounts paid as death benefits or life insurance proceeds are includible in gross income. [Treas. Reg. § 1.457-10(d)]

Q 2:186 How are PS-58/Table 2001 costs reported in a 457(f) trust?

PS-58/Table 2001 costs represent the economic value of the current life insurance protection, if any, purchased under the plan. It is unclear how PS-58/Table 2001 costs are to be reported to participants and the IRS in a 457 trust, if at all (see Q 2:182; see chapter 13). Although the IRS has traditionally treated 457 plan contributions as deferred wages (compensation) reportable on Form W-2, it remains to be seen whether the reporting requirements will apply to the employer, trustee, or both, or whether Form 1099-R will become the form for reporting.

Custodial Accounts Used as 457(g) Trusts

Q 2:187 Who must hold the assets of a custodial account used as a 457(g) trust?

A bank or a qualified nonbank custodian (see Q 2:189) must hold title to all assets in a custodial account used as a 457(g) trust. [I.R.C. § 401(f); Treas. Reg. § 1.457-8(a)(3)]

Q 2:188 What is a bank?

The term *bank* is broadly defined and includes the following:

1. A bank or trust company incorporated and doing business under the laws of the United States (including laws relating to the District of Columbia) or of any state, a substantial part of the business of which consists of receiving deposits and making loans and discounts, or of

exercising fiduciary powers similar to those permitted to national banks under authority of the comptroller of the currency, and which is subject by law to supervision and examination by state, territorial, or federal authority having supervision over banking institutions. This term also includes a domestic building and loan association.

2. A corporation that, under the laws of the state of its incorporation or under the laws of the District of Columbia, is subject to both the supervision of and examination by the authority in the jurisdiction in charge of the administration of the banking laws.

3. An insured credit union. [Federal Credit Union Act § 101(6) (12 U.S.C. § 1752)]

Thus, banks, federally insured credit unions, and savings and loan associations are acceptable. Any other person or entity generally must be approved by the IRS. For this purpose, a custodial account is treated as a trust, and the custodian of the account is treated as the trustee thereof.

Although a bank is required to be the trustee, the participant may be granted the power in the governing instruments to control the investment of the trust funds either by directing investments—including reinvestment, disposal, and exchanges—or by disapproving proposed investments, including reinvestment, disposal, or exchanges. In some cases, the plan may contain provisions whereby the participant appoints a third party, such as a registered investment advisor, to invest and reinvest the assets of the trust.

Q 2:189 Under what criteria will the IRS grant approval for a nonbank custodian?

The trustee may be a person other than a bank if the person demonstrates to the satisfaction of the IRS that the manner in which the person will administer the trust will be consistent with the requirements of Code Sections 457(b) and 457(g). [Treas. Reg. § 1.457-8(a)(3)(iii)(B)] Effective upon approval, the person may act as a nonbank custodian. The person must demonstrate by written application to the IRS that it satisfies the following requirements:

Fiduciary ability. The applicant must demonstrate in detail its ability to act within the accepted rules of fiduciary conduct. Such demonstration must include the following elements of proof:

1. The applicant must ensure the uninterrupted performance of its fiduciary duties notwithstanding the death or change of its owners. Thus, for example, there must be sufficient diversity in the ownership of the applicant to ensure that the death or change of its owners will not interrupt the conduct of its business. If individuals each of whom owns more than 20 percent of the voting stock in the applicant own, in the aggregate, no more than 50 percent of such stock, sufficient diversity in the ownership of an incorporated applicant is demonstrated.

2. The applicant or a parent corporation has issued securities. The securities must be registered under Section 12(b) of the Securities Exchange

Act of 1934 [15 U.S.C. § 781(b)] or under Section 12(g)(1) of that Act [15 U.S.C. § 781(g)(1)].

Sufficient diversity in the ownership of an applicant that is a partnership means that (1) individuals each of whom owns more than 20 percent of the profit interest in the partnership own, in the aggregate, no more than 50 percent of that profit interest, and (2) the individuals each of whom owns more than 20 percent of the capital interest in the partnership own, in the aggregate, no more than 50 percent of that capital interest.

For purposes of determining diversity, the ownership of stock and of capital and profit interests is determined in accordance with the rules for constructive ownership of stock provided in Code Sections 1563(e) and 1563(f)(2).

Established location. The applicant must have an established place of business in the United States where it is accessible during every business day.

Fiduciary experience. The applicant must have fiduciary experience or expertise sufficient to ensure that it will be able to perform its fiduciary duties. Evidence of fiduciary experience must include proof that a significant part of the business of the applicant consists of exercising fiduciary powers similar to those it will exercise if its application is approved. Evidence of fiduciary expertise must include proof that the applicant employs personnel experienced in the administration of fiduciary powers similar to those the applicant will exercise if its application is approved.

Fiduciary responsibility. The applicant must ensure compliance with the rules of fiduciary conduct. The applicant must demonstrate that under applicable regulatory requirements, corporate or other governing instruments, or its established operating procedures:

1. The owners or directors of the applicant will be responsible for the proper exercise of fiduciary powers by the applicant. Thus, all pertinent matters, including the determination of policies, the investment and disposition of property held in a fiduciary capacity, and the direction and review of the actions of all employees utilized by the applicant in the exercise of its fiduciary powers, will be the responsibility of the owners or directors. In discharging this responsibility, the owners or directors may assign to designated employees, by action duly recorded, the administration of such of the applicant's fiduciary powers as it may be proper to assign.

2. A written record will be made of the acceptance and of the relinquishment or closing out of all fiduciary accounts, and of the assets held for each account.

3. If the applicant has the authority or the responsibility to render any investment advice with regard to the assets held in or for each fiduciary account, the advisability of retaining or disposing of the assets will be determined at least once during each 12-month period.

4. All employees taking part in the performance of the applicant's fiduciary duties will be adequately bonded.

5. The applicant will employ or retain legal counsel who will be readily available to pass upon fiduciary matters and to advise the applicant.

6. In order to segregate the performance of its fiduciary duties from other business activities, the applicant will maintain a separate trust division under the immediate supervision of an individual designated for that purpose. The trust division may utilize the personnel and facilities of other divisions of the applicant, and other divisions of the applicant may utilize the personnel and facilities of the trust division, as long as the separate identity of the trust division is preserved.

Adequacy of net worth. In the case of applications received after January 5, 1995, no initial application will be accepted by the IRS unless the applicant has a net worth of not less than $250,000 (determined as of the end of the most recent taxable year). The term *net worth* means the amount of the applicant's assets less the amount of its liabilities, as determined in accordance with generally accepted accounting principles. A special rule is provided for nonbank trustees that are members of the Securities Investor Protection Corporation (SIPC). Thereafter, the applicant must satisfy the adequacy of net worth requirements as follows:

1. No fiduciary account will be accepted by the applicant unless the applicant's net worth (determined as of the end of the most recent taxable year) exceeds the greater of $100,000 or 4 percent (or, in the case of a passive trustee that is a member of SIPC, 2 percent) of the value of all of the assets held by the applicant in fiduciary accounts (determined as of the most recent valuation date).

2. The applicant will take whatever lawful steps are necessary (including the relinquishment of fiduciary accounts) to ensure that its net worth (determined as of the close of each taxable year) exceeds the greater of $50,000 or 2 percent (or, in the case of a passive trustee that is a member of SIPC, 1 percent) of the value of all of the assets held by the applicant in fiduciary accounts (determined as of the most recent valuation date).

Value of assets. The applicant will determine the value of the assets held by it in trust at least once in each calendar year and no more than 18 months after the preceding valuation. The assets will be valued at their fair market value.

Audits. At least once during each 12-month period, the applicant will enable detailed audits of the fiduciary books and records to be made by a qualified public accountant. At that time, the applicant will ascertain whether the fiduciary accounts have been administered in accordance with the law and sound fiduciary principles. The audits must be conducted in accordance with generally accepted auditing standards and must involve whatever tests of the fiduciary books and records of the applicant are considered necessary by the qualified public accountant.

Funds awaiting investment or distribution. Funds held in a fiduciary capacity by the applicant awaiting investment or distribution will not be held uninvested or undistributed any longer than is reasonable for the proper management of the account.

Custody of investments. Except for investments pooled in a common investment fund, the investments of each account will not be commingled with any other property.

Safekeeping. Assets of accounts requiring safekeeping will be deposited in an adequate vault. A permanent record will be kept of assets deposited in or withdrawn from the vault.

Common investment funds. The assets of a 457 plan may be pooled in a common investment fund if the applicant is authorized under applicable law to administer a common investment fund and if pooling the assets in a common investment fund is not in contravention of the plan documents or applicable law, including securities laws. (See chapter 10.)

Financial responsibility. The applicant must exhibit a high degree of solvency commensurate with the obligations it will undertake. Among the factors to be taken into account are the applicant's net worth, its liquidity, and its ability to pay its debts as they come due.

Capacity to account. The applicant must demonstrate in detail its experience and competence with respect to accounting for the interests of a large number of individuals (including calculating and allocating income earned and paying out distributions to payees). Such individuals could include shareholders in a regulated investment company or variable annuity contract holders.

The applicant must demonstrate in detail its experience and competence with respect to other activities normally associated with the handling of retirement funds. Examples of activities normally associated with the handling of retirement funds include (1) receiving, issuing receipts for, and safely keeping securities; (2) collecting income; (3) executing such ownership certificates, keeping such records, making such returns, and rendering such statements as are required for federal tax purposes; (4) giving proper notification regarding all collections; (5) collecting matured or called principal and properly reporting all such collections; (6) exchanging temporary for definitive securities; (7) giving proper notification of calls, subscription rights, defaults in principal or interest, and the formation of protective committees; and (8) buying, selling, receiving, or delivering securities on specific directions.

Special rules. An applicant that undertakes to act only as a passive trustee may be relieved of one or more of the following requirements on clear and convincing proof that such requirements are not germane, under all the facts and circumstances, to the manner in which the applicant will administer any trust. A trustee is a passive trustee only if under the written trust instrument the trustee has no discretion to direct the investment of the trust funds or any other aspect of the business administration of the trust but is merely authorized to acquire and hold particular investments specified by the trust instrument.

Evidence that an applicant is subject to federal or state regulation with respect to one or more relevant factors must be given weight in proportion to the extent that such regulatory standards are consonant with the requirements of Code Section 408(n). Such evidence may be submitted in addition to, or in lieu of, the required specific proofs.

An applicant will be approved to act as a nonbank bank if the following requirements are satisfied:

1. The applicant is a credit union, industrial loan company, or other financial institution designated by the IRS.

2. The investment of the trust assets will be solely in deposits in the applicant.

3. Deposits in the applicant are insured (up to the dollar limit prescribed by applicable law) by an agency or instrumentality of the United States or by an organization established under a special statute the business of which is limited to insuring deposits in financial institutions and providing related services. An applicant that satisfies the requirements concerning fiduciary experience is automatically approved and (notwithstanding the preceding) is not required to submit a written application.

Substitution of trustee. No applicant will be approved unless the applicant undertakes to act as trustee only under trust instruments that contain a provision to the effect that the grantor is to substitute another trustee on notification by the IRS that such a substitution is required because the applicant has failed to comply with the statutory requirements or is not keeping such records, or making the returns, or rendering the statements that are required by forms or regulations.

If the applicant is approved, a written notice of approval will be issued to the applicant. The notice of approval will state the day on which it becomes effective and (except as otherwise provided therein) will remain effective until revoked. Generally, the notice will not be revoked unless the IRS determines that the applicant has knowingly, willfully, or repeatedly failed to administer fiduciary accounts in a manner consistent with the statutory requirements or has administered a fiduciary account in a grossly negligent manner. [I.R.C. § 408(a), (n); Treas. Reg. § 1.408-2(e)]

Q 2:190   Can a governmental retirement board qualify as a nonbank custodian?

The regulations governing such approvals do not seem to forbid it, but it is unclear, at this time whether the IRS will issue any such approvals to government retirement boards.

Distributions and Related Issues

Q 2:191   Must an eligible 457(b) plan specify when benefits are payable from the plan?

Yes. In general, an eligible plan must specify a fixed or determinable time of payment by reference to the occurrence of an event (e.g., retirement) that triggers the individual's right to receive or commence receiving amounts deferred under the plan. The individual can be given the right to make an election as to that time or event (see Qs 2:192, 2:206).

Q 2:192   When can distributions be made from an eligible 457(b) plan?

Benefits cannot be made available to participants before the earliest of the following:

1. The occurrence of an unforeseeable emergency [I.R.C. § 457(d)(1)(A)(iii); TAMRA § 1011(e)];
2. The participant's separation (severance after 2001) (see Qs 1:14, 7:13) from service with the sponsoring employer;
3. Retirement in accordance with the terms of any retirement plan maintained by the sponsoring entity;
4. The participant's attainment of age 70½; or
5. The participant's death.

[I.R.C. § 457(d)(1)]

In addition, minimum distribution requirements apply to eligible plans. (The minimum distribution requirements are more fully discussed in chapter 3. See Q 2:220 for a general discussion of basic minimum distribution concepts.)

Q 2:193   Can an employer offset plan benefits by the amount due from the participant?

Possibly in the case of a nongovernmental 457(b) plan, to the extent that a plan (or applicable law) does not contain a prohibition against alienation or assignment. There is an economic benefit issue raised by an offset; that is, whether the amount of the offset is taxable under the cash equivalency theory (Press and Patchell 1996). As a result of the exclusive benefit rule, a governmental 457(g) trust is not subject to offset, except perhaps for expenses (e.g., administrative, legal) properly chargeable against it as specified in the trust document.

Q 2:194   Can a secured creditor of the employer make a claim on 457 plan assets?

A secured creditor of the employer cannot make a claim on 457 plan assets if the plan is funded, that is, if the plan is a governmental 457 trust. In other cases, it would depend on the status of a secured creditor under applicable law.

Q 2:195   Are plan distributions excludable from the bankruptcy estate?

Contradictory federal court rulings leave this issue unresolved. Creditors' rights and bankruptcy protection are more fully discussed in chapter 9.

A U.S. district court determined that an eligible 457(b) plan is excluded from the bankruptcy estate. [In re Wheat, 149 B.R. 1003 (Bankr. S.D. Fla. 1992)] A different federal court determined that an eligible 457(b) plan is not excluded from the bankruptcy estate. [Pederson v. Public Employees Benefit Services Corp., No. 91-91194 (S.D. Iowa June 16, 1993)]

In-Service Withdrawals

Q 2:196   Under what conditions may a participant receive a distribution while employed?

Except for cash-outs of accounts of less than $5,000 where there have been no contributions for the two years prior to the distribution (see Q 2:215), there are only two conditions under which a participant may request a distribution prior to separation from service with the employer:

1. For an unforeseeable emergency (the plan must contain provisions for allowing such distributions, and the term *unforeseeable emergency* must be defined in the plan documents); or

2. On attainment of age 70½.

The need to pay funeral expenses of a spouse or a dependent may also constitute an unforeseen emergency. [Treas. Reg. § 1.457-6(c)(2)(i)]

Special rules apply to terminated plans (see Q 2:250).

Q 2:197   Can rollovers be ignored for cash-outs?

For years after 2001, a plan will be permitted to ignore amounts attributable to rollover contributions when determining the cash-out amount. [I.R.C. § 457(e)(9)(A)(ii), amended by EGTRRA § 648(b)]

Q 2:198   What constitutes an unforeseeable emergency?

If plan documents provide for distributions on account of an unforeseeable emergency, that term must be defined as follows:

1. Severe financial hardship to the participant resulting from a sudden and unexpected illness or accident of the participant or beneficiary, the participant or beneficiary's spouse, or the participant or beneficiary's dependent; or

2. Loss of the participant's or beneficiary's property because of casualty, or other similar extraordinary and unforeseeable circumstances arising as a result of events beyond the control of the participant or beneficiary.

[Treas. Reg. § 1.457-6(c)(2)]

Q 2:199   What are dependents?

The term *dependent* means any of the following individuals over half of whose support, for the calendar year in which the taxable year of the taxpayer begins, was received from the taxpayer (or is treated under Code Section 152 as received from the taxpayer):

1. A son or daughter of the taxpayer, or a descendant of either;
2. A stepson or stepdaughter of the taxpayer;
3. A brother, sister, stepbrother, or stepsister of the taxpayer;
4. The father or mother of the taxpayer, or an ancestor of either;
5. A stepfather or stepmother of the taxpayer;
6. A son or daughter of a brother or sister of the taxpayer;
7. A brother or sister of the father or mother of the taxpayer;
8. A son-in-law, daughter-in-law, father-in-law, or mother-in-law of the taxpayer;
9. A brother-in-law or sister-in-law of the taxpayer; or
10. An individual (other than an individual who at any time during the taxable year was the spouse—determined without regard to Code Section 7703—of the taxpayer relating to the definition of the term *spouse* for other purposes) who, for the taxable year of the taxpayer, has as his or her principal place of abode the home of the taxpayer and is a member of the taxpayer's household.

[I.R.C. § 152(a)–(e)]

Q 2:200   What other circumstances must exist to grant a withdrawal to a participant with an unforeseeable emergency?

The circumstances that will constitute an unforeseeable emergency will depend on the facts of each case, but in any case payment may not be made to the extent that hardship is or may be relieved (1) through reimbursement or compensation by insurance or otherwise; (2) by liquidation of the participant's assets, to the extent that the liquidation of such assets would not itself cause severe financial hardship; or (3) by cessation of deferrals under the plan. Examples include imminent foreclosure or eviction from the participant or beneficiary's primary residence, the need to pay for medical expenses, and the need to pay for funeral expenses of a spouse or a dependent. [Treas. Reg. § 1.457-6(c)(2)]

Q 2:201   What amounts may be distributed as a result of this withdrawal?

Amounts payable are permitted only to the extent reasonably needed to satisfy the emergency need, including taxes anticipated on the distribution. [Treas. Reg. § 1.457-6(c)(2)(iii)]

Q 2:202   Is an unforeseeable emergency the same as a hardship under the rules applicable to 401(k) plans?

No. It is easy to confuse distributions for unforeseeable emergencies with hardship distributions. Under a 401(k) plan, a sponsor can make distributions for such things as tuition expenses, down payments for houses, or ordinary medical expenses. Because these expenses are foreseeable, they cannot be used as a reason to distribute 457(b) plan assets. Thus, as a general rule, plan money cannot be distributed for an event within the control of the employee. [Treas. Reg. §1.457-6(c)(2)(i)]

Q 2:203   Are any penalties associated with unforeseeable emergency withdrawals?

No statutory penalties are assessed as a result of receiving an unforeseeable emergency withdrawal. Receipt of such a withdrawal, however, results in the later receipt of reduced benefits and can be conditioned on the cessation of future deferrals.

Example. Dorothy is granted a withdrawal by the plan's administrative committee for an unforeseeable emergency. As a condition for receiving this withdrawal, she may be asked to suspend elective deferrals for six months in order to contribute to meeting the emergency need.

Q 2:204   How do unforeseeable emergency withdrawals differ from safe harbor hardship withdrawals from 401(k) plans?

The circumstances that permit hardship withdrawals from a qualified 401(k) plan are broader than the circumstances that permit unforeseeable emergency withdrawals from an eligible 457(b) plan. Under a 401(k) plan, participants can make withdrawals for

1. Expenses for medical care incurred by the employee, spouse, or other dependents;
2. Costs related to the purchase of a principal residence;
3. Payment of tuition, room and board, and related educational expenses for postsecondary education of the employee, spouse, and dependents for the next 12-month period; and
4. Payments necessary to prevent eviction from or foreclosure on the employee's primary residence.

[Treas. Reg. § 1.401(k)-1(d)(2)(iii)]

Example. Andy wants to make a withdrawal from his eligible 457(b) plan account balance to pay postsecondary educational expenses. His reason for requesting a loan would permit him to receive a hardship withdrawal from a 401(k) plan but does not allow him to receive an unforeseeable emergency withdrawal from a 457(b) plan.

Retirement Distributions

Q 2:205   What is normal retirement age?

The determination of a normal retirement age is significant for purposes of the catch-up rule. *Normal retirement age* (NRA) refers to the following:

1. *NRA.* The plan must specify an NRA that is on or after the earlier of age 65 or the minimum NRA age. [Treas. Reg. § 1.457-4(c)(3)(v)]

2. *Minimum NRA.* The earliest age at which the participant has the right to retire without the consent of the employer and immediately to receive unreduced retirement benefits under the employer's basic defined benefit retirement plan, or a money purchase pension plan in which the participant participates, if the participant is not eligible to participate in a defined benefit plan. In the case of qualified plan or firefighters as defined under Section 415(b)(2)(H)(ii)(I), the plan may designate an NRA as early as age 40. [Treas. Reg. § 1.457-4(c)(3)(v)(B)]

3. *Maximum NRA.* The age elected by the participant, which may not be later than the later of age 70½. [Treas. Reg. § 1.457-4(c)(3)(i)(A)]

The plan may also allow the participant to designate his or her NRA within these ages. [Treas. Reg. § 1.457-4(c)(3)(v)]

A participant's election of an NRA is irrevocable once contributions have been made utilizing the three-years catch-up limitation (see Qs 2:100, 2:101).

Q 2:206   Can plan elections affect the determination of normal retirement age?

Should a participant elect to utilize the limited catch-up provision of the plan (see Q 2:100), presumably, the plan may provide that NRA will be no later than the participant's age three years following the commencement of the application of this provision.

Example. Bo has elected the limited catch-up provision at age 63. The plan may provide that Bo's NRA will then be deemed to be age 66 (or sooner if so elected).

Q 2:207   Must a normal retirement age be specified in the plan?

A plan must designate an NRA, but may alternatively provide that a participant may designate his or her NRA, within the permissible ages. [Treas. Reg. § 1.457-4(c)(3)(v)(A)]

Q 2:208   What if a participant works beyond the normal retirement age specified in the plan?

The last three years catch-up election may no longer be used. If the plan allows the participant to elect his or her NRA, the participant should not elect an NRA until he or she is ready to make the contributions, subject to the age 70½ limit.

Q 2:209   When must a plan commence distributions?

For plans of tax-exempt employers, and for plans of governmental employers for years before 2002, amounts deferred under a 457(b) plan will be includible in gross income when made available on or after the participant's severance of employment. [Treas. Reg. § 1.457-7(c)]

The participant may elect to defer commencement of distributions under the plan if the election is made after a permissible distribution event has occurred and prior to the time the amounts would be made available, and he or she has made only one election. [I.R.C. § 457(e)(9)(B)]

For governmental plans, for years after 2001, participant distribution elections may be made in a manner similar to elections for 401(a) and 403(b) plans. [Treas. Reg. § 1.457-7(b)]

Separation from Service and Deferred Distributions

Q 2:210   Can participants who retire early defer the commencement of distributions?

Yes. A plan may contain a provision to allow for the deferral of distributions. Distributions must commence no later than April 1 of the year following the year in which the participant attains age 70½ or retires, whichever is later.

Q 2:211   When must a participant elect when distributions commence?

If participants are given the right to make such an election, they must do so before the funds are made available.

Example. An eligible 457(b) plan provides that benefits are payable on the 60th day following a participant's severance of employment. The plan could allow a different period after severance of employment, but 60 days from severance of employment or 60 days after the close of the plan year in which severance from employment occurred are both common. The participant must make his or her election to commence or not to commence distributions within that period.

Q 2:212   If distributions are deferred, when are these amounts considered to be "made available" to the participant?

For plans of tax-exempt employers, and for plans of governmental employers for years before 2002, that are subject to the "made available" rule, no amount need be made available earlier than the age to which the distribution is deferred or on account of a participant's or beneficiary's right to delay the election of the method of payout. Participants can change the effective date of deferrals prior to commencement of payments. [Treas. Reg. § 1.457-7(c), ex. 6]

Example. Horace makes an irrevocable election to defer distribution of his benefit until age 65, the plan's NRA. He dies at age 63. Horace's beneficiary need not change the method of payment (deferral of the distribution) and can receive the benefit two years hence; the distribution will not be considered to have been made available (taxable as gross income) until it is actually made.

Q 2:213 When is an employee treated as having separated from service under an eligible 457(b) plan for years prior to 2002?

Under the same desk rule, an employee is treated as having separated from service:

1. If there is a separation from service that would constitute a separation from service for purposes of the qualified plan lump-sum distribution rules contained in Code Section 402(e)(4)(A)(iii);
2. On death; or
3. On retirement.

[Prior Treas. Reg. § 1.457-2(h)(2); see chapter 7]

For years after 2001, the same desk rule is repealed. Separation from service as an event of distribution has been changed to severance of employment. [I.R.C. § 457(d)(1)(A)(ii), amended by EGTRRA § 641(a)(1)(C); Treas. Reg. § 1.457-6(b)]

Q 2:214 Would a merger of plan sponsors be considered a separation from service?

A change in the employment relationship as a result of merger or restructuring would not in and of itself constitute a separation from service. [Rev. Rul. 81-26, 1981-1 C.B. 200; see chapter 7 for a discussion of 457 plans and mergers and acquisitions] It might, however, constitute a "severance of employment" for distribution purposes if there is a change in the common-law employer. A more vexing issue may be determining who is the employer.

Q 2:215 Are there special rules for distributions of amounts less than $5,000 from eligible plans?

Yes. Benefits are not treated as made available by reason of certain elections if the total amount payable is $5,000 or less for plan years beginning after August 5, 1997 ($3,500 for plan years beginning before August 6, 1997). The total amount payable to a participant under the plan is not treated as made available if the participant can elect to receive such amount (or the plan can distribute such amount without the participant's consent) and:

1. The amount does not exceed $5,000 for 2000;

2. No amount has been deferred under the plan with respect to the participant during the two-year period ending on the date of distribution;

3. No additional amounts can be deferred by the participant under the
   plan; and

4. There has been no prior distribution under the plan to the participant to
   which this rule applied.

Items 2 and 4 apply only in taxable years beginning after 1996. The $5,000
amount is adjusted for cost-of-living increases after 1997 in $50 increments. [I.R.C.
§ 457(e)(9)(A); SBJPA § 1447(e); TRA 1997 § 1071(a)(2); Treas. Reg. § 1.457-6(e)]

Example. Myra has an account balance of $3,300 in an eligible 457(b) plan
that permits participants with balances of $5,000 or less to elect a lump-
sum payment on separation from service and within 60 days. Myra could
take a distribution of the amount, but she will not be considered to have
constructively received it if she does not elect to take it.

Q 2:216 When must the election be made to receive a lump-sum benefit?

For plans of tax-exempt employers, and plans of governmental employers
for years before 2002, the election must be made before the funds are made
available.

Example 1. Emily terminates employment with the Rosemont Marine Biol-
ogy Institute, a tax-exempt employer, and before such amounts become
payable, she makes an election not to receive a single-sum payment; thus,
no amounts are immediately made available to Emily at the time of her
severance of employment. [Treas. Reg. § 1.457-7(c)(3), ex. 2] Emily may
subsequently be eligible to postpone receipt of her distribution one more
time (see Q 2:72).

Example 2. Joe's 457 plan, sponsored by a tax-exempt employer, provides
for payments to be made on the 60th day following separation from service.
Joe must make his election to defer distributions before benefits commence,
that is, before the 60th day following his separation from service. [I.R.C.
§ 457(d)(1)] Joe may be entitled to make one further election to defer
payments and taxes.

Q 2:217 Can a participant defer commencement of distributions that are already scheduled to begin?

Yes. For plans of tax-exempt employers, and for plans of governmental
employers after 2001, an election to defer commencement of distributions payable to a participant under the plan will not cause the amounts to be made
available provided the election is made after amounts may be available under
the plan in accordance with Code Section 457(d)(1)(A) and before commencement of such distributions. Only one such election may be made. [I.R.C.
§ 457(e)(9)(B); Treas. Reg. § 1.457-7(c)(2)(iii)]

Distributions to Independent Contractors

Q 2:218   What constitutes severance of employment if the participant is an independent contractor?

An independent contractor generally is considered having severance of employment with an employer on the expiration of the contract (or, in the case of more than one contract, all contracts) under which services are performed for the employer maintaining the plan if the expiration constitutes a good-faith and complete termination of the contractual relationship.

An expiration will not constitute a good-faith and complete termination of the contractual relationship if the employer anticipates the renewal of the contractual relationship or the independent contractor's becoming an employee. For this purpose, an employer is considered to anticipate the renewal of the contractual relationship with an independent contractor if it intends to contract again for the services provided under the expired contract and neither the employer nor the independent contractor has eliminated the independent contractor as a possible provider of services under any such new contract. Further, an employer is considered to intend to contract again for the services provided under an expired contract if the employer's doing so is conditioned only on the employer's incurring a need for the services, or the availability of funds, or both. [Treas. Reg. § 1.457-6(b)(2)]

Q 2:219   Is there a safe harbor approach for determining when an independent contractor separates from service?

Yes. A plan will satisfy the requirement that no amount be paid or made available under the plan to an independent contractor before the independent contractor separates from service if the plan provides that:

1. No amount will be paid to the participant before a date at least 12 months after the day on which the contract under which services are performed for the employer expires (or, in the case of more than one contract, all such contracts expire); and

2. No amount payable to the participant on that date can be paid to the participant if, after the expiration of the contract (or contracts) and before that date, the participant performs services for the employer as an independent contractor or an employee.

[Treas. Reg. § 1.457-6(b)(2)(ii)]

Q 2:220   What are the minimum distribution requirements?

Three separate minimum distribution requirements apply to eligible plans:

1. The plan must meet the minimum distribution requirements applicable to qualified plans, such that benefits:

   a. Commence no later than the required beginning date; and

b. Will be distributed over the life of the employee or the lives of the employee and beneficiary, not in excess of the life expectancy of the employee or the joint life expectancies of the employee and beneficiary [I.R.C. § 401(a)(9)(A)].

2. The plan must comply with additional requirements relating to the term of payment for benefits.

3. Distributions payable over a period of more than one year must be paid no less frequently than annually, and the amount of the distributions cannot substantially increase (see Q 3:21).

For years after 2001, these minimum distribution rules for 457(b) plans are conformed to the rules for 401(a) and 403(b) plans. [Treas. Reg. § 1.457-6(d)]

The minimum distribution requirements are more fully discussed in chapter 3.

Plan-Approved Domestic Relations Orders

Q 2:221   What is a plan-approved domestic relations order?

In general, a plan-approved domestic relations order (PADRO) is a state court's judgment, decree, or order that affirms the rights of an alternate payee to a distribution or payment from a governmental plan under Code Section 414(d) or a church plan under Code Section 414(e) and relates to the provision of child support, alimony payments, and/or marital property under the state's domestic relations law. (PADROS are more fully discussed in chapter 13.)

In other words, a PADRO is a domestic relations order that a governmental or church plan arranges (or is required by law) to follow. It need not meet all of the requirements of a "qualified" domestic relations order (QDRO) under Code Section 414(p), although many such plans voluntarily apply the QDRO rules to PADROs. After the amendments to Code Section 414(p) by EGTRRA, the terms *PADRO* and *QDRO* are likely to be used interchangeably in 457(b) plans. [I.R.C. § 414(p)(12)]

Q 2:222   Are 457 plans subject to the QDRO rules?

Prior to EGTRRA, the QDRO rules under Code Section 414(p) did not apply to 457(b) plan distributions; however, a church or governmental 457 plan could make payments to a spouse or former spouse under a PADRO (see Q 2:223). The EGTRRA permits QDRO-based early distributions from 457(b) plans after 2001. [I.R.C. § 414(p)(11); EGTRRA § 635(c); Treas. Reg. § 1.457-10(c)]

Q 2:223   Can payment be made under a PADRO?

A distribution or payment from an eligible church or governmental plan can be made under a PADRO/QDRO; however, the plan must specifically contain provisions that allow for the payment. [I.R.C. § 414(p)(11); P.L.R. 9619029, 9237018, 9145010]

Q 2:224   What form of benefit may the alternate payee receive under a PADRO/QDRO?

The alternate payee may receive the same form of benefit elected or available to the participant or permitted under the provisions of the plan.

Q 2:225   What are the tax consequences of a PADRO/QDRO distribution?

Any distribution to either the participant or an alternate payee will be includible in gross income for the year of distribution. For years before 2002, if the plan is not a church or governmental plan, the distribution is taxable to the participant as ordinary income. If the plan is a church or governmental plan and the payee is a spouse or former spouse, any distribution is taxable to the recipient. [I.R.C. § 414(p)(11)] For years after 2001, all such distributions are taxable to the recipient. [I.R.C. § 414(p)(12), added by EGTRRA § 635(c); Treas. Reg. § 1.457-10(c)(1)]

Q 2:226   When can PADRO amounts be distributed?

Prior to 2002, distribution is not permitted at any time other than upon satisfying the conditions outlined in Q 2:227. [P.L.R. 9145010] The final regulations provide that a distribution may be made before such an event. [Treas. Reg. § 1.457-10(c)(1)]

Q 2:227   Can a distribution from a 457 plan under a PADRO/QDRO be rolled over into an IRA?

Not in years before 2002 (see Q 2:242). Such an amount would be considered to have been "made available," and would be considered a taxable distribution followed by an ordinary contribution to an IRA. [Rev. Rul. 86-103, 1986-2 C.B. 62; P.L.R. 9145010] The rollover issue was discussed in Letter Ruling 9145010. The following is a discussion of that ruling.

Code Section 401(a)(13)(A) provides that a trust does not constitute a qualified exempt trust under that section unless the plan of which the trust is a part provides that benefits provided under the plan cannot be assigned or alienated; however, Code Section 401(a)(13)(B) states that Code Section 401(a)(13)(A) does not apply to a qualified trust if a QDRO creates, assigns, or recognizes a right to any pension benefit payable with respect to a participant. Code Section 402(a) regulates the taxation of the beneficiaries of any employees' exempt trust described in Code Section 401(a). Code Section 402(e)(1)(B) (regarding rollovers) states, in relevant part, that the general rollover rules apply to "the alternate payee who is the spouse or former spouse of the participant by reason of any qualified domestic relations order (within the meaning of section 414(p)). . . ."

Code Section 414(d), in relevant part, defines *governmental plan* as a plan established and maintained for its employees by the government of any state or political subdivision of a state. Code Section 414(p) provides rules defining the term *qualified domestic relations order*. Code Section 414(p)(11), added to the Code by the Omnibus Budget Reconciliation Act of 1989, states that a distribution or payment from a governmental plan (as defined in Code Section 414(d)) is treated as made pursuant to a QDRO if the domestic relations order meets certain requirements. The legislative history of this provision states, "The tax rules relating to transfers of interests in a governmental plan are also amended to conform generally to the tax rules applicable to other qualified plans pursuant to the Retirement Equity Act." [H.R. Rep. No. 101-247, at 1443 (1989)] This strongly implies that Congress was considering only governmental plans that are treated as qualified plans. The Section 414(p)(11) provision was necessary because the original Section 414(p) QDRO provision was applicable only to plans subject to the Section 401(a)(13) anti-alienation rules. By terms of Treasury Regulations Section 1.401(a)-13(a) (applicable only to qualified pension plans), the Section 401(a)(13) rules do "not apply to a governmental plan, within the meaning of section 414(d)." Even if it is assumed "(without so ruling) that a state governmental section 457 plan constitutes a government plan described in section 414(d)," Code Section 457(d)(1)(A), in the absence of a provision similar to Code Section 401(a)(13)(B), does not allow such a plan to remain eligible after a QDRO-ordered withdrawal prior to the earliest date described in Code Section 457(d)(1)(A). Thus, "the legislative scheme devised to permit court-ordered early withdrawals from government plans does not appear to provide for such withdrawals from eligible section 457 plans." The ruling goes on to state: "Since a section 457 plan, such as the one described in your ruling request, is neither an exempt trust nor treated as an exempt trust described in section 401(a), the section 402(e)(1)(B) provision permitting tax-deferred rollovers of QDRO-mandated distributions from an exempt trust to an IRA does not apply to any distributions from a section 457 plan made pursuant to a QDRO." [P.L.R. 9145010]

Transfers Between Plans

Q 2:228   Are amounts transferred from one eligible plan to another required to be included in gross income?

No. The portion of the entire amount payable to a participant solely by reason of the transfer of that portion from one eligible plan to another eligible plan is not included in the participant's gross income provided the amounts are not actually or constructively received prior to the transfer. [I.R.C. § 457(e)(10), added by TRA 1986 § 1107(a); P.L.R. 8946019, 8906066, 8752029, 8330080] Final regulations indicate that such transfers can be made only between like plans (i.e., governmental to governmental, and tax-exempt to tax-exempt), and in the case of governmental plans, only if the plans are in the same state. [Treas. Reg. § 1.457-10(b)]

The effects of mergers and acquisitions on 457 plans are discussed more fully in chapter 7.

Q 2:229   Can contributions made to an eligible plan in which the employee was not eligible to participate be transferred to an eligible plan in which the employee is a participant?

No. If such a transfer occurs, the amount transferred will be treated as wages and subject to the applicable statute of limitations, and unless the employer is exempt, the employer will be liable for the payment of the FICA taxes on the wages received by the employee. In addition, subject to the applicable statute of limitations, each affected employee will be liable for payment to the government of the employee portion of the FICA tax imposed under Code Section 3101 with respect to the wages received by the employee until either the tax is collected from the employee or the employer pays the tax. [P.L.R. 9540057]

Q 2:230   Can transfers be made between eligible plans of employers located in different states?

The statute does not so limit transfers. [I.R.C. § 457(e)(10)] Final regulations do not so limit transfers between plans of tax exempt employers, but in the case of governmental plans only, the regulations provide that transfers prior to a severance of employment may be made only between plans of employers within the same state and only if all plan assets are transferred. [Treas. Reg. § 1.457-10(b)(2)] An exception to this is a transfer to purchase permissive service credit. [Treas. Reg. 1.457-10(b)(4)]

Government Balance Sheet Reporting

Q 2:231   Does Code Section 457 require a specific method of financial reporting?

No. Code Section 457 only provides rules for determining whether the plan and the employer are eligible and the tax treatment of contributions to and distributions from the plan (see chapter 3). For unfunded eligible 457 plans of state and local governments, the Governmental Accounting Standards Board (GASB) has issued special rules (see Q 2:233). These rules do not apply to 457(g) trusts.

Q 2:232   What types of employers are subject to the rules of the Governmental Accounting Standards Board?

In general, GASB pronouncements apply to financial reports of all state and local government activities, including public benefit corporations and authorities, public employee retirement systems, and governmental utilities, colleges, and universities.

Q 2:233 How should a governmental employer report 457 plan assets?

In October 1997, the GASB issued Statement No. 32, which superseded previous Statement No. 2 regarding accounting for 457 plans. In Statement No. 32, the GASB declared that the assets of 457 plans should be treated as expendable trust funds, and thus appear on the governmental entity's balance sheet, if the assets "are held by a governmental unit in a trustee capacity or as an agent for individuals, private organizations, other governmental units, or other funds." [National Council on Governmental Accounting Statement 1, ¶ 26(3)(8); GASB Statement No. 32, app. B, ¶ 17]

Q 2:234 When are 457 plan assets held in a trustee capacity for balance sheet reporting purposes?

GASB Statement No. 32 is deliberately vague in that regard. It intentionally does not provide any definition of trustee capacity, though Statement No. 32 is relatively clear that it is not a reference to whether a trustee capacity exists or does not exist as a matter of trust law. Rather, it appears that it is a concept akin to whether the governmental entity is a fiduciary with respect to the investment of plan assets, and is to be interpreted as a matter of industry practice and judgment. Statement No. 32 recognizes that "governments will need to exercise judgment in determining whether they have fiduciary accountability for section 457 plans and whether they hold the assets in a trustee capacity. . . . The Board believes it is beyond the scope of this project to specify what activities meet the fiduciary criteria in NCGA Statement 1, and, therefore, should be reported." [GASB Statement No. 32, app. B, ¶ 18]

To date, industry practice has apparently been, with at least the tacit agreement of the GASB, for governmental entities not to treat 457 plan assets held in a 457(g) trust on their balance sheet if there is individual participant investment direction of trust assets in investment funds or contracts, such as mutual funds, offered by a third-party provider, even though the governmental entity may hold the assets as a passive trustee and even select which third-party providers' investment funds or contracts may be available for investment.

In contrast, it appears that where the governmental entity is the sole fiduciary for investment purposes, such as in a defined benefit plan, some practitioners believe that those assets probably should appear on the entity's balance sheet, even if they are held by an independent passive custodial trustee, such as a financial institution.

Q 2:235   How should 457 plan assets be valued in financial reports under GASB rules?

Section 457 plan assets are to be reflected at market value because the employer's liability to each participant, at any point in time, generally is measured by that participant's share of the market value of the plan assets. If the employer's obligation is determined by a measurement other than market value (e.g., fixed-rate insurance contracts), the same method used to calculate the obligation (e.g., contract value) should be used to value the contract. [GASB Statement No. 32, app. B, ¶¶ 22, 23]

Q 2:236   Is there any additional disclosure required on the financial reports?

No. GASB Statement No. 32 does not require specific note disclosures. [GASB Statement No. 32, app. B, ¶ 24]

Advantages of a 457(b) Plan

Q 2:237   Is a 401(k) plan better than a 457(b) plan for a nongovernmental tax-exempt employer?

For years before 2002, for nongovernmental tax-exempt organizations that are not eligible to sponsor a 403(b) plan (e.g., Section 501(c)(6) associations), a 401(k) plan clearly is preferable to a 457(b) plan.

A 401(k) plan has numerous advantages. It has a structured plan approval program and provides a wider range of investment options than is generally allowed under a 457(b) plan. Some states tax 457 plan deferrals but not 401(k) plan deferrals. In addition, the requirement to maintain the eligible deferred compensation plan as an unfunded arrangement makes a 457 plan an unacceptable alternative to 401(k) plans for nongovernmental tax-exempt organizations. Finally, the 401(k) plan has higher contribution limits unless the employee is also a participant in an eligible 457(f) plan.

There was no valid policy reason for not making 401(k) plans available to governmental employers. Apparently, while the legislation was being considered by Congress, some local governments and insurance companies opposed the change, so it was dropped. [Letter from David A. Pratt, Albany Law School (Oct. 20, 1996)]

For years after 2002, because the limitations on 457(b) plan contributions are decoupled from those on 403(b) and 401(a) plan contributions, use of a 457(b) plan in addition to a 403(b) or 401(a) plan is a useful option for retirement savings.

Q 2:238   What are the advantages of a 403(b) plan?

If an organization is eligible to sponsor a 403(b) plan, the comparison of a 457 plan to a 401(k) plan or 403(b) plan is more complex. In general, public schools and organizations exempt from tax under Code Section 501(c)(3) can establish a 403(b) plan. The advantages of a 403(b) plan over a 401(k) or 403(b) plan include the following:

1. No ADP (actual deferral percentage) test for employee deferrals;
2. Higher limitations, particularly if the employer also has a qualified plan;
3. Potential exemption from ERISA if the plan is funded solely by employee deferrals; and
4. Less involvement by state government.

Negative Election Plans

Q 2:239 What is a negative election deferral?

Some employers maintain a retirement savings plan under which an employee becomes a participant and makes elective deferrals unless he or she affirmatively opts out by making a written election not to participate in the plan. Under such a negative election plan, the employer gives an employee a special notice of the plan's negative election provisions, informs the employee that he or she has the right to opt out and not allow any salary reduction, and tells the employee that in the absence of receiving the specified opt-out form the employer will take a specific amount or percentage of salary from the employee's pay. In the Treasury Department's view, by not objecting to the salary reduction that the employer said would be made, the employee impliedly elects that salary reduction. Under a series of Treasury Department rulings, such a plan creates a valid elective deferral. [See, e.g., Rev. Rul. 98-30, 1998-1 C.B. 1273]

Q 2:240 Can transfers be made between eligible plans of employers located in different states?

The statute does not so limit transfers. [I.R.C. § 457(e)(10)] Final regulations do not so limit transfers between plans of tax exempt employers, but in the case of governmental plans only, the regulations provide that transfers prior to a severance of employment may be made only between plans of employers within the same state and only if all plan assets are transferred. [Treas. Reg. § 1.457-10(b)(2)] An exception to this is a transfer to purchase permissive service credit. [Treas. Reg. 1.457-10(b)(4)]

Q 2:241 How does the employer or plan trustee invest the negatively enrolled participant's deferrals?

Because a negative election plan involves making contributions for a participant who has not communicated about his or her plan participation, usually the employer, acting as plan administrator, must specify the negatively enrolled participant's investment. For an ERISA plan, when deciding the individual's plan investment the plan administrator must act as an expert fiduciary. For church plans and governmental plans, different state laws may apply (see chapter 4). If the employer lacks sufficient retirement plan investment expertise, it must get expert advice.

A plan administrator should consider that recent survey evidence shows that many negatively enrolled participants stick with the default investment chosen by the plan fiduciary. This may increase the employer's fiduciary liability exposure. The plan fiduciary can meet its fiduciary responsibility (and thereby avoid liability) by using careful procedures to select the default investment (see chapter 4).

Governmental Plan Rollovers

Q 2:242   Are rollovers to and from governmental 457(b) plans permitted?

EGTRRA permits rollovers between the various types of defined contribution arrangements (i.e., 401(a), 403(b), and eligible governmental 457(b) plans) without restriction. [I.R.C. § 457(e)(16)] The provision is effective for distributions made after December 31, 2001. This portability does not extend to rollovers to nongovernmental 457(b) plans. (See Q 1:14.) [I.R.C. § 402(c), amended by EGTRRA § 643(a); Treas. Reg. § 1.457-7(b)(2)]

Caution. It is unclear whether an amount rolled over to an eligible governmental 457(b) plan may be distributed prior to the time specified in Q 2:192. [I.R.C. § 457(d)(1), (e)(16)] Informally the IRS has indicated that they may not be distributed prior to the time permitted under Code Section 457(d)(1). It should be noted, too, that many qualified plans permit immediate availability of funds rolled over from other plans. Arguably, deemed IRAs (see Q 1:14) would be treated differently because they do not take on the characteristics of the recipient plan. Until further guidance is issued, practitioners should exercise caution.

Q 2:243   Can amounts rolled into a governmental 457(b) plan be distributed from the recipient plan without another distributable event?

Yes. In new Revenue Ruling 2004-12 [2004-7 I.R.B. (Feb. 17, 2004)], the IRS has cleared up a controversy that came to the forefront when it issued proposed 457(b) regulations. At that time, representatives of the IRS indicated, informally, that perhaps an eligible rollover distribution that was rolled over into an eligible governmental 457(b) plan could not be distributed from the recipient plan until the participant had a severance from employment with the employer, attained age 70½, or had an unforeseen emergency. Apparently, the IRS originally believed that those restrictions might apply to all assets held

under a plan, including rollovers into the plan, and that in the case of a severance from employment, there had to be a severance of employment with the
employer maintaining the recipient plan.

The new ruling reverses that original informal view and expressly provides
that if an eligible retirement plan separately accounts for amounts attributable
to rollover contributions to the plan, distributions of those amounts are not subject to the restrictions on permissible timing that apply, under the applicable
requirements of the Internal Revenue Code, to distributions of amounts attributable to rollover contributions at any time pursuant to an individual's request.

The ruling also clarifies that distributions of amounts attributable to rollover
contributions are subject to the survivor annuity requirements of Code
Sections 401(a)(11) and 417, the minimum distribution requirements of Section 401(a)(9), and the additional income tax on premature distribution requirements under Section 72(t), to the extent applicable to the receiving plan. The
ruling further states that it does not apply to amounts received by a plan as a
result of a merger, consolidation, or transfer of plan assets under Section 414(l),
nor to plan-to-plan transfers otherwise permitted between 403(b) tax-sheltered
annuities and between 457(b) eligible governmental plans.

Q 2:244   What notice is required for governmental plan rollovers?

A rollover notice is required for distributions from governmental (but not tax-
exempt) 457(b) plans. [I.R.C. § 402(h)] The rollover notice (with respect to all
plans) must include a description of the provisions under which distributions
from the plan to which the distribution is rolled over may be subject to restrictions and tax consequences different from those applicable to distributions from
the distributing plan. (See Q 1:14.) The IRS has provided a model notice. [IRS
Notice 2002-3, 2002-2 I.R.B. 1] The IRS Model Notice does not address the issue
of when such amounts may be distributed from the 457 plan (see Q 2:242).

Q 2:245   Are amounts rolled over to a governmental 457(b)
plan from another plan subject to the 10 percent
excise tax on early withdrawals?

Distributions from governmental 457(b) plans are subject to the 10 percent
early withdrawal tax to the extent that the distribution consists of amounts
attributable to rollovers from another type of plan subject to that tax, such as a
401(a) plan, a 403(b) plan, or an IRA. [I.R.C. § 72(t)(9)] Governmental 457(b)
plans are required to account for such amounts separately.

Q 2:246   Can after-tax monies be rolled over to a governmental
457(b) plan?

After-tax contributions (including nondeductible contributions to an IRA)
cannot be rolled over to a tax-sheltered annuity or governmental 457(b) plan;
however, after 2001, after-tax employee contributions can be included in an

eligible rollover distribution to a qualified plan or an IRA. (See Q 1:14.) [I.R.C. § 402(c)(2), amended by EGTRRA]

Q 2:247 Can a surviving spouse roll over a governmental 457(b) plan distribution?

Yes, after 2001. A surviving spouse can roll over distributions received after 2001 to a qualified plan, 403(b) plan, or another governmental 457(b) plan in which the spouse participates. (See Q 1:14.) [I.R.C. § 402(c), amended by EGTRRA § 641(d)]

Tax and Service Credit for Governmental Plans

Q 2:248 Is the nonrefundable tax credit for certain individuals who make elective contributions to certain types of plans available for governmental 457(b) plan contributions?

Yes. A nonrefundable tax credit for a percentage of elective contributions made by eligible taxpayers to certain types of plans is available from 2002 through 2006. The credit is available with respect to the following:

1. Elective contributions to a 401(k) plan, a 403(b) tax-sheltered annuity, or eligible deferred compensation arrangement of a governmental 457(b) plan, SIMPLE, or SEP;
2. Contributions to a traditional or Roth IRA; and
3. Voluntary after-tax employee contributions to a qualified retirement plan.

The credit does not apply to 457(b) plans of tax-exempt employers.

The maximum annual contribution eligible for the credit is $2,000. The credit rate—0, 10, 20, or 50 percent—depends on the taxpayer's adjusted gross income (AGI). For this purpose, AGI is determined without regard to the exclusion provided by Code Sections 911, 931, or 933.

Only taxpayers filing joint returns with AGI of $50,000 or less, taxpayers filing head of household returns with AGI of $37,500 or less, and taxpayers filing single returns (and married taxpayers filing separate returns) with AGI of $25,000 or less are eligible for the credit. The credit is available to individuals age 18 or over, other than individuals who are full-time students or are claimed as a dependent on another taxpayer's tax return. [I.R.C. § 25B, added by EGTRRA § 618(a)–(b)] (See Q 1:14.) [See also Ann. 2001-160, 2001-44 I.R.B. 416; Ann. 2001-120, 2001-50 I.R.B. 583]

Q 2:249 Can a participant in a governmental defined benefit plan purchase service credit?

Yes. Under state law, state and local government employees often have the option of purchasing credit for prior service (such as for years served in another state). Under EGTRRA, after 2001, state and local government employees can use funds from their 403(b) arrangements or 457 plans to purchase service credits under their defined benefit plans or to repay withdrawals of contributions and earnings. (See Q 1:14.) [I.R.C. § 457(e)(17), added by EGTRRA § 647(b); Treas. Reg. § 1.457-10(b)(4)]

Plan Termination

Q 2:250   Can an eligible plan be frozen or terminated?

Yes. A plan may be amended to eliminate future deferrals (i.e., frozen), and it can be terminated. To be considered terminated, amounts deferred must be distributed to all participants and beneficiaries as soon as practicable after termination of the plan. [Treas. Reg. § 1.457-10(a)]

References

Brisendine, A.T., "Current Issues in Section 457 Deferred Compensation Plans," 9(4) *Benefits L.J.* (Winter 1996).

Harm, K., *State and Local Government Deferred Compensation Programs* (Government Finance Officers Association of the United States and Canada, 1993), at 20, 31.

Lesser, G.S., "SIMPLE Plans Offer Retirement Savings with Less Complex Administrative and Compliance Rules," 5(1) *J. Tax'n Employee Benefits* 3 (May/June 1997).

Lesser, G.S., "State Taxation of Pension Income Curtailed," 4(2) *J. Tax'n Employee Benefits* 88 (July/Aug. 1996).

Mazawey, L.T., and Evans, W.M., "New Federal Limitations on State Taxation of Retirement Income," 22(2) *J. Pension Plan. & Compliance* 1 (Summer 1996).

O'Meara, M.J., and Anderson, T., "Section 457 Plans: Deferred Compensation for Tax-Exempts and Government Organizations," 18(3) *J. Pension Plan. & Compliance* 55 (Fall 1992).

Powell, D.W., and Summers, C.L., "Design and Use of Section 457 Plans," 1(4) *J. Deferred Compensation* 1 (Summer 1996).

Press, C., and Patchell, R.D., "Section 457 Deferred Compensation Plans of State and Local Government and Tax Exempt Employers," *Exempt Organizations Technical Instruction Program for FY 1997* § M (IRS, Washington, D.C. 1996).

Scialabba, A.L., "Defining the Top-Hat Group in Executive Compensation," 4(6) *J. Tax'n Employee Benefits* 243 (Mar./Apr. 1997).

Scialabba, A.L., "Members of the 'Top-Hat' Group for Executive Compensation Planning Are Not Always Easily Identifiable," 5(1) *J. Tax'n Employee Benefits* 19 (May/June 1997).

Scialabba, A.L., Fowler, D.E., and Morrison, G.M., "Will Compliance with USERRA Violate the Code's Qualified Plan Provisions?" 4(2) *J. Tax'n Employee Benefits* 59 (July/Aug. 1996).

Shultz, P., and Hall, L., "The New Source Tax Ban: Key Implications for Nonqualified Plans," *Pension & Benefits Week* (RIA), Jan. 29, 1996.

Chapter 3

Distribution Rules

Joseph A. Zavoda, Esq.
CitiStreet Retirement Services

This chapter explains rules that govern distributions from eligible 457(b) plans, including the rules for early distributions, small account "cash-outs," unforeseeable-emergency distributions, severance from employment, required distributions, rollovers, and other distribution rules, including pre-EGTRRA rules. Chapter 11 explains distributions under ineligible 457(f) plans.

Note. This chapter explains the federal tax law currently in effect for 2002 through 2010. Under current law, provisions of the Internal Revenue Code (Code) added or amended by the Economic Growth and Tax Relief Reconciliation Act of 2001 (EGTRRA) do not apply to tax, plan, or limitation years that begin after December 31, 2010. [EGTRRA § 901] Thereafter, the Code applies as if EGTRRA's provisions and amendments never had been enacted. The law then would be the Code as it was just before EGTRRA's enactment on June 7, 2001. If by the end of the decade Congress has not made permanent or extended EGTRRA's provisions, *457 Answer Book* will include explanations of the pre-EGTRRA and other applicable law.

Overview

Q 3:1 What restrictions apply to distributions from an eligible plan?

An eligible plan is subject to restrictions concerning the following:

1. The earliest time that distributions may be made (the early distribution rule) [I.R.C. § 457(b)(5), (d)(1)(A)] (Q 3:2);
2. When the commencement of benefits may be deferred [I.R.C. § 457(e)(9)(B)] (Q 3:60); and
3. The latest time that distributions must be made (the minimum distribution rule) [I.R.C. § 457(b)(5), (d)(1)(B), (d)(2)].

Also, an eligible plan of a state or local government employer must permit a participant or spouse beneficiary to instruct a direct rollover to another eligible retirement plan. [I.R.C. § 457(b)(5), (d)(1)(C)]

Early Distribution Rule

Q 3:2 What does the early distribution rule require?

The early distribution rule provides that an eligible plan must not allow an amount to be paid or made available under the plan earlier than:

1. The calendar year in which the participant attains age 70½;
2. When the participant has a severance from employment with the employer (see Qs 3:13, 3:14); or
3. When the participant is faced with an unforeseeable emergency (see Qs 3:5, 3:6).

[I.R.C. § 457(d)(1)(A)(i)–(iii); see Treas. Reg. § 1.457-6(a)]

Q 3:3 May an eligible plan permit distributions of small amounts?

Yes, a participant may receive an in-service distribution of an account of small amounts up to $5,000. Under Section 457(e)(9), an amount will not be treated as made available (and thus will not be treated as constructively received nor as running afoul of the early distribution rule) merely because a participant may elect to receive the amount, or a plan may distribute the amount to the participant without his or her consent. This rule applies only if:

1. The participant's total account balance that is not attributable to rollover contributions is no more than $5,000 (for 2004), the dollar limit under Code Section 411(a)(11)(A);
2. No amount has been deferred under the plan for the participant during the two-year period that ends on the date of distribution; and
3. The plan paid no prior distribution to which this special rule applied.

Such a distribution may be made at the participant's election or as an involuntary cash-out. [I.R.C. § 457(e)(9)(A); Treas. Reg. § 1.457-6(e)] (See Q 3:2.)

For years that begin after December 31, 1996, this provision allows for either a voluntary or an involuntary distribution to a participant when his or her account does not exceed $5,000. Further, the plan may provide a *lower* cash-out amount. Alternatively, a plan may provide an amount for involuntary distributions and a different amount for voluntary distributions. Each such amount must be no more than $5,000. A plan may preclude any in-service distribution. [I.R.C. § 457(e)(9)(A)]

Q 3:4   Is there a model amendment that an employer may consider in updating its plan document?

Yes. In Revenue Procedure 98-41, the IRS provided model amendments an employer may consider in updating its plan documents. The model amendments are based on the guidance in Notice 98-8 [1998-4 I.R.B. 6]. Revenue Procedure 98-41 includes a choice of model amendments for an in-service distribution of $5,000 or less. One option is for an involuntary distribution, another for a voluntary distribution, and a third is for a combination of voluntary and involuntary distributions.

Example. The ABC plan provides that an account of $1,500 or less will be automatically cashed out if a participant made no deferrals under the plan during the two-year period that ends on the date of the distribution and no in-service distribution was made to the participant under this provision. If a participant's account balance exceeds $1,500 but does not exceed $5,000, the distribution will be made only with the participant's consent.

Unforeseeable Emergency

Q 3:5   May a plan permit a distribution on account of an unforeseeable emergency?

Yes. A plan may permit a distribution based on a participant's or beneficiary's unforeseeable emergency. A plan must define an *unforeseeable emergency* as a severe financial hardship of a participant or beneficiary that results from:

1. An illness or accident of the participant or beneficiary, the participant's or beneficiary's spouse, or the participant's or beneficiary's dependent (see Q 3:12);
2. A loss of the participant's or beneficiary's property "due to" casualty; or
3. Other similar extraordinary and unforeseeable circumstances arising as a result of events beyond the control of the participant or beneficiary.

Q 3:6   What could an unforeseeable emergency include?

If other conditions are met, an unforeseeable emergency could include:

1. A need to rebuild the participant's or beneficiary's home following damage to it not covered by insurance;

2. An imminent foreclosure on the participant's or beneficiary's primary residence;

3. The participant's or beneficiary's imminent eviction from his or her primary residence;

4. A need to pay medical expenses or for prescription drugs; or

5. A need to pay the funeral expenses of the participant's or beneficiary's spouse or dependent.

[Treas. Reg. § 1.457-6(c)(2)]

Q 3:7   Is every event that is beyond the control of a participant an unforeseeable emergency?

No. A plan administrator must decide whether a participant or beneficiary is faced with an unforeseeable emergency based on the facts and circumstances of each case. [Treas. Reg. § 1.457-6(c)(2)(ii)]

Q 3:8   What if an unforeseeable emergency has been relieved through insurance or other similar compensation?

No matter how severe the circumstances, a plan may not provide a distribution for an emergency that has been or will be relieved through insurance or similar compensation. [Treas. Reg. § 1.457-6(c)(2)(ii)]

Example. Sharon discovered that her daughter Martha will need a lung transplant. Martha has always been a healthy child and has never before shown any symptom of a major medical problem. The expense of the surgery and recuperative care will be $250,000. However, ABC's health plan will pay the entire expense. Although the medical need was sudden and unexpected and involved Sharon's dependent, Sharon does not need a plan distribution because the expense will be paid by ABC's health plan.

Q 3:9   Does the fact that a participant has other money to meet the emergency preclude a distribution?

Maybe. It depends on what money, investments, and other property are readily available and the potential consequences to the participant or beneficiary. Specifically, even if an event is extraordinary and unforeseeable and arises as a result of events beyond the participant's control, the event will not constitute an unforeseeable emergency allowing distribution to the extent that the hardship is or may be relieved by liquidation of the participant's or beneficiary's assets, so long as the liquidation of such assets would not itself cause severe financial hardship; or to the extent that the hardship is or may be relieved by stopping deferrals under the plan. Before a plan may pay a distribution based on an unforeseeable emergency, the plan administrator must decide not only whether the event is an extraordinary and unforeseeable emergency beyond the control of the participant but also whether the need can be met by other resources of the participant. [Treas. Reg. § 1.457-6(c)(2)(ii)]

Q 3:10   Could a participant's divorce be an unforeseeable emergency?

Probably not, in most usual circumstances. Before making or even proposing the current regulations, the IRS held, based on particular facts and circumstances, that a divorce was not an unforeseeable emergency. [P.L.R. 9543010] However, that ruling is not codified in the current regulations. In some circumstances, a participant or beneficiary might persuade a plan administrator that a divorce was unexpected and unforeseeable or was sufficiently related to an illness or accident of the participant or beneficiary, the participant's or beneficiary's spouse, or the participant's or beneficiary's dependent.

Q 3:11   Is there a limit on how much may be distributed to meet an unforeseeable emergency?

Yes. Although no set dollar ceiling (other than the plan participant's account) applies, the amount distributed may not exceed the amount reasonably needed to meet the emergency need. [Treas. Reg. § 1.457-6(c)(2)(iii)] The distribution may include a "gross-up" for reasonably anticipated federal, state, and local taxes "reasonably anticipated to result from the distribution." [Treas. Reg. § 1.457-6(c)(2)(iii)]

Example. Phil is an employee of Big City and a participant in its deferred compensation plan. The evidence (sworn under penalties of perjury) submitted with his claim for an unforeseeable-emergency distribution shows that considering his wife's income, his marginal rate for federal income tax purposes is at least 35 percent. Big City requires its employees to live in Big City. Big City knows that the state's tax rate is 3 percent and that Big City's tax rate for residents is 4 percent. Thus, Phil's marginal tax rate is 42 percent. To meet an emergency need of $10,000, the plan pays Phil $17,241.38.

Tax	Tax rate	Tax on emergency distribution
Federal income tax	35.0000%	$6,034.48
State income tax	3.0000%	$ 517.24
City income tax	4.0000%	$ 689.66
Taxes (total)	42.0000%	$7,241.38

$17,241.38 − $7,241.38 = $10,000.00

Q 3:12   Who is a dependent?

To the extent that an eligible plan's definition of an unforeseeable emergency refers to a dependent, the plan must define *dependent* by reference to Code Section 152(a). [Treas. Reg. § 1.457-6(c)(2)(i)]

Code Section 152(a) provides that each of a participant's or beneficiary's lineal ascendants and descendants, siblings, aunts, uncles, nieces, nephews, in-laws, or several step-relations is a dependent if the participant or beneficiary provides more than half of the person's support. [I.R.C. § 152(a)(8)] Even a person who is not any kind of relative of the participant or beneficiary may nonetheless be the participant's or beneficiary's dependent if the person "has as his [or her] principal place of abode the home of the [participant or beneficiary] and is a member of [that] household." [I.R.C. § 152(a)(9)]

Severance from Employment

Q 3:13   What is a severance from employment?

Whether a severance from employment has occurred depends in part on whether the participant is an employee or an independent contractor.

An employee has a severance from employment if he or she:

- Dies;
- Retires; or
- Has a severance from employment with the eligible employer.

[Treas. Reg. § 1.457-6(b)(1)]

The Section 457 regulations refer to regulations under Code Section 401(k) for "additional guidance concerning severance from employment." [Treas. Reg. § 1.457-6(b)(1)]

Q 3:14   When is an independent contractor severed from employment?

An independent contractor is severed from employment on the expiration of his or her contract (or, in the case of more than one contract, all contracts) under which he or she performs services for the eligible employer. However, the expiration of the contract must be a good-faith and complete end of the contractual relationship. An expiration is not a good-faith and complete end of the contractual relationship if the employer anticipates a renewal of the contractual relationship or that the independent contractor will become an employee.

Q 3:15   When is an employer considered to intend to contract again?

An employer is considered to anticipate the renewal of the contractual relationship if:

1. The employer intends to contract again for the services provided under the expired contract; and
2. Neither the employer nor the independent contractor has ruled out the independent contractor as a possible provider of services under a new contract.

Further, an employer is considered to intend to contract again for the services provided under an expired contract if the employer's doing so is conditioned only on the employer's incurring a need for the services or the availability of money. [Treas. Reg. § 1.457-6(b)(2)(i)]

Q 3:16   What may a plan provide to meet the severance-from-employment rules?

Notwithstanding the general rule on contracting again (see Q 3:15), a plan meets the severance-from-employment rule if the plan provides that:

1. No distribution will be paid (or delivered) to the independent contractor for at least 12 months following the expiration of all contracts with the employer; and

2. No distribution will be paid (or delivered) at that time if, after the expiration of such contracts but before the completion of the 12-month period, the independent contractor again performs services for the employer, whether as an independent contractor or as an employee.

[Treas. Reg. § 1.457-6(b)(2)(ii)]

Q 3:17   May an eligible plan ever provide for in-service distributions?

Yes. If a participant has reached the calendar year in which he or she attains age 70½ or has an unforeseeable emergency (see Q 3:5), a distribution may be made without violating the early distribution rule. [I.R.C. § 457(d)(1)(A)(i), (iii); Treas. Reg. § 1.457-6(a)]

Minimum Distribution Rule

Q 3:18   What is the required-distribution rule?

The required-distribution rule is a rule that applies minimum distribution rules to eligible 457(b) plans. An eligible 457(b) plan meets the required-distribution rule if it meets the minimum distribution rules of Section 401(a)(9). [I.R.C. § 457(d)(1)(B), (d)(2)]

Q 3:19   What do the minimum distribution rules require for pre-death distributions?

For a pre-death distribution, there are two minimum distribution rules:

1. Distribution must be made, or at least begun, no later than the participant's required beginning date.

2. The distribution must meet a specified minimum distribution amount.

Under this rule, if the entire distribution is not made by the participant's required beginning date, distribution must be made: (1) over the life of the participant; (2) over the lives of the participant and the designated beneficiary; (3) over a period not extending beyond the life expectancy of the participant; or (4) over a period not extending beyond the joint life and last survivor expectancy of the participant and the designated beneficiary. [Treas. Reg. § 1.401(a)(9)-2, Q&A 1(a)]

Q 3:20   What is the required beginning date?

The required beginning date is the April 1 next following *the later of* the calendar year in which the participant:

1. Attains age 70½; or
2. Retires.

[I.R.C. § 401(a)(9)(C); Treas. Reg. § 1.401(a)(9)-2, Q&A 2(a)]

The required beginning date for a participant in a for-profit organization is slightly different from the rule for governmental plans. The required beginning date for a participant in a for-profit organization who is a 5 percent owner is the April 1 that next follows the calendar year in which the participant attains age 70½. However, this rule does not apply to governmental plans. [Treas. Reg. § 1.401(a)(9)-2, Q&A 2(d)]

> **Example.** Sam is employed by the Good Fellows Charity and participates in its eligible plan. The plan provides a distribution only after death or severance from employment and does not provide a distribution based on age 70½ or an unforeseeable emergency. Sam's account balance is about $700,000. Sam turns age 71. Although he would like to begin receiving distributions, Sam feels that he is too young to retire. Therefore, unless he retires, dies, or otherwise has a severance from employment from Good Fellows, Sam is precluded from receiving a plan distribution.

Q 3:21   After the initial required distribution, when must distributions be made?

Although the first distribution must be made by the applicable April 1, later payments must be made on or before December 31 of each distribution year. [Treas. Reg. § 1.401(a)(9)-5, Q&A 1(c)] If the distribution is delayed as long as permissible—that is, until the participant's required beginning date—the first two required payments must be made during the calendar year that contains the required beginning date. [Treas. Reg. § 1.401(a)(9)-5, Q&A 1(c)]

Q 3:22   How is life expectancy determined for years beginning with the first distribution year up through the participant's death?

Except for situations in which the spouse is the sole beneficiary, the applicable distribution period for minimum distributions for distribution calendar years up to and including the distribution calendar year that includes the participant's death is determined using the Uniform Lifetime Table. [Treas. Reg. § 1.401(a)(9)-5, Q&A 4(a)] Each year, life expectancy is calculated based on the participant's age as of his or her birthday in the relevant distribution calendar year.

However, if the sole designated beneficiary of the participant is the participant's surviving spouse and the spouse is more than 10 years younger than the participant, the longer distribution period measured by the joint life and last survivor life expectancy of the participant and spouse may be used. [Treas. Reg. § 1.401(a)(9)-5, Q&A 4(b)] Under these circumstances the use of this table results in a longer life expectancy than provided by the Uniform Lifetime Table. A longer life expectancy results in smaller required payments.

The joint life expectancy of the participant and the spouse is determined using the participant's and the spouse's birthdays in the distribution calendar year.

Example. Pat is 70 years old, and her husband, Bob, is 45 years old. Their joint life expectancy is 39.4 years. If the plan administrator used the uniform table, the life expectancy based on Pat's age alone would be 27.4.

Q 3:23 What is the distribution period for years after the year of the participant's death?

For years after the year of the participant's death, the distribution period is generally the remaining life expectancy of the designated beneficiary. The beneficiary's remaining life expectancy is calculated using the age of the beneficiary in the year following the year of the participant's death, reduced by one for each subsequent year. If the participant's spouse is the sole beneficiary, the distribution period during the spouse's life is the spouse's single life expectancy. For years after the year of the spouse's death, the distribution period is the spouse's life expectancy calculated in the year of death reduced by one for each subsequent year. If there is no designated beneficiary, the distribution period is the participant's life expectancy calculated in the year of death, reduced by one for each subsequent year. [Treas. Reg. § 1.401(a)(9)-5, Q&A 5]

Q 3:24 What is the applicable date for determining the designated beneficiary?

The applicable date for determining the designated beneficiary depends on whether a distribution is a pre- or post-death distribution. For a pre-death distribution, whom the designated beneficiary is only affects the minimum required distribution if the sole designated beneficiary is the spouse. A spouse is considered the sole designated beneficiary for distribution during the participant's lifetime only if the spouse is the sole beneficiary of the participant's entire interest at all times during the distribution calendar year. [Treas. Reg. § 1.401(a)(9)-5, Q&A 4(b)]

For a post-death distribution, the time for making this determination is the participant's date of death. [Treas. Reg. § 1.401(a)(9)-4, Q&A 4(a)] The regulations provide exceptions to this general rule.

Q 3:25 In determining the life expectancy, how is a person's current age determined?

A life expectancy is determined using the attained age of the participant—and of the participant's spouse if the spouse is the sole designated beneficiary—as of the birthday of each in the relevant calendar year.

If either element of the life expectancy is recalculated, the applicable life expectancy is redetermined each year using the attained ages as of the birthdays in each year. [Treas. Reg. § 1.401(a)(9)-5, Q&A 4]

Q 3:26 How is a participant's designated beneficiary determined?

A *designated beneficiary* is a person designated as a beneficiary pursuant to the terms of the plan or by or under a participant's beneficiary designation (see chapter 5). [Treas. Reg. § 1.401(a)(9)-4, Q&A 1]

Q 3:27 Whose life expectancy is used if a participant has more than one designated beneficiary?

If a participant named (or the plan designates) more than one person who could be a designated beneficiary as that term is specially defined for the minimum distribution rules, the designated beneficiary with the shortest life expectancy is the designated beneficiary for purposes of determining life expectancy and, in some cases, the distribution period. [Treas. Reg. § 1.401(a)(9)-5, Q&A 7(a)] This person is selected as of the September 30 that next follows the calendar year of the participant's death. [Treas. Reg. § 1.401(a)(9)-4, Q&A 4(a)] For this purpose, someone who is no longer a beneficiary by that date—because he or she was paid or renounced his or her benefit—is not a designated beneficiary.

Q 3:28 Must the designated beneficiary be specified under the plan?

Yes, the designated beneficiary must be specified under the plan. This may take the form of a plan provision that allows a participant to name his or her beneficiary. Alternatively, a plan may state provisions that designate a beneficiary without the participant's choice (or in the absence or failure of a participant's beneficiary designation). If provided by the plan, a default beneficiary is the designated beneficiary for the minimum distribution rules. [Treas. Reg. § 1.401(a)(9)-4, Q&A 2]

Q 3:29   What if a participant's interest passes to someone by operation of applicable law?

That a participant's interest passes to someone by operation of applicable law is not sufficient to give rise to designated beneficiary status unless the individual is designated as a beneficiary under the plan. [Treas. Reg. § 1.401(a)(9)-4, Q&A 1]

Q 3:30   Must a person be specified as a designated beneficiary by name?

No. A person need not be specified by name (either in the plan itself or by the participant) to be a designated beneficiary, as long as the person is identifiable. That the persons named are a class capable of expansion or contraction does not preclude the persons from being identifiable if the plan administrator can identify the class member with the shortest life expectancy. [Treas. Reg. § 1.401(a)(9)-4, Q&A 1]

Q 3:31   May a participant name the participant's estate as his or her designated beneficiary?

Usually, no. If a participant names his or her estate as his or her beneficiary, the participant will be treated as though he or she had no designated beneficiary. [Treas. Reg. § 1.401(a)(9)-4, Q&A 3] Special rules apply to trusts and separate accounts. Usually, an estate will not be a designated beneficiary under these rules.

Q 3:32   May a participant name a trust as his or her designated beneficiary?

Generally, only a natural person will be a designated beneficiary. (See Q 3:26.) There is an exception for a beneficiary designation concerning a trust and trustee that meet special conditions that the regulations provide to find a sufficient measuring life. [Treas. Reg. § 1.401(a)(9)-4, Q&A 5] If the trust that is named as beneficiary meets the special conditions, the beneficiaries under the trust, with respect to the trust's interest in the participant's benefit, may be treated as designated beneficiaries for purposes of determining the distribution period under Section 401(a)(9). Different conditions apply to distributions before death and after death.

Q 3:33   What documents must be furnished to a plan administrator if a trust is named as the designated beneficiary?

The documents that must be furnished to a plan administrator for a beneficiary of a trust to be treated as the designated beneficiary depends on whether the required minimum distribution begins before death (see Q 3:34) or after death (see Q 3:35). The Uniform Lifetime Table now applies for all minimum required distributions before death unless the participant's spouse is more than

10 years younger than the participant. This means that the determination of whom the designated beneficiary is for lifetime distributions is important only if the spouse is the sole beneficiary of the trust and the spouse is more than 10 years younger than the participant.

Q 3:34   What requirements must be met for the beneficiary of a trust to be considered a designated beneficiary for purposes of required minimum distributions that begin before death?

For required minimum distributions that begin before death, if a participant designates a trust as the beneficiary of his or her entire benefit and the participant's spouse is the sole beneficiary of the trust, in order for the spouse to be treated as the sole designated beneficiary, the participant must:

1. Furnish the plan administrator a copy of the trust instrument and agree that if the trust is amended, the participant will provide the plan administrator a copy of the amendment within a reasonable time of the amendment;

2. Furnish the plan administrator a list of all of the beneficiaries of the trust (including contingent and remaindermen beneficiaries with a description of the conditions on their entitlement sufficient to establish that the spouse is the sole beneficiary); and

3. Certify that, to the best of the participant's knowledge, this list is complete and accurate and that the requirements are satisfied.

In addition to what must be furnished to the plan administrator, the participant must agree that if the trust agreement is amended, the participant will, within a reasonable time, provide corrected certifications to the extent any of the information on the previous certifications changed and agree to provide a copy of the trust instrument to the plan administrator on demand. [Treas. Reg. 1.401(a)(9)-4, Q&A 6(a)]

Q 3:35   What requirements must be met for the beneficiary of a trust to be considered a designated beneficiary for purposes of required minimum distributions that begin after death?

For required minimum distributions that begin after death, in order for the beneficiary of a trust to be treated as a designated beneficiary, the trustee must provide documentation to the plan administrator by October 31 of the calendar year immediately following the calendar year in which the participant died. To satisfy this requirement, the trustee must comply with one of the following requirements and furnish the plan administrator either:

1. A final list of all beneficiaries of the trust (including contingent and remaindermen beneficiaries with a description of the conditions of their entitlement) as of September 30 of the calendar year following the calendar year

of the participant's death. The trustee must also certify that to the best of the trustee's knowledge, the list is correct and complete and the requirements are satisfied. Finally, the trustee must agree to provide a copy of the trust instrument to the plan administrator on demand.

2. A copy of the actual trust document for the trust that is named as a beneficiary of the participant under the plan as of the participant's death.

Q 3:36 Will a plan violate the minimum distribution rules because it allows participants to elect the method of payment?

No, an eligible plan does not violate the minimum distributions rules if the method selected meets the distribution rules of Code Sections 457(d) and 401(a)(9).

Q 3:37 May a plan allow a distribution to a participant's spouse or former spouse before the participant's severance from employment or attainment of age 70½ if required by a domestic relations order?

Yes. [I.R.C. § 414(p)(10)–(11)]

Q 3:38 May a plan honor a domestic relations order without violating the minimum distribution rules?

Yes. [I.R.C. § 414(p)(10)–(11)]

For information about domestic relations orders, see chapter 14.

Q 3:39 What minimum distribution rules apply to a post-death distribution?

The minimum distribution rules that apply on the death of the participant depend on whether a distribution is treated as having begun before or after the participant's death. The rules also depend on whether the participant has a designated beneficiary and whether the designated beneficiary is a spousal or nonspouse beneficiary.

Q 3:40 What minimum distribution rules apply if a distribution is treated as having begun before the participant's death?

If a distribution is treated as having begun before the participant's death, but the entire interest had not been distributed before the participant's death, how the remaining portion will be distributed differs depending on whether there is a nonspouse beneficiary, the spouse is the sole beneficiary, or there is no beneficiary. [Treas. Reg. § 1.401(a)(9)-5, Q&A 5(a)]

Nonspouse beneficiary. For years after the year of the participant's death, the distribution period for a nonspouse beneficiary is generally the remaining life expectancy of the designated beneficiary. The beneficiary's remaining life expectancy is calculated using the age of the beneficiary in the year following the year of the participant's death, reduced by one for each subsequent year. Alternatively, the distribution period may be the participant's life expectancy calculated in the year of death, reduced by one for each subsequent year.

Spouse is sole beneficiary. If the participant's spouse is the sole beneficiary, the distribution period during the spouse's lifetime is the spouse's single life expectancy. For years after the year of the spouse's death, the distribution period is the spouse's life expectancy calculated in the year of death, reduced by one for each subsequent year. Alternatively, the distribution period may be the participant's life expectancy calculated in the year of death, reduced by one for each subsequent year.

No designated beneficiary. If there is no designated beneficiary, the distribution period is the participant's life expectancy calculated in the year of death, reduced by one for each subsequent year.

Q 3:41   When is a distribution deemed to begin for purposes of the minimum required distribution rules?

A distribution is deemed to have begun on the participant's required beginning date, even though payments were made before that date. [Treas. Reg. § 1.401(a)(9)-2, Q&A 6] However, if a participant dies before his or her required beginning date, a post-death distribution must be made under the rule (see Q 3:42) that applies if a participant dies before a distribution began. This is so even if a distribution began during the participant's life. Thus, whether a distribution is deemed to have begun cannot be determined, for this purpose, until after a participant's required beginning date.

Q 3:42   What minimum distribution rules apply if distributions are treated as not having begun before the participant's death?

If a participant dies before the participant's required beginning date (and thus before distributions are treated as having begun), the distribution of the participant's entire interest must be made in accordance with the five-year rule [I.R.C. § 401(a)(9)(B)(ii)] or the life expectancy rule [I.R.C. § 401(a)(9)(B)(iii)]. Under the final regulations, the life expectancy rule, not the five-year rule, is the default distribution rule. Which method to use depends on which provisions, if any, the plan has stated concerning the rules and whether the plan has optional provisions or permits participants to elect which method to use.

Q 3:43   What is the five-year rule?

The five-year rule requires that the entire interest of the participant be distributed within five years of the participant's death, regardless of who or what entity receives the distribution. [Treas. Reg. § 1.401(a)(9)-3, Q&A 1(a)]

Q 3:44 When must a participant's entire interest be distributed in order to satisfy the five-year rule?

In order to satisfy the five-year rule, the participant's entire interest must be distributed by the end of the calendar year that contains the fifth anniversary of the date of the participant's death. [Treas. Reg. § 1.401(a)(9)-3, Q&A 2]

Example. If a participant dies on January 1, 2003, the entire interest must be distributed by December 31, 2008.

Q 3:45 What is the life expectancy rule?

The life expectancy rule generally requires that any portion of a participant's interest payable to (or for the benefit of) a designated beneficiary be distributed commencing within one year of the participant's death (see Q 3:48) and continuing over the life expectancy of the beneficiary. Alternatively, it may be paid over a period not extending beyond the life expectancy of the beneficiary. [Treas. Reg. § 1.401(a)(9)-3, Q&A 1(a)]

Q 3:46 When must distributions begin under the life expectancy rule?

The time period when distributions must begin in order to satisfy the life expectancy rule depends on whether the beneficiary is a nonspouse beneficiary or a spousal beneficiary.

Q 3:47 When must distributions begin under the life expectancy rule for a nonspouse beneficiary?

If the designated beneficiary is not the participant's surviving spouse, distributions must begin on or before the end of the calendar year following the participant's death. This rule also applies if another individual, in addition to the participant's surviving spouse, is the beneficiary.

Q 3:48 When must distributions begin for a beneficiary who is the participant's surviving spouse?

If the sole beneficiary is the participant's surviving spouse, distributions must begin under the life expectancy rule by:

- The end of the calendar year following the calendar year in which the participant died; or
- The end of the calendar year in which the participant would have attained age 70½.

[Treas. Reg. § 1.401(a)(9)-3, Q&A 3(b)]

Q 3:49   What if the participant's spouse is the sole designated beneficiary and the spouse dies after the participant dies but before distributions begin?

If the spouse dies after the participant dies but before distributions begin, the five-year rule and the life expectancy rule apply as if the spouse were the participant. [Treas. Reg. § 1.401(a)(9)-3, Q&A 5]

Q 3:50   What transition rule applies to post-death distributions that began under the five-year rule?

The final regulations permitted plans to provide that beneficiaries subject to the five-year rule under the 1987 proposed regulations for Code Section 401(a)(9) could switch to the life expectancy rule. To change methods, all amounts that would have been required under the life expectancy rule were required to be distributed by the earlier of December 31, 2003, or the end of the five-year period following the year of the participant's death. [Treas. Reg. § 1.401(a)(9)-1, Q&A 2(b)(2)]

Q 3:51   What if a plan does not state whether the life expectancy or the five-year rule applies?

If a plan does not specify the method of distribution following the death of a participant, distribution must be made using the life expectancy rule if the participant has a designated beneficiary or using the five-year rule if the participant does not have a designated beneficiary. [Treas. Reg. § 1.401(a)(9)-3, Q&A 4(a)]

Q 3:52   What optional provisions may a plan sponsor adopt?

A plan sponsor may adopt a provision that applies the five-year rule to certain distributions after the death of a participant even if the participant has a designated beneficiary. A plan may also provide that distributions will always be made using the five-year rule. Additionally, a plan may permit participants to elect on an individual basis whether to use the five-year rule or the life expectancy rule. [Treas. Reg. § 1.401(a)(9)-3, Q&A 4(b), (c)]

Q 3:53   What if a participant's benefit is divided into separate accounts?

If a participant's benefit under a defined contribution plan is divided into separate accounts under a defined contribution plan, the separate accounts are aggregated for purposes of satisfying Section 401(a)(9). [Treas. Reg. § 1.401(a)(9)-8, Q&A 2(a)] However, if the beneficiaries of the separate accounts differ and the separate account was established before the last day of the year following the year of the participant's death, the rules under Section 401(a)(9) may be applied separately to each separate account under the plan. [Treas. Reg. § 1.401(a)(9)-8, Q&A 2(b)]

Q 3:54 Is a plan subject to consequences if it fails to comply with the minimum distribution rule?

Yes. A plan that does not provide the minimum distribution rules is not an eligible plan. [I.R.C. § 457(b)(5), (d)(1)] Furthermore, a person who should have received a minimum distribution is subject to an additional 50 percent excise tax on the amount that should have been distributed but was not. [I.R.C. § 4974]

Rollovers

Q 3:55 May distributions from a 457(b) plan be rolled over into another eligible retirement plan?

Yes, if the distribution is from a governmental 457(b) plan defined in Code Section 457(e)(1)(A), the distribution may be an eligible rollover distribution. An eligible rollover distribution is any portion of a distribution to a participant that does not include:

- Corrective distributions;
- Hardship distributions;
- Minimum required distributions, or;
- Substantially equal periodic payments.

A distribution is considered one of a series of substantially equal payments if it is made:

- At least annually;
- For the life (or life expectancy) of the employee or the joint lives (or joint life expectancies) of the participant and the participant's designated beneficiary; or
- For a specified period of 10 or more years.

[I.R.C. §§ 457(e)(16), 402(c)(4)]

Q 3:56 What is an eligible retirement plan?

An eligible retirement plan includes:

- An individual retirement account described under Code Section 408(a);
- An individual retirement annuity described under Code Section 408(b);
- A qualified trust;
- An annuity plan described in Section 403(a);
- An eligible deferred compensation plan maintained by a governmental employer described in Code Section 457(e)(1)(A); and
- An annuity contract described in Code Section 403(b).

[I.R.C. § 402(c)(8)(B)]

However, because the rollover rules were expanded as a result of EGTRRA to permit rollovers between different types of plans, it is unclear how these rules will apply after December 31, 2010, if EGTRRA is not made permanent.

Q 3:57 Why may a participant in a 457(b) plan not want to roll money into another type of eligible retirement plan?

A participant in a 457(b) plan may not want to roll money into another type of eligible retirement plan because the 10 percent additional tax on early distributions does not apply to 457(b) plans (see Q 3:59). If a participant rolls money into another type of plan and later takes a distribution prior to age 59½, it may not be possible for the participant to avoid the 10 percent additional tax on early distributions. [I.R.C. §§ 72(t), 4974(c)] A distribution of amounts attributable to a rollover contribution is subject to the additional income tax on premature distributions under Code Section 72(t), as applicable to the surviving plan. [Rev. Rul. 2004-12, 2004-07 I.R.B. 478]

Q 3:58 If an eligible retirement plan separately tracks rollover contributions, do restrictions on timing of distributions under the Internal Revenue Code otherwise applicable to the plan apply?

No. If an eligible retirement plan separately accounts for amounts attributable to rollover contributions, distributions of those amounts are not subject to the distribution restrictions of the Code otherwise applicable to distributions from the plan. Accordingly, the plan may permit the distribution of amounts attributable to rollover contributions at any time pursuant to an individual's request.

Example. A 457 eligible governmental plan receives amounts attributable to rollovers and maintains those amounts in separate accounts. The 457(b) plan may distribute the rollover amounts at any time, even though distributions of other amounts under the plan are restricted by Code Section 457(d)(1)(A). [Rev. Rul. 2004-12, 2004-07 I.R.B. 478]

Q 3:59 Are distributions from a 457(b) plan subject to the 10 percent additional tax on early distributions?

No. Under Code Section 72(t), the 10 percent additional tax on early distributions applies only to a distribution from a qualified retirement plan as described in Section 4974(c). The definition of qualified retirement plan for purposes of the 10 percent additional tax does not include a 457 plan. It includes only the following:

- 401(a) plan;
- 403(a) annuity;
- 403(b) annuity contract; or
- Individual retirement account or annuity.

Other Distribution Rules

Q 3:60   May a participant elect to defer commencement of a distribution?

A participant may elect to further defer the commencement of a distribution without running afoul of the made-available rule if the participant makes the election after amounts can be distributed under the plan but before commencement of a distribution. It should be noted that the participant can make only one such election. [I.R.C. § 457(e)(9)(B)]

> **Example.** John severs his employment with Gary's Home for Lost Cats in June 2003. He makes an "irrevocable" election to receive his deferred compensation over a 10-year period that would begin January 2004. In December 2003, John changes his previous starting-date election to January 2009. This change will not violate the made-available rule. John may not, however, make another change to that election.

Q 3:61   What is required to meet the payment term provisions of pre-EGTRRA Code Section 457(d)(2)(B)?

This pre-EGTRRA rule does not apply until distributions after 2010.

Q 3:62   Must a distribution be nonincreasing?

No. For the years 2002 through 2010, a pre-EGTRRA rule that previously required some distributions to be "substantially nonincreasing" and paid or delivered no less frequently than annually does not apply. [EGTRRA § 649(a)]

Q 3:63   What are substantially nonincreasing amounts?

None of the current statute, the pre-EGTRRA statute, the current regulations, or the 1982 regulations defines or defined *substantially nonincreasing amounts*. The IRS has suggested that although this phrase does not require the amounts distributed to be equal, they must not be radically or unexplainably dissimilar. [P.L.R. 9631034] In the absence of guidance, some practitioners assume that a specified and generally recognized cost-of-living index might be used without running afoul of the substantially nonincreasing rule that might apply to post-2010 distributions.

Q 3:64   May a plan make distributions in decreasing amounts?

Yes. Even for post-2010 distributions, the substantially nonincreasing rule does not preclude a distribution of *decreasing* amounts, as long as other rules are met.

**Q 3:65   May a participant transfer amounts from his or her deferred
compensation plan to buy service credit under
a governmental pension plan?**

Yes. A participant under a state or local government employer's eligible
plan may, even before his or her severance from employment, transfer an
amount to a governmental defined benefit plan if the transfer is for the participant's purchase of permissive service credit under that defined benefit plan.
[I.R.C. § 457(e)(17)]

Chapter 4

Investments

Peter J. Gulia, Esq.
CitiStreet Retirement Services

A deferred compensation plan may permit a participant's retirement savings to be invested in mutual funds, collective trust funds, fixed and variable annuity contracts, life insurance contracts, and other investments. This chapter describes the different options and an employer's responsibility in selecting plan investment options.

Because many deferred compensation plans provide for participant-directed investment, this chapter includes an explanation of contract and trust law principles that allow an employer to shift some fiduciary responsibility to participants, beneficiaries, and alternate payees, and describes employers' efforts to educate participants on plan investments.

Permitted Investments for Deferred Compensation Plans

Q 4:1 What kinds of investments may be used for a deferred compensation plan?

For a deferred compensation plan of a nongovernmental employer, an employer may use any investment (other than a participant loan). Of course, if a plan is unfunded, an employer need not make any investment.

For a deferred compensation plan of a state or local government employer, state law will regulate what investments may be held for the plan. Frequently, the types of permitted investments are specified by the state's enabling statute (see Q 4:2).

(For background on some widely used deferred compensation plan investment options, refer to Qs 4:3–4:10.)

Q 4:2 What is an enabling statute?

In local government law, a political subdivision of a state, such as a city or county, does not have authority to take action until the state grants it legal power to do so. An enabling statute is a state statute that grants political subdivisions of a state the authority to take a specified action.

In all 50 states, one or more state enabling statutes expressly grant the state's political subdivisions legal power to adopt and implement an eligible deferred compensation plan. In some states, these enabling statutes merely authorize deferred compensation and place few or no restrictions on a municipality in deciding the terms of a plan. In a few states, the enabling statute and the regulations adopted under the authority of the statute broadly regulate the terms of a municipality's deferred compensation plan. [See, e.g., N.J. Admin. Code tit. 5, § 37 (1999); N.Y. Comp. Codes R. & Regs. tit. 9, § 9000 *et seq.*] In some states, an enabling statute restricts a municipality's decisions regarding plan administration services.

Following Section 457(g) of the Internal Revenue Code (Code), most enabling statutes require a state or local government deferred compensation plan sponsor to manage a plan for the exclusive benefit of plan participants and their beneficiaries. [See I.R.C. § 457(g)(1)]

Many state statutes concerning state and local government procurement of goods and services appear to apply to a plan sponsor's or plan administrator's decisions concerning deferred compensation plan investments and services. It seems unlikely, however, that a court would restrain a government official's decision to select plan investment or service providers in a manner contrary to the procurement statute if the official believed that his or her means was necessary to administering a deferred compensation plan in the best interests of participants and their beneficiaries. [See I.R.C. § 457(g)(1)]

For a model enabling statute, see appendix H on the CD-ROM.

Types of Investments

Q 4:3   What is a mutual fund?

Mutual fund is the popular name for what the securities laws call a "registered investment company." The formal name comes from the Investment Company Act of 1940, a federal law that regulates how a mutual fund is operated. (The Code refers to a mutual fund as a "regulated investment company." [I.R.C. § 851(a)])

A mutual fund is a corporation, partnership, or business trust that invests commonly for investors who have selected that fund. Pooling is the key aspect of mutual fund investing; by banding together, the shareholders may get diversification and management that they could not get as individuals.

A mutual fund manager has a fiduciary duty to invest the fund according to the investment objectives and restrictions stated in the fund's prospectus and other governing documents. A fund cannot give any assurance that its objectives will be achieved.

Q 4:4   What is a collective trust fund?

A collective trust fund is an investment fund maintained by a bank or trust company for several investors, all of which are employee benefit plan trusts. [12 C.F.R. § 9.18; Securities Act of 1933 § 3(a)(2), 15 U.S.C. § 77c(a)(2); Securities Exchange Act of 1934 § 3(a)(12)(A)(iv), 15 U.S.C. § 78c(a)(12)(A)(iv); Investment Company Act of 1940 § 3(c)(11), 15 U.S.C. § 80a-3(c)(11); I.R.C. § 581]

The bank or trust company invests commonly for those employee benefit plan trusts that have selected the fund. A collective trust fund manager has a fiduciary duty to invest the fund according to the investment objectives and restrictions stated in the fund's statement of operations and other governing documents.

Q 4:5   What is an annuity contract?

An annuity contract is an insurance company's written promise that it will pay to the contract holder, or to one or more annuitants, a specified amount of money on a regular basis over a specified period. Although a contract holder is not required to choose an annuity option, an insurance company is required to offer annuity options. Because under an annuity option the insurer is obligated to keep paying the specified amount no matter how long the annuitant lives, an annuity contract is a kind of insurance and is regulated by state insurance law.

Annuity contracts are of two kinds: fixed and variable (see Qs 4:6, 4:7).

Q 4:6   What is a fixed annuty contract?

A fixed annuity contract is an annuity contract that has guaranteed minimum interest and typically credits a current interest rate that the insurer declares from time to time (often each month) at the insurer's sole discretion.

Although a fixed annuity holder hopes that the insurer will continue to declare reasonably market-sensitive interest rates, an insurer has no obligation to do so. A fixed annuity is regulated by insurance law, but not by securities law. But a fixed interest option that can become subject to a market value adjustment is regulated by securities law. [Securities Act of 1933 § 3(a)(8), 15 U.S.C. § 77c(a)(8); Securities Act Rule 151]

The contributions received under a fixed annuity contract are commingled with the insurer's other assets in its general account. The insurer must invest its general account assets for the benefit of all contract holders. In addition, the insurer must invest according to state insurance-law requirements.

Q 4:7 What is a variable annuity contract?

A variable annuity contract is an annuity contract that has a "cash value" that goes up or down with the investment performance of separate accounts that are invested in mutual funds, or funds that are diversified but unregistered. An insurance company separate account or subaccount invests in the shares or units of just one fund. Usually, the underlying fund is subject to banking or securities regulation and therefore should be invested as stated by the fund's prospectus or other documents. As with mutual funds, there can be no guarantee that a separate account or subaccount will achieve its stated investment objective. A variable annuity is regulated by both insurance law and securities law. [Securities Act Rule 151]

> **Note.** Concerning a variable annuity contract, an investor cannot pursue a state law claim that alleges misrepresentation or nondisclosure; instead, the investor must rely on federal law claims and such a case may be removed to federal court. [See, e.g., Patenaude v. Equitable Life Assurance Society, No. 00-56913 (9th Cir. May 14, 2002) (construing the Securities Litigation Uniform Standards Act of 1998)]

For information about securities laws, see chapter 10.

Q 4:8 What is a securities account?

A securities account is an account that a broker-dealer keeps for its customer to buy, sell, and hold securities, including nondiversified securities, such as individual stocks and bonds. [See generally National Conference of Commissioners on Uniform State Laws, Uniform Commercial Code § 8-601 (2001)]

Q 4:9 May deferred compensation plan amounts be invested in securities accounts?

Whether deferred compensation plan amounts may be invested in individual stocks and bonds (rather than mutual funds and collective investment funds) turns on the type of plan and, for a state or local government employer's plan, state law.

For a state or local government employer's deferred compensation plan, most states' enabling statutes (see Q 4:2) limit plan investment to bank instruments, insurance company annuity contracts, and mutual funds. Some states permit collective investment funds and group trusts that provide pooled investment. A typical enabling statute does not permit deferred compensation plan investment in individual stocks and bonds. In such a state, if a "brokerage" or securities account (see Q 4:8) can include securities other than mutual fund shares, it is not a permitted investment. California law permits a state or local government employer's deferred compensation plan to invest in individual stocks and bonds. [Cal. Const. art. 16, § 17; Cal. Gov't. Code § 53609]

For an unfunded deferred compensation plan, a nongovernmental employer may invest in any investment it desires (see Q 4:28). A church might limit its investments based on the church's religious beliefs.

Q 4:10   What is a life insurance contract?

A life insurance contract is a contract in which an insurance company agrees to pay the contract owner a sum of money when the *insured* (a specified individual who is the subject of the insurance) dies. Based on information about the insured's age and health, the insurance company will specify the *premium*, or amount of money it requires to accept the risk of being obligated to pay a sum when the insured dies. Life insurance is regulated by state insurance law. [For more information about life insurance contract provisions, refer to G.S. Lesser & L.C. Starr, *Life Insurance Answer Book* ch.5 (New York: Aspen Publishers, 3d ed. 2002, 2003)]

Q 4:11   What is a life insurance illustration?

In many life insurance contracts, many or most of the contract's provisions are "non-guaranteed"—that is, the insurance company has a practice of providing benefits greater than those stated by the terms of the written contract. To show a potential buyer how such a life insurance contract "works" in his or her personal financial planning situation, an insurance agent typically provides a computer-generated life insurance illustration.

A life insurance illustration is an oral or written presentation that is meant to explain the benefits that a contract might provide if the holder called upon the contract's death benefit or "cash value" at a particular future time. The typical life insurance illustration is a personal-computer printout that shows the proposed contract's assumed or hypothetical death benefit and accumulation value for each age or year until a specific age or year, such as normal retirement age or contract termination.

The illustration assumes facts such as the proposed insured's age and risk classification and which policy form is proposed. To show anything beyond minimum contractually obligated benefits, an illustration includes assumptions for one or more of the following: a mortality table or cost of insurance charge that is more favorable to the holder than the table or charge specified by the contract; interest (or dividends) crediting that is greater than what the contract requires; and administration charges that are lower than those specified by the contract.

Insurance regulators' concerns about whether these illustrations had a potential to mislead unknowledgeable consumers led to a model regulation recommended by the National Association of Insurance Commissioners. [For information on that regulation, refer to G.S. Lesser & L.C. Starr, *Life Insurance Answer Book* ch. 26 (New York: Aspen Publishers, 3d ed. 2002, 2003)]

A participant should carefully read a life insurance illustration to understand the difference between what might happen (if all of the illustration's assumptions occur) and what the insurer would be contractually obligated to provide.

Q 4:12 May an eligible deferred compensation plan invest in a participant loan?

For a governmental eligible deferred compensation plan, yes; for a nongovernmental plan, no.

For an unfunded plan of a tax-exempt organization, "[I]f a participant or beneficiary receives (directly or indirectly) any amount deferred as a loan . . ., that amount will be treated as having been paid or made available to the individual as a distribution under the plan, in violation of the distribution requirements of section 457(d)." [Treas. Reg. § 1.457-6(f)(1)]

For an eligible deferred compensation plan maintained by a state or local governmental employer,

> [W]hether the availability of a loan, the making of a loan, or a failure to repay a loan made from a trustee (or a person treated as a trustee under section 457(g)) of an eligible governmental plan to a participant or beneficiary is treated as a distribution (directly or indirectly) for purposes of this section, and . . . whether the availability of the loan, the making of the loan, or a failure to repay the loan is in any other respect a violation of the requirements of section 457(b) and the regulations, depends on the facts and circumstances. Thus, for example, a loan must bear a reasonable rate of interest[.]

[Treas. Reg. § 1.457-6(f)(2); see also I.R.C. § 457(g)(1); Treas. Reg. §§ 1.457-7(b)(3), -8(a)(1)]

The Treasury Department's explanation that was contained in the 2002 proposed regulation stated that "the legislative history to the SBJPA (Small Business Job Protection Act of 1996) indicates that the new statutory provisions should be interpreted as permitting participant loans from the eligible plan trust under the rules applicable to loans from qualified plans." [67 Fed. Reg. 30,826, 30,829 (May 8, 2002)] According to the Treasury Department, "[t]he pre-ERISA requirements applicable to loans from qualified plans require a facts and circumstances analysis of the availability of the loan feature to all participants, the rate of return, the overall prudence of the investment of the trust corpus in the note of an individual participant, and the pattern of repayments." [67 Fed. Reg. 30,826, 30,829 (May 8, 2002), (citing Central Motor Co. v. United States, 583 F.2d 470, 488–91 (10th Cir. 1978); Winger's Department Store v. Commissioner, 82 T.C. 869 (1982); Ma-Tran Corp. v. Commissioner, 70 T.C. 158 (1978); Feroleto Steel Co. v. Commissioner, 69 T.C. 97 (1977); Rev. Rul. 69-494, 1969-2 C.B. 88; Rev. Rul. 67-258, 1967-2 C.B. 68]

The Treasury Department's view that the SBJPA's legislative history calls for pre-ERISA rules is not free from doubt. Congress's report said "that amounts held in trust (or custodial account or annuity contract), [sic] may be loaned to plan participants (or beneficiaries) pursuant to rules applicable to loans from qualified plans (sec. 72(p))." The sentence's reference to qualified-plan rules was qualified by a reference to a particular Code provision. Also, the sentence was further explained by a footnote that summarized the rules of Code Section 72(p). [H.R. Rep. No. 104-737, at 251 & n.35 (1996)] Based on this, some practitioners believe that an eligible plan of a state or local government employer may provide participant loans simply by obeying the Section 72(p) rules.

Protecting the Safety of Investments

Q 4:13 What protects the safety of fixed annuity or life insurance contracts?

An insurer's investment of its general account is regulated by state insurance law (see Q 4:6). In the unlikely event that an insurer becomes insolvent or impaired and cannot meet its obligations, the state's life insurance guaranty association will meet those obligations, subject to state law coverage limits and assessment limits. All states and the District of Columbia have a life insurance guaranty association. The association can protect contract holders, insureds, and annuity participants against an impaired or insolvent insurer's failure to meet its contract obligations by "reinsuring" the covered policies of the impaired insurer or by causing another insurer to assume the policies.

A typical coverage limit per annuitant or insured is $100,000 for cash values and $300,000 for all benefits, but some states provide greater coverage. Most states cover only residents, and some states exclude nonresidents only when they are covered by another state's guaranty law. This rarely matters, because every state has a guaranty association.

All states prohibit any statement regarding the guaranty association, including even reference to its existence, in the context of insurance sales. One state's highest court held on free speech constitutional grounds that such a ban could not be applied to a truthful and nonmisleading statement. [New Mexico Life Insurance Guaranty Ass'n v. Quinn & Co., 111 N.M. 750, 809 P.2d 1278 (1991)] Some states provide for a written notice, given on delivery of an annuity or life insurance contract, that provides a basic explanation of guaranty association coverage.

Q 4:14 What protects the safety of a variable annuity?

A variable annuity carries no insolvency risk. The cash value of each variable annuity contract is supported by the investments of the separate accounts selected by the contract holder. An insurance company separate account is not subject to claims by anyone other than contract holders invested under that separate account. The separate account cannot be reached by other creditors, not even by the insurance company itself. Although such segregation has always been the law of insurance company separate accounts [see, e.g., Conn. Gen. Stat. Ann. § 38a-459], Connecticut's Insurance Commissioner reaffirmed this legal conclusion in a formal declaratory ruling. [Declaratory Rul. No. IC 91-51 (Dec. 17, 1991)]

Q 4:15 What protects the safety of a mutual fund?

A mutual fund (see Q 4:3) is required to keep custody of its money and securities, and the form and manner of custody are regulated by federal securities law. The money and securities of a mutual fund typically are held by a bank custodian. Additionally, the officers and employees of a mutual fund must be bonded against larceny and embezzlement. [Investment Company Act of 1940 § 17(f), (g), 15 U.S.C. § 80a-17(f), (g); Investment Company Act Rules 17f, 17g, 17 C.F.R. §§ 270.17f, 270.17g-1]

Rabbi Trusts

Q 4:16 What is a rabbi trust?

A rabbi trust is a particular kind of grantor trust in which investments are set aside for deferred compensation plan purposes. At all times, the trust investments must be available to the employer if it needs to pay its creditors. [Rev. Proc. 92-64, 1992-2 C.B. 422; P.L.R. 8752013, 8727028]

A rabbi trust does not protect a deferred compensation plan participant against the employer's bankruptcy, insolvency, or other inability to pay deferred compensation. A rabbi trust might help protect a participant against an employer's dishonest refusal to pay its deferred compensation obligation.

Caution. Every rabbi trust provides that an executive officer's notice of the employer's insolvency triggers the trust's provisions for the protection of creditors other than plan participants and beneficiaries. [Rev. Proc. 92-64, 1992-2 C.B. 422] An employer could use that power dishonestly to delay or avoid payment of a deferred compensation obligation.

Q 4:17 Does a rabbi trust have to file a tax return?

No. For federal income tax purposes, a typical rabbi trust is treated as an agency rather than as a trust. Because the trust's assets may be available to the employer, any income of the trust is counted as the employer's income. [I.R.C. §§ 671–677; Treas. Reg. § 301.7701-6(b)(2); P.L.R. 8750046]

Trusts for Governmental Deferred Compensation Plans

Q 4:18   What is a Section 457(g) trust?

Throughout this chapter, the term *Section 457(g) trust* is used to refer to any trust, custodial account, or annuity contract that is intended to meet the exclusive benefit requirement of Code Section 457(g).

For an eligible deferred compensation plan of a state or local government, "all assets and income of the plan [must be] held in trust for the exclusive benefit of [plan] participants and their beneficiaries." [I.R.C. § 457(g)(1); Treas. Reg. § 1.457-8(a)(1)]

In the Treasury Department's view, an exclusive benefit trust "must be established pursuant to a written agreement that constitutes a valid trust under State law. The terms of the trust must make it impossible, prior to the satisfaction of all liabilities with respect to participants and their beneficiaries, for any part of the assets and income of the trust to be used for, or diverted to, purposes other than for the exclusive benefit of participants and their beneficiaries." [Treas. Reg. § 1.457-8(a)(2)(i)]

The exclusive benefit requirement can be met using a custodial account or an annuity contract instead of a trust. [Treas. Reg. § 1.457-8(a)(3)] For the purpose of Code Section 457(g), a life, health, accident, property, casualty, or liability insurance contract is not treated as an annuity contract; therefore, if a state or local governmental deferred compensation plan's investment options include a life insurance contract, the employer must establish an exclusive benefit trust, at least for the life insurance contract. [Treas. Reg. § 1.457-8(a)(3)(iii)] Whenever a plan uses a custodial account or an annuity contract instead of a trust, the account or contract must expressly state the exclusive benefit language. [Treas. Reg. § 1.457-8(a)(3)(i)] If a plan sponsor or administrator wants to use a custodial account instead of a trust, the custodian must be a bank or an IRS-approved nonbank custodian. [Treas. Reg. § 1.457-8(a)(3)(ii)(B)]

A plan can "mix and match" different kinds of exclusive benefit arrangements—trust, custodial account, and annuity contract—as long as every plan asset is held under at least one exclusive benefit arrangement. [Treas. Reg. § 1.457-8(a)(3)(i)]

An exclusive benefit arrangement implies a prompt contribution requirement:

Amounts deferred under an eligible governmental plan must be transferred to a trust within a period that is not longer than is reasonable for the proper administration of the participant accounts (if any). [A] plan may provide for amounts deferred for a participant under the plan to be transferred to the trust within a specified period after the date the amounts would otherwise have been paid to the participant. For example, the plan could provide for amounts deferred under the plan to be contributed to the trust within 15 business days following the month in which these amounts would otherwise have been paid to the participant.

[Treas. Reg. § 1.457-8(a)(2)(ii)]

Q 4:19 What provisions must be included in a Section 457(g) trust?

Under the Code, the only required provision in a Section 457(g) trust is a provision that "all assets and income [will be] held . . . for the exclusive benefit of [plan] participants and their beneficiaries." [I.R.C. § 457(g)(1)] A deferred compensation plan of a state or local government employer cannot qualify for favorable tax treatment unless the exclusive benefit provision is legally enforceable under state law. (See Q 4:18.) Although it is not expressly stated in the Code, the Section 457(g) trust should be irrevocable because the exclusive benefit provision would be ineffective if the trust could be revoked.

Of course, the provisions of the trust, custodial account, or annuity contract must be such that it would be respected as a trust, custodial account, or annuity contract under state law.

Q 4:20 Who can be trustees of a Section 457(g) trust?

In some states, the enabling statute grants a state agency or a municipality power to serve as trustee for its deferred compensation plan. In other states, a state agency's or municipality's incidental or implied powers may be sufficient to permit the agency or municipality to serve as trustee for its deferred compensation plan.

Sometimes, a state agency or municipality may feel more comfortable asking particular individuals to serve as trustees. If a person who is a government official or employee serves as trustee, he or she would be wise to request indemnity, as is customarily provided to government officials concerning their official duties. Even if sovereign immunity, governmental immunity, and public officer immunity (see Qs 4:33–4:35) protect an official from monetary liability, indemnity might be useful to pay or reimburse his or her lawyer's fees if the attorney general or other government lawyer is not required or permitted to defend the official.

In some situations, a plan sponsor might select a bank, trust company, or other IRS-approved custodian. If a plan sponsor is considering an "outside" trustee in an attempt to diminish the sponsor's liability, it should consider that a professional trustee will not accept responsibility for any decision that the trustee did not make. Moreover, for this kind of plan, a professional trustee typically will insist on its own form of trust agreement that provides that the trustee has no discretion and acts only according to the plan sponsor's instructions. If the trustee has no discretion and has a right to rely on instructions, the plan sponsor will not have shifted any liability that might arise from those decisions.

Q 4:21   Is a Section 457(g) trust subject to ERISA's prohibited transaction rules?

An employee benefit plan trust created for a governmental plan is not subject to ERISA's prohibited transaction rules. [ERISA § 4(b)(1); I.R.C. § 4975(g)(2)] A trust used for a state or local government employer's qualified retirement plan may be subject to the prohibited transaction rules that apply to certain tax-exempt organizations. [I.R.C. §§ 503(a)(1)(B), 4975(g)(2); Treas. Reg. § 1.503(a)-1(a)(3)]

Code Section 457(g)(2)(A) states that a state or local government eligible deferred compensation plan's Section 457(g) trust "shall be treated as an organization exempt from taxation under section 501(a)," and Code Section 457(g)(3) states that "custodial accounts and [annuity] contracts described in section 401(f) shall be treated as trusts under rules similar to the rules under section 401(f)." Taken together, these statements suggest that a Section 457(g) trust might be treated as a Section 401(a) trust for federal income tax purposes. If a Section 457(g) trust is treated as a Section 401(a) trust, then a Section 457(g) trust should be subject to the prohibited transaction rules that apply to tax-exempt organizations, including governmental retirement plans.

Q 4:22   What is a prohibited transaction?

A prohibited transaction is a transaction in which the trust engages in one of the following activities with a closely related person (see Q 4:25):

1. The trust lends any part of its income or corpus (without getting adequate security and a reasonable rate of interest) to a closely related person.
2. The trust pays any closely related person compensation in excess of a reasonable allowance for personal services actually rendered.
3. The trust makes its services available to a closely related person on a preferential basis.
4. The trust buys securities or other property from a closely related person for more than adequate consideration in money or money's worth.
5. The trust sells its securities or other property to a closely related person for less than adequate consideration in money or money's worth.
6. The trust engages in any other transaction that results in a diversion of the trust's income or corpus to a closely related person.

[I.R.C. § 503(b)(1)–(6); Treas. Reg. § 1.503(b)-1(a)]

These prohibited transactions are in addition to all other restrictions required by the Code. Any prohibited transaction or other self-dealing transaction will be considered in an evaluation of whether the trust is in fact operated for its stated tax-exempt purpose. [Treas. Reg. § 1.503(a)-1(b)]

Because of the definition of *closely related person* (see Q 4:25), these prohibited transaction rules generally mean that the Section 457(g) trust must not be used to benefit the state or local government entity or a corporation or business controlled by it.

Q 4:23   Is a participant loan a plan investment?

Yes and no. Under a typical annuity contract, a participant loan involves a use of the contract rights and an adjustment in the plan account's value. Under a typical plan, a participant loan is, in form, an investment of the account. In either case, a typical participant loan affects only the account of the participant, who, in effect, is both borrower and lender. [Cf. DOL Reg. § 2550.408b-1(f)]

Q 4:24   Must a plan fiduciary collect repayments on a participant loan?

A typical participant loan affects only the account of the participant, who is, in effect, both borrower and lender. If a plan fiduciary has a duty to manage plan assets, it may use discretion, usually restricted only by an arbitrary and capricious review standard, in collecting on a defaulted loan. [See, e.g., Colaluca v. Climaco, Climaco, Seminatore, Lefkowitz & Garofolo, 1997 U.S. App. LEXIS 2108 (6th Cir. 1997)] A prudent plan fiduciary might ask a borrowing participant to direct that none of the plan fiduciaries collect loan repayments. A plan fiduciary will not be liable for a loss that results from following such a direction. [Cf. ERISA § 404(c)(1)(B)]

Q 4:25   Who is a closely related person?

For purposes of the prohibited transaction rules (see Q 4:22), *closely related person* means any of the following:

1. The state or local government entity;
2. Any person who has made a substantial contribution to the trust;
3. A family member of a substantial contributor;
4. A corporation controlled, directly or indirectly, by a substantial contributor; or
5. A corporation controlled, directly or indirectly, by the state or local government entity.

[I.R.C. § 503(b)]

Substantial contributor is defined for other purposes as a person who contributed more than $5,000 if that amount is more than 2 percent of the total contributions received in a year. [I.R.C. § 507(d)(2)(A); Treas. Reg. § 1.507-6(a)(1)] The term does not include the state or local government entity that creates the Section 457(g) trust. [Treas. Reg. § 1.507-6(a)(1)] The term *contribution* means a charitable contribution. [Treas. Reg. § 1.507-6(c)(1)] Therefore, in normal operation of an eligible deferred compensation plan, a Section 457(g) trust should not have any substantial contributor and the only closely related persons would be the state or local government entity and any corporation or business controlled, directly or indirectly, by the state or local government entity.

Q 4:26   Should the trust document preclude prohibited transactions?

The Code does not require that the trust document preclude prohibited transactions. [I.R.C. § 457(g)] In addition, the mere fact that a trustee has authority under the trust document to enter into transactions that would be prohibited transactions does not by itself cause the trust to lose tax-exempt status as long as the trust does not engage in any prohibited transactions. [Waller v. Commissioner, 39 T.C. 665 (1963)]

Stating the prohibited transaction restriction in the trust document may be helpful guidance to the trustees, especially if they are not professional fiduciaries. Of course, this restriction should be stated without conceding that any prohibited transaction rules apply.

Q 4:27   Does a Section 457(g) trust have to file a tax return?

No. Although IRS Form 5500 is required (and its related Schedule P is permitted) for most qualified retirement plans, this information return is not required for a governmental plan. [Instructions to IRS Form 5500] The Code does not impose a tax return filing requirement on this kind of tax-exempt trust.

Q 4:28   Must a Section 457(g) trust be audited?

Because a governmental plan is not subject to ERISA, ERISA's financial reporting requirements do not apply to a Section 457(g) trust. [ERISA § 4(b)(1)] In addition, the Code does not impose any reporting requirement. [I.R.C. § 6058]

It might be prudent for a trustee to engage an independent certified public accountant to examine and express an opinion on the trust's financial statements. Even if the eligible deferred compensation plan and its related trust provide for participant-directed investment, the trustee still has a legal duty to maintain record ownership of the plan investments. A course of regular audits could help show that the trustee owned the investments that it should have owned.

Employer Responsibility for Plan Investments

Q 4:29   What is the employer's investment responsibility for a nongovernmental or unfunded deferred compensation plan?

If a deferred compensation plan is unfunded, the employer does not have any fiduciary responsibility for the selection of investments. Why? Because the employer is making investments of "amounts, property, and rights" that it owns and cannot set aside specially for the benefit of participants, the employer cannot have a fiduciary duty to invest for the benefit of participants. Of course, the employer remains responsible to pay the deferred compensation provided by the plan or contract.

Q 4:30 What is the employer's investment responsibility for a state or local government eligible deferred compensation plan?

The assets and income of a state or local government eligible deferred compensation plan must be held in a Section 457(g) trust (see Q 4:18). The trustee has only those fiduciary duties that are provided by (1) the trust agreement or declaration and (2) applicable state law. Generally, it should be possible for an employer to create a trust under which the trustee does not have any investment responsibility.

If a plan is designed to provide participant-directed investment, the plan and the trust should say so. Because state law may provide that a trustee ordinarily has a fiduciary duty to invest trust assets, it may be prudent for an employer that creates a Section 457(g) trust to state expressly in the trust agreement or declaration that the trustee has no investment responsibility and instead must follow participants' and beneficiaries' instructions. [See generally Restatement (Third) of Trusts § 227 & cmts. (1992)]

Under Code Section 457(g), the trust or custodial account need not provide any fiduciary duty other than the duty to hold the plan investments "for the exclusive benefit of participants and their beneficiaries." [I.R.C. § 457(g)(1)]

In some states, the state's enabling statute requires the employer to act as a fiduciary in selecting the "menu" of plan investment options within which participants direct investment. [See, e.g., N.Y. Comp. Codes R. & Regs. tit. 9, § 9003.3(a) (implementing N.Y. State Fin. Law § 5)]

Q 4:31 If a trustee has fiduciary responsibility for plan investments, what is that fiduciary duty?

Under modern trust law, a fiduciary must act with the care, skill, prudence, and diligence under the circumstances then prevailing that a prudent person acting as a fiduciary and familiar with deferred compensation plan matters would use in the conduct of managing a deferred compensation plan. This means that the fiduciary must act as an expert would. [See generally Restatement (Third) of Trusts § 227 & cmts. (1992) (prudent investor rule)]

Under the "prudent expert" concept, a fiduciary must make a careful inquiry into the merits of an investment decision. Thus, a fiduciary's lack of familiarity with a form of investment is not an excuse for making an imprudent investment. If a fiduciary does not have sufficient knowledge to evaluate the merits or soundness of a proposed investment, the fiduciary has a duty to obtain expert advice in making the decision. [See, e.g., Katsaros v. Cody, 744 F.2d

270, 279 (2d Cir.), *cert. denied sub nom.* Cody v. Donovan, 469 U.S. 1072, 105 S. Ct. 565, 83 L. Ed. 2d 506 (1984); Marshall v. Glass/Metal Ass'n & Glaziers & Glassworkers Pension Plan, 507 F. Supp. 378, 384 (D. Haw. 1980)] Although a fiduciary has a duty to seek independent advice when it lacks expertise or knowledge, the fiduciary must make its own decision using that advice. [Whitfield v. Cohen, 682 F. Supp. 188, 194–95 (S.D.N.Y. 1988); Donovan v. Tricario, 5 Employee Benefits Cas. (BNA) 2057 (S.D. Fla. 1984), *aff'd,* 768 F.2d 1351 (11th Cir. 1985)] Further, a fiduciary must make sure that the advisor receives complete information so that its advice can be grounded in the relevant purposes, facts, and circumstances. [Cf. Chao v. Hall Holding Co., 285 F.3d 415 (6th Cir. 2002)]

A fiduciary does not have to make the right decision. The fiduciary must merely consider sufficient information. The legal standard is whether the fiduciary's procedure made it possible to make a well-informed decision. If a fiduciary diligently investigated the relevant information, a court will not interfere with and will uphold the fiduciary's judgment. Any review of a fiduciary's decision is based on the circumstances and the analysis conducted at the time that the fiduciary made the decision, and not from the vantage point of "20/20 hindsight." [See, e.g., Metzler v. Graham, 112 F.3d 207 (5th Cir. 1997); Katsaros v. Cody, 744 F.2d 270, 279 (2d Cir.), *cert. denied sub nom.* Cody v. Donovan, 469 U.S. 1072, 105 S. Ct. 565, 83 L. Ed. 2d 506 (1984); Lanka v. O'Higgins, 810 F. Supp. 379 (N.D.N.Y. 1992); Whitfield v. Cohen, 682 F. Supp. 188 (S.D.N.Y. 1988)]

Finally, a fiduciary should make (and regularly update) a written investment policy statement. If the plan provides for participant-directed investment (see Q 4:44), the statement should say that the policy is to make available a broad range of different investment options that have varying degrees of risk and return and that the selection is intended to make it possible for the participant to achieve a diversified, balanced portfolio consistent with modern portfolio theory. Consistent with the trustee's continuing fiduciary duty, the trustee should revise or reapprove the investment policy statement each year.

Q 4:32   What should a plan fiduciary do if the other fiduciaries make a decision that is imprudent?

Under the common law of trusts, any action by fewer than all trustees, even though a majority, is void unless the trust document states that the trustees may act by a majority. [Restatement (Second) of Trusts § 194] In modern retirement plan practice, however, many plan fiduciary committees act by majority vote.

When a plan fiduciary is outvoted, resignation, without further action to protect the interests of participants and beneficiaries, generally is not enough to protect the outvoted fiduciary from personal liability.

While Part 4 of Subtitle B of Title I of ERISA does not apply to any 457 plan, DOL guidance provides a helpful restatement of the common law of trusts. According to the DOL, where a majority of [fiduciaries of one fiduciary body] appear ready to take action [that] would clearly be contrary to the prudence requirement . . ., it is incumbent on the minority [fiduciaries] to take all reasonable and legal steps to prevent the action. Such steps might include preparations to obtain an injunction from [an appropriate] court . . . or to publicize the vote if the decision is to proceed as proposed. If, having taken all reasonable and legal steps to prevent the imprudent action, the minority [fiduciaries] have not succeeded, they will not incur liability for the action of the majority. Mere resignation, however, without taking steps to prevent the imprudent action, will not suffice to avoid liability for the minority [fiduciaries] once they have knowledge that the imprudent action is under consideration.

Likewise, a fiduciary's insistence that his or her "objections and the responses to such objections [(if any)] be included in the record of the meeting" will not be sufficient to protect the outvoted fiduciary. "[R]esignation by the [fiduciary] as a protest against [a fiduciary] breach will not generally be considered sufficient to discharge the [fiduciary's] positive duty . . . to make reasonable efforts under the circumstances to remedy the breach." [DOL ERISA Interpretive Bulletin 75-5, 40 Fed. Reg. 31,599 (July 28, 1975), redesignated at 41 Fed. Reg. 1906 (Jan. 13, 1976), reprinted in 29 C.F.R. § 2509.75-5]

Arguably, a plan fiduciary might be protected from liability if the other fiduciaries' breach was not *clearly* a breach. However, when considering whether any decision is clearly a fiduciary breach, the outvoted fiduciary still must act as an expert fiduciary. The DOL guidance is consistent with the common law of trusts.

An outvoted trustee remains liable for a cotrustee's breach unless the outvoted trustee takes prudent steps to prevent the other trustee's breach or to compel the other trustee to correct the breach. [Restatement (Second) of Trusts §§ 184, 224 (1957); National Conference of Commissioners on Uniform State Laws, Uniform Trust Act § 703(b)(2)] The outvoted trustee has a right to engage independent legal counsel, and (if he or she acts or acted in good faith) a right to have the trust advance or reimburse his or her expenses (including lawyers' fees). [F.M. English, Annotation, *Right of Coexecutor or Trustee to Retain Independent Legal Counsel*, 66 A.L.R.2d 1169 (1959); Lee R. Russ, Annotation, *Award of Attorneys' Fees out of Trust Estate in Action by Trustee against Cotrustee*, 24 A.L.R.4th 624 (1983)]

For a church plan, an outvoted fiduciary who fails to take protective action might nevertheless avoid liability to the extent that the breach would not have been prevented or corrected because a court could not have required the breaching fiduciary to take an action that would have interfered with his or her free exercise of religion. [U.S. Const. amend. I; see generally K.E. North, *Religious Disputes in Secular Courts* (Durham, NC: Carolina Academic Press, 2000)]

For a governmental plan, an outvoted fiduciary who fails to take protective action might be protected by sovereign immunity (see Q 4:33), governmental immunity (see Q 4:34), or public officer immunity (see Q 4:35).

Q 4:33   What is sovereign immunity?

Sovereign immunity is a law or court doctrine that precludes a lawsuit against the government without the government's consent. [Restatement (Second) of Torts § 895B] That consent or "waiver" can be made only by statute. Although most states have expressly waived immunity for specified kinds of claims, any such waiver is strictly and narrowly construed. [See, e.g., Shedrick v. William Penn School District, 654 A.2d 163, 164 (Pa. Commw. Ct.), *appeal denied*, 542 Pa. 682, 668 A.2d 1142 (1995); Bullard v. Lehigh-Northampton Airport Authority 668 A.2d 223 (Pa. Commw. Ct. 1995); DeLuca v. School District of Philadelphia, 654 A.2d 29, 31 (Pa. Commw. Ct. 1994); Kiley v. City of Philadelphia, 537 Pa. 502, 506, 645 A.2d 184, 185–86 (1994)] The author is unaware of any enabling statute (see Q 4:2) that waives sovereign immunity regarding state or local government employers' deferred compensation plans.

In many states, a claim against the state can be submitted only to a special court or tribunal. For example, in Pennsylvania, a claim against the commonwealth can be heard only in Commonwealth Court. [Pa. Const. art. I, § 11] For this purpose, a retirement plan or its trust is treated as "an integral part of the Commonwealth." [See, e.g., United Brokers Mortgage Co. v. Fidelity Philadelphia Trust Co., 26 Pa. Commw. 260, 363 A.2d 817 (1976)]

A state or local government's immunity from many kinds of legal claims also may include immunity from limitations generally imposed on nongovernment persons on the time for or manner of asserting legal claims. For example, a governmental person or entitity may be exempt from a statute of limitations or statute of repose that would preclude a nongovernment person from pursuing a lawsuit. [See, e.g., Kan. Stat. Ann. § 60-521; Kansas Public Employees Retirement System v. Reimer & Koger Associates, 262 Kan. 635 (1997); State Highway Commission v. Steele, 215 Kan. 837, 839, 528 P.2d 1242, 1244 (1974)]

If the state or municipality has sovereign immunity, the government is immune from a tort action, but not from lawsuits based on a proper contract. [Elliot v. Colorado Department of Corrections, 865 P.2d 859 (Colo. Ct. App. 1993), *cert. denied*, No. 93SC386, 1994 Colo. LEXIS 65 (Colo. Jan. 10, 1994); Ager v. Public Employees' Retirement Ass'n, No. 91 CV 346 (Colo. Dist. Ct. Larimer County Apr. 29, 1993), *aff'd in part, rev'd in part, and remanded*, 923 P.2d 133 (Colo. Ct. App. 1995); Pritchard v. Public Employees' Retirement Ass'n, No. 92 CV 65 (Colo. Dist. Ct. Moffat County May 3, 1993)] Further, sovereign immunity cannot defeat a retirement plan right that has been declared or recognized as a constitutional contract right. [See, e.g., Sgaglione v. Levitt, 37 N.Y.2d 507, 337 N.E.2d 592, 375 N.Y.S.2d 79, *reargument denied*, 37 N.Y.2d 924, 340 N.E.2d 754, 378 N.Y.S.2d 1027 (1975)]

An American Indian tribe also enjoys sovereign immunity. [Kiowa Tribe of Oklahoma v. Manufacturing Technologies, Inc., 523 U.S. 751 (1998); United States v. U.S. Fidelity & Guaranty Co., 309 U.S. 506) (1940)]

Caution. A reader should get expert legal advice on how state law applies to a particular state agency or municipality.

Q 4:34   What is governmental immunity?

Even if sovereign immunity does not apply, a state or municipality may be immune from liability for an act (or omission) that is the exercise of an administrative function involving government policy or of a discretionary function. [Restatement (Second) of Torts §§ 895B & cmts., 895C & cmts.]

In Pennsylvania, a municipality and the individuals who serve the municipality with respect to a retirement plan have governmental immunity [42 Pa. Cons. Stat. Ann. § 8541] or official immunity [42 Pa. Cons. Stat. Ann. § 8546] that would preclude any monetary relief from the municipality or the individual. At least one court decision expressly recognized that municipal officials acting as trustees of a retirement plan were entitled to governmental immunity. [Potter v. Springfield Township, 681 A.2d 241 (Pa. Commw. Ct. 1996), *petition for allowance of appeal denied*, 547 Pa. 760, 692 A.2d 568 (1997)]

Caution. A reader should get expert legal advice on how state law applies to a particular state agency or municipality and a particular state or municipal official.

Q 4:35   What is public officer immunity?

Sovereign immunity and governmental immunity refer to the potential liability of the state or local government entity. Sometimes, a lawsuit names a state or local government officer or employee as an individual. In these situations, public officer immunity may protect the individual.

In general, a public officer who acts within the scope of his or her authority is not subject to liability for an administrative act (or omission) taken in the exercise of a discretionary function. [Restatement (Second) of Torts § 895D] This immunity "extends . . . to lower administrative officers when they engage in making a decision by weighing the policies for and against it." [Id. cmt. d]

Caution. A reader should get expert legal advice on how state law applies to him or her. If an official considers the advice of a government lawyer, the official should ask the lawyer to explain any conflicts of interest or other concerns that might restrain the lawyer's readiness to give the official candid advice. Further, an official should consider getting the advice of his or her personal lawyer.

Q 4:36   Does sovereign immunity mean that a participant or beneficiary has no remedy?

Even if sovereign immunity precludes any monetary liability for past actions, a participant or beneficiary may petition a court for a mandamus order that restrains a government official's future conduct. [See Restatement (Second) of Torts ch. 45A, special note on governmental immunity]

Mandamus is a special kind of court order in which a court commands a government official to perform his or her official duty. This special remedy is available only when the government official's legal duty as such is clear and there is no other adequate remedy. [See, e.g., Cohen v. Ford, 19 Pa. Commw. 417, 339 A.2d 175 (1975)] Courts observe that this special remedy should be invoked only in extraordinary situations. [Bankers Life & Casualty Co. v. Holland, 346 U.S. 379, 382–85, 74 S. Ct. 145, 147–49, 98 L. Ed. 106 (1953)] In some states' practice, rather than petitioning for a writ of mandamus, a plaintiff files a complaint or motion in the nature of mandamus. [See, e.g., Mass. R. Civ. P. 81(b)]

If the fiduciary conduct complained of is a poor investment decision, a writ of mandamus or other court order that applies only with respect to future actions may fail to provide complete relief. If, however, a fiduciary's conduct revoked a retirement plan right that the state declared or recognizes as a constitutional contract right, a participant or beneficiary may seek restoration of his or her contract right. [See, e.g., Sgaglione v. Levitt, 37 N.Y.2d 507, 337 N.E.2d 592, 375 N.Y.S.2d 79, *reargument denied*, 37 N.Y.2d 924, 340 N.E.2d 754, 378 N.Y.S.2d 1027 (1975)]

Q 4:37 May an employer limit a deferred compensation plan to socially responsible investments?

Under common-law fiduciary standards, "social investing" is contrary to the fiduciary duty of prudence if the investment or investment program involves subordinating the interests of participants and beneficiaries to any objective other than seeking the maximum feasible investment return. [Restatement (Third) of Trusts §§ 170, 227; National Conference of Commissioners on Uniform State Law, Uniform Prudent Investor Act § 5 official cmt.] Further, even if an investment is prudent, the fiduciary duty of loyalty bars the fiduciary from acting in its own interest or in the interest of a third party rather than according to the exclusive interest of participants and beneficiaries. [Restatement (Third) of Trusts §§ 170, 227]

For a state or local government employer's deferred compensation plan subject to Code Section 457(g), "social investing" is contrary to the exclusive benefit requirement, and therefore could jeopardize the plan's tax-deferred status. [I.R.C. § 457(g)]

A better course may be for the fiduciary to select socially responsible investment funds as plan investment options, in addition to other prudently selected investment options, and allow participants to decide whether socially responsible investing is appropriate.

Q 4:38 Should a deferred compensation plan provide life insurance for all participants?

No. Although some participants might have a suitable use for life insurance, others may have no need for life insurance death proceeds. Because providing a death benefit results in some insurance cost, life insurance should not be used unless the participant has a need to protect a spouse, child, or other person from the consequences of the participant's early death.

A plan sponsor should make life insurance a plan investment option and then allow the participant to decide whether he or she needs life insurance, how much life insurance he or she needs, and whether life insurance should be obtained through the plan or outside the plan. As long as the plan follows applicable participant-directed rules, the plan fiduciaries are relieved from liability for the participant's choice between life insurance and other plan investment options. [See Restatement (Second) of Trusts §§ 216–218 (1959); see also 20 Pa. Cons. Stat. Ann. § 7208 (Supp. 2000); S.C. Code § 62-7-302]

Q 4:39 How does an employer decide whether to include life insurance as an option?

Although it is not feasible (and might not be prudent) to include every option that any participant may desire, the employer should give serious consideration to including an option if it believes that a significant number of participants could benefit from that option.

When considering whether to add or remove a participant-directed option from a plan, the plan sponsor should compare that option's potential benefits to some participants against the plan administration expense attributable to that option. The plan sponsor should also consider that the plan can charge participants' accounts for the expense of carrying out the participants' investment directions. Thus, if there is little additional expense or the incremental expense will be charged to the participants who select a life insurance option, it may be not imprudent to add life insurance as a participant-directed option.

If life insurance is included as a plan option, it should not be one of the core options in a participant-directed plan.

Protection Against Liability

Q 4:40 May a plan exempt a plan fiduciary from liability?

A provision in a plan or trust document may provide that a plan fiduciary does not have a duty that otherwise would be a fiduciary duty. [Restatement (Second) of Trusts § 174 (1957)] Likewise, a plan or trust document may vary a fiduciary's duties. Finally, a provision in a plan or trust document may relieve a plan fiduciary from liability for a breach of fiduciary responsibility. [Restatement (Second) of Trusts § 222 (1957)] Even if a deferred compensation plan (other than a church plan or governmental plan) is governed by ERISA, Part 4 of Subtitle B of Title I of ERISA does not apply to an unfunded plan maintained for a select group of highly compensated management employees. [ERISA § 401(1)] Therefore, ERISA Section 410, which would void a provision that relieves a fiduciary, does not restrain such an unfunded plan's exculpation of a fiduciary.

An exemption clause cannot protect a fiduciary who acts (or fails to act) in bad faith or with reckless indifference to the participants' or beneficiaries' interests. [Restatement (Second) of Trusts § 222(2) (1957)]

A provision that might exempt a fiduciary from liability is strictly construed to limit the potential exemptions from fiduciary responsibility. [Restatement (Second) of Trusts § 222(1) & cmt. a (1957)]

A fiduciary that is a government or who is a government official may be protected by sovereign immunity (see Q 4:33), governmental immunity (see Q 4:34), or public officer immunity (see Q 4:35).

Q 4:41   May an employer indemnify a plan fiduciary?

Yes. Nothing in the common law of trusts precludes a third person from providing indemnification to a fiduciary unless receiving that indemnification is a breach of the fiduciary's duty (if any) to avoid self-dealing with those whose interests may be contrary to the purposes of the trust or the interests of the participants and beneficiaries.

Whether a church will indemnify a deferred compensation plan fiduciary may be further provided by the church's organizing documents.

Whether a state or local government will indemnify a deferred compensation plan fiduciary may be further provided by the enabling statute (see Q 4:2) and other state or local law.

Q 4:42   What limits a charitable organization's ability to provide indemnification to its plan fiduciaries?

A charitable organization may provide indemnification to its employees if the charity's governing body (or a duly authorized delegate) finds that providing indemnification is necessary and appropriate to the organization's ability to attract and retain officers and employees to carry out the business that furthers the organization's charitable purposes. [Treas. Reg. § 1.501(c)(3)-1] In some states, the law presumes that an employee serves as an employee benefit plan fiduciary because his or her job duties require that work. [See, e.g., N.Y. Not-for-Profit Corp. Law § 722(d)] Nevertheless, an employee who serves as a plan fiduciary would be wise to specifically request indemnification.

Notwithstanding any written agreement that purports to provide greater protection, an organization will be unable to provide indemnification unless the employee acted in good faith and reasonably believed that he or she acted in (or not opposed to) the best interests of the organization. [See, e.g., Del. Gen. Corp. Law § 145; N.Y. Not-for-Profit Corp. Law §§ 721, 722; 42 Pa. Cons. Stat. Ann. § 8361 *et seq.* See generally American Bar Ass'n Business Law Section, Revised Model Nonprofit Corp. Act § 8.51] Therefore, since the law might require a deferred compensation plan fiduciary to act in good faith, a cautious fiduciary will take expert legal, investment, actuarial, and accounting advice.

Q 4:43   May a service provider indemnify a plan fiduciary?

No. Accepting a service provider's agreement to provide indemnification to a plan fiduciary is a breach of the fiduciary's duty of loyalty. [Restatement (Third) of Trusts § 170 (1992)] A careful fiduciary should adopt and follow written procedures for avoiding self-dealing and conflicts of interest. [Id. §§ 2, 170; see also 12 C.F.R. § 9.5(c)] A plan fiduciary may accept for the use of the plan a service provider's indemnification that restores the plan's loss arising from the service provider's breach of its own contract services.

Participant-Directed Investment

Q 4:44   Should a nongovernmental deferred compensation plan provide for participant-directed investment?

An employer providing a nongovernmental deferred compensation plan should allow participant-directed investment only if it is prepared to accept the risks involved when participants make bad investment decisions with the employer's assets. The employer should not provide for participant-directed investment until it receives legal opinions that the plan will still be unfunded and tax deferred for participants, and that the plan need not be registered under any securities law or is properly registered.

Q 4:45   Should a governmental eligible deferred compensation plan provide for participant-directed investment?

A state or local government employer's eligible deferred compensation plan should provide for participant-directed investment. An employer does not know the retirement need, time horizon, or risk tolerance of its employee, and therefore cannot make an efficient investment allocation for the individual. Only the participant (or the participant with the help of an investment advisor) can define these needs and make appropriate investment decisions. Therefore, a plan should provide participant-directed investment in a manner similar to other retirement savings plans.

Q 4:46   Does participant-directed investment mean the employer avoids all liability?

No. If a plan provides for participant-directed investment, a plan fiduciary is relieved from responsibility for participants' investment directions (within the choices available); however, the employer might be responsible for its selection (including periodic monitoring) of an appropriate menu of plan investment choices. If an employer has a fiduciary responsibility for plan investment selection (see Q 4:30), it must act prudently in selecting and reviewing the investment options available to the plan participants. In addition, a plan fiduciary might be responsible for providing investment information to participants and promptly implementing participants' investment instructions.

Q 4:47 Should an employer or trustee keep records on participant investment direction procedure and investment information?

Maybe. If a trustee otherwise would have had investment responsibility, that fiduciary must prove that it was not responsible because the participant (or beneficiary) exercised control over investment decisions. Because it may be a long time before all participants retire and receive all payments during retirement, a cautious fiduciary might consider keeping its investment procedure records until at least several years after the plan is terminated and fully distributed, and keeping any investment information (other than prospectuses) until at least several years after delivery of the account statement relating to the period during which the investment could have been made. The particular number of years should be based on the statute of limitations and statute of repose provided by the state whose law governs the trust.

Additionally, the fiduciary should make sure that the plan and trust documents include an account-stated provision and a procedure for a participant or beneficiary to request account corrections.

Q 4:48 What investment information should be furnished to a participant?

If a deferred compensation plan provides for participant-directed investment, the employer should take reasonable steps to ensure that the participant is furnished with and has the opportunity to obtain sufficient information to make informed investment decisions. The plan materials should make clear that the participant (or beneficiary) and not the employer is responsible for the consequences of any investment direction.

Q 4:49 Is the participant taxed when he or she buys a life insurance contract from a state or local government deferred compensation plan trust?

No, a participant does not incur federal income tax when he or she buys a life insurance contract from a state or local government employer's deferred compensation plan trust (see Qs 4:18, 4:19) if the participant pays fair market value for the contract.

To avoid a plan distribution, the participant must pay fair market value for the life insurance contract. Although tax law frequently refers to the concept of fair market value, it is difficult to establish fair market value for an asset that by its terms cannot be sold in any market. In the context of a life insurance contract held under a retirement plan trust, fair market value usually means the amount that puts the plan trust in the same cash position it would have been in if the trustee had surrendered the contract. Thus, a contract's fair market value usually is its surrender value.

If a plan permits a participant to buy a life insurance contract from the plan trust, the plan should preclude such a purchase in circumstances that would have the effect of allowing a participant a distribution before his or her severance from employment. [I.R.C. § 457(a), (b)(5)] But a bona fide purchase for fair market value does not have the effect of a distribution. [Cf. PTCE 92-6]

Q 4:50 May deferred compensation plan amounts be invested in "brokerage" accounts?

Whether deferred compensation plan amounts may be invested in "individual" stocks and bonds (rather than mutual funds and collective investment funds) depends on the type of plan, and for a state or local government employer's plan, on state law.

For a state or local government employer's deferred compensation plan, most states' enabling statutes (see Q 4:2) limit plan investment to bank instruments, insurance company annuity contracts, and mutual funds. Some states permit collective investment funds and group trusts that provide pooled investment. A typical enabling statute does not permit deferred compensation plan investment in individual stocks and bonds. In such a state, if a "brokerage" account (see Q 4:90) can include securities other than mutual fund shares, it is not a permitted investment.

California law permits a state or local government deferred compensation plan to invest in individual stocks and bonds. [Cal. Const. art. 16, § 17; Cal. Gov't Code § 53609]

For an unfunded deferred compensation plan, a nongovernmental employer may invest in any investment it desires that is not precluded by the law and governing documents that apply to the charitable or tax-exempt organization. For a church's deferred compensation plan, the church may invest in any investment permitted by applicable state law. A church may further limit its investments based on the church's religious beliefs.

Providing Investment Education and Investment Advice

Q 4:51 Should an employer provide foreign-language investment materials for its non-English-speaking employees?

For a state or local government deferred compensation plan, a plan fiduciary should provide foreign-language investment materials only if it has determined, based on expert fiduciary prudence, that any expense that would be borne by plan assets is necessary to the administration of the plan. [I.R.C. § 457(g)(1)] In making this determination, the plan fiduciary should consider whether some of those who cannot read English also cannot read any language.

It is difficult for a provider to offer foreign-language materials, because securities law prohibits the use of foreign-language materials unless the issuer also furnishes the complete prospectus in the same foreign language. [Investment Company Act Release No. 6082 (June 23, 1970); American Funds Distributors,

Inc., SEC No-Action Letter (Oct. 16, 1989)] Unless a fund's governing board is presented with responsible evidence that sales to people who read the foreign-language prospectuses would sufficiently benefit the fund in relation to the expense, the fund's directors or trustees may have a duty to disapprove the translation expense. [See generally Investment Company Act § 36, 15 U.S.C. § 80a-35; American Law Institute, Principles of Corporate Governance]

Q 4:52   Does the employer have to give advice to participants?

A plan sponsor, employer, or other plan fiduciary has no duty to provide advice to participants concerning their investment choices. Nonetheless, some employers may want to provide a means by which participants can receive guidance on investment choices. If so, it may be advisable to have these services performed by persons that are appropriately regulated in that conduct, such as a registered investment advisor.

Q 4:53   Should an employer make investment education available to participants?

Probably, if the plan fiduciary makes a carefully considered finding that an improvement to participant decision making is likely to result from the investment education and that the improvement is worth the plan expense to be incurred.

The term *investment education* refers to the idea of helping a participant learn the basics of how different kinds of asset classes have behaved in the past. Typically, investment education includes some explanation of modern portfolio theory. A state or local government employer or nongovernmental plan administrator is under no legal duty to provide investment education or make it available. [Cf. DOL Reg. § 2550.404c-1(b)(2)(i)(B)]

Some practitioners believe that investment information is not meaningful for an individual who has no background to evaluate that information. "While items required by the disclosure provisions, such as risk and return characteristics, historical performance, and prospectuses, are important to making investment decisions, they may be inadequate for someone who has not been given some information about general investment principles or the differences between asset classifications." [*Keith* R. Pyle, "Compliance under ERISA Section 404(c) with Increasing Investment Alternatives and Account Accessibility," 32 *Ind. L. Rev.* 1467, 1486 (1999)]

Although the views of employee benefits and human-resources practitioners vary widely, most employers make some form of investment education available to plan participants.

Q 4:54   If investment education is provided, is the employer liable?

Although an employer has no legal duty to provide participant investment education, it may want to do so to help participants meet their responsibilities.

If an employer chooses to make investment education available to participants, it may be responsible for the quality of the information given. If the employer itself provides the information, it is responsible for the accuracy, completeness, and appropriateness of that information. [Restatement (Second) of Torts § 552]

An employer that selects a service provider for participant investment education may be responsible if it does not make a prudent selection. The selection of a provider or even the selection of an investment advisor to provide investment advice to participants and beneficiaries does not, however, result in liability for a loss that is the direct and necessary result of a participant's or beneficiary's investment decision. Further, if the participant chose the investment education provider, the employer is not responsible.

Q 4:55   Who should pay for investment advice?

If the fees for investment advice are not paid by the employer, a plan fiduciary must consider whether a charge against plan accounts for investment advice would be fair to all participants, beneficiaries, and alternate payees.

Q 4:56   What rules apply to providing investment information?

Whoever chooses to provide any information should do so carefully. Anyone who provides investment information has a legal duty to provide information that is accurate and not misleading. This duty may require that any communication to participants

1. Be based on generally accepted investment theories that take into account the historic returns of standard market indices of different asset classes (such as stocks, bonds, and money market funds) over a defined period of time;
2. Expressly state all relevant facts and assumptions;
3. Expressly state that the participant or beneficiary should consider his or her assets, income, and investments outside the plan;
4. Include a statement that past performance is not an indication of future performance;
5. Calculate or estimate investment performance according to formulas prescribed by the Securities and Exchange Commission (SEC);
6. Display historical investment performance according to certain one-, five-, and 10-year periods ended as of the most recent available quarter-end date; and
7. Include several other disclosures concerning the scope and appropriate use of the information.

Under the common-law tort of negligent communication, whoever provides information knowing that people may rely on it can be liable if the analysis and communication are not as careful, accurate, and thorough as the analysis and communication of a recognized professional would have been. [Restatement (Second) of Torts § 552]

Q 4:57   Should a participant seek investment advice?

According to recurring surveys, even among participants who said that they were knowledgeable in investment matters, majorities continue to give wrong answers to such simple questions as what is the basic difference between stocks and bonds or what kinds of investments are found in a stock fund or a bond fund. These surveys also show that many participant-directed accounts are almost completely invested in a manner that results in little real investment return after considering inflation, even among participants who said they were saving for retirement. A participant who lacks investment expertise may wish to seek professional advice.

Q 4:58   How should a participant evaluate an investment advisor?

Although no regulation can ensure the knowledge or competence of any person, the federal or state law that applies to a registered investment advisor may help a participant get the information needed to evaluate an investment advisor. For example, the federal Investment Advisers Act of 1940 requires a registered investment advisor to deliver a disclosure statement that explains the advisor's methods. The information in the disclosure statement may help an investor decide whether an advisor's methods make sense.

Q 4:59   Should an investment advisor be independent?

A participant deserves to feel comfortable that his or her investment advisor's advice is not compromised by an undisclosed conflict of interest. It may not be necessary, however, to avoid every related interest. For example, if the advisor receives compensation for managing an investment option, the conflict can be cured by providing that such compensation is an offset against the investment advisory fee that the participant pays. [Restatement (Second) of Trusts §§ 216–218; 3 Austin Wakeman Scott & William Franklin Fratcher, *Scott on Trusts* §§ 216–218 (4th ed. 1987); see also Prohibited Transaction Class Exemption 77-4, 42 Fed. Reg. 18,782 (1977)] Alternatively, there might be no conflict if there are other provisions that restrain an investment advisor's opportunity to render its advice with a view to increasing its own (including an affiliate's) compensation.

Q 4:60   May an investment advisor give advice about its own funds?

Yes. Notwithstanding the general principle that a fiduciary must not use its discretionary power with a view to increasing its own compensation, an investment advisor may give a participant, beneficiary, alternate payee, or plan advice about investing in the advisor's (or an affiliate's) funds if:

1. The advisor adjusts its investment advisory fee to subtract the amount of the fee received by each fund manager [see PTCE 77-4; see also PTE 2000-46 (Bank of Oklahoma)]; or

2. The advisor adjusts its investment advisory fee to "level" each combination of investment advisory fees so the advisor has no incentive to favor any fund [see PTE 99-15 (Smith Barney), PTE 97-12 (Wells Fargo)]; or

3. The advisor's investment advisory method reflects the work of an independent consultant and there are significant restraints on the opportunity for the advisor to influence the work of that independent consultant. [See DOL ERISA Adv. Op. 2001-09A]

Of course, a participant, beneficiary, or alternate payee who considers whether to engage an investment advisor on such a basis should read carefully all disclosure information (see Q 4:58) and evaluate whether the investment advisor's methods make sense.

Communicating About a Blackout

Q 4:61   What is the blackout-notice rule?

If an individual-account retirement plan that is governed by Part 1 of Subtitle B of Title I of ERISA will have a blackout (see Q 4:66), the plan administrator must send affected participants, beneficiaries, and alternate payees a notice explaining blackout. [ERISA § 101(i), as added by Sarbanes-Oxley Act of 2002]

Q 4:62   Does the blackout-notice rule apply to a state or local government employer's deferred compensation plan?

No. ERISA does not apply to a governmental plan. [ERISA §§ 3(32), 4(b)(1)]

Practice Pointer. ERISA does not require a governmental plan's trustee or administrator to send a blackout notice. However, a cautious fiduciary might want legal advice about whether a notice is prudent under other law.

Q 4:63   Does the blackout-notice rule apply to a church's deferred compensation plan?

Usually, no. Unless the plan administrator affirmatively elects that a plan be governed by ERISA, ERISA does not apply to a church plan. [ERISA §§ 3(33), 4(b)(2)]

Practice Pointer. ERISA does not require a church plan's administrator to send a blackout notice. However, a cautious fiduciary might want legal advice about whether a notice is prudent under other law.

Q 4:64   Does the blackout-notice rule apply to an unfunded excess-benefit plan?

No. ERISA does not apply to an unfunded excess-benefit plan. [ERISA §§ 3(36), 4(b)(5)]

Q 4:65   Does the blackout-notice rule apply to an unfunded deferred compensation plan for a select group?

Usually, no. If a deferred compensation plan is unfunded and the plan is maintained for a select group of management or highly compensated employees, the plan's administrator may comply with the reporting and disclosure requirements of Part 1 of Subtitle B of Title I of ERISA by filing a statement with the DOL. [DOL Reg. § 2520.104-23(b)] Because ERISA Section 101(i) is in Part 1, the section does not apply if the plan's administrator has made the one-time filing.

Practice Pointer. An employer or plan administrator should make sure that the DOL has recorded the required statement.

Q 4:66   What is a blackout?

A plan has a blackout if participants, beneficiaries, or alternate payees are restrained—for three consecutive business days or more—from giving an investment direction or taking a loan or distribution, if those transactions ordinarily would be permitted. [DOL Reg. § 2520.101-3(d)(1)]

Caution. The regulation does not define the words *business day*.

If the restriction will be for less than three days, it is not a blackout. In counting days, the regulation does not count a Saturday, Sunday, or holiday on which "transactions" would not be processed anyhow. For example, if a plan's customary procedure is that an instruction received on a holiday will be processed on the next business day, the holiday does not count.

A blackout does not include a restriction that results from:

- Applying securities law;
- A regularly scheduled restriction explained in a plan's summary plan description;
- Following a qualified domestic relations order (QDRO);
- Following the plan's procedure for considering whether a court order is a QDRO;
- The participant's, beneficiary's, or alternate payee's act (or failure to act); or
- A third person's claim or action "involving the account of an individual participant."

[DOL Reg. § 2520.101-3(d)(1)]

Example. A plan's procedure provides that a distribution must not become payable until 15 days after a participant initiates an address change. (The plan uses this procedure to provide the participant and the plan administrator an opportunity to detect, by reading a confirmation, that a fraudster impersonated the participant.) The unavailability of a distribution that results from following the procedure is not a blackout, because it results from the participant's instruction.

The most common reason for a blackout is a change in recordkeepers. Another reason is a recordkeeper's computer-system change.

Q 4:67   What must a blackout notice say?

A blackout notice must address at least the following:

- The reason for the blackout;
- An explanation of each investment and other plan rights affected;
- The expected beginning of the blackout;
- The expected ending of the blackout;
- An investment warning (see below); and
- Instructions for obtaining further information from the plan administrator.

[ERISA § 101(i); DOL Reg. § 2520.101-3(b)(1)(iv)–(v)]

A notice may describe a blackout's beginning or ending (or both) by referring to a calendar week rather than a particular day.

If a blackout will restrain the ability of participants, beneficiaries, or alternate payees to give investment directions, the notice must warn a reader that he or she should evaluate the appropriateness of his or her current investment decisions in light of the inability to direct or diversify assets credited to his or her plan account during the blackout.

Also, the notice must be written so that it can be understood by an average participant.

The blackout regulation includes a model notice. If a notice uses paragraphs 4 and 5A from the model notice, such a notice meets the requirements to tell a reader that he or she should evaluate the appropriateness of his or her current investment decisions in light of the inability to direct or diversify assets credited to his or her plan account during the blackout and that the plan administrator must furnish the notice at least 30 days before the blackout begins. Using the model notice does not provide any assurance concerning the regulation's other requirements. [DOL Reg. § 2520.101-3(e)(1)]

The requirements described above meet only the plan administrator's duty under ERISA Section 101(i). A plan fiduciary might have further duties to communicate information that a participant, beneficiary, or alternate payee needs to know.

Q 4:68   Who must a plan administrator send a blackout notice to?

If the blackout notice rule applies (see Qs 4:61–4:65), a plan administrator must send a blackout notice to each participant, beneficiary, or alternate payee who could be affected by an inability to give an investment direction or take a loan or distribution. [DOL Reg. § 2520.101-3(a)]

Q 4:69   When must a plan administrator send the notice?

If the blackout notice rule applies (see Qs 4:61–4:65), a plan administrator must furnish the notice at least 30 days (but no more than 60 days) before the blackout begins. [DOL Reg. § 2520.101-3]

An exception might be available if the blackout results from a corporate merger, acquisition, divestiture, or similar business transaction. In such a case, the plan administrator must furnish notice as soon as "reasonably practicable." [DOL Reg. § 2520.101-3(b)(2)(ii)(C)]

Another excuse from giving the usually-required 30 days' notice might apply if a plan administrator "documents" its decision that there are unforeseeable or extraordinary circumstances beyond its control or that delaying an action would be a breach of its fiduciary duties. Even then, a plan administrator must furnish a blackout notice "as soon as reasonably possible under the circumstances." [DOL Reg. § 2520.101-3(b)(2)(ii)(B)]

Q 4:70   What must a plan administrator do if a blackout does not end as scheduled?

If there is a change in either the beginning or ending of a blackout, the plan administrator must send another notice to affected participants, beneficiaries, and alternate payees as soon as "reasonably practicable." This notice must explain any "material" change in the information furnished in the original (or most recent) notice. [DOL Reg. § 2520.101-3(b)(4)]

Q 4:71   Why should a plan administrator furnish a blackout notice?

If the blackout notice rule applies (see Qs 4:61–4:65), the consequences of failure to furnish a blackout notice might include:

- Responsibility for investment losses caused by the lack of notice;
- Civil penalties; and
- Criminal punishment.

Responsibility for investment losses. Failing to furnish a required blackout notice might be a breach of the employer's or plan administrator's contract or fiduciary duties. Although it might be difficult to prove causation, some lawyers believe a participant, beneficiary, or alternate payee could allege that he or she would have made different investment directions had he or she received the proper notice.

Civil penalty. If a plan administrator fails to furnish a required blackout notice, the DOL may impose a penalty. The penalty is up to $100 *multiplied by* the number of affected participants, beneficiaries, and alternate payees *multiplied by* the number of days that the administrator failed to furnish the notice. [DOL Reg. §§ 2560.502e-5, -7]

Example. Wellness Healthcare Network maintains a select-group deferred compensation plan, and did not file a statement to permit alternative compliance with ERISA's Part 1. The plan has 59 participants. Wellness, as plan administrator, changes the plan's recordkeeper. To do so, it began a blackout as of 4 p.m. January 31, 2003. The "conversion" and reconciliation were completed in three business days and the blackout ended with close-of-business on February 5. Although Wellness should have sent a blackout notice on January 1, it failed to send any notice. In this case, the penalty is $212,400 ($100 × 59 [$5,900] × 36 days).

Criminal punishment. A willful failure to furnish a blackout notice may be punished by a fine up to $500,000 and up to ten years' imprisonment, in addition to punishment for related crimes. [ERISA § 501]

Paying Plan Administration Expenses

Q 4:72   Can the expenses of administering a deferred compensation plan be paid from the plan investments?

For a deferred compensation plan of a nongovernmental employer, the participant's (or beneficiary's) right to future payment of deferred compensation is merely an unsecured promise, and the terms of that promise are stated by the plan. Typically, the plan will permit the payment of all expenses.

For a state or local government employer's eligible deferred compensation plan, a plan may provide that reasonable expenses of administering the plan will be charged against plan assets. *Reasonable* probably means

1. That the employer would not have incurred the expense in the normal course of its government function or services but for its administration of the deferred compensation plan;
2. It was prudent for the plan administrator to incur the expense;
3. The arrangement is not a prohibited transaction; and
4. The arrangement is not made for a purpose other than participants' exclusive benefit.

[I.R.C. § 457(g)(1)] A plan fiduciary can show prudence by charging administration expenses according to a written procedure adopted following the advice of an expert employee benefits lawyer.

Timely Investment of Contributions

Q 4:73   How quickly must the employer invest contributions?

For an unfunded deferred compensation plan, federal law does not regulate the time by which an employer must invest participant contributions. An employer's failure to invest or credit contributions or deferrals in a timely manner may be a breach of an express or implied term of the deferred compensation plan or a salary reduction agreement, and if so, the employer may be liable to the participant for lost investment value plus attorneys' fees and costs. For this reason, an employer should promptly deliver for investment any contributions or deferrals.

For an eligible deferred compensation plan of a state or local government employer, the state's enabling statute or regulations may specify a rule for timely investment of participant deferrals. [See, e.g., N.Y. Comp. Codes R. & Regs. tit. 9, § 9003.8] Further, the IRS interprets the Section 457(g) exclusive benefit requirement as requiring that the investment of a participant's contribution not be unreasonably delayed. Further, to maintain a plan's tax treatment as an eligible plan, an employer cannot hold participant contributions any longer than is reasonable for the proper administration of participants' accounts. (See Q 4:18.)

For employer-provided deferrals (other than salary reduction contributions), the time for making a contribution or crediting a deferral may be specified or implied by the terms of the plan. For example, if a calendar-year plan provides that a matching contribution is provided only for a participant who completed 1,000 hours of service during the year and who was actively employed on December 31, it may be reasonable, even without a plan provision expressly saying so, for the plan administrator to delay allocating the matching contribution until early February because it needs a month to compile the necessary data and because it is prudent to confirm certain factors, such as compensation and elective deferrals, with the employer's Forms W-2 reported on January 31.

Q 4:74   May a plan recover restoration for missing or late contributions from a participant's plan account?

Yes, if an individual responsible to effect an employer's payment of contributions to a plan committed a crime regarding the plan or breached his or her fiduciary duty to a plan, the plan may take restoration by setting off the amount of restoration the individual owes the plan against the plan's obligation to pay deferred compensation to the participant (or his or her beneficiaries). [Cf. I.R.C. § 401(a)(13)(C); see also Gaudet v. Sheet Metal Workers' National Pension Fund, No. Civ. A.01-0718 (E.D. La. Mar. 13, 2002)]

Q 4:75   Is a failure to invest participant contributions promptly a crime?

Yes. Whether for an ERISA plan or a non-ERISA plan, an employer's failure to invest participant contributions promptly is a crime.

For a non-ERISA plan, state laws on embezzlement, conversion, or misapplication of entrusted money make an employer's failure to invest participant contributions promptly a crime.

For example, the Model Penal Code provides as follows:

> A person who purposely obtains property upon agreement, or subject to a known legal obligation, to make specified payment or other disposition, whether from such property or its proceeds or from his own property to be reserved in equivalent amount, is guilty of theft if he deals with the property obtained as his own and fails to make the required payment or disposition. The foregoing applies notwithstanding that it may be impossible to identify particular property as belonging to the victim at the time of the actor's failure to make the required payment or disposition.

[National Conference of Commissioners on Uniform State Laws, Model Penal Code § 223.8 (Theft by Failure to Make Required Disposition of Funds Received)]

This criminal offense has been applied in a wide variety of situations that did not involve direct stealing or embezzlement. [See generally Commonwealth v. Morrissey, 540 Pa. 1, 654 A.2d 1049 (1995); Commonwealth v. Rosenzweig, 514 Pa. 111, 522 A.2d 1088 (1987); Commonwealth v. Stockard, 489 Pa. 209, 413 A.2d 1088 (1980); Commonwealth v. Wood, 432 Pa. Super. 183, 637 A.2d 1335 (1994); State v. Dandy, 243 N.J. Super. 62, 578 A.2d 881 (App. Div. 1990); State v. Kelly, 204 N.J. Super. 283, 498 A.2d 784 (App. Div.), cert. denied, 103 N.J. 496, 497, 511 A.2d 669 (1985); Commonwealth v. Robichow, 338 Pa. Super. 348, 487 A.2d 1000, appeal dismissed, 510 Pa. 418, 508 A.2d 1195 (1985); Commonwealth v. Coward, 330 Pa. Super. 122, 478 A.2d 1384 (1984); Commonwealth v. Fritz, 323 Pa. Super. 488, 470 A.2d 1364 (1983); Commonwealth v. Celane, 311 Pa. Super. 93, 457 A.2d 509 (1982); Commonwealth v. Nappi, 288 Pa. Super. 240, 431 A.2d 1027 (1981); Commonwealth v. Hoffman, 263 Pa. Super. 442, 398 A.2d 658 (1979); Commonwealth v. Austin, 258 Pa. Super. 461, 393 A.2d 36 (1978); Commonwealth v. Bhojwani, 242 Pa. Super. 406, 364 A.2d 335 (1976)] Even when it may be difficult to prove embezzlement, the prosecutor may proceed in showing conversion. [State v. Pritchard, 172 N.J. Super. 578, 412 A.2d 1335 (Law Div. 1979)]

Courts recognize a theft by conversion when the actor was an intermediary between the real parties. [Commonwealth v. Shapiro, 275 Pa. Super. 28, 418 A.2d 594 (1980); Commonwealth v. Austin, 258 Pa. Super. 461, 393 A.2d 36 (1978)] Courts recognize an improper use of money held in a fiduciary capacity as theft by conversion. [In re Wilson, 81 N.J. 451, 409 A.2d 1153 (1979)] An assertion that the actor merely intended to "borrow" rather than steal does not excuse an unauthorized use of money held in a fiduciary capacity; the unauthorized use is no less a crime. [Id.] Moreover, commingling money when a person is under a duty to segregate amounts constitutes theft by conversion. Likewise, court decisions recognize that money is fungible; it does not matter whether it was the money of the complaining witnesses that was not forwarded or put to the proper use. [Commonwealth v. Austin, 258 Pa. Super. 461, 393 A.2d 36 (1978)]

A related provision of the Model Penal Code makes it a crime merely to misapply money that belongs to a financial institution or is entrusted to a person as a fiduciary:

> A person commits an offense if he applies or disposes of property that has been entrusted to him as a fiduciary, or property . . . of a financial institution, in a manner which he knows is unlawful and involves substantial risk of loss or detriment to the owner of the property or to a person for whose benefit the property was entrusted.

[National Conference of Commissioners on Uniform State Law, Model Penal Code § 224.13 (Misapplication of Entrusted Property and Property of Government or Financial Institution)]

This crime is an effective supplement to the crime of theft by conversion. [See generally Commonwealth v. Edwards, 399 Pa. Super. 545, 582 A.2d 1078, *appeal denied*, 529 Pa. 640, 600 A.2d 1258 (1990); State v. Pritchard, 172 N.J. Super. 578, 412 A.2d 1335 (Law Div. 1979)] The crime of misapplication of entrusted property is not a lesser included offense of theft by failure to make required disposition of funds received. [Commonwealth v. Schreiber, 319 Pa. Super. 367, 466 A.2d 203 (1983)]

In a prosecution for misapplication of entrusted property, circumstantial evidence can be sufficient to warrant conviction. [Commonwealth v. Iacino, 265 Pa. Super. 375, 401 A.2d 1355, *aff'd*, 490 Pa. 119, 415 A.2d 61 (1979)]

For an ERISA deferred compensation plan, federal and state law makes an employer's failure to invest participant contributions promptly a crime. Although ERISA generally preempts state laws, it does not preempt state criminal laws. [ERISA § 514(b)(4)] In addition to being the state law crimes explained above, a misuse of plan money or property is a federal crime:

> Any person who embezzles, steals, or unlawfully and willfully abstracts or converts to his own use or to the use of another, any of the moneys, funds, securities, premiums, credits, property, or other assets of any [ERISA] plan, or of any fund connected therewith, shall be fined . . . or imprisoned not more than five years, or both.

[18 U.S.C. § 664]

The regulation that defines when participant contributions become plan assets applies only for fiduciary and prohibited transaction provisions. The fact that a contribution is not yet a plan asset for purposes of Title I of ERISA does not bar either federal or state criminal prosecution. [61 Fed. Reg. 41,220, Preamble 8.b (Aug. 7, 1996)]

Participant contributions withheld from pay, and even employer-provided contributions when required, are plan assets, notwithstanding the fact that the contributions have not been credited to the plan. [See, e.g., United States v. Grizzle, 933 F.2d 943 (11th Cir.), *reh'g denied, cert. denied*, 502 U.S. 897, 112 S. Ct. 271, 116 L. Ed. 2d 223 (1991); In re Consolidated Welfare Fund ERISA Litig., 839 F. Supp. 1068, 1073 (S.D.N.Y. 1993); United States v. Panepinto, 818 F. Supp. 48 (E.D.N.Y. 1993), *aff'd*, 28 F.3d 103 (2d Cir. 1994); Galgay v. Gangloff, 677 F. Supp. 295, 301 (M.D. Pa. 1987), *aff'd without opinion*, 932 F.2d 959 (3d Cir. 1991); United States v. Silva, 517 F. Supp. 727 (D.R.I.), *aff'd*, 644 F.2d 68 (3d Cir. 1980). But see Young v. West Coast Industrial Relations Ass'n, 763 F.

Supp. 64 (D. Del. 1991) (mere failure to contribute amount owed to fund does not constitute embezzlement), *aff'd,* 961 F.2d 1570 (3d Cir. 1992) ("[18 U.S.C.] Section 664 goes beyond the traditional concepts of embezzlement")]

The statute's reference to "any person" has been construed literally; a person need not hold any particular status regarding a plan to be subject to this crime. [United States v. Grizzle, 933 F.2d 943 (11th Cir.), *reh'g denied, cert. denied,* 502 U.S. 897, 112 S. Ct. 271, 116 L. Ed. 2d 223 (1991)] The phrase "to his own use" is a carryover from the common-law action in trover, and does not require any showing that the misapplication was for the personal advantage of the defendant. Any use other than the legally proper deferred compensation plan contribution use can constitute the crime. [United States v. Santiago, 528 F.2d 1130, 1135 (2d Cir.), *cert. denied,* 425 U.S. 972, 96 S. Ct. 2169, 48 L. Ed. 2d 795 (1976)] Further, the statute includes the phrase "or to the use of another." [18 U.S.C. § 664]

Q 4:76   Who investigates crimes concerning an ERISA deferred compensation plan?

The DOL has shared responsibility and authority to detect, investigate, and refer ERISA crimes and other federal crimes relating to an employee benefit plan, including a deferred compensation plan. [ERISA § 506(b)] (A state or local government employer's deferred compensation plan is not governed by ERISA. A church plan is not governed by ERISA unless it so elects.)

The DOL's Pension and Welfare Benefits Administration (PWBA) conducts criminal investigations involving employee benefit plans. The PWBA generally conducts its criminal enforcement program through its 10 regional and 5 district offices. In some instances, the PWBA may conduct joint investigations with other U.S. government agencies, such as the Office of Labor Management Standards, the Office of Labor Racketeering, the Department of Treasury (including the IRS), the Federal Bureau of Investigation, and the Postal Service. Occasionally, the PWBA works with state and local law enforcement agencies.

A PWBA office may open a criminal or "Program 52" investigation if the staff finds credible allegations or evidence of potential criminal violations of the following statutes:

1. Theft or embezzlement from an employee benefit plan [18 U.S.C. § 664];
2. False statements or concealment of facts in relation to documents required under ERISA [18 U.S.C. § 1027];
3. Offer, acceptance, or solicitation to influence the operations of an employee benefit plan [18 U.S.C. § 1954];
4. Prohibition against certain persons holding certain positions [ERISA § 411];
5. Willful violation of ERISA Title I, Part 1 [ERISA § 501];
6. Coercive interference with participant rights [ERISA § 511]; or
7. Other criminal statutes, such as mail fraud, wire fraud, or conspiracy.

A participant, beneficiary, alternate payee, or other person who suspects, or has evidence of, criminal activity involving an employee benefit plan can call his or her local PWBA office to discuss with an investigator or supervisor any information or suspicions he or she has. Many callers prefer to remain anonymous, and the PWBA generally does not reveal the identity of such a source.

When beginning a criminal investigation, the PWBA consults the U.S. Attorney's Office. When the U.S. Attorney's Office states an interest in pursuing the matter, the PWBA continues with the investigation. If the U.S. Attorney's Office is not interested in pursuing the matter, the PWBA may close the investigation, refer it to another agency, or pursue the case with a local law enforcement agency for prosecution under applicable state laws. Remember, although ERISA generally preempts state laws, it does not preempt a state's generally applicable criminal laws. [ERISA § 514(b)(4)] The PWBA can use its findings to pursue remedies for ERISA civil violations.

Q 4:77 Does a service provider have a duty to inform participants about missing or late contributions?

No, a service provider has no duty to inform participants about missing or late contributions.

Consider the following real case:

> In July of 1991, PPI [Pension Professionals, Inc.] was hired by CSA [Computer Software Analysts Inc.] to prepare financial reports and perform other third-party administrative services for the Plan. The terms of the agreement that CSA and PPI entered into (the "Service Agreement") specified that PPI was to provide its services as a third-party administrator and not as a fiduciary of the Plan. . . . Approximately six months into the job, PPI discovered what appeared to be discrepancies between the amount of funds that CSA withheld from employee paychecks for investment in the Plan and the amounts actually deposited in the employee 401(k) retirement accounts. PPI sought to ascertain whether the missing assets were located elsewhere, but suspected embezzlement by the Plan's co-trustee and chief executive officer of CSA, Levi Carey. PPI formally notified the Plan trustees, Carey and Louis King, that the failure to deposit employees' funds into their retirement accounts violated Internal Revenue Service and Department of Labor regulations, and could be classified as both embezzlement and a breach of their fiduciary duties under ERISA. PPI further indicated that it would have to disclose the shortage on the financial reports that it was required to prepare. Carey reassured PPI that CSA intended to bring all Plan assets current, and agreed to a repayment schedule as set out in a March 31, 1993 letter to PPI. Upon consulting with legal counsel, PPI agreed to continue its third-party administration duties for the Plan as long as Carey fulfilled certain "conditions." PPI required Carey to adhere to the repayment schedule that he outlined in his March 31, 1993 letter, and stated that PPI would need to place the following language on all employee participant (the "Plan Participants") account statements: "Contrary to the requirements of the Department of Labor and the Internal Revenue Service, a

portion of the 401(k) benefits have not yet been received by the trust." PPI also required verification of Carey's compliance with the repayments (i.e., copies of deposited checks), and indicated that it would withdraw as third-party administrator of the Plan if Carey failed to follow the repayment schedule. Carey signed a letter witnessing his agreement, and deposited approximately $35,000 of previously missing Plan funds. Carey later told PPI that he would like to modify the repayment schedule. His request was rebuffed by PPI, which again stated that it would discontinue its administrative services unless Carey honored his repayment agreement. In July of 1994, after receiving falsified financial statements from CSA, PPI resigned as third-party administrator of the Plan. PPI did not warn law enforcement authorities or the Plan Participants of Carey's suspected embezzlement after its resignation. In July of 1998, Carey pleaded guilty to embezzling the missing funds [about $750,000].

On October 3, 1996, several former employees of CSA and participants in the Plan filed suit in federal court against PPI, seeking to recover the embezzled funds. [The facts suggest that the breaching plan fiduciary lacked money to make restitution to the plan.] The employees asserted that PPI is liable as a fiduciary under ERISA for the misappropriated money because it exercised authority and control over Plan administration after its discovery of Carey's embezzlement, and failed to take reasonable steps to warn the Plan Participants or governmental authorities of Carey's conduct as trustee.

[CSA 401(k) Plan v. Pension Professionals, Inc., 195 F.3d 1135, 1137–38 (9th Cir. 1999)]

Both the district court and the court of appeals (in a 3–0 decision) found that PPI did not exercise any discretionary authority, was not a fiduciary, and had no duty to inform participants or anyone else concerning the missing contributions. Specifically, the court of appeals found that "the conditions that PPI proposed were designed to assert control over its own engagement, and not to exercise discretionary authority or control over the Plan's management or administration." [Id.; see also Arizona Carpenters Pension Trust Fund v. Citibank, 125 F.3d 715, 722 (9th Cir. 1997); Beddall v. State State Bank & Trust Co., 137 F.3d 12, 21 (1st Cir. 1998)] Further, the court found that a nonfiduciary has no duty to furnish information to or warn participants. [See also Coleman v. Nationwide Life Insurance Co., 969 F.2d 54 (4th Cir. 1992), *cert. denied*, 506 U.S. 1081, 113 S. Ct. 1051, 122 L. Ed. 2d 359 (1993)]

Although the *Pension Professionals* case involved an ERISA plan, the result would be the same for a non-ERISA deferred compensation plan: a service provider has no duty to inform participants about missing or late contributions.

Under the common law, "[t]he fact that the actor realizes or should realize that action on his part is necessary for another's aid or protection does not of itself impose upon him a duty to take such action." [Restatement (Second) of Torts § 314] "Th[is] rule . . . is applicable irrespective of the gravity of the danger to which the other is subjected and the insignificance of the trouble, effort, or expense of giving him aid or protection." [Id. cmt. c] The fact that the service provider may be the only person other than the participants who has knowledge of the fiduciary's embezzlement does not create any duty of the service provider. [See generally Buch v. Amory Manufacturing Co., 69 N.H. 257, 44 A. 809 (1898)]

Unless the service provider has undertaken a special (fiduciary) relationship with the participant, it has no duty to discover or furnish information about another person's wrongdoing. [Restatement (Second) of Torts § 314A; see, e.g., Mid-Cal National Bank v. Federal Reserve Bank, 590 F.2d 761 (9th Cir. 1979)]

Insuring the Deferred Compensation Promise

Q 4:78 Can a participant buy insurance to protect against an employer's inability or refusal to pay deferred compensation?

Yes. This form of casualty insurance might be available from a few insurers. The earliest contracts were sold by Lloyd's of London syndicates; more recently, contracts have been issued by Bermuda and London insurers.

The insurance pays a benefit if the insured's employer refuses to pay or is unable to pay its deferred compensation obligation. In addition, the insurance may cover lawyers' fees that the insured participant incurs to enforce his or her right to deferred compensation.

Executive deferred income insurance or executive compensation insurance might be available to executives of some tax-exempt organizations. The availability and price of a bankruptcy insurance contract depends on the financial soundness of the employer. The insurance might be expensive or unavailable if the employer's credit is not investment grade.

To avoid an appearance of economic benefit that might affect the tax treatment of the deferred compensation, the participant should make the arrangements through the insurance broker and should avoid any unnecessary involvement by the employer. [P.L.R. 9344038; Gary P. Blitz, "Executive Compensation Insurance: What to Make of PLR 9344038," 20(2) *J. Pension Plan. & Compliance* 29 (Summer 1994)]

Q 4:79 Is an employer required to be bonded?

If a deferred compensation plan is governed by ERISA, the employer need not obtain a fidelity bond. ERISA's fidelity bond provision—Section 412(a)—is in Part 4 of Subtitle B of Title I of ERISA. Part 4's provisions do not apply to an unfunded deferred compensation plan maintained for a select group of highly compensated or management employees. [ERISA § 401(1)]

If a deferred compensation plan is not governed by ERISA, state law generally does not require that an employer obtain a fidelity or surety bond to handle deductions from wages.

Practice Pointer. Even if no law requires the employer to be bonded, an employer should consider whether insurance against an employee's dishonesty is useful protection.

Insurance Company Demutualization

Q 4:80 What is demutualization?

Demutualization is a word some insurance practitioners use to describe the transactions that permit a mutual life insurance company to become a stock life insurance company owned by its shareholders.

A mutual insurance company is an insurer meant to be operated solely for the mutual benefit of its contract holders. A stock insurance company, while it also must provide promised benefits to contract holders, usually is operated to produce profits that can help provide dividends or other investment value to stockholders, who need not be insurance contract holders.

With a mutual company, most contract holders are also members. In a sense, the members are the "owners" of the company. On its conversion from a mutual company to a stock company, many (but not all) contract holders receive compensation—in the form of stock, cash, or "policy credits"—in exchange for their membership interests. Seeing to the proper use of this compensation raises various fiduciary and tax implications, some of which are discussed below.

Even though some large insurance companies already have completed a "demutualization," other insurers are considering demutualization.

Q 4:81 What is a reorganization plan?

A reorganization plan is a document in which a mutual insurer states its proposal for what compensation would be provided to members on the extinguishment of members' rights.

Among other requirements, a plan of reorganization must "specify the manner in which the aggregate value of the consideration shall be determined[,] and the method by which the consideration shall be allocated among eligible policyholders." [N.J. Stat. Ann. § 17:17C-3c]

Typically, a reorganization plan provides cash or common stock in the newly organized insurer as most members' compensation for the extinguishment of members' rights. Although the state laws governing demutualization generally require that members receive stock rather than additional insurance, these laws recognize that some exceptions may be appropriate to maintain a member's (and participants') desired federal income tax treatment. [See, e.g., N.J. Stat. Ann. § 17:17C-3c(3)]

When a reorganization plan provides that some members or eligible contract holders may receive demutualization compensation in a form other than stock, the reorganization plan must "include a provision for determining . . . the value of the consideration by means of reference to (a) the estimated market value of the reorganized insurer based upon an independent evaluation by a qualified expert; (b) the per share public market value of the registered common stock of the reorganized insurer or its parent corporation; or (c) by another method acceptable to the [insurance] commissioner." [N.J. Stat. Ann. § 17:17C-3c(3)]

Q 4:82   What are the decisions a contract holder must make?

From the time that an insurer first presents a plan of conversion, a contract holder may face many decisions, including

1. Whether to object to the insurance commissioner's approval of the plan of reorganization;
2. Whether (if qualified to vote) to vote in favor of or against the insurer's plan of reorganization;
3. Whether to use demutualization compensation for plan expenses; and
4. How to allocate demutualization compensation among participants, beneficiaries, and alternate payees.

While these are some of the more common decisions, a contract holder should carefully read the reorganization plan and all demutualization documents to discern the decisions that may be required or permitted.

Q 4:83   Is a contract holder's right to vote for or against a demutualization a plan asset?

Yes, a right to vote that derives from a plan investment is itself a plan investment. [3 Austin Wakeman Scott & William Franklin Fratcher, *Scott on Trusts* § 193 (4th ed. 1987). Cf. DOL Interpretive Bulletin 94-2, codified at 29 C.F.R. § 2509.94-2]

Q 4:84   How should a plan fiduciary decide whether to vote for or against a demutualization?

If a plan's vote will not be instructed by participants', beneficiaries', and alternate payees' investment direction (see Q 4:44), the plan administrator must act as a fiduciary. [3 Austin Wakeman Scott & William Franklin Fratcher, *Scott on Trusts* § 193 (4th ed. 1987). Cf. DOL Interpretive Bulletin 94-2, 29 C.F.R. § 2509.94-2] Therefore, the plan administrator generally has a fiduciary duty to vote. Nevertheless, a plan fiduciary need not vote if the expense of determining the appropriate vote outweighs the benefit that a favorable outcome would provide for the plan. [Cf. DOL Interpretive Bulletin 94-2, codified at 29 C.F.R. § 2509.94-2; DOL letters to Margaret Carroll (Investor Responsibility Research Center, Inc.), Howard D. Sherman (Institutional Shareholder Services, Inc.), J. Michael Farrell (Mar. 9–11, 1994)]

Q 4:85 Is demutualization compensation a plan asset?

If the insurance contract with the reorganizing mutual insurer is a plan asset, the demutualization compensation is a plan asset. [Cf. ERISA § 401(b)(2); DOL Adv. Ops. 94-31A, 92-02A; DOL Information Letter to Groom Law Group (Feb. 15, 2001) (Prudential Insurance Company of America)]

Q 4:86 What kind of plan asset is demutualization compensation?

Many pension practitioners assume that demutualization compensation is an item of investment income. [See P.L.R. 200020048, 200011035, 200002010, 199941023, 199933040, 9847010, 9801030, 9736018, 9540004, 9339024, 9230033]

Q 4:87 Do fiduciary duties apply to demutualization compensation?

Yes. If the demutualization compensation is a plan asset (see Q 4:85), fiduciary duties apply to the plan fiduciary's handling of that asset. [Cf. DOL Information Letter to Groom Law Group (Feb. 15, 2001) (Prudential Insurance Company of America)]

Q 4:88 What is an employer's duty when it makes decisions about a plan's demutualization compensation?

Because demutualization compensation is a plan asset, the contract holder must decide as a fiduciary how to use or allocate the compensation. For an eligible deferred compensation plan of a state or local government employer, plan assets must be used to provide retirement benefits to participants and their beneficiaries or to pay reasonable plan administration expenses. [I.R.C. § 457(g)(1)] For a deferred compensation plan of a tax-exempt organization that is not a state or local government employer, the employer's duty is provided by the plan and state law.

A fiduciary's lack of familiarity with a particular kind of decision is not an excuse for making an imprudent decision. If an employer does not have available within its organization sufficient actuarial, insurance, investment banking, and legal expertise to evaluate whether a particular demutualization is in the best interest of providing retirement income to the plan's participants and their beneficiaries, it should obtain expert advice in evaluating the decision. (See Q 4:91.)

Q 4:89 How must a plan fiduciary make a governmental plan's demutualization decisions?

For most governmental plans, a statute or the common law of trusts and contracts may provide fiduciary duties substantially similar to ERISA fiduciary duties. However, a plan fiduciary may be immune from monetary liability under sovereign immunity (see Q 4:33), governmental immunity (see Q 4:34), or public officer immunity (see Q 4:35).

In making decisions, a plan fiduciary should follow the plan documents, including the plan's investment policy statement. However, a plan fiduciary should not follow the plan documents when a plan provision is inconsistent with an enabling statute (see Q 4:2) or other applicable law.

Q 4:90   How must a plan fiduciary make a church plan's demutualization decisions?

For many church plans, the plan or the common law of trusts and contracts may provide fiduciary duties substantially similar to ERISA fiduciary duties.

A church plan fiduciary that votes on a demutualization plan based on church doctrine or religious beliefs may avoid liability based on freedom of religion grounds. [Basich v. Board of Pensions, Evangelical Lutheran Church in America, 540 N.W.2d 82, 19 Employee Benefits Cas. (BNA) 2231 (Minn. Ct. App. 1995), *review denied* (Minn. Jan. 25, 1996) (unpublished order), *cert. denied*, 519 U.S. 810, 117 S. Ct. 55, 136 L. Ed. 2d 18 (1996); see generally Kenneth E. North, *Religious Disputes in Secular Courts* (Durham, NC: Carolina Academic Press, 2000)]

Q 4:91   When making demutualization decisions, must a fiduciary engage an expert consultant?

The right of a member of a mutual insurer to vote in favor or against a reorganization is itself a plan investment. Therefore, a plan fiduciary generally has a fiduciary duty to evaluate the issues and vote. [Cf. DOL Interpretive Bulletin 94-2, 29 C.F.R. § 2509.94-2] If the group contract holder (usually, the employer) lacks expertise, it should obtain the advice of experts. (See Qs 4:31, 4:34.)

In the author's view, a plan fiduciary need not engage an expert if, after as much prudent diligence as the fiduciary can exercise without incurring imprudent expense, the plan fiduciary makes a written finding that explains its reasonably prudent analysis that the expense of determining the appropriate decision outweighs the benefit that a favorable outcome would provide for the plan. [Cf. DOL Interpretive Bulletin 94-2, codified at 29 C.F.R. § 2509.94-2; DOL letters to Margaret Carroll (Investor Responsibility Research Center, Inc.), Howard D. Sherman (Institutional Shareholder Services, Inc.), J. Michael Farrell (Mar. 9–11, 1994)]

Q 4:92   May demutualization compensation be used to pay plan expenses?

Demutualization compensation may be used to pay reasonably incurred plan administration expenses. [I.R.C. § 457(g)(1)] The use of plan assets to pay expenses must be provided in the plan document. In addition, the expenses must have been necessary for the sound administration of the plan.

A reimbursement of expense payments advanced by the employer is limited to direct expenses.

Q 4:93   How should a plan administrator allocate demutualization compensation among participant accounts?

Most 457 plans are defined contribution or individual account plans. Thus, the plan fiduciary must allocate the demutualization compensation (if not used to pay plan expenses) as provided by the plan documents. If the plan does not state a sufficient allocation method, the plan sponsor should consider adopting a plan amendment before the compensation is to be received. However, the plan sponsor may be content to let the annuity contract's or life insurance contract's provisions state the plan's provisions.

> **Practice Pointer.** For many 457 plans, the plan's only investment options are annuity contracts, life insurance contracts, and custodial accounts holding mutual fund shares. It is common for such a plan to provide that investment gains, losses, and income are allocated as provided by those contracts. In addition, some plans provide that the contracts' provisions are incorporated by reference into the plan to the extent that they are not inconsistent with the plan's other provisions. Following this, if the group contract holder does not give any other instruction, the "default" allocation method that the insurer specifies becomes the plan's allocation provision.

In making any allocation provisions, the plan sponsor should consider what allocations are appropriate for a participant, beneficiary, or alternate payee who directed investment into or from the affected insurance contract after the demutualized insurer's record date and before the plan's allocation date.

Q 4:94   How should a plan administrator allocate demutualization compensation under a plan that provides participant-directed investment?

If the contract of the reorganized insurer is not the only plan investment option, the plan administrator must decide whether to allocate demutualization compensation among all participant accounts or among only those participant accounts that include an eligible contract on a record date that the plan administrator decides.

At least one practitioner has suggested that a plan fiduciary might consider an allocation of demutualization compensation among all participant accounts because that compensation may be based on many years of insurance experience and a participant's account may have included one or more investment options of the reorganized insurer in the past. Although such a view may be inconsistent with the logical consequences of following a participant's investment direction, perhaps "[t]here should be some flexibility in selecting an allocation method, so long as it is reasonable and consistent with the plan documents." [Louis T. Mazawey & Elizabeth T. Dold, *Retirement Plan*

Issues Resulting from Insurance Company Demutualizations, SF19 ALI-ABA 383, 389 (2000)]

In the author's opinion, the better view is that the participant must be presumed to have carefully considered all possible information (including the absence of information and any general or particular uncertainty concerning future events) when making his or her investment direction. [Restatement (Third) of Trusts § 185 (1992)] Thus, the potential loss of demutualization compensation is part of the "total mix" of information that the participant is presumed to have considered in deciding that he or she no longer desired an investment in the reorganized insurer's contract.

Q 4:95   Is the crediting of demutualization policy credits a taxable event?

A contract holder's or participant's "receipt" of a demutualization policy credit does not result in current federal income tax or excise tax because the credit is neither a contribution nor a distribution, but merely an item of investment income. [See P.L.R. 200020048, 200011035, 200002010, 199941023, 199933040, 9847010, 9801030, 9736018, 9540004, 9339024, 9230033] Because a demutualization policy credit is not a distribution, such a credit is not a "designated distribution" subject to tax reporting and withholding. [Id.; see also I.R.C. § 3405(e)(1)(A)]

Q 4:96   What should a plan trustee do if it receives an unlawful investment?

A plan trustee that receives an unlawful investment should sell it as soon as the trustee can do so prudently.

A demutualization may cause a deferred compensation plan trustee to receive an investment that is unlawful for the trustee to hold under the plan trust. For example, a demutualization may cause a plan trustee to receive stock in the reorganized insurer—even if such an investment is unlawful for the plan trustee. A plan trust of a state or local government employer's deferred compensation plan may be restricted by an enabling statute (see Q 4:2) concerning the kinds of investments that are authorized for the plan trust. For example, New Jersey law does not authorize a municipal deferred compensation plan to invest in stocks other than mutual fund shares. [N.J. Stat. Ann. § 3B:15; N.J. Admin. Code tit. 5, § 37-9.1 (1999)]

On receiving an unlawful investment, a plan trustee should sell that investment as soon as the trustee can do so prudently. [See, e.g., Dickerson v. Camden Trust Co., 1 N.J. 459, 64 A.2d 214 (1949), *aff'g* 53 A.2d 225 (N.J. Ch. 1947); Stephens' Executors v. Milnor, 24 N.J. Eq. 358 (Ch. 1874); Ashhurst v. Potter, 29 N.J. Eq. 625 (N.J. 1878); Gates v. Plainfield Trust Co., 121 N.J. Eq. 460, 191 A. 304, *aff'd,* 122 N.J. Eq. 366, 194 A. 65 (Err. & App. 1937); Ross v. Savings Investment & Trust Co., 120 N.J. Eq. 87, 184 A. 183 (Ch. 1936); Macy v. Mercantile

Trust Co., 68 N.J. Eq. 235, 59 A. 586 (Ch. 1904); In re Brown's Estate, 112 N.J. Eq. 499, 164 A. 692 (Prerog. Ct. 1933); see generally Restatement (Second) of Trusts §§ 230–231 (1957); Austin Wakeman Scott & William Franklin Fratcher, *Scott on Trusts* §§ 230–231 (4th ed. 1987); George Gleason Bogert & George T. Bogert, *The Law of Trusts and Trustees* §§ 685–686 (2d ed. rev. 1984)]

If a trustee fails to sell an unlawful investment within a reasonable time, the trustee is liable for the difference between the price actually obtained and what would have been obtained had the trustee sold the investment at the proper time together with the investment earnings that should have been obtained on that difference. [See Restatement (Third) of Trusts § 209 (1992); see also Beam v. Paterson Safe Deposit & Trust Co., 81 N.J. Eq. 195, 11 Buchanan 195, 86 A. 369 (N.J. 1913); Babbitt v. Fidelity Trust Co., 72 N.J. Eq. 745, 2 Buchanan 745, 66 A. 1066 (N.J. 1907)] In addition, a trustee must use due care and act prudently concerning the time and terms of the sale. [See, e.g., Braman v. Central Hanover Bank & Trust Co., 138 N.J. Eq. 165, 47 A.2d 10 (N.J. 1946)]

Customer Identity

Q 4:97   Do anti-money-laundering rules apply to deferred compensation plans?

Yes. Anti-money-laundering rules, which previously applied to banks and subsidiaries of a financial holding company, and customer-identity rules apply to every financial institution, including a bank, trust company, insurance company, or securities broker-dealer. [31 U.S.C. § 5318A, as added, and 31 U.S.C. §§ 5311–5318, as amended by Title III of the Uniting and Strengthening America by Providing Appropriate Tools Required to Intercept and Obstruct Terrorism Act of 2001, 115 Stat. 272 (2001), Pub. L. No. 107-56 (USA PATRIOT Act); see also 67 Fed. Reg. 37,736 (May 30, 2002), 67 Fed. Reg. 21,110 (Apr. 29, 2002)] Because almost every deferred compensation plan involves at least one financial institution, these anti-money-laundering rules apply.

Along with further requirements, a broker-dealer's anti-money-laundering program must establish and implement procedures "that can be reasonably expected to detect and cause the reporting of [suspicious] transactions[.]" [NASD Rule 3011, NYSE Rule 445 (under 15 U.S.C. § 78s(b)(1)); 17 C.F.R. § 240.19b-4] For a broker-dealer's services regarding deferred compensation plans, this rule might be difficult to implement. The nature of a deferred compensation plan makes it difficult to find when (if ever) a contribution or distribution might be suspicious. [See Securities Industry Ass'n Anti-Money Laundering Committee, Preliminary Guidance for Deterring Money Laundering Activity 12–13 (Feb. 2002)]

When processing or accepting contributions, a typical insurer, custodian, or broker-dealer does not accept currency. If a broker-dealer effects a transaction that exceeds $10,000 and involves currency, the broker-dealer must report such a transaction. [17 C.F.R. § 240.17a8]

Chapter 5

Beneficiary Designations and Estate Planning

Peter J. Gulia, Esq.
CitiStreet Retirement Services

A participant's use of his or her valuable right under a deferred compensation plan to name a beneficiary is an important part of estate planning. This chapter explains some of the opportunities and restrictions in making a beneficiary designation, including marriage and family rights that restrain a beneficiary designation. Because a deferred compensation plan benefit is not transferred by a will, a beneficiary designation affects the individual's overall estate plan.

This chapter introduces tax-oriented estate planning because many participants mistakenly assume that they lack enough wealth for estate tax issues to be of concern, even when one or more estate, inheritance, or other transfer taxes likely will apply.

Author's note. Although it is not correct usage, this chapter uses the popular expression *probate* to refer to property that is transferred through a court-supervised administration or succession and *nonprobate* to refer to property that is transferred or contract rights that are provided without such an administration.

For convenience, this chapter uses the term *payor* to refer to any of a trustee, custodian, insurer, plan administrator, or other person responsible to decide or pay a claim under or regarding a deferred compensation plan.

This chapter uses the word *state* in its popular meaning to refer to the District of Columbia or any state, commonwealth, territory, possession, or similar jurisdiction within the United States of America. Because this chapter has many references to state law, this chapter uses only the word *state* (rather than the lawyers' word, *jurisdiction*) for reading ease. For example, although the District of Columbia is not a state, law that applies to an individual because he or she resides in the District is state law, as distinguished from United States law or federal law that applies throughout the United States of America.

Effect of Beneficiary Designation

Q 5:1   Is a deferred compensation plan benefit disposed of by a participant's will?

No. A deferred compensation plan includes a provision by which the participant may name his or her beneficiary or beneficiaries. The beneficiary designation applies even if the participant's will attempts to state a contrary disposition. Although this conclusion results simply from applying the terms of the deferred compensation plan, some jurisdictions for convenience include an explicit provision in the state's probate statute. [See, e.g., Mass. Gen. Laws Ann. ch. 167D, § 30 (LEXIS 1997); N.Y. Est. Powers & Trusts Law § 13-3.2 (McKinney Supp. 2001); 20 Pa. Cons. Stat. Ann. § 8704 (Bisel/West 1975). See generally National Conference of Commissioners on Uniform State Laws, Uniform Probate Code §§ 1-201(4), 6-101(a)(3), 6-104, 6-201 (1998)] Courts have held that a will cannot override a beneficiary designation. [Moss v. Warren, 43 Cal. App. 3d 651, 117 Cal. Rptr. 796 (1974); Strohsahl v. Equitable Life Assurance Society of the United States, 71 N.J. Super. 300, 176 A.2d 814 (Ch. Div. 1962); Cook v. Cook, 17 Cal. 2d 639, 111 P.2d 322 (1941)]

If a deferred compensation plan is not governed by the Employee Retirement Income Security Act of 1974 (ERISA), state law may supplement the plan's provisions concerning the manner of making a beneficiary designation. For example, New York law requires that a beneficiary designation be signed. [N.Y. Est. Powers & Trusts Law § 13-3.2 (McKinney Supp. 2001)]

If a deferred compensation plan is governed by ERISA, only the plan's provisions govern a beneficiary designation. [ERISA § 514; Egelhoff v. Egelhoff, 532 U.S. 141 (2001)]

Q 5:2   Who may make a beneficiary designation?

Ordinarily, only a plan participant may make a beneficiary designation. However, a deferred compensation plan may permit a beneficiary to name a further contingent beneficiary if the participant did not (before his or her death) designate all of the benefit and the plan lacked any other default provision. [See P.L.R. 199936052 (concerning an IRA)]

Such a power to name further beneficiaries can cause the deferred compensation that remains undistributed at each beneficiary's death to be subject to federal estate tax and state inheritance tax, notwithstanding that the same benefit was previously so taxed on the participant's (and each earlier beneficiary's) death. [I.R.C. § 2041(a)(2); Treas. Reg. § 20.2041-1(b)] This second federal estate tax may be postponed if the beneficiary names his or her spouse as the succeeding beneficiary and that spouse has the power to take the entire remaining benefit. [I.R.C. § 2056; P.L.R. 199936052]

A more typical deferred compensation plan default provision pays any undistributed benefit to the personal representative of the participant's estate (see Q 5:9). Although the participant's estate may have been closed before this time, it may be reopened for subsequent administration on the discovery of property that was not disposed of by the previous administration. [See generally National Conference of Commissioners on Uniform State Laws, Uniform Probate Code § 3-1008 (1998)]

Practice Pointer. A prudent participant should make a complete beneficiary designation that contemplates all possibilities. A participant who does not want to specify alternate takers may create a trust, which can include a power of appointment for a beneficiary to name a further beneficiary.

Q 5:3   Why should a participant read a beneficiary-designation form?

Plan administrators design beneficiary-designation forms in anticipation of the possibility that a participant might give incomplete or ambiguous instructions.

For example, many forms provide that—if a participant has not specified the shares—an account will be divided among all beneficiaries in equal shares.

A beneficiary-designation form might include other "gap-fillers" or "default" provisions, some of which might be surprising to a participant. For example, a beneficiary-designation form might provide that a beneficiary change for an account will change the beneficiary for every account with the provider that is classified under the same Internal Revenue Code subsection. Some deferred compensation plans provide as a default beneficiary (see Q 5:9) the person or persons designated under a pension plan. Because provisions of this kind might frustrate one's intent, a careful participant should read the beneficiary-designation form.

Q 5:4   Will a beneficiary designation made under a power of attorney be accepted?

A plan administrator may (but is not required to) accept a beneficiary designation made by an agent under a power of attorney. Typically, a plan administrator will decline to act unless the power-of-attorney document expressly states a power to change beneficiary designations. [See Clouse v. Philadelphia Electric Co., 787 F. Supp. 93, 15 Employee Benefits Cas. (BNA) 1347 (E.D. Pa. 1992); see also Restatement (Second) of Agency § 37 (1957)]

For a church plan or governmental plan that is not governed by ERISA, state law governs whether an employer or plan administrator may or must permit the actions of an agent under a power of attorney. In some states, banking law regulates how a bank or trust company must evaluate whether to honor a power of attorney. [See, e.g., N.Y. Gen. Oblig. Law § 5-1504 (McKinney Supp. 2001)]

Q 5:5   What is the doctrine of substantial compliance?

When recognized, the doctrine of substantial compliance excuses a contract holder's failure to effect a change of beneficiary according to the contract's terms if he or she intended to change his or her beneficiary and did everything reasonably in his or her power to effect the change. [See, e.g., Prudential Insurance Co. v. Withers, 127 F.3d 1106 (9th Cir. 1997); Phoenix Mutual Life Insurance Co. v. Adams, 30 F.3d 554 (4th Cir. 1994); Cipriani v. Sun Life Insurance Co., 757 F.2d 78 (3d Cir. 1985); Provident Mutual Life Insurance Co. of Philadelphia v. Ehrlich, 508 F.2d 129 (3d Cir. 1975); Dennis v. Aetna Life Insurance & Annuity Co., 873 F. Supp. 1000 (E.D. Va. 1995); Prudential Insurance Co. v. Bannister, 448 F. Supp. 807 (W.D. Pa. 1978); Pimentel v. Conselho Supremo de Uniao Portugueza da Estado da California, 6 Cal. 2d 182, 57 P.2d 131 (1936); Saunders v. Stevers, 221 Cal. App. 2d 539, 34 Cal. Rptr. 579 (Dist. Ct. App. 1963); IDS Life Insurance Co. v. Estate of Groshong, 112 Idaho 847, 736 P.2d 1301 (Idaho 1987); State Employees' Retirement System of Illinois v. Taylor, 131 Ill. App. 3d 997, 476 N.E.2d 749, 87 Ill. Dec. 47 (1985); Haynes v. Metropolitan Life Insurance Co., 166 N.J. Super. 308 (App. Div. 1979); Riley v. Wirth, 313 Pa. 362, 169 A. 139 (Pa. 1933); Sproat v. Travelers Insurance Co., 289 Pa. 351, 137 A. 621 (1927); Carruthers v. $21,000,

290 Pa. Super. 54, 434 A.2d 125, 127 (1981); Dale v. Philadelphia Board of Pensions & Retirement, 702 A.2d 1160 (Pa. Commw. Ct. 1997)] Courts find that this equitable doctrine of substantial compliance circumvents "a formalistic, overly technical adherence to the exact words of the change of beneficiary provision in a given [contract]." [Phoenix Mutual Life Insurance Co. v. Adams, 30 F.3d 554, 563 (4th Cir. 1994)]

The doctrine of substantial compliance, which is one manifestation of the doctrine of substantial performance of a contract, has been criticized as defeating freedom of contract. [See, e.g., Grant Gilmore, *The Death of Contract* 74 (1974)]

A payor's interpleader (or other circumstances that make a payor a mere stakeholder do not lessen that a claimant must show the participant's substantial compliance with the plan's procedure for making a beneficiary designation. [See, e.g., McCarthy v. Aetna Life Insurance Co., 704 N.E.2d 557, 681 N.Y.S.2d 790 (N.Y. 1998)]

Q 5:6   Does the doctrine of substantial compliance apply to a non-ERISA plan?

Yes, in most states. If ERISA does not preempt state law, a state court likely would apply the state's doctrine of substantial compliance. (See Q 5:5)

Q 5:7   Does the doctrine of substantial compliance apply to an ERISA plan?

If a plan is governed by ERISA, the doctrine of substantial compliance should apply only if the plan administrator in its discretion decides to use such a concept to aid its own interpretation or administration of the plan.

To determine the beneficiary under an ERISA plan, a court should hold that any state's doctrine of substantial compliance is preempted. [ERISA § 514; see Egelhoff v. Egelhoff, 532 U.S. 141 (2001); see, e.g., Phoenix Mutual Life Insurance Co. v. Adams, 30 F.3d 554, 18 Employee Benefits Cas. (BNA) 2262, Pens. Plan Guide (CCH) ¶ 23901W, 1994 U.S. App. LEXIS 19385 (4th Cir. 1994); Continental Assurance Co. v. Davis, 24 Employee Benefits Cas. (BNA) 2273, 2000 WL 1141434, 2000 U.S. Dist. LEXIS 810 (N.D. Ill. Aug. 11, 2000); Metropolitan Life Insurance Co. v. Hall, 9 F. Supp. 2d 560 (D. Md. 1998); Fortis Benefits Insurance Co. v. Johnson, 966 F. Supp. 987 (D. Nev. 1997); First Capital Life Insurance Co. v. AAA Communications, Inc., 906 F. Supp. 1546 (N.D. Ga. 1995)] However, the Ninth and Tenth Circuits have held that a state's common-law doctrine of substantial compliance supplements an ERISA plan's provisions. [BankAmerica Pension Plan v. McMath, 206 F.3d 821, 24 Employee Benefits Cas. (BNA) 1686 (9th Cir. 2000), *cert. denied subnom.* McMath v. Montgomery, 531 U.S. 952, 121 S. Ct. 358, 148 L. Ed. 2d 288 (2000); Peckham v. Gem State Mutual of Utah, 964 F.2d 1043 (10th Cir. 1992)] The Fourth and Seventh Circuits found that ERISA preempts a state's doctrine of substantial compliance, and instead applied a federal common-law doctrine of substantial compliance. [Phoenix Mutual Life

Insurance Co. v. Adams, 30 F.3d 554, 18 Employee Benefits Cas. (BNA) 2262, Pens. Plan Guide (CCH) ¶ 23901W, 1994 U.S. App. LEXIS 19385 (4th Cir. 1994); Metropolitan Life Insurance Co. v. Johnson, 297 F.3d 558, 28 Employee Benefits Cas. (BNA) 1648 (7th Cir. 2002)] Although some federal courts considering the question have held that ERISA does not necessarily preempt a state's doctrine of substantial compliance, the author's view is that ERISA preempts any such law relating to an ERISA plan. [ERISA § 514]

Practice Pointer. Unless a plan provision is contrary to ERISA, an ERISA plan administrator should administer a plan according to the plan's documents. [ERISA § 503] Therefore, if a plan states that any doctrine of substantial compliance will not apply, the plan administrator must interpret and administer the plan without using such a doctrine.

Further, if a plan grants the plan administrator discretion in interpreting or administering the plan, a court will not interfere with the plan administrator's decision unless it was an abuse of discretion. [See Firestone Tire & Rubber Co. v. Bruch, 489 U.S. 101, 109 S. Ct. 948, 103 L. Ed. 2d 80 (1989); Nelson v. EG&G Energy Measurements Group, Inc., 37 F.3d 1384 (9th Cir. 1994); see, e.g., Clouse v. Philadelphia Electric Co., 787 F. Supp. 93, 15 Employee Benefits Cas. (BNA) 1347 (E.D. Pa. 1992)]

Q 5:8   What should a plan administrator do if it cannot locate a beneficiary designation because the plan's records were destroyed?

Even with prudent efforts to safeguard records, circumstances beyond a plan administrator's control might result in the destruction of plan records. If so, a plan administrator should try to reconstruct a beneficiary designation using the best evidence available to it.

That records are lost or destroyed does not discharge a plan administrator from its duty to administer the plan. When deciding whether to pay any benefit to a potential beneficiary, a plan administrator must act in good faith and must use reasonable procedures, especially when deciding who is a participant's beneficiary. When a record is lost or destroyed, a plan administrator may use the most reliable evidence available to it. For example, a service provider might have a copy of a beneficiary designation. Or a claimant might furnish a copy of a beneficiary designation. A plan administrator might use its discretion to rely on a document that appears to be a copy of a participant's beneficiary designation. But a plan administrator should do so only if it has adopted and uses reasonable procedures designed to detect a forgery. Further, when a claimant submits evidence that he or she is the participant's beneficiary, a plan administrator must take reasonable steps to consider whether the evidence is credible.

[DOL PWBA, FAQs for Plan Sponsors, Fiduciaries and Service Providers Related to the Events of September 11, *www.dol.gov/pwba/faqs/faq_911_3.html*]

Q 5:9   What happens when a participant does not make a beneficiary designation?

A deferred compensation plan usually will state a "default" beneficiary designation that applies when the participant has not made a valid beneficiary designation. A typical provision pays the nondesignated benefit to the executor or personal representative of the participant's probate estate. (This is *not* the provision recommended by the author.)

If, under community property law (see Q 5:41), a portion of the participant's deferred compensation belongs or belonged to the participant's spouse, the spouse (or the spouse's beneficiaries or heirs) might have a claim against the participant's executor for payment of the spouse's community property (see Q 5:44). In Alaska, Arkansas, Colorado, Connecticut, Hawaii, Kentucky, Michigan, New York, Oregon, Virginia, and Wyoming, the Uniform Disposition of Community Property Rights at Death Act may apply. [National Conference of Commissioners on Uniform State Laws, 8 U.L.A. 121 (1971 & Supp. 2001)]

Q 5:10   Does a divorce revoke a beneficiary designation?

Whether a divorce will revoke a deferred compensation plan beneficiary designation turns on the following:

1. Whether the plan is an ERISA-governed plan;
2. Which state law (if any) applies; and
3. What the chosen state law (when applicable) provides.

If a deferred compensation plan is not an ERISA plan, state law may apply. In many states, a divorce will not revoke a beneficiary designation that names the ex-spouse. [In re Declaration of Death of Santos, Jr., 282 N.J. Super. 509, 660 A.2d 1206 (App. Div. 1995); Hughes v. Scholl, 900 S.W.2d 606 (Ky. 1995); Stiles v. Stiles, 21 Mass. App. 514, 487 N.E.2d 874 (1986); O'Toole v. Central Laborers' Pension & Welfare Funds, 12 Ill. App. 3d 995, 299 N.E.2d 392 (1973); Gerhard v. Travelers Insurance Co., 107 N.J. Super. 414, 258 A.2d 724 (Ch. Div. 1969)] Some states have statutory provisions that attempt to provide that a divorce or annulment has the effect of making the former spouse not a beneficiary except as otherwise specified by a court order. [See, e.g., Ohio Rev. Code Ann. § 1339.63 (Anderson 2002); Okla. Stat. Ann. tit. 15, § 178 (West Supp. 2002); Mich. Comp. Laws § 552.101 (West 1988); Minn. Stat. Ann. § 524.2-804 (West 2003); Mo. Rev. Stat. § 461.051(1) (1986 & Supp.); Tex. Fam. Code Ann. § 3.632 (West 1993); see generally National Conference of Commissioners on Uniform State Laws, Uniform Probate Code § 2-804(b) (1998)] Even when the relevant state has such a statute, it may not apply if the plan has contrary provisions, and many plans include a provision that a divorce or anything other than the plan's beneficiary designation form has no effect on the beneficiary designation. Further, the law of the state in which a participant resided is not necessarily the governing law. [See, e.g., Pound v. Insurance Co. of North America, 439 F.2d 1059 (10th Cir. 1971). But see

Travelers Insurance Co. v. Fields, 451 F.2d 1292 (6th Cir. 1971); see generally Restatement (Second) of Conflict of Laws § 187 (1971)] In any case, state law will protect a payor that pays the beneficiary of record unless the payor has received a court order restraining payment or at least a written notice that states a dispute about who the lawful beneficiary is. [See, e.g., Alaska Stat. § 13.12.804(a)(1)(A); Ohio Rev. Code Ann. § 1339.63 (1988 & Supp.); Okla. Stat. Ann., tit. 15, § 178 (1991); Mich. Comp. Laws § 552.101 (1991); 20 Pa. Cons. Stat. Ann. § 6111.2 (1975); Mo. Rev. Stat. § 461.051(1) (1986 & Supp.); Tex. Fam. Code Ann. § 3.632 (Qwar 1993); see generally Uniform Probate Code § 2-804(b)(1998)]

If a deferred compensation plan is an ERISA plan, only the plan's terms will govern whether a divorce or other circumstance has any effect on the plan beneficiary designation, because ERISA preempts all state laws. [ERISA § 514; Egelhoff v. Egelhoff, 532 U.S. 141 (2001); Boggs v. Boggs, 520 U.S. 833, 117 S. Ct. 1754, 138 L. Ed. 2d 45, 65 U.S.L.W. 4418, 21 Employee Benefits Cas. (BNA) 1047, Pens. Plan Guide (CCH) ¶ 23934N, *reh'g denied*, 521 U.S. 1138, 118 S. Ct. 9, 138 L. Ed. 2d 1043, 66 U.S.L.W. 3128 (1997)] A qualified domestic relations order (see chapter 13) does not preclude a participant from continuing a beneficiary designation that provides for his or her former spouse. [See, e.g., LeTourneau v. General Motors Corp., 24 Fed. Appx. 332, 27 Employee Benefits Cas. (BNA) 1120, Pens. Plan Guide (CCH) ¶ 23977F, 2001 WL 1450672, 2001 U.S. App. LEXIS 24537 (6th Cir. Nov. 9, 2001)]

Practice Pointer. A plan sponsor should consider whether it might be helpful for an ERISA deferred compensation plan to state that any annulment, divorce, marital separation, or other event or circumstance has no effect under the plan.

Practice Pointer. After a divorce, a participant should remember to change or confirm his or her beneficiary designation.

Q 5:11   What happens when a beneficiary designation is contrary to an external agreement?

An administrator of a deferred compensation plan pays according to the plan's provisions, and need not consider external documents. If the plan is governed by ERISA, ERISA preempts all state laws that otherwise might control who gets a plan benefit. [ERISA § 514; Egelhoff v. Egelhoff, 532 U.S. 141 (2001); Boggs v. Boggs, 520 U.S. 833, 21 Employee Benefits Cas. (BNA) 1047, Pens. Plan Guide (CCH) ¶ 23934N (1997), *reh'g denied*, 521 U.S. 1138 (1997)] An administrator of a non-ERISA plan also pays according to the plan's provisions, and ordinarily need not consider external documents. However, once a non-ERISA plan has paid the plan beneficiary, a person who has rights under an external agreement may pursue remedies under state law. [See, e.g., Kinkel v. Kinkel, 699 N.E.2d 41 (Ohio 1998). (A custodian correctly paid an IRA participant's designated beneficiary, but the participant's children later recovered from the participant's surviving spouse.)]

Q 5:12   May an executor participate in a court proceeding concerning a disputed benefit?

Often, no. A personal representative of a participant's estate may participate in a court proceeding concerning a disputed benefit only if the personal representative is a bona fide claimant. If a personal representative does not make any claim of right to the benefit, however, such a personal representative has no justiciable claim or standing to participate in a court proceeding. [See, e.g., Deaton v. Cross, 184 F. Supp. 2d 441 (D. Md. 2002)]

Q 5:13   Why would a divorced participant not want to name his or her young child as a beneficiary?

A divorced participant might not want to name his or her young child as a beneficiary if doing so might have the effect of putting money in the hands of the child's other parent—the participant's former spouse.

A deferred compensation plan is a contract. An employer or other payor wants to be sure that a payment is a complete satisfaction of that contract. Ordinarily, a beneficiary's deposit or negotiation of a check that pays a plan distribution is the beneficiary's acceptance of the employer's or payor's satisfaction of the beneficiary's claim under the deferred compensation plan.

A *minor* is a person still young enough that he or she cannot make a binding contract. Although state laws vary, most end an individual's minor status at age 18. [See, e.g., 23 Pa. Cons. Stat. Ann. § 5101 (West 2001)] Usually, a minor's emancipation from his or her parents does not change the minor's lack of power to make binding contracts. [See, e.g., Central Bucks Aero, Inc. v. Smith, 310 A.2d 283 (Pa. 1972)]

Before a child reaches age 18 (or the other age of competence to make binding contracts), his or her guardian or conservator may disaffirm an agreement or promise the child made. After a child reaches age 18 (or the other full age), he or she may disaffirm an agreement or promise he or she made before he or she reached the age of competence to make contracts.

If state law applies, an employer or payor will not take the risk that payment of a plan distribution is not a complete satisfaction of plan obligations. Even if ERISA preempts state law, a plan administrator might be concerned that a court would fashion a federal common-law rule. Thus, plan administrators, employers, and payors almost universally are unwilling to pay deferred compensation to a minor.

To facilitate payment of deferred compensation in these circumstances, most plans permit payment to a minor's conservator, guardian, or Uniform Transfers to Minors Acts custodian. If a participant named his or her child as a beneficiary (rather than naming as beneficiary a custodian), a plan administrator or payor is likely to honor a claim made by the child's conservator or guardian. If a child's other parent is living, most courts would appoint the parent as the child's conservator. In some states, the law presumes that a parent is a child's natural guardian and conservator. [Compare Manley v. Detroit Auto Inter-Insurance Exchange, 127 Mich. App. 444, 339 N.W.2d 205 (1983), *motion denied*, 357 N.W.2d 644 (Mich. App. 1983), *cause remanded on other grounds*, 425 Mich. 140, 388 N.W.2d 216 (1983), with In re Estate of Fisher, 503 So. 2d 962 (Fla. Dist. Ct. App. 1987); see generally National Conference of Commissioners on Uniform State Laws, Uniform Probate Code §§ 5-202, -409 (1998)]

Using Trusts

Q 5:14   May a participant hold his or her deferred compensation in a living trust?

No. Typically, a deferred compensation plan provides that a participant cannot assign or transfer any right he or she has under the plan.

Practice Pointer. There is no particularly good reason to try to put a deferred compensation benefit into a living trust. A right to deferred compensation already is nonprobate property, which will pass according to the plan's beneficiary designation.

Q 5:15   May a trust be a beneficiary under a deferred compensation plan?

Yes. A participant may name a trust as beneficiary under a deferred compensation plan. To make a correct beneficiary designation, a participant must designate the trustee, as trustee of the trust, as beneficiary. Nonetheless, a plan administrator usually treats a designation of a trust as though it were a designation of the duly appointed and then-currently serving trustee of that trust.

The trust must be legally in existence (or completed such that it would be legally in existence on the trustee's receipt of money or property) before the participant makes the beneficiary designation.

A beneficiary of a trust will not be a designated beneficiary to extend life expectancy when measuring minimum distribution and incidental benefit requirements unless the trust meets specified requirements and necessary information is certified to the plan administrator. [Treas. Reg. § 1.401(a)(9)-1, Q&A D-5]

Q 5:16   What is a subtrust?

A subtrust is a portion of a trust that is administered according to provisions different from those that apply to other subtrusts or other portions of the whole trust.

In the context of using life insurance in deferred compensation plans, the word *subtrust* is used by some lawyers to refer to an estate planning concept in which the life insurance contract and subtrust are administered according to trust provisions meant to ensure that the life insurance contract will not be treated as part of the participant-insured's estate for federal estate tax purposes. [For an explanation of this technique, refer to G.S. Lesser & L.C. Starr, *Life Insurance Answer Book* ch.18 (New York: Aspen Publishers, 3d ed. 2002, 2003)]

Family Rights That Restrain a Beneficiary Designation

Q 5:17 Can a participant make a beneficiary designation that does not provide for his or her spouse?

Yes. Even if a deferred compensation plan is governed by ERISA, it is exempt from Part 2 of Subtitle B of Title I of ERISA. Thus, a 457 plan is not subject to the survivor-annuity and spouse's-consent rules that apply to a pension plan. [ERISA § 201; I.R.C. §401(a)(11), (17)] Sometimes, a select-group deferred compensation plan by its express terms provides that the participant's surviving spouse is the beneficiary. A spouse's-consent beneficiary provision is not typical for a state or local government employer's deferred compensation plan.

In the absence of any court order or written notice of a dispute, a plan administrator will give effect to the participant's beneficiary designation. Even when a participant's beneficiary change has an obvious potential to frustrate a divorcing spouse's equitable-distribution rights, a participant remains free to make his or her beneficiary designation unless a court's restraining order binds him or her. [See, e.g., Titler v. State Employees' Retirement Board, 768 A.2d 899 (Pa. Commw. Ct. 2001)] Further, an order that binds a participant might not bind a plan or its administrator.

If a participant's spouse did not receive his or her share provided by state law, a distributee may be liable to the participant's executor to the extent that state law provides for a spouse's elective share to be payable from nonprobate property—that is, property other than property administered by the decedent's executor or personal representative. [See, e.g., Fla. Stat. Ann. § 732.2135 (Westlaw 2002); La. Civ. Code Ann. art. 1505 (West 2000); T.L. James & Co. v. Montgomery, 332 So. 2d 834 (La. 1976); N.Y. Est. Powers & Trusts Law § 5-1.1 (McKinney 1999); see generally National Conference of Commissioners on Uniform State Laws, Uniform Probate Code § 2-204 (1998)]

> **Note.** If a distributee received a plan distribution in one year but paid over an amount to the participant's surviving spouse in a later year, the distributee recognizes income for the year he or she received the distribution and claims a deduction for the year he or she paid restoration to the surviving spouse. [I.R.C. § 1341; United States v. Lewis, 340 U.S. 590 (1951)]

> **Note.** A surviving spouse who is not the participant's named beneficiary and instead receives deferred compensation because of an elective-share law or community-property law is not a designated beneficiary when applying the

plan's minimum distribution provisions. [Treas. Reg. § 1.401(a)(9)-4, A-1] Thus, it might become necessary to compute a minimum distribution by reference to a different person's life.

In Louisiana, the plan administrator may follow the participant's beneficiary designation. [La. Rev. Stat. Ann. §§ 23:638, :652 (West 1998)] A distributee who receives benefits under a nongovernmental and non-ERISA plan—a church plan—must account for and pay over benefits to the participant's surviving spouse to the extent that payment is necessary to satisfy the spouse's community property rights and usufruct. [T.L. James & Co. v. Montgomery, 332 So. 2d 834 (La. 1976)] A distributee who receives benefits under a deferred compensation plan of "any public or governmental employer" is not subject to the claims of forced heirs. [La. Civ. Code Ann. art. 1505 (West 2000)]

Different law may apply for members of a Native American Indian tribe. [Jones v. Meehan, 175 U.S. 1, 20 S. Ct. 1, 44 L. Ed. 49 (1899); see also Davis v. Shanks, 15 Minn. 369 (1870); Hasting v. Farmer, 4 N.Y. 293 (1850); Dole v. Irish, 2 Barb. 639 (N.Y. App. Div. 1848)] However, a Native American Indian tribe's law usually applies between or among members of the tribe, and often cannot be enforced against persons outside the tribe.

Q 5:18   Must a plan administrator tell an ex-spouse when a participant changes his or her beneficiary designation contrary to a court order?

No, in the absence of a court order that commands the plan administrator to furnish specified information, a plan administrator has no duty to furnish information about a particular beneficiary designation change.

> Absent a promise or misrepresentation, the courts have almost uniformly rejected claims by plan participants or beneficiaries that an ERISA administrator has to volunteer individualized information taking account of their peculiar circumstances. This view reflects ERISA's focus on limited and general reporting and disclosure requirements . . . and also reflects the enormous burdens an obligation to proffer individualized advice would inflict on plan administrators[.]

[Barrs v. Lockheed Martin Corp., 287 F.3d 202, 27 Employee Benefits Cas. (BNA) 2409, Pens. Plan Guide (CCH) ¶ 23979F (1st Cir. 2002)]

Even when a plan administrator is governed by ERISA Section 404's greatest fiduciary duties, courts have not required a plan administrator to furnish an alternate payee information beyond that required by an express statutory or plan provision. For an unfunded deferred compensation plan regarding which a plan administrator is not governed by ERISA Section 404, it seems unlikely that a court would impose such a duty. For a governmental deferred compensation plan, it seems unlikely that a court would impose a duty greater than federal courts have applied concerning ERISA plans.

Q 5:19 Can a participant make a beneficiary designation that does not provide for his or her child?

In most states, yes.

In the United States, only Louisiana and Puerto Rico have a forced-share provision for a decedent's children. [See La. Civ. Code Ann. arts. 1493–1514 (West 2000); P.R. Laws tit. 31, §§ 2362, 2411–2463 (1993)] Therefore, a participant usually may disinherit his or her children. In some jurisdictions a family allowance may be required for the decedent's children if there is no surviving spouse. [See generally National Conference of Commissioners on Uniform State Laws, Uniform Probate Code § 2-403 (1998)]

In Louisiana, a plan administrator may follow the participant's beneficiary designation. [La. Rev. Stat. Ann. §§ 23:638, :652 (West 1998)] A distributee who receives benefits under a nongovernmental and non-ERISA deferred compensation plan—a church plan—must account for and pay over benefits to the participant's surviving spouse to the extent that payment is necessary to satisfy his or her community property rights and usufruct and to the participant's children or forced heirs to the extent that payment is necessary to satisfy their légitime (the portion of an estate that children and other close heirs can claim against the decedent's testament). [T.L. James & Co. v. Montgomery, 332 So. 2d 834 (La. 1976)] A distributee who receives benefits under a deferred compensation plan of "any public or governmental employer" is not subject to the claims of forced heirs. [La. Civ. Code Ann. art. 1505 (West 2000)]

Different law may apply for members of a Native American Indian tribe. [Jones v. Meehan, 175 U.S. 1, 20 S. Ct. 1, 44 L. Ed. 49 (1899); see also Davis v. Shanks, 15 Minn. 369 (1870); Hasting v. Farmer, 4 N.Y. 293 (1850); Dole v. Irish, 2 Barb. 639 (N.Y. App. Div. 1848)] However, a Native American Indian tribe's law usually applies between or among members of the tribe, and often cannot be enforced against persons outside the tribe.

Whether it is called légitime, legitimate portions, or compulsory portions in civil-law nations, family provision or family maintenance in nations following English law, or ahl alfara'id under the Koran, in most nations other than the United States of America a person is limited in his or her right or privilege to disinherit his or her children. [See, e.g., Egypt, Law of Testamentary Dispositions of 1946, Law of Inheritance of 1943; England and Wales, Inheritance (Provision for Family and Dependants) Act 1975, as amended; India-Pakistan, Muslim Family Laws Ordinance of 1961] In India, the law of succession of property varies according to the religion professed by the decedent. In Israel, religious courts may take jurisdiction when all parties consent. [Martindale-Hubbell International Law Digests (2000)]

> **Practice Pointer.** A plan participant who resides in a nation other than the United States of America should consult an expert lawyer before he or she makes a beneficiary designation that does not provide for his or her spouse and children.

Pet Animals

Q 5:20 May a participant designate his or her dog or cat as a beneficiary?

No. A beneficiary must be a person, whether a natural person or a non-natural person (such as a corporation), that can endorse a negotiable instrument—for example, the check that pays the plan distribution.

For many people, living with a pet is an important and comforting part of life, and providing for the care of the pet is a real concern. Although it is usually more effective for a pet owner to plan for the care of the pet in the owner's will, some people might have insufficient probate property to provide for the pet's care and instead may use a beneficiary designation.

Under the laws of every state, a person cannot give any part of his or her estate to a nonhuman animal. However, a pet owner may leave a sum of money to a person named to care for the pet, along with a request that the money be used for the pet's care. In these circumstances, the pet owner should select a caretaker whom he or she trusts, because the caretaker often has no legal obligation to use the money for the purpose specified. If there is no suitable relative or friend who would take the pet, the pet owner or guardian might consider a charitable organization that cares for or places companion animals.

Q 5:21 May a trust provide for a pet animal's care?

State laws differ widely concerning whether and how a trust may provide for the care of animals. These differences may be grouped in the following broad categories:

1. In some states, a trust for the support of an animal is invalid because there is no beneficiary. However, a trust for a human beneficiary may include a provision that the trustee may use trust property to pay for the care of an animal, since the animal's care may benefit the human beneficiary.

2. In some states, a person may create a valid trust for an animal (if the trust satisfies other trust law concerning the duration of a trust), but such a trust is an honorary trust. [See, e.g., Mo. Ann. Stat. § 456.055 (Vernon 1992); Tenn. Code Ann. § 35-50-118 (LEXIS 2001); Wis. Stat. Ann. § 701.11(1) (West 1981); Willett v. Willett, 197 Ky. 663, 247 S.W. 739 (1923); In re Estate of Sea Right, 87 Ohio App. 417, 95 N.E.2d 779 (1950); In re Stewart's Estate, 13 Pa. D. & C.3d 488 (Orphans' Ct. 1979); In re Lyon's Estate, 67 Pa. D. & C.2d 474 (Orphans' Ct. 1974); Skrine v. Walker, 3 Rich. Eq. 262 (S.C. 1851); Richberg v. Robbins, 33 Tenn. App. 66, 228 S.W.2d 1019 (1950); see generally Restatement (Second) of Trusts § 124; 2 Austin Wakeman Scott & William Franklin Fratcher, *Scott on Trusts* § 124 (4th ed. 1987)] A court will not order any remedy if the trustee fails to perform the honorary trust.

3. In some states, a trust for an animal's care may be enforced in the courts. [Alaska Stat. § 13.12.907 (LEXIS 2000); Ariz. Rev. Stat. Ann. § 14-2907 (West 1995); Colo. Rev. Stat. Ann. § 15-11-901 (West 1997); Mich. Comp. Laws Ann. § 700.2722 (Westlaw 2002); Mont. Code Ann. § 72-2-1017 (Westlaw 2002); N.M. Stat. Ann. § 45-2-907 (Westlaw 2002); N.Y. Est. Powers & Trusts Law § 7-6.1 (McKinney 1999); N.C. Gen. Stat. § 36A-147 (Westlaw 2002); Utah Code Ann. § 75-2-1001 (Westlaw 2002). See generally National Conference of Commissioners on Uniform State Laws, Uniform Probate Code § 2-907 (1998)] In most states, a trust recognized under category 2 or 3, above, cannot exceed 21 years, even if the life span of a particular animal is longer. [See, e.g., Mo. Ann. Stat. § 456.055 (Vernon 1992); Tenn. Code Ann. § 35-50-118 (LEXIS 2001); see generally National Conference of Commissioners on Uniform State Laws, Uniform Probate Code § 2-907 (1998)] Colorado, however, permits a valid pet trust for the lifetime of the animal and "the animal's offspring in gestation." [Colo. Rev. Stat. Ann. § 15-11-901 (LEXIS 2000)]

A trust does not necessarily mean that the trustee must be the animal's caretaker. If the trustee cannot or prefers not to take physical possession of the animal, a separate person may be named as the caretaker. It is usually more efficient, however, for one individual to serve as both caretaker and trustee.

Q 5:22   How might a participant make a beneficiary designation to provide for his or her pet animal's care?

The following example illustrates how a participant might provide for the care of a pet without using a trust.

Example. Gary wants his cat to be properly cared for after Gary's death. Gary is a man of modest income and little wealth. He anticipates that almost none of his property will pass by his will. Gary has a small balance (to which he no longer contributes) under a retirement plan. To provide for his cat, Gary makes the following provisions:

Beneficiary designation—Mary Johnson 100%

Will

I give my cat, Lady Lucy of Canterbury Tails, and any other animals that I may own at the time of my death, to Mary Johnson (who currently resides at 234 Sunset Road, Indianapolis, Indiana), with the request that she treat them as companion animals. To provide for the care of these animals, I have made a separate financial provision for Mary Johnson, and I request (but do not direct) that she use that money for the care of these animals.

If a participant has relatives who might challenge the beneficiary designation, the participant should consider providing only a reasonable amount of money for the care of any pet. A large sum of money for the pet may prompt relatives to challenge the beneficiary designation.

An unreasonably large bequest, gift, trust, or beneficiary designation in favor of a pet animal may be capricious and therefore legally ineffective. [See, e.g., Wis. Stat. Ann. § 701.11(1) (West 1981); see generally Restatement (Second) of Trusts § 124; 2 Austin Wakeman Scott & William Franklin Fratcher, *Scott on Trusts* § 124 (4th ed. 1987)] Sometimes, a court will reduce the amount set aside for the care of the pet animal. [See, e.g., In re Templeton Estate, 4 Fiduc. Rep. 2d (Bisel) 172 (Pa. Orphans' Ct. 1984); In re Lyon's Estate, 67 Pa. D. & C.2d 474 (Orphans' Ct. 1974); see generally National Conference of Commissioners on Uniform State Laws, Uniform Probate Code § 2-907(c)(6) (1998)]

Q 5:23   Who is taxed on a distribution set aside for the care of a pet animal?

If a distribution is paid to a pet's caretaker who does not serve as a trustee, the distribution is income to that person.

If a distribution is paid to a trustee who serves under a valid trust (see Q 5:21), the distribution is income to the trust. A valid pet trust that is legally unenforceable will nevertheless be treated as a trust for federal income tax purposes.

A pet trust is subject to federal income tax at the rates that apply to a married individual who files a separate return. Although a trust normally has a deduction in the amount of trust distributions, "since the amounts of income required to be distributed . . . and amounts properly paid, credited, or required to be distributed under [the relevant Internal Revenue Code sections] are limited to distributions intended for beneficiaries, a deduction under those sections is not available for distributions for the benefit of a pet animal. Similarly, such distributions are not taxed to anyone. . . ." [Rev. Rul. 76-476, 1976-2 C.B. 192] These rules are consistent with the idea that trust income should be taxed only once.

Charitable Gifts

Q 5:24   May a participant name a charity as a beneficiary?

Yes, a participant may name a charitable organization as a beneficiary.

Although some states previously had statutes that would void some charitable gifts made soon before a donor's death or of more than a specified portion of the donor's estate, those statutes were unconstitutional. [See, e.g., Estate of Cavill, 329 A.2d 503 (Pa. 1974)] States repealed all of these statutes.

Although a charitable organization employer should avoid inappropriately inducing its employees to designate the organization as a beneficiary, an absolute bar is unnecessary. Many people who have worked for a charity or in education are inclined to continue that work by making a gift to a charitable organization.

Practice Pointer. For someone who already has decided to make charitable gifts on death and expects his or her estate to be subject to a significant federal estate tax, some financial planners suggest that using a deferred compensation plan benefit might be an efficient way to provide the gift. They suggest this because deferred compensation is subject to both federal income tax and federal estate tax, while a capital asset enjoys a "stepped-up" basis (except for deaths in 2010) and is not subject to income tax until the beneficiary sells the asset. Other planners point out that the federal income tax deduction for federal estate tax attributable to property that is income in respect of a decedent partially mitigates the "double tax." [See I.R.C. § 691(c)] Along with this, they argue that a deferred compensation plan might permit longer income tax deferral while post-death income on capital assets will subject the beneficiary to income tax. Considering which course might be "right" turns on the donor's and the planner's assumptions. Further, nontax factors might favor a particular approach.

Q 5:25 If a charity is a beneficiary, what is the tax treatment of the deferred compensation?

Although deferred compensation will be included in a participant's taxable estate for federal estate tax purposes, an estate will have a deduction for the amount that properly passes to charity. [I.R.C. § 2055] Further, although distributions from a deferred compensation plan will be included in the distributee's income for federal income tax purposes, a charitable organization does not pay federal income tax on its receipts from charitable gifts. [I.R.C. § 501(a)]

Simultaneous Death; Absentees

Q 5:26 What should a payor do if there is doubt about the order of deaths?

For many deferred compensation plans, the order of deaths between a participant and a beneficiary is irrelevant. A carefully drafted plan should state that a person cannot be a beneficiary if he or she is not living at the time a benefit is to be paid or becomes payable. Even in the absence of such language, an ERISA plan administrator's procedure may adopt the same rule. [See Clouse v. Philadelphia Electric Co., 787 F. Supp. 93, 15 Employee Benefits Cas. (BNA) 1347 (E.D. Pa. 1992)]

If it becomes necessary for an ERISA plan administrator to determine the order of deaths between a participant and a beneficiary and the retirement plan does not provide a presumption concerning the order of deaths, it may be prudent for the plan administrator to follow either the 1940 version of the Uniform Simultaneous Death Act or the Uniform Probate Code.

The "old" Uniform Simultaneous Death Act, adopted by many states, provides that if "there is no sufficient evidence that the persons have died otherwise than simultaneously, the property of each person shall be disposed of as if he [or she] had survived [the other person]." [National Conference of Commissioners on Uniform State Laws, Uniform Simultaneous Death Act § 1 (1940)]

The Uniform Probate Code provides that an individual cannot qualify as an heir unless he or she survives the first decedent for 120 hours. Further, the person who would claim through the heir has the burden of proving the duration that the heir survived the first decedent. [National Conference of Commissioners on Uniform State Laws, Uniform Probate Code §§ 2-104, -702 (1998)] The 1991 version of the Uniform Simultaneous Death Act has a substantially identical rule.

> **Practice Pointer.** For tax planning purposes, a wealthy participant may prefer to vary these "default" rules by express language in his or her beneficiary designation. [See, e.g., Treas. Reg. § 20.2056(e)-2(e)] Even if state law applies to the plan, state law will permit a different provision if it is stated by the plan or the participant's beneficiary designation. [See, e.g., N.Y. Est. Powers & Trusts Law § 2-1.6(e) (Westlaw 2002)]

Alternatively, a common-disaster clause or a delay clause of up to six months does not disqualify property for the federal estate tax marital deduction. [I.R.C. § 2056(b)(3); Treas. Reg. § 20.2056(b)-3(b)]

If it becomes necessary for an ERISA plan administrator to determine the order of deaths between or among potential beneficiaries and the retirement plan does not provide a presumption concerning the order of deaths, it may be prudent for the plan administrator to indulge a presumption that all persons who died within a few days of one another died at the same time and survived to the relevant time.

If a plan administrator decides claims under a non-ERISA plan, the plan administrator may be required to follow state law.

Q 5:27 What should a payor do when someone says a participant or beneficiary is absent and presumed dead?

In ordinary circumstances, a plan administrator or payor should not presume a participant's or beneficiary's death. Instead, a plan administrator or payor should require the claimant (usually, the next beneficiary) to prove the absentee's death by an appropriate court order.

Under the common law, an individual was presumed dead if he or she had been absent for a continuous period of seven years. [See, e.g., 20 Pa. Cons. Stat. Ann. § 5701(b) & cmt. (West Supp. 2002)] Likewise, an absentee's exposure to a specific peril was a sufficient ground for presuming death. [See, e.g., 20 Pa. Cons. Stat. Ann. § 5701(c) & cmt. (West Supp. 2002)] Further, death may be inferred if survival of the absentee would be beyond human expectation or experience. [See, e.g., In re Katz's Estate, 135 Misc. 861, 239 N.Y.S. 722 (Sup. Ct. 1930)] Courts sometimes required considerable evidence of an unexplained absence. For example, an individual's absence from the places where his relatives resided together with his failure to communicate with his relatives was not enough to show that he was absent from his residence without explanation. [Estate of Morrison v. Roswell, 92 Ill. 2d 207, 441 N.E.2d 68, 65 Ill. Dec. 276 (1982)]

In 1939, the Uniform Absence as Evidence of Death and Absentees Property Act reversed the common-law rules: the fact that an individual had been absent for seven years (or any duration) or had been exposed to a specific peril did not set up a presumption of death; instead, these facts were merely evidence for a court or jury to consider in making its own finding of whether the absentee's death had occurred. [See National Conference of Commissioners on Uniform State Laws, Uniform Absence as Evidence of Death and Absentees Property Act § 1 (1939); Armstrong v. Pilot Life Insurance Co., 656 S.W.2d 18 (Tenn. Ct. App. 1983)]

The Uniform Probate Code, portions of which have been adopted in many states, returns to a presumption. An individual is presumed dead after he or she has been absent for a continuous period, such as three, four, five, or seven years. [Cf. Minn. Stat. § 576.141 (West 2001); N.J. Stat. Ann. § 3B:27-1 (West Supp. 2001); N.Y. Est. Powers & Trusts Law § 2-1.7 (McKinney 1998); 20 Pa. Cons. Stat. Ann. § 5701(c) (West Supp. 2002)] However, a person who seeks a declaration of the absentee's death must demonstrate to a court's satisfaction that the absentee has not been heard from after diligent search or inquiry and that his or her absence is not satisfactorily explained. [National Conference of Commissioners on Uniform State Laws, Uniform Probate Code § 1-107(5) (1998); see also 20 Pa. Cons. Stat. Ann. §§ 5702–5705 (West Supp. 2002)]

Unless sufficient evidence proves that death occurred sooner, the end of the five-year period is deemed the date of death. [National Conference of Commissioners on Uniform State Laws, Uniform Probate Code § 1-107(5) (1998); see also Hubbard v. Equitable Life Assurance Society of the United States, 248 Wis. 340, 21 N.W.2d 665 (1946); Hogaboam v. Metropolitan Life Insurance Co., 248 Wis. 146, 21 N.W.2d 268 (1946)]

The presumption of an absentee's death does not necessarily apply to all property in the same way. For example, some states do not use the presumption to provide a life insurance death benefit. [See, e.g., Armstrong v. Pilot Life Insurance Co., 656 S.W.2d 18 (Tenn. Ct. App. 1983)]

Usually, the person who would benefit from the absentee's death bears the burden of proof. [Id.]

Note. The terrorist attacks of September 11, 2001, focused renewed attention on laws that permit a finding of death based on exposure to a specific peril. [See N.J. Stat. Ann. §§ 3B:27-1, -6 (as amended by Pub. L. No. 2001, ch. 247); N.Y. Est. Powers & Trusts Law § 2.17(b); 20 Pa. Cons. Stat. Ann. § 5701(c) (West Supp. 2002); Chiaramonte v. Chiaramonte, 435 N.Y.S.2d 523 (Sup. Ct. 1981); Zucker's Will, 219 N.Y.S.2d 72 (Sup. Ct. 1961); Bobrow's Estate, 179 N.Y.S.2d 742 (Sup. Ct. 1958); Brevoort's Will, 73 N.Y.S.2d 216 (Sup. Ct. 1947)]

An ERISA plan's administrator need not follow state law and instead may make its own rules and use discretion in deciding whether or when a person's death occurred. [See Estate of Slack ex rel. Apostal v. Laborer's Welfare & Pension Fund, 195 F. Supp. 2d 1052, 27 Employee Benefits Cas. (BNA) 2670 (N.D. Ill. 2002)]

Marriage

Q 5:28   Why is understanding the law of marriage important to beneficiary designations?

An important restraint on a beneficiary designation is a spouse's rights. Of course, these rights turn on a person's showing that he or she was a participant's spouse. Although many people are accustomed to thinking of the marriage certificate as evidence that a valid marriage occurred, sometimes it is unclear whether a marriage existed. The questions under this heading explain some basics of marriage, and then explain differences between ceremonial marriage and informal or common-law marriage.

Q 5:29   What is marriage?

Marriage is a civil contract and a relationship or status by which each of two persons agrees to live with the other as spouses, to the exclusion of other persons. States regulate marriage as part of their police power. Most states recognize a marriage contracted in another state, unless the marriage is contrary to public policy.

Q 5:30   What is a void marriage?

A void marriage is one that is invalid from its inception and cannot be made valid. A marriage is void if:

- The parties are too closely related; or
- Either party is married to someone else.

In some states, a later "marriage" becomes valid on the end of an earlier marriage if both parties to the later "marriage" were unaware that the earlier marriage was undissolved when they entered into the later "marriage." In most states, a marriage is void if the parties are of the same sex, and a restriction against such a marriage is not unconstitutional. Either party may "walk away" from a void marriage without waiting for a divorce or annulment.

Q 5:31   What is a voidable marriage?

A voidable marriage is one that is initially invalid but remains in effect unless ended by a court order. For example, a marriage is voidable if either party was underage, drunk, or otherwise legally incompetent. Likewise, a marriage is voidable if one party used fraud, duress, or force to induce the other party to "agree" to the marriage. The parties may ratify an otherwise voidable marriage by words or conduct after the removal of the impediment that made the marriage voidable.

Ceremonial Marriage

Q 5:32 What is a ceremonial marriage?

A ceremonial marriage is a marriage performed according to a state statute. Most people prefer a ceremonial marriage to an informal or common-law marriage because a ceremonial marriage is easier to prove.

A license to marry is required and is furnished by a state court or official upon approval of an application designed to check the parties' eligibility to marry. In most states, an application must state identifying information, information about each prior marriage of either applicant, that neither of the applicants is afflicted with a communicable disease, and other facts necessary to find whether there is a legal impediment to the proposed marriage. A refusal to issue a marriage license is reviewable by a court. An application for a marriage license is a public record.

If either party is a minor or mentally incapacitated, most states require at least a guardian's approval, and sometimes a court's approval.

Most states provide that a judge, government official, or clergyperson may perform a ceremony. Some people use the term "civil marriage" to describe a ceremony led by a judge or government official, as distiguished from one solemnized by a clergyperson. Some states permit the parties to perform their own marriage ceremony. Some states permit (and others prohibit) a proxy marriage—a ceremony in which someone stands in for an absent party.

A failure to comply with statutory rules does not necessarily result in a void marriage. Sometimes a defect makes a marriage voidable rather than void. In a state that permits common-law marriage, a defective ceremonial marriage often results in a valid common-law marriage.

Q 5:33 What is the effect of a marriage certificate?

A person who wants to prove that a marriage exists (or existed until the other person's death) may refer to the marriage certificate as evidence of the marriage's validity. Unless someone else shows persuasive evidence of a defect, a marriage certificate is usually strong evidence that the marriage occurred.

Common-Law Marriage

Q 5:34 What is common-law marriage?

A common-law marriage (perhaps more appropriately called an informal marriage) is a marriage that was not solemnized by a ceremony, but was created by the simple agreement of the parties.

Each individual must:

1. Be legally capable of making a marriage contract;

2. State his or her present agreement to the marriage (or to the relation of husband and wife); and

3. Agree to live with his or her spouse as husband or wife to the exclusion of all others.

Although some people mistakenly assume that a period of cohabitation results in a common-law marriage, that is not true under any state's law. Conversely, no period of cohabitation is necessary; the present agreement to the marriage is all that is needed. [See generally 2 James Kent, *Commentaries on American Law* [1794] 86–87 (New York: O. Halsted, 2d ed. 1832)]

If the law of a state that recognizes common-law marriage (see Q 5:35) applies, the couple may be married, notwithstanding the absence of any ceremony or writing. In an appropriate context, even an implication of consent to a marriage might be sufficient. [In re Garges' Estate, 474 Pa. 237, 378 A.2d 307 (1977)] Also, a marriage ceremony that had a defect is likely to result in a common-law marriage. [See, e.g., In re Larry's Estate, 29 Fiduc. Rep. (Bisel) 298 (Pa. Orphans' Ct. 1979)]

Practice Pointer. Usually, the absence of a ceremony (and the absence of witnesses, other than the parties) makes it difficult to prove that a common-law marriage exists or existed. Often, there is an evidence law rule or presumption against the claimant testifying to the creation of the relationship. [See, e.g., 20 Pa. Cons. Stat. Ann. § 2209 (West Supp. 2002); 42 Pa. Cons. Stat. Ann. § 5930 (West 2000); see also Estate of Stauffer v. Stauffer, 476 A.2d 354 (Pa. 1984); Wagner's Estate, 398 Pa. 531 (1960); Estate of Corace v. Graeser, 527 A.2d 1058 (Pa. Super. Ct. 1987)] Courts consider evidence of how each individual described the relationship to third persons and how third persons understood the relationship. However, either spouse's denial of the marriage in records such as a driver's license, Social Security claims, tax returns, insurance applications, bank accounts, and wage records does not necessarily deny a common-law marriage. [See, e.g., Dal-worth Trucking Co. v. Bulen, 924 S.W.2d 728 (Tex. App. 1996); Estate of Giessel, 734 S.W.2d 27 (Tex. App. 1987)] The burden of proving a common-law marriage is on the person who asserts that it existed. [See, e.g., Driscoll v. Driscoll, 220 Kan. 225, 227, 552 P.2d 629 (1976); In re Estate of Gavula, 490 Pa. 535, 417 A.2d 168 (1980); In re Estate of Stauffer, 315 Pa. Super. 591, 462 A.2d 750 (1983), *rev'd on other grounds*, 504 Pa. 626, 476 A.2d 354 (1983). But see Fiedler v. National Tube Co., 161 Pa. Super. 155, 53 A.2d 821 (1947)]

Q 5:35   Which states recognize common-law marriage?

Table 5-1 shows whether a state recognizes common-law marriage for a marriage made within the state. For states in which a statute expressly provides the date after which common-law marriage cannot be made in the state, the table shows the effective date. For states in which nonrecognition results from a court decision, the date of the court decision may provide guidance concerning the date after which a common-law marriage could not be made in the state.

All states recognize a marriage that, even if it does not meet all requirements of local law, was valid under the laws of the state in which the spouses lived at the time they entered into the marriage. [Restatement (Second) of Conflict of Laws § 283(2) (1969)] Likewise, states recognize a marriage made according to any Native American Indian law or custom. [See, e.g., Buck v. Branson, 34 Okla. 807, 127 P. 436 (1912); Oklahoma Land Co. v. Thomas, 34 Okla. 681, 127 P. 8 (1912); People ex rel. La Forte v. Rubin, 98 N.Y.S. 787 (Sup. Ct. 1905); Kobogum v. Jackson Iron Co., 76 Mich. 498, 43 N.W. 602 (1899); Earl v. Godley, 42 Minn. 361, 44 N.W. 254 (1890); Wall v. Williamson, 8 Ala. 48 (1844); Morgan v. McGhee, 24 Tenn. 13 (1844); Dirion v. Brewster, 20 Ohio App. 298, 151 N.E. 818, 4 Ohio Law Abs. 534 (1925); Industrial Commissioner v. Miller, 18 Ohio Law Abs. 244 (Ohio Ct. App. 1934); Ryan v. Ryan, 84 Ohio App. 139, 6 N.E.2d 44 (1948)] Further, some states that recognize common-law marriage internally recognize a marriage that the spouses entered into while they lived in another state, notwithstanding that the marriage was invalid in the other state. [See, e.g., Dibble v. Dibble, 88 Ohio App. 490, 100 N.E.2d 451 (1950) (before enactment of Ohio Rev. Code Ann. § 3105.12) (Anderson 2000)]

Note. In many states that do not recognize a common-law marriage made in the state, children born during an invalid marriage may nevertheless be presumed to be the children of both the child's mother and the man who would be her common-law husband.

Caution. Because of the recognition that states give to other states' and nations' laws, it is possible for a common-law marriage to exist anywhere in the United States.

Although the states that recognize informal marriage are the minority, the mobility of Americans sometimes makes possible an informal marriage. Even a weekend trip across state lines can result in a marriage. [See, e.g., Tornese v. Tornese, 233 A.D.2d 316, 649 N.Y.S.2d 177 (1996); Carpenter v. Carpenter, 208 A.D.2d 882, 617 N.Y.S.2d 903 (1994)] Further, among those states that currently do not recognize common-law marriage, almost half allowed common-law marriage at a time when persons still living now might have married.

Table 5-1. State Common-Law Marriage Recognition

State	Recognition of Common-Law Marriage Made in the State	Statute or Court Decision
Alabama	Recognized	Ex parte Creel, 719 So. 2d 783 (Ala. 1998)
Alaska	No longer recognized	Alaska Stat. §§ 25.05.011, .311 (West 2000); Edwards v. Franke, 364 P.2d 60 (Alaska 1961); United States v. Lustig, 555 F.2d 737 (9th Cir.), *cert. denied*, 434 U.S. 926 (1977), *cert. denied*, 434 U.S. 1045 (1978)

Table 5-1. State Common-Law Marriage Recognition (*cont'd*)

State	*Recognition of Common-Law Marriage Made in the State*	*Statute or Court Decision*
Arizona	No longer recognized	Levy v. Blakely, 41 Ariz. 327, 18 P.2d 263 (1933)
Arkansas	No longer recognized	Furth v. Furth, 97 Ark. 272, 133 S.W. 1037 (1911); see also Rockefeller v. Rockefeller, 335 Ark. 3, 980 S.W.2d 255 (1998) (informal marriage not recognized, although woman lived with a man over several years, bore three children by him, incurred joint debt with him, jointly leased property with him, and used his name, and the couple described themselves to the community as married)
California	Not recognized since 1895	See Elden v. Sheldon, 46 Cal. 3d 267, 758 P.2d 582, 250 Cal. Rptr. 254 (1988)
Colorado	Recognized	Nugent v. Nugent, 955 P.2d 584 (Colo. Ct. App. 1998); Graham v. Graham, 130 Colo. 225, 274 P.2d 605 (1954); Taylor v. Taylor, 7 Colo. App. 549, 44 P. 675 (1896), *aff'd*, 10 Colo. App. 303, 50 P. 1049 (1897)
Connecticut	No longer recognized	McAnerney v. McAnerney, 165 Conn. 277, 334 A.2d 437 (1973)
Delaware	No longer recognized	Wilmington Trust Co. v. Hendrixson, 31 Del. (1 Harr.) 303, 114 A. 215 (1921)
District of Columbia	Recognized	Berryman v. Thorne, 700 A.2d 181 (D.C. 1997)
Florida	Not recognized if made after Jan. 1, 1968	Fla. Stat. Ann. § 741.211 (West 1997)
Georgia	Not recognized if made on or after Jan. 1, 1997	Ga. Code Ann. § 19-3-1.1 (LEXIS 1999)
Hawaii	No longer recognized	Parke v. Parke, 25 Haw. 397 (Haw. Terr. 1920)
Idaho	Not recognized if made on or after Jan. 1, 1996	Idaho Code § 32-201 (Michie 1996)
Illinois	Not recognized if made after June 30, 1905	750 Ill. Comp. Stat. Ann. 5/214 (1999)

Table 5-1. State Common-Law Marriage Recognition (*cont'd*)

State	Recognition of Common-Law Marriage Made in the State	Statute or Court Decision
Indiana	Not recognized if made after Jan. 1, 1958	Ind. Code Ann. § 31-11-8-5 (West 1999)
Iowa	Recognized	Iowa Dep't of Human Servs. ex rel. Greenhaw v. Stewart, 579 N.W.2d 32 (Iowa 1998)
Kansas	Recognized	Shaddox v. Schoenberger, 19 Kan. App. 2d 361, 869 P.2d 249 (1994); Driscoll v. Driscoll, 220 Kan. 225, 552 P.2d 629 (1976); see also Kan. Stat. Ann. § 60-1609 (1994)
Kentucky	No longer recognized except under workers' compensation	Elkhorn Coal Corp. v. Tackett, 243 Ky. 694, 49 S.W.2d 571 (1932)
Louisiana	No longer recognized	La. Civ. Code Ann. art. 87 (West 1999)
Maine	No longer recognized	Pierce v. Secretary of Dep't of Health, Educ. & Welfare, 254 A.2d 46 (Me. 1969)
Maryland	No longer recognized	Jennings v. Jennings, 20 Md. App. 369, 315 A.2d 816 (Ct. Spec. App. 1974)
Massachusetts	No longer recognized	Davis v. Misiano, 373 Mass. 261, 366 N.E.2d 752 (1977)
Michigan	Not recognized if made after Jan. 1, 1957	Mich. Comp. Laws Ann. § 551.2 (West Supp. 2002); Mich. Stat. Ann. § 25.2
Minnesota	Not recognized if made after Apr. 26, 1941	Minn. Stat. Ann. § 517.01 (West Supp. 2002)
Mississippi	Not recognized if made after Apr. 5, 1956	Miss. Code Ann. § 93-1-15 (1999)
Missouri	No longer recognized	Mo. Ann. Stat. § 451.040 (Vernon 1997)
Montana	Recognized	Mont. Code Ann. § 40-1-403 (Westlaw 2002)
Nebraska	Not recognized if made after 1923	Neb. Rev. Stat. Ann. § 42-104 (Westlaw 2002)

Table 5-1. State Common-Law Marriage Recognition (*cont'd*)

State	Recognition of Common-Law Marriage Made in the State	Statute or Court Decision
Nevada	Not recognized if made after Mar. 29, 1943	Nev. Rev. Stat. Ann. § 122.010 (Westlaw 2002)
New Hampshire	Recognized for survivorship but not for divorce	N.H. Rev. Stat. Ann. § 457:39 (Butterworth 1992)
New Jersey	Not recognized if made after Nov. 30, 1939	N.J. Stat. Ann. § 37:1-10 (West 1968)
New Mexico	No longer recognized	In re Gabaldon's Estate, 38 N.M. 392, 34 P.2d 672 (1934)
New York	Not recognized if made after Apr. 28, 1933	N.Y. Dom. Rel. Law § 11 (McKinney 1999); 1933 N.Y. Laws 606
North Carolina	No longer recognized	N.C. Gen. Stat. § 51-1 (Matthew Bender 2002); State v. Samuel, 19 N.C. 177 (1836)
North Dakota	No longer recognized	1890 N.D. Laws 91; Schumacher v. Great N. Ry., 23 N.D. 231, 136 N.W. 85 (1912)
Ohio	Not recognized if made after Oct. 10, 1991	Ohio Rev. Code Ann. § 3105.12 (Anderson 2000)
Oklahoma	Recognized	Boyd v. Monsey Constr. Co., 959 P.2d 612 (Okla. Ct. App. 1998)
Oregon	No longer recognized	Huard v. McTeigh, 113 Or. 279, 232 P. 658, 39 A.L.R. 528 (1925)
Pennsylvania	Recognized for marriages before Sept. 17, 2003; possibly not recognized by some courts in some matters for marriages after Sept. 17, 2003	23 Pa. Cons. Stat. Ann. § 1103 (West 2001); Staudenmayer v. Staudenmayer, 552 Pa. 253, 714 A.2d 1016 (Pa. 1998); but see PNC Bank v. Workers' Compensation Appeal Bd., 831 A.2d 1269 (Pa. Commw. Ct. 2003)
Rhode Island	Recognized	Lovegrove v. McCutcheon, 712 A.2d 874 (R.I. 1998)
South Carolina	Recognized	Barker v. Barker, 330 S.C. 361, 499 S.E.2d 503 (Ct. App. 1998)
South Dakota	Not recognized if made after June 30, 1959	S.D. Codified Laws § 25-1-29 (LEXIS 1999)

Table 5-1. State Common-Law Marriage Recognition (*cont'd*)

State	Recognition of Common-Law Marriage Made in the State	Statute or Court Decision
Tennessee	No longer recognized	Troxel v. Jones, 45 Tenn. App. 264, 322 S.W.2d 251 (1958)
Texas	Recognized	Tex. Fam. Code Ann. § 1.91-101 (West 1998); DeShazo v. Christian, 191 S.W.2d 495 (Tex. Civ. App. 1946)
Utah	Recognized	Utah Code Ann. § 30-1-4.5 (1998)
Vermont	No longer recognized	Morrill v. Palmer, 68 Vt. 1, 33 A. 829 (1895)
Virginia	No longer recognized	Va. Code Ann. § 20-31 (Westlaw 2002); Offield v. Davis, 100 Va. 250, 4 Va. Sup. Ct. Rep. 206 (1902)
Washington	No longer recognized	In re McLaughlin's Estate, 4 Wash. 570, 30 P. 651, 16 L.R.A. 699 (1892)
West Virginia	No longer recognized	Beverlin v. Beverlin, 29 W. Va. 732, 3 S.E. 36 (1877)
Wisconsin	No longer recognized	Wis. Stat. Ann. § 765.16 (West 1993)
Wyoming	No longer recognized	In re Roberts' Estate, 58 Wyo. 438, 133 P.2d 492 (1943); In re Reeves' Estate, 58 Wyo. 432, 133 P.2d 503 (1943)

Q 5:36 How does common-law marriage affect a non-ERISA benefit?

If a participant has a spouse, state law (or American Indian tribe's law) may provide that some or all of a deferred compensation benefit belongs to the spouse (see Q 5:17). If the law of a state that recognizes common-law marriage (see Q 5:35) applies, a couple might be considered, notwithstanding the absence of any ceremony or writing.

A plan administrator or payor is protected in making a payment according to the beneficiary designation. For a benefit paid under a plan that is not governed by ERISA, the distributee receives any payment subject to the spouse's rights.

Example. George and Carmen lived in Pennsylvania throughout their working lives. George was a railroad conductor. In early 1993, before George met Carmen, George named his brother, Bill, as the beneficiary under George's deferred compensation plan. Even after his marriage to Carmen in late 1993 and the birth of their children, Diana in 1994 and Samuel in 1996, it never occurred to George that he should change his beneficiary designation. He did not even remember making one. After George's retirement, George and Carmen moved to a retirement community in Cazenovia, New York. George died without having made a will. After George died, Bill sent in a claim to the insurance company, which paid Bill all of George's deferred compensation plan balance. On his death, George's deferred compensation balance was $200,000 and his probate assets were $60,000. There was nothing else.

(For ease of illustration, this example omits the family exemption, the homestead allowance, funeral and administration expenses, debts, taxes of all kinds, and lawyers' fees.)

If Carmen does not elect to take an elective share of George's augmented estate, George's estate will be divided as follows:

	DCP Benefit	Probate Assets	Augmented Estate	Share
Carmen	0	$55,000	$55,000	21%
Diana	0	$2,500	$2,500	1%
Samuel	0	$2,500	$2,500	1%
Bill	$200,000	0	$200,000	77%
Totals	$200,000	$60,000	$260,000	100%

[N.Y. Est. Powers & Trusts Law § 4-1.1(a)(1) (McKinney 1998)]

If Carmen elects to take an elective share of George's augmented estate, George's estate will be divided as follows:

	Augmented Estate	Share of Augmented Estate
Carmen	$86,666.67	33.33%
Diana	0	
Samuel	0	
Bill	$173,333.33	66.66%
Totals	$260,000.00	100%

[N.Y. Est. Powers & Trusts Law §5-1.1-A(a)(2), (c) (McKinney 1999); see also National Conference of Commissioners on Uniform State Laws, Uniform Probate Code §§ 2-201, -202 (1998)]

Because George's probate estate is insufficient to pay Carmen the amount to which she is entitled, Bill must pay Carmen $26,666.67 ($86,666.67 – $60,000.00). [N.Y. Est. Powers & Trusts Law § 5-1.1-A(c) (McKinney 1999); see also National Conference of Commissioners on Uniform State Laws, Uniform Probate Code § 2-203 (1998)]

Dower or curtesy (if recognized by state law) might provide additional or related rights to a spouse. Many states, however, abolished dower and curtesy. [See, e.g., N.J. Stat. Ann. § 3B:28-1; Pa. Act of June 7, 1917, Pub. L. No. 429; see generally National Conference of Commissioners on Uniform State Laws,

Uniform Probate Code § 2-113 (1998)] In other states, a spouse's election of an elective share is "in lieu of" all dower and curtesy rights. [See, e.g., N.Y. Est. Powers & Trusts Law § 5-1.1-A(c)(8) (McKinney 1999)]

Q 5:37 How does common-law marriage affect a beneficiary designation under an ERISA plan?

An ERISA-governed deferred compensation plan need not but may provide that some or all of a plan benefit belongs to a spouse.

If a couple lived (or even traveled) in a state that recognizes (or recognized) common-law marriage (see Q 5:35), the couple may be married, notwithstanding the absence of any ceremony or writing. A recognized common-law marriage is no less a marriage than is a ceremonial marriage. [See 5 C.F.R. § 630.1202]

Example. Harold and Wendy lived together in Alabama. Harold never made any beneficiary designation under his employer's ERISA-governed deferred compensation plan. Although not required to by ERISA, the plan provides that a surviving spouse is entitled to the participant's account. When Wendy calls the human resources office to ask about this plan benefit, the manager tells Wendy that the employer has no record that Wendy is Harold's spouse. Wendy files the plan's claim form, and attaches to it an affidavit that states facts that, if correct, would constitute a common-law marriage under Alabama law. Because the employer, acting as plan administrator, does not receive any contrary information, it decides that Wendy is Harold's surviving spouse. The plan administrator instructs the custodian to pay the full benefit as Wendy requested.

Practice Pointer. An ERISA-governed plan's administrator must act as an expert when deciding plan claims. In administering a church plan or governmental plan, a plan administrator or employer must act at least in good faith when deciding plan claims. Therefore, a plan administrator should obtain expert legal advice to evaluate a person's claim that he or she is or was the common-law spouse of a participant.

Q 5:38 How does the common-law marriage of a same-sex couple affect a beneficiary designation?

If a participant has a spouse, state law may provide that some or all of a deferred compensation benefit belongs to his or her spouse (see Q 5:17). If a couple lived (or even traveled) in a state that recognizes (or recognized) common-law marriage, the couple may be married, notwithstanding the absence of any ceremony or writing. Many states recognize common-law marriage (see Q 5:35).

Most people assume—and at least one court has found—that common-law marriage does not apply to a couple in which both persons are of the same sex. [DeSanto v. Barnsley, 328 Pa. Super. 181, 476 A.2d 952 (1984)] However, such a discrimination might be unconstitutional, and therefore of no effect. [See U.S. Const. art. IV, § 1, & amend. V; Saenz v. Roe, 526 U.S. 489 (1999); Romer v. Evans, 517 U.S. 620 (1996); Loving v. Virginia, 388 U.S. 1 (1967)]

According to a federal statute, if either spouse of a same-sex couple pursues his or her rights in a state other than the state in which they married, the forum state need not recognize the marriage established in the other state:

> No State . . . shall be required to give effect to any public act, record, or judicial proceeding of any other State . . . respecting a relationship between persons of the same sex that is treated as a marriage under the laws of such other State . . . , or a right or claim arising from such relationship.

[28 U.S.C. § 1738C]

It is unclear whether this statute is the law, because it might be unconstitutional. [See U.S. Const. art. IV, § 1, & amend. V; Saenz v. Roe, 526 U.S. 489 (1999); Romer v. Evans, 517 U.S. 620 (1996); Loving v. Virginia, 388 U.S. 1 (1967)]

Practice Pointer. A participant in a non-ERISA plan who is part of a same-sex couple and wants to name a beneficiary other than his or her spouse should seek expert legal advice.

Q 5:39 How does a Vermont civil union of a same-sex couple affect a beneficiary designation?

If a participant is or was a party to a Vermont civil union, state law might provide that, after the participant's death, some or all of a plan benefit must be provided to the other party to the civil union to the extent necessary to provide such a spouse his or her property rights. (See Q 5:17.)

Vermont law provides that same-sex couples must have the opportunity to obtain the same benefits and protections afforded by Vermont law to married opposite-sex couples. [Vermont Const. ch. I, art. 7; Baker v. Vermont, 744 A.2d 864, 1999 Vt. LEXIS 406 (1999)] Under Vermont statute, the same-sex parties to a civil union have the same benefits, protections, and responsibilities as are provided for spouses in any other marriage. [Vt. Stat. Ann. tit. 15, §§ 1201(2), 1204(a) (Westlaw 2002)] This rule applies whether the source of law is statute, administrative regulation, court rule, policy, common law, or any other source of civil law. [Vt. Stat. Ann. tit. 15, § 1204(a) (Westlaw 2002)] Further, a party to a civil union is included in any definition or use of the term "spouse" as that term is used in any Vermont law. [Vt. Stat. Ann. tit. 15, § 1204(b) (Westlaw 2002)]

Vermont law provides that a surviving spouse has a right to at least one-third of his or her spouse's personal estate. [Vt. Stat. Ann. tit. 14, §§ 401–402 (Westlaw 2002)] If a church plan or governmental plan is not governed by ERISA, a court has power to enter an order relating to nonprobate property, such as a deferred compensation plan benefit, when necessary to give effect to a surviving spouse's property rights. [Vt. Stat. Ann. tit. 14, § 1721 (Westlaw 2002)]

Thus, a participant who is a party to a Vermont civil union and wants to name a beneficiary other than his or her spouse should seek expert legal advice.

Q 5:40   What happens if a participant has two spouses?

Although most Americans assume that it is impossible for a person to have more than one legitimate spouse at the same time, this is not necessarily so if he or she married in another nation. While a state may choose not to recognize a marriage that it finds contrary to its strong public policy, a state may give deference to the customs and laws of another nation. At least one state court has held that a decedent can have more than one spouse for inheritance purposes. [Estate of Dalip Singh Bir, 83 Cal. App. 2d 256, 188 P.2d 499 (1948) (more than 50 years before the decedent's death in California, two women had married him in Punjab Province of British India "according to the law and manner of the Jat community")] However, a court might find that a relationship or status that is recognized under another nation's law or custom is not the same kind of relationship or status that the U.S. state recognizes as marriage or spouse, respectively.

Community Property

Q 5:41   What is community property?

Community property is a term that lawyers use to refer to a regime that treats each item of property acquired by either spouse of a married couple during the marriage and while the couple is domiciled in a community property state (see Q 5:42) as owned equally by each spouse. Each spouse's ownership exists presently, notwithstanding that the other spouse currently may hold title to or have control over the property. Under these laws, deferred compensation generally is community property to the extent that deferrals were made while the participant was married and domiciled in a community property jurisdiction.

In a separate property system, which prevails in 41 states and all U.S. possessions other than Puerto Rico, an item of property normally belongs to the person who has title to it, paid for it, earned it, or otherwise acquired it. Although any property owned by a married person may become subject to equitable distribution on a divorce or other marital dissolution, the property belongs completely to the person who owns it until a court orders otherwise. For information on domestic relations orders, see chapter 14.

Q 5:42   Which states are community property states?

Currently, Arizona, California, Idaho, Louisiana, Nevada, New Mexico, Texas, Washington, and Wisconsin are community property states. Puerto Rico, a possession of the United States, also is a community property jurisdiction.

Alaska allows a choice between a separate property and a community property regime. The separate property regime applies unless the married couple agrees to use a community property regime. If the couple chooses community property, they may use a written community property agreement or a community property trust to vary some of the state law provisions that otherwise would govern their community property. [Alaska Stat. § 34.77.020 et seq.]

California law permits a married couple to accept a conveyance as "community property with right of survivorship." [Cal. Civ. Code § 682.1]

In Texas, community property law is a right protected by the State Constitution. [Tex. Const. [1845], art. VII, § 19]

Although American community property regimes are based primarily on the Spanish system, community property law varies considerably from state to state. (Wisconsin is the only state to adopt any form of the Uniform Marital Property Act recommended by the National Conference of Commissioners on Uniform State Laws.) For example, if all deferrals were made before the participant was married but investment earnings accrued after the marriage, some states would classify all of the deferred compensation (including investment earnings) as separate property, while others might classify the investment earnings that accrued after the marriage as community property.

Q 5:43 How does community property law affect payment of benefits under a deferred compensation plan governed by ERISA?

Not at all. ERISA preempts state laws that relate to an ERISA-governed plan. [ERISA § 514]

Q 5:44 How does community property law affect payment of benefits under a deferred compensation plan that is not governed by ERISA?

If a participant names a beneficiary other than his or her spouse for more than the participant's separate property plus community property in his or her deferred compensation, the spouse may have a right under state law to obtain a court order invalidating the beneficiary designation, or at least as much of it as would leave the spouse with less than the spouse's community property in the deferred compensation.

Nevertheless, a plan administrator may pay based on the beneficiary designation it has on record until it receives a court order restraining payment or a written notice that the spouse asserts his or her rights.

Tenancy by the Entirety

Q 5:45 What is tenancy by the entirety?

A tenancy by the entirety is a form of concurrent property ownership that recognizes the special unity of a married couple. [John V. Orth, *Tenancy by the*

Entirety: The Strange Career of the Common-Law Marital Estate, 1997 B.Y.U. L. Rev. 35 (1997); Thomas F. Bergin & Paul G. Haskell, *Estates in Land and Future Interests* 55 (2d ed. 1984); Robert Kratovil, *Real Estate Law* 198 (6th ed. 1974); 2 William Blackstone, *Commentaries* 179–80 (1765–69)]

A tenancy by the entirety may be created only if required unities of title, interest, possession, time, and person (a valid marriage) all exist. [Restatement (First) of Property § 67] Two individuals can become cotenants in a tenancy by the entirety only if they are legally married and meet other requirements. [See, e.g., In re Estate of Suggs, 405 So. 2d 1360 (Fla. Dist. Ct. App. 1981)] In some states, there is a presumption that a husband and wife take property in a tenancy by the entirety. [See, e.g., Klenke's Estate (No. 1), 210 Pa. 572, 60 A. 166 (1904); see also Stuckey v. Keefe's Executors, 26 Pa. 397 (1856)] Under a tenancy by the entirety, unlike other kinds of joint tenancy, each of the two spouses owns all of the property; however, neither spouse acting alone can dispose of the property. [See, e.g., In re Estate of Reigle, 438 Pa. Super. 361, 652 A.2d 853 (1995); Massie v. Yamrose, 169 B.R. 585 (W.D. Va. 1994); Beall v. Beall, 291 Md. 224, 434 A.2d 1015 (1981); Sawada v. Endo, 57 Haw. 608, 561 P.2d 1291 (1977); Elko v. Elko, 187 Md. 161, 49 A.2d 441 (1946)] Any tenancy by the entirety ends on the death of either spouse, or on the divorce or other dissolution of the marriage. [See, e.g., Cordova v. Mayer (In re Cordova), 177 B.R. 527 (E.D. Va. 1995), *aff'd*, 73 F.3d 38 (4th Cir. 1996); Sebold v. Sebold, 444 F.2d 864 (D.C. Cir. 1971); Dobbyn v. Dobbyn, 471 A.2d 1068 (Md. Ct. Spec. App. 1984); In re Estate of Ikuta, 64 Haw. 236, 639 P.2d 400 (1981); Travis v. Benson, 360 A.2d 506 (D.C. 1976); Madden v. Madden, 44 Haw. 442, 355 P.2d 33 (1960); Chock v. Chock, 39 Haw. 657 (Terr. 1953); Sbarbaro v. Sbarbaro, 3 B. Stockton 101, 88 N.J. Eq. 101, 102 A. 256 (Ch. 1917). But see 23 Pa. Cons. Stat. Ann. § 3507 (West 2001); In re Sharp's Estate, 11 Pa. D. & C.3d 371 (Orphans' Ct 1979)]

Of the states that recognize tenancy by the entirety as an available form of property ownership, some allow it only for real property (such as a couple's home), and some allow it for both real property and personal property.

Q 5:46 Why might someone want to own property in a tenancy by the entirety?

Because neither spouse alone can dispose of the property, a tenancy by the entirety may provide useful protection against the claims of creditors.

For example, if only one of the two spouses is bankrupt, the bankruptcy trustee generally cannot reach property held in a tenancy by the entirety. [See, e.g., Blodgett v. United States, 161 F.2d 47 (8th Cir. 1947). But see 11 U.S.C. § 110. For a detailed explanation of creditor protections that may arise from tenancy by the entirety, see L.D. Solomon & L.J. Saret, *Asset Protection Strategies* §§ 7.2–7.7 (New York: Aspen Publishers, 1999)]

A deferred compensation plan participant might not need the protection that tenancy by the entirety ownership, when available, could provide. A benefit under an ERISA plan is not subject to the claims of a participant's creditors (other than the plan itself). [ERISA §§ 206(d)(1), 514] Likewise, a benefit under an ERISA plan is excluded from the participant's bankruptcy estate. [11 U.S.C. § 541(c)(2); ERISA §§ 206(d)(1), 514; Patterson v. Shumate, 504 U.S. 753, 112 S. Ct. 2242, 119 L. Ed. 2d 519 (1992)] Depending on state law, a non-ERISA deferred compensation plan might or might not be subject to the claims of the participant's creditors. Likewise, a non-ERISA deferred compensation benefit might or might not be excluded from the participant's bankruptcy estate. [11 U.S.C. § 541(c)(2); see, e.g., In re Johnson, 191 B.R. 75 (Bankr. M.D. Pa. 1996) ("TDA" excluded from bankruptcy administration)]

Finally, a married person might prefer tenancy by the entirety ownership simply because it reflects his or her beliefs about the nature of marriage.

Q 5:47   May a participant transfer a deferred compensation benefit into a tenancy by the entirety?

No. A participant will be unable to transfer his or her rights under a deferred compensation plan into a tenancy by the entirety for one or more of the following reasons:

1. State law does not recognize tenancy by the entirety.
2. The deferred compensation plan rights are personal property that cannot be the subject of a tenancy by the entirety.
3. State law precludes a conveyance of property into a tenancy by the entirety.
4. The plan provides that its benefit cannot be assigned or alienated.

At common law, a married couple cannot hold personal property (property other than land and the buildings fixed onto the land) in a tenancy by the entirety. This is still the rule in some states. [See, e.g., Hawthorne v. Hawthorne, 192 N.E.2d 20 (N.Y. 1963); In re Blumenthal's Estate, 141 N.E.2d 911 (N.Y. 1923)]

Also at common law, one spouse who solely owns property cannot convey that property into a tenancy by the entirety. Although some states now allow such a transfer [see, e.g., Mass. Ann. Laws ch. 184, § 8; N.J. Stat. Ann. § 37:2-18; Nicholson v. Shipp, 486 S.W.2d 691 (Ark. 1972); Kluck v. Metsger, 349 S.W.2d 919 (Mo. 1961)], those provisions are of no use to a participant because he or she lacks the power to transfer his or her rights under a deferred compensation plan.

To obtain tax treatment as a deferred compensation plan, even a non-ERISA deferred compensation plan will provide that benefits cannot be assigned, alienated, or transferred. [I.R.C. §§ 451, 457(b)] Thus, even in states that recognize tenancy by the entirety as a form of property ownership, it cannot apply to a deferred compensation plan because the participant cannot transfer his or her rights under such a plan.

Premarital Agreements

Q 5:48   What is a premarital agreement?

A premarital agreement is an agreement made between two persons who are about to marry concerning property rights that arise from marriage. Typically, a premarital agreement provides that one or both of the soon-to-be spouses waive one or more of the property rights that a spouse otherwise would have. A premarital agreement may waive a spouse's right to a share of the other's estate. Within limits required by public policy and basic fairness, a premarital agreement can specify how property will be divided if the marriage ends by divorce or when it ends by death.

Under the Uniform Premarital Agreement Act, the parties to a premarital agreement may contract concerning property rights, the support of a spouse or former spouse, making a will or trust, and "[t]he ownership rights in and disposition of the death benefit from a life insurance policy." [National Conference of Commissioners on Uniform State Laws, Uniform Premarital Agreement Act § 3(a)(6) (1983)] About half the states have adopted similar provisions.

Generally, a premarital agreement must be written. In New York, a premarital agreement must be in writing signed by the parties, and must be acknowledged by the parties in the presence of a notary public or similar officer. [See, e.g., N.Y. Dom. Rel. Law § 236B(3) (McKinney 1999)] Minnesota law further provides that a premarital agreement cannot be made by an attorney-in-fact. [Minn. Stat. Ann. § 519.11(2) (West 2002)]

Many state statutes or court decisions add additional requirements. Typically, each party should fully disclose his or her financial circumstances to the other. In some states, an individual need not disclose an asset that is not subject to his or her control. [See, e.g., In re Perelman Estate, 438 Pa. 112, 263 A.2d 375 (1970)] The better practice is for each party to get the advice of a lawyer of his or her choosing.

In states that do not regulate premarital agreements by statute, courts apply ordinary contract law principles, but with extra scrutiny, recognizing the confidential relationship of those engaged to marry. [See generally, Restatement of Property (Wills and Other Donative Transfers) § 9.4 (2003)]

A premarital agreement that makes reasonable provision for the surviving spouse will be enforced even in the absence of full and fair disclosure. [See, e.g., In re Groff's Estate, 341 Pa. 105, 19 A.2d 107 (1941)] An unreasonable agreement will be enforced only if there was full and fair disclosure. [See, e.g., In re Vallish Estate, 431 Pa. 88, 244 A.2d 745 (1968). See generally National Conference of Commissioners on Uniform State Laws, Uniform Premarital Agreement Act § 6(a)(2)] A court will not enforce an agreement to the extent that it would cause a spouse to become eligible for public assistance. [See generally National Conference on Commissioners on Uniform State Laws, Uniform Premarital Agreement Act § 6(b) (1983)]

Q 5:49 Can a premarital agreement waive a spouse's right to a deferred compensation plan benefit?

Yes. Even if a surviving spouse is entitled to an elective share of a decedent's estate, community property, or other protective rights under state law, an expertly prepared premarital agreement (see Q 5:48) should be sufficient to eliminate or waive the rights (if any) a surviving spouse might have concerning a participant's deferred compensation plan benefit. [See generally National Conference of Commissioners on Uniform State Laws, Uniform Probate Code § 2-207 (1998); Uniform Premarital Agreement Act § 3 (1983)] In New York, a premarital agreement (along with other requirements) must be in writing, signed by the parties, and acknowledged by the parties in the presence of a notary or similar officer. [N.Y. Dom. Rel. Law § 236B(3)]

Marital Agreements

Q 5:50 What is a marital agreement?

A marital agreement is an agreement made between two persons who already are spouses concerning property rights that arise from their marriage. Typically, a marital agreement provides that one or both of the spouses waive one or more of the property rights that a spouse otherwise would have. A marital agreement can waive a spouse's right to a share of the other's estate. Within limits required by public policy and basic fairness, a marital agreement can specify how property will be divided if the marriage ends in divorce. [See generally 41 Am. Jur. 2d *Husband and Wife* § 134]

Generally, a marital agreement must be written. In New York, a marital agreement must be in writing signed by the parties, and must be acknowledged by the parties in the presence of a notary public or similar officer. [See, e.g., N.Y. Dom. Rel. Law § 236B(3)] Minnesota law further provides that a marital agreement cannot be made by an attorney-in-fact. [Minn. Stat. Ann. § 519.11(2)]

Many state statutes or court decisions add additional requirements meant to ensure basic fairness. Typically, each party should fully disclose his or her financial circumstances to the other. The better practice is for each party to get the advice of a lawyer of his or her choosing. Some states require that a marital agreement be fair and equitable. [See, e.g., Pacelli v. Pacelli, 319 N.J. Super. 185 (App. Div. 1999)]

In Minnesota, a marital agreement is valid only if:

1. Each spouse has titled in his or her name property with a net worth of $1.2 million;

2. Each spouse has the advice of a lawyer of his or her choosing (except that each spouse must be "represented by separate legal counsel"); and

3. Neither party begins a divorce proceeding within two years of the date of the agreement's execution.

[Minn. Stat. Ann. § 519.11(1a)]

In Louisiana, a marital agreement must be approved by a judge (following the parties' joint petition). [La. Civ. Code Ann. arts. 2325–2333] Likewise, in North Carolina a marital agreement must be approved by a judge or other certifying officer under the court's supervision. [N.C. Gen. Stat. § 52-10]

In Hawaii, a marital agreement is valid only if the terms are equitable at the time of the divorce. [Haw. Rev. Stat. Ann. § 560:2-204]

A marital agreement is void if it was signed under a threat of a divorce. [See, e.g., In re Sharp's Estate, 11 Pa. D. & C.3d 371 (C.P. 1979)]

Q 5:51   Can a marital agreement waive a spouse's right to a deferred compensation plan benefit?

Yes. Even if a surviving spouse is entitled to an elective share of a decedent's estate, community property, or other protective rights under state law, an expertly prepared marital agreement (see Q 5:50) should be sufficient to eliminate or waive those rights. [See generally National Conference of Commissioners on Uniform State Laws, Uniform Probate Code § 2-207 (1998)]

Disclaimers

Q 5:52   What is a disclaimer?

A disclaimer (also called a renunciation in some states) is a writing in which a beneficiary states that he or she does not want to receive a benefit. To be legally effective and, if desired, to achieve tax planning purposes, the disclaimer document must carefully state certain requirements (see Q 5:57).

Q 5:53   Is a disclaimer permitted under a deferred compensation plan?

A deferred compensation plan generally will not permit a participant to disclaim his or her benefit, because a deferred compensation plan typically provides that a participant cannot assign or give away any right he or she has under the plan.

A plan might permit a disclaimer made by a beneficiary. Although there is no tax ruling that is specific to a deferred compensation plan, other rulings provide some guidance. [GCM 39,858 (Sept. 9, 1991); P.L.R. 9226058, 9037048, 8922036] Under reasoning similar to that used in these rulings, a beneficiary's disclaimer of a deferred compensation plan benefit should be permitted. A plan administrator may (but is not required to) accept a beneficiary's disclaimer.

Q 5:54   What is the effect of a beneficiary's disclaimer?

If a beneficiary makes a valid disclaimer that the plan administrator accepts, the benefit will be distributed as though the beneficiary/disclaimant had died before the participant's death.

Q 5:55   Why would a beneficiary want to make a disclaimer?

Although most people do not lightly turn down money, sometimes there may be a good reason to make a disclaimer. A typical reason for making a disclaimer is to complete tax-oriented estate planning. For example, a beneficiary may prefer to make a disclaimer to help accomplish one or more of the following estate planning objectives:

- Changing a restricted transfer in favor of the beneficiary into an unrestricted transfer to the same beneficiary;
- Changing an unrestricted transfer to the beneficiary into a restricted transfer in favor of the same beneficiary;
- Limiting a transfer to a child or other nonspouse to permit the participant's spouse to delay the required beginning date (see Q 3:20);
- Limiting a transfer to a child or other nonspouse to permit the participant's spouse to make a rollover;
- Limiting a transfer to a child or other nonspouse to increase the marital deduction;
- Limiting a transfer to a spouse as needed to "equalize" the effective transfer tax rate of each spouse;
- Limiting a transfer to a spouse as needed to fully use the generation-skipping tax exemption of the first spouse to die;
- Limiting a transfer to a spouse as needed to avoid an estate transfer surtax [I.R.C. § 2001(c)(2)]; or
- Providing a designated beneficiary (see Qs 3:24–3:35) so as to lengthen tax deferral for the deferred compensation and thereby increase a gift to charity.

If a beneficiary makes a valid disclaimer that also meets all requirements of Code Section 2518, the disclaimed benefit will not be in the disclaimant's estate for federal estate tax purposes, and will not be the disclaimant's income for federal income tax purposes. [I.R.C. § 2518; Treas. Reg. § 25.2518-1] Most states have a similar rule for state death tax purposes.

Another frequent reason for making a disclaimer is to correct a "wrong" beneficiary designation.

Example. Matthew, a hospital technician, saved for retirement under his county's deferred compensation plan. When he enrolled in the plan, he was single, and he named his father and mother as his plan beneficiaries. Recently, Matthew married Laura. Shortly after returning from their honeymoon,

Matthew was killed in an accident at the hospital's emergency room. Matthew's parents believe that if Matthew had thought about it, he would have wanted his wife to be his beneficiary. Therefore, each of them files a disclaimer with the plan administrator. Although the parents cannot directly control who gets the benefit, their lawyer advises them that, by operation of the plan's default provision (see Q 5:9) and their state's intestacy law, Laura will get the benefit. All family members feel that this is a morally sound result and what Matthew would have wanted. The use of disclaimers allows the family to achieve this result.

Caution. A beneficiary should not make a disclaimer unless he or she first gets his or her lawyer's advice that doing so will not be a federal health care crime. [See 42 U.S.C. § 1320a-7b(a)(6)]

Q 5:56   Can a beneficiary's executor or agent disclaim?

If a plan permits a beneficiary to disclaim a plan benefit, whether that power can be exercised only by the beneficiary personally or by the beneficiary's executor, personal representative, guardian, or attorney-in-fact as a fiduciary depends on the plan's language. At least one court decision suggests that unless the plan document states that a power to disclaim can be exercised by an executor, personal representative, guardian, or attorney-in-fact, only the beneficiary personally may exercise the power to disclaim. [Nickel v. Estate of Estes, 122 F.3d 294, 21 Employee Benefits Cas. (BNA) 1762, Pens. Plan Guide (CCH) ¶ 23937U (5th Cir. 1997)] In some states, a personal representative may disclaim an interest and the disclaimer relates back to the disclaimant's death or even to the death of the person making the disclaimant a beneficiary. [See, e.g., Tex. Prob. Code Ann. § 37A; Rolin v. IRS, 588 F.2d 368 (2d Cir. 1978) (applying New York law)]

Even if a fiduciary has power under applicable law to make a disclaimer, such a disclaimer might not be a qualified disclaimer for federal tax purposes. [Compare P.L.R. 200013041, 9615043, 9609052 (disclaimer recognized), with P.L.R. 9437042 (disclaimer not recognized); see also Rev. Rul. 90-110, 1990-2 C.B. 209 (disclaimer by trustee not a qualified disclaimer)]

Q 5:57   What are the requirements for a valid disclaimer?

To be effective for federal tax purposes, a disclaimer must meet all of the following requirements:

1. The disclaimer must be made before the beneficiary accepts or uses any benefit.
2. The benefit must pass without any direction by the disclaimant.
3. The disclaimer must be in writing and must be signed by the disclaimant.
4. The writing must state an irrevocable and unqualified refusal to accept the benefit.

5. The writing must be delivered to the plan administrator.

6. The writing must be so delivered no later than nine months after (a) the date of the participant's death or (b) the date the beneficiary attains age 21, whichever is later.

7. The disclaimer must meet all requirements of applicable state law.

[I.R.C. § 2518; Treas. Reg. § 25.2518-2; GCM 39,858 (Sept. 9, 1991). See generally National Conference of Commissioners on Uniform State Laws, Uniform Disclaimer of Property Interests Act, 8A U.L.A. 151 (1993)]

State law may provide additional requirements. For example, in some states a disclaimer must state the disclaimant's belief that he or she has no creditor that could be disadvantaged by the disclaimer. In some situations, especially when the beneficiary is a minor or an incapacitated person, a disclaimer may require court approval. [See, e.g., N.Y. Est. Powers & Trusts Law § 2-1.11(c) (McKinney 1998); 20 Pa. Cons. Stat. Ann. § 6202] Even when court approval is not required, state law may require that a disclaimer is not valid unless it is filed in the appropriate probate court. [See generally National Conference of Commissioners on Uniform State Laws, Uniform Probate Code § 2-801 (1998)]

In addition to state and tax law requirements, the deferred compensation plan may impose further requirements.

Government Claims

Q 5:58 Is deferred compensation counted as an asset for Medicaid eligibility purposes?

A deferred compensation plan benefit probably is counted as an "available resource" for Medicaid eligibility purposes to the extent that the patient or his or her spouse currently has a legal right to get payment under the plan. [42 U.S.C. § 1396a–p]

A participant might consider not selecting as his or her beneficiary a person likely to need Medicaid benefits if a more appropriate beneficiary designation can be made. A beneficiary should not make a disclaimer without first getting his or her lawyer's advice that doing so will not be a federal health care crime. [See 42 U.S.C. § 1320a-7b(a)(6)]

Q 5:59 Is a participant's deferred compensation counted as an asset for purposes of determining his or her spouse's Medicaid eligibility?

After the community spouse resource allowance is used, a participant's deferred compensation plan benefit probably is counted as an available or includible resource for purposes of determining his or her spouse's Medicaid eligibility. [See, e.g., Mistrick v. Division of Medical Assistance & Health

Services, 154 N.J. 158, 712 A.2d 188 (1998). See generally 42 U.S.C. §§ 1396–1396v; N.J. Stat. Ann. §§ 30:4D-1 to 19.1]

Q 5:60 Can an IRS levy take a participant's plan benefit?

Yes. Although a participant's retirement benefits should not be available to ordinary creditors, a U.S. tax lien or levy applies to deferred compensation plan amounts. [I.R.C. § 6334(a); see, e.g., United States v. Sawaf, 74 F.3d 119 (6th Cir. 1996); Shanbaum v. United States, 32 F.3d 180, 183 (5th Cir. 1994); Hyde v. United States, 93-2 U.S. Tax Cas. (CCH) ¶ 50,432 (D. Ariz. 1993), *reconsideration denied,* 1993 U.S. Dist. LEXIS 12669 (D. Ariz. Aug. 30, 1993), *aff'd per curiam,* 1994 U.S. App. LEXIS 12646 (9th Cir. May 27, 1994); Ameritrust Co. v. Derakhshan, 830 F. Supp. 406, 410–11 (N.D. Ohio 1993); Travelers Insurance Co. v. Rattermann, 1996 WL 149332, 77 A.F.T.R.2d (RIA) 96-956, 96-1 U.S. Tax Cas. (CCH) ¶ 50,143 (S.D. Ohio Jan. 12, 1996); Palmore v. United States ex rel. IRS (In re Palmore), 71 A.F.T.R.2d (PH) 93-1588 (N.D. Okla. 1993); Schreiber v. United States (In re Schreiber), 163 B.R. 327, 334 (Bankr. N.D. Ill. 1994); Raihl v. United States (In re Raihl), 152 B.R. 615, 618 (B.A.P. 9th Cir. 1993); Jacobs v. IRS (In re Jacobs), 147 B.R. 106, 108–09 (Bankr. W.D. Pa. 1992); In re Perkins, 134 B.R. 408, 411 (Bankr. E.D. Cal. 1991); In re Reed, 127 B.R. 244, 248 (Bankr. D. Haw. 1991); see also ERISA § 514(d); I.R.C. § 6334(c); Treas. Reg. § 1.401(a)-13(b)(2)]

A U.S. tax lien or levy supersedes any anti-alienation provision of a deferred compensation plan or state statute. [I.R.C. § 6334(a)] However, a levy extends only to property rights that exist at the time of the levy. [Treas. Reg. § 301.6331-1(a); see also IRS Internal Legal Memo. 200102021]

Q 5:61 When will the IRS levy on a participant's plan benefit?

If a participant has not yet severed from employment or otherwise completed the conditions that entitle him or her to deferred compensation, the IRS usually will not levy on the participant's deferred compensation plan benefit. [IRS Legal Memo. 2000-32-004 (May 18, 1998)] Instead, the IRS will levy on a participant's retirement benefit only if the participant has been unusually abusive. A levy on retirement savings requires the approval of an IRS supervisor. [IRM ¶ 5.11.6.2]

Q 5:62 When will the IRS levy on a beneficiary's plan benefit?

Because a levy regarding a beneficiary, especially a nonspouse beneficiary, does not involve disturbing retirement income in the same way that a levy regarding a participant would, the IRS might be less reluctant to levy on a plan benefit that a beneficiary has become entitled to after the participant's death.

Practice Pointer. If a participant knows that a person whom the participant might prefer to designate as beneficiary has shown irresponsibility in handling money by failing to meet tax obligations, the participant might consider naming as beneficiary a responsible trustee under a spendthrift trust.

Unclaimed Property

Q 5:63   Is an ERISA plan governed by a state's unclaimed property law?

No. Because an unclaimed property law would, if applicable, require delivery of plan assets and liabilities, such a law relates to the plan and its administration, and thus is preempted by ERISA. [ERISA §§ 403(c)(1), 514(b)(7); Commonwealth Edison Co. v. Vega, 174 F.3d 870, 22 Employee Benefits Cas. (BNA) 2794 (7th Cir.), *cert. denied sub nom.* Topink v. Commonwealth Edison Co., 120 S. Ct. 176, 145 L. Ed. 2d 149, 23 Employee Benefits Cas. (BNA) 1888 (1999); Manufacturers Life Ins. Co. v. East Bay Restaurant & Tavern Retirement Plan, 57 F. Supp. 2d 921 (N.D. Cal. 1999)] However, unclaimed property law might apply to the operations of a bank, insurance company, or securities broker-dealer. [See Aetna Life Insurance Co. v. Barges, 869 F.2d 142 (2d Cir.), *cert denied*, 493 U.S. 811, 100 S. Ct. 57, 107 L. Ed. 2d 25 (1989)]

Q 5:64   Is a state or local government employer's plan distribution governed by that state's unclaimed property law?

It depends. If the state's unclaimed property law is based on the uniform acts, the "[state] government or political subdivision, public corporation, public authority, . . . trust, . . . or any . . . legal . . . entity" is subject to that unclaimed property law. [National Conference of Commissioners on Uniform State Laws, Revised Uniform Disposition of Unclaimed Property Act § 1(g), Uniform Disposition of Unclaimed Property Act § 1(g)]

A typical unclaimed property law requires any person in possession of intangible property that is unclaimed by its owner for a specified number of years to transfer that property to the custody of the state. [See, e.g., 765 Ill. Comp. Stat. Ann. 1025] Each of the 50 states (and the District of Columbia and U.S. possessions) has a law regulating abandoned or unclaimed property.

Q 5:65   When is a deferred compensation benefit considered abandoned?

The waiting period that sets up a legal presumption that property is abandoned or unclaimed varies by state law. Under a typical state law, however, the waiting period starts when the benefit "became payable or distributable." [See National Conference of Commissioners on Uniform State Laws, Revised Uniform Disposition of Unclaimed Property Act §§ 7–9, Uniform Disposition of Unclaimed Property Act §§ 7–9] Under many deferred compensation plans, a benefit usually is paid within a month from the date that the benefit became distributable. Therefore, as a practical matter many governmental plan administrators start the waiting period on the check date.

Tax-Oriented Estate Planning

Q 5:66   What is the federal estate tax?

The federal estate tax is a tax on the right to transfer property on death. This tax is imposed on a decedent's taxable estate, which includes nonprobate property and rights. The tax rates begin at 18 percent and go as high as 50 percent. [I.R.C. § 2001(c)] An unlimited marital deduction allows a person to transfer any amount to his or her surviving spouse (if the spouse is a U.S. citizen) without federal estate tax at the individual's death, but tax may apply when the survivor dies. [I.R.C. § 2056] A tax credit allows a person to transfer about $1 million for 2003 without federal estate tax. [I.R.C. § 2010(b)] The generation-skipping transfer tax exemption amount for any calendar year is the same as the applicable exclusion amount for federal estate tax purposes for that year.

Q 5:67   Who should be concerned about estate tax planning?

Many people have more wealth (at least for tax purposes) than they think. Normally, an estate will not incur federal estate tax unless the estate is worth more than the applicable amount shown in the following table:

For Estates of Decedents Dying During	Exemption
2001	$675,000
2002	$1,000,000
2003	$1,000,000
2004	$1,500,000
2005	$1,500,000
2006	$2,000,000
2007	$2,000,000
2008	$2,000,000
2009	$3,500,000
2010	No federal estate tax
2011	$1,000,000 not indexed

For estate tax purposes, a taxable estate includes all nonprobate property, such as the following:

- A home;
- Any personally owned life insurance benefits;
- Any employment-based life insurance benefits; and
- Any retirement benefits.

Example. Because Harry and Sally have young children and it takes both paychecks to run the household, they hold a term life insurance contract on the life of each parent; each death benefit is $1 million. They own their house, which is worth $200,000. Harry's deferred compensation plan account balance is $400,000. (Although Harry does not consider himself wealthy, his estate for federal estate tax purposes is at least $1.5 million.) If either Harry or Sally dies, there will be no federal estate tax as long as all property passes to the surviving spouse. If, however, the second parent dies in 2004, there will be a federal estate tax (assume no deductions or credits), almost $555,800 of which could have been avoided if the first parent had planned gifts or trusts that would transfer some property or rights to the children before or on the death of the first parent to die.

Q 5:68   What is a state death tax?

A state death transfer tax is a tax imposed by a state on the transfer of wealth at an individual's death. Every state except Nevada imposes some form of death transfer tax.

An estate tax is a tax on the privilege of transferring property from a decedent. An inheritance tax is a tax on the privilege of receiving property from a decedent, including even property that an individual did not own at the time of his or her death. Unlike the federal estate tax, an inheritance tax or a state estate tax may apply even when the beneficiary is the decedent's spouse. In some states, the amount of the state death tax is the maximum amount for which the state death tax credit is available under federal estate tax law. [See I.R.C. § 2011] In other states, the state death taxes may be greater. Connecticut, Louisiana, New York, North Carolina, Tennessee, and Puerto Rico have a state gift tax.

Q 5:69   Is deferred compensation subject to federal estate tax?

Yes. The value of the participant's account as of the date of his or her death or, if payments have begun, the value of the remaining payments (if any) is included in the participant's estate for federal estate tax purposes. [I.R.C. §§ 2033–2046; Goodman v. Granger, 243 F.2d 264 (3d Cir. 1957)]

Q 5:70   Is deferred compensation subject to state death tax?

An explanation of the states' inheritance or estate taxes is beyond the scope of this book. Some states tax deferred compensation for death transfer tax purposes according to rules similar to those for the federal estate tax, but often without an exemption amount. Other states have their own rules. In several states, the tax varies based on the relationship of the beneficiary to the participant-decedent.

Q 5:71 Does a beneficiary designation of the spouse qualify for the marital deduction?

Yes, as long as the spouse is the only person who can benefit, at least until his or her death. [I.R.C. § 2056; P.L.R. 199936052]

Q 5:72 Should a plan administrator follow securities laws when it compiles plan investment information?

Yes. When a plan fiduciary communicates about participant-directed investment choices, ERISA requires such a plan fiduciary to communicate using the same expertise that someone in the business of communicating about consumer investment choices would use. [ERISA § 404(a)(1)] Although an ERISA plan fiduciary that is not a securities broker-dealer or investment adviser might not be regulated by securities laws, those laws may be used as evidence of what a careful expert would do in presenting investment information.

Practice Pointer. Not all employee benefits lawyers are experienced in securities laws. If a plan fiduciary prepares any communication concerning plan investment options, it might consider asking its regular employee benefits lawyer to consult with a securities lawyer about the form, content, and accompanying disclosures for such a communication.

Q 5:73 Does a beneficiary designation of a qualified terminable interest property trust qualify for the marital deduction?

Yes, if the trust agreement is carefully worded to include necessary provisions (explained below) and the executor and the trustee properly make the election, a qualified terminable interest property (QTIP) trust qualifies for the marital deduction.

In addition to the usual requirements for a marital deduction or QTIP trust, the participant and his or her estate planning lawyer should make sure that the trust (or at least the subtrust that will hold the retirement plan benefit) provides all of the following:

1. During the spouse's life, no one (including the spouse) can have any power to appoint any part of the retirement plan benefit or QTIP property resulting from it to anyone other than the surviving spouse.
2. The trustee has power to make the retirement benefit and any trust property resulting from it productive or income-earning.
3. The spouse has a right to require the trustee to make the retirement benefit and any trust property resulting from it productive or income-earning.

4. The trust document does not change the definition of principal and income in a way that might result in less income distributable to the spouse.

5. The trustee must have the power under the trust and the right under the deferred compensation plan to get a distribution of the retirement benefit, at least for the amount described in condition 10, below.

6. The surviving spouse must have the right to require the trustee to get a plan distribution, at least for the amount described in condition 10, below.

7. The QTIP trust's fiduciary accounting income must include the deferred compensation plan benefit's income.

8. To ensure the spouse's right to all of the income, the trust must provide that any administrative expenses normally charged to corpus (including any income tax payable with respect to the distribution of principal) be charged to corpus and not to income.

9. If necessary to administer the trust, the trustee must calculate the deferred compensation plan benefit's fiduciary accounting income and the QTIP trust's fiduciary accounting income.

10. If (for a year) the surviving spouse exercises his or her right to get all of the trust's fiduciary accounting income, the QTIP trustee must claim a distribution from the deferred compensation plan in an amount not less than the greater of the Section 401(a)(9) minimum distribution (including any incidental benefit required distribution) or the QTIP trust's fiduciary accounting income attributable to the retirement plan benefit.

11. The participant-decedent's executor and the trustee of the QTIP trust must make the QTIP election for the QTIP trust and for the deferred compensation plan benefit as well.

[I.R.C. § 2056(b)(7); Treas. Reg. §§ 20.2056(b)-5(f)(8), -7; Rev. Rul. 2000-2, 2000-3 I.R.B. 305] For condition 6, it is enough that the surviving spouse has the right to get the deferred compensation plan benefit's and the QTIP trust's income, and it does not invalidate QTIP treatment that the surviving spouse chooses not to exercise that right.

If it otherwise meets the requirements of the Code, a QTIP trust need not conform to all elements of the design described above, and instead may use different provisions to cause a retirement benefit to be treated as QTIP. [See, e.g., N.B. Choate, *Life and Death Planning for Retirement Benefits* (Boston: Ataxplan Publications, 2003)]

Practice Pointer. In making QTIP trust provisions, an estate planning lawyer should recognize that a deferred compensation plan does not state provisions for determining fiduciary accounting income. Therefore, the QTIP trust must provide for its trustee to make its own calculation of fiduciary accounting income based on the information available to it. If the trust is governed by the law of a jurisdiction that has adopted some form of the Uniform Principal and Income Act, a particular rule applies to "rights to receive payments on a contract for deferred compensation." [See, e.g., N.Y. Est. Powers & Trusts Law § 11-2.1(c)(4), (j) (McKinney Supp. 2002). See generally National Conference of Commissioners on

Uniform State Laws, Uniform Principal and Income Act § 4] However, such a provision may do little more than tell the trustee to decide what is equitable. [See, e.g., N.Y. Est. Powers & Trusts Law § 11-2.1(a)(1)(C) (McKinney Supp. 2002)]

Caution. A surviving spouse who does not exercise his or her right to obtain all of the plan benefit's and thereby the QTIP trust's income should consider whether his or her waiver or nonexercise of that right constitutes a taxable gift of a future interest.

Practice Pointer. A careful drafter of a QTIP trust should consider provisions that would preclude (or at least not authorize) an excessive trustee fee. When a trustee is a family member who is a natural object of the QTIP trust beneficiary's bounty, an excessive trustee fee is a taxable gift from the surviving spouse to the trustee. [TAM 200014004. See generally Merill v. Fahs, 324 U.S. 308 (1945); Commissioner v. Wemyss, 324 U.S. 303, 306 (1945); Harwood v. Commissioner, 82 T.C. 239, 259 (1984); Estate of Reynolds v. Commissioner, 55 T.C. 172 (1970); Estate of Anderson v. Commissioner, 8 T.C. 706, 720 (1947); Estate of Hendrickson v. Commissioner, T.C. Memo. 1999-357] In addition to gift tax on the portion of the trustee's fee that is in excess of reasonable compensation, a surviving spouse's acquiescence in an excessive fee calls into question whether the surviving spouse truly had a right to all of the trust's income, and thereby whether the trust is or was a QTIP trust. [I.R.C. § 2056(b)(7)]

Q 5:74 When would a participant want to name a QTIP trust as beneficiary?

A QTIP trust might be desirable when the participant wants the federal estate tax marital deduction but does not want his or her spouse to receive the deferred compensation plan benefit directly.

Example 1. Bob and Cathy, a married couple, have no children together, but Bob has children from a previous marriage. A QTIP trust can allow Bob to provide for Cathy during Cathy's life, while preserving some of the benefit for Bob's children from his previous marriage.

Example 2. Annabelle cares very much for her husband, Jim, and wants her deferred compensation plan benefit to provide for Jim if she dies first. But Annabelle believes that Jim is irresponsible in handling money and prefers that a professional trustee manage his financial needs. A QTIP trust can allow Annabelle to provide for Jim without putting all the money in his hands.

Qualified Domestic Trusts for Aliens

Q 5:75 How is the marital deduction different when a decedent's spouse is an alien?

Normally, an unlimited deduction is available for property passing to a decendent's surviving spouse. [I.R.C. § 2056] This deduction can apply to all or a portion of the value of a plan benefit to the extent that it becomes payable to the participant's surviving spouse or becomes held under a QTIP trust for the spouse's benefit. If a participant's spouse is an alien, however, the availability of the marital deduction is severely restricted. These restrictions apply even if the alien spouse resides in the United States. [I.R.C. §§ 2056, 2056A]

Q 5:76   How can a participant preserve the marital deduction when his or her spouse is an alien?

The federal estate tax marital deduction is not available for an alien spouse unless the property passing to the spouse is provided through a "qualified domestic trust." [I.R.C. § 2056(d)(2)] Estate planners use the acronym QDOT.

Q 5:77   What is a qualified domestic trust?

A qualified domestic trust, or QDOT, is a trust that holds assets for the benefit of (but not subject to the control of) the spouse during the spouse's life. The trust must restrict distributions during the spouse's life to trust income and hardship distributions; if it does not, it must pay a special tax on any other distribution. [I.R.C. § 2056A(b)] A QDOT must have at least one trustee who is a U.S. citizen, or a U.S. corporation must be responsible for paying any federal estate tax due from the trust. [I.R.C. § 2056A] The Treasury regulations specify many other conditions. [Treas. Reg. § 20.2056A-1 et seq.]

Q 5:78   How can a participant obtain QDOT treatment?

It is unlikely that a deferred compensation plan by its own terms will satisfy the conditions for a surviving spouse's benefit to be treated as a QDOT.

A participant who wants QDOT treatment for his or her spouse's benefit should, with his or her estate-planning lawyer's advice, select an appropriate trustee and create a QDOT. To cause any plan benefit remaining on the participant's death to pass into the QDOT, the participant should change his or her plan beneficiary designation.

Although the participant should act only on the advice of his or her expert estate-planning lawyer, the following is a sample beneficiary designation:

> Thomas Tertius, or the duly appointed and then currently serving U.S. trustee of my Qualified Domestic Trust dated February 2, 1991

The parties and the trustee should be careful to follow any additional requirements particular to QDOT treatment for a plan. [See, e.g., P.L.R. 9713018 (involving a 403(b) arrangement)]

Q 5:79   How can a surviving spouse obtain QDOT treatment?

To preserve the marital deduction for a benefit passing to an alien spouse, the spouse must "transfer" his or her plan distribution to a QDOT before the decedent's estate's federal estate tax return is filed. [I.R.C. § 2056(d)(2)(B)(i)] Of course, a beneficiary cannot assign or transfer a plan distribution. But if an alien spouse receives a lump-sum distribution and pays the proceeds into a QDOT before the estate tax return is filed, it might qualify for the marital deduction.

The regulations also provide a special rule for annuity payments, but this rule is unlikely to be helpful concerning a deferred compensation benefit. [Treas. Reg. § 20.2056A-4]

Seeking Advice About Making a Beneficiary Designation

Q 5:80 May a financial services representative give advice about a beneficiary designation?

A financial-services representative may give practical advice about how to fill in the beneficiary information requested by the application for an annuity or life insurance contract or a custodial account. He or she must not give advice about the legal effect of a beneficiary designation.

Except when done by a properly admitted lawyer, giving legal advice, even for free, is a crime in every state of the United States. Even if the nonlawyer explicitly states that he or she is not a lawyer, it is still a crime to give legal advice.

Of course, any criminal punishment is in addition to the nonlawyer's liability to his or her "client" for any inappropriate advice. Courts have not hesitated to impose liability on a nonlawyer for giving incorrect or even incomplete advice. [Buscemi v. Intachai, 730 So. 2d 329 (Fla. Dist. Ct. App. 1999) (nonlawyer financial planner who gave legal advice could be held liable for failure to do so properly), *review denied*, 744 So. 2d 452 (Fla. 1999); Banks v. District of Columbia Department of Consumer & Regulatory Affairs, 634 A.2d 433 (D.C. 1993); Cultum v. Heritage House Realtors, Inc., 694 P.2d 630 (Wash. 1985); Bowers v. Transamerica Title Insurance Co., 675 P.2d 193 (Wash. 1983); Webb v. Pomeroy, 655 P.2d 465 (Kan. Ct. App. 1982); Biakanja v. Irving, 49 Cal. 2d 647, 320 P.2d 16 (1958)] A nonlawyer is held to the same standard of care and expertise as a lawyer. [Williams v. Jackson Co., 359 So. 2d 798 (Ala. Civ. App. 1978), *writ denied*, 359 So. 2d 801 (1978); Wright v. Langdon, 274 Ark. 258, 623 S.W.2d 823 (Ark. 1981); Biakanja v. Irving, 49 Cal. 2d 647, 320 P.2d 16 (1958); Ford v. Guarantee Abstract & Title Co., 553 P.2d 254 (Kan. 1976); Torres v. Fiol, 110 Ill. App. 3d 9, 441 N.E.2d 1300, 65 Ill. Dec. 786 (1982); Latson v. Eaton, 341 P.2d 247 (Okla. 1959); Bowers v. Transamerica Title Insurance Co., 675 P.2d 193 (Wash. 1983); Mattieligh v. Poe, 57 Wash. 2d 203, 356 P.2d 328 (1960). See also Correll v. Goodfellow, 125 N.W.2d 745 (Iowa 1964); Brown v. Shyne, 151 N.E. 197 (N.Y. 1926)] This duty, even for a nonlawyer, includes a duty to have and use specialist expertise, or to refer one's "client" to an appropriate specialist.

A nonlawyer plan administrator also will be liable for incorrect or incomplete advice. Although a lawsuit against a plan administrator or other ERISA fiduciary grounded on state-law claims, such as negligent misrepresentation or negligent communication, is preempted [Griggs v. E.I. DuPont de Nemours & Co., 237 F.3d 371 (4th Cir. 2001); Farr v. US West, Inc., 151 F.3d 908 (9th Cir. 1998)], a plan administrator's incorrect statement might be a breach of its fiduciary duty to furnish accurate and nonmisleading information. [See Griggs v. E.I. DuPont de Nemours & Co., 237 F.3d 371 (4th Cir. 2001)]

Many deferred compensation plan participants believe they cannot afford legal advice. Although a financial services representative should urge a participant to obtain an expert lawyer's advice, it may be impractical to avoid participants' questions asked in the course of filling out a plan's participation agreement. Perhaps it is not the unauthorized practice of law to furnish widely known general information that does not involve applying the law to a specific factual situation.

Practice Pointer. If a participant expresses a desire to make a beneficiary designation that would provide anything less than 100 percent of his or her death benefit for his or her spouse, a nonlawyer financial planner should urge the participant to seek the advice of an expert lawyer.

Q 5:81   Can written materials give guidance about beneficiary designations?

Maybe. In Texas, any restriction against the unauthorized practice of law does not preclude "written materials, books, forms, computer software, or similar products if the products clearly and conspicuously state that the products are not a substitute for the advice of an attorney." [Tex. Gov't Code Ann. § 81.101(c)]

In other states, it is unclear whether such publications would be so protected. Notwithstanding U.S. constitutional protections for free speech, courts have upheld prosecutions and granted injunctions finding that mere written publications, without oral communication, constituted the crime of the unauthorized practice of law. [See, e.g., Unauthorized Practice of Law Committee v. Parsons Technology, Inc., No 3:97CV-2859H, 1999 WL 47235 (N.D. Tex. Jan. 22, 1999) (before enactment of Tex. Gov't Code Ann. § 81.101(c)), *vacated,* 179 F.3d 956 (5th Cir. 1999)]

ERISA does not preempt criminal laws, such as a prohibition against the unauthorized practice of law. [ERISA § 514(b)(7)]

Q 5:82   Does the lawyer who drafts an individual's will need to know about his or her beneficiary designation?

Professor John Langbein, an authority on the law of wills, trusts, and estates, observed that many Americans die with several "wills"—perhaps one that was written in a lawyer's office and a dozen others that were filled out on standard forms. For most people, beneficiary designations dispose of far more money and property than the will does. [John Langbein, "The Nonprobate Revolution and the Future of the Law of Succession," 97 *Harv. L. Rev* 1108 (1984); Carrico, "Public Knowledge and Attitudes About Property Distributions at Death and Will Substitutes in Indiana," *Am. B. Found. Res. J.* (1984); See also Carrico, "Uniform, 'Super Will' Legislation Project," 14 *Prob. & Prop.* 45 (1986)]

Making a beneficiary designation under a deferred compensation plan is an important part of estate planning. Although a deferred compensation plan benefit will not be transferred by a will (see Q 5:1), a deferred compensation plan beneficiary designation will affect the individual's overall estate plan. A participant should make sure his or her lawyer knows what beneficiary designation the participant made under a deferred compensation plan, and should ask for the lawyer's advice about whether to consider changing any beneficiary designation.

Q 5:83   What are some of the common mistakes people make with beneficiary designations?

Because people enroll in deferred compensation plans quickly, they sometimes make beneficiary designations that are less than carefully considered. Below is an explanation of some common mistakes:

1. *Failing to coordinate a beneficiary designation's provisions with those made in other non-probate designations, trusts, and a will.* Although a beneficiary designation's provisions need not be the same as those of a participant's will or other dispositions, if they are different the maker should understand why he or she has made different provisions and whether they are likely to add up to a combined result that he or she wants.

2. *Failing to consider whether a beneficiary designation is consistent with tax-oriented planning.* A participant might have had a lawyer's advice about how to leave his or her estate, including both probate and non-probate property, to achieve a desired tax outcome. Making a beneficiary designation without counting its effect on the maker's tax-oriented plan could result in an unanticipated tax.

3. *Making a beneficiary designation that a plan administrator, insurer, or custodian will refuse to implement.* For example, a participant might try to make a beneficiary designation that refers to terms that may be used in a will or trust but are precluded by his or her plan. A plan administrator's interpretation of the beneficiary designation without the offending terms might result in a disposition quite different from what the participant would have wanted.

4. *Trying to name beneficiaries by writing "all my children, equally" or describing a class.* Whenever a beneficiary designation refers to information not in a plan's records, a plan administrator might decide that the participant did not make a beneficiary designation, or may allow a claimant an opportunity to name every person in the class and prove that there are no others. Since it is difficult to prove the non-existence of an unidentified person, even the opportunity to correct the participant's beneficiary designation would result in significant frustration and delay.

5. *Neglecting to use a beneficiary's Social Security Number or Individual Taxpayer Identification Number, especially for a daughter.*

Example. Harold Smith named his three children—Reed Smith, Catherine Smith, and Alice Smith—as his beneficiaries, and used only their names. By the time of Harold's death many years later, Reed and Alice had married. Reed had no special difficulty claiming his benefit. But Alice Carpenter was required to submit proof that she is the same person as Alice Smith. Because an identifying number assigned by the Social Security Administration or Internal Revenue Service is unique, this burden could have been avoided had Harold put Alice's number on the beneficiary-designation form.

6. *Naming a minor as a beneficiary without considering who the minor's guardian would be.* For example, a divorced participant might not want to name his or her young child as a beneficiary if doing so might have the effect of putting money in the hands of the child's other parent—the participant's former spouse. (See Q 5:13.) Instead, a participant might name a suitable trustee or custodian.

7. *Naming a child as a beneficiary without considering his or her prudence.*

Example. Philip names his daughter, Britney, as beneficiary of Philip's custodial account. When Philip dies, Britney is 19 years old and no longer is a minor under applicable law. Although Britney should pay her sophomore year's $25,000 tuition at the Newark College of Fashion Arts, Britney buys a new car and then neglects to pay the second insurance premium. When the uninsured car is stolen, Britney has nothing left from her father's gift.

A participant who wants to benefit his or her child might consider that person's maturity, and consider whether it could help to choose a suitable trustee to manage the child's benefit.

8. *Forgetting to give a copy of the beneficiary designation to the beneficiary.* A plan administrator, insurer, or custodian has no duty or obligation to contact a participant's beneficiaries to invite them to submit a claim. Indeed, many service providers particularly avoid doing so because such a communication might invite fraudulent claims. A beneficiary might not claim a benefit if he or she is unaware that he or she is a beneficiary. Likewise, a beneficiary might face difficulty in claiming a benefit if he or she does not know the name of the plan administrator, insurer, or custodian.

9. *Naming one's estate as beneficiary.* Some participants think that naming one's estate as beneficiary is a way to avoid inconsistency in his or her estate plan. While such a beneficiary designation might fulfill a goal of avoiding inconsistency, it bears other consequences, which might be disadvantageous. Amounts paid or payable to an executor or personal representative for the estate are available to a decedent's creditors. And a benefit's "run" through an estate might, because of accounting and timing differences, result in income taxes greater than the income tax

that would result if the recipient received the benefit directly. [I.R.C. §§ 1, 72, 641–691]

10. *Failing to make a beneficiary designation.* A participant who has difficulty making up his or her mind about a beneficiary designation is unlikely to have read a plan's terms carefully enough to understand the effect of the plan's "default" provision. Although a young person might assume that death is far away, the point of a beneficiary designation is to provide for the possibility of death.

Practice Pointer. A planner might suggest that the risks of failing to make a beneficiary designation outweigh the risks of a less than perfectly considered beneficiary designation. In those circumstances, a planner might remind the participant that a typical plan allows a participant to change his or her beneficiary designation at any time.

11. *Forgetting to review one's beneficiary designation.* A participant should review his or her beneficiary designations periodically and whenever there is a significant change in his or her family or wealth.

Example. Martha named her husband, John, as her beneficiary under an ERISA plan. Although Martha wanted to make sure that her children would be provided for, she trusted her husband to take care of the whole family. Martha and John divorced, and Martha neglected to change her beneficiary designation. After Martha's death, John submits his claim to the plan administrator. The plan administrator follows the plan's terms, which do not revoke a beneficiary designation because of a participant's divorce. (See Q 5:10) The plan pays John, and he spends the money without considering any needs of Martha's children.

The examples and common mistakes explained above are only a few of the many ways a participant might make an unwise beneficiary designation. Although deferred compensation is meant to be consumed mostly during a participant's retirement years, death always is possible. So a participant should use his or her valuable right to name a beneficiary, and use that right with care.

Chapter 6

ERISA, Its Exemptions, and Other Non-Tax Considerations for 457 Plans

David W. Powell, Esq.
Groom Law Group, Chartered

This chapter discusses the application of the Employee Retirement Income Security Act of 1974 (ERISA) to 457 plans, including the possible exemptions from ERISA, simplified reporting and disclosure requirements for top-hat plans, and the treatment of excess benefit plans and severance and welfare plans. Also addressed are the ERISA consequences of a funded 457 plan and the income tax consequences for such a plan's funding vehicle. Finally, the chapter briefly discusses certain securities and insurance law issues.

ERISA in General

Q 6:1   What requirements does ERISA impose on 457 plans?

The Employee Retirement Income Security Act of 1974 (ERISA) imposes a number of significant requirements on employee pension plans. These include reporting and disclosure requirements. For example, the plan administrator must provide summary plan descriptions (SPDs), summaries of material modifications (SMMs), and summary annual reports (SARs). The plan administrator must also file annual information returns (on Form 5500 or (for plan years beginning prior to January 1, 1999) Form 5500-C/R, including schedules; but see the special top-hat plan rules discussed in Q 6:24). [ERISA § 101 et seq.] There are also participation and vesting rules [ERISA § 201 et seq.]; minimum funding requirements [ERISA § 301 et seq.]; fiduciary, trust, and prohibited transaction requirements [ERISA § 401 et seq.]; and enforcement provisions [ERISA § 501 et seq.].

Q 6:2   What are the consequences to a 457 plan of being subject to ERISA?

The Internal Revenue Code (Code) requires that an eligible deferred compensation plan be unfunded. [I.R.C. § 457(b)(6)] An employee pension plan subject to ERISA must be funded unless it comes within one of the exemptions from the funding requirements. [ERISA §§ 301, 302] Accordingly, a 457 plan that must comply with ERISA's funding requirements will automatically fail to be an eligible deferred compensation plan under Code Section 457(b). Furthermore, because of ERISA's vesting requirements, there can be no substantial risk of forfeiture of ERISA plan assets. Accordingly, contributions to a funded 457 plan will be immediately taxable. Although there may be situations where it is desirable to create a non-tax-deferred 457 plan, both employers and employees generally want to defer income tax until plan benefits are paid, making it important to determine whether an exemption may be available.

Governmental plans are not subject to Title I of ERISA and thus are not subject to ERISA's funding requirements; however, the Small Business Job Protection Act of 1996 (SBJPA) added a requirement that assets of governmental 457(b) plans be held in trust effective August 20, 1996, for new plans and January 1, 1999, for existing plans. Such trusts will be tax-exempt, and benefits will not be taxable until paid. [I.R.C. § 457(g); IRS Notice 98-8, 1998-4 I.R.B. 6]

Q 6:3   What exemptions from ERISA are available?

Governmental plans are exempt from Title I of ERISA. [ERISA § 4(b)(1)] Church plans are also exempt from Title I of ERISA, provided the plan administrator has not made an election under Code Section 410(d). [ERISA § 4(b)(2)] Exemptions from some provisions of ERISA are available to other types of plans, including the so-called top-hat exemption for unfunded plans that exist for the benefit of a "select group of management or highly compensated employees" (see Q 8:1) and an exemption for excess benefit plans that provide benefits in excess of the limits on annual additions under Code Section 415. These exemptions are more fully discussed in Qs 6:4–6:29.

Governmental Plans

Q 6:4   What is a governmental plan exempt from ERISA?

ERISA defines *governmental plan* as a plan established or maintained for its employees by the government of the United States, by the government of any state or political subdivision thereof, or by any agency or instrumentality of the foregoing. It also includes any plan to which the Railroad Retirement Act of 1935 or the Railroad Retirement Act of 1937 applies and that is financed by contributions required under either of those Acts, and any plan of any international organization that is exempt from taxation under the provisions of the International Organizations Immunities Act. [ERISA § 3(32)] A parallel definition exists in Code Section 414(d). Rulings or advisory opinions on governmental plan status are available from the IRS and the Department of Labor (DOL). The degree to which the government controls an employer is significant in determining governmental plan status.

Q 6:5   How much of a relationship with a governmental unit must a plan sponsor have to be a governmental plan?

A plan will not be considered a governmental plan merely because the sponsoring organization has a relationship with a governmental unit or a quasi-governmental entity. One of the most important factors to be considered in determining whether an organization is an agency or instrumentality of the United States or any state or political subdivision thereof is the degree of control that the federal or state government has over the organization's everyday operations. Other factors include the following:

1. Whether there is specific legislation creating the organization;
2. The source of funds for the organization;
3. The manner in which the organization's trustees or operating board is selected; and
4. Whether the applicable governmental unit considers the employees of the organization to be employees of the applicable governmental unit.

Although all of these factors are considered in determining whether an organization is an agency of a government, the mere satisfaction of one or all of the factors is not necessarily determinative. [Rev. Rul. 89-49, 1989-1 C.B. 117]

Church Plans

Q 6:6   What is a church plan exempt from ERISA?

ERISA Section 3(33) and Code Section 414(e) provide identical definitions of the term *church plan*. Within the meaning of those provisions, a church plan that has not made the election under Code Section 410(d) is exempt from all of Title I of ERISA. As a result, plans of churches (within the meaning of Code Section 3121(w)(3)(A); see Q 6:7) and qualified church-controlled organizations (within the meaning of Code Section 3121(w)(3)(B); see Q 6:8) that are not subject to Code

Section 457 (see Q 6:3), as well as plans of nonqualified church-controlled organizations (e.g., church hospitals, colleges, universities, and nursing homes) that are subject to the constraints of Code Section 457, are exempt from Title I of ERISA.

Thus, 457 plans of nonqualified church-controlled organizations, including Section 501(c)(3) organizations that share common religious bonds and convictions with a church or a convention or association of churches or a religious denomination (e.g., church hospitals, colleges, universities, and nursing homes), may be able to maintain eligible 457(b) plans exempt from ERISA.

Q 6:7 What does *church* mean under Code Section 3121(w)(3)(A)?

Under Code Section 3121(w)(3)(A), *church* means a church, a convention or association of churches, or an elementary or secondary school that is controlled, operated, or principally supported by a church or a convention or association of churches.

Q 6:8 What does *qualified church-controlled organization* mean under ERISA?

Qualified church-controlled organization means any church-controlled tax-exempt organization described in Code Section 501(c)(3) except an organization that

1. Offers goods, services, or facilities for sale, other than on an incidental basis, to the general public, other than goods, services, or facilities that are sold at a nominal charge that is substantially less than the cost of providing such goods, services, or facilities; and

2. Normally receives more than 25 percent of its support from either (a) government sources or (b) receipts from admissions, sales of merchandise, performance of services, or furnishing of facilities in activities that are not unrelated activities, or both.

[I.R.C. § 3121(w)(3)(B)]

As a result of these exceptions under Code Section 3121(w)(3), certain church-related organizations that are separate from a church—including many colleges, universities, hospitals, and nursing homes—typically do not qualify as qualified church-controlled organizations. Thus, they may establish an eligible 457 plan.

Q 6:9 What is required of a plan before it qualifies as a church plan?

A plan will qualify as a church plan if it establishes that

1. Substantially all of its covered employees are employees or "deemed" employees of a church or a convention or association of churches [I.R.C. § 414(e)(1), (2); ERISA § 3(33)(A), (B)];

2. It is not primarily for the benefit of employees (or their beneficiaries) who are employed in connection with one or more unrelated trades or businesses (within the meaning of Code Section 513) [I.R.C. § 414(e)(2); ERISA § 3(33)(B)(i)]; and

3. It is established or maintained for employees by

    a. A church or a convention or association of churches that is exempt from tax under Code Section 501 [I.R.C. § 414(e)(1); ERISA § 3(33)(A)]; or

    b. An organization described in Code Section 414(e)(3)(A) and ERISA Section 3(33)(C)(i).

Q 6:10   How does ERISA define *church*?

Although there is no definition of *church* in the Code, ERISA, or the regulations thereunder, the IRS has published in its Exempt Organizations Examination Guidelines Handbook a list of characteristics it considers in evaluating whether an entity is a church. These include the following:

1. A distinct legal existence;
2. A recognized creed and form of worship;
3. A definite and distinct ecclesiastical government;
4. A formal code of doctrine or discipline;
5. A distinct religious history;
6. A membership not associated with any other church or denomination;
7. A complete organization of ordained ministers ministering to their congregations;
8. Ordained ministers selected after completing prescribed courses of study;
9. A literature of its own;
10. An established place of worship;
11. Regular congregations;
12. Regular religious services;
13. Schools for the religious instruction of the young;
14. Schools for the preparation of its ministers; and
15. Other facts and circumstances that may bear on the organization's claim for church status.

[IRM 7(10)69, Exempt Organizations Examination Guidelines Handbook § 321.3 (Apr. 5, 1982)]

For purposes of Code Section 414 only, the term *church* also includes a religious order or a religious organization if that order or organization is an integral part of a church and is engaged in carrying out the functions of a church, whether it is a civil-law corporation or otherwise. [Treas. Reg. § 1.414(e)-1(e)]

Q 6:11   What individuals who are not employees of a church or a convention or association of churches may nevertheless be covered by a church plan as deemed employees?

Code Section 414(e)(3)(C) provides that a church that is exempt from tax under Code Section 501 shall be deemed the employer of any individual included as an employee under Code Section 414(e)(3)(B). That provision defines *employee* as including a duly ordained, commissioned, or licensed minister of a church in the exercise of his or her ministry, regardless of the source of the minister's compensation, and an employee of an organization that is exempt from tax under Code Section 501 and that is controlled by or associated with a church or a convention or association of churches. Together with Code Section 414(e)(5), this permits chaplains, regardless of their employer, and employees of church-related entities, such as church hospitals, universities, nursing homes, and publishing houses (provided they are controlled by or associated with a church or a convention or association of churches), to participate in a church plan. The provisions just described relate to the definition of the term *church plan* as defined in Code Section 414(e).

For years beginning after December 31, 1996, the SBJPA has clarified that a self-employed minister can participate in a Section 403(b)(9) retirement income account program in a manner similar to ministers who are employees, and that a minister serving in a specialized ministry (e.g., chaplains) may also contribute (or the minister's employer may contribute) to the minister's denominational church plan (whether that plan is a Section 401(a) qualified plan or a Section 403(b)(9) retirement income account program). [I.R.C. § 414(e)(5)]

Q 6:12   When is an organization controlled by a church or a convention or association of churches?

The regulations under Code Section 414(e) state that "an organization, a majority of whose officers or directors are appointed by a church's governing board or by officials of a church, is controlled by a church. . . ." [Treas. Reg. § 1.414(e)-1(d)(2)]

Q 6:13   When is an organization associated with a church or convention or association of churches?

In some cases, the IRS has recognized that an organization listed in a particular church directory is associated with the church. [P.L.R. 8824049; GCM 39,832 (Oct. 12, 1990); GCM 39,007 (July 1, 1983)]

Furthermore, an organization may be associated with a church within the meaning of Code Section 414(e)(3)(D) by reason of the common religious bonds and convictions it shares with that church. This may, for example, be evidenced by operating under church principles, by operating under articles of incorporation and bylaws that require the organization to incorporate in its policies and practices the moral teachings of the church, by maintaining a chapel where services are conducted, by employing chaplains, and by performing sacerdotal functions. One of the principal reasons that church plans that cover employees of an associated organization request private letter rulings (or DOL opinions interpreting ERISA Section 3(33)) is to determine the applicability of the "associated with" criterion. For example, the sponsor of a pension plan that covered the employees of a nonprofit organization providing mental health and counseling services and psychotherapy that were "Christian in their vision" requested a letter ruling from the IRS that the plan was a church plan under Code Section 414(e). The IRS concluded that the organization was associated with a church or convention of churches primarily because it was listed in the official church directory. [P.L.R. 9521038] Plans may request determinations from both the IRS and the DOL for greatest certainty.

Q 6:14   May a church plan cover employees employed in an unrelated trade or business?

Yes, to an extent, but the plan may not be primarily for the benefit of employees who are employed in connection with one or more unrelated trades or businesses (within the meaning of Code Section 513).

Q 6:15   When is an employee employed in an unrelated trade or business?

An employee is employed in connection with one or more unrelated trades or businesses of a church if a majority of the employee's duties and responsibilities are directly or indirectly related to carrying on such trades or businesses.

Q 6:16   How is it determined that a plan is established or maintained primarily for employees of an unrelated trade or business?

A plan established after September 2, 1974, is established primarily for the benefit of employees who are not employed in connection with one or more unrelated trades or businesses if, on the date the plan is established, the number of employees employed in connection with the unrelated trades or businesses eligible to participate in the plan is less than 50 percent of the total number of employees of the church eligible to participate in the plan. [Treas. Reg. § 1.414(e)-1(b)(2)(i)(A)]

A plan in existence on September 2, 1974, is considered to be established primarily for the benefit of employees who are not employed in connection with one or more unrelated trades or businesses if, in either of its first two plan years ending after September 2, 1974, it meets the requirements, described below, for determining whether a plan is maintained primarily for the benefit of such employees. [Treas. Reg. § 1.414(e)-1(b)(2)(i)(B)]

A plan will be considered maintained primarily for the benefit of employees of a church who are not employed in connection with one or more unrelated trades or businesses if (1) in four out of five of its most recently completed plan years less than 50 percent of the persons participating in the plan (at any time during the plan year) consist of employees employed in connection with an unrelated trade or business and (2) in the same year less than 50 percent of the total compensation paid by the employer during the plan year (if benefits or contributions are a function of compensation) to employees participating in the plan is paid to employees employed in connection with an unrelated trade or business.

A determination that a plan is not a church plan will apply to the second year for which the plan fails to meet these two requirements and all plan years thereafter, unless, after taking into account all the facts and circumstances, the plan is still considered a church plan. Such facts and circumstances may include the following:

1. The margin by which the plan failed the 50 percent tests; and
2. Whether the failure resulted from a reasonable mistake as to what constituted an unrelated trade or business or whether a particular person or group of persons was employed in connection with one or more unrelated trades or businesses.

[Treas. Reg. § 1.414(e)-1(b)(2)]

Q 6:17 When a nondenominational employer employs a minister, what is the effect on that employer's pension plan?

If a minister who participates in a church plan is employed by an employer ineligible to participate in a church plan, and the services provided by such minister are "in the exercise of his or her ministry," the employer may exclude that minister from being treated as an employee of that employer for purposes of the nondiscrimination rules applicable to either a Section 401(a) qualified plan or a Section 403(b)(9) retirement income account program. [I.R.C. § 414(e)(5)(C)]

Q 6:18 When is a plan established and maintained by a church or a convention or association of churches or by an organization described in Code Section 414(e)(3)(A)?

Under the third test of Code Section 414(e), a church plan must be established and maintained for its employees and their beneficiaries by a church or a convention or association of churches exempt from taxes under Code Section 501(a) or an organization described in Code Section 414(e)(3)(A).

An organization described in Code Section 414(e)(3)(A) includes an organization the principal purpose or function of which is the administration or funding of a plan or program for the provision of retirement or welfare benefits for the employees (or deemed employees) of a church or convention if the organization is controlled by or associated with a church or convention. Such an organization is commonly either a pension board of a religious denomination or, in the case of individual church hospitals, church universities, and other organizations controlled by or associated with a church or a convention or association of churches that maintain their own plans, a retirement plan committee appointed by the church or convention or association of churches, the sole purpose of which is to control and manage the operation and administration of the plan.

Q 6:19 How can a church plan elect to be covered under ERISA?

An election under Code Section 410(d) can be made only by the plan administrator by attaching a statement to

1. The annual return (Form 5500 series) or amended annual return that is filed for the first plan year for which the election is effective; or
2. A written request for a determination letter relating to qualification of the plan.

The statement must indicate that the election is made under Code Section 410(d) and the first plan year for which it is effective. [Treas. Reg. § 1.410(d)-1(c)] In practice, Section 410(d) elections are rare, probably because of the additional administrative burdens of being covered by ERISA.

Inadvertent elections of Section 410(d) coverage brought about by conforming to ERISA and Code requirements applicable to nonchurch plans should not normally occur, because Code Section 410(d)(1) and the legislative history of that section provide that such an election is to be made "in a form and manner to be prescribed in regulations." As noted previously, the regulations provide only one form for such an election and only two ways to notify the IRS of the election. For example, in Private Letter Ruling 8536041, a church adopted a prototype plan for the benefit of its employees. Despite the fact that the prototype plan was apparently drafted to comply with all post-ERISA aspects of the Code and the plan received a favorable determination letter to this effect, the IRS concluded that the plan as adopted by the church for the benefit of its employees was a church plan within the meaning of Code Section 414(e). Similarly, in Advisory Opinion 85-32 the DOL determined that a pension plan for a Catholic hospital qualified as a church plan under ERISA Section 4(b) despite the fact that a plan administrator had filed a Form 5500 for the 1982 plan year and had submitted to the Pension Benefit Guaranty Corporation (PBGC) premium payment forms and payments for plan years 1981 and 1982.

Q 6:20 What are the consequences if a plan fails to meet the requirements for being a church plan?

If a plan fails to meet the requirements of Code Section 414(e), a special remedial period will apply during which the plan may correct its faults and be deemed to meet the requirements of Code Section 414(e) for the year of correction and prior years. If a correction is not made during the correction period, the plan will fail to meet the requirements of Code Section 414(e) beginning with the date on which the earliest failure to meet one of the requirements occurred.

The correction period is the latest to end of the following:

1. The period ending 270 days after the date of mailing by the IRS of a notice of default with respect to the plan's failure to meet one or more of the Section 414(e) requirements;

2. Any period set by a court of competent jurisdiction after a final determination that the plan fails to meet such requirements (if the court does not specify the period, any reasonable period may be determined by the IRS on the basis of the facts and circumstances, but no less than 270 days after the court determination becomes final); or

3. Any additional period that the IRS determines is reasonable or necessary for the correction of the fault.

[I.R.C. § 414(e)(4)]

Q 6:21   Are nonelecting church plans required to file annual information returns?

Although nonelecting church plans are not subject to the reporting requirements of ERISA, there is no church plan exception under Code Section 6058 to the requirement of filing annual information returns with the IRS; however, the IRS has administratively relieved nonelecting church retirement plans from the requirement of filing the Form 5500 series. [Ann. 82-146, 1982-47 I.R.B. 53]

Top-Hat Plans

Q 6:22   What is a *top-hat plan* under ERISA?

Top-hat plan is the colloquial term for an unfunded plan for the benefit of "a select group of management or highly compensated employees." [ERISA §§ 201(2), 301(a)(3)]

Q 6:23   What does *select group* mean under ERISA?

The DOL has not defined the term *select group* by regulation, but DOL representatives have informally indicated that it depicts a higher threshold than *highly compensated employees* under Code Section 414(q). The DOL has issued a few advisory opinions on particular factual situations. [DOL Adv. Ops. 75-63, 75-64, 85-37] In one case, the term has been held not to apply to a group comprising one-fifth of the workforce. [Darden v. Nationwide Mutual Insurance Co., 717 F. Supp. 388 (E.D.N.C. 1989), aff'd, 922 F.2d 203 (4th Cir. 1991), rev'd on other grounds, 503 U.S. 318 (1992)] The definition of *top-hat group* is more fully discussed in chapter 8.

Q 6:24   What are the reporting and disclosure requirements for top-hat plans?

Top-hat plans are subject to the reporting and disclosure requirements of Title I of ERISA, Section 101 et seq. Those sections would normally require that 457 plans file annual reports using Form 5500 and schedules and provide SARs, SPDs, and SMMs to participants. The DOL by regulation has, however, established an "alternative method of compliance" for top-hat plans. An employer that maintains a top-hat plan may use this alternative method by filing with the DOL a single statement that includes the employer's name, address, and identification number, a declaration that the employer maintains the plan primarily for the purpose of providing deferred compensation for a select group of management or highly compensated employees, the number of such plans maintained by the employer, and the number of employees in each plan. [DOL Reg. § 2520.104-23] For plans in existence as of May 4, 1975, statements were required to be filed before August 31, 1975. For new plans, the statement has to be filed within 120 days of the plan's establishment. If an employer fails to make the one-time filing within the 120-day period, the plan will be subject to the normal Title I reporting and disclosure requirements.

Q 6:25   What are the consequences if an employer has failed to make the one-time top-hat plan filing?

For an employer that has failed to make the one-time filing for a 457 plan subject to ERISA, the DOL has instituted an amnesty program (see Q 8:9). Under the program, the sponsor of a top-hat plan that failed to file the necessary statement within the 120-day filing limit can get back into compliance by paying a flat penalty of $750 (without regard to the number of plans), filing the overdue Forms 5500 for prior years, and filing the one-time informational statement. [Vol. 67, No. 60 Fed. Reg. 15053 (Mar. 28, 2002)]

Excess Benefit Plans

Q 6:26   What is an excess benefit plan as defined under ERISA?

An excess benefit plan is defined in ERISA Section 3(36) as an employee benefit plan maintained solely for the purpose of providing benefits in excess of the limitations imposed by Code Section 415.

Q 6:27   How is an excess benefit plan treated under ERISA?

An excess benefit plan is exempt from all of Title I of ERISA if it is unfunded [ERISA § 4(b)(5)] or if it is a governmental plan. An excess benefit plan is exempt from the participation, vesting, and funding requirements if it is funded (but is still subject to the reporting and disclosure, fiduciary responsibility, administration, and enforcement provisions if it is funded). [ERISA § 201(7)] Under the SBJPA, effective for years after 1994, certain governmental excess benefit arrangements are not subject to the Section 457 limits. [I.R.C. §§ 415(m)(3), 457(e)(14); see also P.L.R. 200322019, 200317047]

Severance and Welfare Plans

Q 6:28 Are severance pay plans, death benefit plans, and other types of benefit arrangements subject to ERISA?

Code Section 457(e)(11) explicitly excludes certain types of plans from being subject to Code Section 457, including bona fide vacation leave (presumably including leaves of absence), sick leave, compensatory time, severance pay, disability pay, and death benefit plans; therefore, plans are occasionally structured as one of these types of plans in hopes that the Section 457 limits will not apply to them. In addition, many requirements of ERISA, including the participation, vesting, and funding requirements, do not apply to welfare plans under ERISA. [ERISA §§ 201(1), 301(a)(1)] Welfare plans under ERISA include plans providing any of the following:

1. Medical, surgical, or hospital care or benefits;
2. Benefits in the event of sickness, accident, disability, death, or unemployment;
3. Vacation benefits;
4. Apprenticeship or other training programs;
5. Day care centers;
6. Scholarship funds;
7. Prepaid legal services; or
8. Any benefit described in Section 302(c) of the Labor Management Relations Act of 1947 (other than pensions on retirement or death and insurance to provide such pensions), which includes holiday, severance, and similar benefits.

[DOL Reg. § 2510.3-1(a)]

Q 6:29 What is a severance plan under ERISA?

Regulations promulgated by the DOL provide that a severance plan will be considered to be a welfare plan, and not a pension plan, for purposes of ERISA if total payments under the plan do not exceed the equivalent of twice the employee's annual compensation and if payments must be completed within 24 months of the employee's termination. [DOL Reg. § 2510.3-2(b)] The IRS has not promulgated any rules on what constitutes a severance plan. IRS views of what constitutes a bona fide severance pay plan have been informally expressed in "Severance Pay Plans of State and Local Government and Tax

Exempt Employers," by Cheryl Press and Thomas Brisendine, which was Topic H of the materials for the IRS Exempt Organizations Technical Institute Program for Fiscal Year 1998. (These materials were substantially reprinted in the Spring 1997 issue of *Deferred Compensation.*) The IRS apparently does not view treatment for ERISA purposes as dispositive, focusing instead on the nature of the events that will give rise to payments (e.g., whether on voluntary or involuntary termination). [Lima Surgical Ass'n VEBA v. United States, 20 Cl. Ct. 674, 12 Employee Benefits Cas. (BNA) 1641 (1990), *aff'd*, 14 Employee Benefits Cas. (BNA) 1346 (Fed. Cir. 1991); see also Booth v. Commissioner, 108 T.C. 524 (1997). Cf. Treas. Reg. § 31.3121(v)(2)-1(b)(4)(iv) (severance plan exception for FICA purposes)]

Selected Securities and Insurance Law Issues for 457 Plans

Q 6:30   Are there securities law issues for a 457 plan?

Yes. Representatives of the Securities and Exchange Commission (SEC) have begun to question whether certain nonqualified deferred compensation arrangements constitute securities that should be registered unless an exemption from registration applies, such as for a private placement. In addition, the inclusion of 457 plan assets of nongovernmental plans in a group trust, although not causing the group trust to fail to be tax-exempt under Code Section 401(a)(24), would appear to be a violation of the securities law because the relevant exemption from the securities law for group trusts extends only to qualified plans and governmental plans. [Securities Act of 1933 § 3(a)(2)(A)] Securities law issues are more fully discussed in chapter 10.

The National Securities Markets Improvement Act of 1996 [Pub. L. No. 104-290 (H.R. 3005)], enacted on October 11, 1996, exempts church plans within the meaning of Code Section 414(e) from many provisions of federal and state securities law, and requires that certain disclosures regarding these exemptions be provided to plan participants and beneficiaries.

Q 6:31   Are church plans subject to the securities laws?

Before the enactment of the National Securities Markets Improvement Act of 1996, there was some uncertainty about the scope of exemptions for church retirement plans from federal and state securities law, particularly for church Section 403(b) retirement programs. The National Securities Markets Improvement Act provided the desired clarification for church plans, and now such plans (and the investment pools maintained by church benefit programs in connection with such plans) are not subject to the Investment Company Act of 1940 or the Securities Act of 1933 (as well as certain requirements imposed under the Securities Exchange Act of 1934, the Investment Advisers Act of 1940, and the Trust Indenture Act of 1939). Significantly, state "blue sky" laws that require registration or qualification of securities have also been preempted in the case of church plans, as have any state laws applicable to investment companies or to brokers, dealers, investment advisors, or agents.

Church plans utilizing these exemptions from federal and state securities law are required to give plan participants notice of such exemptions and inform them that they will therefore "not be afforded the protection of these provisions." This notice is to be given to new participants "as soon as practicable" after beginning participation and to all participants annually. The SEC can also require church plans to file a notice with the SEC containing such information as the SEC may prescribe. It should be emphasized that these notices are required (or can be required, in the case of notices to the SEC) only for plans relying on the new exemption. Plans, such as Section 401(a) qualified plans, that can rely on another securities law exemption are not required to give these notices.

Q 6:32   Are there insurance law issues for a non-ERISA 457 plan?

State insurance laws vary from state to state and are often vague and broadly worded. At the time ERISA was enacted, there was some concern that state insurance regulators would seek to impose state insurance laws on self-insured employee benefit plans. [State ex rel. Farmer v. Monsanto, 517 S.W.2d 129 (Mo. 1974); West & Co. v. Sykes, 515 S.W.2d 635 (Ark. 1974)] It is for this reason that the so-called deemer clause was added to ERISA. This clause provides that "[n]either an employee benefit plan . . ., nor any trust established under such a plan, shall be deemed to be an insurance company or other insurer . . . or to be engaged in the business of insurance . . . for purposes of any law of any State purporting to regulate insurance companies, [or] insurance contracts. . . ." [ERISA § 514(b)(2)(B)]

As a result, although attention to the issue has lessened considerably since the passage of ERISA in 1974, plans that are not subject to ERISA preemption of state and local laws, such as church and governmental plans and excess benefit plans, should be reviewed carefully as to whether, by, for example, offering benefits in the form of a life annuity, they may be considered subject to some of the insurance laws of the state in which they provide benefits and whether any exemptions from such state insurance laws may apply.

ERISA and Tax Consequences of Funded 457(f) Plans

Q 6:33   Can an employer maintain a funded ineligible 457 plan?

If an ineligible 457 plan is funded, the amounts will be taxable to the participants in accordance with Code Section 457(f), and ERISA will apply to the plan unless the plan is a nonemployee plan such as a director plan. [DOL Reg. § 2510.3-3] Thus, for example, the participation, vesting, reporting and disclosure, benefit accrual and minimum funding requirements, qualified joint and preretirement survivor annuity (QJSA/QPSA) requirements, and fiduciary requirements of ERISA all apply. Because ERISA imposes a requirement that assets be held in trust [ERISA § 403], the assets cannot be subject to a substantial risk of forfeiture for purposes of Code Section 457(f). Therefore, contributions are likely immediately taxable. Because the Code does not provide a tax exemption for such a nonqualified trust, an ordinary trust, known as a secular trust, must be created.

Q 6:34   How is a secular trust taxed?

Under numerous private letter rulings based on Code Section 402(b), the IRS has held that nonqualified secular trusts are treated as regular trusts subject to trust taxation. [P.L.R. 9302017, 9207010, 9206009] In addition, the income is currently taxed to highly compensated employees (within the meaning of Code Section 414(q)) under Code Section 402(b)(4)(K). Hence, the income can be subject to double taxation.

Under a secular trust, the trustee files Form 1041. A deduction is allowed for distributable net income (DNI) [I.R.C. § 661], so the trust tax can be avoided by annual distribution of income. Since capital gains are not considered DNI unless paid, credited, or required to be distributed to any beneficiary under the trust during the current year, the trust agreement should address capital gains. [I.R.C. § 643(a)(3)]

There is no trust-level tax if life insurance is used for the investment of trust assets; but, because of Code Section 72(u), if an annuity is the funding vehicle, unless the employee is considered the owner of the trust, the annual income on the policy is taxable to the trust. [P.L.R. 9204010]

The trustee must also file Schedules K-1 with respect to distributions. Distributions from a secular trust are subject to the Section 72 rules. Under those rules, a pro rata rule applies for annuity distributions. [I.R.C. § 72(b)] For other forms of distribution, the taxable portion comes out first. [I.R.C. § 72(e)(2)] The Section 72(q) 10 percent excise tax applies to distributions before age 59½.

Besides annual distribution of trust income, another method considered to avoid the issue of double taxation of income to highly compensated employees is the use of an employee-grantor trust (see Q 6:35).

Q 6:35   Can a funded 457(f) plan hold assets in an employee-grantor trust?

An employee-grantor trust may be created if the funds are distributed to the employee first and then contributed to the trust. [P.L.R. 8841923, 8843021] Alternatively, use of "Crummey" types of powers may also suffice. To ensure that the employee will contribute the funds to the trust, it is apparently permissible to make future payments under the plan contingent on the contribution to the trust of prior payments. [P.L.R. 9316018] There is some question as to whether such an arrangement constitutes an employee benefit plan subject to ERISA; such a determination would likely depend on the facts of the situation.

Q 6:36   Can a 457(f) plan be funded by a secular annuity?

A nonqualified 457(f) plan can be funded by an annuity. In that event, the annuity is known as a secular annuity. The value of the contract (i.e., the cash surrender value) is taxable to the employee when vested. [I.R.C. § 403(c)] The employee must be the owner of the annuity to avoid current taxation under Code Section 72(u). In addition, secular annuities are subject to the minimum distribution rules of Code Section 72(s), which are similar to those of Code Section 401(a)(9) (see chapter 3).

Chapter 7

Mergers and Acquisitions

David W. Powell, Esq.
Groom Law Group, Chartered

Mergers and acquisitions are less common in the tax-exempt community than among for-profit corporations. In certain sectors (particularly health care), however, sponsors of 457 and 403(b) plans are increasingly combining with or becoming part of other tax-exempt, governmental, and for-profit employers in a variety of arrangements, including mergers, acquisitions, and privatizations. The new configurations can give rise to many concerns, including plan terminations, severance pay, and distributions, that require unique responses. In addition, the Economic Growth and Tax Relief Reconciliation Act of 2001 (EGTRRA) has added some flexibility to these arrangements but raises some new issues as well.

457 Plan Considerations

Q 7:1 What happens if an employer sponsoring a 457(b) plan is acquired by another tax-exempt or governmental employer?

When a tax-exempt organization such as a hospital is merged with another tax-exempt employer, the acquiree's 457(b) plan may continue to be maintained, but it is advisable to review the terms of the plan to ensure that such terms will apply as intended under the post-merger entity.

Similarly, when a governmental employer maintaining a 457(b) plan is acquired by another governmental employer, the successor employer may continue to maintain the 457(b) plan. However, when a tax-exempt employer acquires a governmental employer's 457(b) plan, the differences between the 457 rules for governmental sponsors and tax-exempt sponsors in funding, distribution election and rollover rules effectively preclude continued operation of the plan by a nongovernmental entity. In such cases, recently proposed regulations provide that the governmental 457(b) plan assets must be transferred to another governmental 457(b) plan of the same state, or the plan may be terminated, with distributions made as soon as administratively practicable. Otherwise, the governmental plan trust will cease to be a tax-exempt trust. [Treas. Reg. § 1.457-10(a)(2)]

If a governmental plan sponsor acquires a tax-exempt entity sponsoring a 457(b) plan, the result is less clear. The proposed regulations indicate that assets of an eligible plan of a tax-exempt entity may not be transferred to a governmental plan and Code Section 457(f) will then apply. This would suggest that the 457(b) plan of the tax-exempt employer should be terminated. [Treas. Reg. § 1.457-10(b), (a)(2)(i)] However, it is not clear how the ability of a governmental plan to make retroactive corrections may affect this result.

Special attention should also be paid to whether the plans under the pre- or post-merger entities may be top-hat (see Q 8:1) or church or governmental plans (see Q 2:1) and whether they may gain or lose such status as a result of the merger or acquisition, because retention of non-Employee Retirement Income Security Act of 1974 (ERISA) status is usually crucial to the compliance of such plans with the Internal Revenue Code (Code). In some types of business combinations, such as joint ventures, the status of a plan may not be at all clear, and the facts may require careful evaluation.

Q 7:2 What happens to an acquiree's 457(b) plan if the acquiror is not tax exempt or governmental?

When a tax-exempt organization is acquired by a for-profit organization, important issues arise. First, it should be noted that Code Section 457 does not in fact confer advantages to nonqualified plans of tax-exempt employers (other than perhaps to avoid constructive receipt upon making a payout election, and even that is questionable), but, rather, generally serves to restrict nonqualified deferrals. The proposed regulations indicate that the constructive receipt rules of Code Section 451 would then apply, but unhelpfully do not indicate how those rules would apply. An example would be whether an election to defer made after separation from service but before the distribution is made available would give rise to constructive receipt. [Treas. Reg. § 1.457-10(a)(2)(i)]

Thus, there is likely to be little advantage in deferring additional compensation in compliance with the terms of a 457(b) plan if the surviving entity is a for-profit corporation. The ordinary rules applicable to nonqualified arrangements not subject to Code Section 457 are likely to be much more beneficial; therefore, termination of the 457(b) plan and the creation of a new nonqualified deferred compensation arrangement may be advisable.

Where the acquiree's plan was a governmental plan, as noted above, the different rules for governmental 457(b) plans will preclude it from being maintained by a nongovernmental entity without violating numerous Code and ERISA requirements.

Q 7:3   What should be done with the acquiree's 457(b) plan if the acquiror is not tax exempt or governmental?

Inasmuch as nonqualified plans principally operate to defer compensation that has not yet been earned, the most common way for a non-tax-exempt or governmental acquiror to deal with a tax-exempt acquiree's 457(b) plan has been simply to freeze (i.e., amend to not permit future deferrals) the plan, make no more deferrals under it, and continue to pay out previously accrued amounts under the terms of the plan. The regulations indicate that the constructive receipt rules would apply to the plan (see Q 7:2). Although the IRS has issued no guidance on the continued administration of a nongovernmental 457(b) plan when the sponsor is no longer tax exempt, presumably, continuation is permissible provided that the 457(b) plan must continue to operate in a manner exempt from ERISA. Again, it is not possible for a governmental 457(b) plan to be taken over by a nongovernmental sponsor. It will be necessary for the 457(b) plan to be terminated or frozen and maintained by another governmental entity.

A different result may occur if the 457 plan sponsored by the tax-exempt sponsor was an ineligible plan. Presumably, additional deferrals of post-merger compensation under what had been a 457(f) plan (i.e., a plan not meeting the requirements of Code Section 457(b) and therefore either treating benefits as subject to a substantial risk of forfeiture or currently taxable) will operate to defer taxation pursuant to the ordinary nonqualified plan rules rather than the rules of Code Section 457(f). Of course, it will always be advisable to review the terms of the ineligible plan to determine whether any changes in plan design may be called for, such as changes in distribution elections. It is unclear whether the deferrals made while the plan was subject to Code Section 457(f) must remain subject to a substantial risk of forfeiture to defer taxation even if the plan is no longer subject to Code Section 457, although the regulations appear to suggest that this is so. [See, e.g., Treas. Reg. § 1.457-11(a)(1)]

Q 7:4   Can an acquiree's 457 plan be terminated or frozen?

If the terms of the plan so permit, an acquiree's 457 plan can be terminated after the acquisition, with immediate distribution and taxation of benefits to the participants and beneficiaries as the result. Section 457(b) plans may also be frozen but the sponsor must remain an eligible employer of the same type for the plan to remain an eligible plan. [Treas. Reg. § 1.457-10(a)]

Q 7:5 Can 457(b) plans be merged?

Although there is no formal guidance, presumably, 457(b) plans may be merged, inasmuch as transfers from one 457(b) plan to another are permitted under the Code. [I.R.C. § 457(e)(10); P.L.R. 9901014] However, the proposed regulations would suggest that such mergers can only be made where a transfer is permissible, for example, between plans of tax-exempt employers or between plans of governmental employers within the same state. [Treas. Reg. § 1.457-10(b)]

Q 7:6 Does the merger or acquisition of a 457(b) plan sponsor constitute a separation from service or severance of employment that would permit distributions?

Before June 7, 2001, probably not. As in the case of 403(b) plans, the same desk rule applied to the merger or acquisition of a 457(b) plan sponsor (see Q 7:13). A change in the tax-exempt status of the employer was apparently not a separation from service. [I.R.C. § 457(d)(1)(A)(ii); P.L.R. 9901014] However, effective June 7, 2001, under EGTRRA, the reference to a "separation from service" in order to permit a distribution was amended to a "severance of employment" for the purpose of eliminating the same desk rule. Thus, upon a change in the common law employer of the participant, a distribution may be permissible unless the plan terms themselves are more restrictive. See, by analogy, IRS Notice 2002-4. [2002-2 I.R.B. 1]

403(b) Considerations

Q 7:7 What happens if a for-profit entity acquires a tax-exempt organization that maintains a 403(b) plan?

There is no formal guidance for dealing with a tax-exempt entity that maintains a 403(b) plan that is acquired by a for-profit entity. Nevertheless, it should be possible to either terminate or freeze the 403(b) plan in such a case. That should be accomplished through appropriate corporate action, such as a board resolution (see Q 7:9).

To bolster the argument that a plan termination has occurred, it may be advisable, if the 403(b) contract is a group contract, to distribute individual annuity contracts or certificates incorporating the appropriate 403(b) plan distribution rules and restrictions (subject to the $5,000 small account cash-out rule) to the participants, as would be done in the termination of a qualified defined benefit plan (see Q 7:9).

Of course, no contributions to the acquiree's 403(b) plan can be made by the new employer, and at least under current law, the assets of the 403(b) plan cannot be merged with a 401(k) or other qualified 401(a) plan maintained by the acquiring entity. However, when a participant has a distributable event, such as a separation from service or attainment of age 59½, it is possible, after 2001, for eligible rollover distributions to be rolled over or transferred directly to a 401(a) plan at the election of the participant. Termination of the plan is not a distributable event permitting a distribution from the plan in the case of a 403(b) plan, however, unlike a 401(k) plan. Compare Code Section 403(b)(11) to 401(k)(10)(A).

If the acquiree's 403(b) plan is subject to Title I of ERISA, a fiduciary must continue to administer the distribution of the contracts and continue to file Forms 5500 for all periods during which there continue to be plan assets, that is, until all accounts have been distributed in cash or through distribution of individual annuity contracts or certificates (see Q 7:10).

As an alternative to terminating the acquiree's 403(b) plan, the acquiror may freeze the plan and administer the 403(b) contracts or accounts on a wasting basis (see Q 7:11).

Q 7:8   What happens if a tax-exempt organization eligible to maintain a 403(b) plan acquires another tax-exempt organization that maintains a 403(b) plan?

When a tax-exempt organization that sponsors a 403(b) plan is acquired by another tax-exempt organization, the acquiror should carefully review the acquiree's plan documents, Form 5500 filings, and other relevant information to determine whether the plan is in compliance with the Code and, if applicable, ERISA. The acquiror will also want to consider whether the design of the acquiree's plan is in accord with its own retirement plan objectives. Depending on the results of those examinations, the acquiror may choose to continue, correct, merge, freeze, or even terminate the acquiree's 403(b) plan (see Qs 7:9, 7:11, 7:15). Whether the acquisition may result in a partial termination and vesting of accounts of affected participants under the acquiree's plan should also be considered.

If the acquiree becomes part of the same controlled group as the acquiror, careful attention should be paid to the impact of controlled group status on the application of nondiscrimination rules, such as the 403(b) plan nondiscrimination safe harbors of IRS Notice 89-23 [1989-1 C.B. 654], on the continued operation of the plans of either entity. Where transactions involve church or governmental entities, careful attention must also be paid to whether the post-transaction plans will be or will continue to be church or governmental plans in order to be certain which Code, or, if applicable, ERISA requirements must be met. [See, e.g., P.L.R. 9717039]

When it is found that the acquiree's 403(b) plan has failed to satisfy the requirements of Code Section 403(b), it may be advisable for the plan to be frozen or terminated. Choosing either of those courses will depend on the degree of continuing responsibility that the acquiror wishes to have for the acquiree's plan. The acquiror may want for some reason (often, to meet employee expectations regarding the benefits that will continue to be available) to assume responsibility for the acquiree's 403(b) plan. Once the acquiree's 403(b) plan is corrected to meet the requirements of Code Section 403(b) (e.g., through the Self-Correction Program (SCP) or the Voluntary Correction for the Tax-sheltered Annuities (VCT) program under IRS Revenue Procedure 2003-44 [2003-25 I.R.B. 1051] (see Q 7:17)), the acquiror may either merge the acquiree's plan into its own 403(b) plan or simply assume operations of the plan.

In any event, any defects that would cause the acquiree's plan to fail to meet the requirements of Code Section 403(b), such as violations of the nondiscrimination requirements of Code Section 403(b)(12), must be given serious consideration: a merger of plans before appropriate correction that includes a plan that does not meet those requirements might cause the merged plan also to fail to satisfy Code Section 403(b). Other defects that may cause particular contracts not to satisfy Code Section 403(b) may be of concern if found in numerous contracts or in group contracts. [See Examination of 403(b) Plans, Guidelines Promulgated by the IRS, May, 1999] Defects that merely cause an inclusion of excess amounts in taxable income, such as violations of the maximum exclusion allowance (MEA) (repealed after 2001) and the Section 415 limit, are presumably of lesser concern because they would not affect the status of the merged plan as a 403(b) plan. Nevertheless, they may, unless corrected, carry significant potential withholding tax or FICA tax liability for the acquiring employer.

Q 7:9   Can an acquiree's 403(b) plan be terminated?

Neither the IRS nor the Department of Labor (DOL) has issued guidance on whether an acquiree's 403(b) plan can be terminated. Nonetheless, it should be possible to do so. At a minimum, it would require a corporate action to terminate the plan. [See, e.g., Ann. 94-101, 1994-35 I.R.B. 53]

Possibly, by analogy to the process established by the Pension Benefit Guaranty Corporation (PBGC) for terminating a qualified defined benefit plan that offers annuities, the acquiree's 403(b) plan may be terminated by distributing plan assets in the form of individual annuity contracts (or certificates under a group contract) that provide for the applicable distribution restrictions and other requirements of Code Section 403(b) and, in the case of plans subject to ERISA, the applicable spousal consent requirements. [See ERISA § 205] Any Section 403(b)(7) (i.e., mutual fund) monies and Section 403(b)(1) monies attributable to salary reduction contributions must continue to be subject to the applicable withdrawal restrictions. Unlike termination of a 401(k) plan, when it is sometimes possible to make distributions even though a separation from service or other event permitting a distribution under the general rules prohibiting in-service withdrawals has not occurred, termination of a 403(b) plan is not an event that in itself permits distributions earlier than such withdrawal restrictions would otherwise allow. Compare Code Section 403(b)(11) to Section 401(k)(10)(A). Of course, some transactions may result in an actual separation from service that may in turn permit distribution (see Q 7:13). If the withdrawal restrictions do allow a distribution, accounts that are subject to ERISA and are valued at less than $5,000 may be distributed without the participant's consent, as long as the 403(b) contract or account also so permits. Participants may be allowed to elect distributions of larger accounts upon a plan termination, if such distributions are permitted under the withdrawal restrictions and spousal consent requirements. The 10 percent excise tax under Code Section 72(t) on early distributions may apply to such distributions if they are not rolled over to another 403(b) plan or individual retirement account (IRA), or after 2001, a 401(a) or governmental 457(b) plan.

If the acquiror also sponsors a 403(b) plan and is sufficiently convinced that the acquiree's plan has complied with Section 403(b) requirements in the past, the acquiror may allow participants to directly roll over (if a distribution is permitted) or to directly transfer benefits to the acquiror's 403(b) plan, as specified in Revenue Ruling 90-24. [1990-1 C.B. 97]

Q 7:10 Can an acquiror refuse to accept responsibility for an acquiree's 403(b) plan?

Possibly. If an acquiree's 403(b) plan is a non-ERISA 403(b) plan, such as a salary-reduction-only plan under DOL Regulations Section 2510.3-2(f), the acquiror may be able to refuse to accept responsibility for the acquiree's plan and simply cease to deduct contributions from employees' salaries. If the acquiree's 403(b) plan is subject to ERISA, however, the duties of the plan administrator and other fiduciaries do not disappear when a plan sponsor ceases to exist. Those duties must devolve to other persons, and it is the responsibility of the fiduciaries of the terminating plan (one of which is usually the employer) to see that they are assumed. As a result, where the acquiree's obligations are generally assumed by the acquiror, as would be the case in a typical merger, any fiduciary obligations of the acquiree would also presumably transfer to the acquiror.

If the acquiree's 403(b) plan is terminated, the acquiror's responsibility to administer that plan should end with the final distribution and the filing of a final Form 5500, indicating that the plan has been terminated. The final Form 5500 is due on the last day of the seventh month (with an extension of two and one-half months if Form 5558 is filed) after the date of the last distribution, which is also the close of the final plan year. [See Rev. Rul. 69-157, 1969-1 C.B. 115; Rev. Rul. 89-87, 1989-2 C.B. 81]

Q 7:11 Can an acquiror freeze an acquiree's 403(b) plan?

There is no formal guidance on the issue of whether an acquiror can freeze an acquiree's 403(b) plan. If the acquiror wishes to cease making contributions to the acquiree's plan but does not wish to terminate it, it can be argued that the acquiror may freeze the acquiree's plan by taking appropriate corporate action, such as a board of directors' resolution, and may continue to administer the plan for those monies already contributed. Even if the acquiree's plan is frozen, however, the acquiror would assume the acquiree's responsibility for administering the acquiree's plan, including the obligation to continue to file Forms 5500 for as long as plan assets exist (see Q 7:10).

Q 7:12   Are there constraints on changes to an acquiree's 403(b) plan by the acquiror?

Very possibly. Promises made to participants in anticipation of a merger or contractual agreements under the merger agreement might constrain the successor employer's ability to alter a 403(b) plan that is subject to ERISA. Although the anti-cutback rule of Code Section 411(d)(6) does not apply to 403(b) plans, the parallel provision of ERISA Section 204(g) does apply to any 403(b) plan subject to ERISA. The provision does not permit an amendment that has the effect of eliminating or reducing an optional form of benefit with respect to benefits attributable to service before the amendment. This provision was recently liberalized by regulations issued in 2000. [See Treas. Reg. § 1.411(d)-4] If the acquiree's 403(b) plan was a money purchase pension plan, it should also be noted that a Section 204(h) notice must be provided to applicable individuals and employee organizations. Before EGTRRA, the notice had to be given after adoption—and at least 15 days before the effective date—of the resolution to cease or lower accruals. For plan amendments after the date EGTRRA was enacted (June 7, 2001), this notice period was changed by EGTRRA to be within a "reasonable time" before the effective date of the amendment. [See Prop. Reg. § 54.4980F-1]

Freezing a plan, as opposed to terminating it, will not normally result in immediate vesting of accounts of affected participants subject to the application of the partial termination rules or, in the case of profit-sharing plans, the rules regarding a complete discontinuance of contributions.

Q 7:13   Does acquisition of a 403(b) plan sponsor constitute a separation from service or severance of employment that would permit distributions?

Before EGTRRA, it probably did not, but the answer may be different after EGTRRA. Generally, salary reduction contributions to a 403(b) plan and contributions to a 403(b)(7) custodial account cannot be distributed before one of the following: attainment of age 59½, separation from service (before 2002), death, disability, or hardship (and no income may be distributed on account of hardship). EGTRRA amended the Code to substitute the term *severance of employment* for *separation from service* after 2001. The legislative history indicates that the purpose of this change was to eliminate the "same desk" rule, regardless of when the severance of employment occurred. [I.R.C. § 403(b)(7)(A)(ii), (b)(11)] Under the pre-EGTRRA rule, there was little authority on what constituted a separation from service for purposes of a 403(b) plan; however, the concept had been discussed by the IRS in other situations, such as the distribution rules applicable to 401(k) plans and the pre-1993 rules that applied to the rollover of in-service distributions. In rulings in those two contexts, the IRS has generally held that an employee would be considered separated from the service of his or her employer only upon death, retirement, resignation, or discharge, and not when he or she continued in the same position for a different employer as a result of the liquidation, merger, consolidation, change of form, or transfer of ownership of his or her former employer. [Rev. Rul. 77-336, 1977-2 C.B. 202; Rev. Rul. 80-129, 1980-1 C.B. 86; Rev. Rul. 81-141, 1981-1 C.B. 204; P.L.R. 9443041] This stance was known as the "same desk rule." In at least one letter ruling, the IRS has applied its 401(a) plan rulings regarding the same desk rule to 403(b) plans. [P.L.R. 8617125]

Thus, under the pre-EGTRRA rule, whether the acquisition of a 403(b) plan sponsor would constitute a separation from service that would permit a distribution depended on the facts of the situation, with particular emphasis on whether the employee under consideration was continuing in the same job. It was also important to consider how the acquisition was treated for other benefits purposes (e.g., under the Consolidated Omnibus Budget Reconciliation Act of 1985 (COBRA) health care continuation coverage).

It may be noted that the rules permitting distribution upon separation from service in the context of 401(k) plans had been earlier amended by the Tax Reform Act of 1986 (TRA '86) specifically to permit distributions upon the disposition by a corporation of substantially all of its assets, upon the disposition by a corporation of its interest in a subsidiary, or upon plan termination, if certain additional requirements are met. [I.R.C. § 401(k)(10)] Similar provisions were not added to Code Section 403(b), however, and thus these exceptions to the same desk rule were not available to 403(b) plans.

After EGTRRA, a severance of employment with the common law employer, such as in an asset acquisition, may be sufficient to permit distributions if the plan so provides. This, if the acquiror does not continue to maintain the 403(b) plan, would make it possible for the affected participants to take eligible rollover distributions that might be rolled over to an acquiror's 401(k) plan, for example. [See, by analogy, IRS Notice 2002-4, 2002-2 I.R.B. 1] However, distributions before age 59½ may still be subject to the 10 percent tax on early distributions under Code Section 72(f). In other cases, for example, where the acquiror may wish to take a transfer of a portion of the acquiror's 403(b) plan attributable to acquired participants into the acquiror's own 403(b) plan, it may be desirable to amend the 403(b) plan to not permit distributions upon severance of employment before age 59½.

Q 7:14 If an acquiror maintains a 403(b) plan, should it count its new employees' service with the acquiree for plan purposes?

There is little authority regarding counting service with prior employers for 403(b) plan purposes. In the case of a corporate merger or acquisition, it appears that the surviving entity may count service with the predecessor employer for 403(b) plan purposes (e.g., for the pre-2002 MEA calculation). [See P.L.R. 9802043, 9451063, 9451082, 8617125] If, however, the prior entity (entity A) continues to exist separately, unrelated to the entity that acquired the employees (entity B), and B merely hired some of A's employees, it would appear that B may not count service with A for purposes of its 403(b) plan MEA limit. Yet, counting prior service with A for vesting or eligibility might be permissible, subject to the nondiscrimination rules of Code Section 403(b)(12)(i).

Q 7:15 Can 403(b) plans be merged?

Probably. If the acquiror is sufficiently convinced that the acquiree's 403(b) plan has complied with the requirements of Code Section 403(b), an alternative to freezing or terminating the plan may be to merge it into the acquiror's 403(b) plan. At a minimum, corporate resolutions should authorize the merger of the two plans, with the agreements, contracts, and other documents constituting the acquiror's plan serving as the surviving plan documents. Assuming that the 403(b) funding vehicle(s) of the acquiree's plan so permits, acquiree plan assets would then be directed by the acquiror to be transferred to the acquiror's 403(b) plan funding agent(s) (subject to the "anti-cutback" requirements; see Q 7:12), together with all information necessary to carry over the accounts—provided that the terms of the applicable annuity contract(s) and custodial account(s) permit the employer to transfer account balances without participant consent. Otherwise, it may be necessary for each participant to direct his or her transfer.

All acquiree plan documents should be carefully reviewed as to the manner of making the transfer and any changes; plan documents may need to be amended. Presumably, Treasury Regulations Section 1.414(l)-1 will be satisfied because each participant will retain his or her full account balance in the merged plan; therefore, no Form 5310-A need be filed. Any withdrawal restrictions on Section 403(b)(7) monies or salary reduction amounts, however, must be carried over to the new contract or plan in accordance with Revenue Ruling 90-24. [1990-1 C.B. 97]

The acquiree's 403(b) plan should also be reviewed to determine whether there is a vesting schedule or there are any exclusions from participation that may be affected by the merger. In addition, Form 5500 must be filed (a merger is currently reflected in item 10 of the form, though that is not an item that must be completed by a 403(b) plan).

The equivalent of Code Section 414(l) would apply to ERISA-covered plans through the operation of ERISA Section 208. Further, if ERISA applies, ERISA Section 204(g) generally prohibits amending a plan to eliminate certain optional forms of benefit, though these rules were substantially liberalized in 2000. [See Treas. Reg. § 1.411(d)-4]

Prior to EGTRRA, after-tax monies could not be directly rolled over to another 403(b) plan in a direct rollover distribution (though they could be transferred in a plan merger or a plan-to-plan asset transfer, via a direct transfer pursuant to Revenue Ruling 90-24). [1990-1 C.B. 97] Effective in 2002, however, after-tax monies may be rolled over into another 403(b) plan. See IRS Notice 2002-3. [2002-2 I.R.B. 289]

Q 7:16   Can 403(b) plans and 401(a) plans be merged?

Not under current law. [See P.L.R. 9021047, 200317022] However, much of the authority governing plan-to-plan transfers and mergers are found in revenue rulings. [See, e.g., Rev. Ruls. 67-213; 1967-2 C.B. 149; 90-24, 1990-1 C.B. 97] It was not clear whether the IRS would extend the rationale of those rulings to plan-to-plan transfers and mergers between 401(a) and 403(b) plans in light of the liberalizing changes to rollovers and increased portability of plan assets under EGTRRA. (See Qs 1:14, 2:227, 2:242, 2:244, 2:245, 2:246, 2:247.) However, the IRS has recently declined to do so. [P.L.R. 200317022]

Q 7:17   What happens if an acquiree's 403(b) plan is found to have defects?

Many defects of a 403(b) plan may be corrected under the VCT program. The VCT program, however, can require a time-consuming submission process. Further, under SCP, many operational defects can be corrected without involving the IRS. There is a requirement that corrections be completed by the end of the second year after the year the violation occurred unless the defect was "insignificant." [Rev. Proc. 2003-44, 2003-25 I.R.B. 1051] Generally, if the acquiror's 403(b) plan is not also defective, it will often be advisable to keep the acquiror's plan and the acquiree's plan separate until any deficiencies in the acquiree's 403(b) plan are resolved.

Severance Pay and 403(b) Plans

Q 7:18   Could severance pay be deferred under a 403(b) plan as a salary reduction contribution under the law in effect before 1996?

Prior IRS authority indicated that the ability of employees to defer severance pay under a 403(b) plan was significantly limited. Under the law in effect before August 20, 1996 (the effective date of the Small Business Job Protection Act of 1996 (SBJPA)), IRS regulations provided that a salary reduction agreement was effective "only to the extent such amounts are earned by the employee after the agreement becomes effective." [Treas. Reg. § 1.403(b)-1(b)(3)(i)] In the context of severance payments, the IRS has held that amounts will be treated as earned in the year "when the services are performed which give rise to the employee's entitlement to the terminal pay," not when the severance pay vests. [See GCM 39659 (Sept. 8, 1987) (considering terminal pay based on accumulated leave and service that vested only on retirement or death, to be earned each year in which services were performed, rather than upon vesting)]

The IRS's position on this matter was also articulated in its Guidelines for Examination of 403(b) Plans published by the IRS in May 1999. The guidelines similarly apply the "earned when services performed" concept in the analogous context of determining includible compensation for Section 403(b)(2) MEA purposes, which also requires that compensation be earned within the year. [See also Treas. Reg. § 1.403(b)-1(e)(1)(I)]

It should be noted that neither the regulations nor the guidelines address how to determine how much severance pay was earned in each year, a practical problem with the IRS's position. For example, in the case of a newly established severance pay plan, it is simply unclear whether a portion of severance pay based on years of service performed before the establishment of the plan may be attributable to such earlier years or whether such retroactive amount is considered earned in the year the plan is established.

Q 7:19   Can severance pay be deferred under a 403(b) plan as a salary reduction contribution under the law in effect after 1995?

Probably, but with limitations. Under SBJPA, effective for taxable years after December 31, 1995, "the salary to which [a salary reduction] agreement may apply . . . shall be determined under the rules applicable to a cash or deferred election under section 401(k). . . ." [SBJPA § 1450(a)(1)]

The general rule under Code Section 401(k) is that a cash or deferred election may be made only with respect to amounts not "currently available." The regulations under Code Section 401(k) provide that compensation is currently available to an employee if (1) it has been paid to the employee, or (2) the employee is able to currently receive the compensation at his or her direction. [Treas. Reg. § 1.401(k)-1(a)(3)(iii)] Assuming that the employee does not have the right to immediate payment at the time of the election to defer, severance pay should be considered not currently available for this purpose. Recently, the IRS has issued letter rulings permitting the deferral of accumulated leave pay under governmental 403(b) plans. [P.L.R. 200252095, 200249009]

Nevertheless, several other considerations may limit the employee's ability to defer such severance amounts. First, the IRS has on a number of occasions informally indicated that, because Treasury Regulations Section 1.401(k)-1(a)(2)(i) provides that a cash or deferred election may be made only by an employee, defined as someone performing services for the employer [Treas. Reg. §§ 1.401(k)-1(g)(5), 1.410(b)-9], such an election cannot be made after the person ceases to be an active employee. It is unclear whether the IRS would take the position that an election made to defer compensation while the employee was an active employee does not apply with respect to amounts paid after the person ceases to be an active employee.

Further, for years prior to 2002, severance pay is treated as includible compensation for MEA purposes only to the extent it was earned in the year of service (see Q 7:18). Thus, if the severance pay formula is such that only $2,500 of the total severance pay of $18,000 was earned in the year in question, only $2,500 of the $18,000 would be treated as includible compensation for purposes of the MEA. [Examination Guidelines for 403(b) Plans, May 1999, at V.C., ex. 23] Such a result, of course, could limit the amount deferred. The MEA has been repealed by EGTRRA, however, for years after 2001.

Section 415 Considerations

Q 7:20 Is severance pay added to compensation for purposes of the Section 415 limit?

Representatives of the IRS have informally indicated that severance pay may not be treated as compensation for purposes of the limitations on annual additions under Code Section 415 if paid in a limitation year in which an employee-employer relationship no longer exists. IRS personnel have also informally questioned whether severance pay may not constitute amounts received "for personal services actually rendered in the course of employment" so as to be treated as compensation under Treasury Regulations Section 1.415-2(d)(2)(i). (This argument, however, would seem to be contradicted by an example in the 403(b) examination guidelines, which clearly indicates that at least the portion of severance pay accrued in the year of termination is treated as earned in that year (see Q 7:19).)

There are certainly arguments against such informal IRS positions, including the following:

1. Taxable fringe benefits are includible in Section 415 compensation [Treas. Reg. § 1.415-2(d)(2)(i)], and severance pay may be considered a fringe benefit.
2. Unfunded deferred compensation payments, which are often of a similar nature to severance pay, are treated as Section 415 compensation in the year includible in the employee's gross income. [Treas. Reg. § 1.415-2(d)(3)(i)]
3. Employers may opt to use W-2 compensation, which would certainly seem to include severance pay, as an alternative definition of compensation for Section 415 purposes. [Treas. Reg. § 1.415-2(d)(11)(i)]

It should be kept in mind that, despite the informally announced IRS positions, there is simply no formal authority discounting severance pay as compensation for Section 415 purposes.

Chapter 8

Defining a Top-Hat Plan in Connection with 457 Plans

Anthony L. Scialabba, Esq.
Scialabba & Associates, P.C.

At first glance, there is some conflict between Section 457 of the Internal Revenue Code (Code) and the Employee Retirement Income Security Act of 1974 (ERISA). Under Title I of ERISA, plans that cover a broad spectrum of employees must be funded, but under Code Section 457 a plan generally must be unfunded. An exception from most of ERISA's burdensome requirements exists for certain unfunded plans that are established and maintained primarily for the purpose of providing deferred compensation for a select group of management or highly compensated employees. This chapter focuses on the determination of whether a plan meets the objective of being primarily for a select group of management or highly compensated employees.

This chapter was prepared with the assistance of Geoffrey M. Strunk, Esq., a partner at Scialabba & Associates, P.C., in Marlton, New Jersey.

457 Plans and ERISA

Q 8:1   In general, what is a top-hat plan?

The Employee Retirement Income Security Act of 1974 (ERISA) provides that a top-hat plan is an arrangement maintained "primarily for a select group of management or highly compensated employees." These individuals are known as the top-hat group. ERISA exempts top-hat plans from many of its requirements. [See ERISA §§ 201(2), 301(a)(3), 401(a)(1); DOL Reg. § 2520.104-23(a)]

Q 8:2   What are the ERISA requirements to which top-hat plans are subject?

Top-hat plans are subject to ERISA's enforcement rules and to limited reporting and disclosure requirements (see Q 8:3). They are exempt from ERISA's participation, vesting, funding, and fiduciary requirements.

Q 8:3   What are the limited reporting and disclosure requirements?

Within 120 days following a top-hat plan's adoption, the administrator of the plan must file with the Department of Labor (DOL) a brief statement that contains the following:

1. The employer's name and address;
2. The employer's identification number (EIN) assigned by the IRS;
3. A declaration that the employer maintains a plan or plans primarily for the purpose of providing deferred compensation for a select group of management or highly compensated employees;
4. A statement of the number of such plans and the number of employees in each; and
5. A statement agreeing to provide the DOL plan documents on the DOL's request.

[DOL Reg. § 2520.104-23(b)] (See appendix I.)

Q 8:4   How often must the top-hat statement be filed?

The statement need be filed only once for each employer maintaining one or more plans. [DOL Reg. § 2520.104-23(b)(2)]

Q 8:5   Who is the administrator of a 457 plan?

The term *administrator* means one of the following:

1. The person specifically so designated by the terms of the instrument under which the plan is operated;
2. If an administrator is not so designated, the plan sponsor; or

3. In the case of a plan for which an administrator is not designated and a plan sponsor cannot be identified, such other person as the Secretary of the Treasury may by regulation prescribe.

Q 8:6 Who is the plan sponsor of a 457 plan?

The term *plan sponsor* means either of the following:

1. In the case of a plan established or maintained by a single employer, the employer; or
2. In the case of a plan established or maintained by two or more employers or jointly by one or more employers, the association, committee, joint board of trustees, or other similar group of representatives of the parties who establish or maintain the plan.

Q 8:7 Do the limited reporting and disclosure requirements apply to all employers that maintain deferred compensation plans?

No. The limited reporting and disclosure requirements apply only to employee pension benefit plans that

1. Are maintained by an employer primarily for the purpose of providing deferred compensation for a select group of management or highly compensated employees; and
2. Pay benefits as needed solely from the general assets of the employer and/or provide benefits exclusively through insurance contracts or policies that are issued by an insurance company or similar organization that is qualified to do business in any state and the premiums for which are paid directly by the employer from its general assets.

Q 8:8 Where is the top-hat statement filed?

Statements may be filed with the Secretary of Labor by mailing them addressed to: Top-Hat Plan Exemption, Pension and Welfare Benefits Administration, Room N-5644, U.S. Department of Labor, 200 Constitution Avenue NW, Washington, DC 20210

Statements may also be delivered during normal working hours to the Division of Reports, Office of Program Services, Pension and Welfare Benefits Administration, Room N-5644, U.S. Department of Labor, 200 Constitution Avenue NW, Washington, DC 20210. [DOL Reg. § 2520.104-23(c)]

Q 8:9 What happens if the (top-hat) statement is not filed with the DOL?

If the (top-hat) statement is not filed with the DOL, the plan may be subject to ERISA's full reporting and disclosure requirements for failure to comply with the one-time filing requirement. In *Barrowclough v. Kidder, Peabody & Co.* [752 F.2d 923 (3d Cir. 1985)], a former participant in a deferred compensation plan was entitled to an accounting because the employer did not comply with the one-time filing requirements.

One of the responsibilities of nongovernmental employers under the full reporting and disclosure requirements of ERISA is the annual filing of IRS Form 5500—Annual Return/Report of Employee Benefit Plan (Form 5500). [ERISA §§ 104, 4065] Therefore, the failure of a nongovernmental employer to file a top-hat declaration with the DOL could obligate the employer to comply with the annual Form 5500 filing requirements.

The DOL can assess an unlimited $1,100 per day penalty for a failure to timely file the annual Form 5500. [ERISA § 502(c)(2); 29 C.F.R. 2575.502c-2] In addition, the IRS can assess concurrent penalties of $50 per day up to a maximum of $15,000 per late-filed return. [I.R.C. § 6652(e)] The DOL has indicated that if a delinquent filer (with regard to Form 5500) voluntarily files that form and follows certain procedures set forth under the Delinquent Filer Voluntary Compliance (DFVC) Program, the penalty will be $750 without regard to the number of plans maintained by the same plan sponsor and without regard to the number of participants. [67 Fed. Reg. 15,053 (Mar. 28, 2002)] Prior to the March 28, 2002, notice, the penalty amount under DFVC was $2,500. [60 Fed. Reg. 20,874 (Apr. 27, 1995)] In addition, the IRS has generally agreed to refrain from assessing penalties associated with the late filing of Form 5500 in situations where DFVC is used.

Note. The DOL allowed a grace period for filing the top-hat letter from March 23, 1992, until September 30, 1992, during which the penalty was $50 per day, up to a maximum of $1,000.

Q 8:10 Why is the top-hat plan exemption under ERISA important for 457 plans?

ERISA generally requires that retirement and deferred compensation plans have a trust to pay for the benefits that individuals receive from such plans. [ERISA § 403(a)] If a *nongovernmental* 457 plan used a trust, the individual beneficiaries of the trust would be in constructive receipt of the assets placed in the trust. [I.R.C. §§ 451, 457(a), 457(g)] Thus, participants in an eligible deferred compensation plan under Code Section 457(a) would receive income in an amount equal to the amount of benefits placed in the trust. On the other hand, top-hat plans are not required to use a trust. Thus, a trust need not be used for an eligible deferred compensation plan that satisfies the top-hat plan provisions, and the requirement that a nongovernmental 457 plan be unfunded would be satisfied. Therefore, participants in such a plan would not have their plan benefits included in gross income, and federal income taxation on those benefits would be deferred.

ERISA subjects retirement and deferred compensation arrangements to vesting requirements. [ERISA § 203] In general, the use of a certain vesting schedule satisfies those requirements. The timing of taxation with respect to an ineligible deferred compensation arrangement under Code Section 457(f) is governed by the doctrine of substantial risk of forfeiture. [I.R.C. § 457(f)(1)(A)] Thus, the benefits of a participant in such a plan are treated as gross income for federal income tax purposes once the participant has nonforfeitable rights to the benefits. If ERISA's vesting requirements applied to a 457(f) plan, a participant's benefits would be subject to federal income taxation once the participant satisfied the vesting requirements of the arrangement. Because a top-hat plan is not subject to those vesting requirements, an ineligible deferred compensation arrangement that is a top-hat plan need not use a vesting schedule. Such a plan could delay the time when a participant's benefits would no longer be subject to a substantial risk of forfeiture. The plan would thus delay the time when the benefits of the participant would be included in gross income for federal income tax purposes.

Q 8:11   What type of 457 plan does the top-hat plan exemption affect?

Tax-exempt organizations can maintain a 457 plan. [I.R.C. § 457(b), (e), (f)] The top-hat plan exemption is an exemption from certain ERISA requirements. [ERISA §§ 201(2), 301(a)(3), 401(a)(1); DOL Reg. § 2520.104-23(a)] Plans of governmental employers, church plans, and excess benefit plans (e.g., plans that are designed to provide benefits in excess of Section 415 limits) are not subject to ERISA. [ERISA § 4(b)] Thus, 457 plans sponsored by tax-exempt entities that are not one of the three aforementioned types of plans can be top-hat plans provided the top-hat plan exemption requirements are met.

Top-Hat Group

Q 8:12   What is the meaning of the words used under ERISA to describe a top-hat plan?

ERISA does not specify the meaning of the phrase "primarily for the purpose of providing deferred compensation for a select group of management or highly compensated employees" with respect to top-hat plans (see Q 8:1). Moreover, the DOL has never issued regulations that define these words.

The issue of what constitutes deferred compensation for purposes of a top-hat plan was addressed in *Duggan v. Hobbs* [95 F.3d 307 (10th Cir. 1996)]. The *Duggan* court held that *deferred compensation* means compensation that is paid substantially after the date the services to which the compensation relates are performed.

Advisory Opinions and Case Law

Q 8:13   What DOL advisory opinion guidance can be used to determine the meaning of the words used under ERISA to describe a top-hat plan?

The DOL's advisory opinions restricted top-hat groups to administrative, supervisory, or professional employees or to employees earning more than a stated amount. In the absence of regulations, the DOL generally issues an advisory opinion on an issue if the answer seems to be clear from the application of ERISA to the facts. [ERISA Proc. 76-1 § 5.03(a)] Conversely, the DOL generally does not issue an advisory opinion on an issue that involves a factual determination. Since the DOL rulings on top-hat groups involved a question of fact rather than of law, in 1976 the DOL stopped issuing rulings on the question of whether a group constituted a top-hat group. In addition, the DOL announced that it would formally rescind all its pre-1980 advisory opinions on top-hat plans because they no longer reflected the government's position on the top-hat plan exemption from most ERISA requirements.

In *Belka v. Rowe Furniture Corp.* [571 F. Supp. 1249, 1253 (D. Md. 1983) (citing Goodman & Stone, "Exempt Compensation Arrangements under ERISA," 28 *Cath. U.L. Rev.* 445, 464 (1979))], the court cited to a law review article that indicated, according to a DOL official, some tests that could be used to determine whether a group consisted of management or highly compensated employees. The official stated that these tests included a "facts and circumstances" test, a "straight-dollar" approach, a "functional and dollar" test, a "percentage" test, a "percentage" test with a "dollar floor," and a "lowest mass" test. The *Belka* court stated that under these tests the plan at bar covered a select group of "highly paid or executive-employee level" employees. Because the *Belka* court used these tests to some degree, they have precedential value.

There is a question whether the DOL is still considering the use of these tests. First, these comments were made before 1980. When the DOL rescinded its pre-1980 advisory opinions on top-hat plans, it may have also "rescinded" all pre-1980 thoughts on the matter. Second, comments made before 1980 are old. Third, the DOL never formally stated that any of these tests could be used. It therefore is doubtful that the DOL is still considering the use of the "Goodman and Stone" tests.

Q 8:14   What guidance exists on what constitutes a select group of management or highly compensated employees?

The determination of whether a select group of management or highly compensated employees exists is generally based on either an analysis of the size of the group in relation to the size of the total workforce of an employer or an analysis of the salaries of the group in relation to the salaries of the total workforce of an employer. In *Belka v. Rowe Furniture Corp.* [571 F. Supp. 1249 (D. Md. 1983)], for example, a district court compared covered employees to total employees. The court relied on the fact that (1) the average compensation level of covered employees was more than three times the average compensation of noncovered employees and (2) specific individuals having compensation below this three-to-one ratio were in management-level positions. The *Belka* court held that a select group of management or highly compensated employees existed because the plan covered 73 present and former employees, constituting at most 4.6 percent of the employer's workforce during any single year.

[Id. at 1252; see DOL Adv. Op. 98-02A ("[W]e note that due to the inherently factual nature of such request, advisory opinions generally will not be issued on the status of a particular plan as a so-called 'top-hat' plan within the meaning of sections 201(2), 301(a)(3), and 401(a)(1) of ERISA.")]

In *Simpson v. Ernst & Young* [879 F. Supp. 802 (S.D. Ohio 1994)], a district court examined whether an employee was part of a group of "highly compensated employees" because he made $194,092. The court ruled that because no evidence was presented on the average compensation of all employees covered by the plan, the plan could not receive a top-hat exemption; however, the court intimated that even though a participant in the plan earned what would commonly be thought of as a high salary ($194,092), that by itself did not mean he was highly compensated compared with the other employees covered by the plan. Thus, if the average salary of the other employees covered by a plan is significantly higher than that of the employee who is the subject of the determination, no matter how much an employee earns he or she may not be considered to be highly compensated.

In Advisory Opinion 85-37A, issued on October 25, 1985, the DOL analyzed an unfunded pension plan covering employees on the sponsoring company's "executive payroll," which covered 50 of 750 employees. This group consisted of the higher-paid individuals of the company, whose average compensation was $29,255, as compared with the 10 highest-paid hourly employees, whose average compensation was $10,442. The executive payroll covered a broad range of management employees, including past presidents and a chairman of the board, cost accountants, controllers, foremen, a superintendent, an assistant in the cost department, an order department clerk, an expediter, a time study position, and an insurance position. The DOL held that a top-hat plan did not exist because the plan included employees with a broad range of salaries and positions.

The Oklahoma Supreme Court confronted the issue of whether a deferred compensation plan should be treated as a top-hat plan for purposes of ERISA. [Loffland Bros. Co. v. CA Overstreet, 785 P.2d 813 (Okla. 1988)] In determining whether the plan was maintained for a select group of management or highly compensated employees, the court ruled that the plan could be considered to have been established primarily for such a select group because the number of participants was relatively small compared with the total number of employees of the company. In arriving at the *Loffland* decision, the court rejected the DOL's position that a plan is not a top-hat plan if it includes employees who are neither management nor highly compensated.

In *Darden v. Nationwide Insurance Co.* [717 F. Supp. 388 (E.D.N.C. 1989), aff'd, 922 F.2d 203 (4th Cir. 1991)], the court examined a plan covering insurance agents and sponsored by an insurance company. The plan covered more than 18 percent of the company's workforce; the participants' average income (after deducting their business expenses) was comparable to other employees' incomes. The *Darden* court concluded that the plan was not a top-hat plan because it was not maintained for a select group of highly compensated employees. The rationale for this position was explained in *Kemmerer v. ICI*

Americas, Inc. [70 F.3d 281 (3d Cir. 1995)], where the court stated that, usually, top-hat plan participants are high-level executive employees who "retain sufficient bargaining power to negotiate particular terms and rights under the plan and therefore do not need ERISA's substantive rights and protections." [Id. at 288] That being said, "it would be absurd to deny such individuals the ability to enforce the terms of their plans." [Id. (internal quotations omitted)] Such a denial would likely render top-hat plan participants unable to negotiate much more than illusory promises. [Id.; Koenig v. Waste Management, 76 F. Supp. 2d 908, 914 (N.D. Ill. 1999)]

DOL Advisory Opinion 90-14A, issued on May 8, 1990, stated:

> It is the view of the Department that in providing relief for top-hat plans from the broad remedial provisions of ERISA, Congress recognized that certain individuals, by virtue of their position or compensation level, have the ability to affect or substantially influence, through negotiation or otherwise, the design and operation of the deferred compensation plan, taking into consideration any risks attendant thereto, and, therefore, would not need substantive rights and protections under Title I [of ERISA].

The DOL's statements in the advisory opinion indicate that Congress and the DOL believe that the select group must be fully informed of the risks of the arrangement. Thus, a risk consideration would be another requirement for identifying the top-hat group if this is a correct interpretation of the advisory opinion.

Some limited guidance on the meaning of the term *top-hat plan* is provided in the legislative history of ERISA. The conference report to ERISA gives as an example of a top-hat plan a phantom stock or shadow stock plan established solely for the officers of a corporation. Similarly, the House floor explanation of ERISA states that Title I of ERISA would not cover "unfunded deferred compensation schemes of top executives." The DOL never cited this portion of the legislative history in its advisory opinions. These definitions may have been too broad by DOL standards.

In deference to DOL Advisory Opinion 90-14A, the Second Circuit stated in *Demery v. Extebank Deferred Compensation Plan* [2000 WL 772039 (2d Cir. June 15, 2000)] that the ability of the participants of a plan to negotiate the terms of a plan is an important component of a top-hat plan. No question of fact was raised by the court with respect to this issue, however, because of a lack of evidence submitted in connection with it.

In *Starr v. JCI Data Processing, Inc.* [757 F. Supp. 390 (D.N.J. 1991), *opinion vacated in part on reconsideration*, 767 F. Supp. 633 (D.N.J. 1991)], the U.S. District Court for the District of New Jersey analyzed a factor not considered in previous cases. Because participation in the plan was predicated on whether an employee had previously worked for a former parent company of the employer, the court held that the plan was not for the benefit of a select group of management or highly compensated employees. [Id. at 394] The criteria for eligibility to participate in the plan resulted in participation of employees from many levels of the company, from nonsupervisory clerical positions (38 percent) to line supervisors (25 percent) to upper management (38 percent), with salaries ranging from $12,000 to $336,000. [Id.] Thus, to determine whether a top-hat group existed, the court in *Starr* considered why the plan's eligibility provisions were established. The *Starr* court held that the plan did not cover a top-hat group, since participation was never based on an employee's compensation level or management status.

Another factor not previously considered was examined in *Demery* and in *Carrabba v. Randalls Food Markets, Inc.* [38 F. Supp. 2d 468 (N.D. Tex. 1999)]. These cases considered the intent of the employer with regard to the provision of benefits to a "select" portion of management or highly compensated employees. The *Carrabba* court stated that the mere fact that the employer intends the plan to be a reward to "key" employees does not satisfy the degree of selectivity contemplated by ERISA. It interpreted ERISA to require that a top-hat plan be only for the benefit of "high-ranking employees." In contrast to the *Carrabba* court, the *Demery* court specifically noted the intent of the company to provide benefits to certain "valuable" employees. The court stated that this factor weighed in favor of classifying the plan as a top-hat plan.

Duggan v. Hobbs [99 F.3d 307 (10th Cir. 1996)] provides additional guidance with respect to what constitutes a select group of highly compensated employees. In *Duggan,* a company provided a plan for one of its 23 employees. The employee had persuaded the company to provide him with the plan and the employee was the only employee of the company ever to be covered by such a plan.

The court analyzed two factors in holding that the arrangement was for a select group of highly compensated employees. First, the court noted that other courts had addressed the issue of what constituted a select group and found that such a group existed when the plan was limited to a small percentage of the employer's workforce. The *Duggan* court noted that the employee who received the plan was the only employee who was covered by the company retirement plan. In addition, the court stated that because the employee was one of 23 employees of the company that sponsored the plan, he represented less than 5 percent of the company's workforce. The *Duggan* court concluded that "numerically" the employee qualified as a "select group" of employees.

The *Duggan* court stated that mere statistical analysis was not enough to determine who is part of a select group of highly compensated employees. The court also relied on DOL Advisory Opinion 90-14A's "exertion of influence" standard. In this regard, the court found determination for the fulfillment of the requirement that the employee covered by the plan was the only employee ever to be covered by such a plan.

There are three points that can be made with respect to *Duggan*. First, a court not only will consider the standard set forth in DOL Advisory Opinion 90-14A but also will examine a statistical analysis. Second, with respect to a statistical standard, less than 5 percent of an employer's workforce may be a "safe harbor." [See A. Kroll, *Deferred Compensation Arrangements,* 385-3d Tax Mgmt. (BNA) A-42] Third, the court's adoption of the "exertion of influence" standard set forth in DOL Advisory Opinion 90-14A may be a problem because many top-hat plans cover employees who do not exert such "influence." [Id.]

The definition of *select group* was also considered in *Demery*. In *Demery*, a company provided a plan for the benefit of over 15 percent of its employees. The Second Circuit held that, although this percentage was probably at or near the upper limit of the acceptable size for a select group, this factor alone did not make the participation in the plan too broad for the plan to be a top-hat plan without considering the positions and average salaries of the plan participants.

Courts generally have taken a restrictive view of what constitutes a select group of management or highly compensated employees. [See, e.g., Carrabba v. Randalls Food Markets, Inc., 38 F. Supp. 2d 468, 478 (N.D. Tex. 1999) ("When applying ERISA, the Court must take into account that the act is a remedial statute to be liberally construed in favor of employee benefit fund participants, and that exemptions from ERISA's coverage should be confined to their narrow purpose.")]

Q 8:15 Can an employer's label cause a group to be a top-hat group?

Under DOL Advisory Opinion 85-37A, merely labeling a group as executive does not satisfy the select-group requirement. Conversely, employees who are not labeled as managers or executives may still be part of the select group if they meet the DOL's requirements for being management or highly compensated employees.

Q 8:16 What does the term *primarily* as used under ERISA mean?

DOL Advisory Opinion 90-14A provides that the term *primarily* as used in the phrase "primarily for the purpose of providing deferred compensation for a select group of management or highly compensated employees" (see Q 8:1) refers to the purpose of the plan (i.e., the benefits provided) as opposed to the participant composition of the plan. Thus, a plan would not constitute a top-hat plan for purposes of Title I of ERISA if it extends coverage beyond a select group of management or highly compensated employees. [See Hollingshead v. Burford Equipment Co., 747 F. Supp. 1421 (M.D. Ala. 1990)] Because the term *primarily* does not modify the composition group (the select group of management or highly compensated employees), there is no authority to include any outsiders in the top-hat group.

The interpretation that DOL Advisory Opinion 90-14A adopted with respect to the term *primarily* in the context of "primarily for the purpose of providing deferred compensation for a select group of management or highly compensated employees" is supported by the interpretation of that word in *Duggan v. Hobbs* [99 F.3d 307 (10th Cir. 1996)]. In *Duggan*, the court noted that a plan was established to provide severance pay to an employee who retired and to provide that employee with payments so the employee would not compete. In holding that the plan was a plan of deferred compensation and not a plan to compensate an employee for ongoing services, the court stated that *primarily* meant "'primarily' for the purpose of providing deferred compensation," not exclusively for that purpose.

In contrast to DOL Advisory Opinion 90-14A and the Tenth Circuit, the Second Circuit interpreted the term *primarily* as defining the participant composition of the plan as opposed to the purpose of the plan. [Demery v. Extebank Deferred Compensation Plan, 2000 WL 772039 (2d Cir. June 15, 2000)] *Demery* interpreted the word *primarily* in the context of "primarily for the purpose of providing deferred compensation for a select group of management or highly compensated employees" to mean that if a plan was principally intended for management and highly compensated employees, it would not be disqualified from top-hat status simply because a small number of the participants did not meet those criteria, or met one of the criteria but not the other.

Other Definitional Issues

Q 8:17   What is the definition of *management employees*?

Little guidance exists on what the term *management employees* means. A facts-and-circumstances determination is required. Some commentators suggest that the DOL would probably define *management employees* to include the individuals who are active in controlling the entire organization rather than only one part of it (e.g., a branch or subsidiary); however, some larger companies have employees who are not permitted to manage the entire company but who still possess substantial management authority. Moreover, professional service organizations (e.g., law firms and accounting firms) may have an employee who supervises a secretary. Thus, the determination of whether an employee who manages in this situation could be eligible to be in the select group of management employees is unclear.

The legislative history of ERISA gives a phantom stock or shadow stock plan established solely for officers of a corporation as an example of a top-hat plan (see Q 8:14). This suggests that Congress intended that *management employees* be interpreted broadly. The DOL ruled in Advisory Opinion 85-37A that a select group of management or highly compensated employees did not exist where a plan covered all employees on an employer's executive payroll because of the broad range of salaries and positions held by the employees. In that opinion, the DOL took a narrow approach with regard to the meaning of the term *management employees*.

Whether the select group of management employees must be a group with a certain degree of management responsibility is another question that arises with respect to the definition of *management employees*. In *Gallione v. Flaherty*

[70 F.3d 724, 728 (2d Cir. 1995)], a union was the plan sponsor. The union's management was composed of 63 officers plus five other employees. Of these 68 individuals, only 22 were entitled to participate in the plan. The full-time employees who were not officers and the 41 part-time officers were not eligible to participate in the plan. The eligible employees of the plan were full-time officers whose primary duties consisted of managing ongoing operations, establishing union policy, and negotiating collective bargaining agreements. The Second Circuit, in concluding that a group of managers is a top-hat group with respect to a plan, noted that the plan sponsor had a management that was hierarchical and that the group consisted of the "upper echelon of management." If this is a factor in determining whether a group is a select group of management employees, and if various levels of management employees exist, this question arises: Must the group at issue be the group of employees with the greatest amount of management responsibility or simply a group with greater management responsibility than another group that also possesses management responsibility?

Q 8:18   What is the definition of *highly compensated employees* under ERISA?

Little guidance exists on the definition of *highly compensated employees.* A facts-and-circumstances determination is required. In the preamble to Treasury regulations promulgated under Code Section 414(q) on the definition of *highly compensated employees* for retirement plan purposes, the Treasury Department essentially stated that the definition in Code Section 414(q) is not determinative with respect to the ERISA provisions on top-hat plans. [53 Fed. Reg. 4967 (Feb. 19, 1988)] The preamble also noted that the Treasury Department and DOL essentially agree that a broad extension of Code Section 414(q)'s definition of *highly compensated employees* to a top-hat determination would be inconsistent with the tax and policy objective of encouraging employers to sponsor tax-qualified plans that provide rank-and-file employees with meaningful benefits.

In *Belka v. Rowe Furniture Corp.* [571 F. Supp. 1249 (D. Md. 1983)], a question arose as to whether an average salary or a median salary should be used to determine the amount of compensation required for a group of employees to be considered a highly compensated group of employees. [Id. at 1253] The compensation amount may be skewed by high salaries of a few employees if an average salary is used. The *Belka* court did not resolve the issue, essentially stating that in either case the group of employees at issue was highly compensated.

Q 8:19   Is the word *or* in the phrase "select group of management or highly compensated employees" conjunctive?

Whether the word *or* in the phrase "select group of management or highly compensated employees" is conjunctive is another issue with regard to identifying a top-hat group. A group would have to be both management and highly compensated if *or* is conjunctive. In *Belka v. Rowe Furniture Corp.* [571 F. Supp.

1249 (D. Md. 1983)], the district court stated that some covered participants were not both highly compensated and management-level employees [id. at 1252] and ruled that the arrangement was a top-hat plan because the top-hat exemption was for plans that were "'primarily' designed for those individuals who are either management or highly compensated." Since the *Belka* decision was rendered, however, the DOL has interpreted the word *primarily* as modifying the phrase "for the purpose of providing deferred compensation." [DOL Adv. Op. 90-14A] The DOL position on this issue used in *Hollingshead v. Burford Equipment Co.* [747 F. Supp. 1421, 1430 (M.D. Ala. 1990)]. Therefore, whether *Belka* can be relied on for the proposition that participants in a top-hat plan need not be both management employees and highly compensated is unclear.

In response to a question from the American Bar Association's Joint Committee on Employee Benefits in May 1988, the DOL informally stated that the word *or* in the phrase "select group of management or highly compensated employees" is disjunctive; that is, participants in a top-hat plan need not be both management employees and highly compensated employees to preserve a plan's status as a top-hat plan. A DOL official agreed with this position at a later conference. [See M. Kleven, *Top Hat Plans*, ALI-ABA, Oct. 12–14, 1995, at 782]

Q 8:20   What does the term *select* mean?

The meaning of the term *select* as it is used in "a select group of management or highly compensated employees" is ambiguous. Specifically, whether it applies to all management or highly compensated employees or only to some portion of such employees is unclear. Only a portion of management or highly compensated employees could be in the top-hat group if the literal meaning of the term *select* is used. In addition, if *select* is interpreted to mean *portion*, it is uncertain how large a portion is meant.

The decision in *Gallione v. Flaherty* [70 F.3d 724 (2d Cir. 1995)] may provide some guidance on this issue. In *Gallione* an entity had 68 management employees, of which 22 were entitled to participate in a plan. [Id. at 728] In holding that a top-hat group consisted of management employees, the Second Circuit stated that the upper echelon of management was entitled to participate in the plan at issue. The conclusion that *select* means that only a portion of the employees who meet the definition of management employees can be in a top-hat group based on management employees could be implied from this decision.

This issue continued to be considered in *Carrabba v. Randalls Food Markets, Inc.* [38 F. Supp. 2d 468 (N.D. Tex. 1999)]. In *Carrabba*, the employer allowed every management-level employee and every employee who received an income over a specific amount to participate in the plan. In that regard, the court determined that all of the participants in the plan were management or highly compensated employees in the context of a top-hat plan. The court also stated, however, that the word *select* must be given some meaning. Thus, although the court did not articulate the meaning of the word *select*, it held that a top-hat plan did not exist because the participants in the plan were not a select group out of the broader group of management or highly compensated employees.

Q 8:21   What does the term *select group* mean?

The term *select group* is ambiguous because it is unclear whether it applies to both management and highly compensated employees. One periodical stated that the DOL considered the term to apply only to management employees. [17 *TMCPJ* 81 (Apr. 7, 1989)] Thus, a top-hat group must consist only of "selected management" employees and highly compensated employees if the interpretation in the periodical is correct.

Future DOL Guidance

Q 8:22   Is there likely to be any future DOL guidance on this issue?

A DOL official wrote in a textbook to a recent retirement plan seminar that the Pension and Welfare Benefits Administration (PWBA) staff reviewed the inventory of advisory opinions to determine if there were any requests that would give the DOL an opportunity to provide guidelines on top-hat plans. [M. Kleven, *Top Hat Plans*, ALI-ABA, Oct. 12–14, 1995, at 781] In the absence of regulations, the DOL generally issues an advisory opinion on an issue if the answer seems to be clear from the application of ERISA to the facts. [ERISA Proc. 76-1 § 5.03(a)] Conversely, the DOL generally does not issue an advisory opinion on an issue that involves a factual determination. The DOL official stated that a factual determination was required as to the existence of a select group of management or highly compensated employees in pending advisory opinion requests. Thus, the official wrote that little guidance could be provided by the DOL without the promulgation of regulations.

The DOL initiated a regulation project on top-hat plans. [17 *TMCPJ* 81 (Apr. 7, 1989)] DOL employees indicated recently, however, that no regulations with respect to top-hat plans are forthcoming. [A. Kroll, *Deferred Compensation Arrangements*, 385-3d Tax Mgmt. (BNA) A-39] These employees claimed that the DOL would consider the number of employees covered by a plan and the relative salaries of these employees in making a top-hat group determination. [Id.]

Applying the Rules

Q 8:23   What are the general rules for determining the existence of a top-hat group?

Only a few general rules for determining the existence of a top-hat group can be set forth because there is little guidance on the meaning of the phrases "primarily for the purpose" and "select group of management or highly compensated" employees. The rules that can be set forth include the following:

1. A plan cannot extend coverage beyond a select group of management or highly compensated employees.
2. The group must be small in comparison to the total workforce, and less than 18 percent of a company's workforce can be covered.
3. The average income of participants must be higher than the average income of other employees.
4. The eligible participants must be employees who, by virtue of their position or compensation level, have the ability to affect or substantially influence the design and operation of their deferred compensation plan.
5. Participation in a plan must be based on an employee's compensation level or management status.

Q 8:24   What groups of employees would be considered to be part of a top-hat group?

The following groups of employees probably would be considered part of a top-hat group:

1. Employees whose decisions may affect the entire company;
2. The chief executive officer and the chief financial officer of a business;
3. The president, deans, and department chairs of a university; and
4. The executive board of a union.

Q 8:25   What groups of employees would not be considered to be part of a top-hat group?

The following groups of employees probably would not be considered to be part of a top-hat group, because of each group's broad range of salaries and positions:

1. All faculty members of a university;
2. All partners of a law or accounting firm; and
3. All professional staff members at a hospital or nursing home (e.g., physicians, therapists, and nurses).

Chapter 9

Creditors' Rights

Lynn B. Witte, Esq.
Seyfarth Shaw

David R. Levin, Esq.
Wiley Rein & Fielding LLP

Lynn Witte passed away in 2002. Lynn was co-author of this chapter; she was my colleague and friend of many years. To paraphrase and quote from John Donne, who was one of Lynn's favorite authors: In her passing, we remember that all of us are of one Author and of one volume. When one person dies, "one chapter is not torn out of the book, but translated into a better language; and every chapter must be so translated." So it has been with Lynn. We will miss her.

Eligible Section 457 plans are tax-qualified plans, but not "qualified plans" under Section 401(a) of the Internal Revenue Code, and many of them are not subject to Title I of the Employee Retirement Income Security Act of 1974 (ERISA). These facts affect how benefits in these plans may be protected from, or available to, the creditors of participants and those of sponsors. The Economic Growth and Tax Relief Reconciliation Act of 2001 (EGTRRA) did not have an effect on the material contained in this chapter. Ineligible plans are more fully discussed in chapter 11.

It is important to note that none of the rules for protection of benefits discussed in this chapter apply to any claims made by the IRS. The IRS has access to retirement benefits regardless of these rules. [I.R.C. § 6334(a), (c)]

Shumate and ERISA Qualified Plans

Q 9:1   What was the holding of *Patterson v. Shumate*?

Patterson v. Shumate [504 U.S. 753, 112 S. Ct. 2242, 119 L. Ed. 2d 519 (1992)] is the seminal case for the protection of plan participants' retirement benefits from the claims of creditors in bankruptcy. The decision held that (1) any relevant nonbankruptcy law, including federal law such as the Employee Retirement Income Security Act of 1974 (ERISA), is applicable nonbankruptcy law under Section 541(c)(2) of the U.S. Bankruptcy Code (Bankruptcy Code) and (2) a participant-debtor's benefit in an "ERISA qualified" pension plan that contains an anti-alienation provision as required by ERISA Section 206(d)(1) and Section 401(a)(13) of the Internal Revenue Code (Code) is excluded from the property of the participant-debtor's bankruptcy estate pursuant to Bankruptcy Code Section 541(c)(2) and therefore is not available to his or her creditors.

Q 9:2   What does *ERISA qualified* mean?

The U.S. Supreme Court did not define *ERISA qualified* when it used the term in *Patterson v. Shumate* [504 U.S. 753, 112 S. Ct. 2242, 119 L. Ed. 2d 519 (1992)]; however, in *Shumate,* the Supreme Court listed, in footnote 1, a number of cases in which the lower courts had found, in the years preceding the *Shumate* decision, that pension plans were "ERISA qualified."

For example, the Supreme Court referred to *In re Daniel* [771 F.2d 1352, 1359 (9th Cir. 1985) (analyzing whether "ERISA qualified plans are properly excluded or exempted" under the Bankruptcy Code)] as one of the cases involving an "ERISA qualified pension plan" that had led to the split among the circuits about whether pension benefits were available to bankruptcy creditors. In *Daniel,* the debtor was a plan participant who had controlling interest in the corporation that had established the pension plan. He also managed the plan and borrowed $75,000 from it. When his loan came due, he rolled it over and did not make payments on it. Obviously, in referring to the case as one that involved an "ERISA qualified plan," the Supreme Court could not have defined the term *ERISA qualified plan* to mean a plan in full compliance with ERISA and the Code, because an unsecured personal loan constitutes a prohibited transaction under ERISA Section 406, which subjects the perpetrator to an excise tax under Code Section 4975 (although, of course, the prohibited transaction does not remove a plan from coverage under Title I of ERISA or qualification under the Code).

Since *Shumate* was decided, the lower courts have failed to consider the definition of *ERISA qualified* developed by the courts before *Shumate*. In fact, there has been no general agreement on the meaning of the term since *Shumate* was decided. Instead, one meaning expounded by some courts is that to be ERISA qualified a plan must be subject to Title I of ERISA. [See, e.g., In re Witwer, 148 B.R. 930 (Bankr. C.D. Cal. 1992), aff'd, 163 B.R. 614 (B.A.P. 9th Cir. 1994)] Others have held that an ERISA qualified plan is a plan that is both subject to ERISA Title I and qualified under Code Section 401(a). [See, e.g., In re Nolen, 175 B.R. 214 (Bankr. N.D. Ohio 1994)] Finally, some cases have found that a plan is ERISA qualified if it is simply qualified under Code Section 401(a). [See, e.g., In re Reed, 985 F.2d 1026 (9th Cir. 1993)]

Shumate and 457 Plans Before the SBJPA

Q 9:3   Can a 457 plan be ERISA qualified?

Under Code Section 457 as constituted before the enactment of the Small Business Job Protection Act (SBJPA) on August 20, 1996, no 457 plans—neither those sponsored by governmental entities nor those sponsored by tax-exempt organizations—truly fit any of the proposed definitions of *ERISA qualified*. The 457 plans sponsored by governmental entities could not be ERISA qualified because governmental plans are not subject to Title I of ERISA. [ERISA § 4(b)(1)] A 457 plan sponsored by a tax-exempt organization must be a top-hat plan for Title I purposes (because it is required by Code Section 457 to be unfunded), and therefore it is not subject to ERISA Section 206(d)(1), found in Title I. Further, neither 457 plans sponsored by governmental entities nor those sponsored by tax-exempt entities are qualified plans subject to Code Section 401(a). Therefore, a 457 plan could not meet any of the definitions of *ERISA qualified* devised by the courts (see Q 9:2).

Perhaps most important for bankruptcy cases, Bankruptcy Code Section 541(c)(2) by its terms applies only to a "beneficial interest held *in trust*" (emphasis added). [For an interesting, informative discussion of this Bankruptcy Code Section 541(c)(2) requirement, see In re Barnes, 264 B.R. 415 (Bankr. E.D. Mich. 2001) (concerning debtor's interests in Code Section 403(b) annuities).] Under the law in effect before August 20, 1996, all 457 plans were required by the terms of Code Section 457 to be unfunded and, therefore, not to have a trust. (Although a 457 plan might have a grantor trust, sometimes called a rabbi trust, established in connection with it, such "trusts" are not traditional employee benefit plan trusts because their assets have long been recognized to be available to the employer's creditors.) Therefore, a 457 plan would not, by the terms of its very existence, have the benefits of a participant-debtor excluded from the bankruptcy estate under Bankruptcy Code Section 541(c)(2), because assets of 457 plans could not be held in trust. [See, e.g., In re Kingsley, 181 B.R. 225 (Bankr. W.D. Pa. 1995)]

Nonetheless, at least one court found a participant-debtor's benefits in a 457 plan to be excluded from his or her estate pursuant to Bankruptcy Code Section 541(c)(2). The court in *In re Wheat* [149 B.R. 1003 (Bankr. S.D. Fla. 1992)] reasoned that the anti-alienation provision in the plan was tantamount to the anti-alienation provisions in Code Section 401(a)(13) and ERISA Section 206(d)(1), as was the case in the *Shumate* plan. In addition, the court found that this anti-alienation provision in the 457 plan was enforceable under Code Section 457(b)(6). The court did not, however, explain the mechanism by which this enforcement was available. It simply stated its conclusion. More important, the court did not make clear why it was able to disregard the fact that the participant-debtor's benefits under the 457 plan were not held in trust, a threshold requirement for the application of Bankruptcy Code Section 541(c)(2). Consequently, *In re Wheat* does not constitute persuasive precedent for protection of benefits in a 457 plan.

Shumate and 457 Plans After the SBJPA

Q 9:4   Does the SBJPA affect the applicability of *Shumate* to 457 plans?

There is no case law yet; the SBJPA became effective on August 20, 1996. Furthermore, the important SBJPA change applies solely to 457 plans sponsored by governmental entities—*not* to those sponsored by tax-exempt entities.

Q 9:5   What change did the SBJPA make with respect to 457 plans?

Code Section 457(g) now provides that any 457 plan sponsored by a governmental entity is required to hold all plan assets in trust "for the exclusive benefit of participants and their beneficiaries." Moreover, Code Section 457(g) now provides that this trust "shall be treated as an organization exempt from taxation under section 501(a)." Further, Code Section 457(b)(6) now provides that the requirement that plan assets remain the assets of the employer sponsoring the plan does *not* apply to 457 plans sponsored by governmental entities.

The significance of the "trust" requirement can be seen in the recent case of *Rhiel v. Adams* [In re Adams, No. 03-8011 (B.A.P. 6th Cir. Dec. 10, 2003), involving annuity plans under Code Section 403(b). The reasoning of the court would seem to support the protection of post-SBJPA Section 457 plans granted under the requirement in Bankruptcy Code Section 541(c)(2) that the assets be held in "trust" if they are to be protected from alienation.

This trust requirement has different effective dates, depending on whether the plan is a new one or an existing one. A plan adopted by an employer after August 20, 1996 (a "new" plan), must have a trust from its inception. A plan adopted on or before August 20, 1996, was required to establish a trust not later than January 1, 1999.

Q 9:6   For purposes of the availability of benefits to creditors, are government-sponsored 457 plans now exactly like qualified retirement plans under Code Section 401(a)?

No. Even if a governmental entity that sponsors a 457 plan has adopted a trust—whether for a new plan or an existing one—that plan and trust still are not subject to either Code Section 401(a)(13) or ERISA Section 206(d)(1). Those two sections are the anti-alienation provisions on which the Supreme Court relied in *Patterson v. Shumate* [504 U.S. 753, 112 S. Ct. 2242, 119 L. Ed. 2d 519 (1992)].

Some practitioners may argue that because Code Section 457(g) requires that the trust for a government-sponsored 457 plan be treated as a trust under Code Section 501(a)—the same section that governs trusts for plans qualified under Code Section 401(a)—a government-sponsored 457 plan is, technically, subject to Code Section 401(a)(13). Code Section 501(a) provides that "[a]n organization described in . . . section 401(a) shall be exempt from taxation under this subtitle." Of course, an "organization described in section 401(a)" is a qualified retirement plan, which, to be qualified, must contain an anti-alienation provision and be administered in accordance with that provision. The argument would therefore be that, to be treated as a Section 501(a) trust, a government-sponsored 457 plan must meet the requirements of Code Section 401(a)(13); however, this argument proves too much. If the government-sponsored 457 plan were treated as being required to comply with Code Section 401(a)(13), it would have to be treated as being required to comply with all the other requirements of Code Section 401(a). Those would include all the nondiscrimination and distribution requirements, and 457 plans simply are not required to comply with those provisions. Therefore, under this argument, it is unlikely that government-sponsored 457 plans would be found to be subject to the anti-alienation provision in Code Section 401(a)(13).

Q 9:7   Is there any other way that a participant's benefits in a government-sponsored 457 plan may be excluded from his or her bankruptcy estate under *Shumate* and Bankruptcy Code Section 541(c)(2)?

One other argument may be made to exclude 457 plan benefits from a participant's bankruptcy estate. Code Section 457(g) now requires that 457 plan assets of a governmental employee must be held in trust "for the exclusive benefit of participants and their beneficiaries" (see Q 2:37). This "exclusive benefit rule" is substantially similar to that included in the first paragraph of Code Section 401(a). Yet, this is not a direct anti-alienation provision, like those in Code Section 401(a)(13) and ERISA Section 206(d)(1).

It is important to remember that to be excluded from the bankruptcy estate under Bankruptcy Code Section 541(c)(2), the benefits in the plan must be subject to a restriction on transfer that is enforceable under applicable nonbankruptcy law. This is not an easy standard to meet, because any funds meeting it never become part of the bankruptcy estate of the debtor and are, therefore, completely unavailable to the bankruptcy creditors.

Nevertheless, a practitioner might argue that the benefits were required to be held in the trust exclusively for the participant and his or her beneficiaries and that this requirement was enforceable under state spendthrift trust law or an applicable state statute. This is by no measure a foolproof argument, because a court might find that the exclusive benefit provision was not tantamount to the anti-alienation provisions of ERISA and the Code. Moreover, spendthrift trust laws vary from state to state. In some states, assets in a trust are not protected under the spendthrift trust rules if the trust is "self-settled"— that is, if the participant-debtor himself or herself puts the money into the trust and has substantially unlimited access to the trust assets. Thus, because participants in 457 plans defer compensation into the 457 plan themselves, the spendthrift trust rules might not make the exclusive benefit rule enforceable in states such as Florida, where no self-settled trust is protected.

With the same caveats about the vagaries of state spendthrift trust laws, the argument could nevertheless be made that any explicit anti-alienation provision that is in the 457 plan document is enforceable under the applicable state's spendthrift trust laws or an applicable state statute. (Note: Under the Bankruptcy Code, the applicable state law will likely be that of the state in which the debtor resides.)

In *In re Domina* [274 B.R. 829, 2002 Bankr. LEXIS 222 (Bankr. N.D. Iowa Mar. 4, 2002)] an Iowa bankruptcy court found that the debtor's interest in the State of Iowa's retirement plan established pursuant to Code Section 457 was excluded from his bankruptcy estate. The plan in this case was accompanied by a trust. Both the "plan" and the "trust" were established pursuant to Iowa statutes. The statutes establishing the plan and the trust included an anti-alienation provision similar to that found in Code Section 401(a)(13) and an exclusive benefit rule provision similar to that found in Code Section 401(a). The court concluded that Code Section 457(f) and the Iowa statute constituted applicable nonbankruptcy law "that creates enforceable restrictions on the debtor's transfer of his beneficial interest." The court did not specifically discuss the source of the authority to enforce the anti-alienation provision. However, the court cited with approval another case, *In re Wilcox* [(Taunt v. General Retirement System of Detroit), 233 F.3d 899 (6th Cir. 2000)], which extensively discusses the enforceability aspect.

Q 9:8   Are a participant's rights to benefit from a 457(g) trust any different from those in an unfunded plan?

Arguably, yes. Such a trust is not subject to ERISA; therefore, there is no ERISA requirement that the trust contain the kind of anti-alienation language reviewed by the Supreme Court in *Patterson v. Shumate*. [504 U.S. 753, 112 S. Ct. 2242, 119 L. Ed. 2d 519 (1992)] On the other hand, including anti-alienation language in the trust, along with an obligation by the trustee to enforce the terms of the trust (including the anti-alienation language), may afford protection to the benefits. [See In re Moses, 21 Employee Benefits Cas. (BNA) 2446 (B.A.P. 9th Cir. 1997)] In *Moses*, the court ruled that for a pension plan that is not ERISA qualified the enforceability of the anti-alienation provision must be determined under the applicable state law. In that particular case, the court ruled that a Keogh plan was excluded from the property of the estate under Bankruptcy Code Section 541(c)(2) because the anti-alienation provision contained in the plan was enforceable under state law.

Conversely, a Florida bankruptcy court found that no Florida statute was "applicable non-bankruptcy law" that would protect the retirement benefit held in trust by a debtor's governmental employer. [In re Turner, 261 B.R. 767 (Bankr. M.D. Fla. 2001)] The court's basis for its opinion is that the plan was "a non-ERISA qualified plan and, in turn, [could] not be excepted" under the applicable Florida statutes.

A bankruptcy court in the Eastern District of New York came to a contrary conclusion using a totally different analysis and applying a New York state law [N.Y. Debt. & Cred. Law (McKinney 2001) (DCL)] that was not even mentioned in the Western District's *Johnson* decision. In *In re Ruffo* [261 B.R. 580, 586 (Bankr. E.D.N.Y. 2001)], the Chapter 7 trustee objected to the debtor's claimed exemption under DCL Section 282(2)(e) for his interest in a 457 plan sponsored by his employer, the City of New York. The court ruled that if the plan qualified under Code Section 457 and made payments on account of "illness, disability, death, age, or length of service," those payments were exempt under DCL Section 282(2)(e).

Subsequent to and consistent with the ruling in the case of *In re Ruffo*, a district court affirmed a bankruptcy court ruling that a debtor's interest in her 457 plan was exempt and, therefore, protected from her creditors under New York state law. [Ring v. Maurer, 28 Employee Benefits Cas. (BNA) 1736 (W.D.N.Y. 2002)] The court held that the 457 plan benefits were protected, because the benefits were "payable from a plan or contract similar to a stock bonus, pension or profit sharing plan; the right to receive benefits depended on illness, disability, death, age or length of service"; and, the plan did not fail to qualify under Code Section 457. With respect to the last point, the court held that the plan was "'qualified' . . . via a ruling of the Internal Revenue Service. . . ."

A bankruptcy court in the Western District of New York had ruled a debtor's 457 plan benefit was not exempt from her estate, on the ground that the trust in which the assets were held was a self-settled trust because it was her decision to have the amounts deferred to the plan. [In re Johnson, 254 B.R. 786 (Bankr. W.D.N.Y. 2000 (Johnson I)] However, in light of the decision of the bankruptcy court in *In re Mauer* [268 B.R. 339 (Bankr. W.D.N.Y. 2001)] and arguments made in the *Mauer* case but not made in *Johnson I*, the court vacated its decision and ruled that the 457 plan benefits are exempt under New York state law and protected from creditors. [In re Johnson, 268 B.R. 341 (Bankr. W.D.N.Y. 2001) (Johnson II), vacating Johnson I].

In *In re Atwood* [259 B.R. 158, 161 n.4 (B.A.P. 9th Cir. 2001)], the bankruptcy appellate panel affirmed a bankruptcy court's ruling that the interest of husband and wife debtors in a 457 plan was not property of the estate. The panel found that (1) the debtor husband's employer had created the trust; (2) the debtors did not exercise excessive control over the trust; (3) an unrelated party administered the trust; and (4) it was not a self-settled trust because the employer, not the debtors, was the settlor. The fact that the debtor contributed part of his compensation to the plan was, the panel held, insufficient to cause the trust to be self-settled. The debtors could access the funds only at age 70½, at the time of separation of service, on death, or for an unforeseeable emergency. Although the plan's terms permitted loans that were secured by the funds in the account, the employer had adopted a resolution preventing such loans. Based on the foregoing, the panel affirmed the holding that the 457 plan's trust was a valid spendthrift trust under California law. The panel acknowledged that the 457 plan allowed the debtors to change their contribution on a monthly basis. However, it found to be significant the absence of any evidence in the record that the debtors had attempted to manipulate their contributions to the plan by increasing those contributions. The panel concluded that, "[i]n any event, even monthly changes in the amount of Debtors' contributions would not constitute control over the res as the funds in the Section 457 plan would still be subject to all the restrictions governing access by participants."

It is worthy of note that in *Atwood* the bankruptcy trustee urged the panel to follow the rulings in *In re Dunn* [215 B.R. 121 (Bankr. E.D. Mich. 1997)] and *In re Leadbetter* [111 B.R. 640 (Bankr. N.D. Ohio 1990)]. In those cases, the bankruptcy courts held that the 457 plans were property of the estate. The panel rejected the trustee's urgings, pointing first to the fact that in 1996 Code Section 457 was amended to require that plan assets be held in trust "for the exclusive benefit of participants and their beneficiaries." [I.R.C. § 457(g)] *Dunn* and *Leadbetter* dealt with 457 plans established prior to and not modified pursuant to the 1996 amendments; neither case involved a 457 plan that held assets in a trust. Of more importance to the panel, though, was that both cases have been overruled, "either directly or indirectly, and are no longer good law." The decision in *Leadbetter* was vacated when the Supreme Court granted certiorari and remanded the case to the Sixth Circuit for further consideration in light of *Patterson v. Shumate*. [See Ohio Public Employees Deferred Compensation Program v. Sicherman, 505 U.S. 1202 (1992)]

Similarly, *Dunn* was recently overruled by the Sixth Circuit, because its reasoning conflicted with *Shumate*. [See Taunt v. General Retirement System of Detroit (In re Wilcox), 233 F.3d 899, 904 (6th Cir. 2000)]

Q 9:9 Can 457 plan benefits have the same protection from creditors that is now available to ERISA qualified plans under *Shumate* and its progeny?

Perhaps. In 1998, both houses of Congress passed bankruptcy reform legislation that would have, among other things, extended protection to benefits in 457 plans, as well as in individual retirement accounts (IRAs). The President did not sign the legislation, so it did not become law.

In addition, it is possible that some courts may find exclusion under existing law. A bankruptcy court in Maryland found that a debtor's benefit in the plan sponsored by her governmental employer, whose plan's assets were held in trust, was excluded from her bankruptcy estate on the ground that the 457 plan was a "tax-qualified plan under Internal Revenue Code [Section] 457" and that Maryland Code Annotated, Courts and Judicial Proceedings Section 11-504(h) was applicable nonbankruptcy law that protected the retirement benefit from the reach of creditors. [In re Mueller, 256 B.R. 445, 455–56 (Bankr. D. Md. 2000)] The court did not explain the significance under Maryland law that the plan be a "tax-qualified" plan, and the longevity of this ruling may depend on the court's interpretation of that detail. In a similar vein, in *In re Ruffo* [261 B.R. 580 (Bankr. E.D.N.Y. 2001)], the Chapter 7 trustee conceded that a plan was a "qualified plan" under Code Section 457.

The term *tax-qualified* generally is not used in connection with 457 plans. Rather, it generally refers to plans qualified under Code Section 401(a). However, the trust required of governmental plans under Code Section 457(g) is specifically designated as tax-exempt pursuant to Code Section 501(a), and that fact could perhaps support the interpretation that a 457 plan is tax-qualified.

Exemptions from the Bankruptcy Estate

Q 9:10 Even if a 457 plan participant's benefits are not excluded from his or her bankruptcy estate under Bankruptcy Code Section 541(c)(2) and *Shumate*, may the benefits still be protected from bankruptcy creditors?

Yes. Whether a debtor's 457 benefits will be exempt property depends on the law of the state in which the debtor resides. The exemption provisions may apply to a 457 plan sponsored by a tax-exempt entity, as well as to one sponsored by a governmental entity.

If a bankruptcy debtor's benefits are not excluded under Bankruptcy Code Section 541(c)(2) (see Qs 9:3, 9:7), the benefits in the 457 plan would be considered part of his or her bankruptcy estate. The debtor may argue, however, that the benefits should be *exempted* from his or her bankruptcy estate. (Note: "Excluded property" never comes into the bankruptcy estate and is, therefore, never available to creditors. "Exempt property" initially comes into the bankruptcy estate and then is protected in whole or in part.)

Bankruptcy Code Section 522(b) sets out two alternate provisions for exempting property from a debtor's bankruptcy estate. The first alternative is in Bankruptcy Code Section 522(b)(1). That section exempts property listed in Bankruptcy Code Section 522(d) unless the state in which the debtor resides has "opted out" of the provision by enactment of a statute to that effect. Most states have opted out of this exemption. [2 King, *Collier Bankruptcy Manual* § 522.01 n.6 (3d ed. 1996)] Bankruptcy Code Section 522(d) does not currently contain any exemption applicable to 457 plan benefits.

The second alternative exemption is set out in Bankruptcy Code Section 522(b)(2)(A), which states that it exempts from the estate any property that is exempt under federal law (other than the statutory federal law exemption) or under any state or local law.

Thus, if a bankruptcy debtor either (1) elects the state exemptions or (2) lives in a state that has opted out of the statutory federal law exemption, the state law will apply to determine whether the debtor's 457 plan benefits are exempt from his or her bankruptcy estate.

In *In re Ridgway* [11 Employee Benefits Cas. (BNA) 2596 (N.D. Okla. 1989)], the court ruled that a participant's benefits in a 457 plan were protected under Oklahoma law. The court also ruled that the same Oklahoma law protected IRA benefits, and that this law was not preempted by ERISA. [See also In re Nielsen, 1998 WL 3379 (Bankr. D. Minn. 1998) (discussing the Minnesota state exemption for 457 plan benefits)]

Similarly, California has a statute that exempts from creditors

> all amounts held, controlled, or in process of distribution by a public entity derived from contributions by the entity or by an officer or employee of the public entity for public retirement benefit purposes, and all rights and benefits accrued or accruing to any person under a public retirement system. . . .

[Cal. Civ. Proc. Code § 704.110(b)]

This section would apply to a California-domiciled bankruptcy debtor to determine whether his or her 457 plan benefits were exempt from the bankruptcy estate.

Judgment Creditors in Nonbankruptcy Situations

Q 9:11 Even if a creditor is unable to reach a participant's interest in his or her benefits from the 457 plan, can the creditor force the plan to make the contributions available to the participant's estate?

Perhaps. This issue was raised in *In re Ruffo*. [261 B.R. 580 (Bankr. E.D.N.Y. 2001)] The Chapter 7 trustee alleged that the debtor's contributions to the plan might have been avoidable as fraudulent conveyances under Bankruptcy Code Section 548 and DCL Section 273 et seq. The court declined to resolve the issue until the Chapter 7 trustee actually commenced a proceeding to recover any payments. Without expressing any opinion on the merits of this claim, the court agreed to consider the issue at such time as the Chapter 7 trustee filed an adversary proceeding to recover the alleged fraudulent conveyances. [See Fed. R. Bankr. P. 7001 (requiring such an action to be brought by adversary proceeding)]

Creditors have used fraudulent conveyance and preference arguments with mixed success in trying to recover contributions to plans qualified under Code Section 401(a). The Sixth Circuit held that when contributions to a partnership's profit sharing plan were not made in accordance with the terms of the plan document, certain plan contributions could be garnished by the bankruptcy trustee and were not protected by ERISA's anti-alienation provisions. [In re Bell & Beckwith, 5 F.3d 150 (6th Cir. 1993)] A bankruptcy court in Nebraska, however, ruled that a Chapter 7 debtor's voluntary contributions to an ERISA-qualified plan were not transfers for or on account of an antecedent debt and, therefore, were not preferences; the court also ruled that the debtor received reasonably equivalent value for the contributions, so they could not be avoided as constructively fraudulent transfers. [In re Loomer (Butler v. Loomer), 222 B.R. 618 (Bankr. D. Neb. 1998)]

Q 9:12   When a 457 plan participant has not filed for bankruptcy, but a creditor has a court judgment against him or her, are the 457 plan benefits available to the creditor?

It depends on the law of the state in which the participant resides. The same state law that would apply to exempt a bankruptcy debtor's 457 plan benefits from his or her bankruptcy estate (see Q 9:10) would likely apply when a debtor who is a participant in a 457 plan, whether sponsored by a governmental entity or by a tax-exempt entity, has not filed for relief under the Bankruptcy Code. That is, the participant would turn to the law of the state in which he or she lives.

Specific state statutes, like state spendthrift trust laws (see Qs 9:7, 9:10), vary tremendously. [*Accord* Orlando Police Pension Board of Trustees v. Langford, 29 Employee Benefit Cas. (BNA) 2512 (Fla. Dist. Ct. App. 2002) (whether state's anti-alienation provision for municipal pension plan assets conflicts with state's equitable distribution laws)] Therefore, whether a participant's 457 plan benefits are protected under state law in a particular situation will depend on the laws of the state involved.

Consequences of Availability of Benefits to Creditors

Q 9:13   If a participant's 457 plan benefits are determined to be available to his or her creditors, will the participant be taxed on the benefits?

Yes. The amount of the benefits distributed to any creditors would be taxable to the participant under Code Section 457(a), the constructive receipt doctrine, the economic benefit doctrine, and/or Code Section 83.

Q 9:14 If a participant's 457 plan benefits are paid to his or her creditors at a time when that participant is not eligible to receive a distribution under Code Section 457(d), will the plan retain its designation as an eligible deferred compensation plan under Code Section 457?

Although it is unclear precisely what the consequence to the plan would be if benefits were paid out to a participant's creditors at a time when the participant was not eligible for a distribution, it is likely that the IRS would find that the plan was no longer an eligible deferred compensation plan. As a consequence, all participants in the plan would be subject to immediate taxation on the amount of their benefits under the plan. This point—that an IRS determination adverse to all participants can flow from the alienation of one participant's benefit under the plan—was of significance to the Supreme Court in *Patterson v. Shumate* in reaching its decision that the benefit could not be alienated. [504 U.S. 753, 760 n.3, 112 S. Ct. 2242, 2247 n.3, 119 L. Ed. 2d 519 n.3 (1992)]

Consequences of the Bankruptcy of the Plan Sponsor

Q 9:15 What happens if the sponsor of the 457 plan files for bankruptcy relief?

The answer to this question depends on when the sponsor files for bankruptcy relief and what type of entity the sponsor is.

If the sponsor of the 457 plan is a tax-exempt entity, all the assets associated with the 457 plan are available to the entity's creditors. As discussed in Q 9:5, this results because the tax-exempt entity cannot have a typical employee benefit trust, but instead must have only a grantor trust. By definition, the assets associated with a grantor trust are available to the sponsor's creditors.

If the sponsor of the 457 plan is a governmental entity, then 457 plan assets are required to be held in trust (see Q 9:6).

The trust of a 457 plan established by a governmental entity is required to hold all assets for the exclusive benefit of participants and their beneficiaries. The trust is established as an entity separate from the governmental entity itself. Therefore, if the governmental entity files for bankruptcy relief, the trust assets held for the 457 plan should be unaffected and should remain protected and available only to pay the retirement benefits of the participants.

Chapter 10

Application of Federal Securities Law to 457 Plans

David S. Goldstein, Esq.
Sutherland Asbill & Brennan LLP

Of the several federal laws that pertain to securities, three have particular relevance for 457 plans: the Securities Act of 1933, the Securities Exchange Act of 1934, and the Investment Company Act of 1940. This chapter discusses the general relevance of these laws to 457 plans. It includes a discussion of their applicability to ineligible 457 plans under Section 457(f) of the Internal Revenue Code, to eligible public employer plans under Code Sections 457(b) and 457(e)(1)(A), and to eligible tax-exempt employer plans under Code Sections 457(b) and 457(e)(1)(B), as well as the implications for 457 plans of the Small Business Job Protection Act of 1996.

Federal Securities Laws and 457 Plans Generally

Q 10:1   What federal securities laws may apply to 457 plans?

Three federal securities laws may apply to 457 plans:

1. The Securities Act of 1933 (1933 Act) is the principal federal securities law that may apply to 457 plans. The 1933 Act requires that every offer and/or

sale of a security by U.S. mail or through interstate commerce be registered with the Securities and Exchange Commission (SEC) unless an exemption from this requirement is available for the security or the transaction. [1933 Act § 5] The 1933 Act also prohibits the use of U.S. mail or interstate commerce to employ a scheme to defraud or obtain money or property by means of material misstatements or omissions in the offer or sale of a security (an antifraud provision). [Id. § 17] Because, as explained in Qs 10:5–10:7, securities could be deemed to be issued in connection with certain 457 plans in certain circumstances, the 1933 Act and rules thereunder could apply to 457 plans or persons operating such plans.

2. The Securities Exchange Act of 1934 (1934 Act) also contains an antifraud provision that would cover the offer or sale of a security deemed to be issued in connection with a 457 plan. [1934 Act § 10]

3. The Investment Company Act of 1940 (1940 Act) imposes numerous requirements on collective or pooled investment vehicles that come within its definition of an investment company unless an exclusion from this definition is available.

Q 10:2 Are all federal securities laws and rules addressed in this chapter?

Not necessarily. Although federal securities laws and related rules and regulations not addressed in this chapter may come into play in connection with 457 plans, their sponsors or administrators, or collective or pooled investment vehicles supporting 457 plans (or sponsors of such vehicles), such laws and related rules and regulations would apply only in unusual circumstances and therefore are not addressed in this chapter.

Q 10:3 Are the federal securities laws applicable to 457 plans well developed?

No. Little legal authority exists regarding the applicability of the federal securities laws to 457 plans or, for that matter, to nonqualified deferred compensation plans of any kind. Much of the analysis in this chapter is therefore an interpretation of authority established in connection with qualified plans and other types of employee benefit plans.

Q 10:4 When might the 1933 Act, 1934 Act, or 1940 Act apply to 457 plans?

The registration requirements of the 1933 Act and its rules could apply whenever a 457 plan, an employer sponsoring such a plan, or a collective investment vehicle supporting such a plan is deemed to have issued a security in connection with the plan. The antifraud provisions of both the 1933 Act and the 1934 Act could apply whenever a security issued in connection with a 457 plan is offered or sold. The 1940 Act could apply to any collective or pooled investment vehicle used to support a 457 plan. Generally, however, exemptions or exclusions are available under each of these statutes (or under SEC staff interpretations of them) for most 457 plans and related persons.

Q 10:5 What type of security might be issued in connection with a 457 plan?

Generally, three types of securities might be issued in connection with any employee benefit plan, including a 457 plan:

1. A security issued by the employer and held as an asset of the plan (or directly by an employee or plan participant pursuant to the plan);
2. A security representing a participant's interest in the plan (or a related trust or investment vehicle supporting the plan); and
3. A security representing the plan's interest in a collective or pooled investment vehicle in which the plan invests.

The most common type of security issued in connection with employee benefit plans of ordinary industrial corporations is, of course, stock in the corporation. Obviously, this type of security is not issued in connection with a 457 plan.

Most other types of securities issued in connection with employee benefit plans generally, and 457 plans in particular, arise from the existence of an investment contract. The definition of a security under the 1933 Act contains a list of instruments that are securities, including an investment contract. [1933 Act § 2(1)] An investment contract exists when an investment is made in a common venture with a reasonable expectation that profits will be made from the entrepreneurial or managerial efforts of others. [SEC v. W.J. Howey Co., 329 U.S. 819, 67 S. Ct. 27, 91 L. Ed. 697 (1946)]

Although the SEC staff has not specifically addressed 457 plans, it has informally taken the position in recent years that nonqualified deferred compensation plans generally give rise to a security issued by the employer called a deferred compensation obligation. Although this position appears to have been taken in connection with top-hat plans and excess benefit plans rather than 457 plans, informal discussions between private practitioners and SEC staff members suggest the use of a two-step analysis by the SEC staff that is equally applicable to 457 plans:

1. Because of the unfunded nature of nonqualified deferred compensation plans, participants in such plans rely on the employer's promise to pay; therefore, if an investment contract exists, it is a contract issued by the employer.
2. Absent an appropriate exemption (see Q 10:11), deferred compensation obligations generally are subject to the registration requirements of the 1933 Act when such plans have an investment as well as tax planning goal that might be viewed as an investment contract. In recent years, a number of companies have registered deferred compensation obligations under the 1933 Act (on Form S-8) in connection with top-hat and excess benefit plans.

The SEC staff's position regarding deferred compensation obligations is based on the idea that the plan is not a separate issuer. Under this analysis, a nonqualified deferred compensation plan generally would not be a separate issuer unless it limited participants' rights against the employer (e.g., limited the participants' rights to a specific pool of assets). For example, use of a rabbi trust to fund plan obligations should not make the plan a separate issuer, but use of a secular trust for this purpose probably would make the trust or the plan a separate issuer (see Q 10:17).

Q 10:6   How does the SEC staff analysis of nonqualified deferred compensation plans differ from its analysis of qualified plans?

The SEC staff also has historically relied on the investment contract test to reach the conclusion that participants' interests in qualified plans often are securities. After the Supreme Court concluded in 1980 that participant interests in involuntary, noncontributory pension plans are not securities under the 1933 Act or 1934 Act, the SEC staff issued two releases in which it expressed the view, based on the investment contract analysis, that participant interests in plans that are both voluntary and contributory generally come within the definition of a security under the 1933 Act. [SEC Rel. No. 33-6188 (Feb. 1, 1980); SEC Rel. No. 33-6281 (Jan. 15, 1981)] The SEC staff also indicated in these releases that plans that are involuntary, and plans that are voluntary but not contributory, generally are not securities under the 1933 Act.

Federal courts have not always agreed with the SEC staff that participant interests in voluntary contributory plans are securities. Since 1981, several lower federal courts have concluded that participant interests in different types of qualified plans (including voluntary contributory plans) are not securities. Generally, these federal courts gave considerable weight to two factors that the SEC staff did not consider significant: (1) contribution to retirement plans is not a traditional investment decision; and (2) the Employee Retirement Income Security Act of 1974 (ERISA) provides comprehensive regulation of qualified plans.

The SEC staff also relied on the investment contract analysis to conclude that a qualified plan's interest in a collective or pooled investment vehicle is a security under the 1933 Act. [SEC Rel. No. 33-6188 (Feb. 1, 1980)]

Although registration under the 1933 Act generally would be required of securities arising from participant interests in qualified plans and from such plans' interests in collective or pooled investment vehicles, exemptions from this requirement usually are available (see Q 10:11).

Q 10:7   What conclusions may be drawn about 457 plans specifically?

The federal courts have not decided and the SEC and its staff have not published any position as to whether a 457 plan participant's interest in a 457 plan is a security or whether such a plan's interest in a collective or pooled investment vehicle is a security. Nevertheless, it is probable that based on an investment contract analysis, the SEC staff would conclude that a 457 plan's investment in a collective or pooled investment vehicle is a security, and that where participant interests in a 457 plan are not securities issued by the employer (i.e., are not deferred compensation obligations), interests in the plan may nonetheless be securities (see Q 10:5).

Q 10:8   What is the definition of *offer and sale* under the 1933 Act?

The answer to this question is complex and depends on a number of factors. Generally, the SEC staff considers participation in a voluntary contributory employee benefit plan to be the result of an offer and sale to the participant of any security issued by the plan or the employer. Although the SEC staff has never addressed this question in the context of a 457 plan, it seems likely that a 457 plan would be deemed to be voluntary and contributory and that any security issued in connection with a 457 plan would not escape the registration requirements of the 1933 Act on the ground that there was no offer or sale.

Q 10:9   Are definitions under the 1934 Act different from those under the 1933 Act?

As it might relate to a 457 plan, the term *security* has the same definition under the 1934 Act as it would under the 1933 Act, and the antifraud provisions of the 1934 Act would apply where an offer and sale, as defined in the 1933 Act, occurs.

Q 10:10   What entities might be investment companies subject to the 1940 Act in connection with a 457 plan?

Any collective or pooled investment vehicle that is deemed under the investment contract analysis to issue a security to a 457 plan (or, for that matter, a qualified plan) would likely come within the definition of an investment company under the 1940 Act. Although registration of such an entity under the 1940 Act generally would be required, exclusions from the definition of an investment company usually are available for vehicles that offer their securities solely to qualified plans and governmental plans (see Qs 10:5, 10:12). In addition, if the collective or pooled investment vehicle is an agency, authority, or instrumentality of a state, or a political subdivision of a state, the vehicle is not subject to the 1940 Act at all.

Q 10:11   What exemptions are available from the registration requirements of the 1933 Act?

A number of exemptions from the registration requirements of the 1933 Act are potentially available for securities issued in connection with 457 plans or for transactions through which such securities are offered or sold. Even if an exemption is available, the offer and sale of the security is still subject to the antifraud provisions of the 1933 Act and the 1934 Act.

Government and municipal securities. The most important exemption is found in Section 3(a)(2) of the 1933 Act. Section 3(a)(2) exempts from the registration requirements of the 1933 Act any security issued by the United States or any territory thereof, or by the District of Columbia, or by any state of the United States, or by any political subdivision of a state or territory, or by any public instrumentality of one or more states or territories, or by any person controlled or supervised by and acting as an instrumentality of the government of the United States pursuant to authority granted by Congress. In other words, government and most municipal securities are exempt from the registration requirements of the 1933 Act.

Employee benefit plans. Section 3(a)(2) also exempts both participant interests in most employee benefit plans and interests of such plans in collective or pooled investment vehicles. Specifically, Section 3(a)(2) exempts from the registration provisions of the 1933 Act any interest or participation in a single or collective trust maintained by a bank, or any security arising out of a contract issued by an insurance company, which interest, participation, or security is issued in connection with any of the following:

1. A plan that qualifies under Code Section 401;
2. An annuity plan that meets the requirements for the deduction of the employer's contributions under Code Section 404(a)(2); or
3. A governmental plan as defined in Code Section 414(d).

Section 3(a)(2) does, however, carve out the following from these exempt securities:

1. Interests in single trust funds and separate accounts maintained by an insurance company for a single employer that invest more than the amount of the employer's contribution in securities issued by the employer or its affiliates;
2. Plans covering individuals who are employees within the meaning of Code Section 401(c); and
3. Plans funded by Section 403(b) annuity contracts.

Nonprofit organizations. Section 3(a)(4) of the 1933 Act exempts from the Act's registration requirements any security issued by a person (such as a corporation) organized and operated exclusively for religious, educational, benevolent, fraternal, charitable, or reformatory purposes, and not for pecuniary profit, if no part of the net earnings of the organization inures to the benefit of any person, private stockholder, or individual. Section 3(a)(4) also exempts any security issued by a collective or pooled investment vehicle that is excluded from the definition of an investment company by Section 3(c)(10) of the 1940 Act (see Q 10:12).

Intrastate transactions. Section 3(a)(11) of the 1933 Act exempts from the Act's registration requirements any security that is part of an issue offered and sold only to persons resident within a single state or territory, where the issuer of that security is a person resident and doing business within, or, if a corporation, incorporated by and doing business within, that state or territory.

Private offerings. Section 4(2) of the 1933 Act exempts from the Act's registration requirements any transaction not involving a public offering. Commonly known as the private offering exemption, Section 4(2) covers offerings made to a limited number of investors who are assumed to be sophisticated in business matters and have access to the types of information about an issuer that otherwise would be obtained through a registration statement under the 1933 Act. Legal authority regarding the scope of a private offering versus a public offering generally is limited, and is extremely limited in the context of any deferred compensation plan obligations. To the author's knowledge, no such authority exists regarding a 457 plan. Regulation D under the 1933 Act [1933 Act Rules 501–508] does provide safe harbors for several specific types of private offerings, but these would likely be impractical for most 457 plans. Because of the complexity of the private offering exemption, expert securities counsel should be consulted before reliance is placed on this exemption.

Limited amount transactions. Rule 701 under the 1933 Act provides an exemption from the Act's registration requirements for offers and sales of securities pursuant to written compensatory benefit plans or written contracts by issuers that are not subject to the reporting requirements of Section 13 or 15(d) of the 1934 Act and are not investment companies.

The SEC amended Rule 701 to increase the rule's utility to many issuers of deferred compensation obligations, including some employers offering 457 plans. [SEC Rel. No. 33-7645 (Feb. 25, 1999)] Rule 701 no longer limits the amount of securities that can be offered and sold in reliance on it. Other changes included the elimination of the $5 million aggregate offering price ceiling and a change in the maximum amount of securities that may be sold in a year to the greatest of $1 million, 15 percent of the issuer's total assets, or 15 percent of the outstanding securities of the class being sold. Another change was the addition of certain required disclosures to plan participants relating to information about the plan, descriptions of the risk factors associated with investment in securities being offered, and provision of financial statements of the employer.

Nevertheless, as with the private offering exemption, Rule 701 transactions may still be impractical for many 457 plans. For example, it is not at all clear how one should measure an issuer's "outstanding securities" as that term might be applied in the context of deferred compensation obligations. Rule 701 has a number of other complex requirements, and expert securities counsel should be consulted before reliance is placed on this exemption.

Q 10:12 What exemptions are available from the registration and other requirements of the 1940 Act?

Section 2(b) of the 1940 Act provides that the Act does not apply to states, political subdivisions of states, or agencies, authorities, or instrumentalities of states or their political subdivisions. Therefore, a collective or pooled investment vehicle that is an authority or instrumentality of a state, or a political subdivision of a state, is not subject to the 1940 Act.

Section 3(c)(10) of the 1940 Act excludes from the definition of an investment company any of the persons described in Section 3(a)(4) of the 1933 Act, as well as a list of other pools of assets related to charitable entities (see Q 10:18).

Section 3(c)(11) of the 1940 Act excludes the following from the definition of an investment company under the Act:

1. Any employees' stock bonus, pension, or profit-sharing trust that qualifies under Code Section 401;

2. Any governmental plan described in Section 3(a)(2)(C) of the 1933 Act;

3. Any collective trust fund maintained by a bank consisting solely of assets of such trusts or governmental plans, or both; or

4. Any insurance company separate account containing assets derived solely from

   a. Contributions under plans qualifying under Code Section 401 and/or contributions meeting the requirements for deduction of an employer's contribution under Code Section 402(a)(2);

   b. Contributions under governmental plans in connection with which interests, participations, or securities are exempted from the registration requirements of the 1933 Act by Section 3(a)(2)(C) of the 1933 Act; and

   c. Advances made by an insurance company in connection with the operation of such a separate account.

Any collective or pooled investment vehicle excluded from the definition of an investment company under the 1940 Act is essentially exempted from all of the provisions of the Act (see Q 10:10).

Q 10:13   What exemptions are available from the requirements of the 1934 Act?

Section 3(a)(12) of the 1934 Act includes in its list of exempted securities those securities exempted by Sections 3(a)(2)(A) to 3(a)(2)(C) of the 1933 Act (see Q 10:11).

Eligible Public Employer 457 Plans Under Code Sections 457(b) and 457(e)(1)(A)

Q 10:14   What exemptions or exclusions generally apply to public employer 457 plans?

The exemption under Section 3(a)(2) of the 1933 Act for government securities should be available for deferred compensation obligations deemed to be issued by a Section 457(e)(1)(A) employer (a public employer) (see Q 10:11). A recent SEC staff no-action letter indicates that the government securities exemption under Section 3(a)(2) usually is available to interests in a collective or pooled investment vehicle that is an authority or instrumentality of a state or local government and probably is available to interests in the plan or trust itself to the extent that the plan or trust is a separate issuer (see Q 10:5). [Public Employees' Retirement Board of the State of Oregon, SEC No-Action Letter (Mar. 3, 1998)]

In addition, under the terms of another SEC staff no-action letter, Sections 3(a)(2) of the 1933 Act, 3(a)(12) of the 1934 Act, and 3(c)(11) of the 1940 Act (hereinafter, the exemptive and exclusionary provisions) should apply to 457(b) plans of a public employer and to nongovernmental collective or pooled investment vehicles in which such plans invest. [Massachusetts Mutual Life Insurance Co., SEC No-Action Letter (Aug. 10, 1998)] (See Q 10:17.)

Q 10:15   What is a no-action letter?

In a no-action letter, a party writes to the SEC staff and requests that the staff take a position that it will not recommend enforcement action to the SEC under specific statutory provisions and related rules if the writer proceeds in the manner described. The writer almost always provides a legal analysis supporting its assertion that the requested position is consistent with (or at least not inconsistent with) pertinent statutory provisions and related rules, as well as with any SEC or SEC staff interpretations thereof (e.g., prior no-action positions). Because the SEC staff usually takes no-action positions without agreeing or disagreeing with the writer's legal analysis, readers often must draw inferences concerning the staff's views about this analysis from the request letter and the staff's response. Often no-action positions are subject to various conditions, and one can usually infer a fair amount about the SEC staff's thinking from the conditions. Although a court may give weight to a no-action position, such positions are not, strictly speaking, interpretations of law by the SEC or its staff and are not binding on anyone (e.g., a private litigant) except the staff.

Q 10:16   Under what circumstances might an SEC no-action position be sought?

No-action letters often are sought by a party to obtain confirmation that its interpretation of a law or regulation is reasonable in a particular set of circumstances. For the reasons described below, parties have sought confirmation of their belief that the exemptive and exclusionary provisions apply to certain 457 plans.

The exemption under Section 3(a)(2) of the 1933 Act for government securities would cover only deferred compensation obligations issued by a public employer and interests in collective or pooled investment vehicles that are state or local government authorities or instrumentalities. Section 3(a)(2)(C) of the 1933 Act, however, exempts from the registration requirements of the Act both participant interests in governmental plans described therein (if any exist) and the interests of such plans in nongovernmental collective or pooled investment vehicles (see Q 10:11). Moreover, Section 3(c)(11) of the 1940 Act excludes from the definition of *investment company* any governmental plan described in Section 3(a)(2)(C) of the 1933 Act and any collective or pooled investment vehicle containing assets derived solely from contributions from such governmental plans and/or plans qualified under Code Section 401 (see Q 10:12). Section 3(a)(12) of the 1934 Act exempts from the registration requirements of the Act any security exempted from the registration requirements of the 1933 Act under Section 3(a)(2)(C) (see Q 10:13). Therefore, if eligible 457 plans of public employers are governmental plans as described in Section 3(a)(2)(C) of the 1933 Act, the exemptive and exclusionary provisions would relieve such plans, employers sponsoring such plans, third-party administrators administering such plans, and financial institutions (e.g., banks, insurance companies, and mutual fund organizations) that provide investment vehicles for such plans from most of the federal securities law regulation that would otherwise burden their operations.

Unfortunately, the exemptive and exclusionary provisions do not explicitly reference 457 plans. Although many people believe that the reference in Section 3(a)(2)(C) to "a governmental plan as defined in Section 414(d) of the Code" was always meant by Congress to apply to 457 plans, prior to the Small Business Job Protection Act of 1996 (SBJPA) enough doubt existed that sponsors of collective or pooled investment vehicles wishing to rely on the exemptive and exclusionary provisions sought and obtained no-action letters from the SEC staff beginning in 1988.

A 457 plan could, of course, be "a governmental plan as defined in Section 414(d) of the Code"; however, the portion of the exemptive and exclusionary provisions relating to governmental plans contains language that limits its scope to governmental plans that do not permit plan assets to be used for, or diverted to, any purpose other than the exclusive benefit of the employees for whom the plan was established and is maintained. For example, Section 3(a)(2)(C) encompasses only a governmental plan (as defined in Code Section 414(d)) that has been established by an employer for the exclusive benefit of its employees (or their beneficiaries) for the purpose of distributing to such employees (or their beneficiaries) the corpus and income of the funds accumulated under the plan if, under the plan, it is impossible, prior to the satisfaction of all liabilities with respect to such employees and their beneficiaries, for any part of the corpus or income to be used for, or diverted to, purposes other than the exclusive benefit of such employees or their beneficiaries.

Prior to the SBJPA, this language appeared to exclude nearly all eligible public employer 457 plans, because the assets of such plans would have been available to satisfy the claims of general creditors of the employer. The no-action positions were conditioned on a number of factual representations about the plans to which the collective or pooled investment vehicles were offered that the SEC staff believed limited the likelihood that plan assets could be diverted (particularly by the employer) to purposes other than providing benefits under the plan. The last of these letters contained new conditions imposed by the SEC staff and supplanted a long line of earlier no-action positions. [State Street Bank & Trust Co., SEC No-Action Letter (Aug. 1, 1996)] The SBJPA made these letters moot after January 1, 1999 (see Q 10:17).

Q 10:17   How does the SBJPA affect the applicability of Section 3(a)(2)(C) of the 1933 Act to eligible public employer 457 plans?

The SBJPA requires, among other things, that all amounts deferred under eligible 457 plans of public employers be held in a trust, custodial account, or annuity contract, where the documents establishing the trust or custodial account, or the provisions of the annuity contract, operate to ensure that assets and income of the plan are used for the exclusive benefit of employees participating in the plan and their beneficiaries. If held in such a trust, custodial account or annuity contract, the exclusive benefit requirement found in subparagraph (2)(C) of Section 3(a) of the 1933 Act would be met because it would be impossible, prior to the satisfaction of all liabilities with respect to employees participating in a 457 plan using such a trust and their beneficiaries, for any part of the corpus or income of the plan to be used for, or diverted to, purposes other than the exclusive benefit of such employees or their beneficiaries. The 457 plan would, therefore, clearly be a governmental plan of the type described in subparagraph (2)(C). The SEC staff has confirmed this position. [Massachusetts Mutual Life Insurance Co., SEC No-Action Letter (Aug. 10, 1998)]

The fact that the assets of these plans generally are insulated from the liabilities of their sponsoring employer and that participants' rights against the employer generally are limited to the plan's assets likely makes the plan or trust a separate issuer in relation to the employer. Thus, it is unlikely in this scenario that the SEC staff would consider the employer to be issuing deferred compensation obligations (see Q 10:5).

Eligible Tax-Exempt Employer 457 Plans Under Code Sections 457(b) and 457(e)(1)(B)

Q 10:18   What exemptions or exclusions generally apply to tax-exempt employer 457 plans?

The exemption under Section 3(a)(4) of the 1933 Act should be available for deferred compensation obligations deemed to be issued by many eligible tax-exempt employers, such as Section 501(c)(3) organizations (see Q 10:11).

Section 3(a)(4) of the 1933 Act exempts from the Act's registration requirements any security issued by a person (such as a corporation) organized and operated exclusively for religious, educational, benevolent, fraternal, charitable, or reformatory purposes, and not for pecuniary profit, if no part of the net earnings of the organization inures to the benefit of any person, private stockholder, or individual. Section 3(a)(4) also exempts any security issued by a collective or pooled investment vehicle that is excluded from the definition of an investment company by Section 3(c)(10) of the 1940 Act (see Q 10:12). Section 3(c)(10) of the 1940 Act excludes from the definition of investment company any of the persons described in Section 3(a)(4) of the 1933 Act, as well as a list of other pools of assets related to charitable entities or organizations.

Unfortunately, eligible tax-exempt employers other than the charitable organizations described in Section 3(a)(4) of the 1933 Act or Section 3(c)(10) of the 1940 Act may not rely on these two exemptive and exclusionary provisions. Unless they can rely on Section 3(a)(11) or 4(2) of the 1933 Act or Rule 701 thereunder, such employers may have to consider registration of deferred compensation obligations under the 1933 Act (see Q 10:11).

Noneligible 457 Plans Under Code Section 457(f)

Q 10:19   What exemptions or exclusions generally apply to noneligible 457 plans?

The exemption under Section 3(a)(2) of the 1933 Act for government securities should be available for deferred compensation obligations deemed to be issued by a public employer, even in connection with a 457(f) plan (see Qs 10:11, 10:14).

The exemption under Section 3(a)(4) of the 1933 Act should be available for deferred compensation obligations deemed to be issued by many tax-exempt employers, such as Section 501(c)(3) organizations (see Qs 10:11, 10:18).

The exemptions under Sections 3(a)(2) and 3(a)(4) are only exemptions from the registration requirements of the 1933 Act (see Q 10:11). Even if an exemption is available, the offer and sale of the subject security is still subject to the antifraud provisions of the 1933 Act and the 1934 Act.

Chapter 11

Ineligible Plans Under 457(f)

David A. Pratt
Albany Law School

This chapter discusses plans designed to provide benefits to executives of tax-exempt and governmental organizations beyond the dollar limits applicable to plans that are "eligible" under Section 457 of the Internal Revenue Code (Code). These plans generally are referred to as "ineligible" plans, or as Section 457(f) plans because their tax consequences are set out in Code Section 457(f). The principal issues in designing these plans are the timing and amount to be included in the employee's income, under the rules of that Code Section. This chapter deals with how to design these plans for the most favorable federal income, estate, and payroll tax consequences. Plan design issues focus on the tax rules relating to the concept of a substantial risk of forfeiture. The chapter also discusses constraints imposed by the Employee Retirement Income Security Act of 1974 (ERISA) and other nontax rules. The effect of the final regulations under Code Section 457 and how Code Section 457(f) may affect split-dollar plans are also discussed.

The author would like to acknowledge the contribution of John J. McFadden, who was the author of prior versions of this chapter.

General Rules

Q 11:1 What is a 457(f) plan?

A 457(f) plan (or an "ineligible Section 457 plan") is a plan:

1. That is maintained by an "eligible employer" (see Q 11:2); and

2. That is not excluded or exempted from the application of Section 457 (see Q 11:3); and

3. That fails (intentionally or inadvertently) to satisfy one or more of the requirements for an eligible plan under Section 457(b).

An eligible plan that satisfies the requirements of Section 457(b) is often set up in tandem with an ineligible plan that is subject to Section 457(f). For example, assume that an employer and an employee want a $100,000 total deferral for 2004. The Section 457(b) maximum for 2004 (generally $13,000) would be deferred under the eligible portion of the plan, and the balance would be deferred under the ineligible portion. (For rulings approving tandem plans, see P.L.R. 200321002, 199916037.)

Generally, a 457(f) plan is a plan or agreement under which a tax-exempt or governmental employer provides nonqualified deferred compensation to an employee, typically an executive or key employee, in excess of the annual dollar/percentage limitation applicable to eligible plans (see chapter 2). However, it is also possible for a plan that is intended to be an eligible plan to be or become a Section 457(f) plan because it fails, at any time, to satisfy all of the requirements for an eligible plan. For example, if any amount deferred is subject to a substantial risk of forfeiture, then the regulations provide that it is taken into account (adjusted to reflect gain or loss allocable to the deferred amount) in the year when that risk lapses. [Treas. Reg. § 1.457-2(b)(1), (2)] Assume that, beginning in 2004, a private tax-exempt employer deposits $9,000 per year on behalf of an employee under a 457 plan that has a three-year cliff vesting schedule. The employee's account becomes fully vested in 2006. Under the proposed regulations, the entire $27,000 deposited to date (plus earnings) would be taken into account in 2006. This exceeds the maximum deferral ($15,000) allowed in that year, so the entire plan becomes ineligible. [Treas. Reg. § 1.457-4(e)(3)]

The rule (as to when favorable amounts are taken into account) does not appear in Section 457(b) and should, as the statute provides [I.R.C. § 457(f)], be limited to deferrals under ineligible plans. Deferrals under an eligible plan should be taken into account in the year deferred, regardless of whether they are vested. This rule would be much simpler to administer and would reduce the risk of the plan's inadvertently becoming ineligible. Besides being difficult to administer, the rule in the regulations is not consistent with the Section 415 rules, applicable to qualified plans and 403(b) plans, under which annual additions are taken into account even if they are not vested.

The tax rules for 457(f) plans are less favorable than those for deferred compensation plans that comply with the dollar/percentage limitation (eligible plans). The tax treatment of 457(f) plans also is less favorable than that of nonqualified deferred compensation plans of private non-tax-exempt employers. Generally, under Section 457(f) of the Internal Revenue Code (Code), deferral of taxation on compensation cannot be extended beyond the year in which the employee's rights to the compensation are no longer subject to a substantial risk of forfeiture, even if actual payment is made in a later year (see Q 11:10).

Q 11:2   What is an "eligible employer" under Section 457?

In order to sponsor a 457 plan, the employer must be one of the following:

1. A nongovernmental organization other than a church [I.R.C. § 457(e)(13)] that is tax-exempt under the Code. Section 457 applies to an organization that is exempt under any paragraph of Section 501, such as a chamber of commerce. [I.R.C. § 501(c)(6)] By contrast, a tax-sheltered annuity (403(b)) arrangement is available only to an organization that is tax-exempt under Section 501(c)(3).

2. A state, a political subdivision of a state, or an agency of either. Section 457 plans differ from Section 403(b) plans in that participation is not limited to governmental employees who perform services for an educational organization.

For this purpose, *church* is defined in Code Section 3121(w)(3)(A) and includes a qualified church-controlled organization, as defined in Section 3121(w)(3)(B). A church within the meaning of Code Section 3121(w)(3)(A) means a church, a convention or association of churches, or an elementary or secondary school that is controlled, operated, or principally supported by a church or a convention or association of churches. This definition is less broad than the definition of *church* in Code Section 414, which also includes a religious order or a religious organization if that order or organization is an integral part of a church and is engaged in carrying out the functions of a church. [Treas. Reg. § 1.414(e)-1(e)]

A *qualified church-controlled organization* means any church-controlled tax-exempt organization described in Section 501(c)(3) except an organization that:

1. Offers goods, services, or facilities for sale, other than on an incidental basis, to the general public, other than goods, services, or facilities that are sold at a nominal charge that is substantially less than the cost of providing such goods, services, or facilities; and

2. Normally receives more than 25 percent of its support from either (a) government sources or (b) receipts from admissions, sales of merchandise, performance of services, or furnishing of facilities in activities that are not unrelated activities, or both.

[I.R.C. § 3121(w)(3)(B)]

Accordingly, the term *church-controlled organization* does not include hospitals or universities with a religious affiliation. Such organizations are subject to Section 457 and may establish an eligible or ineligible 457 plan.

If a plan or arrangement is maintained by an employer that is not an eligible employer, as described above, then the plan *cannot* be subject to Section 457 and thus cannot be either an eligible 457 plan or a 457(f) plan. [Treas. Reg. § 1.457-2(h)] The plan sponsor's conversion from taxable to tax-exempt does not cause its frozen nonqualified deferred compensation plans to become subject to Section 457. [P.L.R. 200302015] The regulations discuss the consequences if an employer ceases to be an eligible employer and the plan is not terminated. [Treas. Reg. § 1.457-10(a)(2)(i)]

The current rules for 457 plans maintained by state and local government employers ("governmental plans") differ significantly from the rules governing 457 plans maintained by private tax-exempt employers ("private plans").

Q 11:3   What types of benefits are subject to the restrictions of Code Section 457?

Determining whether an arrangement is subject to Section 457 is crucially important. If the arrangement is subject to Section 457, then, unless it satisfies the requirements for an "eligible deferred compensation plan," it is subject to unfavorable tax treatment under Section 457(f). If the arrangement is not subject to Section 457, then its tax consequences to the individual participant will be governed by other sections of the Code (such as Sections 83 and 402), which typically permit deferral of all or most of the taxable income until benefits are actually or constructively received. Unfortunately, the scope of some of the key exemptions is far from clear.

Section 457 generally applies to *any* plan of an eligible employer that provides for the deferral of compensation. The IRS has taken the position that Section 457 applies to all forms of nonqualified deferred compensation, including nonelective deferred compensation and arrangements with a single individual [IRS Notice 87-13, 1987-1 I.R.B. 432; IRS Notice 88-8, 1988-1 C.B. 477], subject to the following statutory exceptions:

1. A qualified plan, or an annuity plan or contract described in Section 403. [I.R.C. § 457(f)(2)(A), (B)]

2. That portion of any plan that consists of a transfer of property "described in" Section 83. [I.R.C. § 457(f)(2)(C)] (For further discussion, see Q 11:4)

3. That portion of any plan that consists of a trust to which Section 402(b) applies. [I.R.C. § 457(f)(2)(D)] In general, Section 402(b) applies to a

funded trust (or to a portion of a funded trust) that is not exempt from tax under Section 501(a). Section 402(b) does not apply to a trust, custodial account, or annuity established for a governmental 457 plan under Section 457(g). [I.R.C. § 457(g)(2)(B)]

4. A qualified governmental excess benefit arrangement described in Section 415(m). [I.R.C. § 457(f)(2)(E)] A qualified governmental excess benefit arrangement is a plan forming part of a governmental qualified plan [I.R.C. § 414(d)] that provides benefits in excess of the Section 415 limits applicable to qualified plans. [I.R.C. § 415(m)(3)] The Section 415 limit applicable to governmental plans limits annual benefits to $165,000, as indexed for inflation. [I.R.C. § 415(b)(11)]

5. Any "bona fide" vacation leave, sick leave, compensatory time, severance pay, disability pay, or death benefit plan. [I.R.C. § 457(e)(11)(A)(i)] (For further discussion, see Qs 11:5 and 11:6.) In Private Letter Ruling 200351002, the IRS ruled that a state's comprehensive leave program was a bona fide plan that qualified for this exception.

6. Any plan paying solely length-of-service awards to bona fide volunteers (or their beneficiaries) who provide firefighting and prevention services, emergency medical services, or ambulance services. [I.R.C. § 457(e)(11)(A)(ii); see also Rev. Rul. 2003-47, 2003-19 I.R.B. 866] The aggregate amount of length-of-service awards accruing with respect to any year of service for any volunteer may not exceed $3,000. [I.R.C. § 457(e)(11)(B)(ii)]

7. Nonelective deferred compensation of non-employees [I.R.C. § 457(e)(12)], but only if (a) all individuals who have satisfied any initial service requirement and who have the same relationship with the payor are covered under the same plan and (b) there are no individual variations or options under the plan. If independent contractors can individually elect the amount of compensation to be deferred, the exception does not apply. [See P.L.R. 9809038 (holding that plan qualified for this exception)]

8. Any qualified state judicial plan described in Section 131(c)(3)(B) of the Revenue Act of 1978, enacted by Section 252 of TEFRA [§ 1107(c)(4) of TRA '86, as amended]. Such a plan is qualified if:

   a. The plan has been continuously in existence since December 31, 1978;

   b. All judges eligible to benefit under the plan are required to participate and to contribute the same fixed percentage of their basic or regular rate of compensation;

   c. A judge's retirement benefit under the plan is a percentage of the compensation of judges of the state holding similar positions;

   d. Benefits for any year do not exceed the benefit limitation for a qualified defined benefit plan (generally, for 2004, the lesser of $165,000 or 100 percent of the participant's average compensation over the three highest paid years) [I.R.C. § 415(b), (d)]; and

   e. No judge has an option concerning contributions or benefits that, if exercised, would affect the amount of the participant's currently includible compensation. [TEFRA 1982 § 252]

Unfortunately, the final regulations under Section 457 do not provide specific guidance on arrangements that are not subject to Section 457, such as bona fide death benefits and severance plans. Guidance would be helpful, as there is considerable uncertainty with regard to the scope of some of these arrangements.

Clearly, SEPs and SIMPLE IRAs are not intended to be subject to Section 457, but they are not specifically exempted by the statute. Pending enactment of a technical correction, it would be helpful to have guidance from the IRS clarifying that they will not be considered to be subject to Section 457.

Apparently, however, Code Section 457 may apply to split-dollar plans. Specifically, the Preamble to the recent split-dollar regulations states that an "equity split-dollar life insurance arrangement governed by the economic benefit regime constitutes a deferred compensation arrangement." Accordingly, an employee of a tax-exempt organization or of a state or local government may have to include an amount in gross income attributable to an equity split-dollar life insurance arrangement even if the employee does not have current access to the policy cash value under these regulations. Section 457 will apply to the split-dollar arrangement if (1) the employer is an eligible employer and (2) the arrangement is not exempt as a "bona fide" death benefit plan. If the arrangement fails to satisfy one or more of the requirements for an eligible 457 plan (e.g., the annual deferral exceeds the dollar limit), then Code Section 457(f) taxation will apply. As a result, a nonowner may have to include an amount in gross income under an equity split-dollar life insurance arrangement at a time earlier than would normally be required under those regulations. For example, Code Section 457(f) generally requires an employee of a tax-exempt organization (other than a church organization under IRC Section 3121(w)(3)) or of a state or local government to include deferred compensation in gross income when the employee's rights to the deferred compensation are not subject to a substantial risk of forfeiture. [Preamble, T.D. 9092, 68 Fed. Reg. 54,336, 54,340 (Sept. 17, 2003)]

Q 11:4   What is a transfer of property "described" in Section 83?

Section 457 does not apply to that portion of any plan that consists of a transfer of property "described" in Section 83. [I.R.C. § 457(f)(2)(C)] Accordingly, tax-exempt organizations have sought to avoid the deferral limitations on eligible deferred compensation plans under Section 457(b) and the substantial risk of forfeiture requirement for deferral of tax on benefits under a Section 457(f) plan by offering third-party options to their executives. A third-party option is an option issued by an employer to an employee that allows the employee to acquire securities or property (e.g., mutual fund shares).

Third-party option arrangements generally provide options with a deep discount. The amount of the discount reflects the amount of compensation the employee wishes to defer. For instance, if an employee wants to defer $75,000, the employer could reduce the employee's compensation by $75,000 and grant an option to acquire $100,000 worth of corporate stock, mutual fund shares, or other property (valued at the date of grant) for a $25,000 exercise price.

Options are property, taxable under the rules of Section 83. Under Section 83(e)(3) and (4), if an option has a readily ascertainable fair market value when granted, the recipient must recognize ordinary income at the time of grant, but not at the time of exercise or disposal. If an option does not have a readily ascertainable fair market value when granted, the recipient must recognize ordinary income at the time of exercise or disposal, but not at the time of grant. Accordingly, the argument made by proponents of third-party option arrangements is that the grant of a third-party option should not be subject to Section 457, because the options are "described" in Section 83.

Under the final 457 regulations, Section 457(f) applies if the date on which there is no longer a substantial risk of forfeiture (the *vesting date*) occurs before the date on which there is a transfer of property subject to Section 83 (the *transfer date*). Section 457(f) does not apply if the vesting date is on or after the transfer date. [Treas. Reg. § 1.457-11(d)] This rule is clearly intended to eliminate mutual fund option plans and similar arrangements, and applies to options granted after May 8, 2002 (regardless of when the option plan was adopted). [Treas. Reg. § 1.457-12(d)]

The regulations include the following example:

> Example 3. (i) Facts. In 2004, Z, a tax-exempt entity, grants an option to acquire property to employee C. The option lacks a readily ascertainable fair market value, within the meaning of section 83(e)(3), has a value on the date of grant equal to $100,000, and is not subject to a substantial risk of forfeiture (within the meaning of section 457(f)(3)(B) and within the meaning of section 83(c)(1)). Z exercises the option in 2012 by paying an exercise price of $75,000 and receives property that has a fair market value (for purposes of section 83) equal to $300,000.

> (ii) Conclusion. In this Example 3, under section 83(e)(3), section 83 does not apply to the grant of the option. Accordingly, C has income of $100,000 in 2004 under section 457(f). In 2012, C has income of $125,000, which is the value of the property transferred in 2012, minus the allocable portion of the basis that results from the $100,000 of income in 2004 and the $75,000 exercise price. [Treas. Reg. § 1.457-11(d)(2)]

Q 11:5   What is a *bona fide death benefit plan*?

Section 457 does not apply to any bona fide death benefit plan. [I.R.C. § 457(e)(11)(A)(i)] There is no guidance as to what this means, but this exclusion has been used as the justification for tax-exempt organizations providing to their senior executives very large amounts of cash value life insurance. Typically, the marketing materials for these programs do not focus on the amount of the death benefit but rather on the amount of the cash value accumulation at the executive's anticipated retirement age. These arrangements share more characteristics with deferred compensation arrangements than with death benefit plans, so many commentators believe that they should be taxed as deferred compensation plans.

Further, the words *bona fide* must mean something. They could mean (1) a plan under which the death benefit is at least as important as any other benefit (e.g., lifetime withdrawals) available to the executive under the plan; and/or (2) a plan under which the amount of the death benefit is reasonably comparable to the life insurance benefits customarily provided to active employees and retirees under a plan (e.g., a group-term life insurance plan) for employees generally.

These life insurance programs were generally provided on a split-dollar basis, because prior to the changes recently announced by the IRS, the taxable cost of a split-dollar arrangement to an executive was typically much less than its true economic value. The Department of Labor (DOL) has ruled that split-dollar plans are classified as welfare plans (rather than pension plans) under ERISA [ERISA Op. Ltr. No. 77-23], and this has been used to support the argument that they are exempt from Section 457 as bona fide death benefit plans. It appears that the DOL ruling, even if correct, has no bearing on the 457 issue.

Q 11:6 What is a *bona fide severance pay plan*?

Section 457 does not apply to any bona fide severance pay plan. [I.R.C. § 457(e)(11)(A)(i)] Again, the Code does not define *severance plan* for this purpose. The severance pay plan exception was first announced in IRS Notice 88-8, 1988-1 C.B. 477, which was subsequently clarified by Notice 88-68, 1988-1 C.B. 556, and then codified in Section 457(e)(11) by TAMRA.

Unfortunately, the legislative history of TAMRA gives no guidance as to the intended scope of the exception and, as the IRS has acknowledged, there is currently no authoritative guidance defining the term *bona fide severance pay plan* for purposes of Section 457(e)(11). It is not clear whether other definitions of *severance plan*, which were developed for different purposes and in different contexts, should be extended to Section 457(e)(11).

Many plan sponsors have relied on the DOL regulation under ERISA [29 C.F.R. § 2510.3-2(b)], which treats a severance plan as a welfare plan (rather than a pension plan) if:

1. Payments are not contingent, directly or indirectly, on the employee's retiring;
2. The total amount of the payments does not exceed the equivalent of twice the employee's annual compensation during the year immediately preceding termination of service; and
3. All payments are generally completed within 24 months.

However, the DOL acknowledges that this definition is merely a safe harbor, and that "in appropriate circumstances a severance pay plan not meeting the conditions [set forth in the regulations] might also be deemed not to be an employee pension benefit plan. . . ." [DOL Adv. Op. 99-01A].

Treasury Regulations Section 31.3121(v)(2)-1(b)(4)(iv)(B) discusses when an arrangement constitutes severance pay (rather than deferred compensation) for purposes of the rules governing employment taxation of nonqualified deferred compensation arrangements. If the arrangement satisfies the requirements of the DOL regulations, then it is treated as severance pay for this purpose. If not, then

> whether those benefits are severance pay within the meaning of this paragraph (b)(4)(iv) depends upon the relevant facts and circumstances. For this purpose, relevant facts and circumstances include whether the benefits are provided over a short period of time commencing immediately after (or shortly after) termination of employment or for a substantial period of time following termination of employment and whether the benefits are provided after any termination or only after retirement (or another specified type of termination). Benefits provided under a severance pay arrangement (within the meaning of section 3(2)(B)(i) of ERISA) are in all cases severance pay within the meaning of this paragraph (b)(4)(iv) if the benefits payable under the plan upon an employee's termination of employment are payable only if that termination is involuntary.

The IRS has taken the position that an unanticipated set of circumstances is required to trigger a bona fide severance payment. In one ruling, the IRS concluded that although the benefits provided were labeled "severance pay," they did not differ in any meaningful manner from deferred compensation. Thus, the contract was not a bona fide severance pay plan under Section 457(e)(11) but rather a Section 457(f) ineligible deferred compensation arrangement. Amounts payable to a teacher at retirement under the contract were includible in income in the year in which the teacher satisfied a "rule of 73" eligibility requirement, making the future payment no longer subject to a substantial risk of forfeiture, regardless of whether he or she retired at that time:

> Generally, the term "severance pay" connotes payment to an employee because of his or her termination of employment under an unanticipated set of circumstances, rather than compensation that has been unconditionally deferred until termination of employment. Severance plans have as their basic function the payment of benefits on account of a separation from service due to a contingency beyond the control of the employee. For example, employees who are laid off or dismissed due to corporate downsizing or restructuring would be paid these benefits, while those that held their jobs would have no rights to those funds. Thus, these arrangements generally provide payments to employees because employment has terminated, not simply when employment terminates. Payments regarded as severance may also include payments made to employees who voluntarily terminate employment, most often before attaining retirement age, as part of a window-type early retirement incentive program.

[TAM 199903032]

Similarly, in *Wellons v. Commissioner* [T.C. Memo. 1992-704, *aff'd*, 31 F.3d 569 (7th Cir. 1994)], the court reviewed whether an employer's plan constituted a severance pay plan or a plan of deferred compensation for purposes of the employer's deduction under Code Section 404(a)(5). Under the plan, a participant who terminated employment was entitled to a benefit equaling 21 weeks of average weekly compensation for each year of service. The maximum allowable benefit was two times the annual salary of the participant for the year immediately preceding termination. Benefits were paid under the plan within 24 months of the severance. The Seventh Circuit, in affirming the Tax Court, determined that the plan was a plan of deferred compensation. Similar to a pension plan, the benefits vested after five years of employment and were commensurate with salary and length of service.

On December 23, 1999, the IRS issued Announcement 2000-1, 2000-1 I.R.B. 1, to provide interim guidance on the reporting requirements for the school district in TAM 199903032 and other similarly situated employers. State and local governments need not report amounts deferred, under a plan that has consistently been treated as a severance plan, for any year prior to the year in which the participant or beneficiary is in actual or constructive receipt of these amounts, if the amounts are provided under a plan that meets certain requirements. The IRS and the Treasury Department requested comments on "what types of plans maintained by state and local government and tax-exempt employers are properly considered bona fide severance pay plans for purposes of section 457."

The preamble to the final regulations under Section 457 also requests comments on an appropriate definition.

Q 11:7   Are some existing nonqualified deferred compensation plans of tax-exempt and governmental employers grandfathered?

Originally, Section 457 applied only to governmental employers. TRA '86 extended it to private tax-exempt employers, and certain existing plans were grandfathered. [I.R.C. § 457(e)(1)] A plan that is grandfathered is not subject to Section 457 and is governed by other Code sections (primarily Sections 72 and 402(b)) as long as it remains grandfathered. The following types of plans received grandfather protection.

Nongovernmental plan, pre-1987 deferrals. Amounts deferred under a nongovernmental plan, by an individual covered by the plan on August 16, 1986, from compensation that would have been paid or made available in a taxable year beginning before January 1, 1987, are grandfathered. [TRA '86 § 1107(c)(3)(B)(i), as amended]

Nongovernmental plan, post-1986 deferrals. Deferrals of compensation under a nongovernmental plan, by an individual covered by the plan on August 16, 1986, that would have been paid or made available in a taxable year beginning after 1986, are grandfathered if such deferrals were fixed (a fixed amount or fixed formula) pursuant to an agreement that was in writing on August 16, 1986. Any modification of the fixed amount or formula will cause the plan to cease to be eligible for grandfather protection. [TRA '86 § 1107(c)(3)(B)(i), as amended; IRS Notice 87-13, Q&A 28, 1987-1 C.B. 432; P.L.R. 9538021]

Grandfathered amounts are taken into account in applying Section 457 to amounts deferred under any other deferred compensation plan. [See I.R.C. § 457 legislative history; TRA '86 § 1107(c)(3)(B), as amended by TAMRA § 1011(e)(6); S. Rep. No. 100-445, 100th Cong., 2d Sess. 148 (1988); IRS Notice 87-13, Q&A 28, 1987-1 C.B. 432]

Nonelective governmental plans in existence on July 14, 1988. Because of uncertainty as to the applicability of Section 457 to nonelective (as opposed to elective) contributions, a grandfather rule was enacted for nonelective governmental plans in existence on July 14, 1988. Amounts deferred under such a plan before July 14, 1988, are not subject to Section 457. Amounts deferred under such a plan after July 13, 1988, are also not subject to Section 457, but only if there was a written agreement on July 14, 1988. The agreement must provide either (1) for deferral of a fixed amount or (2) for deferral of an amount determined under a fixed formula, and must cover the individual for whom the agreement was made. Grandfathered amounts are taken into account in applying Section 457 to amounts deferred under any eligible 457(b) plan. [TAMRA § 6064(d)(3)] Section 457 will apply to any tax year that ends after the effective date of a written agreement that increases a benefit by modifying either the fixed amount or the formula. Thus, a reduction of a fixed amount or formula amount is permissible.

Nonelective collectively bargained plans in existence on December 31, 1987. Nonelective deferred compensation under a plan in existence on December 31, 1987, and maintained pursuant to one or more collective bargaining agreements, is grandfathered until the effective date of any material modification to the plan agreed to after December 31, 1987. IRS Notice 88-98 called for a January 1, 1991, cutoff date to be provided in regulations, but regulations were not issued, and the January 1, 1991, date does not appear in the statute. [TAMRA § 6064(d)(2)] For this purpose, a nonelective plan is a plan that covers a broad group of employees and under which the covered employees earn nonelective deferred compensation under a definite, fixed, and uniform benefit formula. [TAMRA § 6064(d)(2)(B)]

If such a plan is modified to reflect changes in the benefit formula or to expand the class of participants included in the pre-1988 plan definition, then Section 457 will apply. Such modifications do not include arrangements under which qualified plans with offsetting nonelective plan benefits are modified and the nonelective deferred compensation plan is modified to provide benefits that the qualified plan would have provided before its modification. If, on December 31, 1987, participation extended to a broad group of nonunion employees on the same terms as union employees, then the transitional rules will continue to apply as long as the union employees constitute at least 25 percent of total participants. [TAMRA § 6064(d)(2); IRS Notice 88-98, 1988-2 C.B. 421]

These grandfather provisions generally require that the plans remain unmodified in order to take advantage of the grandfather provision; however, in Private Letter Ruling 9549003, it was held that the adoption of a qualified plan by a tax-exempt employer and reduction (offsetting) of amounts payable under the nonqualified plan by qualified plan benefits payable to the participant did not destroy the grandfather protection of the nonqualified plan. Similarly, Private Letter Ruling 9822038 held that a change of investment funds and the addition of another mode of distribution did not destroy the grandfather protection. (See Qs 2:17, 2:18, and 2:19 for additional information on the grandfather rules.)

Q 11:8 What kind of benefit formulas can be provided under a 457(f) plan?

Subject to the limitations described in Q 11:3, the Code does not impose any restrictions on the type of benefit payment formula or arrangement provided under a 457(f) plan. Typical benefit formulas are discussed below.

Account balance plans. Under this approach, the plan document or agreement specifies the annual amount that will be deferred, either through a salary reduction agreement by the employee or as an employer contribution or bonus. The amount payable at the end of the deferral period is equal to the total of the principal amounts deferred, increased or decreased by investment results. The investment results can be based on actual investment return on assets set aside by the employer or rabbi trust, a stated interest rate, or a rate of return based on a specified index. [See, e.g., P.L.R. 199943008]

Defined benefit formula. This type of plan pays a fixed benefit amount, or a formula benefit based on compensation or years of service. Such a plan raises the issue of determining whether the annual limitation for eligible plans has been met or exceeded for the amount of compensation deferred. The annual deferral for the taxable year is the present value of the increase in the participant's vested benefit for the year (disregarding any increase attributable to prior annual deferrals). Present value must be determined using "reasonable" actuarial assumptions and methods, as determined by the IRS. [Treas. Reg. § 1.457-2(b)(3)]

Excess benefit formula. This type of formula is designed to restore benefits lost by an employee whose qualified plan amount is limited by the rules of Code Section 415. Such plans are advantageous because, if unfunded, they are exempt from Title I of the Employee Retirement Income Security Act of 1974 (ERISA). [ERISA § 4(b)(5)] (See Qs 11:24, 11:25, 11:30, 11:31.)

However, an excess plan can only replace benefits lost as a result of the Section 415 limitations. [See ERISA § 3(36)] It cannot replace benefits lost as a result of any other provision, such as the Code Section 401(a)(17) limit on the amount of compensation that can be taken into account under a qualified plan.

Distribution Requirements

Q 11:9 Are there limitations on or requirements for distributions from 457(f) plans?

Because these plans are not eligible plans under Code Section 457, they are not subject to the distribution requirements of Code Section 457(d); therefore, distributions can be made at any time and are not limited to distributions at age 70½, on separation from service, or on the occurrence of an unforeseeable emergency. Similarly, distributions from 457(f) plans are not subject to the minimum distribution requirements or minimum distribution penalties. A 457(f) plan can therefore permit amounts to be accumulated after age 70½ or retirement.

Income Tax Considerations

Q 11:10 When is deferred compensation in a 457(f) plan subject to federal income tax?

Year of inclusion. Deferred compensation under Section 457(f) is includible in the income of the participant or beneficiary for the first taxable year in which there is no substantial risk of forfeiture of the rights to such compensation. [I.R.C. § 457(f)(1)(A); Treas. Reg. § 1.457-11(a)] (See Q 11:11 for discussion of "substantial risk of forfeiture.")

If the earnings on the compensation deferred are subject to a substantial risk of forfeiture, the amount includible in gross income includes earnings to the date on which there is no substantial risk of forfeiture. However, the regulations can be read as providing that if the earnings on the deferred compensation are not forfeitable, these earnings are not taxable until actually paid or made available to the participant or beneficiary, if the plan is unsecured (i.e., the participant's or beneficiary's interest is "not senior to the [sponsoring] entity's general creditors." [Treas. Reg. § 1.457-11(a)(3)]

This language suggests the possibility that in an account balance type of plan, the amount includible in the year the account becomes vested could be valued in some manner other than adding to the principal amount the earnings credited to the account under the plan.

Based on this distinction, some planners have suggested that plan earnings can be deferred over a longer period than the principal amounts are deferred. Under their approach, the plan provides immediate vesting of plan earnings (i.e., earnings become vested as they are earned) while the principal amounts deferred are subject to a substantial risk of forfeiture for a longer period. It is asserted that as long as the plan is unfunded these earnings will not be taxed to the employee until actually paid. [Treas. Reg. § 1.457-11(a)(3)] Principal amounts would be taxable in the first year in which they are not subject to a substantial risk of forfeiture.

The regulation quoted above was promulgated in 2003. There was similar language on this issue in the earlier (1982) regulations, but in some rulings issued under the earlier regulations, the IRS did not seem to accept this approach to the extended deferral of plan earnings. In Private Letter Ruling 9628020, one conclusion was "[a] participant that irrevocably elects install-ment payments of all or a part of the deferral amount will nevertheless include the *entire deferral account balance* [emphasis added] in gross income on the distribution date [the date of vesting under the terms of the plan] because such amount is no longer subject to a substantial risk of forfeiture." The ruling fur-ther concluded that earnings that accumulate *after* the risk of forfeiture expires are includible in the year when paid or made available. This is a more reasonable reading of Treasury Regulations Section 1.457-11(a)(3).

Amount includible. If the plan distributes property other than cash, includ-ing a distribution of an annuity contract, the fair market value of the property in excess of the participant's basis is includible in his or her income in the year of distribution. [H.R. Rep. No. 1445, 95th Cong., 2d Sess. at 53, 1978-3 C.B. (vol. 1) 227]

The amount to be included when the forfeiture risk expires before benefits are actually paid is the present value of the benefits promised under the plan. [See Treas. Reg. § 1.457-11(c)] For example, suppose a plan provides for a pay-ment of $100,000 in 2020 and the forfeiture risk expires in 2010 when the present value of the $100,000 payment is $50,000. In 2010 the participant includes $50,000 in income.

Distributions after forfeiture risk expires. Distributions from 457(f) plans are subject to the rules of Code Section 72. [I.R.C. § 457(f)(1)(B); Treas. Reg. § 1.457-11(a)(4)] Code Section 72 provides a method of recovering a partici-pant's basis (including amounts previously taxed) from plan distributions. An amount previously included in income in the year in which a forfeiture risk expired would constitute basis to be recovered under Code Section 72. If the benefit is distributed as periodic payments, a portion of each payment is treated as a tax-free recovery of basis under the rules of Code Section 72 and the regulations thereunder, relating to annuities. [I.R.C. § 72(b)] If the payment is not made as an annuity (e.g., paid in a lump sum), only the amount in excess of basis is taxable. [I.R.C. § 72(e)] Thus, in the example from the preceding paragraph, when the participant receives the $100,000 payment in 2020, he or she will have $50,000 includible in income (i.e., the $100,000 payment less the participant's $50,000 basis).

Coordination with Section 83. Under the regulations, Code Section 457(f) applies to an arrangement (if it is an ineligible plan) in which vesting of bene-fits occurs before property is transferred, whereas Code Section 83 applies if property is transferred on or after the date of vesting. [Treas. Reg. § 1.457-11(d)]

For example, suppose a participant agrees to defer a specified amount of com-pensation to an ineligible plan in Year 1, with no substantial risk of forfeiture, in return for a commensurate payment of property in Year 5. This transaction would be governed by Code Section 457(f) and the participant would be taxable in Year 1 in an amount equal to the present value of the 2005 payment. However, if equivalent property was transferred to the participant in Year 1, subject to a substantial risk of forfeiture that expired in Year 5, the transaction would be governed by Code Section 83 and the participant would be taxed in Year 5 in an amount equal to the then fair market value of the property. The regulations include the following example:

> Example 4. (i) Facts. In 2010, X, a tax-exempt entity, agrees to pay deferred compensation to employee D. The amount payable is $100,000 to be paid 10 years later in 2020. The commitment to make the $100,000 payment is not subject to a substantial risk of forfeiture. In 2010, the present value of the $100,000 is $50,000. In 2018, X transfers to D property having a fair market value (for purposes of section 83) equal to $70,000. The transfer is in partial settlement of the commitment made in 2010 and, at the time of the transfer in 2018, the present value of the commitment is $80,000. In 2020, X pays D the $12,500 that remains due.

> (ii) Conclusion. In this Example 4, D has income of $50,000 in 2010. In 2018, D has income of $30,000, which is the amount transferred in 2018, minus the allocable portion of the basis that results from the $50,000 of income in 2010. (Under section 72(e)(2)(B), income is allocated first. The income is equal to $30,000 ($80,000 minus the $50,000 basis), with the result that the allocable portion of the basis is equal to $40,000 ($70,000 minus the $30,000 of income).) In 2020, D has income of $2,500 ($12,500 minus $10,000, which is the excess of the original $50,000 basis over the $40,000 basis allocated to the transfer made in 2018).

See also the discussion of this issue in Q 11:4.

Substantial Risk of Forfeiture

Q 11:11   What constitutes a substantial risk of forfeiture for purposes of Code Section 457(f)?

Code Section 457(f)(3)(B) states:

> The rights of a person to compensation are subject to a substantial risk of forfeiture if such person's rights to such compensation are conditioned upon the future performance of substantial services by any individual.

Recent letter rulings have indicated that the following constituted substantial risks of forfeiture under this test:

> The participant's benefits are forfeited if the participant terminates employment with the employer or if he is discharged by the employer prior to the distribution date (a stated date no sooner than two years from the effective date of the deferral agreement). [P.L.R. 9628020] Employer contributes a stated monthly sum to a book account for the

participant. The participant (or his beneficiary in the event of death) is entitled to the full amount in his book account upon death, termination of employment due to disability, or the completion of five continuous years of service. The participant will forfeit the entire amount in his book account if he does not complete five continuous years of service, except in the case of his death or disability. [P.L.R. 9627007] A participant vests in his benefit upon his remaining in the employer's employ until his normal retirement age, his death, or his separation from service due to disability prior to that age. [P.L.R. 9623027, 200321002]

Many earlier letter rulings have similar themes, so in general it is not difficult to design a service-based, or "earn-out," type of forfeiture provision. The provision must require that the person earn the rights to the deferred compensation by performing substantial future services. Because of the substantial possibility that this requirement will not be fulfilled, taxation of the benefit is postponed until the condition is completed and the benefit is vested. Presumably, the provisions allowing benefit payments on death or disability (without fulfilling the full-service requirement) do not sufficiently weaken the substantial risk of forfeiture, because death or disability during the forfeiture period is only a possibility.

Q 11:12 What constitutes a substantial risk of forfeiture for purposes of Code Section 83?

Code Section 83 provides a "substantial risk of forfeiture" test to determine the year of taxation for property transferred to an employee with restrictions that is similar to the definition in Code Section 457(f)(3)(B) (see Q 11:11). The authorities under Code Section 83 provide a basis for arguments based on analogy. In fact, it can be argued that these authorities are directly applicable to 457(f) plans. In recent letter rulings, the IRS has cited authorities under Code Section 83 in interpreting the risk of forfeiture, one ruling even stating that "Section 83(c) of the Code, concerning compensatory transfers of property, includes the same definition of substantial risk of forfeiture as section 457(e)(3) [(now section 457(f)(3))]." [P.L.R. 9627007]

The regulations under Code Section 83 provide illustrations that may be relevant to 457(f) plans.

Discharges for cause. The regulations state that a requirement that the property be returned to the employer if the employee is discharged for cause or for committing a crime will not be considered to result in a substantial risk of forfeiture. [Treas. Reg. § 1.83-3(c)(2)]

Noncompetition and consulting provisions. The Section 83 regulations in effect create a presumption against the existence of a substantial risk of forfeiture where the forfeiture will occur only if the employee accepts a job with a competing firm. In that case, a "facts and circumstances" test will apply. Factors taken into account in determining whether the noncompetition covenant constitutes a substantial risk of forfeiture include the age of the employee, the availability of alternative employment opportunities, the likelihood of the employee's obtaining such other employment, the degree of skill possessed by the employee, the employee's health, and the employer's practice (if any) of enforcing such covenants. Similarly, the regulations state that property transferred to a retiring employee, subject to the sole requirement that the property will be returned unless the employee renders consulting services on the request of the former employer, will not be considered subject to a substantial risk of forfeiture unless the participant is, in fact, expected to perform substantial services. [Id.]

Organizational performance. Where an employee receives property from an employer subject to a requirement that it be returned if the total earnings of the employer do not increase, such property is subject to a substantial risk of forfeiture. [Id.] As applied to a tax-exempt or governmental employer, a provision related to some quantifiable index of organizational performance arguably would serve the same purpose as the earnings increase provision.

Q 11:13   Can conditions or restrictions beyond the requirement that services be performed defer taxation under Code Section 457(f)?

A general issue is whether a condition or restriction other than the requirement that services be performed can defer taxation under Code Section 457(f). Although Code Section 457(f)(3)(B) does not mention anything but a service-based requirement (see Q 11:11), it does not contain the word *only* or state that it is the exclusive test. There is little or no authority on this issue that relates directly to Code Section 457(f). The regulations under Code Section 83 define the term *substantial risk of forfeiture* using the same language as that in Code Section 457(f)(3)(B) (which also appears in Code Section 83(c)(1)), but add the phrase "or the occurrence of a condition related to a purpose of the transfer." [Treas. Reg. § 1.83-3(c)(1)]

It therefore appears that forfeiture provisions not directly related to service are valid under Code Section 83, at least if the condition of forfeiture is related to the purpose of the transfer. The earnings increase provision in the example from the Section 83 regulations discussed in Q 11:12 under "Organizational performance" may hint at the meaning of *related to a purpose of the transfer.*

Robinson v. Commissioner [805 F.2d 38 (1st Cir. 1986), *rev'g* 82 T.C. 444 (1984)] dealt with a provision under which stock was transferred to an employee on a condition that if he wanted to dispose of it within one year, he had to sell it back to the employer at the original cost. The court viewed this as a substantial risk of forfeiture and noted that this provision served the substantial corporate purpose of avoiding insider trading. This is a further step away from a purpose related to the transfer specifically.

Finally, the committee reports for Code Section 83 state: "In other cases [besides those involving service conditions] the question of whether there is a substantial risk of forfeiture depends upon the facts and circumstances." [H.R. Rep. No. 91-413 (pt. 1), at 88 (1969); S. Rep. No. 91-552, at 121 (1969)]

Q 11:14   Can a forfeiture provision be postponed to extend the deferral of compensation?

In Private Letter Ruling 9431021, the IRS ruled that a postponement of the forfeiture risk did not trigger current taxation to the employee. The case concerned a restricted stock plan under which the vesting period was postponed (before the stock had become vested) for 17 to 33 months. This ruling dealt with a Section 83 issue and did not involve a 457(f) plan, but the IRS might likely reach a similar result under Code Section 457(f) in view of its apparent current ruling position (see Q 11:12) that the same rules apply under Code Section 457 as under Code Section 83.

At tax practitioner meetings, the IRS has informally expressed concern about the use of "rolling" risks of forfeiture. Rolling risks of forfeiture occur where the plan has a relatively short period of forfeiture and covered employees extend the forfeiture provision periodically just before it goes into effect. A single extension of a forfeiture provision may not be cause for undue concern, but any series of extensions could attract an IRS challenge. For a discussion of this issue, see Berquist, "Nonqualified Deferred Compensation for Tax-Exempt Employers—Avoiding Section 457," 20 *J. Pension Plan. & Compliance* 48 (1994). See also Michael A. Laing, "Section 457(f) Planning," ALI-ABA Course of Study Materials, Retirement, Deferred Compensation, and Welfare Plans of Tax-Exempt and Governmental Employers, Sept. 2003, Course No. SJ017.

Some commentators have made a distinction between a unilateral right of the participant to extend a forfeiture provision and a bilateral renegotiation of the agreement by which both parties agree to extend the forfeiture provision and the employee continues to provide services to the employer during the period of extension. The bilateral extension appears to provide a sounder basis for recognizing an extension for Section 457(f) purposes.

Q 11:15   Can a 457(f) plan be designed to extend a risk-of-forfeiture provision beyond retirement to avoid having all deferred compensation taxed in the year of retirement?

When participants retire, they generally have finished performing services for the employer. Consequently, it is difficult to condition entitlement to deferred compensation payments on the future performance of substantial services, as provided in Code Section 457(f)(3)(B).

One approach to complying with the Code is to establish a consulting provision, that is, a provision that deferred compensation benefits will be forfeited unless the participant renders consulting services on the request of the former employer; however, as noted in Q 11:12, the regulations under Code Section 83 in effect create a presumption against the validity of such a provision, and the provision will not be considered to create a substantial risk of forfeiture unless the participant can show that he or she is in fact expected to perform substantial services. [Treas. Reg. § 1.83-3(c)(2)] In many, if not most, practical situations this burden would be difficult to meet.

Life Insurance Contracts

Q 11:16 What is the federal income tax treatment of life insurance contracts held by the employer under a 457(f) plan?

If the plan is unfunded (see Q 11:24) and the employer holds life insurance contracts to provide a source of funds to pay benefits under the plan, the employee is not in receipt of income when the contract is purchased because the insurance contract is the employer's asset, subject to the claims of the employer's creditors. [Rev. Rul. 72-25, 1972-1 C.B. 127; Rev. Rul. 68-99, 1968-1 C.B. 193] In addition, there is no current life insurance cost (generally the Table 2001 cost; see Qs 2:179–2:186) to employees as long as the employer retains all incidents of ownership in the policies. The employer is the sole beneficiary under the policies and is under no obligation to transfer them or pass through their proceeds. This result applies even if the contracts are purchased at the option of participants. [P.L.R. 9008043] Benefits to participants and their beneficiaries, including death benefits, are not excludable as life insurance proceeds even if plan funds originate with life insurance policies. [See Treas. Reg. § 1.457-10(d)— although this section of the regulations applies to eligible plans, there is no reason why the result should be different for an ineligible, or 457(f), plan]

Estate Tax Considerations

Q 11:17 What is the federal income and estate tax treatment of benefits paid to beneficiaries under a 457(f) plan?

All amounts paid under a 457(f) plan are taxable as ordinary income, including benefits paid to a beneficiary on the death of the participant. Even if the funds for the death benefit derive from life insurance contracts held by the employer, the amount is fully taxable and not eligible for the exclusion under Code Section 101(a). A beneficiary is not taxed on any basis the employee had in the distribution.

> **Example.** An employee paid tax on a benefit worth $50,000 in 2003 (the year in which forfeiture provisions expired), but no distribution was made in 2003. If the total account grows to $60,000 in 2006 and is distributed to the beneficiary in that year on the employee's death, the beneficiary has $10,000 of taxable income in 2006 as a result.

Death benefits paid to a participant's beneficiaries are includible in the participant's estate for federal estate tax purposes unless the plan was designed solely to pay a death benefit and the beneficiary designation was irrevocable. [See discussion of death-benefit-only plans in S. Leimberg & J. McFadden, *Tools and Techniques of Employee Benefit and Retirement Planning* (Cincinnati, Ohio: National Underwriter Co., 7th ed. 2001)]

A 457(f) death benefit includible in the participant's estate is income in respect of a decedent under Code Section 691, and the recipient is allowed an income tax deduction for the federal estate tax paid on the amount. [I.R.C. § 691(c)]

Transfers and Rollovers

Q 11:18   Can distributions from a 457(f) plan be rolled over or directly transferred, tax-free, to an individual retirement account or annuity (IRA)?

No. Such distributions are not eligible for the IRA rollover provisions. [I.R.C. § 402(c)(8)]

Q 11:19   Can distributions from one 457(f) plan be rolled over or directly transferred, tax-free, to another 457(f) plan?

No. The provisions for Section 457 plan-to-plan transfers apply only to eligible 457 plans. [I.R.C. § 457(e)(10)]

Social Security and Medicare Taxes

Q 11:20   How is Section 457(f) deferred compensation taxed for FICA and FUTA purposes?

If a 457(f) plan qualifies as an "exempt governmental deferred compensation plan" under Code Section 3121(v)(3), benefits are exempt from FICA and FUTA. [See P.L.R. 200247040] However, not all 457(f) plans are eligible for this exemption, so the general rules will be discussed here.

Year of inclusion. The year of inclusion for FICA and FUTA taxes generally is governed by Code Section 3121(v)(2)(A), under which nonqualified deferred compensation is included as of the later of the year "when the services are performed or when there is no substantial risk of forfeiture of the rights to such amount." The determination of whether a substantial risk of forfeiture exists is made under the principles of Code Section 83 and the regulations thereunder. [Treas. Reg. § 31.3121(v)(2)-1(e)(3)] Therefore, for practical purposes under most 457(f) plans, deferred compensation is included in the Social Security tax base in the same year in which the amount is included in income for federal income tax purposes (see Q 11:10).

Most executives covered by 457(f) plans are relatively highly compensated, so in most years they will have regular compensation greater than the taxable wage base; therefore, inclusion of deferred compensation in that year will not increase the regular Social Security tax. The Medicare tax base is unlimited, so inclusion will result in a liability for Medicare taxes (1.45 percent employee share, 1.45 percent employer share).

Amount includible. In an account balance plan the amount deferred that is includible in the FICA tax base includes income earned on the account through the date on which the principal amount is required to be included. [Treas. Reg. § 31.3121(v)(2)-1(c)] For nonaccount balance plans (plans using a defined benefit type of formula, which is uncommon in 457(f) plans), the employer can use any reasonable actuarial method and assumptions to determine the amount includible. [Treas. Reg. § 31.3121(v)(2)-1(c)(2)] These rules are more definite than the rules for the amount includible in taxable income under Code Section 457(f) (see Q 11:10).

Deferred compensation is included in the Social Security tax base only once, and the amount included is not taxable in a subsequent year. For example, if an amount is includible in 2001, then paid to the employee in a later year, say 2004, the amount originally includible in 2001 is not includible in the Social Security base for 2004. In addition, after the amount has been included, income attributable to the amount is not subject to further Social Security taxes even if it is payable at a later date. [I.R.C. § 3121(v)(2)(B)]

> **Example.** An employee defers $10,000 of compensation in 1998, subject to a substantial risk of forfeiture. In 2003, the forfeiture provision expires but no actual payment is made to the employee. As of 2003, the original $10,000 has grown to $12,500 as a result of interest earnings (which the plan credits to the employee's account). In 2003, the amount includible in the FICA and FUTA tax base is $12,500. In 2006, the employee's account balance of $15,000 is paid to the employee. If $12,500 was taxed in 2003, the 2006 payment produces $2,500 of additional income subject to income tax ($15,000 distribution − $12,500 basis). The 2006 payment does not, however, result in any additional inclusion in the employee's Social Security tax base.

State Tax

Q 11:21   How do states tax benefits from 457(f) plans?

The specifics of individual state tax laws as applied to 457(f) plans are beyond the scope of this book; however, many states do not make the federal income tax law's distinction between 457(f) plans and other types of deferred compensation.

Federal law prohibits a state from imposing an income tax on any "retirement income" of an individual who is neither a resident nor a domiciliary of the state, as determined under that state's laws. [4 U.S.C. § 114, enacted by § 1(a) of Pub. L. No. 104-95, 104th Cong., 2d Sess.] The term *state* includes any political subdivision of a state, the District of Columbia, and the possessions of the United States. [See generally Louis T. Mazawey & William M. Evans, "New Federal Limitations on State Taxation of Retirement Income," 22 *J. Pension Plan. & Compliance* (No. 2) 1 (1996)]

For this purpose, any "retirement income" includes:

1. Income from a qualified plan, a SEP, a 403(a) annuity plan, a 403(b) plan, an IRA, a 457(b) eligible plan, a governmental plan (including, apparently, a governmental 457(f) plan), or a 501(c)(18) trust;

2. Certain payments received from a nonqualified deferred compensation plan described in Section 3121(v)(2)(C); and

3. Retired or retainer pay of a member or former member of a uniformed service. [see 10 U.S.C. § 1401 et seq.]

Many states grant preferential treatment to retirement income paid to their own retirees. In its 1989 *Davis* decision [*Davis v. Michigan Department of Treasury*, 489 U.S. 803 (1989) (wherein the plaintiff challenged a Michigan statute that exempted Michigan state and local governmental pensions from income taxation, but taxed all other pensions, including federal pensions)], the U.S. Supreme Court held that any state that does so must grant similar treatment to federal retirees. In 1992, the Court extended this rule to U.S. military pensions. [*Barker v. Kansas*, 503 U.S. 594 (1992)] The state is not required to grant similar favored treatment to retirees of other states. [*Sherman v. Department of Revenue*, Or. T.C. No. 4547 (Aug. 9, 2002)]

According to a recent study by the National Conference of State Legislatures (NCSL) [Fiscal Affairs Program—State Personal Income Taxes on Pensions and Retirement Income: Tax Year 2001 (Jan. 24, 2002), available at *www.ncsl.org*]:

1. Nine states (Alaska, Florida, Nevada, New Hampshire, South Dakota, Tennessee, Texas, Washington, and Wyoming) do not tax pension income at all.

2. Of the 41 remaining states, 34 offer some type of pension exclusion, or a broad income exclusion or tax credit targeted at the elderly. The seven states that do not offer any exclusion are California, Connecticut, Indiana, Nebraska, Rhode Island, Vermont, and Wisconsin, although previous Wisconsin exclusions are still available to some taxpayers. The District of Columbia excludes public pensions.

3. Ten states (Alabama, Hawaii, Illinois, Kansas, Louisiana, Massachusetts, Michigan, Mississippi, New York, and Pennsylvania) exclude all federal, state, and local pension income from taxation.

One threshold issue under these state statutes is whether benefits from a 457(f) plan are characterized as wage income (as they would be for federal income tax withholding purposes) or as pension income. Note also that some states, including New Jersey, tax 457 deferrals even though they do not tax 401(k) deferrals.

Participation in Other Plans

Q 11:22 Does deferral of compensation under a 457(f) plan limit the participant's contributions to other types of retirement plans sponsored by the employer?

No. If the participant also participates in a 401(k) plan or 403(b) plan, the $13,000 (as indexed) salary reduction limitation is not reduced as a result of deferral of compensation (either by salary reduction or by direct employer contribution) under a 457(f) plan. Code Section 402(g)(3) lists the types of plans causing a reduction, and 457 plans are not included.

Q 11:23 Do employee contributions to a 457(f) plan have to be reduced if the participant makes salary reduction contributions to a 403(b) plan, 401(k) plan, or SIMPLE arrangement?

No. Code Section 457 once had a provision (now repealed) reducing the dollar/percentage limitation in these situations [I.R.C. § 457(c)(2)], but it was relevant only to eligible 457 plans governed by the dollar/percentage limitation and did not require a reduction in amounts contributed to an ineligible, or 457(f), plan.

Funding Requirements and ERISA Considerations

Q 11:24 Must benefits under a 457(f) plan be funded under the ERISA funding standards?

Tax-exempt organizations. Churches and church-related organizations are not subject to Title I of ERISA, which includes the funding requirements. [ERISA § 4(b)(2)] Other nongovernmental tax-exempt organizations are subject to ERISA Title I.

The ERISA Title I funding requirements, including the minimum funding standards and the requirement of holding plan assets in trust for participants and beneficiaries, do not apply to "a plan which is unfunded and is maintained by an employer primarily for the purpose of providing deferred compensation for a select group of management or highly compensated employees." [ERISA §§ 301(a)(3), 401(a)(1)] Consequently, a plan for this "top-hat" group (see Q 11:26) does not need to be funded.

Other exemptions to the funding requirements include excess benefit plans [ERISA § 301(a)(9)], which are plans maintained solely to provide benefits in excess of the Section 415 limitations on qualified plans. [ERISA § 3(36)]

Governmental organizations. Governmental plans (federal, state, or local) are not subject to Title I of ERISA. [ERISA § 4(b)(1)] Consequently, there is no funding, vesting, or other ERISA Title I requirement for 457(f) plans maintained by governmental employers. Code Section 457(g) requires that an eligible plan of a governmental employer hold assets and income of the plan in trust for the exclusive benefit of participants and beneficiaries, but this provision does not apply to ineligible, or 457(f), plans.

Q 11:25   Are 457(f) plans subject to the ERISA vesting standards?

Tax-exempt organizations. Title I of ERISA, which includes the vesting requirements, does not apply to churches or church-related organizations, or to excess benefit plans (see Q 11:24). Otherwise, the ERISA vesting requirements apply unless the plan is unfunded and maintained by an employer primarily for the purpose of providing deferred compensation for the top-hat group—a select group of management or highly compensated employees (see Q 11:26). [ERISA § 201(2)]

If the plan is subject to the ERISA vesting requirements, plan benefits must vest at least as rapidly as they would under either of two standards: (1) vesting of the full benefit after five years of service or (2) vesting of 20 percent of the accrued benefit after three years of service, with an additional 20 percent vesting each year thereafter and full vesting after seven years of service. [ERISA § 203(a)]

Governmental organizations. Governmental organizations (federal, state, or local) are not subject to Title I of ERISA, which includes the vesting requirements. [ERISA § 4(b)(1)]

Q 11:26   Who constitutes the top-hat group?

If an unfunded plan of a tax-exempt organization is limited to the top-hat group—a "select group of management or highly compensated employees"—it generally avoids coverage by the ERISA funding and vesting requirements and has simplified reporting and disclosure requirements (see Qs 11:24, 11:25, 11:30).

The Department of Labor (DOL) has not provided any detailed guidance on this provision, so the issue generally cannot be settled definitively in any situation. The DOL considers that the Section 414(q) definition of *highly compensated employee* for qualified plan purposes does not apply here. [DOL Adv. Op. 85-37A] In 1985 the DOL announced a regulations project that would provide a definition, but that project appears to be inactive.

There are a few old DOL rulings that offer some dubious guidance. In Advisory Opinion 75-63, the DOL ruled that a plan covering certain exempt employees (exempt from the Fair Labor Standards Act) earning more than $18,200 was a top-hat plan. Another opinion approved as a top-hat plan a plan covering 4 percent of the workforce, where those employees had an average salary of $28,000 as compared with $19,000 for all managerial employees. [DOL Adv. Op. 75-64] By contrast, in a case where a plan covered 50 out of 750 employees, with participants' salaries averaging $30,000 or three times the highest hourly compensation, the DOL ruled that the plan was not a top-hat plan because the plan's participants covered a broad range of salaries and positions. [DOL Adv. Op. 85-37A] One U.S. district court found that there was a top-hat group where the plan covered between 1.6 percent and 4.6 percent of the employees. [Belka v. Rowe Furniture Corp., 571 F. Supp. 1249 (D. Md. 1983)] More favorably, in a significant recent case, *Demery v. Extebank Deferred Compensation Plan* [2000 WL 772039 (2d Cir. June 15, 2000)], the Second Circuit held that a nonqualified deferred compensation plan made available to a middle-management group consisting of 15.34 percent of the company's employees met the ERISA top-hat exception.

In light of this uncertainty, most practitioners advise caution when a plan covers more than a few very highly paid employees. The idea behind the top-hat exemption is apparently that because select management employees do not need the protection of the DOL and ERISA, top-hat plans ought perhaps to be confined to employees who are in a position to influence or dictate the terms of their deferred compensation agreements. See the most recent DOL ruling (itself now 14 years old), Adv. Op. 90-14A. For a good discussion of these rules, see Edward J. Rayner, "ERISA's Top-Hat Exemption: A Primer," *Tax Notes Today*, Apr. 8, 2003, 2003 T.N.T. 67-33.

Q 11:27 Should a 457(f) plan be funded?

To fund a plan means to set aside assets irrevocably in a trust or equivalent arrangement for plan participants and beneficiaries, and to fund vested benefits. In a funded plan such assets are beyond the reach of the employer's creditors. [Dependahl v. Falstaff Brewing Corp., 653 F.2d 1208 (8th Cir. 1981); DOL Adv. Op. 92-01A] Funding appears attractive to employees because it secures benefits by raising their status above that of mere unsecured contractual obligations of the employer.

For a tax-exempt employer, if the plan is funded, it becomes subject to various provisions of ERISA, because the exemptions for unfunded top-hat plans (see Qs 11:24, 11:25) are not applicable. The plan would have to meet the ERISA three-to-seven-year or five-year vesting standard (see Q 11:25). [ERISA § 203(a)] This would generally make it impossible to extend tax deferral for more than seven years in a funded plan, because in a 457(f) plan taxation of deferred compensation occurs in the year in which the benefits become vested. Furthermore, the funding standards of ERISA are applicable. [ERISA § 302] These standards impose specific annual funding obligations, subject to penalties for noncompliance. For these reasons, funded 457(f) plans for employees of tax-exempt employers are impracticable.

For governmental employers, the absence of ERISA restrictions may make funding more flexible and therefore more attractive.

Q 11:28 Can an employee direct the investments of deferred compensation amounts under a 457(f) plan?

In general, as discussed in Q 11:27, there is no requirement for the employer to set assets aside for purposes of a 457(f) plan. If an employer has assets set aside for plan purposes, where all assets are the property of the employer and not protected against creditors of the employer (so the plan remains unfunded in the tax sense), employee investment direction does not defeat tax deferral under an eligible 457 plan. Treasury Regulation § 1.457-7(c)(1) includes a provision stating that "[a]mounts deferred under an eligible plan of a tax-exempt entity will not be considered made available to the participant solely because the participant is permitted to choose among various investments under the plan." The IRS has ruled that the same rationale applies to an ineligible, or 457(f), plan that is unfunded. [P.L.R. 9805030, 9815039]

Where employers maintain reserve accounts to provide assets for future payment of nonqualified deferred compensation, the general IRS position is that any employee investment direction with regard to those assets should be advisory only, not binding on the employer or other fundholder such as a rabbi trust. [See P.L.R. 9332028; AALU Washington Report, May 13, 1994 (regarding IRS position)]

Q 11:29   Can a 457(f) plan be indirectly funded using a rabbi trust?

A rabbi trust is a revocable or irrevocable trust that holds assets that will be used to satisfy all or part of an employer's obligation to pay deferred compensation benefits. The employer gives up the use of these assets, and if and when the trust becomes irrevocable, it cannot get them back. The assets are dedicated solely to the provision of deferred compensation benefits for specific employees, with one major exception: To maintain the plan's status as an unfunded plan, the rabbi trust's assets must be available to the employer's creditors. That is, the employee covered under the plan must not have any interest in the rabbi trust that is superior to that of the employer's creditors. The term *rabbi trust* arose because an early IRS ruling in this area involved a trust for the benefit of a rabbi.

The purpose of using a rabbi trust is to provide better security for the payment of benefits to the employee. If a rabbi trust is used, an employee may be able to receive benefits without litigation even if the organization's management becomes hostile toward the employee; however, a rabbi trust cannot protect the employee against the possibility of the organization's bankruptcy or insolvency. In that event, the position of the employee is the same as that of any unsecured creditor.

Currently, the IRS will rule favorably, except in rare and unusual circumstances, only if the rabbi trust documents conform with an IRS model agreement. [Rev. Proc. 92-64, 1992-2 C.B. 422] Even if the parties do not consider it necessary to obtain a formal IRS ruling on the arrangement, use of the model agreement is advisable to avoid an IRS challenge.

In many Private Letter Rulings, the IRS has ruled favorably on 457(f) plans using rabbi trust arrangements. [E.g., P.L.R. 9212011, 9236014, 9623027, 9628020, 9839008, 200009009, 200229001 (the IRS model trust was used in most of these rulings)]

Q 11:30   What are the ERISA reporting and disclosure requirements applicable to 457(f) plans?

Governmental plans, church plans, and unfunded excess benefit plans are not subject to Title I of ERISA and therefore not subject to the reporting and disclosure requirements. [ERISA § 4(b)(1), (2), (5)]

If these exemptions do not apply, an unfunded top-hat plan (see Q 11:27) is subject only to limited reporting and disclosure requirements. The plan must file with the DOL a statement including the name and address of the employer and the employer identification number, a declaration that the employer maintains a plan or plans primarily for the purpose of providing deferred compensation for a select group of management or highly compensated employees, and a statement of the number of such plans and the number of employees in each. In addition, the employer must provide plan documents to the DOL on request. [DOL Reg. § 2520.104-23]

Plans not meeting the exemptions or eligibility for the limited reporting and disclosure requirements are subject to the full reporting and disclosure requirements, including the filing of annual reports (Form 5500 series) and the providing of summary plan descriptions to employees and the DOL.

ERISA Administration and Enforcement

Q 11:31   What are the ERISA administration and enforcement provisions applicable to 457(ff) plans?

Governmental plans, church plans, and unfunded excess benefit plans are not subject to Title I of ERISA and therefore not subject to ERISA's administration and enforcement provisions. [ERISA § 4(b)(1), (2), (5)]

Other plans are subject to the administration and enforcement provisions of Title I, Part 5, of ERISA. In particular, there is a requirement that the plan have a claims procedure providing written notice of claims denials and allow the participant an opportunity for a review of any claim denial. [ERISA § 503]

Q 11:32   Are benefits under 457(f) plans protected against the participant's creditors in the event of the participant's bankruptcy?

The U.S. Supreme Court held that assets of a plan covered by ERISA's anti-assignment and anti-alienation provisions [ERISA § 206(d); I.R.C. § 401(a)(13)] cannot be part of the participant's estate in bankruptcy. [Patterson v. Shumate, 504 U.S. 753, 112 S. Ct. 2242, 119 L. Ed. 2d 519 (1992)] Many if not most 457(f) plans, however, are not covered by the ERISA anti-alienation provisions because (1) they are not qualified plans covered by Code Section 401(a)(13), (2) they are plans of a governmental entity or church plans not subject to Title I of ERISA [ERISA §§ 4(b)(1), (2)], or (3) they are unfunded top-hat plans not subject to

ERISA Section 206(d) [ERISA § 201(2)]. Therefore, the basis for excluding such plans from the bankruptcy estate is uncertain.

There are at least two diverging bankruptcy cases on this issue. [Compare *Pedersen v. Public Employees Benefit Services Corp.*, No. 91-91194 (S.D. Iowa June 16, 1993), with *In re Wheat*, 149 B.R. 1003 (Bankr. S.D. Fla. 1992)] Many believe that the Supreme Court did not decide this issue definitively for plans not subject to ERISA's anti-alienation provisions.

In order to maximize the likelihood of 457(f) plan benefits, being excluded from the participant's bankruptcy estate under Section 541(c)(2) of the Bankruptcy Code, the benefits should be informally funded through a rabbi trust, and the plan document and the trust agreement should include an enforceable anti-alienation clause. For a detailed discussion of the treatment of 457 plan benefits in bankruptcy, see Robert B. Chapman, "A Matter of Trust, Or Why 'ERISA-Qualified' Is 'Nonsense Upon Stilts': The Tax and Bankruptcy Treatment of Section 457 Deferred Compensation Plans as Exemplar," 40 *Willamette L. Rev.* 1 (2004).

Federal Securities Law

Q 11:33   Must a 457(f) plan be registered under federal securities law?

Securities issued by state, local, or federal governmental organizations are not subject to registration. [Securities Act of 1933 § 3(a)(2)] Therefore, this issue concerns only plans of tax-exempt organizations.

A 457(f) plan, like any pension plan, arguably meets the definition of *security* in the securities law and could therefore be subject to a registration requirement. [Securities Act of 1933 § 2(1)] The Supreme Court has held that an interest in an involuntary, noncontributory defined benefit plan does not constitute a security. [International Brotherwood of Teamsters v. Daniel, 439 U.S. 551, 99 S. Ct. 790 (1979)] In addition, qualified plans are exempt from registration if no amount in excess of employer contributions can be invested in employer securities. [Securities Act of 1933 § 3(a)(2)]

The exemptions described above do not appear to cover all 457(f) plans or other nonqualified plans. Nevertheless, the Securities and Exchange Commission (SEC) has traditionally taken the position that interests in unfunded, nonqualified plans are not subject to registration, as indicated in past no-action letters. [McKesson Corp., SEC No-Action Letter (Jan. 9, 1990); Monsanto Co., SEC No-Action Letter (Apr. 4, 1985)] At recent practitioner meetings, however, SEC officials indicated that their no-action position on nonqualified plans was based on the assumption that the plans in question covered only a few top executives and that the plans therefore constituted a private offering (exempt from registration) for securities law purposes. [SEC Rule 506 (35 or fewer investors)] In this view, a plan covering a broader group of employees would require registration.

Because plans of tax-exempt organizations generally are confined to the top-hat group to avoid the ERISA funding requirements (see Q 11:24), the exposure to possible SEC enforcement on this issue is relatively small. The private offering exemption probably would generally apply. In addition, because the tax-exempt organization generally is not a publicly held company, SEC Rule 701 would allow the employer to offer up to $5 million a year, or 15 percent of the issuer's assets if less, in unregistered interests to employees.

See chapter 10 for additional information on the application of federal securities law.

Chapter 12

IRS Form Reporting and Related Issues

Joseph A. Zavoda, Esq.
CitiStreet Retirement Services

Federal tax law requires that specific forms be filed to report contributions to and distributions and deemed distributions from 457 plans. This chapter explains federal tax reporting requirements that generally apply to employers, trustees, custodians, and other payors. Further, the chapter explains how Federal Insurance Contributions Act (FICA) and Federal Unemployment Tax Act (FUTA) taxes apply to 457 plans and explains how the 1099-R, W-2, and related forms and notices report information about 457 plans. It also explains how to obtain additional form-filing information and get copies of IRS forms and publications. Also, this chapter addresses the governmental exemption and the select-group simplified compliance exception to the Employee Retirement Income Security Act of 1974 (ERISA) filing requirements.

Note. This chapter explains the federal tax law currently in effect for 2002 through 2010. Under current law, Code provisions added or amended by the Economic Growth and Tax Relief Reconciliation Act of 2001 (EGTRRA) do not apply to tax, plan, or limitation years that begin after December 31, 2010. [EGTRRA § 901] Thereafter, the Internal Revenue Code applies as if EGTRRA's provisions and amendments never had been enacted. The law then would be the Internal Revenue Code as it was just before EGTRRA's enactment on June 7, 2001. If by the end of the decade Congress has not made permanent or extended EGTRRA's provisions, *457 Answer Book* will include explanations of the pre-EGTRRA and other applicable law.

General Information

Q 12:1 How may additional information about form reporting be obtained?

Additional information about form reporting may be obtained through the methods described below.

Telephone queries. The IRS operates a centralized call site to answer questions about reporting on Forms W-2, W-3, and 1099 and other information returns. For questions related to reporting on information returns, call 1-866-455-7438 (toll free) or 1-304-263-8700, Monday through Friday, 8:30 A.M to 4:30 P.M., Eastern Standard Time. For questions about magnetic media filing of Form W-2, contact the Social Security Administration (SSA) at 1-800-772-6270, Monday through Friday, 7 A.M. to 7 P.M., Eastern Standard Time.

Websites. Both the IRS and the SSA provide websites that provide helpful information for organizations.

The IRS website, located at *www.irs.gov*, provides a source for forms and publications. It also provides helpful information for individuals, businesses, charities and nonprofits, government entities, tax professionals, and retirement plans. In addition, the website includes answers to frequently asked questions.

The SSA website is located at *www.socialsecurity.gov/employer*. The website includes magnetic media filing information, some IRS and SSA publications, information on electronic filing, and general topics of interest about annual wage reporting. The SSA's Business Services Online also provides answers to questions about wage reporting.

The SSA's Business Services Online can be accessed with a personal computer and a modem to electronically report wage data. For questions about using SSA's Business Services Online website for filing Forms W-2 electronically, go to *www.socialsecurity.gov/bso/bsowelcome.htm*, call 1-888-772-2970, fax: 1-410-597-0237, or e-mail *eso.support@ssa.gov*.

Forms and publications. To order IRS forms and publications, call 1-800-TAX-FORM (1-800-829-3676).

Q 12:2   What if a compliance deadline falls on a weekend or legal holiday?

Generally, if the due date for a specific act of compliance or filing a return falls on a Saturday, Sunday, or legal holiday, the compliance or filing is considered timely if it is performed on the next day that is not a Saturday, Sunday, or legal holiday. [I.R.C. § 7503; Treas. Reg. § 301.7503-1(a)]

Q 12:3   What is a legal holiday?

For federal tax compliance deadlines, a *legal holiday* refers to a legal holiday in the District of Columbia. [Internal Revenue Manual 25.6.17.2] A list of legal holidays can be found in Section 28-2701 of the District of Columbia Code. Currently, the holidays are the following:

- New Year's Day, January 1
- Dr. Martin Luther King, Jr.'s Birthday, the third Monday in January
- Inauguration Day (every fourth year), January 20
- Washington's Birthday (Presidents' Day), the third Monday in February
- Memorial Day, the last Monday in May
- Independence Day, July 4
- Labor Day, the first Monday in September
- Columbus Day, the second Monday in October
- Veterans Day, November 11
- Thanksgiving Day, the fourth Thursday in November
- Christmas Day, December 25

When one of these holidays other than Inauguration Day falls on a Saturday, the preceding day is a holiday.

[I.R.C. § 7503; Treas. Reg. § 301.7503-1(b); D.C. Code Ann. § 28-2701]

Q 12:4   Are any other holidays considered legal holidays?

Yes. For an act, return, statement, or other document required to be filed at a regional or local office of the IRS, a *legal holiday* includes, in addition to the legal holidays in the District of Columbia (see Q 12:3), any statewide legal holiday of the state where the IRS office in which the act is required to be performed is located. Likewise, if the applicable IRS office is located in a U.S.

territory or possession, a holiday that is recognized throughout that territory or possession is a legal holiday. [Treas. Reg. § 301.7503-1(b)]

Q 12:5 When is a document or payment that is mailed deemed filed or paid?

Generally, a document or payment is considered filed or paid on the date of the postmark stamped on the cover in which it was properly mailed (see Q 12:9). Thus, if the cover containing the document or payment bears a timely postmark, the document or payment is considered timely filed or paid, even if it is received after the normal due date. [I.R.C. § 7502; Treas. Reg. § 301.7502-1]

Q 12:6 Are the dates recorded or marked by a designated delivery service covered under the "timely mailing is timely filing" rule?

For this "timely mailing is timely filing" rule, any reference to a postmark by the U.S. Postal Service includes any date recorded or marked by a "designated delivery service." A designated delivery service is any delivery service provided by a trade or business if that service is so designated by the Secretary of the Treasury. The Secretary may designate a delivery service only if the Secretary finds that the service:

1. Is available to the general public;
2. Is at least as timely and reliable on a regular basis as the U.S. mail;
3. Records electronically to its database, kept in the regular course of its business, or marks on the cover in which any item referred to in Section 7502(f) of the Internal Revenue Code (Code) is to be delivered, the date on which it received that item for delivery; and
4. Meets such other criteria as the Secretary may prescribe.

The Secretary may provide a rule similar to the "timely mailing is timely filing" rule for any service provided by a designated delivery service that is substantially equivalent to U.S. registered or certified mail. [I.R.C. § 7502(f)]

Q 12:7 What private delivery services may a filer use to have the delivery date treated as the postmark date?

The IRS has designated four private delivery companies that last-minute filers may use in accordance with the same rule as those who use the U.S. Postal Service (i.e., that a payment or return mailed on time will be considered paid or filed on time). The most recent IRS list of the designated delivery services was published in September 2002. It includes only the following:

- Airborne Express (Airborne)—Overnight Air Express Service, Next Afternoon Service, and Second Day Service
- DHL Worldwide Express (DHL)—DHL "Same Day" Service and DHL USA Overnight

- Federal Express (FedEx)—FedEx Priority Overnight, FedEx Standard Overnight, FedEx 2Day, FedEx International Priority, and FedEx International First
- United Parcel Service (UPS)—UPS Next Day Air, UPS Next Day Air Saver, UPS 2nd Day Air, UPS 2nd Day Air A.M., UPS Worldwide Express Plus, and UPS Worldwide Express

Only these delivery *services* qualify; other services offered by the same companies do not qualify.

The date on which an item given to Airborne, DHL, FedEx, or UPS is recorded electronically to the delivery service's database is treated as the postmark date. At least concerning these services, the company must maintain its electronic database for six months. [Rev. Proc. 97-19, 1997-1 C.B. 644; IRS Notice 97-26, 1997-17 I.R.B. 6; IRS Notice 2002-62, 2002-39 I.R.B. 574]

Q 12:8 What rule applies if a document or payment is not timely filed or paid?

If a document or payment is not timely filed or paid, it is not deemed to have been filed or paid on the date of the postmark stamped on the cover in which it was mailed. To compute any penalties and additions to tax, the date on which the document or payment is *received* will be the date on which the document or payment is filed or paid.

Q 12:9 Must a document be received to be considered delivered?

Not always. For a document (but not a payment) sent by registered or certified mail, proof that the document was properly registered or that a postmarked certified mail sender's receipt was properly issued for it and that the envelope or wrapper was properly addressed to an agency, officer, or office is evidence that the document was delivered to that agency, officer, or office.

Q 12:10 Must a payment be received to be considered paid?

Yes. Whether a payment is made in the form of currency or other money, it is not treated as paid unless it is actually received and accounted for. For example, if a check is used as a form of payment, the check is not treated as payment unless it is honored on presentation.

Q 12:11 What are the requirements for a valid mailing?

A document or payment must be mailed in accordance with the following requirements:

1. It must be contained in an envelope or other appropriate wrapper and be properly addressed to the agency, officer, or office with which the document is required to be filed or to which the payment is required to be made.

2. Sufficient postage must be affixed.

3. It must be deposited within the prescribed time in the mail with the domestic mail service of the U.S. Postal Service (including mail transmitted within, among, and between the United States, its possessions, and Army-Air Force (APO) and Navy (FPO) post offices). [See 39 C.F.R. § 2.1]

Q 12:12 Does a valid mailing include the use of mail services of another nation?

No, a valid mailing does not include the use of the mail services of another nation.

As an alternative, certain designated courier services may be used (see Q 12:7).

Q 12:13 What rule applies if the postmark date is wrong or illegible?

If a postmark date is wrong or illegible, the person who must file the document or make the payment has the burden of proving when the postmark was made. Further, if the cover containing a document or payment bearing a timely postmark is received later than when a document or payment postmarked and mailed at that time would ordinarily be received, the sender may be required to prove that it was timely mailed.

Special rules apply if the postmark on the envelope or wrapper is made by a foreign postal service. When the document or payment is received later than it would have been if it had been duly mailed and postmarked, it is treated as having been received when a document or payment so mailed and so postmarked would ordinarily be received; however, the person required to file must establish that it was actually and timely deposited in the mail before the last collection of the mail from the place of deposit. The person must also show: (1) that the delay in receipt was caused by a delay in the transmission of the mail; and (2) the cause of that delay.

Q 12:14 How may one overcome the risk that the document or payment will not be postmarked on the day it is deposited?

The risk may be overcome by using registered or certified mail.

Q 12:15 What rules apply to U.S. registered mail?

If a document or payment is sent by U.S. registered mail, the date of its registration is treated as the postmark date.

Q 12:16   What rules apply to U.S. certified mail?

If a document or payment is sent by U.S. certified mail and the sender's receipt is postmarked by the postal employee to whom the document or payment is presented, the date of the U.S. postmark on the receipt is treated as the postmark date.

General 457 Reporting Rules

Q 12:17   Have the rules for reporting some eligible plan distributions changed in light of the 1996 Act's exclusive benefit trust requirement?

Yes. A distribution under a state or local government employer's eligible 457 plan is reported on Form 1099-R. [I.R.C. § 3401(a)(12)(E); I.R.S. Notice 2003-20, 2003-19 I.R.B. 894 (May 12, 2003)] However, distributions from a non-governmental tax-exempt employer's 457(b) plan are wages and are reported on Form W-2, Wage and Tax Statement, as provided in the form's instructions. [I.R.S. Notice 2003-20, 2003-19 I.R.B. 894]

Q 12:18   Will the IRS change the forms used for a governmental 457(b) plan's reporting purposes?

Yes. The IRS generally updates its forms on an ongoing basis and updates Forms 1099-R and W-2 and each form's instructions annually.

ERISA Reporting Requirements

Q 12:19   What ERISA reporting and disclosure requirements apply to 457 plans?

Generally, 457 plans are either governmental plans not governed by ERISA (see Q 12:20) or unfunded plans for a select group of highly compensated or management employees that can use the alternative method of compliance (see Q 12:21). The only kind of 457 plan that is subject to ERISA is a nongovernmental tax-exempt organization for other than a select group of management or highly compensated employees. (See chapters 6 and 8.)

Q 12:20   Must the ERISA disclosure and reporting requirements be met by a state or local government's 457 plan?

No. A governmental plan is not governed by ERISA. [ERISA § 4(b)(1)] Therefore, ERISA's reporting and disclosure requirements do not apply to a governmental plan.

Q 12:21   Do the ERISA disclosure and reporting requirements apply to an unfunded plan for a select group of highly compensated or management employees?

Yes, but only a limited, one-time filing is necessary. If a plan is an unfunded plan maintained by an employer for a select group of management or highly compensated employees (sometimes called a top-hat plan), a one-time, one-page filing with the Department of Labor (DOL) frees it from further ERISA reporting requirements. In addition, the plan administrator is required to furnish copies of the plan documents, if any, to the Secretary of Labor on request. [DOL Reg. § 2520.104-23(b)]

Q 12:22   What information must be included in the one-time filing for a select group of employees?

The one-time filing with the DOL for a select group of highly compensated or management employees must include:

1. The name and address of the employer;
2. The Employer Identification Number (EIN) assigned by the IRS;
3. A declaration that the employer maintains the plan or plans primarily for the purpose of providing deferred compensation for a select group of highly compensated employees; and
4. A statement of the number of plans and the number of employees in each.

[DOL Reg. § 2520.104-23(b)(1)]

Q 12:23   Do the ERISA disclosure and reporting requirements apply to a plan maintained by a nongovernmental tax-exempt organization for other than a select group of employees?

Yes. A plan of a nongovernmental tax-exempt organization for other than a select group of employees is not exempt from ERISA's reporting and disclosure requirements under the governmental exemption and cannot use the alternative method of compliance for a select group of management or highly compensated employees. (See chapters 6 and 8.)

Q 12:24   What reporting and disclosure requirements are avoided by plans that are not governed by ERISA or can use the alternate method of compliance?

Plans that are not governed by ERISA (see Q 12:20) or can use the alternate method of compliance (see Q 12:21) avoid the detailed reporting that applies to plans subject to ERISA's reporting and disclosure requirements. Except for 457 plans maintained by a nongovernmental tax-exempt organization for other than a select group of management or highly compensated employees (see Q 12:23), the following reporting and disclosure requirements can be avoided:

1. Periodically furnishing a summary plan description to each employee [ERISA §§ 101(a), 102(a), 104];

2. Providing a summary of material modifications to the terms of the plan or any previously filed information [ERISA § 102(a)(2), (b)(3)];

3. Filing annual reports (Form 5500) containing specific financial and demographic information about the plan [ERISA §§ 103, 104(b)(4)];

4. Providing a summary annual report to participants [ERISA § 104(b)(3)];

5. Filing terminal and supplementary reports in the event of plan termination [ERISA § 101(c)].

Q 12:25   Why is it important to be sure that a plan is not governed by ERISA or that the alternative method of compliance is satisfied?

Whether a plan is not governed by ERISA or has met the alternative method of compliance is extremely important. If an exception does not apply, the plan administrator is responsible for filing Form 5500. [ERISA § 103]

If a plan is governed by ERISA, serious penalties for noncompliance may apply. The following is a list of some of the more serious penalties that could apply:

1. If a person willfully violates ERISA and is convicted, he or she may be fined up to $100,000 or imprisoned for up to 10 years, or both, or, if the violator is not an individual, the violator may be fined up to $500,000 [ERISA § 501];

2. A penalty of up to $10,000, five years' imprisonment, or both, may be imposed for making any false statement or representation of fact, knowing it to be false, or for knowingly concealing or not disclosing any fact required by ERISA;

3. A penalty of $1,100 per day may be imposed for failing to file a complete Form 5500, unless reasonable cause can be shown [ERISA § 502(c)(2)];

4. A penalty of $25 a day (up to $15,000) may be imposed for not filing certain returns regarding deferred compensation, trusts and annuities, and bond purchase plans [I.R.C. § 6652(e)];

5. A penalty of $1 a day (up to $5,000) may be imposed for each participant for whom a registration statement (Schedule SSA (Form 5500)) is required but not filed [I.R.C. § 6652(d)(1)].

FICA and FUTA

Q 12:26   Is compensation deferred by an employee into a 457 plan subject to FICA taxes?

Yes. Unless exempt (see Q 12:31), an employer must report each employee's FICA wages and pay FICA taxes on those wages. In addition, each affected employee is liable for payment to the government of the employee portion of the FICA taxes imposed on his or her wages until the tax is collected from the employee or paid by the employer. [P.L.R. 9540057]

Q 12:27   Are deferrals made in the form of matching or nonelective contributions FICA wages subject to FICA taxes?

Yes, unless the employment is not treated as service subject to FICA taxes. The exemption from FICA taxes for state and local governments is explained in Q 12:31.

Example. X is a tax-exempt governmental employer pursuant to Code Section 115. X maintains an eligible plan and makes a 5 percent matching contribution. X's employees are currently covered by Social Security. Code Section 3121(v)(3) provides that an *exempt governmental deferred compensation plan* does not include any plan to which Code Section 457(a) or 457(f)(1) applies. Thus, X's matching contribution to the eligible plan is not excludable from *wages* for purposes of FICA taxes. [P.L.R. 9024069, modified by P.L.R. 9025067]

Q 12:28   Are deferrals made to a 457 plan in the form of matching or nonelective contributions FUTA wages subject to the Federal Unemployment Tax Act?

If an employer is not exempt from FUTA, deferrals made to a 457(b) plan in the form of matching or nonelective contributions are subject to FUTA. However, an employer that is a state or political subdivision or a charitable organization described in Code Section 501(c)(3) is exempt from FUTA (see Q 12:34).

Q 12:29   When are deferrals to a 457 plan treated as wages for FICA tax purposes?

Deferrals under an eligible or ineligible plan are wages for FICA tax purposes when the participant's deferred compensation no longer is subject to an employment-based substantial risk of forfeiture. [I.R.C. §§ 3121(a)(5), 3121(v)(2), 3306(b)(5), 3306(r); Treas. Reg. §§ 31.3121(v)(2)-1, 31.3306(r)(2)-1; I.R.S. Notice 2003-20, 2003-19 I.R.B. 894 (May 12, 2003)]

Q 12:30   What is the FICA tax rate?

The FICA tax rate is 7.65 percent. Both the employer and its employee pay this tax, for a combined rate of 15.3 percent. The 7.65 percent tax rate has two components: Old Age, Survivors, and Disability Insurance (OASDI) tax and Hospital Insurance (HI). These are computed as follows:

- *OASDI tax*—6.2 percent of FICA wages, up to a limit.
- *HI*—1.45 percent of FICA wages, without any limit.

[I.R.C. §§ 3101, 3111, 3121]

Q 12:31 When does employment, for FICA purposes, include service as an employee for a state or local government employer?

For FICA purposes, service as an employee for a state or local government employer is included unless the employee is a "member of a retirement system" with respect to service performed after July 1, 1991 (see Q 12:32). Effective July 2, 1991, Congress generally made FICA coverage mandatory for state and local government employees who are not covered by a Section 218 Agreement and are not participants in a public retirement system. Thus, wages for services performed after July 1, 1991, that are received by an employee of a state or local government employer who is not a member of a qualifying retirement system usually will be subject to FICA taxes.

Q 12:32 What is a qualifying retirement system?

A retirement system may include any pension, annuity, retirement, or similar fund or system within the meaning of Section 218 of the Social Security Act [42 U.S.C. § 418] if the plan is maintained by a state, political subdivision, or instrumentality of a state or political subdivision to provide retirement benefits to its employees who are participants. The definition of *retirement system* is limited. Under the regulations, for service in the employ of a state or local government employer to qualify for the exception from employment under Code Section 3121(b)(7), the employee must be a member of a qualifying retirement system that provides certain minimum retirement benefits to that employee. An eligible plan may meet this requirement and serve as a "FICA alternative" plan.

Q 12:33 Are Medicare taxes reduced under a FICA alternative plan?

No. Under a FICA alternative plan, the OASDI portion, but not the HI portion, of FICA taxes is eliminated.

IRS Form 940—Employer's Annual FUTA Tax Return

Q 12:34 Are all employers subject to federal unemployment tax?

No. Payment for service performed in the employ of a state or political subdivision or in the employ of a religious, educational, or other charitable organization described in Code Section 501(c)(3) does not constitute wages for FUTA purposes. [I.R.C. § 3306(c)(7), (8)] Other exemptions from FUTA might apply. [I.R.C. § 3306(c)(6)–(10)] Such payments might be subject to FICA taxes.

Q 12:35 How is FUTA tax reported?

An annual return must be filed by the employer on Form 940 by January 31 following the close of the calendar year for which FUTA tax is due. The employer may have to make deposits of the tax before filing the return. If the employer deposits the tax on time and in full, the employer has an extra 10 days to file—until February 10. In some cases, Form 940-EZ, a simplified version of Form 940, may apply.

Q 12:36   What is the FUTA tax rate?

The FUTA tax rate is 6.2 percent of the first $7,000 in wages paid annually to each employee. A credit of up to 5.4 percent applies to the state unemployment tax that is paid, unless the credit reduction applies (see Q 12:37). If for any reason the employer is exempt from state unemployment tax, the full 6.2 percent rate applies.

Q 12:37   When does the FUTA tax credit reduction apply?

A credit of up to 5.4 percent is given for the state unemployment tax that is paid; however, the credit is reduced if the state's unemployment fund borrows from the federal government and keeps an outstanding balance for two or more years. The net tax rate may, therefore, be as low as 0.8 percent (6.2% − 5.4%) if the state is not subject to a credit reduction. If the state tax rate (experience rate) is less than 5.4 percent, an employer is allowed the full 5.4 percent credit; however, an employer may not take the credit for any state taxes that it fails to pay.

Reporting Distributions on Form 1099-R

Q 12:38   Are distributions from governmental 457(b) plans reported on Form 1099-R?

Distributions from a governmental 457(b) plan are reported on Form 1099-R, including those to employees and former employees for years after 2001. For years prior to 2002, Form W-2 reporting rules described in Qs 12:87–12:120 for tax-exempt entity 457(b) plans applied to governmental plan distributions. A distribution to a deceased participant's beneficiary is also reported on Form 1099-R. Distributions to an employee from a nonqualified plan or a nongovernmental 457(b) plan are reported on Form W-2, not Form 1099-R.

Q 12:39   Will the IRS enforce the 1099-R reporting rules for distributions made in 2002 and 2003?

The IRS will not enforce the Form 1099-R reporting rules for distributions made in 2002 or 2003 if the rules in Notice 2000-38 are followed. [I.R.S. Notice 2003-20, 2003-19 I.R.B. 894] Therefore, reporting a distribution on Form W-2 in accordance with Notice 2000-38 should not be treated as a reporting failure, even though the distribution should have been reported on Form 1099-R. This is because Form 1099-R and Code Section 3405 were not addressed in Notice 2000-38 [2000-33 I.R.B. 174], which was replaced by Notice 2003-20 [2003-19 I.R.B. 894].

Q 12:40   What information about the payor is reported on Form 1099-R?

Form 1099-R reports the payor's name, address, and federal identification number.

Q 12:41   What information about the recipient is reported on Form 1099-R?

Form 1099-R reports the recipient's name, address, and identification number, which is a Social Security number or, for an alien, an individual taxpayer identification number.

Q 12:42   What information about a distribution is reported on Form 1099-R?

Form 1099-R has 17 boxes that are used to report detailed information about the distribution. The boxes report the following information:

Box 1—"Gross distribution" (see Q 12:43)

Box 2a—"Taxable amount" (see Q 12:44)

Box 2b—"Check boxes for Taxable amount not determined and Total distribution" (see Qs 12:45 and 12:46)

Box 3—"Capital gain (included in box 2a)" (see Q 12:50)

Box 4—"Federal income tax withheld" (see Q 12:51)

Box 5—"Employee contributions or insurance premiums" (see Q 12:55)

Box 6—"Net unrealized appreciation in employer securities" (see Q 12:56)

Box 7—"Distribution code(s)" (see Qs 12:57–12:73)

Box 8—"Other" (see Q 12:74)

Box 9a—"Your percentage of total distribution" (see Q 12:75)

Box 9b—"Total employee contributions" (see Q 12:76)

Box 10—"State tax withheld" (see Q 12:77)

Box 11—"State/Payer's state no." (see Q 12:77)

Box 12—"State distribution" (see Q 12:77)

Box 13—"Local tax withheld" (see Q 12:77)

Box 14—"Name of locality" (see Q 12:77)

Box 15—"Local distribution" (see Q 12:77)

Q 12:43   What does the payor report in box 1, "Gross distribution," of Form 1099-R for governmental plans?

In box 1 of Form 1099-R, report distributions to plan participants from governmental plans. Report the total amount of the distribution before income tax or other deductions were withheld, but do not include certificate of deposit penalties for early withdrawal. For employer securities and other property, report the fair market value at the time of distribution.

Q 12:44   What does the payor report in box 2a, "Taxable amount," of Form 1099-R?

Generally the payor reports the same amount in box 2a as in box 1, if the distribution was not paid as a direct rollover. If the entire distribution was a direct rollover, report 0 in box 2a. If part of the distribution was a direct rollover and part was distributed to the participant, issue two Forms 1099-R to report each part.

Q 12:45   How are corrective distributions of excess deferrals from governmental plans reported?

The instructions for Form 1099-R do not specifically address corrective distributions from governmental 457 plans. However, the instructions generally provide that the amount of excess deferrals is reported in box 2a. Corrective distributions of an excess plus earnings are reported on Form 1099-R for the year of distribution regardless of when the distribution is taxable to the participant. The code entered in box 7 indicates the taxable year. If the excess and earnings are taxable in two different years, issue two Forms 1099-R to designate the year each part of the distribution is taxable. The instructions to Form 1099-R state that participants must also be told at the time of the distribution the year, or years, in which the distribution is taxable and that it may be necessary to file an amended return for a prior year.

Q 12:46   What if a participant has a deemed distribution of a loan?

If a loan is treated as a deemed distribution, report it on Form 1099-R using the normal taxation rules of Section 72, including basis recovery. The 10 percent early distribution penalty does not apply, because 457 plans are not subject to the excise tax penalties under Code Section 4975. Deemed distributions are not eligible for rollover. Interest that accrues after a deemed distribution is not an additional loan and is not reported on Form 1099-R.

Q 12:47   What if a participant's loan is reduced (offset) to repay the loan?

If a participant's accrued benefit is reduced (offset) to repay the loan, the amount of the offset is an actual distribution. Report it the same as any other actual distribution and do not enter Code L in box 7. Loan offset amounts are eligible for rollover if the participant makes up the offset loan amount from other sources.

Q 12:48 When does a payor check box 2b, "Taxable amount not determined"?

If a payor is unable to reasonably obtain the data needed to compute the taxable amount, the payor may enter an X in box 2b, "Taxable Amount not Determined."

Q 12:49 When does a payor check box 2b, "Total distribution"?

If the distribution reported in box 1 is a total distribution, the payor should enter an X in box 2b, "Total distribution." A total distribution is one or more distributions within one tax year in which the entire balance of the account is distributed. If periodic or installment distributions are made, mark this box in the year in which the final distribution is made.

Q 12:50 Does box 3, "Capital Gain (included in box 2a)," apply to governmental plans?

No, this box is used to report certain lump-sum distributions from qualified plans that are eligible for a capital gain election. However, it does not apply to 457 plans.

Q 12:51 What does a payor report in box 4, "Federal income tax withheld"?

Use this box to report any federal income tax withheld. Such withholding is subject to the deposit rules and the withholding tax return Form 945, Annual Return of Withheld Federal Income Tax. No withholding is required until the annual aggregate distribution exceeds $200.

Q 12:52 What mandatory withholding rules apply to eligible rollover distributions?

Eligible rollover distributions from a *qualified plan, 403(b) plan, or govern-mental 457(b)* plan that are not paid as a direct rollover are subject to mandatory withholding at the rate of 20 percent. If part of an eligible rollover distribution is paid in a direct rollover and the other part is distributed to the participant, the portion distributed is subject to the 20 percent mandatory withholding on the taxable amount.

Q 12:53 What withholding rules apply to distributions that are not eligible rollover distributions?

A distribution from a qualified plan, 403(b) plan, and governmental 457(b) plan that is not an eligible rollover distribution is subject to either 10 percent withholding (for nonperiodic distributions) or to the wage tables in Circular E (for periodic distributions).

Q 12:54   What if the payee fails to furnish his or her tax identification number?

For *all plans*, if a payee fails to furnish his or her taxpayer identification number (TIN), or if the IRS provides notice before any distribution that the TIN furnished is incorrect, the payee may not claim exemption from these withholding requirements (see Qs 12:84–12:86). Backup withholding under Section 3406 does *not* apply to any retirement plan distribution.

Q 12:55   What does a payor report in box 5, "Employee contributions or insurance premiums"?

The payor reports in box 5 after-tax employee contributions or insurance premiums that the employee may recover tax free this year based on the method used to determine the taxable amount reported in box 2a. If a total distribution is made, the total employee contributions or insurance premiums available to be recovered tax free must be reported only in this box 5. However, if any previous distributions were made, any amount recovered tax free in prior years must not be reported here. If the information necessary to compute the taxable amount is not reasonably obtainable, leave box 2a and box 5 blank, and mark the first box, "Taxable amount not determined," in box 2b.

Q 12:56   Does box 6, "Net unrealized appreciation in employer securities," apply to governmental plans?

No, this box does not apply, because governmental 457 plans cannot invest in employer securities.

Q 12:57   What information is reported by the distribution codes that are used in box 7?

The distribution codes reported in box 7 provide a great deal of information about the type of distribution that is being reported. The IRS uses the codes to determine whether the recipient has properly reported the distribution. The following is a list of the distribution codes that are used on the 2003 Form 1099-R:

1—"Early distribution, no known exception"

2—"Early distribution, exception applies as defined in section 72(q), (t) or (v)"

3—"Disability"

4—"Death"

5—"Prohibited transaction"

6—"Section 1035 exchange"

7—"Normal distribution"

8—"Excess contributions plus earnings/excess deferrals (and/or earnings) taxable in 2003"

9—"Cost of current life insurance protection"

A—"May be eligible for 10-year tax option"

D—"Excess contribution plus earnings/excess deferrals taxable in 2003"

E—"Excess annual additions under section 415/certain excess amounts under section 403(b) plans"

F—"Charitable gift annuity"

G—"Direct rollover and rollover contribution"

J—"Early distribution from a Roth IRA, no known exception"

L—"Loans treated as deemed distributions under section 72(p)"

N—"Recharacterized IRA contribution made for 2004—Qualified distribution from a Roth IRA"

P—"Excess contributions plus earnings/excess deferrals taxable in prior year (2003)"

Q—"Qualified distribution from a Roth IRA"

R—"Recharacterized IRA contribution made for 2002 and recharacterized in 2003"

S—"Early distribution from a SIMPLE IRA in the first 2 years, no known exception"

T—"Roth IRA distribution, exception applies 10 percent penalty"

Q 12:58   May more than one code be reported on box 7?

Yes, when applicable a payor may enter both a numeric and an alpha code.

Example. If a direct rollover from a governmental 457(b) to a traditional IRA for the surviving spouse of a deceased participant was made, the double code 4G would be reported.

However, only three numeric combinations are permitted: codes 8 and 1, 8 and 2, or 8 and 4. If two other numeric codes apply, the payor must file more than one Form 1099-R. If both alpha and numeric codes are used, there is no required ordering of the codes.

Q 12:59   When is code 1, "Early Distribution, no known exception," used?

Code 1 is used to report that the employee/taxpayer is under age 59½ and none of the exceptions to the additional 10 percent tax on an early distribution is known to apply. Distributions from a governmental Section 457(b) plan are not subject to the 10 percent tax on early distributions. However, if a governmental Section 457(b) is rolled over to another plan (such as a plan described in Code Section 401(a)) that is subject to that tax, subsequent distributions from the plan that received the 457(b) assets will be subject to the 10 percent tax on early distributions. [Rev. Rul. 2004-12, 2004-7 I.R.B. 478]

Q 12:60   When is code 2, "Early distribution, exception applies as defined in section 72(q), (t) or (v)," used?

Use code 2, if the recipient has not reached age 59½, to report that an exception under Section 72(q), (t), or (v) applies. It is unclear whether 457(b) distributions are reported using code 2 or code 7.

Q 12:61   When is code 3, "Disability," used?

Use code 3 if the payor knows that the participant is disabled.

Caution. The instructions for Form 1099-R do not define *disability* for purposes of using code 3. Many employer plans define *disability* differently from the disability definition under Section 72(m)(7) that would avoid the 10 percent tax on early distributions. It is unclear whether this code is used for 457 distributions.

Q 12:62   When is code 4, "Death," used?

Use code 4, regardless of the age of the deceased participant or beneficiary, to report that the distribution was made to the decedent's beneficiary, including an estate or trust. If applicable, use one of the codes 8, D, G, L, or P in addition to code 4.

Q 12:63   When is code 5, "Prohibited transaction," used?

Use code 5 to report an improper use of the account that is a prohibited transaction (see Q 2:165).

Q 12:64   Is code 6, "Section 1035 exchange," used to report distributions from governmental 457(b) plans?

No. Code 6 is used to report the tax-free exchange of life insurance, annuity, or endowment contracts under Section 1035.

Q 12:65   When is code 7, "Normal distribution," used?

Use code 7 for a normal distribution from a 457 plan to the participant to indicate that the taxpayer is age 59½ or older, unless another code applies. Also use code 7 to report a distribution from a life insurance, annuity, or endowment contract and for reporting income from a failed life insurance contract. If no other code applies to the distribution, code 7 generally should be used.

Q 12:66   When is code 8, "Excess contributions plus earnings/excess deferrals (and/or earnings) taxable in 2003," used?

Use code 8 to report corrective distributions of excess deferrals unless code D or P applies. These types of corrective distributions may be taxable in more than one year. If this occurs, separate Forms 1099-R must be issued reporting the year each part is taxable and using code 8, D, or P as applicable. If applicable, use code 1, 2, or 4 in addition to code 8.

Q 12:67   When is code 9, "Cost of current life insurance protection," used?

Use code 9 to report premiums paid by a trustee or custodian under an employer's plan for current life insurance protection taxable to plan participants or their beneficiaries. Life insurance costs are reported in box 1 and box 2a. However, life insurance costs and a distribution should not be reported on the same Form 1099-R. No other code should be used with code 9.

Q 12:68   Is code A, "May be eligible for 10-year tax option," used for distributions from a 457(b) plan?

No, the 10-year option method of computing the tax on lump-sum distributions does not apply to 457(b) plans.

Q 12:69   When is code D, "Excess contributions plus earnings/excess deferrals taxable in 2001," used?

Use code D to indicate a corrective distribution made in 2003 that is taxable in 2001. In most cases, this type of excess amount is taxed the year it was deferred, but the earnings are taxed in the year of distribution. Thus, depending on when the excess was corrected in relation to the year it was deferred, two Forms 1099-R are required to properly report when each part of the corrective distribution is taxable.

Under the current instructions, code D only applies to the following types of plans: Section 401(k), Section 403(b), and Section 408(k)(6) SARSEPs. Code D does not apply to traditional IRAs, regular SEP IRAs, SIMPLE IRAs, Roth IRAs, or Coverdell Education Savings Accounts. Also, these types of corrective distributions are *generally* not subject to withholding and are never eligible for rollover treatment. The IRS suggests that the trustee advise the participant at the time of the distribution of the year or years in which the distribution is taxable and that it may be necessary to file an amended return for a prior tax year. If applicable, use one of the following codes in addition to code D: code 1, 2, or 4.

Q 12:70   When is code G, "Direct rollover and rollover contribution" used?

Use code G for a direct rollover from a qualified plan (including a governmental Section 457(b) plan) or tax-sheltered annuity to an eligible retirement plan. An eligible retirement plan includes a qualified plan, a tax-sheltered annuity, a governmental Section 457(b) plan, or an IRA.

If part of a distribution is paid as a direct rollover to an eligible retirement plan and part is distributed to the participant, issue two Forms 1099-R to report the different parts. Also, do not use code G with any other code, except for code 4, "Direct Rollover to a Qualified Plan, Section 403(b) or governmental 457(b)."

Q 12:71 When is code L, "Loans treated as deemed distributions under section 72(p)," used?

Use code L to report a deemed distribution of a participant loan that fails to meet the requirements of Section 72(p). Do not use code L to report a loan off-set amount (see Q 12:47) under the box 2a description for the difference between a deemed distribution and a loan offset amount. If applicable, use one of the following codes in addition to code L: code 1 or 4.

Q 12:72 When is code P, "Excess contributions plus earnings/excess deferrals taxable in 2003,"used?

Use code P to report that the distribution is taxable in the prior year (see Q 12:45 and previous discussions for box 2a and code 8).

Q 12:73 What letter codes are not used to report distributions from a governmental 457(b) plan?

Codes J, N, Q, R, S, and T are not used to report distributions from 457(b) plans. These codes are used to report on the type of IRA distribution or the recharacterization of a contribution.

Q 12:74 What does a payor report in box 8, "Other"?

Box 8, "Other," is used to report the current actuarial value of an annuity contract that is part of a lump-sum distribution. This value is not reported in box 1 or 2a.

Q 12:75 What does a payor report in box 9a, "Your percentage of total distribution"?

If the distribution is made to more than one person, report the percentage received by the person whose name appears on Form 1099-R

Q 12:76 What does a payor report in box 9b, "Total employee contributions"?

This optional box is used to report total employee contributions, which may be helpful to the recipient. However, a 457 plan that is correctly designed and administered never has employee (after-tax) contributions.

Q 12:77   Are boxes 10–15, "State and local information," required to be completed?

No. These boxes are provided for convenience only. They are not required by the IRS. The boxes may be used to report distributions and taxes for up to two states or localities.

Rollover Distribution Notice

Q 12:78   Must recipients of distributions from a governmental 457(b) plan eligible for rollover treatment be furnished a written explanation?

Yes. No more than 90 days and no fewer than 30 days before making an eligible rollover distribution (or before the annuity starting date), the plan administrator of a governmental 457(b) plan must furnish a written explanation to each recipient. [I.R.C. § 402(f)]

Q 12:79   May a plan administrator ever make a distribution fewer than 30 days after the notice was provided?

Yes. If the recipient who received the Section 402(f) notice affirmatively elects a distribution, the administrator will not fail to satisfy the timing requirements merely because the plan administrator made the distribution fewer than 30 days after the notice was provided as long as the requirements of Treasury Regulations Section 1.402(f)-1, Q&A-2, are met.

Q 12:80   May a plan administrator provide a 402(f) notice more than 90 days before a distribution?

A plan administrator may provide the 402(f) notice more than 90 days before a distribution if the plan administrator provides a summary of the notice during the 30- to 90-day period before the distribution.

Q 12:81   What must the 402(f) notice provide?

The notice must explain the rollover rules, the special tax treatment for lump-sum distributions, the direct rollover option (and any default procedures), the mandatory 20 percent withholding rules and an explanation of how distributions from the plan to which the rollover is made may have different restrictions and tax consequences than the plan from which the rollover is made.

Q 12:82   May the notice and summary be made electronically?

The notice and summary are permitted to be sent either as a written paper document or through an electronic medium reasonably accessible to the recipient. [See Treas. Reg. § 1.402(f)-1, Q&A-5]

Q 12:83   What notice rules apply to periodic distributions?

For periodic distributions that are not eligible rollover distributions, the plan administrator must provide the notice before the first distribution and at least once a year as long as the distributions continue. IRS Notice 2002-3, 2002-2 I.R.B. 289, contains model notices that the plan administrator can use to satisfy the notice requirement.

Taxpayer Identification Numbers

Q 12:84   Are there penalties for missing or incorrect Taxpayer Identification Numbers (TINs)?

Yes. Form 1099-R was first included in the Identification Returns Name/TIN Matching Program beginning in tax year 1996. In IRS Announcement 98-73 [1998 I.R.B. 14], the IRS granted penalty relief for missing or incorrect TINs for Forms 1099-R issued for 1996, 1997, and 1998. The Announcement also provided that the Notice 972CG to the payor with respect to TIN errors would not constitute a "notice" under Section 3405(e)(12) for purposes of income tax withholding on future retirement distributions for that payee.

A penalty for missing or incorrect name/TIN will be assessed to the filer.

Q 12:85   What actions must a filer take for missing TINs?

To address the problem of missing TINs, the filer of a Form 1099-R or payor must:

1. Complete an initial solicitation at the time the account is opened.
2. Withhold federal income tax from any retirement plan distribution as normally would be done based on the type of plan and frequency of distribution, if a response is not given to the initial solicitation. For example, eligible rollover distributions from an employer's plan that are not paid as a direct rollover to another eligible plan are subject to withholding at the rate of 20 percent, and the payee may not elect out of this withholding requirement.
3. Complete a first annual solicitation by December 31 of the calendar year in which it receives a Notice 972CG providing notification of a missing TIN, if a TIN is not received as a result of the initial solicitation.
4. Complete a second annual solicitation by December 31 of the year immediately following the calendar year in which it receives a Notice 972CG, providing notification of a missing TIN, if the payor does not receive a TIN as a result of the first annual solicitation.

Q 12:86   What actions must a filer take for incorrect TINs?

To address the problem of incorrect TINs, the filer of a Form 1099-R or payor must:

1. Complete an initial solicitation when the payee opens the account.

2. Complete a first annual solicitation by the later of:

   a. 30 business days from the date on a Notice 972CG in which the IRS provides notification of an incorrect name/TIN combination; or

   b. 30 business days from the date of receipt of a Notice 972CG.

3. Continue to treat as valid any withholding election the payee previously made by completing Form W-4P (or a substitute form), if the payee responds to the first annual solicitation within 45 days and confirms that the name/TIN combination in the payor's records is correct. To notify the payor regarding the amount to be withheld from future distributions, the payee must submit a new withholding election by completing Form W-4P (or a substitute form).

4. Withhold at the appropriate rate, depending on the type of plan and the frequency of the distributions, until the new withholding election is received. The new withholding election is effective on the date provided in Treasury Regulations Section 35.3405-1, Q&A D-21 (no later than January 1, May 1, July 1, or October 1 after it is received, as long as it is received at least 30 days before that date).

5. Withhold from any distribution at the appropriate rate, if the payee does not respond to the first annual solicitation within 45 days. Alternatively, upon receipt of a Notice 972CG in which the IRS provides notification of an incorrect name/TIN combination, the payor may instead choose to disregard any prior withholding elections made by the payees whose name/TIN combinations are identified as incorrect in the Notice 972CG. In that event, the payor should consider these payees to have no withholding election in effect until receipt of new withholding elections.

6. Complete a second annual solicitation within the same time frame as required for the first annual solicitation, if the payor is notified of an incorrect name/TIN combination in any calendar year following the first notification. [I.R.S. Publication 1586 (rev. 7-99)]

IRS Form W-2—Wage and Tax Statement

Q 12:87   Which persons must file Form W-2?

Distributions from a nongovernmental tax-exempt employer's 457(b) plan are wages and are reported on Form W-2, Wage and Tax statement, as provided in the form's instructions. [I.R.S. Notice 2003-20, 2003-19 I.R.B. 894]

An employer must file Form W-2 for each employee from whom it withheld federal income or FICA taxes. In addition, an employer must file Form W-2 for each employee from whom it would have withheld federal income tax had the employee claimed no more than one withholding allowance or not claimed exemption from withholding (usually on Form W-4, Employee's Withholding Allowance Certificate; see Q 12:124).

Q 12:88   When and how must Form W-2 be filed?

The entries on Form W-2 must be based on a calendar year. Copy A of Form W-2 must be filed with the entire first page of Form W-3, Transmittal of Wage and Tax Statements, by the last day of February following the calendar year reported. If an extension of time to file Form W-2 is needed, the employer should see "When to File" in the instructions for Form W-3.

Q 12:89   What records must an employer maintain for Forms W-2 it files?

An employer must keep copy D (For Employer) of Forms W-2 with its records for four years.

Q 12:90   What if the employee copy of Form W-2 is undeliverable?

Any employee copies of Form W-2 that could not be delivered must be kept for four years. Undeliverable Forms W-2 should not be sent to the SSA.

Q 12:91   When is magnetic media filing required?

If an employer has 250 or more Forms W-2 to file, magnetic media filing usually is required. (See Form W-2, Instructions, Magnetic Media Reporting.)

Q 12:92   What information is reported on Form W-2?

Form W-2 is a wage and tax statement that an employer must file for wages paid to each employee from whom income tax, Social Security tax, or Medicare tax was withheld or income tax would have been withheld if the employee had claimed no more that one withholding allowance.

Q 12:93   What information about the employer is reported on Form W-2?

Information about the employer that is reported on Form W-2 includes:

Box b—Employer identification number

Box c—Employer's name, address, and ZIP code

Q 12:94   What information about the employee is reported on Form W-2?

Information about the employee that is reported on Form W-2 includes:

Box d—Employee's Social Security number

Box e and f—Employee's name and address

Q 12:95   What boxes are included on Form W-2 for reporting income and information?

Form W-2 is a wage and tax statement. The information it is used to report includes:

Box 1—"Wages tips, other compensation"

Box 2—"Federal income tax withheld"

Box 3—"Social security wages"

Box 4—"Social security tax withheld"

Box 5—"Medicare wages and tips"

Box 6—"Medicare tax withheld"

Box 7—"Social security tips"

Box 8—"Allocated tips"

Box 9—"Advanced EIC payment"

Box 10—"Dependent care benefits"

Box 11—"Nonqualified plans"

Box 12—Codes (used to report specific information)

Box 13—Checkboxes (used to report statutory employees, retirement plan, third-party sick pay)

Box 14—"Other" (used to report other information to employees)

Boxes 15 through 20—State and local income tax

The discussion of Form W-2 contained in this chapter is limited to information relating to unfunded deferred compensation plans.

Q 12:96   What period is used for reporting information on Form W-2?

The entries on Form W-2 must be based upon the calendar year.

Q 12:97   How are unfunded deferred compensation amounts reported on Form W-2?

For a nongovernmental employer's eligible plan, amounts subject to Social Security and Medicare taxes are reported on 2004 Form W-2 in boxes 3, 5, and 12. Distributions are reported in boxes 1 and 11.

For an ineligible plan, amounts are reported on 2004 Form W-2 in boxes 1, 3, 5, and 11.

A distribution from a state or local government employer's eligible plan is reported on Form 1099-R.

Q 12:98   Is Form W-2 used to report distributions to beneficiaries?

No. A distribution to a participant's beneficiary is reported on Form 1099-R, Distributions From Pensions, Annuities, Retirement or Profit-Sharing Plans,

IRAs, Insurance Contracts, Etc. [Rev. Rul. 86-109, 1986-2 C.B. 196; I.R.S. Notice 2003-20, 2003-19 I.R.B. 894 (May 12, 2003)] No federal income tax withholding is required. [See Rev. Rul. 59-64, 1959-1 C.B. 31] A distribution to a beneficiary is reported in boxes 1 and 2a, and code 4 is used in box 7 of Form 1099-R.

Q 12:99   How often must FICA and FUTA taxes be withheld on deferred compensation?

An employer must withhold applicable FICA and FUTA taxes with respect to nonqualified deferred compensation treated as wages on each date it treats such an amount as paid. As a rule of convenience, the amount may be withheld on any date that is later than, but within the same calendar year as, the actual date on which an amount deferred is otherwise required to be taken into account. An employer may choose to treat amounts deferred under a nonqualified deferred compensation plan as wages paid on a pay-period, quarterly, semiannual, annual, or other basis, provided the amounts are treated as paid no less frequently than annually. The employer must deposit the withheld taxes under the regular rules for tax deposits. [IRS Notice 94-96, 1994-2 C.B. 564; Treas. Reg. § 31.3121(v)(2)-1(e)(5)]

Example. If services are considered performed periodically throughout a year, the employer may nevertheless treat the services as performed on December 31 of that year.

Q 12:100   May deferred compensation be credited as wages more than once?

No. Deferred compensation is credited as wages for FICA tax purposes only once. [I.R.C. §§ 3121(v)(2)(B), 3306(r)(2)(B); Treas. Reg. § 31.3131(v)(2)-1(a)(2)(iii); I.R.S. Notice 2003-20, 2003-19 I.R.B. 894 (May 12, 2003)]

Q 12:101   Are distributions from a 457(b) plan of a nongovernmental tax-exempt entity subject to the special pension and deferred compensation withholding and election rules?

No. Amounts paid under a 457(b) plan of a nongovernmental tax-exempt entity are wages under Code Section 3401(a). [I.R.S. Notice 2003-20, 2003-19 I.R.B. 894 (May 12, 2003)] Thus, they are not designated distributions, which are subject to the special pension withholding and election rules. [I.R.C. § 3405(e)(1)(B)(i); Temp. Treas. Reg. § 35.3405-1T, Q&A A23] As a result, a participant may not elect to waive withholding on periodic payments. A participant may use Form W-4 to adjust his or her wage withholding (see Q 12:124).

Q 12:102 Is a 457 plan distribution treated as income earned in the current year for purposes of the Social Security earnings test?

No. A distribution from an eligible plan or an ineligible plan is treated as income earned in a prior year for purposes of a Social Security earnings test (if any). [42 U.S.C. §§ 411, 1382, 1382a] Thus, the information contained in box 11 of Form W-2 helps the SSA verify they have properly applied the Social Security earnings test and paid the correct amount of benefits.

Q 12:103 How is box 4 on Form W-2, "Social security tax withheld," completed?

The total employee portion (not the employer's share) of Social Security tax withheld or paid by the employer for the employee for the year is reported in box 4. The amount reported should not exceed 6.2 percent of the taxable wage base.

Q 12:104 How is box 5 on Form W-2, "Medicare wages and tips," completed?

The wages subject to HI or "Medicare" tax is the same as the wages subject to OASDI or "Social Security" tax (boxes 3 and 7), except that there is no wage base limit for Medicare tax. Total HI wages are entered in box 5. If an employer pays an employee's share of taxes, the amount must be included as wages in box 1.

Q 12:105 How is box 6, "Medicare tax withheld," completed?

In box 6 (Medicare tax withheld), total the employee portion (not the employer's share) of Medicare tax withheld by the employer for the employee for the year that is entered. A federal, state, or local government agency with employees who pay only the 1.45 percent Medicare tax enters the Medicare tax in this box.

Q 12:106 What is the purpose of box 11, "Nonqualified plans," on Form W-2?

Box 11 is used by the SSA to determine whether any portion of the amount reported in box 1 (wages, tips, and other compensation) or boxes 3 and 5 (Social Security and Medicare wages) for a year was earned in a prior year. The determination is essential for proper application of a Social Security earnings test, if any. The results of this test may reduce Social Security benefits for a year if a Social Security recipient's income exceeds a certain level.

Q 12:107   What is included in box 11?

Box 11 includes distributions made from nonqualified plans, such as a non-governmental eligible or an ineligible 457(b) plan. The amount entered is also included in box 1. Box 11 also includes a "contribution" by an employer under a nongovernmental deferred compensation plan that is included in box 3 (up to the Social Security wage base) or box 5.

Q 12:108   How are deferred compensation "contributions" identified in box 11, if no distributions were made during the year?

If no distributions were made during the year, enter in box 11 deferrals (plus earnings) under a nonqualified or any 457 plan that became taxable for Social Security and Medicare taxes during the year (but were for prior year services) because the deferred amounts were no longer subject to a substantial risk of forfeiture. Also report this amount in boxes 3 and 5 as Social Security wages and Medicare wages. Report an amount in box 11 only if it is also included in box 1, 3, or 5. Do not include deferrals in box 11 that are included in box 3, "Social security wages," and/or box 5, "Medicare tax withheld," that are for current year services.

Q 12:109   Should box 11 be completed if an amount was distributed and deferrals are reported in boxes 3 and/or 5?

If an amount was distributed and deferrals are reported in boxes 3 and/or 5, do not complete box 11 (see IRS Publication 957, Reporting Back Pay and Special Wage Payments to the Social Security Administration, and Form SSA-131, Employer Report of Special Wage Payments, for instructions on reporting these and other kinds of compensation earned in prior years). However, do not file Form SSA-131 if contributions and distributions occur in the same year and the employee will not be age 62 or older by the end of that year. The purpose of box 11 is for the SSA to determine if any part of the amount reported in box 1 or boxes 3 and/or 5 was earned in a prior year.

Q 12:110   How are distributions from a nonqualified plan or a nongovernmental plan identified in box 11?

Distributions to an employee from a nonqualified plan or a nongovernmental 457(b) plan are identified with code G in box 11, "Nonqualified plans." The code should be entered as a capital letter; at least one space should be left blank after the code; and the dollar amount should be entered on the same line. Decimal points should be used, but not dollar signs or commas.

Example. To report a $4,000 distribution from a 457 plan, the entry in box 11 would be G 4000.00.

Q 12:111   What if a payor must report a distribution from both a nonqualified plan and a 457 plan?

Distributions from both a nonqualified plan and a 457 plan should be reported as a single amount in box 12, but do not use code G. Only one entry is permitted to be made in box 11. The distribution is also reported in box 1.

Q 12:112   Are distributions from a governmental 457(b) plan reported on Form W-2?

No. Report distributions from a governmental 457(b) plan on Form 1099-R.

Q 12:113   What is reported in box 12?

Any item listed as codes A through W in Q 12:115 is reported in box 12. Employer "pick-up" contributions under Code Section 414(h)(2) (relating to certain state or local plans) under a governmental qualified plan that are made to qualified plans are not reported in box 12. No more than four codes should be entered in this box. If more than four items need to be reported in box 12, a separate Form W-2 or a substitute Form W-2 must be used to report the additional items.

Q 12:114   How are amounts entered in box 12?

The codes shown in Q 12:115 are used with the dollar amount. The code should be entered as a capital letter, at least one space should be left blank after the code, and the dollar amount should be entered on the same line. Decimal points should be used, but not dollar signs or commas. For example, to report a $6,000 deferral to an eligible plan, the entry in box 12 would be G 6000.00.

Unlike other plans—for which an employer reports only elective deferrals (the portion of his or her wages that the employee did not receive because of the deferral) in box 12—for code-G-eligible 457 plans the employer includes both elective and nonelective deferrals in box 12. Do not report ineligible plan amounts under Code Section 457(f) that are subject to a substantial risk of forfeiture.

Q 12:115   What are the box 12 deferred compensation codes?

Some of the box 12 deferred compensation codes that are used for retirement or deferred compensation plans include:

D—"Elective deferrals to a Section 401(k) cash or deferred arrangement (including SIMPLE 401(k) elective deferrals)"

E—"Elective deferrals under a Section 403(b) salary reduction agreement"

F—"Elective deferrals under a Section 408(k)(6) salary reduction SEP"

G—"Elective and nonelective deferrals to a Section 457(b) eligible deferred compensation plan (state and local government and tax-exempt employers)"

H—"Elective deferrals to a Section 501(c)(18)(D) tax-exempt organization plan"

S—"Elective salary reduction contributions under a Section 408(p) SIMPLE IRA"

Q 12:116   When is box 13 checked?

Box 13 includes three check-off boxes for:

- "Statutory employee"
- "Third-party sick pay"
- "Retirement plan"

Q 12:117   When is the "Statutory employee" box checked?

This statutory employee box is checked only if the payee is a statutory employee (as the Code defines that term for this purpose) whose earnings are subject to Social Security and Medicare taxes, but not subject to federal income tax withholding. The statutory employee box is not checked for common-law employees.

Q 12:118   When is the "Third-party sick pay" box checked?

Third-party sick pay filers check this box if they are filing a W-2 for an insured's employee. Employers check the box to report sick pay payments made by a third party.

Q 12:119   When is the "Retirement plan" box checked?

The retirement plan box is checked if the employee was an active participant (for any part of the year) in any of the following:

- A qualified plan described in Code Section 401(a) (including a 401(k) plan);
- An annuity plan described in Code Section 403(a);
- An annuity contract or custodial account described in Code Section 403(b);
- A simplified employee pension (SEP) plan described in Code Section 408(k);
- A SIMPLE retirement account described in Code Section 408(p);
- A trust described in Code Section 501(c)(18); or
- A plan for employees of a federal, state, or local government or an agency or instrumentality thereof (other than a 457 plan)

This box is not checked for contributions made to a nonqualified plan or any 457 plan.

Q 12:120   How are boxes 15 through 20 used?

Boxes 15 through 20 are used to report state and local income tax information. They may be used to report wages and taxes for two states and two localities. Each state's and locality's information should be kept separated by the broken line. If information needs to be reported for more than two states or localities, more Form W-2s must be filed.

The two-letter abbreviation for the name of the state is used to identify the state. Individual states assign an employer its state identification number.

IRS Form W-3—Transmittal of Wage and Tax Statements

Q 12:121   Who must file Form W-3?

An employer that filed Form W-2 must file Form W-3 to transmit copy A of Forms W-2. A transmitter or sender may sign Form W-3 for the employer or payor only if the sender:

1. Has authorization to sign by an agency agreement (whether oral, written, or implied) that is valid under state law; and
2. Writes "For (name of payor)" next to the signature.

Q 12:122   What amounts are reported on Form W-3?

The amounts reported on Form W-3 are the totals of the amounts that are reported on Form W-2.

For Box 11—Nonqualified plans, enter the total reported in box 11 on Forms W-2.

For Box 12—Deferred compensation, enter the total of all amounts reported on Forms W-2 with codes D through H and S. Do not enter a code on Form W-3.

Q 12:123   What records must an employer maintain for Forms W-3 it files?

An employer must keep a copy of Form W-3 with its records for four years.

IRS Form W-4—Employee's Withholding Allowance Certificate

Q 12:124   How may a participant adjust the amount of wages withheld?

An employee may use Form W-4, Employee's Withholding Allowance Certificate, to adjust the amount of wages withheld. Because an individual's tax situation may change, an individual may need to refigure withholding each year.

IRS Form W-4P—Withholding Certificate for Pension or Annuity Payments

Q 12:125   May a deferred compensation recipient use Form W-4P to inform a payor whether income tax is to be withheld and on what basis?

No. Form W-4P may not be used for that purpose, because the payments are already defined as wages subject to income tax withholding. [I.R.C. § 3405(e)(1)(B)(i)] (But see Qs 12:97, 12:99.)

IRS Form 5329—Additional Taxes Attributable to Qualified Retirement Plans (Including IRAs), Annuities, and Modified Endowment Contracts

Q 12:126   When must Form 5329 be filed?

A taxpayer must file Form 5329 if he or she did not receive the minimum distribution under a retirement plan, including an eligible 457(b) plan. If a minimum distribution was not made, an excise tax applies. The excise tax is equal to 50 percent of the difference between the amount that was required to be distributed and the amount that was distributed. [I.R.C. § 4974(a)]

A taxpayer may also need to file Form 5329 if a governmental 457(b) plan distribution included amounts rolled over from a plan other than a governmental 457(b) plan and the amount of the distribution attributable to the rollover is subject to the additional tax on early distributions (see Q 12:131). The instructions to IRS Form 5329 state that a taxpayer must file Form 5329 if code 1 is not correctly shown in box 7 of Form 1099-R.

IRS Form 1040—Individual Income Tax Return

Q 12:127   How are the amounts reported in box 1 of Form W-2 reported on the individual's Form 1040?

A "distribution" from a nongovernmental 457 plan that is reported in box 1 of Form W-2 is included on line 7, "Wages, salaries, tips, etc." of the payee's federal income tax return (Form 1040).

Q 12:128   How do 457 plans affect the IRA worksheets for Form 1040?

A distribution received from a tax-exempt organization's 457(b) plan that is included in box 1 of Form W-2 should not be included in the IRA worksheet, which is contained in the Instructions to Form 1040 (line 24). The distribution should be reported in box 11 of Form W-2.

A 457(b) plan participant is not required to check "yes" to line 1a of the IRA Worksheet, "Were you covered by a retirement plan?", because the taxpayer was a participant in a 457(b) plan. The "retirement plan" box in line 13 of Form W-2 should not be checked for contributions to a 457 plan (see Q 12:119).

Q 12:129   How are excess 457 plan contributions reported?

The amount deferred must be reported in box 12 of Form W-2. However, if an employee's Form W-2 is incorrect, the employee/taxpayer still must correctly report his or her federal income tax wages (reduced only by proper deferrals) on Form 1040, line 7.

Q 12:130   May a deferral reported in box 12 of Form W-2 be deducted by the individual?

No. Elective deferrals to a 457 plan may not be deducted. These amounts are included as income in box 1 of Form W-2. However, a participant in a 457(b) plan may be able to take the retirement savings contribution credit if the participant and spouse (if filing jointly) made contributions to a governmental 457(b) plan (see IRS Form 8880).

Q 12:131   How is a distribution from a governmental 457(b) plan that is reported on a Form 1099-R reported on a taxpayer's Form 1040?

The taxable amount of pension and annuity distributions reported on Form 1099-R is reported in line 16b of Form 1040. If a distribution is fully taxable, an entry is not made on line 16a.

Generally, distributions from a governmental 457(b) plan are not subject to the 10 percent additional tax on early distributions. However, the 10 percent additional tax on early distributions does apply to distributions from a 457(b) plan to a participant who is under age 59½ at the time of a distribution if the distribution is attributable to an amount transferred or rolled over from a qualified retirement plan (other than a 457(b) plan). Such a transfer or rollover must be accounted for separately and must be reported separately [I.R.C. 72(t)(9); Rev. Rul. 2004-12, 2004-7 I.R.B. 478] The 10 percent additional tax on early distributions is reported on line 57 of Form 1040.

IRS Form 990—Return of Organization Exempt from Income Tax

Q 12:132   Must a tax-exempt organization file a Form 990?

Yes. A tax-exempt organization must report annual deferrals and distributions to certain participants in their Section 457 plans on Form 990—Return of

Organization Exempt from Income Tax, as specified by Form 990 instructions. [I.R.S. Notice 2003-20, 2003-19 I.R.B. 894]

Q 12:133   Must a governmental 457(g) trust file a Form 990?

No. A governmental 457(g) trust is not required to file Form 990—Return of Organization Exempt from Income Tax. [I.R.S. Notice 2003-20, 2003-19 I.R.B. 894]

IRS Form 990-T—Exempt Organization Business Income Tax Return

Q 12:134   Is a governmental 457(g) trust required to file Form 990-T?

Maybe. A governmental 457(g) trust may have to file Form 990-T—Exempt Organization Business Income Tax Return. (See Treas. Reg. §§ 1.6012-2(e) and 1.6012-3(a)(5) for the filing requirements for Form 990-T.)

Chapter 13

Plan-Approved Domestic Relations Orders

Peter J. Gulia, Esq.
CitiStreet Retirement Services

Although a deferred compensation plan is intended to provide payments to a participant, domestic relations law in all states recognizes interests in employment-based compensation plans as property subject to division on the dissolution of a marriage. Although nothing in federal law requires a deferred compensation plan to honor a domestic relations order that provides for a spouse or any person other than a participant, some plans, especially plans of state and local government employers, include provisions designed to create a workable regime to permit accounting and distributions to meet marital property expectations. Because federal law sets up a norm of a qualified domestic relations order that may be used with a qualified retirement plan, some deferred compensation plans voluntarily include somewhat similar requirements and procedures.

There is no statutory name for the kind of domestic relations order that might be recognized under a deferred compensation plan, but some plans refer to such an order as a plan-approved domestic relations order. Just as employee benefits and family law practitioners use the term QDRO as shorthand for a qualified domestic relations order, this chapter uses PADRO to refer to a court order that meets the requirements of a deferred compensation plan that contains provisions for recognizing a domestic relations order.

The plans that include such provisions try to balance the non-participant alternate payee's right to get a marital property distribution with the plan administrator's need for administrative efficiency and certainty.

Author's note. For reasons explained in this chapter, the qualified domestic relations order or QDRO moniker is not helpful to a reader's analysis of the law that governs whether a deferred compensation plan administrator will act according to a court order. For any 457 deferred compensation plan— whether eligible or ineligible, and whether maintained by a state or local government employer or by a nongovernmental tax-exempt organization—ERISA's QDRO requirement does not apply. For an ineligible deferred compensation plan, QDRO tax treatment is not available. For an eligible deferred compensation plan, a special provision of the Internal Revenue Code (Code) governs whether a payment will be treated as made under a domestic relations order for federal income tax purposes.

Therefore, this chapter uses the following special terms for domestic relations orders:

1. *Domestic relations order* (DRO) means a court order made under state domestic relations law that provides marital property rights, alimony, or child support to a participant's spouse, former spouse, child, or other dependent.

2. *Plan-approved domestic relations order* (PADRO) means a court order (usually a DRO) that meets any conditions specified by the plan such that the plan administrator will administer the plan following the order.

3. *Deemed qualified domestic relations order* (deemed QDRO) has the meaning provided by Code Section 414(p), including Code Section 414(p)(11). Thus, an order that otherwise would not be a qualified domestic relations order might nonetheless be deemed a QDRO if it is a DRO and an eligible deferred compensation plan paid a distribution following the order. Whether a court order is a deemed QDRO might be important in determining the federal income tax treatment of a participant or alternate payee, and in determining whether an eligible plan may pay a distribution before the participant's severance from employment.

4. *Qualified domestic relations order* (QDRO) has the meaning provided by Code Section 414(p) without regard to Code Section 414(p)(11).

This chapter's explanations of federal income tax law refer to the law in effect for a domestic relations order distribution after December 31, 2001 and before January 1, 2011.

In this chapter, the word state, when used to refer to state law, includes the 50 states of the United States, the District of

Columbia, American Samoa, Guam, Northern Mariana Islands, Puerto Rico, Virgin Islands, and other possessions and islands.

Reason for Retirement Plan Domestic Relations Orders

Q 13:1   Why did Congress create the qualified domestic relations order?

Before 1984, many plan administrators refused to honor state court orders that purported to assign a participant's benefit to the participant's spouse or former spouse. They refused because they believed that a plan's provisions that prohibited alienation of the participant's benefit precluded the plan from permitting payment to a person other than the participant. Likewise, many plan administrators of nongovernmental plans believed that a state court order directed to a plan governed by the Employee Retirement Income Security Act of 1974 (ERISA) was preempted by ERISA. [ERISA § 514] To preclude a participant from evading family support responsibilities that he or she could not pay by other means, many courts decided that a statute did not mean what it said: "[A] literal interpretation [*sic*] of the words of a statute is not always a safe guide to [the statute's] meaning and [the words] should be disregarded when [reading the words] defeats the manifest purpose of the statute as a whole." [Cartledge v. Miller, 457 F. Supp. 1146, 1154 (S.D.N.Y. 1978); see generally Lewis Carroll, *Through the Looking-Glass and What Alice Found There* 70 (1986 reprint Ariel/Borzoi Alfred A. Knopf, Inc. 1896)] Courts differed on whether there was an unwritten exception to ERISA's anti-alienation rule. [Compare AT&T Co. v. Merry, 592 F.2d 118 (2d Cir. 1979), and Carpenters Pension Trust v. Kronschnabel, 460 F. Supp. 978 (C.D. Cal. 1978), *aff'd*, 632 F.2d 745 (9th Cir. 1980), *cert. denied*, 453 U.S. 922 (1981), with Monsanto Co. v. Ford, 534 F. Supp. 31 (E.D. Mo. 1984), and Francis v. United Technology Corp., 458 F. Supp. 84 (N.D. Cal. 1978)]

To provide a workable solution, the Retirement Equity Act of 1984 [Pub. L. No. 98-397] (REA) enacted an ERISA provision requiring a plan governed by Part 2 of Subtitle B of Title I of ERISA to provide for payment on a qualified domestic relations order (QDRO). Also, REA amended ERISA to provide that payment following a QDRO is an exception to ERISA's anti-alienation requirement. [ERISA § 206(d)(3)(A)] Along with these ERISA changes, REA made a corresponding exception to the Internal Revenue Code (Code) rule that prohibits assignment or alienation of benefits under a nongovernmental retirement plan. [I.R.C. § 401(a)(13)(B)] Further, REA added to the Code a provision that shifts the federal income tax on a QDRO distribution from the participant to the alternate payee. [I.R.C. § 402(e)(1)]

Q 13:2   Must a 457 plan follow a QDRO?

No. Federal law does not require a 457 plan to recognize any domestic relations order (DRO).

A deferred compensation plan—whether an eligible plan or an ineligible plan—of a nongovernmental employer must be unfunded; that is, the participant has a contract right to the deferred compensation but all plan investments are the property of the employer and must be available to the employer's creditors. [I.R.C. § 457(b)(6), (f)] Under ERISA, a deferred compensation plan (other than a church plan or governmental plan) may be unfunded only if participation is restricted to "a select group of management or highly compensated employees." [ERISA §§ 201(2), 301(a)(3), 401(a)(1)] If plan participation is so limited, Part 2 of Subtitle B of Title I of ERISA does not apply to the plan. [ERISA § 201(2)] If Part 2 does not apply, ERISA Section 206 does not apply, which means that ERISA's QDRO rule does not apply. [See ERISA § 206(d)(3)]

A deferred compensation plan that is a church plan that has not elected to be governed by ERISA is not governed by any ERISA provision. [ERISA § 4(b)(2)] Thus, ERISA's QDRO rule does not apply to a nonelecting church plan.

A governmental plan is not required by ERISA to recognize a QDRO or any kind of DRO. [ERISA § 4(b)(1)] But since ERISA does not apply, state law is not preempted. Although a governmental plan is not required to follow ERISA's QDRO rule, popular awareness of QDROs affects governmental plan participants' and spouses' expectations concerning the way in which any retirement plan might recognize DROs. Many governmental retirement plans permit some recognition of a DRO to provide rights to a nonparticipant alternate payee. In many states, state law provides for many governmental plans to recognize a DRO that meets the requirements of a statute or plan provision that is similar to the federal QDRO provision.

Before 2002, a state or local government employer's eligible deferred compensation plan might include a provision for segregation of a separate account for a nonparticipant and payment to such an alternate payee following a DRO that meets plan-specified conditions. These provisions may have been furthered by the release of a few IRS rulings. [P.L.R. 9729013, 9619029, 9543010, 9237018, 9049036, 9024075] For 2002–2010, a state or local government employer's eligible deferred compensation plan may permit a distribution to an alternate payee without waiting for the participant's severance from employment. [I.R.C. § 414(p)(10); but see Q 13:27]

Q 13:3   Can a 457(b) plan be the subject of a QDRO?

Yes, for distributions paid in 2002–2010; no, for distributions paid before 2002 or after 2010.

For distributions paid in 2002–2010, an eligible deferred compensation plan may (but is not required to) pay a distribution to an alternate payee according to a DRO that is a deemed QDRO. [I.R.C. § 414(p)(11)]

For distributions paid before 2002 (or after 2010), an eligible deferred compensation plan cannot be the subject of a QDRO, at least according to the Internal Revenue Service (IRS). Before 2002, Code Section 414(p), which defines a QDRO for federal income tax purposes, applied only to a qualified plan subject to the anti-alienation requirement of Code Section 401(a)(13) or a governmental plan. [I.R.C. § 414(p)(11), before amendment by EGTRRA § 635] The IRS construed this provision to include only governmental plans that are similar to "other qualified plans" by including an anti-alienation provision. [P.L.R. 9145010. See generally H.R. Rep. No. 101-247, at 1443 (1989)]

For a state or local government employer's eligible deferred compensation plan, it is unclear whether such a construction was correct if the plan limited a plan-approved domestic relations order (PADRO) to payments after the participant's separation from service or other distributable event and the plan included an exclusive benefit provision as required by Code Section 457(b)(6). [See I.R.C. § 457(g)]. That the QDRO definition might be available for an order directed to a state or local government employer's eligible deferred compensation plan does not mean that a plan must recognize such an order. (See Q 13:2.)

Following Revenue Ruling 2002-22, whether an order directed to an eligible deferred compensation plan was or is a QDRO has almost no practical significance. (See Q 13:54.)

Q 13:4   What other plans do not recognize a QDRO?

While this chapter is limited to an explanation of domestic relations orders (DROs) directed to a Section 457(b) eligible deferred compensation plan or a Section 457(f) ineligible deferred compensation plan, divorce lawyers often work in a context that involves dividing pensions, deferred compensation, and other benefits under other laws, plans, and arrangements.

A plan governed by Part 2 of Subtitle B of Title I of ERISA must follow ERISA's QDRO rules.

A governmental plan need not follow QDRO rules. [For an explanation of these rules as applied to governmental plans, see C.V. Calhoun et al., *Governmental Plans Answer Book* ch. 13 (New York: Aspen Publishers, 2002)]

A Section 403(b) annuity contract or custodial account usually follows QDRO rules. [For an explanation of these rules as applied to Section 403(b) arrangements, see D.R. Levy et al., *403(b) Answer Book* ch. 13 (New York: Aspen Publishers, 6th ed. 2002)]

The Federal Employee Retirement System and the Civil Service Retirement System each has its own rules for a Court Order Acceptable for Processing (COAP). The rules are much more strict than the QDRO rules. [5 C.F.R. pt. 838] Even if there is no actuarial cost to providing a survivor annuity, a court order is not a COAP unless it expressly permits the Office of Personnel Management to reduce the annuity amounts under a formula provided by federal law. [5 U.S.C. §§ 8339(j)(4), 8419] A retiree may provide a former spouse a survivor annuity only if the retiree's current spouse consents. [5 C.F.R. §§ 831.614, 831.618] Also, a retiree may not elect a survivor annuity if doing so would cause the total of the current-spouse survivor annuity and former-spouse annuities to exceed 55 percent of the annuity the retiree would have been entitled to had he or she not provided any survivor annuities.

Under the Uniformed Services Former Spouses' Protection Act, a state court cannot divide a nonresident military member's retirement pay unless the member specifically consents to personal jurisdiction on the retirement pay issue. [10 U.S.C. § 1408(c)] This rule is strictly applied; for example, a nonresident's acceptance of service, general appearance, and participation in discovery matters (concerning matters other than military retirement pay), and attendance at a support hearing did not show consent. [Wagner v. Wagner, 768 A.2d 1112 (Pa. 2001)]

Q 13:5   What happens if a nonparticipant spouse fails to get a PADRO?

In the absence of a PADRO, a nonparticipant spouse might have little or no ability to protect his or her marital property rights.

Example. Debbie married Chet. They lived together for several years until they separated. Debbie and Chet signed a separation agreement. That agreement provided that Debbie "shall receive half of Chet's deferred compensation." Later, the court acted on Debbie's divorce petition and granted a final divorce decree. The divorce decree stated that the property settlement agreement was not merged into the divorce decree.

Debbie sent a copy of the separation agreement and the divorce decree to the plan administrator, asking that the plan set aside her half of Chet's deferred compensation. The plan administrator sent Debbie a formal claim denial letter, which explained that the separation agreement was not a PADRO or even a DRO because it was not part of a court order.

Soon after this, Chet left his job and took a distribution of his entire account. Chet did not pay Debbie any portion of the deferred compensation proceeds. Chet spent all the money he received from the plan distribution.

Debbie sued the plan administrator. The plan administrator answered that there had been no PADRO delivered to it before it decided to pay Chet's plan benefit. Further, the plan administrator had no duty or authority to put a "stop" on paying Chet's benefit once it had decided that the order furnished to it was not a DRO. Finally, Debbie did not have any rights as a spouse, because she was not Chet's spouse at the time he claimed his distribution. The court dismissed Debbie's lawsuit. In addition, the court ordered Debbie to reimburse the plan administrator's attorneys' fees.

Practice Pointer. Because a plan administrator usually has no duty or authority to restrain distribution of a participant's benefit except during the time that the plan administrator is deciding whether a DRO is a PADRO, a potential alternate payee should act diligently to make sure that the domestic relations court makes an order, and to deliver the court order to the plan administrator.

Elements of a Domestic Relations Order

Q 13:6   What is a domestic relations order?

Federal tax law defines *domestic relations order*, which practitioners sometimes call a DRO, as a court order made under state domestic relations law that provides marital property rights, alimony, or child support to a participant's spouse, former spouse, child, or other dependent. [I.R.C. § 414(p)(1)(B)]

A DRO must be a court order. A private agreement between spouses is not a DRO. [Stinner v. Stinner, 523 A.2d 1161 (Pa. 1987), *cert. denied*, 492 U.S. 919, 109 S. Ct. 3245, 106 L. Ed. 2d 591 (1989)]

A DRO must be an order "made pursuant to a State domestic relations law." [I.R.C. § 414(p)(1)(B)(ii)] In appropriate circumstances, community property law might be domestic relations law to classify a court order as a DRO. [Id.] However, plan administrators recognize a court order made under community property law only insofar as state law uses community property law to determine property division in divorce or similar domestic relations proceedings.

Q 13:7   Can a foreign nation's court order be a DRO?

Probably not. Because many state laws follow the Code's QDRO and DRO definitions, typically a DRO is described as an order made "pursuant to" a state domestic relations law. [See I.R.C. § 414(p)(1)(B)(ii)]

Although the definition of the word *state* is unclear, its use in context suggests that the term includes any state of the United States, the District of

Columbia, Puerto Rico, Virgin Islands, American Samoa, Guam, and other U.S. possessions, but does not include any foreign nation. [See, e.g., I.R.C. § 7701(a)(10); ERISA § 3(10); 43 U.S.C. §§ 1331–1343]

If a state court recognizes a foreign nation's judgment in a marriage or similar domestic relations matter and makes its own order, that state court order might be a DRO that could be a PADRO. For example, the *Uniform Interstate Family Support Act* sometimes provides for a state court's enforcement of a child support order made by a foreign nation's court. [See, e.g., N.J. Stat. Ann. § 2A:4-30.65 et seq.] Under that Act, a state court will enforce such an order under specified conditions that include an appropriate basis for personal jurisdiction. [See, e.g., N.J. Stat. Ann. § 2A:4-30.68] Most states exercise personal jurisdiction over a nonresident defendant to the extent permitted by the U.S. Constitution's protection of due process of law. Thus, if the defendant was not personally present before the foreign nation's court, he or she must have had some contact with the foreign nation such that a legal proceeding against him or her there "does not offend traditional notions of fair play and substantial justice." [See International Shoe Co. v. State of Washington, 326 U.S. 310 (1946)] If the Uniform Interstate Family Support Act does not apply, a state court will not enforce an order of a foreign nation's court unless the foreign court had both jurisdiction over the subject matter and a procedure that does not offend the current forum state's public policy. [See, e.g., Fantony v. Fantony, 21 N.J. 525 (1956); see generally Uniform Enforcement of Foreign Judgments Act of 1964, 9A U.L.A. 488 (1965)]

The law and procedure of marital dissolution in other nations might be significantly different from the law of a U.S. state. [C.V. Calhoun & G.L. Needles, "The Division of Pensions Across Borders," 13 *J. Am. Acad. Matrim. L.* 211 (1996)]

Elements of a Plan-Approved Domestic Relations Order

Q 13:8   What is a plan-approved domestic relations order?

State law and plan provisions concerning a DRO directed to a governmental plan differ from the rules that apply for a QDRO directed to an ERISA plan. Likewise, plan provisions concerning a DRO directed to a nongovernmental plan that is not required to, but chooses to, recognize some orders differ from the qualified-plan QDRO rules. In an effort to communicate to divorce lawyers the possibility of significant differences, some state or local laws create a different label for the form of order that will be accepted by a state or local government employer's deferred compensation plan (see Q 13:31), and some plans create a specially defined label.

Q 13:9   What makes an order a PADRO?

Because federal law does not require a 457 plan to recognize any DRO (see Q 13:2), a deferred compensation plan (if it recognizes DROs at all) states its own provisions for what requirements an order must meet to be recognized as a PADRO.

Under typical plan provisions, a PADRO is a court order that:

1. Is made under a state's domestic relations law;

2. Relates to the provision of property rights or alimony to a spouse or former spouse;

3. Specifies the plan to which the order applies (and applies to only one plan);

4. Specifies the name, last known mailing address, and taxpayer identifying number of the participant;

5. Specifies the name, last known mailing address, and taxpayer identifying number of the alternate payee (and applies to only one alternate payee);

6. Recognizes, creates, or assigns to the alternate payee a right to receive all or a portion of the participant's deferred compensation under the specified plan;

7. Specifies a fixed or determinable amount of the participant's benefit or account balance payable to the alternate payee;

8. Does not require the plan administrator to determine any amount other than according to its regular account records and valuation procedures;

9. Specifies the number of payments or the period to which the order applies, or specifies that the alternate payee elects his or her distribution option;

10. Does not require the plan to provide additional vesting;

11. Does not require the plan to provide additional benefits;

12. Does not require the plan to provide any form of benefit not provided under the plan;

13. Does not require the plan to pay to the alternate payee benefits that are required to be paid to another alternate payee under a previously determined PADRO;

14. Does not permit a distribution to the alternate payee before the participant's severance from employment unless the plan expressly provides otherwise;

15. Does not permit the alternate payee to designate a beneficiary;

16. Specifies that the order cannot affect the plan administrator's or payor's tax reporting and withholding duties; and

17. Specifies that the order cannot affect either the participant's or the alternate payee's taxes.

[See generally I.R.C. § 414(p)(1)–(3); Treas. Reg. § 1.401(a)-13(g)]

An order that is in substantial compliance with these rules is not a PADRO; instead, a PADRO "must include" *every* PADRO element. [Cf. Metropolitan Life Insurance Co. v. Pettit, 164 F.3d 857 (4th Cir. 1998)]

Under most plans, a PADRO cannot require the plan to pay a joint and survivor annuity for the life of the alternate payee and his or her later spouse or beneficiary. [See I.R.C. § 414(p)(4)(A)(iii)]

A typical deferred compensation plan provides that a child or other dependent of the participant cannot be an alternate payee. For an ineligible plan, a plan sponsor does not provide for a nonspouse alternate payee to remain consistent with IRS rulings. [P.L.R. 9729013, 9619029, 9543010, 9237018, 9049036, 9024075] Other plans do not provide for a nonspouse alternate payee simply to avoid inappropriate burdens that would be faced by the plan administrator.

Q 13:10 May a PADRO provide for a putative spouse from a void marriage?

No, but practically yes for the reasons explained below.

To be a PADRO an order first must be a DRO. A DRO must provide alimony payments, child support, or marital property rights to a spouse or former spouse. [I.R.C. § 414(p)(1)(B)(i)] Because a void marriage means that the purported marriage never existed, the putative spouse never was a spouse. If an order provides for a person other than a participant's spouse, child, or other dependent, such an order is not a DRO. Although some might argue that "[a]n individual . . . who . . . has as his [or her] principal place of abode the home of the [participant] and is a member of the [participant's] household" is a dependent, "[a]n individual is not a member of the [participant's] household if the relationship between such individual and the [participant] is [or was] in violation of local law." [See I.R.C. § 152(a)(9)] Thus, it is doubtful that a putative spouse in a void marriage is a participant's dependent.

A putative spouse is someone who participates, in good faith, in a void marriage.

A marriage might be void if:

1. Either of the parties was married to someone else when the purported marriage took place;
2. The parties are too closely related to one another;
3. Either of the parties was unable to consent to a marriage because he or she was insane or under a mental disability;
4. Either of the parties was unable to consent because he or she had not attained a sufficient age;
5. A party did not truly consent because he or she was fraudulently induced to enter into the purported marriage;
6. Either of the parties was under the influence of alcohol or drugs;
7. Either of the parties failed to satisfy a necessary health condition; or
8. The ceremony or agreement failed to meet necessary formalities.

[See, e.g., 23 Pa. Cons. Stat. Ann. §§ 1302, 1304, 1702, 3303–3305 (West 2001)]

Even when a court annuls a marriage or otherwise finds that a purported marriage was a nonmarriage, a putative spouse who acted in good faith usually is entitled to alimony and child support. [See, e.g., Steadman v. Turner, 357 Pa. Super. 361, 516 A.2d 21 (1986); see also 20 C.F.R. §§ 440.345, .346] In some states, finding a nonmarriage means that equitable distribution does not apply. In other states, equitable distribution is incident to either a divorce action or an annulment action. [See, e.g., 23 Pa. Cons. Stat. Ann. § 3502 (West 2001). But see 23 Pa. Cons. Stat. Ann. § 3501 (West 2001)] Except as expressly provided by a domestic-relations court order, the termination or nonexistence of a marriage defeats a property right that depends on the existence of a marriage. [See, e.g., 23 Pa. Cons. Stat. Ann. § 3503 (West 2001)] This rule matters because some rights, such as rights under an ERISA plan, cannot be changed by state law.

Although an order that provides for a putative spouse is not a DRO, some lawyers suggest that a plan administrator may rely on the court order's description of the alternate payee. In practice, a domestic relations court that enters an order directing a retirement plan to provide for a putative spouse often misdescribes that as a spouse. If a plan administrator decides to assume the risks of relying on a domestic relations court's description of a person as a spouse or former spouse, such a plan administrator might prefer to design its procedures to avoid receiving information other than the court order.

Also, a putative spouse is not entitled to a death benefit that turns on being a participant's surviving spouse. [See Boyd v. Waterfront Employers ILA Pension Fund, 182 F.3d 907 (4th Cir. 1999) (A woman who had not divorced her first husband was therefore not married to her second "husband" and so was not entitled to a survivor annuity.)] Even a putative spouse who is blameless and was a victim of fraud is not entitled to a death benefit as a surviving spouse, especially if there is an undivorced spouse who has a claim. [See Grabois v. Jones, 89 F.3d 97 (2d Cir. 1996) (A participant concealed his first marriage when he "married" a second "wife." Notwithstanding over 20 years of "marriage" with the second "wife," the first (and only) wife received a benefit and the second "wife" was not so entitled).]

Ordinarily, an undivorced spouse does not lose any rights merely because he or she has knowledge of his or her spouse's "marriage" to another. However, one court suggested that a spouse who did not object to a participant's "marriage" to another over many years might be barred by laches from asserting a right to a survivor benefit. [Croskey v. Ford Motor Co.-UAW, No. 01-Civ-1094 (S.D.N.Y. May 2, 2002)] In the author's view, the court was wrong because ERISA Section 205 states the exclusive means by which a participant and his or her spouse make a qualified election against a survivor benefit.

Q 13:11   May a PADRO be used to pay claims based on marital torts?

No. To be a PADRO an order first must be a DRO. A DRO must provide alimony payments, child support, or marital property rights to a spouse or former spouse. [ERISA § 206(d)(3)(B)(ii)(I); I.R.C. § 414(p)(1)(B)(i)] Although the dignitary torts of alienation of affections, seduction, and criminal conversation could occur only in the context of a marriage, it is doubtful that damages from such a tort are marital-property rights. A spouse's right against interference with his or her marriage is a right based on his or her personal dignity. That recovery is provided only to the wronged spouse reveals that such a right is not marital property.

Q 13:12   May a PADRO be used to pay child support?

Maybe. A PADRO is a DRO that provides for an alternate payee and meets form requirements. [I.R.C. § 414(p)(1)(A)] A DRO includes an order that "relates to the provision of child support[.]" [I.R.C. § 414(p)(1)(B)(i)] Several court decisions have recognized the use of a DRO to pay child support. [See, e.g., In re Marriage of LeBlanc, 944 P.2d 686 (Colo. Ct. App. 1997); Rohrbeck v. Rohrbeck, 318 Md. 28, 566 A.2d 767 (1989); Baird v. Baird, 843 S.W.2d 388 (Mo. 1992); Arnold v. Arnold, 154 Misc. 2d 715, 586 N.Y.S.2d 449 (Sup. Ct. Onondaga Cty. 1992); Stinner v. Stinner, 523 A.2d 1161 (Pa. 1987)]

If a child's custodial parent is the participant's spouse or former spouse, receiving child support payments following a QDRO might be disadvantageous to the custodial parent if he or she (rather than the child) is the alternate payee. Child support payments received usually are not income. [I.R.C. § 71(c)] However, an alternate payee who is the participant's spouse or former spouse is, for federal income tax purposes, the distributee of a QDRO distribution. [I.R.C. § 402(e)(1)(A)]

Practice Pointer. If a custodial parent uses a PADRO to collect child support payments, his or her lawyer should make sure that the court order specifies that the child (rather than the custodial parent) is the payee.

Q 13:13   Is an income-withholding notice issued by a child support enforcement agency a DRO?

Maybe, if such a notice is an order under applicable state law and is made under a state domestic relations law.

To be a PADRO, an order first must be a DRO. A domestic relations order is "any judgment, decree, or order . . . [that] relates to the provision of child support, alimony payments, or marital property rights to a spouse, former spouse, child, or other dependent of a participant, and is made pursuant to a State domestic relations law (including a community property law)." [I.R.C. § 414(p)(1)(B)]

The Code does not define the word *order*. Because the context refers to state domestic relations law, it seems likely that a plan administrator's finding on whether a document is an order should be grounded in state law. If it is unclear whether a document is an order, a plan administrator should get expert legal advice.

On a request from the Division of Child Support Enforcement of the New York State Office of Temporary and Disability Assistance, the DOL stated its view that an income withholding notice issued by that office is a domestic relations order. [DOL ERISA Adv. Op. 2001-06A] According to the text of the Advisory Opinion, the DOL did not consider whether the notice described by the applicant was any kind of order under New York law or whether such notices are made under a domestic relations law.

Note. Under New York law, an income execution probably is a supplemental order based in a court's inherent power to enforce its own orders. [N.Y. C.P.L.R. § 5241] Because the provisions are stated in New York's Civil Practice Law and Rules, however, it is unclear whether an income execution "is made pursuant to a State domestic relations law[.]"

Because none of the deferred compensation plans described in this book is governed by ERISA Section 206, a plan administrator cannot rely on this ERISA Advisory Opinion. Further, it is doubtful that a prudent plan administrator could consider the Advisory Opinion as persuasive authority because the text does not state any reasoning in support of its conclusion. Instead, a plan administrator should get its own lawyer's advice on whether an income withholding notice is a DRO.

Caution. Even if an income withholding notice issued by a child support enforcement agency is a DRO, a plan administrator still must decide whether the order is a PADRO.

A typical income execution is not a PADRO because such an order often does not "clearly specif[y]" either the amounts to be paid or "the number of payments or period to which [the] order applies[.]" (See Q 13:9.)

Q 13:14   Is a court order to refrain from changing a beneficiary a PADRO?

Usually not. In a divorce proceeding, a court sometimes makes (or is deemed to have made) an order that restrains one or both of the divorcing parties from taking actions that could frustrate the court's ability to divide property between the parties. For example, a court might order a participant to refrain from changing his or her beneficiary designation under a deferred compensation plan.

Unless such an order specifies a payment to an alternate payee and meets the other requirements of the plan's PADRO rule (see Q 13:9), it is not a PADRO. If an order is not a PADRO, a plan administrator has no obligation to act following the order.

Example. In their divorce proceeding, a domestic relations court ordered JoAnn and Kenneth not to dispose of or transfer any marital assets while the proceeding was pending. In violation of this order, Kenneth changed the beneficiary designation under a governmental deferred compensation plan from JoAnn to his children by a previous marriage. After Kenneth's death, the plan benefit was properly payable to the designated beneficiaries. Because the domestic relations court's order was not a PADRO, the plan administrator did not follow it.

ERISA preempts any state law that otherwise might require a plan administrator or employer to follow a court order that is contrary to the plan's provisions. [See, e.g., Central States, Southeast & Southwest Areas Pension Fund v. Howell, 227 F.3d 672 (6th Cir. 2000)]

Even if a court order relates to a non-ERISA plan (and thus is not preempted), a plan administrator, insurer, or custodian need not follow an order if it was not named in the court proceeding, served with legal process, and afforded a court hearing. Further, to comply with a plan's anti-alienation provision, a plan administrator must make a reasonable effort to resist a court order that is not a PADRO, unless the plan provides that it is the participant's responsibility to enforce that provision.

Q 13:15   Is a court order to refrain from taking a distribution a PADRO?

Usually not. In a divorce proceeding, a court sometimes makes an order that restrains one or both of the divorcing parties from taking actions that could frustrate the court's ability to divide property between the parties. For example, a court might order a participant to refrain from taking a distribution-under a deferred compensation plan.

Unless such an order specifies a payment to an alternate payee and meets the other requirements of the PADRO rule (see Q 13:9), it is not a PADRO. If an order is not a PADRO, the plan administrator has no obligation to act following the order.

Example. In their divorce proceeding, a domestic relations court ordered Jack and Jill not to dispose of or transfer any marital assets while the proceeding was pending (but did not yet provide any payment to either of them). In violation of this order, Jack took a full distribution from his deferred compensation plan. Soon after receiving this payment, he spent all the money. When Jill tried to sue the plan for paying Jack when the plan administrator knew that Jack was restricted by a court order, the court dismissed Jill's lawsuit and ordered her to pay the plan's attorney's fees because she should have known that her lawsuit was frivolous.

Caution. A person who receives money that was paid based on a divorcing person's act in violation of a court order might be subject to a constructive trust in favor of the eventual rightful owners of the property.

Practice Pointer. For reasons suggested by the caution described above, a divorce lawyer should not accept a fee payment from his or her client if the lawyer knows (or should know) based on the surrounding circumstances that the client became able to pay the fee because of a violation of a court order.

Q 13:16   Must a plan administrator tell an ex-spouse when a participant changes his or her beneficiary designation contrary to a court order?

No. A court order that, if followed, would interfere with plan administration (other than by providing for payments to an alternate payee) will not be a PADRO.

> Absent a promise or misrepresentation, the courts have almost uniformly rejected claims by plan participants or beneficiaries that an ERISA administrator has to volunteer individualized information taking account of their peculiar circumstances. This view reflects ERISA's focus on limited and general reporting and disclosure requirements . . . and also reflects the enormous burdens an obligation to proffer individualized advice would inflict on plan administrators[.]

[Barrs v. Lockheed Martin Corp., No 01-1203 (1st Cir. Apr. 24, 2002)]

Even when a plan administrator is governed by ERISA Section 404's greatest fiduciary duties, courts have not required a plan administrator to furnish an alternate payee information beyond that required by an express statutory or plan provision. For an unfunded deferred compensation plan regarding which a plan administrator is not governed by ERISA Section 404, it seems unlikely that a court would impose such a duty. For a governmental deferred compensation plan, it seems unlikely that a court would impose a duty greater than federal courts have applied concerning ERISA plans.

Q 13:17   Could a participant's bad acts affect an alternate payee's PADRO rights?

Yes. A PADRO must not require a plan to provide additional benefits. (See Q 13:9.) An unfunded deferred compensation plan may provide that a participant's obligations to the employer will be an offset against the participant's deferred compensation. If such an offset reduces a participant's plan account before the alternate payee is paid, the employer's obligation to pay the alternate payee might be reduced or extinguished. [Cf. Gaudet v. Sheet Metal Workers' National Pension Fund, No. 01-0718 (E.D. La. Mar. 13, 2002)]

Q 13:18   Must a plan administrator reject an order that is missing identifying information?

Usually, yes. Whether a plan administrator must reject a DRO that is missing identifying information depends on the plan's procedures and applicable state law.

Many plans impose identifying information requirements under plan procedures or applicable state law. A plan administrator's failure to follow state law or plan procedures might be a breach of a duty to administer the plan according to its terms. For an ERISA-governed plan, a plan administrator's failure to follow the plan's claims procedures might be an ERISA violation [ERISA

§ 503], and might permit a claimant to start a court proceeding without waiting to exhaust plan remedies. [DOL Reg. § 2560.503-1(l)] For a church plan or governmental plan, a failure to follow the plan's claims procedures might be a breach of the employer's contract duty of good faith and fair dealing.

Further, if a plan is a state or local government employer's eligible deferred compensation plan, following an order that is missing identifying information might violate the plan's exclusive-benefit provision. [I.R.C. § 457(b)(6), (g)] A pattern of not applying the plan's exclusive-benefit provision, even if non-application was ordered by a court, might mean that the plan does not have an effective exclusive-benefit provision and therefore is not an eligible plan. [I.R.C. § 457(b)]

In addition to a plan administrator's duty to ensure that it pays the correct person and tax-reports the payment to the correct taxpayer identifying number, some plans use identifying information checks as part of the plan's controls against fraud.

Q 13:19   What should a plan administrator do if an order is ambiguous?

If an order is ambiguous, a plan administrator should reject it. If an order is ambiguous, it is likely that the order fails to meet one or more requirements of the plan's procedures. If a plan administrator is in doubt about how to give effect to an order, it is likely that the order is not a PADRO.

Because many divorce lawyers submit defective orders and teaching those lawyers how to correct the orders may burden the plan administrator, a plan administrator might be tempted to decide that a defective order is a PADRO. Since the plan administrator's effort to "correct" or "resolve" a defect might adversely affect one of the parties, yielding to this temptation sometimes leads to further litigation. [See, e.g., Hullett v. Towers Perrin Forster & Crosby, Inc., 38 F.3d 107, 18 Employee Benefits Cas. (BNA) 2340, Pens. Plan Guide (CCH) ¶ 23,901Q (3d Cir. 1994)] If an order's defect relates to a death benefit or survivor annuity, the participant's death and the claims of other spouses and beneficiaries may make litigation more difficult to resolve.

Q 13:20   May a PADRO direct payment to the alternate payee's lawyer?

No. A DRO cannot create or recognize a right for any person other than an alternate payee. [I.R.C. § 414(p)(1)(A)] An alternate payee cannot be anyone other than a spouse, former spouse, child, or other dependent of the participant. (See Q 13:9.) Therefore, a PADRO cannot direct payment to the alternate payee's lawyer. Even if a plan sponsor desired to permit such a payment, a plan provision that allowed this would destroy the plan's tax treatment. [I.R.C. §§ 414(p)(10), 457(b)(5), 457(f); P.L.R. 9729013, 9619029, 9543010, 9237018, 9049036, 9024075. Cf. Johnson v. Johnson, Pens. Plan Guide (CCH) ¶ 23,957T (N.J. Super. Ct. 1999)] An order may direct payment to an alternate payee in an amount that reflects attorney fees within the marital property division ordered. [Cf. Trustees of the Directors Guild America-Producer Pension Benefit Plans v. Tise, 234 F.3d 415 (9th Cir. 2000)]

For an ERISA deferred compensation plan, ERISA preempts state laws, and a court order other than a PADRO can have no effect. [ERISA § 514(b)(7)] If a state court persists in making orders that purport to bind an ERISA plan or its plan administrator, a federal court will issue an injunction nullifying the acts of the state court. [AT&T Management Pension Plan v. Tucker, 902 F. Supp. 1168, 64 U.S.L.W. 2224, 19 Employee Benefits Cas. (BNA) 2129, Pens. Plan Guide (CCH) ¶ 23,917C (C.D. Cal. 1995)]

For a non-ERISA deferred compensation plan, a plan administrator normally will refuse to comply with an order that is not a PADRO. In most states, a domestic relations court will not have jurisdiction over the state or local government organization responsible for a deferred compensation plan. Therefore, the domestic relations court's order may bind the divorcing parties, but usually cannot bind the governmental employer or plan administrator.

Even if an order that provides for a payment to a lawyer may be recognized under a particular plan, a participant may have tax reasons to object to such an order. Although a deferred compensation plan may recognize an order that does not meet the Code's definition of a QDRO or even a DRO, a payment under such an order is the participant's income for federal income tax purposes. (See SQ 13:43.) In addition, because many states base the state income tax on federal income or on federal income tax, a payment under such an order may be the participant's income for state income tax purposes.

Q 13:21 May a church plan or governmental plan recognize a court order that provides for a spouse in a same-sex couple?

Yes. Because a church plan or governmental plan is not governed by ERISA, such a plan need not limit the persons recognized as a potential alternate payee under a PADRO to those who could be recognized under a QDRO governed by ERISA requirements. [ERISA §§ 4(b)(1), 206(d)(3)]

A Vermont governmental plan must recognize an order relating to parties to a same-sex civil union to the same extent that the plan recognizes an order relating to opposite-sex spouses (see Q 13:32).

It is unclear whether Vermont law could require a church plan to recognize an order relating to parties to a same-sex civil union. [U.S. Const. amend. I. Cf. Basich v. Board of Pensions, Evangelical Lutheran Church in America, 540 N.W.2d 82, 1995 Minn. App. LEXIS 1446, 19 Employee Benefits Cas. (BNA) 2231 (Minn. Ct. App. 1995), review denied, 1996 Minn. App. LEXIS 97 (Minn. Jan. 25, 1996) (unpublished order), cert. denied, 519 U.S. 810, 117 S. Ct. 55, 136 L. Ed. 2d 18 (1996); see generally Kenneth E. North, Religious Disputes in Secular Courts (Durham, NC: Carolina Academic Press, 2000)]

To preserve its tax treatment, a plan must not provide a distribution to a same-sex spouse until after the participant's severance. [I.R.C. § 457(b)(5), (f); see Q 13:27]

Q 13:22   Must an ERISA deferred compensation plan follow a court order that provides for a spouse in a same-sex couple?

No. Because ERISA Section 206 does not apply to an unfunded plan, an ERISA deferred compensation plan need not have any provision concerning domestic relations orders. [ERISA § 206] Further, if an ERISA plan has a provision that recognizes some DROs, any state law that otherwise might require a person to avoid discrimination between same-sex and opposite-sex marriages is preempted. [ERISA § 514]

Q 13:23   May an ERISA deferred compensation plan follow a court order that provides for a spouse in a same-sex couple?

Yes. Because an ERISA deferred compensation plan is unfunded and need not be for a participant's exclusive benefit, a plan may provide for an alternate payee beyond those recognized by ERISA Section 206. [ERISA § 401]

To preserve its tax treatment, a plan must not provide a distribution to a same-sex spouse until after the participant's severance. [I.R.C. § 457(b)(5), (f); see Q 13:27]

Q 13:24   Can an order made after the participant's death be a PADRO?

Maybe. For an ERISA-governed defined benefit plan, an order made after the participant's death, even if the order "relates back" to the time of an earlier court order for state law purposes, is not a QDRO because following such an order would require the plan to provide increased benefits. [See Samaroo v. Samaroo, 193 F.3d 185, 23 Employee Benefits Cas. (BNA) 1761 (3d Cir. 1999), cert. denied, 529 U.S. 1062 (2000); see also Hopkins v. AT&T Global Information Solutions Co., 105 F.3d 153, 20 Employee Benefits Cas. (BNA) 2418, Pens. Plan Guide (CCH) ¶ 23,931C (4th Cir. 1997). But see Patton v. Denver Post Corp., 179 F. Supp. 2d 1232 (D. Colo. 2002) (federal court reasoned that state court order made in 1999 was "effective" in 1988); Payne v. GM/UAW Pension Plan, No. 95-CV73554DT, 1996 WL 943424, 1996 U.S. Dist. LEXIS 7966 (E.D. Mich. May 7, 1996)] Although the ERISA provision that precludes a QDRO from providing increased benefits does not apply to a deferred compensation plan, the plan usually imposes a similar requirement.

Those benefit soundness concerns usually are not relevant to a defined contribution plan that permits a participant to designate any beneficiary to receive his or her undistributed account. As long as the participant's account has not been distributed and the order does not interfere with the rights of a surviving spouse, an order made after the participant's death might nonetheless be a PADRO. Of course, an order must meet all PADRO requirements (see Q 13:9).

The unpleasantness and expense of needless litigation may be avoided if the alternate payee's lawyer obtains an appropriate order before the participant's death.

PADRO Distribution Before a Participant's Severance

Q 13:25   May an ineligible deferred compensation plan permit a distribution to an alternate payee before the participant's severance?

Probably not. Deferred compensation under an ineligible deferred compensation plan is included in gross income as soon as "there is no substantial risk of forfeiture of the rights to such compensation." [I.R.C. § 457(f)(1)(A)] To meet this condition, an ineligible plan typically provides that a participant must perform substantial services over a significant period of years before he or she becomes entitled to the plan's deferred compensation. [See I.R.C. § 457(f)(3)(B)] Until a participant completes his or her service condition, there is no present right to deferred compensation. A PADRO cannot provide to a spouse or former spouse compensation to which the participant is not yet entitled.

Q 13:26   May an eligible deferred compensation plan permit a distribution to an alternate payee before the participant's severance?

Yes, except as explained below and in Q 13:27.

Before 2002, an eligible deferred compensation plan—even if funded with an exclusive benefit trust—could not permit a participant's spouse or former spouse to take a distribution until after the participant's death or separation from service. [P.L.R. 9729013, 9619029, 9543010, 9237018, 9049036, 9024075]

Following the Economic Growth and Tax Relief Reconciliation Act of 2001 (EGTRRA), an eligible deferred compensation plan may permit a distribution to an alternate payee (such as the participant's spouse or former spouse) before the participant's severance from employment. [I.R.C. § 414(p)(10)] An eligible plan may permit such a preretirement PADRO distribution for distributions paid in 2002–2010. [EGTRRA §§ 635, 901]

For an alternate payee to get this exception from a 457(b) plan's distribution restriction, the court order need not be a QDRO as long as it is a deemed QDRO. A DRO must be an order made under a state domestic relations law, which includes community property law insofar as state law uses community property law to determine alimony, child support, and property division in divorce, child support, or similar domestic relations proceedings. [I.R.C. § 414(p)(1)(A)(i)] A DRO must be a court order; a private agreement between spouses is not a DRO. The court order must specify sufficient information for the plan administrator to implement the order. For most plans, an order must meet additional requirements designed to protect the plan.

Practice Pointer. Nothing in federal law obligates an eligible deferred compensation plan to honor a DRO. Many employers' plans do not include any provision for recognizing DROs.

Some plan sponsors permit an immediate distribution to an alternate payee, believing that this is simpler than keeping an order "open" for many years while waiting for a participant to reach retirement. Other plan sponsors decide that it is inappropriate to pay an alternate payee before the participant becomes entitled to receive a distribution. Whether an eligible deferred compensation plan should permit a PADRO distribution before the participant's severance is a plan design choice.

The rule that precludes a distribution to an alternate payee until the participant's severance (unless the plan expressly specifies otherwise) is strictly construed. [Cf. Dickerson v. Dickerson, 803 F. Supp. 127, 15 Employee Benefits Cas. (BNA) 2630 (E.D. Tenn. 1992); Stott v. Bunge Corp., 800 F. Supp. 567 (E.D. Tenn. 1992)]

Q 13:27   May an eligible deferred compensation plan permit a preretirement distribution to an alternate payee who is or was a same-sex spouse?

Probably not.

An eligible deferred compensation plan may (but need not) permit a distribution to an alternate payee (such as the participant's spouse or former spouse) before the participant's severance from employment (see Q 13:26). To get this exception from a 457(b) plan's distribution restriction, the court order must be a DRO. [I.R.C. § 414(p)(1)(A)(i), (p)(10)–(11)] In defining a DRO, the Code refers to a *spouse*. [I.R.C. § 414(p)(1)(B)]

Although a marriage of a same-sex couple may be recognized under state law, a marriage of a same-sex couple might not be recognized in applying the Code because a general U.S. statute defines the word *spouse* as follows:

> In determining the meaning of any Act of Congress . . . , the word "marriage" means only a legal union between one man and one woman as husband and wife, and the word "spouse" refers only to a person of the opposite sex who is a husband or a wife.

[1 U.S.C. § 7] If this statute is not unconstitutional, an order that provides for a same-sex spouse is not a DRO for federal income tax purposes. [I.R.C. § 414(p)(1)(A)(i). But see U.S. Const. art. IV, § 1, amend. V; Saenz v. Roe, 526 U.S. 489, 119 S. Ct. 1518, 143 L. Ed. 2d 689 (1999); Romer v. Evans, 517 U.S. 620, 116 S. Ct. 1620, 134 L. Ed. 2d 855 1996)]

Further, a DRO may provide for a dependent of the participant. [I.R.C. § 414(p)(1)(B)(i)] If the participant provides (or provided) sufficient support for his or her same-sex spouse, that spouse or former spouse might be a dependent. [See I.R.C. § 152]

Caution. A person is not a participant's dependent if the relationship violates state law. Code Section 152(a)(9) includes as a possible dependent "[a]n individual . . . who . . . has as his principal place of abode the home of the taxpayer and is a member of the taxpayer's household." However, Code Section 152(b)(5) states that "[a]n individual is not a member of the taxpayer's household if . . . the *relationship* between [the] individual and the taxpayer is in violation of local law.

While a majority of U.S. states have statutes that might make adultery, cohabitation, fornication, or sodomy a crime (if such a statute is not unconstitutional), it is unclear whether a prohibition of a particular sex act causes a *relationship* to be in violation of state law. Moreover, the legislative history of this rule suggests that Congress meant to deny a tax deduction only when a taxpayer and his or her dependent failed to act according to law when a lawful way to legitimate a relationship was available to them. [See S. Rep. No. 85-1983 (to accompany Technical Amendments Act of 1958, Pub. L. No. 85-866) (I.R.C. § 152(b)(5) "would make it clear that an individual who is a 'common-law wife' where the applicable state law does not recognize common-law marriages would not qualify as a dependent of the taxpayer"); see also John J. Untermann, 38 T.C. 93 (1962); Turnipseed v. Commissioner, 27 T.C. 758 (1957) (construing 1954 Code before the 1958 revision of I.R.C. § 152(b)(5)); Nicholas v. Commissioner, 1991 T.C.M. (CCH) ¶ 393; Eichbauer v. Commissioner, No. 6987-70SC, T.C.M. 1971-133, 30 T.C.M. (CCH) ¶ 581 (1971)]

Further, in many states it is unclear whether a relationship (if any) between the spouses of a same-sex couple can be said to be unlawful if there is no lawful relation to be had. [See Succession of Bacot, 502 So. 2d 1118 (La. Ct. App.), *writ denied*, 503 So. 2d 466 (La. 1987)] In Vermont, the relationship of same-sex spouses does not violate state law because Vermont law expressly recognizes that relationship.

Practice Pointer. A plan administrator may rely on a participant's written statement that his or her same-sex spouse is the participant's dependent for federal income tax purposes if the plan administrator has formed a good-faith belief that the same-sex spouses' relationship does not violate state law. [See P.L.R. 200108010]

If a plan permits a PADRO to provide for an alternate payee who is the participant's dependent and the participant shows the plan administrator that the divorced or separated same-sex spouse *is* the participant's dependent, an eligible deferred compensation plan may (if it so provides) pay a distribution to such an alternate payee before the participant's severance from employment. [I.R.C. § 414(p)(1)(A)(i), (p)(10), (p)(11)]

Caution. Many employers' plans provide that only a spouse or former spouse can be an alternate payee.

Note. By the time a couple have divorced or separated, it seems unlikely that the dependent spouse still lives in the participant's home.

Death or Survivor Benefits; Loans; Special Provisions

Q 13:28   May a PADRO provide survivor benefits to the alternate payee?

Usually, yes, if the plan has a survivor benefit. For many plans, a PADRO may provide that an alternate payee who is a former spouse of the participant is treated as the participant's surviving spouse for all or some purposes. [See generally I.R.C. § 414(p)(5); Treas. Reg. § 1.401(a)-13(g)(4)] If used, such a provision may have the effect of wholly or partly depriving the participant's current spouse of survivor benefits to which he or she otherwise might become entitled. [See I.R.C. § 414(p)(5)(A); Treas. Reg. § 1.401(a)-13(g)(4)(iii)(B), (C)] But if a former spouse who is treated as a current spouse dies before the participant's benefit commences, the actual current spouse of the participant is treated as the current spouse, except as otherwise provided by another PADRO. [See Treas. Reg. § 1.401(a)-13(g)(4)(iii)(C)]

In the absence of an express statement in an order that the former spouse is treated as the participant's surviving spouse and beneficiary, an alternate payee might not be entitled to any benefit if the participant dies before becoming entitled to receive retirement benefits. [See, e.g., Dugan v. Clinton, No. 86-C-8492, 1987 WL 11640, 8 Employee Benefits Cas. (BNA) 2065 (N.D. Ill. May 22, 1987)] Therefore, if a divorce practitioner is not certain that a PADRO distribution will be paid immediately, he or she should make sure that the court order states that the alternate payee is the surviving spouse and beneficiary to the extent of the amount owing to the alternate payee. While an order may compel the participant to designate his or her former spouse as beneficiary, such an order binds only the participant—not the plan administrator or the plan.

Q 13:29   Can an alternate payee designate a beneficiary?

Usually, no. A lawyer who prepares a court order directed to a deferred compensation plan should carefully inquire into the plan's provisions and the plan's administration procedure.

Even for an ERISA-governed retirement plan that is subject to ERISA's QDRO rule, it is unclear whether such a plan must permit an alternate payee to designate a beneficiary to receive any benefit provided by a QDRO that is not distributed before the alternate payee's death. [Compare Shelstead v. Shelstead, 66 Cal. App. 4th 893, 78 Cal. Rptr. 2d 365, 22 Employee Benefits Cas. (BNA) 1906 (1998), with Treas. Reg. § 1.401(a)-13(g)(4)(iii)(B)]

If a plan allows an alternate payee to designate a beneficiary, the alternate payee's right to designate a beneficiary cannot be any greater than the participant's right to designate a beneficiary. [See Treas. Reg. § 1.401(a)-13(g)(4)(iii)(B)]

Caution. Some plans provide that on an alternate payee's death before payment any undistributed benefit is restored to the participant.

Practice Pointer. Many plans do not permit an alternate payee to designate a beneficiary but permit the alternate payee's executor or personal representative to become entitled to the undistributed benefit. Although a divorce lawyer usually does not become involved in his or her client's estate planning, a divorce lawyer should suggest that an alternate payee revise his or her will.

To find out whether an alternate payee may designate a beneficiary or use other rights instead, the alternate payee and his or her lawyer should carefully read the plan.

Q 13:30 What happens if a participant's account is loaned out and there is no money to pay the alternate payee?

Because a PADRO cannot require a plan to provide additional benefits (see Q 13:9), a PADRO cannot order a payment to an alternate payee that the plan would not be obligated to pay the participant.

Example. Larry, who is age 61 and retired, is a participant in the State of Euphoria Deferred Compensation Plan, a defined contribution plan that permits participant loans. Larry's account is currently valued at $27,000. That $27,000 balance includes $6,000 worth of mutual fund shares and a $21,000 plan loan receivable over five years. The loan was within the plan's limit when made, but Larry has since been an unlucky investor. If a court enters a DRO directing an immediate payment of $13,500 (50 percent of $27,000) to Fiona, Larry's former spouse, the order is not a PADRO because the plan trustee could raise only about $6,000 by selling mutual fund shares and the loan agreement provides for level repayments quarterly over five years. Instead, the court could order an immediate payment of $6,000 and a $7,500 interest in the account (including the loan receivable), with distributions payable only after the plan receives loan repayments.

If a plan account is loaned out, an alternate payee may want to get a court order directing the participant to inform the alternate payee when the participant fails to meet any scheduled loan repayment. An alternate payee should not seek an order directing the plan administrator to inform the alternate payee that the participant has failed to meet a loan repayment, because such an order is not a PADRO (see Q 13:9). For a governmental plan, a domestic relations court's order would not be binding on the plan administrator if state law requires that claims against the state be brought only in a special jurisdiction court. [See, e.g., Pa. Const. art. I, § 11; United Brokers Mortgage Co. v. Fidelity Philadelphia Trust Co., 26 Pa. Commw. 260, 363 A.2d 817 (1976)] For an ERISA-governed plan (even if the plan is not subject to ERISA's QDRO rule), a state court's order is preempted by ERISA. [ERISA § 514(a)]

State Variations

Q 13:31 Have states made special names for a PADRO?

Yes. State law and plan provisions concerning a DRO directed to a state or local government employer's plan may differ from the rules that apply to a

QDRO directed to an ERISA-governed qualified plan. In an effort to communicate to divorce lawyers the possibility of significant differences, some state or local laws create a different label for the form of order that will be accepted by a state or local government employer's plan.

In several states, the state's or commonwealth's deferred compensation plan recognizes a PADRO. In New York, the Deferred Compensation Plan for Employees of the State of New York and Participating Public Jurisdictions recognizes a plan-certified domestic relations order, or PCDRO.

Q 13:32   Must a plan of a Vermont state or local government employer recognize a court order that provides for a party to a civil union?

Usually, yes. The Vermont Constitution and Vermont's civil union law for same-sex couples require a governmental plan to recognize an order relating to parties to a civil union to the same extent that the plan recognizes an order relating to opposite-sex spouses.

Vermont law provides that same-sex couples must have the opportunity to obtain the same benefits and protections afforded by Vermont law to opposite-sex couples. [Vt. Const. ch. I, art. 7; Baker v. State, 744 A.2d 864 (Vt. 1999)] Under the Vermont statute, the same-sex parties to a civil union have the same benefits, protections, and responsibilities as Vermont law provides for spouses in any marriage. [Vt. Stat. Ann. tit. 15, §§ 1201(2), 1204(a)] This rule applies whether the source of law is a statute, administrative regulation, court rule, policy, common law, or any other source of civil law. [Vt. Stat. Ann. tit. 15, § 1204(a)] Further, a party to a civil union is included in any definition or use of the terms *spouse* and *dependent* as those terms are used in any Vermont law. [Vt. Stat. Ann. tit. 15, § 1204(b)] A party to a civil union is responsible for the support of the other party "to the same degree and in the same manner as prescribed under law for married persons." [Vt. Stat. Ann. tit. 15, § 1204(c)] Likewise, "[t]he law of domestic relations, including annulment, separation and divorce, child custody and support, and property division and maintenance shall apply to parties to a civil union." [Vt. Stat. Ann. tit. 15, § 1204(d)] Vermont's family court has jurisdiction over all proceedings relating to the dissolution of civil unions, and the dissolution of a civil union is according to the same laws and procedures that govern the dissolution of a marriage. [Vt. Stat. Ann. tit. 4, § 454(17); Vt. Stat. Ann. tit. 15, § 1206] Although the Vermont legislature adopted the term of art, *civil union*, and avoided the common word, *marriage*, in this author's view a Vermont civil union is a marriage for all Vermont law purposes.

Because a deferred compensation plan need not follow the federal law QDRO rules, Vermont law alone governs whether an order directed to a Vermont governmental plan is a PADRO. For orders directed to governmental plans, Vermont law defines an alternate payee not as a spouse or dependent but simply as "any individual who is recognized by a DRO as having a right to receive all, or a portion of, another individual's payment rights in the retirement system." [Vt. Stat. Ann. tit. 3, §§ 468, 476a; Vt. Stat. Ann. tit. 4, § 451; Vt. Stat. Ann. tit. 16, §§ 1941, 1946b; Vt. Stat. Ann. tit. 24, §§ 5060, 5066a]

Because Vermont's civil union statute provides that the general law of domestic relations applies to parties to a civil union, an alternate payee (for governmental plan purposes) can include a party (or former party) to a civil union.

Even if a PADRO is effective to permit a distribution to a participant's same-sex spouse, any such PADRO distribution is not treated as a deemed QDRO and therefore is treated as a distribution to the participant for federal income tax purposes. Further, a PADRO distribution paid to a participant's same-sex spouse cannot be rolled over for federal income tax purposes. Because the same-sex alternate payee is treated as a nonspouse for federal income tax purposes, the plan administrator or payor must withhold from the PADRO distribution as if the participant were the distributee. (See Q 13:45.) This overview of the federal income tax treatment of a PADRO distribution to a same-sex spouse alternate payee assumes that the federal law definitions of marriage and spouse are not unconstitutional.

Vermont income tax "appl[ies] to parties to a civil union and surviving parties to a civil union as if federal income tax law recognized a civil union in the same manner as Vermont law." [Vt. Stat. Ann. tit. 32, § 5812] Thus, a PADRO distribution to a same-sex spouse alternate payee will be the participant's income for federal income tax purposes but the alternate payee's income for Vermont income tax purposes. While this tax principle seems simple enough, it is unclear how Vermont will apply it to a rollover that is not recognized for federal income tax purposes but might be recognized for Vermont income tax purposes.

Deciding Whether an Order Is a PADRO

Q 13:33   Who decides whether an order is a PADRO?

The plan administrator decides whether an order is a PADRO. In some cases, the plan administrator may permit a service provider to perform this function, subject to the plan administrator's oversight.

Q 13:34   Who is the plan administrator?

For a governmental plan, state law provides what agency or which official serves as the plan administrator. For a nongovernmental plan, usually the plan specifies that the employer is the plan administrator. In the unusual situation in which the plan document and state law fail to name a plan administrator, the Code presumes that the employer is the plan administrator. [I.R.C. § 414(g)(2)(A); Treas. Reg. § 1.414(g)-1(b)(1)]

Q 13:35   Why is it desirable for a plan administrator to adopt a written procedure?

A prudent plan administrator may desire to use a written procedure to demonstrate to divorcing parties and their lawyers the correctness of the plan administrator's decisions. Further, an absence of a written procedure might make it difficult for a court to defer to a plan administrator's finding.

Further, a plan administrator might be liable to a disappointed alternate payee or person who sought to become an alternate payee if efforts to pursue a PADRO were frustrated by the plan administrator's lack of procedures. [See, e.g., Stewart v. Thorpe Holding Co. Profit Sharing Plan, 207 F.3d 1143 (9th Cir. 2000)]

Q 13:36   Is deciding whether an order is a PADRO a fiduciary activity?

It depends on whether ERISA or state law applies, and, if state law applies, which state's law governs the plan.

For an ERISA-governed deferred compensation plan, in deciding whether an order is a PADRO an employer is not governed by ERISA's fiduciary responsibility provisions. [ERISA § 401(a)(1)] Further, because ERISA preempts state law, any state law that otherwise might impose a fiduciary responsibility does not apply. [ERISA § 514]

For a church plan, in deciding whether an order is a PADRO an employer usually is subject only to a common contract duty of good faith and fair dealing.

Many governmental plan administrators assume—usually mistakenly—that deciding whether an order is a PADRO is a fiduciary activity. Most state laws do not provide such a fiduciary duty, and many state laws are ambiguous on this point. However, for an eligible deferred compensation plan of a New York state or local government employer, in finding whether an order is a PADRO the employer is governed by a state law fiduciary duty. [N.Y. Comp. Codes R. & Regs. tit 9, § 9001 et seq.]

Q 13:37   Should a plan administrator retain a lawyer to advise it concerning whether an order is a PADRO?

Maybe. Although deciding whether an order is a PADRO might not be a fiduciary activity (see Q 13:36), a plan administrator nonetheless should act in good faith and with prudence in finding whether an order is a PADRO. It is doubtful whether a nonlawyer may be presumed to possess expert skill in making any legal determination. Therefore, it might be appropriate for the plan administrator to obtain expert legal advice. In addition, an administrator that reasonably relies on written legal advice usually is protected against an allegation of breach of duty.

On the other hand, some plan administrators believe that nonlawyers are equally or even better prepared to find whether an order is a PADRO. If a plan administrator is permitted to rely on a court's findings about family law issues, the remaining issues involve plan administration. For understanding the relevant deferred compensation plan, a nonlawyer might know as much as a lawyer. And when considering whether an order is workable, a nonlawyer might have more practical experience than some lawyers.

Plan Administration Procedures

Q 13:38 How does a plan administrator decide whether an order is a PADRO?

A plan administrator should establish reasonable procedures for (1) deciding whether an order submitted to the plan administrator is a PADRO, and (2) administering any distribution required under a PADRO.

A plan administrator might want to include in the written procedure a provision that, during the time the plan administrator evaluates an order proposed as a PADRO, the participant continues to have any investment direction rights he or she ordinarily would have. [See Schoonmaker v. Employee Savings Plan of Amoco Corp., 987 F.2d 410 (7th Cir. 1993)]

For plans governed by ERISA's QDRO rule, the Department of Labor (DOL) has expressed its view that a plan administrator need not evaluate the correctness of a state court's determination that a person is or was a spouse under state domestic relations law. [DOL Adv. Op. 92-17A. But see ERISA § 206(d)(3)] The DOL's view does not apply to a deferred compensation plan. Nonetheless, the usual practice of most plan administrators is to accept a court's statement that a person is or was a spouse, child, or other dependent of the participant unless the plan administrator has actual knowledge to the contrary.

Practice Pointer. It is less clear what a plan administrator should do when a court order is internally inconsistent. For example, if a court order declares a void marriage annulled but also declares that one of the parties to the nonmarriage is a former spouse, one of those findings cannot be correct. The better practice may be to require the claimant who submitted the order to the plan administrator to request that the court correct its order.

Q 13:39 Should a plan administrator furnish confidential information to a prospective alternate payee?

No, a plan administrator should not disclose a participant's confidential information until it receives the participant's written consent or an appropriate subpoena or other court order that at least binds the participant. Conversely, a plan administrator has no duty to a prospective alternate payee other than the duty (if any) to decide whether an order submitted to the plan administrator is a PADRO. A prudent plan administrator will adopt procedures that do not require it to disclose information without adequate protection.

Q 13:40 May a plan administrator or service provider give a participant or alternate payee legal advice about a DRO?

No. For an employee of a plan administrator or service provider who is not a lawyer, giving legal advice is the unauthorized practice of law, which is a crime or offense in every U.S. state. A plan administrator might have a duty to furnish plan documents, including a plan administration procedure, on a proper request. But the plan administrator has no duty to provide advice.

If an employee of a plan administrator or service provider is a lawyer, he or she must not give legal advice to a person who is not his or her client. [Restatement of the Law Governing Lawyers §§ 98–103 (2001); American Bar Ass'n, Model Rules of Prof'l Conduct R. 1.7 (2003)] If a participant, alternate payee, or claimant has a lawyer, another lawyer (including an employee of a plan administrator or service provider) must talk only with the participant's, alternate payee's, or claimant's lawyer. [American Bar Ass'n, Model Rules of Prof'l Conduct R. 4.2 (2003); Restatement of the Law Governing Lawyers § 99 (2001); see also J. Leubsdorf, "Communicating with Another Lawyer's Client: The Lawyer's Veto and the Client's Interest," 127 *U. Pa. L. Rev.* 683 (1979)] If a participant, alternate payee, or claimant does not have a lawyer, a lawyer employed by a plan administrator or service provider must not give that person any advice. [American Bar Ass'n, Model Rules of Prof'l Conduct R. 1.7, 4.3 (2003)] The lawyer may (but is not required to) urge the person to engage a lawyer.

A lawyer or nonlawyer employed by a plan administrator or service provider may give information to the participant's, alternate payee's, or claimant's lawyer. At least one advisory opinion recognizes that "[when] it furthers the interest of the [plan administrator] for [its lawyer] to assist representatives of [participants] or their spouses in the preparation of court orders acceptable to the [plan administrator]," the lawyer may (but is not obligated to) do so. [N.Y. County Ethics Op. 713 (1996)] If an employee of a plan administrator or service provider gives a lawyer information, the employee should remind the lawyer that any information provided is not legal advice.

Even when talking with a participant's or proposed alternate payee's lawyer, a plan administrator or service provider should caution the lawyer not to rely on the administrator's or provider's assistance. At least one court held that a lawyer could pursue a state law claim (such as, the tort of negligent communication) against a nonlawyer that gave legal advice to the divorce lawyer. [Templeman v. Dahlgren, 1990 WL 117451, 12 Employee Benefits Cas. (BNA) 2275 (D. Or. July 31, 1990); see generally Restatement of the Law Governing Lawyers § 51 (2001); Restatement (Second) of Torts § 552 (1957)]

Practice Pointer. Some practitioners recommend that if a plan administrator or service provider employee has a conversation with only one of the two lawyers engaged in a domestic relations matter, the employee confirms the conversation in an evenhanded letter delivered to both lawyers. Others suggest that information should be limited to furnishing (to whichever lawyer asks) a model PADRO, with no more than a written explanation of the assumptions used in drafting that model PADRO. In any communication to divorce lawyers, a plan administrator or service provider should avoid suggesting that any information is for the benefit of either of the divorcing parties.

Q 13:41   Should a plan administrator provide a model PADRO?

Whether a plan administrator should provide a model PADRO turns on whether the plan administrator's convenience in avoiding inadequate court orders outweighs its concern about potential liability to divorce lawyers (see Q 13:40).

Although there is no requirement that anyone do so, some plan administrators find it convenient to make available a model PADRO. Because many divorce lawyers are unfamiliar with PADRO rules or deferred compensation plan provisions, it might be convenient to make available a model PADRO to avoid the expense of rejecting defective court orders and then reconsidering amended orders.

If a plan administrator makes available a model PADRO, it should furnish the model PADRO only to a duly licensed lawyer. Because of the significant possibility that a nonlawyer might perceive a model PADRO as legal advice, furnishing it may constitute the unauthorized practice of law, which is a crime or offense in every U.S. state. Worse, if an individual who has no lawyer relies on a model PADRO that is not suitable to that person's needs and circumstances and the plan administrator knew or should have known that the individual might rely on the model PADRO as suitable for his or her use, the plan administrator might be responsible to the individual. [Restatement (Second) of Torts § 552] However, sovereign immunity, governmental immunity, or public officer immunity might protect a governmental plan administrator from liability for money damages.

Q 13:42   May a plan charge a special fee for processing an order?

Yes. In handling any claims under a plan (including deciding whether an order is or is not a PADRO), a plan administrator must make a correct decision so the plan may avoid making any improper distribution (or improperly reducing the participant's benefit) or failing to make a proper distribution. Therefore, the expense (such as the fees of a lawyer advising the plan administrator) incurred in determining whether an order is a PADRO is a plan administration expense chargeable against plan assets. Following this, a plan may provide that the prudent expense incurred in deciding whether an order is a PADRO is an expense chargeable to the participant's accrued benefit or account under the plan. [Cf. DOL Field Assistance Bulletin 2003-3 (May 19, 2003)]

Q 13:43   Does a plan administrator have a duty to question a fraudulent divorce?

Maybe. When faced with circumstances that strongly suggest the "divorcing" parties' perjury, a plan administrator may inquire about a court order to consider whether it is a DRO; however, it is unclear whether a plan administrator must do so.

A DOL ERISA advisory opinion described a situation in which the plan administrator noticed information that suggested fraudulent DROs. The plan administrator received several orders within a very short period, including several from the same lawyer. Each of these orders identically provided for an assignment to an alternate payee of all of the participant's benefit in the defined contribution plans but made no division of any pension plan benefit. In each of the orders, the alternate payee and participant were shown as having the same address. The plan administrator was aware of recent circulation of a pamphlet entitled "Retirement Liberation Handbook." That pamphlet advocated, as a method of obtaining a retirement plan distribution before the participant's separation from service, that a participant and his or her spouse obtain a "divorce" for the sole purpose of entering a "QDRO." Thereafter, the participant and his or her spouse might "remarry." After reading the pamphlet, the plan administrator found that several orders had significant similarities to the format promoted by the pamphlet, including an error repeated consistently in most of the orders. Further, all of the questioned orders related to employees who resided in the same geographic area, were in related work groups, and had common atypical characteristics, including prompt "remarriage" and continued use of employer-provided fringe benefits for spouses. [DOL Adv. Op. 99-13A]

Because information suggesting that an order was fraudulently obtained calls into question whether the order was issued under state domestic relations law, a plan administrator's duty to determine whether an order submitted to it is a DRO may require it to make some effort to avoid acquiescing in an obvious fraud. Although a plan administrator might prefer to rely on the ostensible order, a plan administrator may possess more information than the court had before it.

When the plan involved is a defined contribution plan and the plan does not require that a participant complete a forfeiture condition to become entitled to deferred compensation, it might seem strange to take action when the perjuring participant would harm no plan account but his or her own. Nevertheless, to protect the plan's tax treatment a plan administrator must act to avoid a distribution or payment that calls into question the plan provisions that support the plan's tax deferral. [I.R.C. § 457(b), (f)] Further, a governmental plan administrator must act according to applicable state law and for the exclusive purpose of providing deferred compensation plan benefits to participants and their beneficiaries. [I.R.C. § 457(g)]

If the state court finds that the "divorcing" parties committed perjury, a plan administrator should consider whether it would be productive (or more wasteful) for the plan to sue the participant and spouse for restoration of the expenses incurred in handling the fraud.

A lawyer who observes a divorce lawyer's participation in a fraudulent "divorce" may have an obligation to report that lawyer to the state supreme court or other body that has disciplinary authority over the divorce lawyer. [American Bar Ass'n Model Rules of Prof'l Conduct, Rule 8.3 (2003)] In most cases, however, the lawyer's observation will be a client confidence, which the lawyer is prohibited from disclosing without his or her own client's consent. [American Bar Ass'n, Model Rules of Prof'l Conduct R. 1.6 (2003)] (See Q 13:71.)

Finally, the perjurers may face criminal penalties and imprisonment. Because perjury in a court proceeding is (in most states) a felony, each of the "divorcing" parties may be subject to a substantial fine or imprisonment. [See, e.g., 18 Pa. Cons. Stat. Ann. § 4902; see generally Model Penal Code § 241.1]

Tax Treatment of a Deemed QDRO

Q 13:44   What is a deemed QDRO?

A deemed QDRO is a DRO directed to a governmental plan—including a state or local government employer's eligible deferred compensation plan—that for federal income tax purposes is treated as a QDRO.

The Code provides that Code Section 414(p) "shall not apply to any plan to which section 401(a)(13) does not apply." [I.R.C. § 414(p)(9)] Because the Section 401(a)(13) anti-alienation condition does not apply to an eligible or ineligible deferred compensation plan, the QDRO rule does not apply to such a plan.

Instead, the Code provides that a distribution from an eligible deferred compensation plan is treated as made "pursuant to" a QDRO if it is made following an order that the Code defines as a DRO. [I.R.C. § 414(p)(11)]

Q 13:45   What is the tax treatment of a deemed QDRO?

If an order is a deemed QDRO, an alternate payee who is the spouse or former spouse of the participant is treated as a distributee for a distribution paid to him or her under the deemed QDRO. [I.R.C. § 402(e)(1)(A)] The spouse or former spouse is taxed even if the court order states that the participant will be liable for the tax. [Clawson v. Commissioner, 72 T.C.M. (CCH) ¶ 814 (1996)]

A distribution to a nonspouse alternate payee, even if it is made following a deemed QDRO, is taxed to the participant. [IRS Notice 89-25, 1989-1 C.B. 662]

Q 13:46   May an alternate payee roll over a PADRO distribution?

If a spouse alternate payee is treated as a distributee (see Q 13:45), he or she may make a rollover (including a direct rollover) to an individual retirement account or annuity (IRA) or to another eligible retirement plan. [I.R.C. § 402(c)(1), (e)(1)(B)]

A nonspouse alternate payee is not treated as a distributee and cannot make a rollover. [I.R.C. § 402(c), (d)(4)(J), (e)(1)(A); IRS Notice 89-25, Q&A-4, 1989-1 C.B. 662]

Q 13:47 Must a plan administrator furnish a rollover notice to an alternate payee?

Usually, yes, for a spouse alternate payee; no, for a nonspouse alternate payee.

If a distribution made following a deemed QDRO is an eligible rollover distribution (see Q 2:242), the plan administrator must deliver to the distributee, within a reasonable time (at least 30 days) before paying the distribution, a written explanation of the plan's direct rollover provisions and the tax withholding that applies if the distributee does not elect a direct rollover. [I.R.C. § 402(f)(1)]

If a spouse alternate payee wants to make a direct rollover (and thereby avoid mandatory federal income tax withholding), he or she should make sure the court order states the required explanation together with the alternate payee's acknowledgment that he or she received that explanation and waives the 30 days' time that the plan administrator or payor must give him or her to consider whether to make a rollover. [Temp. Treas. Reg. § 1.402(c)-2T, Q&A-13; IRS Notice 93-26, 1993-1 C.B. 308]

Q 13:48 May an alternate payee roll over a PADRO distribution?

If (because an order is a deemed QDRO) a spouse alternate payee is treated as a distributee (see Q 13:45) and the form of a distribution is an eligible rollover distribution, he or she may make a rollover (including a direct rollover) to an eligible retirement plan. [I.R.C. § 402(c), (e)(1)(B)]

An *eligible retirement plan* refers to:

1. An individual retirement account or annuity (IRA);
2. A Section 401(a) qualified plan (including such a plan funded by annuity contracts);
3. A Section 403(b) annuity contract or custodial account; and
4. An eligible deferred compensation plan maintained by a state or local government employer.

[I.R.C. § 402(c)(8)(B)]

A nonspouse alternate payee is not treated as a distributee and cannot make a rollover. [I.R.C. § 402(c), (d)(4)(J), (e)(1)(A); IRS Notice 89-25, Q&A 4, 1989-1 C.B. 662]

Q 13:49 Can a participant use a DRO to obtain QDRO tax treatment for a distribution already made?

No. The tax rule that treats a spouse alternate payee as the distributee for federal income tax purposes applies only if the distribution is made "pursuant to" a QDRO or deemed QDRO. If a distribution is made first and a court order "ratifies" the distribution already made, QDRO tax treatment does not apply. [Karem v. Commissioner, 100 T.C. 521, 16 Employee Benefits Cas. (BNA) 2728, Tax Ct. Rep. (CCH) ¶ 49,091 (1993)]

Q 13:50   What is the federal income tax treatment of life insurance protection held by an alternate payee?

If a participant has a life insurance contract as part of his or her deferred compensation plan account, the participant's separated or former spouse might want to obtain rights to a portion of that contract. Even if a PADRO does not permit the alternate payee to designate a beneficiary, usually a PADRO may provide that the alternate payee's benefit becomes payable to his or her estate (see Q 13:29).

If a spouse or former spouse obtains rights as an alternate payee under a PADRO that is a deemed QDRO, that alternate payee "shall be treated as the distributee of any distribution or payment made to the alternate payee under [the] qualified domestic relations order." [I.R.C. § 402(e)(1)(A)] Because this provision is not limited to a payment and includes "any distribution," it should be construed literally to refer to *any* distribution, including a deemed distribution, as long as it is made *under* the deemed QDRO. If a court order awards the alternate payee the right to have life insurance protection on the participant's life, the deemed distribution arising from that right is made under the court order. Further, the general income tax principle that income follows a person's property or rights suggests that an alternate payee should be treated as the distributee of the deemed distribution that arises from the life insurance protection.

> **Example.** Hubert and Wendy divorced in 2001. Hubert's deferred compensation plan account included mutual fund shares and a life insurance contract. The life insurance contract had a "face amount" death benefit of $100,000, which is not scheduled to increase. The policy year is the calendar year.

> The plan does not permit payment to an alternate payee before the participant's severance. Hubert is 35 years old, and he does not intend to leave work until he reaches age 55. Therefore, unless Hubert quits his job or is fired, Wendy might be required to wait 20 years or more for a PADRO to provide a payment.

> Wendy obtained a court order that granted her a half interest in all rights (to the fullest extent permitted under the plan), including the life insurance contract, measured as of December 31, 2001, with 8 percent interest on the mutual fund's value and 6 percent interest on the life insurance cash value after that date. The court order provides that any amount not paid to Wendy is payable to her executor.

> The court order restrains Hubert from taking any action to cancel, lapse, or surrender the life insurance contract, and commands him to continue his

contributions in an amount sufficient to meet the scheduled premium of the life insurance contract. The order expressly states that the last two provisions bind only Hubert, and do not affect the plan administrator.

On January 2, 2002, the plan administrator made a written determination that the court order is a PADRO. On December 31, 2001, the life insurance contract's face amount death benefit was $100,000 and its cash value was $3,000. On January 1, 2002, Hubert was age 35. On December 31, 2002, the life insurance contract's face amount death benefit was $100,000 and its cash value was $3,157.

Because it is unclear whether the "net amount at risk" measurement of life insurance protection refers to the insurer's risk or the insured's benefit, there are at least two alternative methods of figuring each individual's deemed distribution.

If "net amount at risk" refers to the insurer's risk, the following chart illustrates each individual's federal income tax treatment of the life insurance protection during 2002:

	Total Policy	Hubert's "Half"	Wendy's "Half"
Death benefit	$100,000	$50,000	$50,000
Cash value	$3,157		
"Net amount at risk"	$96,843	$48,421.50	$48,421.50
"Cost" per $1	× 0.00321	× 0.00321	× 0.00321
Deemed distribution	$310.87	$155.43	$155.43
Marginal tax rate		× 0.28	× 0.28
Federal income tax		$43.52	$43.52

If "net amount at risk" refers to the insured's benefit, the following chart illustrates each individual's federal income tax treatment of the life insurance protection during 2002:

	Total Policy	Hubert's "Half"	Wendy's "Half"
Death benefit	$100,000	$50,000	$50,000
Cash value	$3,157	$1,567	$1,590
"Net amount at risk"	$96,843	$48,433	$48,410
"Cost" per $1	× 0.00321	× 0.00321	× 0.00321
Deemed distribution	$310.87	$155.47	$155.40
Marginal tax rate		× 0.28	× 0.28
Federal income tax		$43.53	$43.51

In the second table, Wendy's deemed distribution is less than Hubert's because Wendy owns a greater share of the contract's cash value and, therefore, arguably has less economic benefit from life insurance protection.

The cost of life insurance protection is greater with each year of older age the insured attains. The cost of life insurance for a 55-year-old is much greater than for a 35-year-old. Thus, with either measurement, over 20 years Wendy might pay almost $3,000 in federal income tax if the life insurance contract remains in force and Hubert does not die.

Because of the tax cost, an alternate payee who has a choice should negotiate for a division that does not include a death benefit unless the alternate payee has an economic need for protection in the event of the participant's death. However, life insurance might be useful if the participant's alimony, child support, and other obligations to the alternate payee continue for a period of years and do not end on the participant's death.

If an alternate payee prefers a division that does not include a death benefit, he or she should consider whether the continuing term life insurance aspect of a life insurance policy has any value. Courts differ about whether it is possible to value life insurance. In California, appeals courts for three different districts reached three different conclusions about how to value life insurance. [In re Marriage of Lorenz, 146 Cal. App. 3d 464 (1983) (term life insurance impossible to value); In re Marriage of Gonzalez, 168 Cal. App. 3d 1021 (1985) (term life insurance must be valued); In re Estate of Logan, 191 Cal. App. 3d 319 (1987) (term life insurance not to be valued unless the insured has become uninsurable)]

Q 13:51 What is the tax treatment of an order that is not a deemed QDRO?

If a plan makes a payment following an order that is not a deemed QDRO but is incident to divorce, the payment is not the participant's income and instead is the former spouse's income. (See Q 13:54.)

If an eligible deferred compensation plan makes a payment following an order that is not a deemed QDRO and is not incident to divorce, several undesirable tax consequences regarding the participant, the payee, and the plan follow.

Participant consequences. Because the payee is not treated as a distributee, the participant will be taxed on the amount paid to the nonparticipant. [I.R.C. § 402(e)(1)(A); Karem v. Commissioner, 100 T.C. 521, 16 Employee Benefits Cas. (BNA) 2728, Tax Ct. Rep. (CCH) ¶ 49,091 (1993). Cf. Rev. Rul. 2002-22, 2002-19 I.R.B. 849]

If the participant has not yet reached age 59½, the 10 percent penalty tax on an early distribution from the portion of the plan account that reflects amounts contributed as a rollover from an eligible retirement plan other than a 457(b) plan will apply. [I.R.C. § 72(t)(2)(C)]

Payee consequence. Because the payee is *not* treated as a distributee, such a payee cannot make a rollover to an IRA or to a retirement plan. [I.R.C. § 402(c)(1), (e)(1)(B)]

Plan consequences. A payment to a nonparticipant—under an order that is not a deemed QDRO—before the participant has a distributable event (such as severance from employment) might be a breach of the plan's provision that precludes a distribution before the participant's severance from employment or other distributable event. [I.R.C. § 457(d)(1)(A)(ii)]

For a state or local government employer's plan, a payment to a nonparticipant—under an order that is not a deemed QDRO—before the participant has a distributable event (such as severance from employment) might be a breach of the plan's exclusive benefit provision. [I.R.C. § 457(g)(1); see Rev. Rul. 91-8, 1991-1 C.B. 281; Rev. Rul. 80-27, 1980-1 C.B. 85; see, e.g., Francis v. United Technologies Corp., 458 F. Supp. 84 (N.D. Cal. 1978)]

Q 13:52   May a payee assert that an order was not a deemed QDRO for tax purposes?

Probably not. A plan's definition of a PADRO usually is more strict than the Code's definition of a deemed QDRO. Following this, a payee's acquiescence (without appeal or a petition for a stay) in what was proposed to the court as a PADRO may estop him or her from taking a contrary position in his or her federal income tax return (as long as the payee had a due process opportunity to seek a decision that the order was not a PADRO). This may be so even if all the state court and plan administrator decisions were wrong as a matter of law. [See generally Brotman v. Commissioner, 105 T.C. 141, 19 Employee Benefits Cas. (BNA) 1850, Tax Ct. Rep. (CCH) ¶ 50,860, Pens. Plan Guide (CCH) ¶ 23,912U, Tax Ct. Rep. Dec. (RIA) 105.12 (1995)] However, when an underlying case litigated only whether an order was a QDRO, collateral estoppel would not preclude a taxpayer from litigating the issue of the qualified status of the plan. [Brotman v. Commissioner, 105 T.C. 141, 19 Employee Benefits Cas. (BNA) 1850, Tax Ct. Rep. (CCH) ¶ 50,860, Pens. Plan Guide (CCH) ¶ 23,912U, Tax Ct. Rep. Dec. (RIA) 105.12 (1995)] Thus, regarding a nongovernmental plan a payee might assert that deemed QDRO tax treatment does not apply because the plan was not an eligible plan.

Q 13:53   Is a same-sex spouse taxed in the same way as an opposite-sex spouse?

Probably not. Even if a PADRO is effective to permit a distribution to a participant's same-sex spouse, such a PADRO might not shift federal income tax to the alternate payee.

Although a marriage of a same-sex couple may be recognized under state law or the governmental plan, a marriage of a same-sex couple might not be recognized in applying the Code because a general U.S. statute defines the word *spouse* as follows:

> In determining the meaning of any Act of Congress . . ., the word "marriage" means only a legal union between one man and one

woman as husband and wife, and the word "spouse" refers only to a person of the opposite sex who is a husband or a wife.

[1 U.S.C. § 7]

If this statute is not unconstitutional, a PADRO that provides for a same-sex spouse is not a DRO for federal income tax purposes. [I.R.C. § 414(p)(1)(B). But see U.S. Const. art. IV, § 1, amend. V; Saenz v. Roe, 526 U.S. 489, 119 S. Ct. 1518, 143 L. Ed. 2d 689 (1999); Romer v. Evans, 517 U.S. 620, 116 S. Ct. 1620, 134 L. Ed. 2d 855 (1996)]

Only an alternate payee who is the participant's spouse or former spouse (as the United States Code defines that term) is treated as a distributee. Any other distribution is treated as a distribution to the participant. Further, a PADRO distribution paid to an alternate payee who is not the participant's spouse or former spouse (as the United States Code defines a spouse) cannot be rolled over. [I.R.C. § 402(c), (d)(4)(J), (e)(1)(A); IRS Notice 89-25, Q&A-4, 1989-1 C.B. 662]

If the alternate payee is not a spouse for federal income tax purposes, the plan administrator or payer must "withhold from the [PADRO] distribution as if the . . . participant were the payee . . . ." [IRS Notice 89-25, Q&A-3, 1989-1 C.B. 662] The participant may make his or her withholding certificate on IRS Form W-4P if the plan is a governmental plan, or on IRS Form W-4 for a distribution from a nongovernmental plan.

Q 13:54   What is the federal income tax treatment of a distribution that is incident to a participant's divorce?

If a distribution to a participant's spouse or former spouse is paid or made available following a court order (including an order's reference to a property settlement agreement) and incident to a participant's divorce, the former spouse (and not the participant) must include in his or her income the amount paid or made available. [I.R.C. § 1041; Temp. Treas. Reg. § 1.1041-1T; Rev. Rul. 2002-22, 2002-19 I.R.B. 849; see also Meisner v. United States, 133 F.3d 654 (8th Cir. 1998); Kenfield v. United States, 133 F.3d 654 (10th Cir. 1986); Hempt Bros., Inc. v. United States, 490 F.2d 1172 (3d Cir.), *cert. denied*, 419 U.S. 826 (1974); Rubin v. Commissioner, 429 F.2d 650 (2d Cir. 1970); Cofield v. Koehler, 207 F. Supp. 73 (D. Kan. 1962); Balding v. Commissioner, 98 T.C. 368 (1992); Schulze v. Commissioner, T.C.M. 1983-263 (1983)]

According to the Treasury Department, this income-shifting rule does not apply if at the time of the transfer to the former spouse, the participant's right to deferred compensation is not yet nonforfeitable or otherwise is subject to a substantial contingency. [Rev. Rul. 2002-22, 2002-19 I.R.B. 849; see Kochansky v. Commissioner, 92 F.3d 957 (9th Cir. 1996)]

A transition rule might apply to a distribution made following a property settlement agreement or court order made before November 9, 2002. According to the Treasury Department, if such an agreement or order specifically states that the participant must report gross income "attributable to the transferred interest," the deferred compensation paid or made available to the participant's former spouse is the participant's income. Likewise, if a participant has returned as his or her income an amount paid or made available to the participant's former spouse, the income so reported is the participant's income. [Rev. Rul. 2002-22, 2002-19 I.R.B. 849]

Tax Treatment of a PADRO Distribution from an Ineligible Plan

Q 13:55   When does income arise from deferred compensation under an ineligible plan?

Deferred compensation under an ineligible plan is "included in the gross income of the participant or beneficiary for the [first] taxable year in which there is no substantial risk of forfeiture of the rights to such compensation." [I.R.C. § 457(f)(1)(A)]

Q 13:56   What is the tax treatment of a PADRO distribution from an ineligible plan?

It is unclear whether the participant or the alternate payee counts as income the payments made to an alternate payee under a PADRO.

Some tax lawyers believe that a PADRO distribution that is not governed by Code Section 414(p) (see Q 13:44) or Revenue Ruling 2002-22 (see Q 13:54) may nonetheless result in a tax-free transfer incident to divorce, and that following such a transfer each payment to the alternate payee is the alternate payee's income. [See I.R.C. § 1041(a); Temp. Treas. Reg. § 1.1041-1T; Balding v. Commissioner, 98 T.C. 368 (1992)] So far, the IRS has rejected that view. [P.L.R. 9340032, 9024075. See generally Lucas v. Earl, 281 U.S. 111 (1930)] The 1990 and 1993 rulings are somewhat inconsistent with earlier IRS positions. [See Rev. Rul. 87-112, 1987-2 C.B. 207; P.L.R. 8813023, disagreed with in Balding v. Commissioner, 98 T.C. 368 (1992). See generally United States v. Davis, 370 U.S. 65 (1962)] The IRS's rulings and positions have been criticized as suffering from less than entire consistency. [D.A. Geier, "Form, Substance, and Section 1041," 60 *Tax Notes* 519 (July 26, 1993); see also D.A. Geier, "Interpreting Tax Legislation: The Role of Purpose," 2 *Fla. Tax Rev.* 492 (1995)] The Treasury Department's ruling providing transfer-incident-to-divorce treatment for deferred compensation does not apply "to the extent [that] such . . . rights are unvested [or] are subject to substantial contingencies . . . at the time of [the] transfer[.]" [See Kochansky v. Commissioner, 92 F.3d 957 (9th Cir. 1996); Rev. Rul. 2002-22, 2002-19 I.R.B. 849]

Some lawyers suggest that a payment made following a bona fide PADRO should be treated as a transfer incident to divorce and not under the assignment-of-income doctrine. Because a divorce settlement is a division of marital property made for a legitimate purpose and is not a voluntary transfer susceptible of manipulation for tax avoidance purposes, the assignment-of-income doctrine should not apply. [Kenfield v. United States, 783 F.2d 966 (10th Cir. 1986); Schulze v. Commissioner, 46 T.C.M. (CCH) ¶ 143 (1983)] At least one court has observed that "resort to 'common law' doctrines of taxation . . . may occasionally be useful in connection with 'transactions heavily freighted with tax motives' which cannot be satisfactorily handled in other ways . . ., but they have no place where, as here, there is a statutory provision adequate to deal with the problem presented." [Rubin v. Commissioner, 429 F.2d 650, 894–95 (2d Cir. 1970)] Almost all tax scholars and practitioners who have published on this point say that the assignment-of-income doctrine should not override the statutory rule for transfers incident to divorce. [See, e.g., S. Dods, "*Kochansky v. Commissioner*: The Assignment of Income Doctrine, Community Property Law, and I.R.C. § 1041," 72 *Wash. L. Rev.* 873 (1997); C.S. McCaffrey & M.G. Salten, *Structuring the Tax Consequences of Marriage and Divorce* § 604 (1995); D.A. Geier, "Form, Substance, and Section 1041," 60 *Tax Notes* 519 (July 26, 1993); M.J.R. Hoffman & K.N. Orbach, "Assignment of Income and Divorce," 23 *Tax Adviser* 601 (1992); J.A. Miller, "Federal Income Taxation and Community Property Law: The Case for Divorce," 44 *Sw. L.J.* 1087, 1121–30 (1990); W.H. Nunnallee, "The Assignment of Income Doctrine as Applied to Section 1041 Divorce Transfers: How the Service Got It Wrong," 68 *Or. L. Rev.* 615 (1989); M. Asimow, "The Assault on Tax-Free Divorce: Carryover Basis and Assignment of Income," 44 *Tax L. Rev.* 65, 84–112 (1988); R.L. Hjorth, "Divorce, Taxes, and the 1984 Tax Reform Act: An Inadequate Response to an Old Problem," 61 *Wash. L. Rev.* 151, 165–66 n.68 (1986); N.J. Brown, Comment, "Domestic Relations Tax Reform," 20 *Gonz. L. Rev.* 251, 261–62 (1985); W.P. Kean, Note, "Federal Income Tax Consequences of Dissolving the Marital Community Upon Divorce," 44 *La. L. Rev.* 1823, 1829 n.43 (1984). But see L. Gabinet, "Section 1041: The High Price of Quick Fix Reform in Taxation of Interspousal Transfers," 5 *Am. J. Tax Pol'y* 13, 21–26 (1986)]

If a participant and his or her spouse resided in a community property state (see Q 5:26) when the deferred compensation was earned, the participant may argue that the rights or property awarded to the spouse alternate payee reflects what already was the alternate payee's share of the community property. [See United States v. Mitchell, 403 U.S. 190 (1971)] Following this, income arising from such property or rights is the alternate payee's income. [I.R.C. § 66. See generally Helvering v. Horst, 311 U.S. 112, 61 S. Ct. 144, 85 L. Ed. 75, 1940-2 C.B. 206 (1940) (income from property is taxable to the owner of the property)]

Q 13:57   How does a payor report and withhold on payments to an alternate payee?

For payments made in 2002–2010, a payment under a state or local government employer's Section 457(b) plan is governed by the tax–reporting and withholding rules that apply to retirement plans. [I.R.C. § 3401(a)(12)(E), and added by EGTRRA § 641(a)(1)(D)(i)] This means that a payment is reported on Form 1099-R. Likewise, the withholding rules are those that apply for pension distributions, including mandatory withholding on an eligible rollover distribution that is not directly rolled over to another eligible retirement plan.

A payment under a nongovernmental employer's Section 457(b) plan is wages. This means that a payment is reported on Form W-2, and the wage withholding rules apply. Along with other provisions, this means that ordinarily a payee cannot properly choose to avoid withholding. [I.R.C. § 3405(1)(B)(i); Temp. Treas. Reg. § 35.3405-1T Q&A A-23] Likewise, a payment under an ineligible deferred compensation plan is governed by the tax-reporting and withholding rules for wages [I.R.C. § 3401(a)] If the payor chooses to apply the withholding rule for supplemental wages, the amount withheld toward federal income tax will be 27 percent of the payment. [Omnibus Budget Reconciliation Act of 1993 § 13273 (1993-3 C.B. 1, 130); Treas. Reg. § 31.3402(g)-1(a); Rev. Rul. 82-46, 1982-1 C.B. 158; IRS Notice 2000-38, 2000-2 C.B. 174, 2000-33 I.R.B. 1]

Whether to tax-report an alternate payee's payment as the alternate payee's or the participant's wages or income turns on:

1. Whether the plan is a governmental plan that reports distributions on Form 1099-R or a nongovernmental plan that reports wages on Form W-2;
2. Whether plan is an eligible or ineligible deferred compensation plan, and thereby whether a court order might be a QDRO or deemed QDRO;
3. Whether a payment might be a transfer incident to divorce; and
4. If neither QDRO nor transfer-incident-to-divorce treatment applies, whether the payor believes the payment more likely is the alternate payee's or the participant's income.

Except for QDRO or deemed QDRO distribution under a state or local government employer's eligible plan, the IRS has not provided a clear tax-reporting rule. There is no Treasury Regulation, Revenue Ruling, Revenue Procedure, or even an Internal Revenue Service Notice that states a reporting rule for deferred wages paid to a person who is not a participant or a beneficiary. [See IRS Notice 2000-38, 2000-2 C.B. 174, 2000-33 I.R.B. 1] Neither Form W-2 nor Form 1099-R states the manner of reporting payments made to a former spouse or other alternate payee. In the absence of clear authority, many practitioners consider it reasonable to report deferred wages paid to an alternate payee as though paid to the individual that the payor believes is more likely than not the one who has an amount of gross income because of the payment. If a payor believes that a payment to an alternate payee is includible only in the gross income of that former spouse, there might be substantial authority to assume that the alternate payee's court-ordered right is not the participant's wages. If so, it should be reasonable to assume that a payment following the court-ordered right is not reportable on the participant's Form W-2. [I.R.C. §§ 3401–3402, 6041, 6051] Of course, consistency with such a reporting position would require the payor to report those payments as the former spouse's income. Internal Revenue Code Section 6724(a) provides that the penalties imposed under section 6721 or 6722 do not apply if the failure that otherwise would result in a penalty is "due to reasonable cause and not to willful neglect." [I.R.C. § 6724(a)] In the absence of an IRS rule, it might be reasonable to assume that, if there is substantial authority to support a position that an item is not includible in the participant's gross income, the failure to report that item on the participant's Form W-2 should be excused as based on "reasonable cause." [Cf. I.R.C. § 6664(c)]

While none of the answers is certain, the following is a summary of the likely tax-reporting decisions a payor might make until the IRS provides further guidance.

Governmental 457(b) plan

If a payment is made to an alternate payee who never was the participant's spouse, the payment is the participant's income. (See Q 13:45.) Report the payment on Form 1099-R as a distribution to (or for the use of) the participant.

If an alternate payee is or was the participant's spouse and a payment is made under a QDRO or deemed QDRO, the payment is the alternate payee's income. (See Q 13:45.) Report the payment on Form 1099-R as a distribution to the alternate payee.

If an alternate payee is or was the participant's spouse and a payment is made as a transfer incident to divorce, the payment is the alternate payee's income. (See Q 13:54.) Report the payment on Form 1099-R as a distribution to the alternate payee.

If a payment to an alternate payee is not treated as under a QDRO or deemed QDRO or as a transfer incident to divorce, the payment might be the participant's income. (See Qs 13:51, 13:53, 13:56.) Report the payment on Form 1099-R as a distribution to the participant, unless the payor finds that there is substantial authority for a position that no portion of the payment is the participant's income. If the payment is only the former spouse alternate payee's income, report the payment on Form 1099-R as a distribution to the alternate payee.

Nongovernmental 457(b) plan

If a payment is made to an alternate payee who never was the participant's spouse, the payment is the participant's income. (See Q 13:45.) Report the payment on Form W-2 as the participant's wages.

If an alternate payee is or was the participant's spouse and a payment is made under a QDRO or deemed QDRO, the payment is the alternate payee's income. (See Q 13:45.) Report the payment as the alternate payee's income.

If an alternate payee is or was the participant's spouse and a payment is made as a transfer incident to divorce, the payment is the alternate payee's income. (See Q 13:54.) Report the payment as the alternate payee's income.

If a payment to an alternate payee is not treated as under a QDRO or deemed QDRO or as a transfer incident to divorce, the payment might be the participant's income. (See Qs 13:51, 13:53, 13:56.) Report the payment on Form W-2 as the participant's wages, unless the payor finds that there is substantial authority for a position that no portion of the payment is the participant's income. If the payment is only the former spouse alternate payee's income, report the payment as the alternate payee's income.

Ineligible deferred compensation plan

If a payment is made to an alternate payee who never was the participant's spouse, the payment is the participant's income. (See Q 13:45.) Report the payment on Form W-2 as the participant's wages.

If an alternate payee is or was the participant's spouse and a payment is made as a transfer incident to divorce, the payment is the alternate payee's income. (See Q 13:54.) Report the payment as the alternate payee's income.

If a payment to an alternate payee is not a transfer incident to divorce, the payment might be the participant's income. (See Qs 13:51, 13:53, 13:56.) Report the payment on Form W-2 as the particpant's wages, unless the payor finds that there is substantial authority for a position that no portion of the payment is the participant's income. If the payment is only the former spouse alternate payee's income, report the payment as the alternate payee's income.

Practice Pointer. Whenever there is significant doubt about what tax-reporting is required, a payor should get its lawyer's advice and keep written evidence of why a reporting position was reasonable.

Q 13:58   What could a lawyer do to protect a participant from tax on payments to an alternate payee?

Because of the significant possibility that the IRS and other tax authorities might treat payments to an alternate payee as the participant's income, some family law practitioners recommend a settlement agreement provision by which the alternate payee must reimburse the participant for all taxes that the participant incurs on payments made to the alternate payee.

Example. Priscilla is a participant in the Springfield Community Hospital Section 457(f) deferred compensation plan. The plan recognizes a domestic relations order that meets the plan's PADRO rules. Stephen divorces Priscilla in September 2002. At that time, Priscilla's plan account was worth $400,000. The PADRO provides that $100,000 worth of the potential deferred compensation right is set aside for Stephen, and $300,000 worth remains Priscilla's right. By 2006, Priscilla has met all of the plan's conditions to become entitled to her deferred compensation without any forfeiture. Priscilla retires and both Priscilla and Stephen take an immediate distribution. Following investment returns, Priscilla's portion is $360,000 and Stephen's portion is $120,000

The plan administrator treats the $120,000 payment to Stephen as supplemental wages, and therefore withholds $30,000 (25 percent) and pays Stephen the net proceeds of $90,000. (Springfield is in the state of Utopia, which has no state income tax.) In January 2007, the plan administrator sends Priscilla a Form W-2 for the payment made to Stephen during 2006.

Priscilla feels that it is unfair for her to be taxed when she has not received any cash, so on her Form 1040 she takes the position that the plan's payment to Stephen is not her income. Because the state of Utopia (in which Priscilla and Stephen have resided at all times) is not a community property state, the IRS examines Priscilla's Form 1040 and determines that the $120,000 payment to Stephen is Priscilla's income. Priscilla challenges the IRS determination, but the court upholds the IRS. For calendar tax year 2006, Priscilla's marginal income tax rate is 35 percent. Because the divorce settlement includes a reimbursement provision, Priscilla demands that Stephen pay her $12,000 ($42,000 − $30,000) plus interest.

As illustrated by the example, the effect of a tax reimbursement provision is to reimburse the participant for the difference between the tax withheld and the tax ultimately determined.

A family law practitioner should consider that a fair tax reimbursement provision might require the participant to reimburse the alternate payee if the tax withheld is greater than the tax ultimately assessed against both parties.

Q 13:59 Can an alternate payee roll over into a retirement plan or IRA an amount paid in an ineligible plan's PADRO distribution?

No. First, an ineligible plan's PADRO distribution cannot be treated as a QDRO distribution for federal income tax purposes. [P.L.R. 9145010] Only a QDRO or deemed QDRO can give a participant's spouse the opportunity to make a rollover. [I.R.C. § 402(e)(1)(B)] Further, only a governmental eligible deferred compensation plan is an eligible retirement plan for rollover purposes. [I.R.C. § 402(c)(8)]

Q 13:60 What is the federal estate tax treatment of deferred compensation transferred in a pre-2002 PADRO distribution?

It is unclear whether a transfer of rights made by a PADRO will be effective to remove the value of those rights from the participant's estate for federal estate tax purposes. Although this specific question has not been litigated, one case suggests the possibility that the IRS could assert that the transferred rights are included in the participant's estate for federal estate tax purposes. [Estate of Waters, Jr. v. Commissioner, T.C. Memo. 1994-194]

A decedent's gross estate generally consists of the property and rights that the decedent possessed at his or her death. [I.R.C. §§ 2031–2042] Thus, a participant's executor might argue that the participant did not possess rights that had been transferred to his or her former spouse. Many federal estate and gift tax provisions, however, include in a decedent's gross estate amounts that had been transferred before death, and the IRS might assert that the participant-decedent "assigned" his or her deferred compensation. Yet again, the Treasury

Department's view on a related income tax question suggests that the IRS might not argue that an involuntary transfer incident to a divorce is an assignment. [See Rev. Rul. 2002-22, 2002-19 I.R.B. 849]

In this author's view, the better view is that a PADRO (if it provides for a former spouse) effects a transfer incident to divorce [I.R.C. § 1041], and general tax principles of consistency should mean that the portion set aside for the alternate payee no longer is the participant's property or rights.

For an eligible plan's PADRO distribution paid in 2002–2010, such a distribution should make the property distributed no longer part of the participant's estate.

Bankruptcy

Q 13:61 Does a participant's bankruptcy before a PADRO is entered affect an alternate payee's property right in deferred compensation plan benefits?

No. An alimony, maintenance, support, or similar property settlement debt incurred in a divorce proceeding is nondischargeable. [11 U.S.C. § 523(a)(5), (15), (18); see, e.g., Bush v. Taylor, 912 F.2d 989 (8th Cir. 1990); In re Debolt, 177 B.R. 31 (Bankr. W.D. Pa. 1994); In re Bennett, 175 B.R. 181 (Bankr. E.D. Pa. 1994)] However, a participant's bankruptcy might impair the participant's obligations other than a property settlement debt. [See, e.g., In re Ellis, 72 F.3d 628 (8th Cir. 1995); Bush v. Taylor, 912 F.2d 989 (8th Cir. 1990), *vacating* 893 F.2d 962 (8th Cir. 1990)]

Practice Pointer. A non-participant's lawyer should work promptly to get a PADRO completed. In the absence of a QDRO or similar order, courts have discharged a bankrupt participant from responsibility for meeting marital-property expectations. [See, e.g., In re Varrone, 269 B.R. 475 (Bankr. D. Conn. 2001); In re King, 24 B.R. 69 (Bankr. D. Conn. 1997)]

Q 13:62 Does a participant's bankruptcy affect a plan administrator's duty to administer a PADRO?

No. Although a bankruptcy may impair a participant's obligations other than a divorce property settlement, a participant's bankruptcy does not affect a plan administrator's obligations. [See, e.g., In re Gendreau, 122 F.3d 815, 21 Employee Benefits Cas. (BNA) 1533, Pens. Plan Guide (CCH) ¶ 23,936M, Bankr. L. Rep. ¶ 77,497 (9th Cir. 1997), *cert. denied*, 523 U.S. 1005, 118 S. Ct. 1187, 140 L. Ed. 2d 318 (1998); see also Trustees of the Directors Guild America-Producer Pension Benefits Plans v. Tise, 234 F.3d 415, 25 Employee Benefits Cas. (BNA) 2683, Pens. Plan Guide (CCH) ¶ 23,967J (9th Cir. 2000); In re McCafferty, 96 F.3d 192 (6th Cir. 1996). But see In re King, 214 B.R. 69 (Bankr. D. Conn. 1997)]

Practice Pointer. If there is a significant risk that the participant might become bankrupt, his or her spouse or former spouse should prefer (in the absence of other factors) a PADRO over a personal obligation that might be discharged in bankruptcy.

Divorce Negotiation

Q 13:63   Should a divorce lawyer engage an actuary when dividing a defined benefit plan?

Yes. For a defined benefit plan (including a deferred compensation plan that specifies the plan's benefit in defined benefit form), a divorce lawyer should be aware that there are many different ways to value the portion of the unknown future benefits that may be assumed to have accrued during a marriage. Likewise, there are many different ways to value the effect that unknown subsequent events might have on the benefits that may be provided. [J. Reiss,"Dividing Pension Rights: Exposing the Myths and the Malpractice," *Fair$hare,* Mar. 1997, at 2; G.S. Finley, "Assigning Defined Benefits—The Great QDRO Challenge," *Fair$hare,* Jan. 1997, at 2; J.P. Weinstein, "The Use and Abuse of Economic Experts in Divorce Litigation," *Fair$hare,* Mar. 1995, at 12; M. Snyder, "Early Retirement Pension Benefits in Divorce," *Fair$hare,* July 1992, at 11; J.T. Friedman, "Questions to Trap the Expert," *Family Advocate,* Fall 1985, at 24]

Q 13:64   Should a divorce lawyer engage an actuary when dividing a defined contribution plan?

Maybe. Whether a divorce lawyer should engage an actuary when dividing a defined contribution plan turns on

1. Whether the couple's divorce will affect rights that cannot be divided;
2. How much economic damage the divorce will cause the lawyer's client;
3. The likelihood that the lawyer's client could obtain a right that will compensate him or her for all or some of that economic damage; and
4. Whether a failure to obtain a compensating right would outweigh the actuary's fee.

Many divorce lawyers assume that it is a relatively simple matter to divide an account balance, especially if the plan permits a distribution to the alternate payee before the participant's severance. However, the couple may have other pension rights that cannot be divided so easily, and may have other rights that cannot be divided at all.

Some rights cannot be divided at all. For example, a domestic relations court cannot alter either individual's Social Security benefits. [42 U.S.C. §§ 405–407; Boulter v. Boulter, 930 P.2d 112 (Nev. 1997)] Further, Social Security benefits may not be community property or marital property. [See generally McCarty v. McCarty, 453 U.S. 210, 101 S. Ct. 2728, 69 L. Ed. 2d 589 (1981); Hisquierdo v. Hisquierdo, 439 U.S. 572, 99 S. Ct. 802, 59 L. Ed. 2d 1 (1979); Free v. Bland, 369 U.S. 663, 82 S. Ct. 1089, 8 L. Ed. 2d 180 (1962); Wissner v.

Wissner, 338 U.S. 655, 70 S. Ct. 398, 94 L. Ed. 424 (1950)] Moreover, a divorce can substantially reduce or even eliminate a nonemployed spouse's Social Security benefits. [42 U.S.C. §§ 402–416; 20 C.F.R. § 404.310–.346]

On the other hand, nothing precludes the divorcing parties from negotiating a settlement agreement that provides an "unequal" division of another retirement plan or other property to reflect an impairment that arises from pension rights or Social Security benefits that are difficult or impossible to divide. To do so, a divorce lawyer may need an actuary's evaluation of such an impairment to support a negotiating position.

As explained in Q 13:63, a divorce lawyer should be aware that there are many different ways to value the portion of the unknown future benefits that can be assumed to have accrued during a marriage.

Lawyer's Professional Conduct

Q 13:65   Is it malpractice for a lawyer to fail to prepare a PADRO?

Whether it is malpractice for a lawyer to fail to prepare a PADRO turns on the scope of the client's engagement of the lawyer.

A lawyer must exercise the competence and diligence normally exercised by lawyers in similar circumstances. A lawyer may choose to act only within the scope of the representation and the client's proper instructions. A lawyer who informs a client that the lawyer will undertake a specifically described activity is required to do so. If the client properly instructs the lawyer to take a particular step, the lawyer must do so. An informed client can agree that the lawyer will provide services only within a budget or according to an agreed-upon timetable. [See generally Restatement (Third) of the Law Governing Lawyers §§ 30–32, 74–76 (2001); Restatement (Second) of Torts § 299A (1997)]

If the client instructed (and agreed to pay for) the lawyer to prepare a PADRO and the lawyer received sufficient information in time, the lawyer is obliged to prepare a PADRO.

It is unclear whether a lawyer must prepare a PADRO if the client failed to instruct the lawyer to do so. The better view is that a lawyer must, before the entry of a divorce decree or a court order approving a property settlement, prepare a PADRO or confirm the absence of any need for a PADRO.

A lawyer is liable for failing to give advice about well-established principles of domestic relations law. [McMahon v. Shea, 657 A.2d 938 (Pa. Super. Ct. 1995)]

Q 13:66   Is it malpractice for a lawyer to prepare an order intended as a PADRO that is not a PADRO?

Yes. Ordinarily, a lawyer who does not suggest that he or she is a specialist is required to exercise only the skill and knowledge normally possessed by other lawyers. [Restatement (Second) of Torts § 299A (1977)] But showing that the average practitioner or even all practitioners regularly perform incompetently will not excuse a lack of reasonable prudence. If a minimum standard of care is necessary to protect the client and is not unreasonably burdensome to the profession, the law requires that standard of care even if it is unusual among the profession's practitioners. [Hall v. Hilbun, 466 So. 2d 856 (Miss. 1985); Helling v. Carey, 83 Wash. 2d 514, 519 P.2d 981 (1974); An Attorney v. Mississippi State Bar Ass'n, 481 So. 2d 297 (1985); In re Wines, 370 S.W.2d 328 (Mo. 1963); The TJ Hooper, 60 F.2d 737, 740 (2d Cir. 1932) ("a whole calling may have unduly lagged"); Texas & Pac. Ry. v. Behymer, 189 U.S. 468, 470, 23 S. Ct. 622, 623 (1903) ("what ought to be done is fixed by a standard of reasonable prudence, whether it is usually complied with or not"); United States v. Carroll Towing Co., 159 F.2d 169 (2d Cir. 1947)]

Preparing a PADRO should be easy. In many states, the only legal research needed is reading a short statute along with a plan summary routinely furnished by the plan administrator. Many plan administrators furnish model PADRO forms for the divorce lawyer's convenience. With only modest effort, any lawyer can prepare a PADRO that would be approved by the plan administrator.

Q 13:67   What responsibility does a client have to help a lawyer prepare a PADRO?

Notwithstanding the lawyer's duty to use sensible care (see Qs 13:65, 13:66), a lawyer's failure to prepare a PADRO can be the client's fault instead of the lawyer's. A lawyer is not responsible if the bad outcome resulted solely or primarily from the client's negligence. [Restatement (Third) of the Law Governing Lawyers § 76 (2001)] If a client fails to give his or her lawyer necessary information, the client cannot blame the lawyer for a bad outcome. [See, e.g., Carmel v. Clapp & Eisenberg, PC, 960 F.2d 698 (7th Cir. 1992); Nika v. Danz, 556 N.E.2d 873 (Ill. App. Ct. 1990)]

A lawyer must make a reasonable effort to remedy a client's weaknesses—for example, a client's failure to read or understand a document—that in another context would be contributory negligence. [See, e.g., Kushner v. McLarty, 300 S.E.2d 531 (Ga. Ct. App. 1983); Cicorelli v. Capobianco, 453 N.Y.S.2d 21 (App. Div. 1982)]

Example. Martha engages Linda to handle Martha's divorce from John. Martha explains to Linda that it is important that Martha get a fair portion of John's deferred compensation. Martha is a smart client and gives Linda a copy of John's summary plan description. The booklet explains that the plan does not permit a distribution to anyone until the participant's retirement. Ignoring Martha's effort to furnish information, Linda does not read the booklet. Instead, Linda instructs her secretary to use the word processing file of the last DRO she prepared and just change the names. That order was for a plan that permitted an early distribution to an alternate payee. The plan administrator rejects the order Linda submitted. Because Martha took action to make sure that her lawyer had useful information, Linda is liable for her failure to prepare a PADRO.

A lawyer is not responsible for inaccuracy in preparing a DRO if the lawyer curtailed his or her work because the client did not pay the lawyer's fee. [See generally Restatement (Third) of the Law Governing Lawyers § 29 (2001)]

Q 13:68 Does a PADRO malpractice claim require expert testimony?

Maybe not. Usually, a legal malpractice claim requires that the plaintiff submit expert witness testimony to show that the defendant did not meet the professional standard of care. However, expert testimony might be unnecessary if the malpractice is obvious:

> [E]xpert testimony is not required when an ordinary person is equipped by common skill and knowledge to judge the issue. . . . [E]xpert testimony is not required where an ordinary and reasonable person would recognize error upon discovering that there was no preparation or filing of a QDRO. Plaintiff's QDRO malpractice claim is within the common knowledge of laymen. Accordingly, plaintiff is not required to produce expert testimony.

[Williams v. Law Firm of Cooch & Taylor, No. 92C-03-024, 1994 WL 234000 (Del. Super. Ct. May 11, 1994); see generally Restatement (Third) of the Law Governing Lawyers §§ 74–76 (2001)]

Q 13:69 Should a lawyer engaged to redo a defective order sue the former lawyer?

Usually, yes. Although the lawyer engaged to prepare a PADRO usually should first attend to preparing and obtaining the PADRO, prompt action may be necessary to avoid losing the client's claim based on the former lawyer's malpractice. "[A]n attorney's notice or knowledge of facts affecting the rights of his client will be considered notice to the client." [Burton v. Guarnieri, No. 60428, 1991 WL 58412 (Ohio Ct. App. Apr. 18, 1991); Raible v. Raycel, 162 Ohio 25 (1954); Gerl Construction Co. v. Medina County Board of Commissioners, 24 Ohio App. 3d 59 (1985)]

A claim for malpractice accrues when the client discovers or should have discovered that his or her injury was caused by the lawyer's act (or failure to act). Thus, the statute of limitations begins to run when the newly engaged lawyer discovers the previous lawyer's malpractice.

Even if the newly engaged lawyer is successful in obtaining a PADRO before the client suffers harm, a malpractice claim may be appropriate to help the client recover his or her expenses for the "redo."

Q 13:70 May a lawyer take a contingent fee for a PADRO matter?

Generally, no. American public policy discourages divorce and favors reconciliation. [See generally Restatement (Second) of Contracts § 332(3) (Tentative Draft 1997); 93 A.L.R.3d 523 (1996)] Because a lawyer engaged under a contingent fee might have an incentive to discourage reconciliation, the common law generally prohibits a contingent fee in divorce matters. [See, e.g., Dotsko v. Dotsko, 244 N.J. Super. 668, 583 A.2d 395 (App. Div. 1990); Davis v. Taylor, 81 N.C. App. 42, 344 S.E.2d 19 (1986); Meyers v. Handlon, 479 N.E.2d 106 (Ind. Ct. App. 1985); In re Wright, 89 Ill. 2d 498, 434 N.E.2d 293, 61 Ill. Dec. 140 (1982); Guenava v. Burke, 387 Mass. 802, 443 N.E.2d 892 (1982); Husband F v. Wife F, 432 A.2d 331 (Del. 1981); Osborne v. Osborne, 384 Mass. 591, 428 N.E.2d 810 (1981); Florida Bar v. Perry, 377 So. 2d 712 (Fla. 1979); Aucoin v. William, 195 So. 2d 868 (La. Ct. App. 1974); Burns v. Stewart, 290 Minn. 289, 188 N.W.2d 760 (1971); Avant v. Whitten, 253 So. 2d 394 (Miss. 1971); Barelli v. Levin, 144 Ind. App. 576, 247 N.E.2d 847 (1969); Coons v. Kary, 263 Cal. App. 2d 650, 68 Cal. Rptr. 712 (1968); Hay v. Erwin, 244 Or. 488, 419 P.2d 32 (1966); In re Smith, 42 Wash. 2d 188, 254 P.2d 464 (1953); Dannenberg v. Dannenberg, 151 Kan. 600, 100 P.2d 667 (1940); Jordan v. Westerman, 62 Mich. 170, 28 N.W. 826 (1886)]

In most states, the Rules of Professional Conduct provide that "[a] lawyer shall not enter into an arrangement for, charge, or collect any fee in a domestic relations matter, the payment or amount of which is contingent upon the securing of a divorce or upon the amount of alimony or support, or property settlement in lieu thereof." [American Bar Ass'n, Model Rules of Prof'l Conduct R. 1.5(d)(1) (2003)]

South Carolina permits a contingent fee in a divorce matter if:

1. Reconciliation is not likely;
2. The matter involves only property division and not support for either spouse or any child;
3. The client cannot afford to retain a lawyer at a usual hourly rate;
4. The matter will produce a fund out of which the fee can be paid; and
5. The lawyer believes that the contingent fee is in the client's best interest.

[S.C. Ethics Op. 87-4 (1987). But see Glasscock v. Glasscock, 403 S.E.2d 313 (S.C. 1991)]

Because a DRO must relate to paying alimony, support, or a property settlement, the majority rule prohibits a contingent fee as a means of compensating a lawyer for his or her work in obtaining or defending a PADRO. [Kan. Bar Ass'n Ethics Op. 91-04 (1991); see also Ariz. Ethics Op. 87-6 (1987); Me. Ethics Op. 75, 13 Fam. L. Rep. (BNA) 1217 (1986); N.Y. County Ethics Op. 660 (1984); Va. Ethics Op. 189 (1984)] But if the divorce is fully concluded and the only issue is the enforcement of a previously ordered property settlement, a contingent fee might be permitted in carefully limited circumstances. [See generally Ronald Williams P.A. v. Garrison, 411 S.E.2d 633 (N.C. Ct. App. 1992); Roberds v. Sweitzer, 13 Fam. L. Rep. (BNA) 1175 (Mo. Ct. App. 1987); In re Cooper, 81 N.C. App. 27, 344 S.E.2d 27 (1986); Grayson v. Pyles, 184 Kan. 116, 334 P.2d 341 (1959); Grasen v. Grasen, 182 Kan. 287 (1958); Costigan v. Stewart, 76 Kan. 355 (1907); Fla. Bar Ethics Op. 87-3 (1987); Va. Ethics Op. 667 (1985); N.Y. County Ethics Op. 660 (1984); Kan. Ethics Op. 83-17 (1983); Miss. Ethics Op. 88 (1983); Va. Ethics Op. 405 (1983); Ariz. Ethics Op. 82-9 (1982); Mich.

Ethics Op. CI-620 (1981); Mont. Ethics Op. 23 (1981); Md. Ethics Op. 80-34 (1980)] Of course, any fee must be reasonable under the circumstances. [American Bar Ass'n, Model Rules of Prof'l Conduct R. 1.5(a) (2003)] For a matter in which liability already has been established, a contingent fee is presumed inappropriate unless the client cannot afford to pay the lawyer's time charge. [Kan. Ethics Op. 84-5 (1984)]

If one of the divorced parties files an independent lawsuit for fraud in obtaining a DRO, a lawyer might be permitted to handle that separate lawsuit under a contingent fee. [See generally Committee on Professional Ethics v. McCullough, 468 N.W.2d 458 (Iowa 1991); Ariz. Ethics Op. 82-9 (1982)]

A lawyer who makes an improper contingent fee arrangement is subject to disciplinary action, including disbarment. [See, e.g., In re Steere, 217 Kan. 271, 536 P.2d 54 (1975)] A lawyer who has nonconfidential knowledge of another lawyer's acceptance of an improper contingent fee might have a duty to report the other lawyer's misconduct. [See generally American Bar Ass'n, Model Rules of Prof'l Conduct R. 8.3 (2003)]

Q 13:71 Does a lawyer who has knowledge that another lawyer failed to prepare a PADRO have a duty to report the other lawyer's misconduct?

Probably not. Although a lawyer generally has a duty to report another lawyer's serious misconduct, that duty does not apply if the observing lawyer's client instructs him or her to keep the information confidential or does not consent to the lawyer's disclosure of the information.

Consider the situation in the following examples.

Example 1. The State of Anxiety maintains an eligible deferred compensation plan. A participant and his spouse are divorcing. The plan requires a PADRO for the spouse to preserve her rights in the plan. In the state court that issues the divorce decree, judges usually expect the claiming spouse's lawyer to prepare a PADRO.

The spouse's lawyer prepares a draft order, and asks the plan administrator's lawyer for a presubmission review. The plan administrator's lawyer finds several defects in the draft order, and provides a list of those defects and suggested corrections to the spouse's lawyer.

The plan administrator does not receive either a court order or another draft order. The plan administrator's lawyer suspects that the spouse's lawyer has neglected the spouse's need for a PADRO.

Example 2. The facts are the same as in Example 1, with the addition of the following.

The plan administrator's lawyer receives a copy of a divorce decree that dissolves the marriage of the participant and his former spouse. The divorce decree refers to but does not incorporate a property settlement agreement.

The property settlement agreement (a full copy of which was enclosed with the divorce decree) states that the spouse's lawyer "shall prepare a qualified [*sic*] DRO and serve [*sic*] such order upon [the plan administrator] forthwith." Based on a reading of the property settlement agreement, it is obvious that the spouse cannot have intended a property division that did not claim a portion of the deferred compensation plan benefit; indeed, the agreement expressly states that the spouse is entitled to "50 percent of Husband's State of Anxiety deferred compensation plan account." Although it is now several months after the date of the divorce, the plan administrator has not received any order that the spouse or her lawyer submits as a PADRO.

What professional conduct duties do the spouse's lawyer and the plan administrator's lawyer have?

Spouse's lawyer. Under the Rules of Professional Conduct, the spouse's lawyer may not accept or continue employment in a divorce matter if the lawyer knows or should know that he or she is incompetent to handle the matter. [American Bar Ass'n, Model Rules of Prof'l Conduct R. 1.1 (2003)] To determine competence, the spouse's lawyer must consider all relevant circumstances, including the spouse's need for a valid PADRO. In addition, the spouse's lawyer must not neglect the representation. [American Bar Ass'n, Model Rules of Prof'l Conduct R. 1.3 (2003)] Neglect includes "inattentiveness involving a conscious disregard for the responsibilities owed to a client or clients." [See, e.g., Tex. Disciplinary Rules of Professional Conduct, Rule 1.01(c)] A lawyer must correct material defects in his or her work for a client, especially if the defect is called to the lawyer's attention at a time when correction is possible. [Tex. Ethics Op. 534, 63 *Tex. B.J.* 808, 809 (2000)] In both examples stated above, the spouse's lawyer has a duty to prepare a correct PADRO or refer the spouse to a lawyer who can do so.

Plan administrator's lawyer. In the above examples, the plan administrator's lawyer (unless governed solely by California's or Kentucky's rules) might, depending on the circumstances, have a duty to inform the appropriate lawyer disciplinary authority about the other lawyer's misconduct. [American Bar Ass'n, Model Rules of Prof'l Conduct R. 8.3(a) (2003); accord N.Y. Code of Prof'l Responsibility D.R. 1-103(A)] This duty applies only if the plan administrator's lawyer *knows* that the spouse's lawyer has improperly taken no action to correct the defective draft order. [See, e.g., Doe v. Federal Grievance Committee, 847 F.2d 57 (2d Cir. 1988) (lawyer must clearly know, rather than merely suspect, misconduct of other lawyer)] In the first example, the observing lawyer may not know this because it is possible that the divorcing parties have reconciled or that the spouse otherwise decided not to pursue divorce. Likewise, the divorcing parties might have negotiated a property division that involved awarding the spouse property other than a portion of the deferred compensation plan benefit.

A lawyer is not expected to report a mere suspicion. [See, e.g., Pa. Bar Ass'n Prof'l Guidance Comm., Guidance Op. 97-3 (1997)] While a lawyer cannot close his or her eyes to the obvious [Bar Ass'n City of N.Y., Formal Op. 1990-3

(1990)], the reporting duty applies only if "[t]he supporting evidence [is] such that a reasonable lawyer under the circumstances would have formed a firm opinion that the conduct in question had more likely than not occurred." [Attorney U v. Mississippi Bar, 678 So. 2d 963, 972 (Miss. 1996)] In the second example, an observing lawyer might more readily form a belief that the spouse's lawyer's misconduct seems likely.

Even if the misconduct is obvious, a lawyer has a duty to inform on another's misconduct only if the observing lawyer's knowledge of the other's misconduct "raises a substantial question as to that [other] lawyer's honesty, trustworthiness[,] or fitness as a lawyer in other respects." [American Bar Ass'n, Model Rules of Prof'l Conduct R. 8.3(a) (2003)] Whether a question about a lawyer's fitness is "substantial" refers to the seriousness of the viola-tion and not the quantum of evidence of which the observing lawyer is aware. [American Bar Ass'n, Model Rules of Prof'l Conduct R. 8.3 cmt. 4 (2003)] At least one court has suggested that fitness, in this context, does not refer to pro-fessional competence; rather, an unfit lawyer is one whose conduct diminishes public confidence in the lawyers' profession. [Iowa Supreme Court Board of Professional Ethics & Conduct v. Marcucci, 543 N.W.2d 879, 882 (Iowa 1996)] However, a breach of the duty of competence, the duty of diligence, or the duty to charge no more than a reasonable fee usually calls into serious question the breaching lawyer's fitness. [See, e.g., In re Puterbaugh, 694 N.E.2d 281 (Ind. 1998); Kentucky Bar Ass'n v. Wells, 967 S.W.2d 585 (Ky. 1998); In re Frank, 706 A.2d 927 (R.I. 1998); People v. Kotarek, 941 P.2d 925 (Colo. 1997); In re Disciplinary Action Against Ramirez, 577 N.W.2d 480 (Minn. 1997); Toledo Bar Ass'n v. Batt, 677 N.E.2d 349 (Ohio 1997); In re Disciplinary Proceedings Against Awen, 564 N.W.2d 326 (Wis. 1997); People v. Motsenbocker, 926 P.2d 576 (Colo. 1996); In re Lassen, 672 A.2d 988 (Del. 1996); In re Comstock, 664 N.E.2d 1165 (Ind. 1996); In re Brown, 931 P.2d 664 (Kan. 1996); Florida Bar v. Herzog, 521 So. 2d 1118, 1120 (Fla. 1988); State Bar of Ariz. Comm. on Rules of Prof'l Conduct, Op. 94-09, at 7 (1994). But see Conn. Bar Ass'n Comm. on Prof'l Ethics, Informal Op. 97-8 (1997) (lawyer malpractice alone does not trigger misconduct-reporting duty)]

In Ethics Opinion 534, the Texas State Bar Committee on Professional Responsibility held that "[i]f [the plan administrator's lawyer] determines that the circumstances described in [Texas] Rule 8.03(a) are present, [the plan administrator's lawyer] is required by that Rule to report [the spouse's lawyer's] violation to the appropriate disciplinary authority, subject to the limitation of [Texas] Rule 8.03(d)(1) that such report is not required to include disclosure of confidential information relating to [the observing lawyer's] client (the [plan administrator]) in violation of Rule 1.05." [Tex. Ethics Op. 534, 63 *Tex. B.J.* 808, 809 (2000)]

A careful application of the lawyers' Rules of Professional Conduct often will mean that the observing lawyer is precluded from reporting the miscon-duct. The misconduct-reporting rule itself states that "[t]his Rule does not require disclosure of information otherwise protected by Rule 1.6" and "[a] report about misconduct is not required where it would involve violation of

Rule 1.6." [American Bar Ass'n, Model Rules of Prof'l Conduct R. 8.3(c) & cmt. 2 (2003); accord N.Y. Code of Prof'l Responsibility D.R. 1-103(A)] The rule for preserving a client's confidences states that "[a] lawyer shall not reveal information relating to representation of a client unless the client consents after consultation." [American Bar Ass'n, Model Rules of Prof'l Conduct R. 1.6(a) (2003); accord N.Y. Code of Prof'l Responsibility D.R. 1-103(B); see also Restatement of the Law (Third) Governing Lawyers § 5(3) & cmt. i (2001). But see Ill. Rev. Stat. ch. 110A, Rule 1-103(a) (a lawyer "possessing *unprivileged* knowledge of a violation . . . shall report such knowledge") (emphasis added); In re Himmel, 125 Ill. 2d 531, 533 N.E.2d 790, 127 Ill. Dec. 708 (1988)] Nothing in this rule requires that the information be privileged or even confidential. If the observing lawyer received information about the spouse's lawyer's misconduct in the course of the observing lawyer's work for the plan administrator, the observing lawyer should presume that the information is a client confidence or at least is related to the lawyer's representation of the plan administrator. Bar association ethics opinions hold that an observing lawyer cannot report another's misconduct unless the observing lawyer's client so instructs or consents. [Pa. Bar Ass'n Prof'l Guidance Comm., Op. 97-12 (1997); Pa. Bar Ass'n Prof'l Guidance Comm., Guidance Op. 96-6 (1996); Conn. Bar Ass'n Comm. on Prof'l Ethics, Informal Op. 95-17, 1995 WL 389626 (1995); Philadelphia Bar Ass'n Prof'l Guidance Comm., Guidance Op. 93-28, 1994 WL 32641 (Jan. 1994); In re Ethics Advisory Panel Op. No. 92-1, 627 A.2d 317 (R.I. 1993); State Bar of Mich. Comm. on Prof'l and Judicial Ethics, Op. RI-88 (1991); Or. State Bar Ass'n Bd. of Governors, Formal Op. 1991-95 (1991); Md. State Bar Ass'n Comm. on Ethics, Op. 89-46, 5 *Law Manual Pro. Conduct* 186 (1989); Conn. Bar Ass'n Comm. on Prof'l Ethics, Informal Op. 89-14, 5 *Law Manual Pro. Conduct* 186 (1989); see also American Bar Ass'n, Formal Op. 94-383 (1994). But see Pa. Bar Ass'n Comm. on Legal Ethics and Prof'l Responsibility, Informal Op. 95-123 (1996) (information also received from nonclient third party is not "confidential" and must be reported)]

Some lawyers have considered an anonymous report as a way of vindicating a lawyer's moral duty to report misconduct while preserving his or her client's confidences. However, most jurisdictions require a complainant reporting lawyer misconduct to identify himself or herself. [C.L. Gendry, Comment, "Ethics—An Attorney's Duty to Report the Professional Misconduct of Co-Workers," 18 *S. Ill. U. L.J.* 603, 611 (1994)] Further, a report that sufficiently describes the breaching lawyer's conduct would almost always have the effect of revealing the identity of the observing lawyer's client.

In contrast to the view that a lawyer's primary duty of loyalty is to his or her client, some lawyers may believe that it is feasible to report another lawyer's misconduct. These lawyers suggest that a lawyer may follow his or her professional or moral duty to report another lawyer's misconduct if the observing lawyer can do so without disadvantaging his or her client's interests and without revealing any confidential information. According to the American Law Institute, "[t]he duty to disclose wrongdoing by another lawyer . . . does not require [or permit] disclosure of confidential client information" and an observing lawyer can report the wrongdoing of another *only* when its revelation would either (1) not be materially adverse to the interests of the client whose information would be involved in the disclosure, or (2) involve only non-confidential information. [Restatement of the Law (Third) Governing Lawyers § 5 & cmt. i (2001)] If there is any doubt, the lawyer must obtain the client's informed consent that a report will not be adverse to the client's interests. [American Bar Ass'n, Model Rules of Prof'l Conduct R. 1.4 (2003)]

If an observing lawyer reports another lawyer's misconduct, most states provide absolute immunity against liability that otherwise might arise from a report of a lawyer's misconduct. [See, e.g., Hecht v. Levin, 613 N.E.2d 585 (Ohio 1993); San Diego County Bar Ass'n Comm. on Legal Ethics and Unlawful Practice, Op. 1992-2 (1992) (although a California lawyer has no duty to report another lawyer's misconduct, a lawyer who does report is absolutely privileged from liability); Jarvis v. Drake, 830 P.2d 23 (Kan. 1992); Stone v. Rosen, 348 So. 2d 387 (Fla. Dist. Ct. App. 1977). Cf. Weber v. Cueto, 568 N.E.2d 513 (Ill. App. Ct.), *cert. denied*, 575 N.E.2d 925 (Ill. 1991)] A law firm cannot terminate a lawyer's employment because he or she reported another lawyer's misconduct. Instead, courts presume that adherence to the lawyers' rules of professional conduct is an implied term of every contract of employment between a lawyer and a law firm. [See, e.g., Wieder v. Skala, 80 N.Y.2d 628, 609 N.E.2d 628 (1992)] However, a lawyer who is an employee of his or her client is less likely to be protected against dismissal based on the lawyer's law-abiding conduct. [Compare GTE Products Corp. v. Stewart, 653 N.E.2d 161 (Mass. 1995), General Dynamics Corp. v. Superior Court (Rose), 7 Cal. 4th 1164, 876 P.2d 487 (1994), Balla v. Gambro, Inc., 584 N.E.2d 104 (Ill. 1992), Willy v. Coastal Corp., 647 F. Supp. 116 (S.D. Tex. 1986), and Herbster v. North America Co., 501 N.E.2d 343 (Ill. App. Ct. 1986), with Nordling v. Northern Power Co., 478 N.W.2d 498 (Minn. 1991), and Mourad v. Automobile Club Insurance Ass'n, 465 N.W.2d 395 (Mich. Ct. App. 1991)]

Chapter 14

Miscellaneous Issues

Carol V. Calhoun, Esq.
Calhoun Law Group, P.C.

This chapter discusses issues involving the eligibility of international organizations, firefighters, bar associations, independent contractors, and American Indian tribes to establish 457(b) plans. In addition, the chapter covers state statutory and constitutional issues involving the investment of plan assets and restrictions that may apply, as well as other matters pertaining to matching contributions, the reduction of future benefits, the consequences of a failed eligible 457(b) plan, and plan-type alternatives to a 457(b) plan.

Agencies, Tribes, and International Organizations

Q 14:1 Can a federal government agency or instrumentality, an international organization, or an American Indian tribe have an eligible 457(b) plan?

No. A governmental employer is an eligible employer for purposes of Section 457 of the Internal Revenue Code (Code) only if it is a state or local government employer (see Qs 2:4, 2:5, 2:22). [I.R.C. § 457(e)(1)] Although Code Section 7871 treats an American Indian tribal government as a state government for purposes of certain sections of the Code, Code Section 457 is not one of the enumerated sections.

A governmental agency, other than a state or local government agency, can maintain an unfunded deferred compensation plan for employees. Such a plan, unlike an unfunded deferred compensation plan of an employer covered by the Employee Retirement Income Security Act of 1974 (ERISA), can cover rank-and-file employees. Moreover, such a plan is not subject to the dollar or percentage-of-compensation limits of Code Section 457. Neither, however, is such a plan subject to Code Section 457(g)(2)(B), which allows an eligible 457(b) plan of a state or local government to fund a 457(b) plan formally without causing participants to be immediately taxable on vested amounts.

Q 14:2 Is there an alternative to an eligible 457(b) plan for a federal government agency, an international organization, or an American Indian tribe?

Yes. One alternative to an eligible 457(b) plan for a federal government agency (see Q 2:22), an international organization (within the meaning of the International Organizations Immunities Act) [22 U.S.C. §§ 288–288f], or an American Indian tribe would be a 401(k) plan. Code Section 401(k)(4)(B) does not bar federal government agencies and international organizations from maintaining 401(k) plans. Code Section 401(k)(4)(B)(iii) specifically permits American Indian tribal governments to maintain 401(k) plans.

Q 14:3 Can a bar association ever have an eligible 457(b) plan that includes rank-and-file employees?

Yes, if it qualifies as an arm or instrumentality of state or local government. The Department of Labor (DOL) has recognized that an integrated bar may so qualify in appropriate circumstances. [DOL Adv. Op. 94-02A]

Q 14:4 Can an eligible 457(b) plan cover volunteers, such as volunteer firefighters, who receive no payment for their services?

No. One of the limits on deferrals in Code Section 457 is 100 percent of compensation. Thus, for someone who has no compensation, the limit would be zero.

An eligible employer can establish a plan paying solely length-of-service awards to bona fide volunteers (or their beneficiaries) for the "qualified services" they perform. [I.R.C. § 457(e)(11)(A)(ii)] For this purpose, qualified services are fire fighting and prevention services, emergency medical services, and ambulance services. Such a plan can be structured similarly to an eligible 457(b) plan, except that (1) the maximum annual deferral is $3,000; (2) the governmental 457(b) plan trust requirement does not apply to such plans; and (3) because volunteers have no salary from which to make deferrals, the employer must make all contributions on a nonelective basis.

Independent Contractor Problems

Q 14:5 Can covering independent contractors in an eligible governmental 457(b) plan create problems?

Yes. Although Code Section 457 permits independent contractors to participate in an eligible 457(b) plan, the definition of governmental plan in ERISA Section 3(32) includes only a plan for employees. Thus, the DOL has taken the position that including independent contractors of a governmental entity in a 457(b) plan could jeopardize its status as a governmental plan, potentially subjecting it to ERISA (see Q 6:1). [See DOL Adv. Op. 94-02A n.1]

Q 14:6 Will covering independent contractors always cause problems for an eligible governmental 457(b) plan?

No. In several advisory opinions (e.g., DOL Adv. Ops. 2000-01A, 2000-04A, 2000-06A, and 2000-08A), the DOL has taken the position that a governmental plan can include a de minimis number of individuals who are not employees of a governmental entity. This seems to be particularly true if their employer has some connection to a governmental entity (e.g., a union that represents employees of a governmental unit) or if the nongovernmental employees were formerly employees of a governmental unit (e.g., in a privatization situation). To the extent that independent contractors represent a de minimis percentage of the employees of an eligible governmental 457(b) plan (particularly if they also perform services for a governmental entity or are former employees of a governmental entity), the same rules should apply to them.

Q 14:7 How can an eligible governmental employer cover independent contractors in an eligible 457(b) plan without creating problems for the plan?

It appears that creating separate 457(b) plans, one for employees and one for independent contractors, avoids the problem regardless of whether the 457(b) plan for independent contractors covers more than a de minimis number of such individuals. The plan for employees would presumably be exempt from ERISA under ERISA Section 3(32). The plan for independent contractors would presumably also be exempt from ERISA, because it would not cover any employees. [DOL Reg. § 2510.3-3(b)]

Failed 457(b) Plans; Restrictions on Investments of Eligible Plans

Q 14:8   What are the tax and withholding consequences of a failed eligible 457(b) plan?

A covered employee must pay income taxes in the year in which the amounts vest. The employer must deduct and pay FICA (Federal Insurance Contributions Act) taxes in the year in which the amounts become reasonably ascertainable; however, the employer need not deduct and pay income tax withholding before it actually or constructively pays the wages. Thus, income taxes, income tax withholding, and FICA taxes may occur in three separate years.

The IRS has not provided guidance on whether or why the employer would need to deduct and pay income tax withholding even in the year in which it paid the amounts to a participant if the participant had already paid income taxes on the amounts in a prior year. [TAM 199903032 (Oct. 2, 1998)]

Q 14:9   What common state statutory provisions restrict the investments of a nongovernmental eligible 457(b) plan?

Because a nongovernmental employer cannot formally fund an eligible 457(b) plan [I.R.C. § 457(b)(6)], the primary investment rules to be taken into account are the rules governing the employer's own investments. For example, Section 6 of the Uniform Management of Institutional Funds Act (UMIFA), which 46 states have adopted, states as follows:

> SECTION 6. [Standard of Conduct] In the administration of the powers to appropriate appreciation, to make and retain investments, and to delegate investment management of institutional funds, members of a governing board shall exercise ordinary business care and prudence under the facts and circumstances prevailing at the time of the action or decision. In so doing they shall consider long and short term needs of the institution in carrying out its educational, religious, charitable, or other eleemosynary purposes, its present and anticipated financial requirements, expected total return on its investments, price level trends, and general economic conditions.

These rules would, for example, restrict the investments of a charitable organization held for purposes of paying benefits under its 457(b) plan to the same extent as they would restrict other investments of a charitable organization.

Q 14:10   What common state constitutional provisions restrict the investments of an eligible governmental 457(b) plan?

Many courts have held that federal or state constitutional provisions dealing with impairment of contracts require that governmental pension funds invest prudently. For example, *Sgaglione v. Levitt* [37 N.Y.2d 507, 337 N.E.2d 592, 375 N.Y.S.2d 79, *reargument denied*, 37 N.Y.2d 924, 340 N.E.2d 754, 378 N.Y.S.2d 1027 (1975)] interpreted Article 5, Section 7, of the New York Constitution, which states as follows:

> After July first, nineteen hundred forty, membership in any pension or retirement system of the state or of a civil division thereof shall be a contractual relationship, the benefits of which shall not be diminished or impaired.

Sgaglione dealt with a state statute that required the New York Common Retirement Fund, which funded the New York State & Local Retirement Systems (the Systems), to invest in obligations of the Municipal Assistance Corporation for the City of New York (MAC). By its terms, the statute did not modify the benefit structure under the Systems. Moreover, the state of New York remained fully liable for the benefits promised under the Systems even if no assets were available in the Common Retirement Fund to pay for them. The New York Attorney General therefore argued that the state statute did not violate the constitutional provision, because it was "limited to the 'benefits' to which members and retired members of the retirement systems are entitled."

The court rejected the attorney general's argument. It held that the constitutional provision prevented a state statute from mandating that the Systems invest in MAC bonds to the extent that the statute impaired methods designed to ensure that public employees receive benefits.

Q 14:11   What common state statutory provisions may restrict the investments of an eligible governmental 457(b) plan?

States generally exercise a high degree of regulation over governmental plans of state and local governments. Because Code Section 457(g) now requires governmental employers to fund their 457(b) plans, courts may increasingly apply such statutes to governmental 457(b) plans.

Besides the requirements imposed by the common law of trusts and state constitutional provisions, states often impose additional fiduciary requirements. As of 2000, 36 states imposed a "prudent investor" rule similar to that of ERISA either by statute or by court interpretation of common law. Nine followed a more lenient "prudent person" rule, requiring that a fiduciary invest as prudently as a prudent person would for his or her own account, rather than as prudently as a professional investor would. Four of the remaining five use other variants of the prudence rule, and one uses a "best interests of beneficial owners" standard. [See C. Moore, *Protecting Retirees' Money: Fiduciary Duties and Other Laws Applicable to State Retirement Systems* (Sacramento: National Council on Teacher Retirement (NCTR), 4th ed. 2000)] The remainder of the states used some variant or combination of these rules (see Q 4:1).

As of 1995, 35 states had conflict of interest rules, which are often quite extensive. Most states also had codes of ethics, which frequently apply to public officials who manage pension funds.

Twenty-six states had some kind of "legal list" statute, which limits the types of investments in which governmental plans can invest. These ranged from statutes totally forbidding equity interests by public pension funds to statutes prohibiting certain kinds of investments deemed speculative. Although the trend is to eliminate legal list statutes in favor of a more generalized prudence standard, such statutes are obviously still a factor with which to contend.

The Uniform Management of Public Employee Retirement Systems Act (UMPERSA) may affect the investments of governmental 457 trusts. Although only one state, South Carolina, has approved UMPERSA to date, UMPERSA appears likely to influence future legislative changes at the state level. Section 6 of UMPERSA states as follows:

> SECTION 6. GENERAL DUTIES OF TRUSTEE AND FIDUCIARY. Each trustee and other fiduciary shall discharge duties with respect to a retirement system: (1) solely in the interest of the participants and beneficiaries; (2) for the exclusive purpose of providing benefits to participants and beneficiaries and paying reasonable expenses of administering the system; (3) with the care, skill, prudence, and diligence under the circumstances then prevailing which a prudent person acting in a like capacity and familiar with such matters would use in the conduct of an activity of like character and purpose; (4) impartially, taking into account any differing interests of participants and beneficiaries; and (5) in accordance with law governing the retirement program and system.

The reporter's notes on this section say that it is intended to track the fiduciary standards of ERISA.

In 1998, the Nebraska, Washington, and Oklahoma legislatures considered UMPERSA, but none of them took action on it. No state appears to have considered UMPERSA since 1998.

Governmental Form Filings

Q 14:12   Does an eligible 457(b) plan have to file Form 5500?

A governmental 457(b) plan does not have to file Form 5500, Return/Report of Employee Benefit Plan (see Q 4:27). [Ann. 82-146, 1982-47 I.R.B. 53] Because a nongovernmental 457(b) plan can cover only highly compensated and management employees, it can use the alternative (simplified) annual reporting requirements of Labor Regulations Section 2520.104-23 instead of the Form 5500 requirements. Chapter 8 more fully discusses the alternate reporting requirements.

Q 14:13   Does an eligible 457(b) plan have to file Form 990?

No. According to the instructions to Form 990, Return of Organization Exempt from Income Tax, any "state institution whose income is excluded from gross income under section 115" need not file Form 990. An eligible nongovernmental 457(b) plan cannot include a trust, other than a grantor trust, so it also would not file Form 990.

Matching Contributions

Q 14:14 Can a state or local government employer make matching contributions to an eligible 457(b) plan?

Yes, but doing so will seriously limit the total amount that the employer and employees can contribute. A governmental employer may want to consider making its matching contributions to a Section 401(a) qualified plan instead.

Example 1. Government X adopts an eligible 457(b) plan under which each employee can make a contribution of up to the maximum permitted by law and Government X will match each employee's contribution at a 100 percent rate. Employee A earns $50,000. The maximum contribution A can make for 2003 is $6,000 (assuming that A is not eligible to make catch-up contributions). At that level, A's own contribution plus X's match will equal $12,000, which is the maximum permitted by law.

Example 2. Suppose instead that Government X adopts an eligible 457(b) plan under which each employee can make a contribution of up to the maximum permitted by law, and adopts a qualified plan to which Government X will contribute an amount equal to the employee's 457 plan contribution. Under this scenario, A can contribute $12,000 to the 457(b) plan, and X can contribute another $12,000 to the qualified plan.

Code Section 401(m)(4)(A)(ii) specifically contemplates a contribution being made to a qualified plan as a match to a 457(b) plan, so such a structure is lawful. Of course, each plan must comply with all of the legal requirements, including the Section 415 limits applicable to qualified defined contribution plans.

This arrangement works only for a governmental organization. For a tax-exempt organization that is subject to ERISA, the 457(b) plan could cover only highly compensated and management employees, and this would cause the matching contributions to violate the nondiscrimination rules of Code Section 401(m). Thus, if such an organization wants a plan to which rank-and-file employees can make matched contributions, it should consider a 401(k) plan (or, in the case of an eligible organization, a 403(b) plan) rather than an eligible 457(b) plan. If it wants a 457(b) plan only for highly compensated employees, it will need to allow for any match in setting the maximum level of contributions.

Benefit Reductions

Q 14:15 Can an employer reduce future benefits under an eligible 457(b) plan?

In a nongovernmental plan, the plan document would govern this question. Typically, it would provide that the employer could reduce or eliminate future benefit accruals, although it could not cut back on past benefit accruals.

In a governmental plan, state constitutional restrictions typically will preclude the diminution of future benefit accruals for existing employees. [See, e.g., Betts v. Board of Administration of the Public Employees' Retirement System, 21 Cal. 3d 859 (1978)] Thus, any reduction of future benefit accruals under an eligible governmental 457(b) plan may have to exclude existing employees.

Q 14:16 Can an employer distribute benefits to participants before they would otherwise be entitled to distributions on the termination of an eligible 457(b) plan?

Yes. Under regulations issued July 11, 2003 [68 FR 41230; Treas. Dec. Int. Rev. 9075], an eligible 457(b) plan is permitted to have provisions whereupon amounts can be distributed on plan termination without violating the distribution requirements of section 457(b). Indeed, an eligible 457(b) plan is considered terminated only if all amounts deferred under the plan are paid to participants as soon as administratively practicable. If the amounts deferred under the plan are not distributed, the plan is treated as a frozen plan and must continue to comply with all of the applicable statutory requirements necessary for plan eligibility.

Plan Choice Alternatives

Q 14:17 What are some considerations in choosing between an eligible 457(b) plan and a 403(b) plan or 401(k) plan?

The attractiveness of a 457(b) plan as compared with a 403(b) plan or a 401(k) plan may vary greatly depending on the circumstances. For example, a state or local government entity other than a public school or university may need to have a 457(b) plan, because it cannot normally have either of the other types of plans. A private university that is tax exempt under Code Section 501(c)(3) but maintains a health maintenance organization that is tax exempt under Code Section 501(c)(4) and/or taxable research subsidiaries may prefer a 401(k) plan, so that it can cover all employees under the same plan. A private school that does not have affiliates, and wants to provide only for salary reduction contributions, may find that a 403(b) plan gives it the greatest ability to cover rank-and file employees while minimizing administrative requirements. A public or private nonprofit school or university that maintains a qualified defined contribution plan may want to have a separate 403(b) plan as well, since it need not combine 403(b) contributions with contributions to its qualified plans in applying the Section 415(c) limits.

With the passage of the Economic Growth and Tax Relief Reconciliation Act of 2001 (EGTRRA), under which 457(b) plan deferrals no longer have to be coordinated with 401(k) or 403(b) deferrals, more employers may want to consider maintaining more than one type of plan to maximize total permitted deferrals. This is particularly true because EGTRRA permits 457(b) and 403(b) plan money, as well as 401(k) plan money, to be used to purchase certain types of service credit under a defined benefit plan.

The following chart sets forth some primary differences among the different types of plans:

	457(b) plan	401(k) plan	403(b) plan
Can it be maintained by a state or local governmental employer?	Yes.	No, unless it is a grandfathered 401(k) plan, or unless it is a rural cooperative as defined in I.R.C. § 401(k)(7)(B).	Only if it is a public school or university, a portion of another agency that is treated as an educational institution (e.g., an educational program for convicts that is part of a state prison system), or a governmental instrumentality that also has 501(c)(3) status.
Can it be maintained by a church employer that has not made an election under I.R.C. § 410(d) to be subject to ERISA ("nonelecting church")?	A nonelecting church is exempt from I.R.C. § 457(b). Thus, it can maintain an unfunded deferred compensation plan but is not subject to the I.R.C. § 457(b) requirements and cannot maintain a funded arrangement.	Yes.	Yes.
Can it be maintained by a tax-exempt employer, other than a government or nonelecting church?	Only for highly compensated and management employees.	Yes.	Only if it is a § 501(c)(3) organization.
Can it include related taxable entities?	No, although an unfunded deferred compensation plan can be maintained for highly compensated and management employees of taxable affiliates.	Yes.	No.
Are there maximum limits on elective deferrals?	Yes. Except to the extent a catch-up applies, for 2003 the limit is the lesser of (a) $12,000 as indexed or (b) 100% of pre-plan compensation. The $12,000 limit rises $1,000 each year until it reaches $15,000 in 2006. Beginning in 2007, the limit is adjusted for changes in the cost of living. 457(b) plans need be	Yes. Except to the extent a catch-up applies, for 2003 the limit is $12,000, with the limit rising $1,000 for each year until it reaches $15,000 in 2006. Beginning in 2007, the limit is adjusted for changes in the cost of living. 401(k) plans need only be combined with	Yes. Except to the extent a catch-up applies, for 2003 the limit is $12,000, with the limit rising $1,000 for each year until it reaches $15,000 in 2006. Beginning in 2007, the limit is adjusted for changes in the cost of living. 403(b) plans need only be combined with other 403(b) plans or 401(k) plans (not 457(b)

	457(b) plan	401(k) plan	403(b) plan
	combined only with other 457(b) plans, not 403(b) or 401(k) plans, in applying limits.	other 401(k) plans or 403(b) plans (not 457(b) plans) in applying limits.	plans) in applying limits.
Are catch-ups available to increase the maximum amount of elective deferrals?	A catch-up is available under 457(b)(3) for one or more of the participant's last three taxable years ending before he or she attains normal retirement age under the plan. A catch-up is available under 457(e)(18) and 414(v) for governmental plans *only*, for participants age 50 or over. If both catch-ups apply, only the higher of the two, not both of the two, may be taken.	A catch-up is available under 402(g) and 414(v), for participants age 50 or over.	A catch-up is available under 402(g) and 414(v), for participants age 50 or over. A catch-up is available under 402(g)(7) for employees who have at least 15 years of service with certain organizations. If both catch-ups apply, the individual can take the sum of the two.
Are there maximum limits on total contributions?	Yes, the lesser of (a) $12,000 for 2003, rising by $1,000 a year until 2006, and indexed for 2007 and later years, or (b) 100% of pre-plan compensation. Other 457(b) plans (but not qualified or 403(b) plans) are combined in determining the limit.	Yes, the lesser of (a) $40,000 as indexed or (b) 100% of pre-plan compensation. Other qualified plans are combined in determining the limit. 457(b) plans are never combined with 401(a) (including 401(k)) plans in applying limits. A 403(b) plan is combined with a 401(a) plan in applying the limit only if the employee is in control of the business that maintains the 401(a) plan.	Yes, the lesser of (a) $40,000 as indexed or (b) 100% of pre-plan compensation. Other 403(b) plans are combined in determining the limit. 457(b) plans are never combined with 403(b) plans in applying limits. A 403(b) plan is combined with a 401(a) plan in applying the limit only if the employee is in control of the business that maintains the 401(a) plan.
Are loans available?	Yes, in the case of a governmental 457(b) plan, subject to maximum limits under 72(p) to avoid taxation of the participant; loans from other 457(b) plans will give rise to participant taxation.	Yes, subject to maximum limits under 72(p) to avoid taxation of the participant.	Yes, subject to maximum limits under 72(p) to avoid taxation of the participant.
Is there excise tax on excess contributions?	No.	Tax-exempt (including governmental and	Only if the 403(b) contract is a custodial account described in

	457(b) plan	401(k) plan	403(b) plan
		church) plans are exempt.	I.R.C. § 403(b)(7), as opposed to an annuity contract.
Are there other effects of violating maximum limits on total contributions?	In the case of a governmental plan that includes the limits in the plan, but violates them administratively, the plan continues to be considered a 457(b) plan until the first day of the first plan year that begins more than 180 days after the date the IRS notifies the employer of the problem, and will continue to be a 457(b) plan then if the employer has fixed the problem. In the case of other 457(b) plans, it appears (but is not certain) that the whole plan could be disqualified.	Disqualification of the plan.	Only the amount in excess of the maximum limits is taxable.
Can money be rolled in from a 401(k) or other qualified plan?*	No for nongovernmental employers; yes for governmental employers.	Yes.	Yes.
Can money be rolled in from a 403(b) plan?*	No for nongovernmental employers; yes for governmental employers.	Yes.	Yes.
Can money be rolled in from a 457(b) plan?*	No for nongovernmental employers; yes for governmental employers. A direct transfer can be made from one 457(b) plan to another, even if either or both of them are nongovernmental.	No for nongovernmental employers; yes for governmental employers.	No for nongovernmental employers; yes for governmental employers.
Can taxes be deferred on distributions by rolling them into another plan or an IRA?*	No for nongovernmental plans; yes for governmental plans. For nongovernmental plans, taxes can be deferred only by direct transfer to another 457(b) plan.	Yes.	Yes.
Is there a trust requirement?	Yes, it is required for governmental employers; however, it is forbidden for nongovernmental employers.	Yes, unless the plan is fully insured.	No, but must have annuity contracts, custodial accounts, or § 403(b)(9) retirement income accounts.
Is there protection	Only if provided under "applicable	Yes, unless a governmental	Only if provided under "applicable

	457(b) plan	401(k) plan	403(b) plan
from creditors of employees?	nonbankruptcy law" (e.g., state trust spendthrift rules). These would typically be applicable only if the plan were a governmental plan that maintained a trust under I.R.C. § 457(g). See Section 26 of the Uniform Management of Public Employee Retirement Systems Act (UMPERSA), which applies the protections of UMPERSA to a 457(b) plan only after such plan becomes subject to § 457(g).	employer or a nonelecting church employer maintains the plan. For a governmental employer or a nonelecting church employer, protection would be available, if at all, only under "applicable nonbankruptcy law." Because a 401(k) plan always includes a trust, however, state spendthrift trust laws are more likely to be available.	nonbankruptcy law" (state trust spendthrift rules). The I.R.C. § 401(g) nonalienation requirement may help.
Is there a prohibition on discrimination in favor of highly compensated employees?	No. In fact, in the case of a plan that is not a governmental plan, discrimination in favor of management and highly compensated employees is required.	Yes, except in the case of a plan of a state or local government. However, IRS Notice 2001-46, 32 I.R.B. 122 (Aug. 6, 2001) delayed the application of these rules until 2003 in the case of a governmental entity other than a state or local government (e.g., a federal government agency or an international organization), and until at least 2003 in the case of a church. These rules include restrictions on the actual level of contributions as well as on the opportunity to contribute. The rules do not apply, however, if no highly compensated employees participate in the plan.	In the case of salary reduction contributions, simplified rules measure only availability of a right to make contributions, not actual contribution levels. In the case of other contributions, state and local government and nonelecting church entities are not subject to the rules, but other employers are. IRS Notice 2001-46, 32 I.R.B. 122 (Aug. 6, 2001) delayed the application of these rules until 2003 in the case of a governmental entity other than a state or local government (e.g., an educational institution operated by a federal government agency). For this purpose, a church-controlled organization is not a church.
Do top heavy rules apply?	No.	Technically the rules are applicable to	No.

	457(b) plan	401(k) plan	403(b) plan
		plans other than governmental or nonelecting church plans, but few plans of tax-exempt organizations are in practice subject to them.	
Are there salary reduction distribution restrictions?	Yes.	Yes.	Such restrictions apply to elective deferrals made after December 31, 1988, and to earnings accrued after December 31, 1988, on both pre-1989 and post-1988 deferrals.
Are there exceptions to salary reduction distribution restrictions for plan terminations?	Yes.	Yes.	Unclear. In instances in which a plan is funded through individually owned contracts, as opposed to a group annuity or custodial account contract or a § 403(b)(9) church retirement income account, the employees can continue to hold their own contracts. Thus, the inability to make distributions upon plan terminations primarily affects plans in which participants do not hold individual contracts.
Is there 10% additional tax on most early distributions?	No, except to the extent a distribution is derived from money rolled over from a 401(a) or 403(b) plan, or an IRA.	Yes.	Yes.
Are there I.R.C. § 401(a)(9) required distributions?	Yes.	Yes.	Yes, but pre-1987 account balances are subject to less stringent rules under which distributions need not commence until the later of termination of employment or the date on which the employee attains (or, in the case of a deceased employee, would have attained) age 75.
Is there ERISA coverage?	None for plans of governmental or	Yes, except in the case of a	No, in the case of a salary-reduction-only

	457(b) plan	401(k) plan	403(b) plan
	nonelecting church-controlled organizations; extremely limited for other plans.	governmental or nonelecting church plan.	plan that meets certain requirements, or a governmental or church plan; yes in other instances.
Do prohibited transaction rules apply?	No for nongovernmental plans, unless provided under state law in the case of a nonelecting church plan. Cross-reference to 401(a) in 457(g) may make I.R.C. § 503(b) prohibited transaction rules applicable to governmental plans.	Strict prohibited transaction rules under I.R.C. § 4975 apply to plans other than governmental or nonelecting church plans. Looser prohibited transaction rules under I.R.C. § 503(b) apply. In addition, some states apply prohibited transaction rules to governmental plans.	No, although the exclusive benefit requirement may impose similar rules on plans that are subject to I.R.C. § 403(b)(9).
Are IRS determination letters available?	Only possible through National Office private letter ruling; no prototype submissions.	Determination letters available; prototype submissions possible.	Only possible through National Office private letter ruling; no prototype submissions.
Is there IRS audit activity?	IRS is targeting 457(b) plans for audit.	No specific focus on 401(k) plans.	IRS is targeting 403(b) plans for audit.
Are there correction programs?	EPCRS available for governmental 457(b) plans, but not for other 457(b) plans until the IRS has had a chance to study the issues.	EPCRS.	EPCRS.
Are there state income tax considerations?	Typically none.	Typically none.	Some states (e.g., New Jersey and Pennsylvania) impose income taxes on all 403(b) contributions.
Are there practical considerations?	457(b) plans are not really understood as a 401(k) equivalent. Fewer entities provide services to 457(b) plans than to 401(k) or 403(b) plans. In many instances, the investment choices readily available are much less favorable. 457(b) plans have become quite attractive as a supplement to 401(k) or 403(b) plans,	Overwhelming popularity makes 401(k) plans a recognizable commodity to most individuals. Good software and support materials are available. Better understanding in vendor community.	403(b) plans are not really understood as a 401(k) equivalent. Good 403(b) software is not as available. In many instances, vendor software is either inaccurate or requires such sophisticated information from employees as to make it virtually unusable. Vendor understanding

457(b) plan	401(k) plan	403(b) plan
if an employer wishes to provide for larger tax deferred contributions.		of 403(b) plans is more limited.

---

* The rules for rollovers (including direct rollovers when a distribution is otherwise available from the plan) are more flexible than the rules for direct transfers. A direct transfer can be made only (a) from a 403(b) or governmental 457(b) plan to a governmental *defined benefit* 401(a) plan for certain purchases of service credit, or (b) from one plan to another plan described in the same section of the Internal Revenue Code (e.g., a 401(a) plan to another 401(a) plan). Thus, for example, although a direct rollover can be made from a 403(b) plan to a 401(k) plan, a direct transfer cannot. Moreover, although the statute refers to direct transfers from 403(b) plans to defined benefit plans (without specifically limiting the transferor 403(b) plans to governmental 403(b) plans), Publication 571 takes the position (based on legislative history not reflected in the statute) that only governmental 403(b) plans can make such transfers.

Q 14:18   What is a mutual fund option plan?

A mutual fund option plan is a plan under which the employer provides the employee with an option to purchase shares in a mutual fund at a particular strike price. Regulations under Code Section 83 provide that an option is not taxed if it does not have a readily ascertainable fair market value. Although, traditionally, stock option plans have involved stock of an employer corporation, some nonprofit organizations have in the past set up plans that provide options in mutual funds unrelated to the employer.

Q 14:19   Can a mutual fund option plan be used to avoid the limitations of Section 457(f)?

No. Regulations under Code Section 457 have effectively ended the use of mutual fund option plans as a tax-deferral mechanism for tax-exempt organizations. The regulations provide that the Section 457(f) limitations apply to mutual fund options and options on other property if the options are not conditioned on the executive's future performance. [Treas. Reg. § 1.457-11] The Section 457 regulations apply to options issued after May 8, 2002. [Treas. Reg. § 1.457-12(d)]

Q 14:20   What is split-dollar life insurance?

Split-dollar life insurance is an arrangement under which an employer purchases life insurance with a cash value. In some instances, the premiums paid by the employer are returned to the employer when the policy is cashed out or when a death benefit is paid. In other instances, the employee is taxed on the premiums as they are paid. The policy, however, will typically provide for a cash value that includes the original premiums plus some sort of an earnings element, and will provide for a death benefit that is higher than the cash value. The intent has been to defer taxes on the earnings buildup in the policy until the policy is cashed in, and to avoid them entirely under Code Section 101 if the contract pays out a death benefit.

Q 14:21   Can split-dollar life insurance be used to avoid the limitations of Section 457(f)?

No. Regulations issued on September 17, 2003 [T.D. 9092, 68 Fed. Reg. 54,336 (Sept. 17, 2003)] and Revenue Ruling 2003-105, 2003-40 I.R.B. 1, greatly diminish the tax benefits of split-dollar life insurance arrangements for all employers by taxing the value of such arrangements under either an economic benefit or a loan theory, depending on whether the employee or the employer is the owner of the policy. Moreover, the Preamble to the regulations suggests that Section 457(f) may apply to an "equity split-dollar life insurance arrangement" in which the employer is the owner of the split-dollar policy. (See Q 11:3.)

Q 14:22   What other concerns apply to split-dollar life insurance?

The Sarbanes-Oxley Act of 2002 [Pub. L. No. 107-204], which became law on July 30, 2002, banned company loans to executives. Even before the IRS issued the revenue ruling and regulations referenced in Q 14:19 many analysts were concerned that the premiums on split-dollar policies could be considered interest-free loans to the extent the corporation is eventually reimbursed for them. The uncertainty over the policies virtually halted their sale in 2002, and has even created uncertainty as to whether premiums can continue to be paid on existing contracts. ["Insurance Plans of Top Executives Are in Jeopardy," *N.Y. Times*, Aug. 29 2002, Business sec.]

Leave Conversion Plan

Q 14:23   What is a leave conversion plan?

In many instances, public employees are entitled to a payment for accrued but unused vacation, sick, or other leave at the time of retirement. However, if the employer pays such amounts to the employee, the amounts are taxable as wages. Thus, employers have sought ways to enable employees to defer taxes on such amounts by having the amounts contributed to a retirement plan.

Q 14:24   If an employee is permitted to choose whether to receive payment for unused leave immediately in cash, or to have the amount contributed to a 457(b) plan, will the employee who chooses a 457(b) plan contribution be immediately taxable on the amount of the contribution?

Yes. This is comparable to the situation in Revenue Ruling 75-539, 1975-2 C.B. 45, in which employees were permitted to choose whether to receive leave payments in cash, or to have them contributed to a medical/health plan. The IRS held that even those employees who elected the plan contribution would be considered to have constructively received the cash, and therefore would be taxed on it.

Q 14:25   Can taxes on accumulated but unused leave be deferred if an employee makes an election to have the payment for such leave contributed to a retirement plan?

Probably not. Elective contributions to a 457(b) plan cannot be made out of compensation the employee would not have received but for the termination of employment. In most instances, an employee cannot elect to cash out accrued but unused leave unless he or she is terminating employment.

Q 14:26   What alternatives are there for permitting an employee to choose between receiving cash or increased retirement benefits in exchange for accumulated unused leave?

One option is to have the amount contributed to the plan on a nonelective basis. Private Letter Ruling 9840006 (June 23, 1998) excludes from income sick leave used to increase the employee's account in a defined benefit plan if payment for the sick leave could not have been received in cash.

In recent years, many employers have recognized that they can in effect permit employees to choose between accumulated leave and 457(b) plan benefits by having unused leave automatically contributed to a 457(b) plan (with no employee election), but permitting a lump-sum distribution from the 457(b) plan upon termination of employment equal to the amount of the leave contribution. Because an employee typically receives unused leave only in connection with a termination of employment, such an arrangement may result in very little delay to the employee in receiving the cash. In Private Letter Ruling 200301032 (Jan. 13, 2003), the IRS approved such a plan.

Rollovers

Q 14:27   Are there any special pitfalls to making a rollover to a 457(b) plan?

Yes. A rollover can be made only if a participant is entitled to an immediate distribution. However, at least under the current IRS position, rolled-over assets become subject to all of the distribution restrictions of the 457(b) plan that receives them.

The preamble to the 457 regulations states as follows:

> These regulations do not permit an eligible governmental plan to distribute rolled-in assets to a participant who is not yet eligible for a distribution until future guidance of general applicability is published that addresses this issue. Treasury and the IRS intend to issue, in the near future, guidance of general applicability resolving this issue in coordination with the applicable rules for qualified plans and section 403(b) contracts.

Appendix A

Extracts from Relevant Code Sections

> **Note.** This appendix reflects additions or amendments to the Code made by the Economic Growth and Tax Relief Reconciliation Act of 2001 (EGTRRA) and the Job Creation and Worker Assistance Act of 2002 (JCWAA), which generally are effective in 2002.

President Bush signed into law the Job Creation and Worker Assistance Act of 2002 (Pub. L. No. 107-147) on March 9, 2002. The changes made by this new law, in the form of technical corrections, are also reflected in this appendix.

A Code section can be divided into several parts. The § symbol is frequently used to abbreviate the word section. For example, the parts to the citation § 72(a)(1)(A)(i)(I) are as follows:

§ 72 (a) (1) (A) (i) (I)

72 Section

(a) Subsection

(1) Paragraph

(A) Subparagraph

(i) Clause

(I) Subclause

Code Section 72(t): 10-Percent Additional Tax on Early Distributions from Qualified Retirement Plans

Code Section 72(t)(9)—Special Rules for Rollovers to Section 457 Plans

(9) SPECIAL RULE FOR ROLLOVERS TO SECTION 457 PLANS.—For purposes of this subsection, a distribution from an eligible deferred compensation plan (as defined in section 457(b)) of an eligible employer described in section 457(e)(1)(A) shall be treated as a distribution from a qualified retirement plan described in 4974(c)(1) to the extent that such distribution is attributable to an amount transferred to an eligible deferred compensation plan from a qualified retirement plan (as defined in section 4974(c)).

Code Section 83: Property Transferred in Connection with Performance of Services

Code Section 83—Property Transferred in Connection with Performance of Services

(a) GENERAL RULE.—If, in connection with the performance of services, property is transferred to any person other than the person for whom such services are performed, the excess of—

(1) the fair market value of such property (determined without regard to any restriction other than a restriction which by its terms will never lapse) at the first time the rights of the person having the beneficial interest in such property are transferable or are not subject to a substantial risk of forfeiture, whichever occurs earlier, over

(2) the amount (if any) paid for such property shall be included in the gross income of the person who performed such services in the first taxable year in which the rights of the person having the beneficial interest in such property are transferable or are not subject to a substantial risk of forfeiture, whichever is applicable. The preceding sentence shall not apply if such person sells or otherwise disposes of such property in an arm's length transaction before his rights in such property become transferable or not subject to a substantial risk of forfeiture.

(b) ELECTION TO INCLUDE IN GROSS INCOME IN YEAR OF TRANSFER.—

(1) IN GENERAL.—Any person who performs services in connection with which property is transferred to any person may elect to include in his gross income for the taxable year in which such property is transferred, the excess of—

(A) the fair market value of such property at the time of transfer (determined without regard to any restriction other than a restriction which by its terms will never lapse), over

(B) the amount (if any) paid for such property.

If such election is made, subsection (a) shall not apply with respect to the transfer of such property, and if such property is subsequently forfeited, no deduction shall be allowed in respect of such forfeiture.

(2) ELECTION.—An election under paragraph (1) with respect to any transfer of property shall be made in such manner as the Secretary prescribes and shall be made not later than 30 days after the date of such transfer. Such election may not be revoked except with the consent of the Secretary.

(c) SPECIAL RULES.—For purposes of this section—

(1) SUBSTANTIAL RISK OF FORFEITURE.—The rights of a person in property are subject to a substantial risk of forfeiture if such person's rights to full enjoyment of such property are conditioned upon the future performance of substantial services by any individual.

(2) TRANSFERABILITY OF PROPERTY.—The rights of a person in property are transferable only if the rights in such property of any transferee are not subject to a substantial risk of forfeiture.

(3) SALES WHICH MAY GIVE RISE TO SUIT UNDER SECTION 16(b) OF THE SECURITIES EXCHANGE ACT OF 1934.—So long as the sale of property at a profit could subject a person to suit under section 16(b) of the Securities Exchange Act of 1934, such person's rights in such property are—

(A) subject to a substantial risk of forfeiture, and

(B) not transferable.

(d) CERTAIN RESTRICTIONS WHICH WILL NEVER LAPSE.—

(1) VALUATION.—In the case of property subject to a restriction which by its terms will never lapse, and which allows the transferee to sell such property only at a price determined under a formula, the price so determined shall be deemed to be the fair market value of the property unless established to the contrary by the Secretary, and the burden of proof shall be on the Secretary with respect to such value.

(e) APPLICABILITY OF SECTION.—This section shall not apply to—

(1) a transaction to which section 421 applies,

(2) a transfer to or from a trust described in section 401(a) or a transfer under an annuity plan which meets the requirements of section 404(a)(2),

(3) the transfer of an option without a readily ascertainable fair market value,

(4) the transfer of property pursuant to the exercise of an option with a readily ascertainable fair market value at the date of grant, or

(5) group-term life insurance to which section 79 applies.

(f) HOLDING PERIOD.—In determining the period for which the taxpayer has held property to which subsection (a) applies, there shall be included only the period beginning at the first time his rights in such property are transferable or are not subject to a substantial risk of forfeiture, whichever occurs earlier.

(g) CERTAIN EXCHANGES.—If property to which subsection (a) applies is exchanged for property subject to restrictions and conditions substantially similar to those to which the property given in such exchange was subject, and if section 354, 355, 356, or 1036 (or so much of section 1031 as relates to section 1036) applied to such exchange, or if such exchange was pursuant to the exercise of a conversion privilege—

(1) such exchange shall be disregarded for purposes of subsection (a), and

(2) the property received shall be treated as property to which subsection (a) applies.

(h) DEDUCTION BY EMPLOYER.—In the case of a transfer of property to which this section applies or a cancellation of a restriction described in subsection (d), there shall be allowed as a deduction under section 162, to the person for whom were performed the services in connection with which such property was transferred, an amount equal to the amount included under subsection (a), (b), or (d)(2) in the gross income of the person who performed such services. Such deduction shall be allowed for the taxable year of such person in which or with which ends the taxable year in which such amount is included in the gross income of the person who performed such services.

Code Section 219: Limitation on Deductions for Active Participants in Certain Plans

Code Section 219—Retirement Savings

(g) LIMITATION ON DEDUCTIONS FOR ACTIVE PARTICIPANTS IN CERTAIN PLANS.—

(1) IN GENERAL.—If (for any part of any plan year ending with or within a taxable year) an individual or the individual's spouse is an active participant, each of the dollar limitations contained in subsections (b)(1)(A) and (c)(1)(A) for such taxable year shall be reduced (but not below zero) by the amount determined under paragraph (2).

(2) AMOUNT OF REDUCTION.—

(A) IN GENERAL.—The amount determined under this paragraph with respect to any dollar limitation shall be the amount which bears the same ratio to such limitation as—

(i) the excess of—

(I) the taxpayer's adjusted gross income for such taxable year, over

(II) the applicable dollar amount, bears to

(ii) $10,000 ($20,000 in the case of a joint return for a taxable year beginning after December 31, 2006).

(B) NO REDUCTION BELOW $200 UNTIL COMPLETE PHASE-OUT.—No dollar limitation shall be reduced below $200 under paragraph (1) unless (without regard to this subparagraph) such limitation is reduced to zero.

(C) ROUNDING.—Any amount determined under this paragraph which is not a multiple of $10 shall be rounded to the next lowest $10.

(3) ADJUSTED GROSS INCOME; APPLICABLE DOLLAR AMOUNT.—For purposes of this subsection—

(A) ADJUSTED GROSS INCOME—Adjusted gross income of any taxpayer shall be determined—

(i) after application of sections 86 and 469, and

(ii) without regard to sections 135, 137, 221, 222, and 911 or the deduction allowable under this section.

(B) APPLICABLE DOLLAR AMOUNT.—The term "applicable dollar amount" means the following:

(i) In the case of a taxpayer filing a joint return:

For taxable years beginning in:	The applicable dollar amount is:
1998	$50,000
1999	$51,000
2000	$52,000
2001	$53,000
2002	$54,000
2003	$60,000
2004	$65,000
2005	$70,000
2006	$75,000
2007 and thereafter	$80,000

(ii) In the case of any other taxpayer (other than a married individual filing a separate return):

For taxable years beginning in:	The applicable dollar amount is:
1998	$30,000
1999	$31,000
2000	$32,000
2001	$33,000
2002	$34,000

For taxable years beginning in:	The applicable dollar amount is:
2003	$40,000
2004	$45,000
2005 and thereafter	$50,000

(iii) In the case of a married individual filing a separate return, zero.

(4) SPECIAL RULE FOR MARRIED INDIVIDUALS FILING SEPARATELY AND LIVING APART.—A husband and wife who—

(A) file separate returns for any taxable year, and

(B) live apart at all times during such taxable year, shall not be treated as married individuals for purposes of this subsection.

(5) ACTIVE PARTICIPANT.—For purposes of this subsection, the term "active participant" means, with respect to any plan year, an individual—

(A) who is an active participant in—

(i) a plan described in section 401(a) which includes a trust exempt from tax under section 501(a),

(ii) an annuity plan described in section 403(a),

(iii) a plan established for its employees by the United States, by a State or political subdivision thereof, or by an agency or instrumentality of any of the foregoing,

(iv) an annuity contract described in section 403(b),

(v) a simplified employee pension (within the meaning of section 408(k)), or

(vi) any simple retirement account (within the meaning of section 408(p), or

(B) who makes deductible contributions to a trust described in section 501(c)(18).

The determination of whether an individual is an active participant shall be made without regard to whether or not such individual's rights under a plan, trust, or contract are nonforfeitable. An eligible deferred compensation plan (within the meaning of section 457(b)) shall not be treated as a plan described in subparagraph (A)(iii).

(6) CERTAIN INDIVIDUALS NOT TREATED AS ACTIVE PARTICIPANTS.—For purposes of this subsection, any individual described in any of the following subparagraphs shall not be treated as an active participant for any taxable year solely because of any participation so described:

(A) MEMBERS OF RESERVE COMPONENTS.—Participation in a plan described in subparagraph (A)(iii) of paragraph (5) by reason of service as a member of a reserve component of the Armed Forces (as defined in section 10101 of title 10, unless such individual has served in excess of 90 days on active duty (other than active duty for training) during the year.

(B) VOLUNTEER FIREFIGHTERS.—A volunteer firefighter—

(i) who is a participant in a plan described in subparagraph (A)(iii) of paragraph (5) based on his activity as a volunteer firefighter, and

(ii) whose accrued benefit as of the beginning of the taxable year is not more than an annual benefit of $1,800 (when expressed as a single life annuity commencing at age 65).

(7) SPECIAL RULE FOR SPOUSES WHO ARE NOT ACTIVE PARTICIPANTS.—If this subsection applies to an individual for any taxable year solely because their spouse is an active participant, then, in applying this subsection to the individual (but not their spouse)—

(A) the applicable dollar amount under paragraph (3)(B)(i) shall be $150,000; and

(B) the amount applicable under paragraph (2)(A)(ii) shall be $10,000.

(h) CROSS REFERENCE.—For failure to provide required reports, see section 6652(g).

Code Section 402: Taxability of Beneficiary

Code Section 402(g)—Limitation on Exclusions for Elective Deferrals

[Caution. Code Section 402(g)(1), below, applies to years beginning after 2001 and before 2006.]

(1) IN GENERAL.—

(A) LIMITATION.—Notwithstanding subsections (e)(3) and (h)(1)(B), the elective deferrals of any individual for any taxable year shall be included in such individual's gross income to the extent the amount of such deferrals for the taxable year exceeds the applicable dollar amount.

(B) APPLICABLE DOLLAR AMOUNT.—For purposes of subparagraph (A), the applicable dollar amount shall be the amount determined in accordance with the following table:

For taxable years beginning in calendar year:	The applicable dollar amount is:
2002	$11,000
2003	$12,000
2004	$13,000
2005	$14,000
2006 or thereafter	$15,000

(C) CATCH-UP CONTRIBUTIONS.—In addition to subparagraph (A), in the case of an eligible participant (as defined in section 414(v)), gross income shall not include elective deferrals in excess of the applicable dollar amount under subparagraph (B) to the extent that the amount of such elective deferrals does not exceed the applicable dollar amount under section 414(v)(2)(B)(i) for the taxable year (without regard to the treatment of the elective deferrals by an applicable employer plan under section 414(v)).

[Caution. Code Section 402(g)(1), below, applies to tax years beginning after 2005.]

(1) IN GENERAL.—

(A) LIMITATION.—Notwithstanding subsections (e)(3) and (h)(1)(B), the elective deferrals of any individual for any taxable year shall be included in such individual's gross income to the extent the amount of such deferrals for the taxable year exceeds the applicable dollar amount. The preceding sentence shall not apply the portion of such excess as does not exceed the designated Roth contributions of the individual for the taxable year.

(B) APPLICABLE DOLLAR AMOUNT.—For purposes of subparagraph (A), the applicable dollar amount shall be the amount determined in accordance with the following table:

For taxable years beginning in calendar year:	The applicable dollar amount is:
2002	$11,000
2003	$12,000
2004	$13,000
2005	$14,000
2006 or thereafter	$15,000

(C) CATCH-UP CONTRIBUTIONS.—In addition to subparagraph (A), in the case of an eligible participant (as defined in section 414(v)), gross income shall not include elective deferrals in excess of the applicable dollar amount under subparagraph (B) to the extent that the amount of such elective deferrals does not exceed the applicable dollar amount under section 414(v)(2)(B)(i) for the taxable year (without regard to the treatment of the elective deferrals by an applicable employer plan under section 414(v)).

(2) DISTRIBUTION OF EXCESS DEFERRALS.—

[Caution. Code Section 402(g)(2)(A), below, applies to tax years beginning before 2006.]

(A) IN GENERAL.—If any amount (hereinafter in this paragraph referred to as "excess deferrals") is included in the gross income of an individual under paragraph (1) for any taxable year—

[Caution. Code Section 402(g)(2)(A), applies to tax years beginning after 2005.]

(A) IN GENERAL.—If any amount (hereinafter in this paragraph referred to as "excess deferrals") is included in the gross income of an individual under paragraph (1) (or would be included but for the last sentence thereof) for any taxable year—

(i) not later than the 1st March 1 following the close of the taxable year, the individual may allocate the amount of such excess deferrals among the plans under which the deferrals were made and may notify each such plan of the portion allocated to it, and

(ii) not later than the 1st April 15 following the close of the taxable year, each such plan may distribute to the individual the amount allocated to it under clause (i) (and any income allocable to such amount).

The distribution described in clause (ii) may be made notwithstanding any other provision of law.

(B) TREATMENT OF DISTRIBUTION UNDER SECTION 401(k).—Except to the extent provided under rules prescribed by the Secretary, notwithstanding the distribution of any portion of an excess deferral from a plan under subparagraph (A)(ii), such portion shall, for purposes of applying section 401(k)(3)(A)(ii), be treated as an employer contribution.

(C) TAXATION OF DISTRIBUTION.—In the case of a distribution to which subparagraph (A) applies—

(i) except as provided in clause (ii), such distribution shall not be included in gross income, and

(ii) any income on the excess deferral shall, for purposes of this chapter, be treated as earned and received in the taxable year in which such income is distributed. No tax shall be imposed under section 72(t) on any distribution described in the preceding sentence.

(D) PARTIAL DISTRIBUTIONS.—If a plan distributes only a portion of any excess deferral and income allocable thereto, such portion shall be treated as having been distributed ratably from the excess deferral and the income.

(3) ELECTIVE DEFERRALS.—For purposes of this subsection, the term "elective deferrals" means, with respect to any taxable year, the sum of—

(A) any employer contribution under a qualified cash or deferred arrangement (as defined in section 401(k)) to the extent not includible in gross income for the taxable year under subsection (e)(3) (determined without regard to this subsection),

(B) any employer contribution to the extent not includible in gross income for the taxable year under subsection (h)(1)(B) (determined without regard to this subsection),

(C) any employer contribution to purchase an annuity contract under section 403(b) under a salary reduction agreement (within the meaning of section 3121(a)(5)(D)), and

(D) any elective employer contribution under section 408(p)(2)(A)(i).

An employer contribution shall not be treated as an elective deferral described in subparagraph (C) if under the salary reduction agreement such contribution is made pursuant to a one-time irrevocable election made by the employee at the time of initial eligibility to participate in the agreement or is made pursuant to a similar arrangement involving a one-time irrevocable election specified in regulations.

(4) COST-OF-LIVING ADJUSTMENT.—In the case of taxable years beginning after December 31, 2006, the Secretary shall adjust the $15,000 amount under paragraph (1)(B) at the same time and in the same manner as under section 415(d), except that the base period shall be the calendar quarter beginning July 1, 2005, and any increase under this paragraph which is not a multiple of $500 shall be rounded to the next lowest multiple of $500.

(5) DISREGARD OF COMMUNITY PROPERTY LAWS.—This subsection shall be applied without regard to community property laws.

(6) COORDINATION WITH SECTION 72.—For purposes of applying section 72, any amount includible in gross income for any taxable year under this subsection but which is not distributed from the plan during such taxable year shall not be treated as investment in the contract.

(7) SPECIAL RULE FOR CERTAIN ORGANIZATIONS—

(A) IN GENERAL.—In the case of a qualified employee of a qualified organization, with respect to employer contributions described in paragraph (3)(C) made by such organization, the limitation of paragraph (1) for any taxable year shall be increased by whichever of the following is the least:

(i) $3,000,

(ii) $15,000 reduced by amounts not included in gross income for prior taxable years by reason of this paragraph, or

(iii) the excess of $5,000 multiplied by the number of years of service of the employee with the qualified organization over the employer contributions described in paragraph (3) made by the organization on behalf of such employee for prior taxable years (determined in the manner prescribed by the Secretary).

(B) QUALIFIED ORGANIZATION.—For purposes of this paragraph, the term "qualified organization" means any educational organization, hospital, home health service agency, health and welfare service agency, church, or convention or association of churches. Such term includes any organization described in section 414(e)(3)(B)(ii). Terms used in this subparagraph shall have the same meaning as when used in section 415(c)(4) (as in effect before the enactment of the Economic Growth and Tax Relief Reconciliation Act of 2001).

(C) QUALIFIED EMPLOYEE.—For purposes of this paragraph, the term "qualified employee" means any employee who has completed 15 years of service with the qualified organization.

(D) YEARS OF SERVICE.—For purposes of this paragraph, the term "years of service" has the meaning given such term by section 403(b).

(8) MATCHING CONTRIBUTIONS ON BEHALF OF SELF-EMPLOYED INDIVIDUALS NOT TREATED AS ELECTIVE EMPLOYER CONTRIBUTIONS.—Except as provided in section 401(k)(3)(D)(ii), any matching contribution described in section 401(m)(4)(A) which is made on behalf of a self-employed individual (as defined in section 401(c) shall not be treated as an elective employer contribution under a qualified cash or deferred arrangement (as defined in section 401(k) for purposes of this title.

Code Section 414(o): Avoiding Discrimination Through Separate Organizations and Leasing Arrangements

Code Section 414—Definitions and Special Rules

(o) REGULATIONS.—The Secretary shall prescribe such regulations (which may provide rules in addition to the rules contained in subsections (m) and (n)) as may be necessary to prevent the avoidance of any employee benefit requirement listed in subsection (m)(4) or (n)(3) or any requirement under section 457 through the use of—

(1) separate organizations,

(2) employee leasing, or

(3) other arrangements.

The regulations prescribed under subsection (n) shall include provisions to minimize the recordkeeping requirements of subsection (n) in the case of an employer which has no top-heavy plans (within the meaning of section 416(g)) and which uses the services of persons (other than employees) for an insignificant percentage of the employer's total workload.

Code Section 414(u): Veterans' Reemployment Rights Under USERRA

Code Section 414—Definitions and Special Rules

(u) SPECIAL RULES RELATING TO VETERANS' REEMPLOYMENT RIGHTS UNDER USERRA.—

(1) TREATMENT OF CERTAIN CONTRIBUTIONS MADE PURSUANT TO VETERANS' REEMPLOYMENT RIGHTS.—If any contribution is made by an employer or an employee under an individual account plan with respect to an employee, or by an employee to a defined benefit plan that provides for employee contributions, and such contribution is required by reason of such employee's rights under chapter 43 of title 38, United States Code, resulting from qualified military service, then—

(A) such contribution shall not be subject to any otherwise applicable limitation contained in section 402(g), 402(h), 403(b), 404(a), 404(h), 408, 415, or 457, and shall not be taken into account in applying such limitations to other contributions or benefits under such plan or any other plan, with respect to the year in which the contribution is made,

(B) such contribution shall be subject to the limitations referred to in subparagraph (A) with respect to the year to which the contribution relates (in accordance with rules prescribed by the Secretary), and

(C) such plan shall not be treated as failing to meet the requirements of section 401(a)(4), 401(a)(26), 401(k)(3), 401(k)(11), 401(k)(12), 401(m), 403(b)(12), 408(k)(3), 408(k)(6), 408(p), 410(b), or 416 by reason of the making of (or the right to make) such contribution.

For purposes of the preceding sentence, any elective deferral or employee contribution made under paragraph (2) shall be treated as required by reason of the employee's rights under such chapter 43.

(2) REEMPLOYMENT RIGHTS UNDER USERRA WITH RESPECT TO ELECTIVE DEFERRALS.—

(A) IN GENERAL.—For purposes of this subchapter and section 457, if an employee is entitled to the benefits of chapter 43 of title 38, United States Code, with respect to any plan which provides for elective deferrals, the employer sponsoring the plan shall be treated as meeting the requirements of such chapter 43 with respect to such elective deferrals only if such employer—

(i) permits such employee to make additional elective deferrals under such plan (in the amount determined under subparagraph (B) or such lesser amount as is elected by the employee) during the period which begins on the date of the reemployment of such employee with such employer and has the same length as the lesser of—

(I) the product of 3 and the period of qualified military service which resulted in such rights, and

(II) 5 years, and

(ii) makes a matching contribution with respect to any additional elective deferral made pursuant to clause (i) which would have been required had such deferral actually been made during the period of such qualified military service.

(B) AMOUNT OF MAKEUP REQUIRED.—The amount determined under this subparagraph with respect to any plan is the maximum amount of the elective deferrals that the individual would have been permitted to make under the plan in accordance with the limitations referred to in paragraph (1)(A) during the period of qualified military service if the individual had continued to be employed by the employer during such period and received compensation as determined under paragraph (7). Proper adjustment shall be made to the amount determined under the preceding sentence for any elective deferrals actually made during the period of such qualified military service.

(C) ELECTIVE DEFERRAL.—For purposes of this paragraph, the term 'elective deferral' has the meaning given such term by section 402(g)(3); except that such term shall include any deferral of compensation under an eligible deferred compensation plan (as defined in section 457(b)).

(D) AFTER-TAX EMPLOYEE CONTRIBUTIONS.—References in subparagraphs (A) and (B) to elective deferrals shall be treated as including references to employee contributions.

(3) CERTAIN RETROACTIVE ADJUSTMENTS NOT REQUIRED.—For purposes of this subchapter and subchapter E, no provision of chapter 43 of title 38, United States Code, shall be construed as requiring—

(A) any crediting of earnings to an employee with respect to any contribution before such contribution is actually made, or

(B) any allocation of any forfeiture with respect to the period of qualified military service.

* * *

(6) INDIVIDUAL ACCOUNT PLAN.—For purposes of this subsection, the term 'individual account plan' means any defined contribution plan (including any tax-sheltered annuity plan under section 403(b), any simplified employee pension under section 408(k), any qualified salary reduction arrangement under section 408(p), and any eligible deferred compensation plan (as defined in section 457(b)).

(7) COMPENSATION.—For purposes of sections 403(b)(3), 415(c)(3), and 457(e)(5), an employee who is in qualified military service shall be treated as receiving compensation from the employer during such period of qualified military service equal to—

(A) the compensation the employee would have received during such period if the employee were not in qualified military service, determined based on the rate of pay the employee would have received from the employer but for absence during the period of qualified military service, or

(B) if the compensation the employee would have received during such period was not reasonably certain, the employee's average compensation from the employer during the 12-month period immediately preceding the qualified military service (or, if shorter, the period of employment immediately preceding the qualified military service).

(8) USERRA REQUIREMENTS FOR QUALIFIED RETIREMENT PLANS.—For purposes of this subchapter and section 457, an employer sponsoring a retirement plan shall be treated as meeting the requirements of chapter 43 of title 38, United States Code, only if each of the following requirements is met:

(A) An individual reemployed under such chapter is treated with respect to such plan as not having incurred a break in service with the employer maintaining the plan by reason of such individual's period of qualified military service.

(B) Each period of qualified military service served by an individual is, upon reemployment under such chapter, deemed with respect to such plan to constitute service with the employer maintaining the plan for the purpose of determining the nonforfeitability of the individual's accrued benefits under such plan and for the purpose of determining the accrual of benefits under such plan.

(C) An individual reemployed under such chapter is entitled to accrued benefits that are contingent on the making of, or derived from, employee contributions or elective deferrals only to the extent the individual makes payment to the plan with respect to such contributions or deferrals. No such payment may exceed the amount the individual would have been permitted or required to contribute had the individual remained continuously employed by the employer throughout the period of qualified military service. Any payment to such plan shall be made during the period beginning with the date of reemployment and whose duration is 3 times the period of the qualified military service (but not greater than 5 years). . . .

Code Section 414(v)—Catch-Up Contributions For Individuals Age 50 or Over

(v) CATCH-UP CONTRIBUTIONS FOR INDIVIDUALS AGE 50 OR OVER—

(1) IN GENERAL.—An applicable employer plan shall not be treated as failing to meet any requirement of this title solely because the plan permits an eligible participant to make additional elective deferrals in any plan year.

(2) LIMITATION ON AMOUNT OF ADDITIONAL DEFERRALS.—

(A) IN GENERAL.—A plan shall not permit additional elective deferrals under paragraph (1) for any year in an amount greater than the lesser of—

(i) the applicable dollar amount, or

(ii) the excess (if any) of—

(I) the participant's compensation (as defined in section 415(c)(3)) for the year, over

(II) any other elective deferrals of the participant for such year which are made without regard to this subsection.

(B) APPLICABLE DOLLAR AMOUNT.—For purposes of this paragraph—

(i) In the case of an applicable employer plan other than a plan described in section 401(k)(11) or 408(p), the applicable dollar amount shall be determined in accordance with the following table:

For taxable years beginning in:	The applicable dollar amount is:
2002	$1,000
2003	$2,000

For taxable years beginning in:	The applicable dollar amount is:
2004	$3,000
2005	$4,000
2006 and thereafter	$5,000

(ii) In the case of an applicable employer plan described in section 401(k)(11) or 408(p), the applicable dollar amount shall be determined in accordance with the following table:

For taxable years beginning in:	The applicable dollar amount is:
2002	$500
2003	$1,000
2004	$1,500
2005	$2,000
2006 and thereafter	$2,500

(C) COST-OF-LIVING ADJUSTMENT.—In the case of a year beginning after December 31, 2006, the Secretary shall adjust annually the $5,000 amount in subparagraph (B)(i) and the $2,500 amount in subparagraph (B)(ii) for increases in the cost-of-living at the same time and in the same manner as adjustments under section 415(d); except that the base period taken into account shall be the calendar quarter beginning July 1, 2005, and any increase under this subparagraph which is not a multiple of $500 shall be rounded to the next lower multiple of $500.

(D) AGGREGATION OF PLANS.—For purposes of this paragraph, plans described in clauses (i), (ii), and (iv) of paragraph (6)(A) that are maintained by the same employer (as determined under subsection (b), (c), (m) or (o)) shall be treated as a single plan, and plans described in clause (iii) of paragraph (6)(A) that are maintained by the same employer shall be treated as a single plan.

(3) TREATMENT OF CONTRIBUTIONS.—In the case of any contribution to a plan under paragraph (1)—

(A) such contribution shall not, with respect to the year in which the contribution is made—

(i) be subject to any otherwise applicable limitation contained in sections 401(a)(30), 402(h), 403(b), 408, 415(c), and 457(b)(2) (determined without regard to section 457(b)(3)), or

(ii) be taken into account in applying such limitations to other contributions or benefits under such plan or any other such plan, and

(B) except as provided in paragraph (4), such plan shall not be treated as failing to meet the requirements of section 401(a)(4), 401(k)(3), 401(k)(11), 403(b)(12), 408(k), 410(b), or 416 by reason of the making of (or the right to make) such contribution.

(4) APPLICATION OF NONDISCRIMINATION RULES.—

(A) IN GENERAL.—An applicable employer plan shall be treated as failing to meet the nondiscrimination requirements under section 401(a)(4) with respect to benefits, rights, and features unless the plan allows all eligible participants to make the same election with respect to the additional elective deferrals under this subsection.

(B) AGGREGATION.—For purposes of subparagraph (A), all plans maintained by employers who are treated as a single employer under subsection (b), (c), (m), or (o) of section 414 shall be treated as 1 plan, except that a plan described in clause (i) of section 410(b)(6)(C) shall not be treated as a plan of the employer until the expiration of the transition period with respect to such plan (as determined under clause (ii) of such section).

(5) ELIGIBLE PARTICIPANT.—For purposes of this subsection, the term "eligible participant" means a participant in a plan—

(A) who would attain age 50 by the end of the taxable year,

(B) with respect to whom no other elective deferrals may (without regard to this subsection) be made to the plan for the plan (or other applicable) year by reason of the application of any limitation or other restriction described in paragraph (3) or comparable limitation or restriction contained in the terms of the plan.

(6) OTHER DEFINITIONS AND RULES.—For purposes of this subsection—

(A) APPLICABLE EMPLOYER PLAN.—The term "applicable employer plan" means—

(i) an employees' trust described in section 401(a) which is exempt from tax under section 501(a),

(ii) a plan under which amounts are contributed by an individual's employer for an annuity contract described in section 403(b),

(iii) an eligible deferred compensation plan under section 457 of an eligible employer described in section 457(e)(1)(A), and

(iv) an arrangement meeting the requirements of section 408(k) or (p).

(B) ELECTIVE DEFERRAL.—The term "elective deferral" has the meaning given such term by subsection (u)(2)(C).

(C) Exception for section 457 plans.—This subsection shall not apply to a participant for any year for which a higher limitation applies to the participant under section 457(b)(3).

Code Section 415: Certain Deferrals Included as Compensation

Code Section 415—Limitations on Benefits and Contributions Under Qualified Plans

(a) GENERAL RULE.—

(1) TRUSTS.—A trust which is a part of a pension, profit sharing, or stock bonus plan shall not constitute a qualified trust under section 401(a) if—

(A) in the case of a defined benefit plan, the plan provides for the payment of benefits with respect to a participant which exceed the limitation of subsection (b), or

(B) in the case of a defined contribution plan, contributions and other additions under the plan with respect to any participant for any taxable year exceed the limitation of subsection (c).

(C) [Stricken]

(2) SECTION APPLIES TO CERTAIN ANNUITIES AND ACCOUNTS.—In the case of—

(A) an employee annuity plan described in section 403(a),

(B) an annuity contract described in section 403(b), or

(C) a simplified employee pension described in section 408(k), such a contract, plan, or pension shall not be considered to be described in section 403(a), 403(b), or 408(k), as the case may be, unless it satisfies the requirements of subparagraph (A) or subparagraph (B) of paragraph (1), whichever is appropriate, and has not been disqualified under subsection (g). In the case of an annuity contract described in section 403(b), the preceding sentence shall apply only to the portion of the annuity contract which exceeds the limitation of subsection (b) or the limitation of subsection (c), whichever is appropriate.

(b) LIMITATION FOR DEFINED BENEFIT PLANS.—* * *

(c) LIMITATION FOR DEFINED CONTRIBUTION PLANS.—

(1) IN GENERAL.—Contributions and other additions with respect to a participant exceed the limitation of this subsection if, when expressed as an annual addition (within the meaning of paragraph (2)) to the participant's account, such annual addition is greater than the lesser of—

(A) $40,000, or

(B) 100 percent of the participant's compensation.

[Caution. The $40,000/100 percent amounts, above, were increased for years beginning after 2001 from $35,000 (adjusted for COLA)/25 percent.]

(2) ANNUAL ADDITION.—For purposes of paragraph (1), the term "annual addition" means the sum for any year of—

(A) employer contributions,

(B) the employee contributions, and

(C) forfeitures.

For the purposes of this paragraph, employee contributions under subparagraph (B) are determined without regard to any rollover contributions (as defined in sections 402(c), 403(a)(4), 403(b)(8), 408(d)(3), and 457(e)(16)) without regard to employee contributions to a simplified employee pension which are excludable from gross income under section 408(k)(6). Subparagraph (B) of paragraph (1) shall not apply to any contribution for medical benefits (within the meaning of section 419A(f)(2)) after separation from service which is treated as an annual addition.

(3) PARTICIPANT'S COMPENSATION.—For purposes of paragraph (1)—

(A) IN GENERAL.—The term "participant's compensation" means the compensation of the participant from the employer for the year.

(B) SPECIAL RULE FOR SELF-EMPLOYED INDIVIDUALS.—In the case of an employee within the meaning of section 401(c)(1), subparagraph (A) shall be applied by substituting "the participant's earned income (within the meaning of section 401(c)(2) but determined without regard to any exclusion under section 911)" for "compensation of the participant from the employer".

(C) SPECIAL RULES FOR PERMANENT AND TOTAL DISABILITY.—In the case of a participant in any defined contribution plan—

(i) who is permanently and totally disabled (as defined in section 22(e)(3)),

(ii) who is not a highly compensated employee (within the meaning of section 414(q)), and

(iii) with respect to whom the employer elects, at such time and in such manner as the Secretary may prescribe, to have this subparagraph apply, the term "participant's compensation" means the compensation the participant would have received for the year if the participant was paid at the rate of compensation paid immediately before becoming permanently and totally disabled. This subparagraph shall apply only if contributions made with respect to amounts treated as compensation under this subparagraph are nonforfeitable when made. If a defined contribution plan provides for the continuation of contributions on behalf of all participants described in clause (i) for a fixed or determinable period, this subparagraph shall be applied without regard to clauses (ii) and (iii).

(D) CERTAIN DEFERRALS INCLUDED.—The term "participant's compensation" shall include—

(i) any elective deferral (as defined in section 402(g)(3), and

(ii) any amount which is contributed or deferred by the employer at the election of the employee and which is not includible in the gross income of the employee by reason of section 125, 132(f)(4), or 457.

(E) ANNUITY CONTRACTS.—In the case of an annuity contract described in section 403(b), the term "participant's compensation" means the participant's includible compensation determined under section 403(b)(3).

(4) [Stricken]

(5) Repealed. [P.L. 97-248, Title II, § 238(d)(5) (Sept. 3, 1982)]

(6) SPECIAL RULE FOR EMPLOYEE STOCK OWNERSHIP PLANS.—* * *

(7) SPECIAL RULES RELATING TO CHURCH PLANS.—* * *

Code Section 457: Deferred Compensation Plans of State and Local Governments and Tax-Exempt Organizations

Code Section 457—Deferred Compensation Plans of State and Local Governments and Tax-Exempt Organizations

[Caution. Code Section 457(a), below, before amendment by EGTRRA, applies to distributions before January 1, 2002.]

(a) YEAR OF INCLUSION IN GROSS INCOME.—In the case of a participant in an eligible deferred compensation plan, any amount of compensation deferred under the plan, and any income attributable to the amounts so deferred, shall be includible in gross income only for the taxable year in which such compensation or other income is paid or otherwise made available to the participant or other beneficiary.

[Caution. Code Section 457(a), below, as amended by EGTRRA, applies to distributions after December 31, 2001.]

(a) YEAR OF INCLUSION IN GROSS INCOME.—

(1) IN GENERAL.—Any amount of compensation deferred under an eligible deferred compensation plan, and any income attributable to the amounts so deferred, shall be includible in gross income only for the taxable year in which such compensation or other income—

(A) is paid to the participant or other beneficiary, in the case of a plan of an eligible employer described in subsection (e)(1)(A), and

(B) is paid or otherwise made available to the participant or other beneficiary, in the case of a plan of an eligible employer described in subsection (e)(1)(B).

(2) SPECIAL RULE FOR ROLLOVER AMOUNTS.—To the extent provided in section 72(t)(9), section 72(t) shall apply to any amount includible in gross income under this subsection.

(b) ELIGIBLE DEFERRED COMPENSATION PLAN DEFINED.—For purposes of this section, the term "eligible deferred compensation plan" means a plan established and maintained by an eligible employer—

(1) in which only individuals who perform service for the employer may be participants,

[Caution. Code Section 457(b)(2), below, before amendment by EGTRRA, applies to years beginning before January 1, 2002.]

(2) which provides that (except as provided in paragraph (3)) the maximum amount which may be deferred under the plan for the taxable year shall not exceed the lesser of—

(A) $7,500, or

(B) 33 percent of the participant's includible compensation,

[Caution. Code Section 457(b)(2), below, as amended by EGTRRA, applies to years beginning after December 31, 2001.]

(2) which provides that (except as provided in paragraph (3)) the maximum amount which may be deferred under the plan for the taxable year (other than rollover amounts) shall not exceed the lesser of—

(A) the applicable dollar amount, or

(B) 100 percent of the participant's includible compensation,

(3) which may provide that, for 1 or more of the participant's last 3 taxable years ending before he attains normal retirement age under the plan, the ceiling set forth in paragraph (2) shall be the lesser of—

[Caution. Code Section 457(b)(3)(A), below, before amendment by EGTRRA, applies to years beginning before January 1, 2002.]

(A) $15,000, or

[Caution. Code Section 457(b)(3)(A), below, as amended by EGTRRA, applies to years beginning after December 31, 2001.]

(A) twice the dollar amount in effect under subsection (b)(2)(A), or

(B) the sum of—

(i) the plan ceiling established for purposes of paragraph (2) for the taxable year (determined without regard to this paragraph), plus

(ii) so much of the plan ceiling established for purposes of paragraph (2) for taxable years before the taxable year as has not previously been used under paragraph (2) or this paragraph,

(4) which provides that compensation will be deferred for any calendar month only if an agreement providing for such deferral has been entered into before the beginning of such month,

(5) which meets the distribution requirements of subsection (d), and

(6) except as provided in subsection (g), which provides that—

(A) all amounts of compensation deferred under the plan,

(B) all property and rights purchased with such amounts, and

(C) all income attributable to such amounts, property, or rights, shall remain (until made available to the participant or other beneficiary) solely the property and rights of the employer (without being restricted to the provision of benefits under the plan), subject only to the claims of the employer's general creditors.

A plan which is established and maintained by an employer which is described in subsection (e)(1)(A) and which is administered in a manner which is inconsistent with the requirements of any of the preceding paragraphs shall be treated as not meeting the requirements of such paragraph as of the 1st plan year beginning more than 180 days after the date of notification by the Secretary of the inconsistency unless the employer corrects the inconsistency before the 1st day of such plan year.

[Caution. Code Sections 457(c) and (d), below, before amendment by EGTRRA, are applicable to years beginning before January 1, 2002.]

(c) INDIVIDUALS WHO ARE PARTICIPANTS IN MORE THAN 1 PLAN.—

(1) IN GENERAL.—The maximum amount of the compensation of any one individual which may be deferred under subsection (a) during any taxable year shall not exceed $7,500 (as modified by any adjustment provided under subsection (b)(3)).

(2) COORDINATION WITH CERTAIN OTHER DEFERRALS.—In applying paragraph (1) of this subsection—

(A) any amount excluded from gross income under section 403(b) for the taxable year, and

(B) any amount—

(i) excluded from gross income under section 402(e)(3) or section 402(h)(1)(B) or (k) for the taxable year, or

(ii) with respect to which a deduction is allowable by reason of a contribution to an organization described in section 501(c)(18) for the taxable year, shall be treated as an amount deferred under subsection (a). In applying section 402(g)(8)(A)(iii) or 403(b)(2)(A)(ii), an amount deferred under subsection (a) for any year of service shall be taken into account as if described in section 402(g)(3)(C) or 403(b)(2)(A)(ii), respectively. Subparagraph (B) shall not apply in the case of a participant in a rural cooperative plan (as defined in section 401(k)(7)).

(d) DISTRIBUTION REQUIREMENTS.—

(1) IN GENERAL.—For purposes of subsection (b)(5), a plan meets the distribution requirements of this subsection if—

(A) under the plan amounts will not be made available to participants or beneficiaries earlier than—

(i) the calendar year in which the participant attains age 70½

(ii) when the participant is separated from service with the employer, or

(iii) when the participant is faced with an unforeseeable emergency (determined in the manner prescribed by the Secretary in regulations), and

(B) the plan meets the minimum distribution requirements of paragraph (2).

(2) MINIMUM DISTRIBUTION REQUIREMENTS.—A plan meets the minimum distribution requirements of this paragraph if such plan meets the requirements of subparagraphs (A), (B), and (C):

(A) Application of section 401(a)(9).—A plan meets the requirements of this subparagraph if the plan meets the requirements of section 401(a)(9).

(B) Additional distribution requirements.—A plan meets the require-ments of this subparagraph if—

(i) in the case of a distribution beginning before the death of the participant, such distribution will be made in a form under which—

(I) the amounts payable with respect to the participant will be paid at times specified by the Secretary which are not later than the time determined under section 401(a)(9)(G) (relating to incidental death benefits), and

(II) any amount not distributed to the participant during his life will be distributed after the death of the participant at least as rapidly as under the method of distributions being used under subclause (I) as of the date of his death, or

(ii) in the case of a distribution which does not begin before the death of the participant, the entire amount payable with respect to the participant will be paid during a period not to exceed 15 years (or the life expectancy of the surviving spouse if such spouse is the beneficiary).

(C) Nonincreasing benefits.—A plan meets the requirements of this subparagraph if any distribution payable over a period of more than 1 year can only be made in substantially nonincreasing amounts (paid not less frequently than annually).

[Caution. Code Sections 457(c) and (d), below, as amended by EGTRRA, are applicable to years beginning after December 31, 2001.]

(c) LIMITATION.—The maximum amount of the compensation of any one individual which may be deferred under subsection (a) during any taxable year shall not exceed the amount in effect under subsection (b)(2)(A) (as modified by any adjustment provided under subsection (b)(3)).

(d) DISTRIBUTION REQUIREMENTS.—

(1) IN GENERAL.—For purposes of subsection (b)(5), a plan meets the distribution requirements of this subsection if—

(A) under the plan amounts will not be made available to participants or beneficiaries earlier than—

(i) the calendar year in which the participant attains age 70½,

(ii) when the participant has a severance from employment with the employer, or

(iii) when the participant is faced with an unforeseeable emergency (determined in the manner prescribed by the Secretary in regulations),

(B) the plan meets the minimum distribution requirements of paragraph (2), and

(C) in the case of a plan maintained by an employer described in subsection (e)(1)(A), the plan meets requirements similar to the requirements of section 401(a)(31).

Any amount transferred in a direct trustee-to-trustee transfer in accordance with section 401(a)(31) shall not be includible in gross income for the taxable year of transfer.

(2) MINIMUM DISTRIBUTION REQUIREMENTS.—A plan meets the minimum distribution requirements of this paragraph if such plan meets the requirements of section 401(a)(9).

(3) SPECIAL RULE FOR GOVERNMENT PLAN.—An eligible deferred compensation plan of an employer described in subsection (e)(1)(A) shall not be treated as failing to meet the requirements of this subsection solely by reason of making a distribution described in subsection (e)(9)(A).

(e) OTHER DEFINITIONS AND SPECIAL RULES FOR PURPOSES OF THIS SECTION.—

(1) ELIGIBLE EMPLOYER.—The term "eligible employer" means—

(A) a State, political subdivision of a State, and any agency or instrumentality of a State or political subdivision of a State, and

(B) any other organization (other than a governmental unit) exempt from tax under this subtitle.

(2) PERFORMANCE OF SERVICE.—The performance of service includes performance of service as an independent contractor and the person (or governmental unit) for whom such services are performed shall be treated as the employer.

(3) PARTICIPANT.—The term "participant" means an individual who is eligible to defer compensation under the plan.

(4) BENEFICIARY.—The term "beneficiary" means a beneficiary of the participant, his estate, or any other person whose interest in the plan is derived from the participant.

[Caution. Code Section 457(e)(5), below, before amendment by JWCAA, applies to years beginning before January 1, 2002.]

(5) INCLUDIBLE COMPENSATION.—The term "includible compensation" means compensation for service performed for the employer which (taking into account the provisions of this section and other provisions of this chapter) is currently includible in gross income.

[Caution. Code Section 457(e)(5), below, after amendment by JWCAA, applies to years beginning after December 31, 2001.]

(5) INCLUDIBLE COMPENSATION.—The term "includible compensation" has the meaning given to the term "participant's compensation" by section 415(c)(3).

(6) COMPENSATION TAKEN INTO ACCOUNT AT PRESENT VALUE.—Compensation shall be taken into account at its present value.

(7) COMMUNITY PROPERTY LAWS.—The amount of includible compensation shall be determined without regard to any community property laws.

(8) INCOME ATTRIBUTABLE.—Gains from the disposition of property shall be treated as income attributable to such property.

[Caution. Code Section 457(e)(9), below, before amendment by EGTRRA, applies to distributions before January 1, 2002.]

(9) BENEFITS NOT TREATED AS MADE AVAILABLE BY REASON OF CERTAIN ELECTIONS, ETC.—

(A) TOTAL AMOUNT PAYABLE IS DOLLAR LIMIT OR LESS.—The total amount payable to a participant under the plan shall not be treated as made available merely because the participant may elect to receive such amount (or the plan may distribute such amount without the participant's consent) if—

(i) such amount does not exceed the dollar limit under section 411(a)(11)(A), and

(ii) such amount may be distributed only if—

(I) no amount has been deferred under the plan with respect to such participant during the 2-year period ending on the date of the distribution and

(II) there has been no prior distribution under the plan to such participant to which this subparagraph applied.

A plan shall not be treated as failing to meet the distribution requirements of subsection (d) by reason of a distribution to which this subparagraph applies.

(B) ELECTION TO DEFER COMMENCEMENT OF DISTRIBUTIONS.—The total amount payable to a participant under the plan shall not be treated as made available merely because the participant may elect to defer commencement of distributions under the plan if—

(i) such election is made after amounts may be available under the plan in accordance with subsection (d)(1)(A) and before commencement of such distributions, and

(ii) the participant may make only 1 such election.

[Caution. Code Section 457(e)(9), below, as amended by EGTRRA, applies to distributions after December 31, 2001.]

(9) BENEFITS OF TAX EXEMPT ORGANIZATION PLANS NOT TREATED AS MADE AVAILABLE BY REASON OF CERTAIN ELECTIONS, ETC.—In the case of an eligible deferred compensation plan of an employer described in subsection (e)(1)(B)—

(A) TOTAL AMOUNT PAYABLE IS DOLLAR LIMIT OR LESS.—The total amount payable to a participant under the plan shall not be treated as made available merely because the participant may elect to receive such amount (or the plan may distribute such amount without the participant's consent) if—

(i) the portion of such amount which is not attributable to rollover contributions (as defined in section 411(a)(11)(D)) does not exceed the dollar limit under section 411(a)(11)(A), and

(ii) such amount may be distributed only if—

(I) no amount has been deferred under the plan with respect to such participant during the 2-year period ending on the date of the distribution and

(II) there has been no prior distribution under the plan to such participant to which this subparagraph applied.

A plan shall not be treated as failing to meet the distribution requirements of subsection (d) by reason of a distribution to which this subparagraph applies.

(B) ELECTION TO DEFER COMMENCEMENT OF DISTRIBUTIONS.—The total amount payable to a participant under the plan shall not be treated as made available merely because the participant may elect to defer commencement of distributions under the plan if—

(i) such election is made after amounts may be available under the plan in accordance with subsection (d)(1)(A) and before commencement of such distributions, and

(ii) the participant may make only 1 such election.

(10) TRANSFERS BETWEEN PLANS.—A participant shall not be required to include in gross income any portion of the entire amount payable to such participant solely by reason of the transfer of such portion from 1 eligible deferred compensation plan to another eligible deferred compensation plan.

(11) CERTAIN PLANS EXCLUDED.—

(A) IN GENERAL.—The following plans shall be treated as not providing for the deferral of compensation:

(i) Any bona fide vacation leave, sick leave, compensatory time, severance pay, disability pay, or death benefit plan.

(ii) Any plan paying solely length of service awards to bona fide volunteers (or their beneficiaries) on account of qualified services performed by such volunteers.

(B) SPECIAL RULES APPLICABLE TO LENGTH OF SERVICE AWARD PLANS.—

(i) Bona fide volunteer.—An individual shall be treated as a bona fide volunteer for purposes of subparagraph (A)(ii) if the only compensation received by such individual for performing qualified services is in the form of—

(I) reimbursement for (or a reasonable allowance for) reasonable expenses incurred in the performance of such services, or

(II) reasonable benefits (including length of service awards), and nominal fees for such services, customarily paid by eligible employers in connection with the performance of such services by volunteers.

(ii) Limitation on accruals.—A plan shall not be treated as described in subparagraph (A)(ii) if the aggregate amount of length of service awards accruing with respect to any year of service for any bona fide volunteer exceeds $3,000.

(C) QUALIFIED SERVICES.—For purposes of this paragraph, the term 'qualified services' means fire fighting and prevention services, emergency medical services, and ambulance services.

(12) EXCEPTION FOR NONELECTIVE DEFERRED COMPENSATION OF NONEMPLOYEES.—

(A) IN GENERAL.—This section shall not apply to nonelective deferred compensation attributable to services not performed as an employee.

(B) NONELECTIVE DEFERRED COMPENSATION.—For purposes of subparagraph (A), deferred compensation shall be treated as nonelective only if all individuals (other than those who have not satisfied any applicable initial service requirement) with the same relationship to the payor are covered under the same plan with no individual variations or options under the plan.

(13) SPECIAL RULE FOR CHURCHES.—The term "eligible employer" shall not include a church (as defined in section 3121(w)(3)(A)) or qualified church-controlled organization (as defined in section 3121(w)(3)(B)).

(14) TREATMENT OF QUALIFIED GOVERNMENTAL EXCESS BENEFIT ARRANGEMENTS.—Subsections (b)(2) and (c)(1) shall not apply to any qualified governmental excess benefit arrangement (as defined in section 415(m)(3), and benefits provided under such an arrangement shall not be taken into account in determining whether any other plan is an eligible deferred compensation plan.

[Caution. Code Section 457(e)(15) below, before amendment by EGTRRA, applies to years beginning before January 1, 2002.]

(15) COST-OF-LIVING ADJUSTMENT OF MAXIMUM DEFERRAL AMOUNT.—The Secretary shall adjust the $7,500 amount specified in subsections (b)(2) and (c)(1) at the same time and in the same manner as under section 415(d), except that the base period shall be the calendar quarter ending September 30, 1994, and any increase under this paragraph which is not a multiple of $500 shall be rounded to the next lowest multiple of $500.

[Caution. Code Section 457(e)(15), below, as amended by EGTRRA, applies to years beginning after December 31, 2001.]

(15) APPLICABLE DOLLAR AMOUNT.—

(A) IN GENERAL.—The applicable dollar amount shall be the amount determined in accordance with the following table:

For taxable years beginning in calendar year:	The applicable dollar amount is:
2002	$11,000
2003	$12,000
2004	$13,000
2005	$14,000
2006 or thereafter	$15,000

(B) COST-OF-LIVING ADJUSTMENTS.—In the case of taxable years beginning after December 31, 2006, the Secretary shall adjust the $15,000 amount under subparagraph (A) at the same time and in the same manner as under section 415(d), except that the base period shall be the calendar quarter beginning July 1, 2005, and any increase under this paragraph which is not a multiple of $500 shall be rounded to the next lowest multiple of $500.

[Caution. Code Section 457(e)(16), below, as added by EGTRRA, applies to distributions after December 31, 2001.]

(16) ROLLOVER AMOUNTS.—

(A) GENERAL RULE.—In the case of an eligible deferred compensation plan established and maintained by an employer described in subsection (e)(1)(A), if—

(i) any portion of the balance to the credit of an employee in such plan is paid to such employee in an eligible rollover distribution (within the meaning of section 402(c)(4)),

(ii) the employee transfers any portion of the property such employee receives in such distribution to an eligible retirement plan described in section 402(c)(8)(B), and

(iii) in the case of a distribution of property other than money, the amount so transferred consists of the property distributed, then such distribution (to the extent so transferred) shall not be includible in gross income for the taxable year in which paid.

(B) CERTAIN RULES MADE APPLICABLE.—The rules of paragraphs (2) through (7) and (9) of section 402(c) and section 402(f) shall apply for purposes of subparagraph (A).

(C) REPORTING.—Rollovers under this paragraph shall be reported to the Secretary in the same manner as rollovers from qualified retirement plans (as defined in section 4974(c)).

[Caution. Code Section 457(e)(17), below, as added by EGTRRA, applies to trustee-to-trustee transfers after December 31, 2001.]

(17) TRUSTEE-TO-TRUSTEE TRANSFERS TO PURCHASE PERMISSIVE SERVICE CREDIT.—No amount shall be includible in gross income by reason of a direct trustee-to-trustee transfer to a defined benefit governmental plan (as defined in section 414(d)) if such transfer is—

(A) for the purchase of permissive service credit (as defined in section 415(n)(3)(A)) under such plan, or

(B) a repayment to which section 415 does not apply by reason of subsection (k)(3) thereof.

(18) COORDINATION WITH CATCH-UP CONTRIBUTIONS FOR INDIVIDUALS AGE 50 OR OLDER—In the case of an individual who is an eligible participant (as defined by section 414(v)) and who is a participant in an eligible deferred compensation plan of an employer described in paragraph (1)(A), subsections (b)(3) and (c) shall be applied by substituting for the amount otherwise determined under the applicable subsection the greater of—

(A) the sum of—

(i) the plan ceiling established for purposes of subsection (b)(2) (without regard to subsection (b)(3)), plus

(ii) the applicable dollar amount for the taxable year determined under section 414(v)(2)(B)(i), or

(B) the amount determined under the applicable subsection (without regard to this paragraph).

(f) TAX TREATMENT OF PARTICIPANTS WHERE PLAN OR ARRANGEMENT OF EMPLOYER IS NOT ELIGIBLE.—

(1) IN GENERAL—In the case of a plan of an eligible employer providing for a deferral of compensation, if such plan is not an eligible deferred compensation plan, then—

(A) the compensation shall be included in the gross income of the participant or beneficiary for the 1st taxable year in which there is no substantial risk of forfeiture of the rights to such compensation, and

(B) the tax treatment of any amount made available under the plan to a participant or beneficiary shall be determined under section 72 (relating to annuities, etc.).

(2) EXCEPTIONS.—Paragraph (1) shall not apply to—

(A) a plan described in section 401(a) which includes a trust exempt from tax under section 501(a),

(B) an annuity plan or contract described in section 403,

(C) that portion of any plan which consists of a transfer of property described in section 83,

(D) that portion of any plan which consists of a trust to which section 402(b) applies, and

(E) a qualified governmental excess benefit arrangement described in section 415(m).

(3) DEFINITIONS.—For purposes of this subsection—

(A) PLAN INCLUDES ARRANGEMENTS, ETC.—The term "plan" includes any agreement or arrangement.

(B) SUBSTANTIAL RISK OF FORFEITURE.—The rights of a person to compensation are subject to a substantial risk of forfeiture if such person's rights to such compensation are conditioned upon the future performance of substantial services by any individual.

(g) GOVERNMENTAL PLANS MUST MAINTAIN SET-ASIDES FOR EXCLUSIVE BENEFIT OF PARTICIPANTS.—

(1) IN GENERAL.—A plan maintained by an eligible employer described in subsection (e)(1)(A) shall not be treated as an eligible deferred compensation plan unless all assets and income of the plan described in subsection (b)(6) are held in trust for the exclusive benefit of participants and their beneficiaries.

(2) TAXABILITY OF TRUSTS AND PARTICIPANTS.—For purposes of this title—

(A) a trust described in paragraph (1) shall be treated as an organization exempt from taxation under section 501(a), and

(B) notwithstanding any other provision of this title, amounts in the trust shall be includible in the gross income of participants and beneficiaries only to the extent, and at the time, provided in this section.

(3) CUSTODIAL ACCOUNTS AND CONTRACTS.—For purposes of this subsection, custodial accounts and contracts described in section 401(f) shall be treated as trusts under rules similar to the rules under section 401(f).

Code Section 818: Definitions Relating to Life Insurance Companies

Code Section 818—Definitions and Special Rules

(a) PENSION PLAN CONTRACTS.—For purposes of this part, the term pension plan contract means any contract—

(5) entered into with trusts which (at the time the contracts were entered into) were individual retirement accounts described in section 408(a) or under contracts entered into with individual retirement annuities described in section 408(b); or

(6) purchased by—

(A) a governmental plan (within the meaning of section 414(d)) or an eligible deferred compensation plan (within the meaning of section 457(b)), or

(B) the Government of the United States, the government of any State or political subdivision thereof, or by any agency or instrumentality of the foregoing, or any organization (other than a governmental unit) exempt from tax under this subtitle, for use in satisfying an obligation of such government, political subdivision, agency or instrumentality, or organization to provide a benefit under a plan described in subparagraph (A).

Code Section 3121(a): Wages for Social Security

Code Section 3121—Definitions

(a) WAGES.—For purposes of this chapter, the term wages means all remuneration for employment, including the cash value of all remuneration (including benefits) paid in any medium other than cash; except that such term shall not include—

(5) any payment made to, or on behalf of, an employee or his beneficiary—

(A) from or to a trust described in section 401(a) which is exempt from tax under section 501(a) at the time of such payment unless such payment is made to an employee of the trust as remuneration for services rendered as such employee and not as a beneficiary of the trust,

(B) under or to an annuity plan which, at the time of such payment, is a plan described in section 403(a),

(C) under a simplified employee pension (as defined in section 408(k)(1)), other than any contributions described in section 408(k)(6),

(D) under or to an annuity contract described in section 403(b), other than a payment for the purchase of such contract which is made by reason of a salary reduction agreement (whether evidenced by a written instrument or otherwise),

(E) under or to an exempt governmental deferred compensation plan (as defined in subsection (v)(3)),

(F) to supplement pension benefits under a plan or trust described in any of the foregoing provisions of this paragraph to take into account some portion or all of the increase in the cost of living (as determined by the Secretary of Labor) since retirement but only if such supplemental payments are under a plan which is treated as a welfare plan under section 3(2)(B)(ii) of the Employee Retirement Income Security Act of 1974,

(G) under a cafeteria plan (within the meaning of section 125) if such payment would not be treated as wages without regard to such plan and it is reasonable to believe that (if section 125 applied for purposes of this section) section 125 would not treat any wages as constructively received,

(H) under an arrangement to which section 408(p) applies, other than any elective contributions under paragraph (2)(A)(i) thereof, or

(I) under a plan described in section 457(e)(11)(A)(ii) and maintained by an eligible employer (as defined in section 457(e)(1)).

Code Section 3121(v): Deferrals Treated as Wages

Code Section 3121—Definitions

(v) TREATMENT OF CERTAIN DEFERRED COMPENSATION AND SALARY REDUCTION ARRANGEMENTS.—

(1) CERTAIN EMPLOYER CONTRIBUTIONS TREATED AS WAGES.—Nothing in any paragraph of subsection (a) (other than paragraph (1)) shall exclude from the term wages—

(A) any employer contribution under a qualified cash or deferred arrangement (as defined in section 401(k)) to the extent not included in gross income by reason of section 402(e)(3), or

(B) any amount treated as an employer contribution under section 414(h)(2) where the pickup referred to in such section is pursuant to a salary reduction agreement (whether evidenced by a written instrument or otherwise).

(2) TREATMENT OF CERTAIN NONQUALIFIED DEFERRED COMPENSATION PLANS.—

(A) IN GENERAL.—Any amount deferred under a nonqualified deferred compensation plan shall be taken into account for purposes of this chapter as of the later of—

(i) when the services are performed, or

(ii) when there is no substantial risk of forfeiture of the rights to such amount.

The preceding sentence shall not apply to any excess parachute payment (as defined in section 280G(b)).

(B) TAXED ONLY ONCE.—Any amount taken into account as wages by reason of subparagraph (A) (and the income attributable thereto) shall not thereafter be treated as wages for purposes of this chapter.

(C) NONQUALIFIED DEFERRED COMPENSATION PLAN.—For purposes of this paragraph, the term nonqualified deferred compensation plan means any plan or other arrangement for deferral of compensation other than a plan described in subsection (a)(5).

(3) EXEMPT GOVERNMENTAL DEFERRED COMPENSATION PLAN.— For purposes of subsection (a)(5), the term exempt governmental deferred compensation plan means any plan providing for deferral of compensation established and maintained for its employees by the United States, by a State or political subdivision thereof, or by an agency or instrumentality of any of the foregoing. Such term shall not include—

(A) any plan to which section 83, 402(b), 403(c), 457(a), or 457(f)(1) applies,

(B) any annuity contract described in section 403(b), and

(C) the Thrift Savings Fund (within the meaning of subchapter III of chapter 84 of title 5, United States Code).

Code Section 3121(w): Exemption of Churches and Qualified Church-Controlled Organizations

Code Section 3121—Definitions

(w) EXEMPTION OF CHURCHES AND QUALIFIED CHURCH-CONTROLLED ORGANIZATIONS.—* * *

(3) DEFINITIONS.—

(A) For purposes of this subsection, the term church means a church, a convention or association of churches, or an elementary or secondary school which is controlled, operated, or principally supported by a church or by a convention or association of churches.

(B) For purposes of this subsection, the term qualified church-controlled organization means any church-controlled tax-exempt organization described in section 501(c)(3), other than an organization which—

(i) offers goods, services, or facilities for sale, other than on an incidental basis, to the general public, other than goods, services, or facilities which are sold at a nominal charge which is substantially less than the cost of providing such goods, services, or facilities; and

(ii) normally receives more than 25 percent of its support from either (I) governmental sources, or (II) receipts from admissions, sales of merchandise, performance of services, or furnishing of faci-lities, in activities which are not unrelated trades or businesses, or both.

Code Section 4974: Penalties on Accumulations in Eligible Plans

Code Section 4974—Excise Tax on Certain Accumulations in Qualified Retirement Plans

(a) GENERAL RULE.—If the amount distributed during the taxable year of the payee under any qualified retirement plan or any eligible deferred compensation plan (as defined in section 457(b)) is less than the minimum required distribution for such taxable year, there is hereby imposed a tax equal to 50 percent of the amount by which such minimum required distribution exceeds the actual amount distributed during the taxable year. The tax imposed by this section shall be paid by the payee.

(b) MINIMUM REQUIRED DISTRIBUTION.—For purposes of this section, the term minimum required distribution means the minimum amount required to be distributed during a taxable year under section 401(a)(9), 403(b)(10), 408(a)(6), 408(b)(3), or 457(d)(2), as the case may be, as determined under regulations prescribed by the Secretary.

(c) QUALIFIED RETIREMENT PLAN.—For purposes of this section, the term qualified retirement plan means—

(1) a plan described in section 401(a) which includes a trust exempt from tax under section 501(a),

(2) an annuity plan described in section 403(a),

(3) an annuity contract described in section 403(b),

(4) an individual retirement account described in section 408(a), or

(5) an individual retirement annuity described in section 408(b).

Such term includes any plan, contract, account, or annuity which, at any time, has been determined by the Secretary to be such a plan, contract, account, or annuity.

(d) WAIVER OF TAX IN CERTAIN CASES.—If the taxpayer establishes to the satisfaction of the Secretary that—

(1) the shortfall described in subsection (a) in the amount distributed during any taxable year was due to reasonable error, and

(2) reasonable steps are being taken to remedy the shortfall, the Secretary may waive the tax imposed by subsection (a) for the taxable year.

Code Section 6051: Form W-2 Reporting Rules

Code Section 6051—Receipts for Employees

(a) REQUIREMENT.—Every person required to deduct and withhold from an employee a tax under section 3101 or 3402, or who would have been required to deduct and withhold a tax under section 3402 (determined without regard to subsection (n)) if the employee had claimed no more than one withholding exemption, or every employer engaged in a trade or business who pays remuneration for services performed by an employee, including the cash value of such remuneration paid in any medium other than cash, shall furnish to each such employee . . . a written statement showing the following:

(1) the name of such person,

(2) the name of the employee (and his social security account number if wages as defined in section 3121(a) have been paid),

(3) the total amount of wages as defined in section 3401(a),

(4) the total amount deducted and withheld as tax under section 3402,

(5) the total amount of wages as defined in section 3121(a),

(6) the total amount deducted and withheld as tax under section 3101,

(7) the total amount paid to the employee under section 3507 (relating to advance payment of earned income credit),

[Caution. Code Section 6051(a)(8), below, before amendment by EGTRRA, applies to taxable years beginning before January 1, 2006.]

(8) the total amount of elective deferrals (within the meaning of section 402(g)(3)) and compensation deferred under section 457,

[Caution. Code Section 6051(a)(8), below, after amendment by EGTRRA, applies to taxable years beginning after December 31, 2005.]

(8) the total amount of elective deferrals (within the meaning of section 402(g)(3)) and compensation deferred under section 457, including the amount of designated Roth contributions (as defined in section 402A),

(9) . . . .

Appendix B

Income Tax Regulations

Compensation Deferred Under Eligible Deferred Compensation Plans

Preamble

Summary: This document contains final regulations that provide guidance on deferred compensation plans of state and local governments and tax-exempt entities. The regulations reflect the changes made to section 457 by the Tax Reform Act of 1986, the Small Business Job Protection Act of 1996, the Taxpayer Relief Act of 1997, the Economic Growth and Tax Relief Reconciliation Act of 2001, the Job Creation and Worker Assistance Act of 2002, and other legislation. The regulations also make various technical changes and clarifications to the existing final regulations on many discrete issues. These regulations provide the public with guidance necessary to comply with the law and will affect plan sponsors, administrators, participants, and beneficiaries.

Effective Date: July 11, 2003.

Applicability Date: These regulations apply to taxable years beginning after December 31, 2001. See "Effective date of the regulations" for additional information concerning the applicability of these regulations.

Background

Section 131 of the Revenue Act of 1978 (92 Stat. 2779) added section 457 to the Internal Revenue Code of 1954. On September 27, 1982, final regulations (TD 7836, 1982-2 C.B. 91) under section 457 (the 1982 regulations) were published in the Federal Register (47 FR 42335). The 1982 regulations provided guidance for complying with the changes to the applicable tax law made by the Revenue Act of 1978 relating to deferred compensation plans maintained by state and local governments and rural electric cooperatives.

Section 1107 of the Tax Reform Act of 1986 (100 Stat. 2494) extended section 457 to tax-exempt organizations. Section 6064 of the Technical and

Miscellaneous Act of 1988 (102 Stat. 3700) codified certain exceptions for certain plans. Notice 88-68, 1988-1 C.B. 556, addressed the treatment of non-elective deferred compensation of nonemployees, and provided an exception under which section 457 does not to apply to certain church plans.

Section 1404 of the Small Business Job Protection Act of 1996 (110 Stat. 1755) added section 457(g) which requires that section 457(b) plans maintained by state and local government employers hold all plan assets and income in trust, or in custodial accounts or annuity contracts (described in section 401(f) of the Internal Revenue Code), for the exclusive benefit of participants and beneficiaries.

Section 1071 of the Taxpayer Relief Act of 1997 (111 Stat. 788) permits certain accrued benefits to be cashed out.

Sections 615, 631, 632, 634, 635, 641, 647, and 649 of the Economic Growth and Tax Relief Reconciliation Act of 2001 (EGTRRA) (115 Stat. 38) included increases in elective deferral limits, repeal of the rules coordinating the section 457 plan limit with contributions to certain other types of plans, catch-up contributions for individuals age 50 or over, extension of qualified domestic relations order rules to section 457 plans, rollovers among various qualified plans, section 403(b) contracts and individual retirement arrangements (IRAs), and transfers to purchase service credits under governmental pension plans.

Section 411(o)(8) and (p)(5) of the Job Creation and Worker Assistance Act of 2002 (116 Stat. 21) clarified certain provisions in EGTRRA concerning section 457 plans, including the use of certain compensation reduction elections to be taken into account in determining includible compensation.

On May 8, 2002, a notice of proposed rulemaking (REG-105885-99) was published in the Federal Register (67 FR 30826) to issue new regulations under section 457, including amending the 1982 regulations to conform them to the legislative changes that had been made to section 457 since 1982.

Following publication of the proposed regulations, comments were received and a public hearing was held on August 28, 2002. After consideration of the comments received, the proposed regulations are adopted by this Treasury decision, subject to a number of changes that are generally summarized below.

Summary of Comments Received and Changes Made

1. Excess Deferrals: The proposed regulations addressed the income tax treatment of excess deferrals and the effect of excess deferrals on plan eligibility under section 457(b). The proposed regulations provided that an eligible governmental plan may self-correct and distribute excess deferrals and continue to satisfy the eligibility requirements of section 457(b) (including the distribution rules and the funding rules) by reason of a distribution of excess deferrals. However, the proposed regulations provided that if an excess deferral arose under an eligible plan of a tax-exempt employer, the plan was no longer an eligible plan.

Commentators objected to the less favorable treatment for eligible plans of tax-exempt employers.

After consideration of the comments received, the regulations extend self-correction for excess deferrals to eligible plans of tax-exempt employers. If there is an excess deferral under such plan, the plan may distribute to a participant any excess deferrals (and any income allocable to such amount) not later than the first April 15 following the close of the taxable year of the excess deferrals, comparable to the rules for qualified plans under section 402(g). In such a case, the plan will continue to be treated as an eligible plan. However, in accordance with section 457(c), any excess deferral is included in the gross income of a participant for the taxable year of the excess deferral. If an excess deferral is not corrected by distribution, the plan is an ineligible plan under which benefits are taxable in accordance with ineligible plan rules.

The income tax treatment and payroll tax reporting of distributions of excess deferrals from eligible section 457(b) governmental plans are similar to the treatment and reporting of distributions of excess deferrals from tax-qualified plans. Such amounts should be reported on Form 1099 and taxed in the year of distribution to the extent of distributed earnings on the excess deferrals. For eligible section 457(b) tax-exempt plans, the excess deferrals are subject to income tax in the year of distribution to the extent of distributed earnings on the excess deferrals and such earnings should be reported on Form W-2 for the year of distribution. See also Notice 2003-20, 2003-19 I.R.B. 894, for information regarding the withholding and reporting requirements applicable to eligible plans generally.

2. Aggregation Rules in the Proposed Regulations: The proposed regulations included several rules that aggregate multiple plans for purposes of meeting the eligibility requirements of section 457(b). These regulations retain all of these rules. For example, the regulations provide that in any case in which multiple plans are used to avoid or evade the eligibility requirements under the regulations, the Commissioner may apply the eligibility requirements as if the plans were a single plan. Also, an eligible employer is required to have no more than one normal retirement age for each participant under all of the eligible plans it sponsors. In addition, all deferrals under all eligible plans under which an individual participates by virtue of his or her relationship with a single employer are treated as though deferred under a single plan for purposes of determining excess deferrals. Finally, annual deferrals under all eligible plans are combined for purposes of determining the maximum deferral limits.

Few comments were received with respect to the aggregation rules under the proposed regulations. However, one commentator requested that, where it is determined that multiple eligible plans maintained by a single employer, which have been aggregated pursuant to the proposed regulations, contain excess deferrals, the employer have the ability to disaggregate those plans solely for the purpose of either (1) distributing the excess deferrals under the self-correcting mechanism or (2) limiting the characterization of such plans as "ineligible" to the one(s) that actually contain the excess deferrals. Taking into account the ability for all eligible plans to self-correct by distribution, these regulations retain without material revision the aggregation rules that were in the proposed regulations.

3. Deferral of Sick, Vacation, and Back Pay: The proposed regulations would have allowed an eligible plan to permit participants to elect to defer compensation, including accumulated sick and vacation pay and back pay, only if an agreement providing for the deferral is entered into before the beginning of the month in which the amounts would otherwise be paid or made available and the participant is an employee in that month. Comments requested that terminating participants be allowed to elect deferral for accumulated sick and vacation pay and back pay even if the participant is not employed at the time of the deferral.

The final regulations retain the rule under which the deferral election must be made during employment and before the beginning of the month when the compensation would have been payable. However, the regulations include a special rule that allows an election for sick pay, vacation pay, or back pay that is not yet payable (subject of course to the maximum deferral limitations of section 457 in the year of deferral). Under the special rule, an employee who is retiring or otherwise having a severance from employment during a month may nevertheless elect to defer, for example, his or her unused vacation pay after the beginning of the month, provided that the vacation pay would otherwise have been payable before the employee has a severance from employment and the election is made before the date on which the vacation pay would otherwise have been payable.

4. Unforeseeable Emergency Distributions: The proposed regulations added examples that would illustrate when an unforeseeable emergency occurred. In particular, one example provided that the need to pay for the funeral expenses of a family member may constitute an unforeseeable emergency. Several commentators requested clarification in the final regulations of the definition of family member. The regulations have been modified to define a family member as a spouse or dependent as defined in section 152(a).

5. Plan Terminations, Plan-to-Plan Transfers, and Rollovers: The regulations include certain rules regarding plan terminations, plan-to-plan transfers, and rollovers. These topics have been affected by the statutory changes that impose a trust requirement on eligible governmental plans. The direct rollovers that were permitted by EGTRRA beginning in 2002 for eligible governmental plans provide participants affected by these types of events the ability to retain their retirement savings in a funded, tax-deferred savings vehicle by rollover to an IRA, qualified plan, or section 403(b) contract. The regulations provide a outline for the different plan termination and plan-to-plan transfer alternatives available to sponsors of eligible governmental plans in these situations.

a. Plan terminations: The regulations allow a plan to have provisions permitting plan termination whereupon amounts can be distributed without violating the distribution requirements of section 457. Under the regulations, an eligible plan is terminated only if all amounts deferred under the plan are paid to participants as soon as administratively practicable. If the amounts deferred under the plan are not distributed, the plan is treated as a frozen plan and must continue to comply with all of the applicable statutory requirements necessary for plan eligibility.

b. Plan-to-plan transfers among eligible governmental plans and purchase of permissive service credit by plan-to-plan transfer: The proposed regulations would have allowed plan-to-plan transfers between eligible governmental plans under new circumstances, as well as the purchase of permissive service credits by transfer from an eligible governmental plan to a governmental defined benefit plan, but only if the transfers were made by plans within the same State. Commentators objected to the requirement under the new transfer rules that the transfers be to plans within the same State.

Upon consideration of the comments received, the regulations allow transfers among eligible governmental plans in three situations. In each case, the transferor plan must provide for transfers, the receiving plan must provide for the receipt of transfers, and the participant or beneficiary whose amounts deferred are being transferred must be entitled to an amount deferred immediately after the transfer that is at least equal to the amount deferred with respect to that participant or beneficiary immediately before the transfer. Transfers are permitted among eligible governmental plans in the following three cases:

- A person-by-person transfer is permitted for any beneficiary and for any participant who has had a severance from employment with the transferring employer and is performing services for the entity maintaining the receiving plan (whether or not the other plan is within the same State).
- No severance from employment is required if the entire plan's assets for all participants and beneficiaries are transferred to another eligible governmental plan within the same State.
- No severance from employment is required for a transfer from one eligible governmental plan of an employer to another eligible governmental plan of the same employer.

The final regulations also allow a plan-to-plan transfer from an eligible governmental plan to a governmental defined benefit plan for permissive service credit, without regard to whether the defined benefit plan is maintained by a governmental entity that is in the same State. In addition, language that was in an example which implied that section 415(n) (which addresses the application of maximum benefit limitations with respect to certain contributions) might apply to such a transfer has been eliminated because Treasury and the IRS have concluded that section 415(n) does not apply to such a transfer in any case in which the actuarial value of the benefit increase that results from the transfer does not exceed the amount transferred.

c. Plan-to-plan transfers among eligible plans of tax-exempt entities: The regulations retain the rule from the 1982 regulations allowing a plan-to-plan transfer after a participant has had a severance from employment.

d. Rollovers: The proposed regulations specified the treatment of amounts rolled into or out of an eligible governmental plan and stated that amounts rolled into the plan are treated as amounts deferred under the plan for purposes of the regulations. Some commentators requested that consideration be given to allowing eligible governmental plans to have the same flexibility that they claimed was permitted for qualified plans with respect to the timing of distributions of rolled-in assets. Specifically, these commentators requested the ability for an eligible governmental plan to allow a participant to receive a distribution of rolled-in assets even though the participant may not yet be eligible for a distribution of other assets held under the plan. Commentators pointed out that, since section 402(c)(10) allows an eligible governmental plan to accept a rollover contribution only if the rolled-in assets from other plan types are separately accounted for (in order to apply the section 72(t) early withdrawal income tax for distributions from these assets), this ability should not cause administrative problems for plan sponsors. Commentators also asserted that the flexibility to design an eligible governmental plan to permit such distributions would be beneficial to its participants.

These regulations do not permit an eligible governmental plan to distribute rolled-in assets to a participant who is not yet eligible for a distribution until future guidance of general applicability is published that addresses this issue. Treasury and the IRS intend to issue, in the near future, guidance of general applicability resolving this issue in coordination with the applicable rules for qualified plans and section 403(b) contracts.

Commentators also requested clarification on the order of accounts for partial distributions to participants who have rolled-in assets that are subject to the early withdrawal income tax. They requested that consideration be given in final regulations to clarifying that the participant may be treated as receiving a partial distribution first from other plan assets to minimize the early withdrawal income tax that would otherwise apply. These regulations clarify that, if a rollover is received by an eligible governmental plan from an IRA, qualified plan, or section 403(b) contract, then distributions from the eligible governmental plan are subject to the early withdrawal income tax in accordance with the plan's method of accounting, i.e., for purposes of applying the section 72(t) early withdrawal income tax, a distribution is treated as made from an eligible governmental plan's separate account for rollovers from an IRA, qualified plan, or section 403(b) contract only if the plan accounts for the distribution as a distribution from that account. Thus, for example, an eligible governmental plan may provide that any unforeseeable emergency withdrawal is made from other accounts to the extent possible, in which event the early withdrawal tax will not apply assuming that the plan only debits such other accounts to reflect the distribution.

The proposed regulations had requested comments on the issue of separate accounting for rolled-in amounts and asked if there are any special characteristics that would be lost if multiple types of separate accounts were not maintained. Commentators asked for the regulations to permit maintenance of a single rollover account for all amounts that are rolled into the eligible governmental plan. These regulations require separate accounting only to the extent mandated by section 402(c)(10), i.e., only for rollovers from IRAs, qualified plans and section 403(b) contracts. Section 72(t)(9) provides that the early withdrawal income tax applies to distributions from rollovers attributable to IRAs, qualified plans, and section 403(b) contracts. Thus, if an eligible governmental plan accepts a rollover from another eligible governmental plan of an amount that was originally deferred under an eligible governmental plan and commingles that rollover in the same separate account that includes a rollover amount from an IRA, qualified plan, or section 403(b) contract, then distributions from that account will be subject to the early withdrawal income tax. Accordingly, in order to avoid this result, eligible governmental plans may choose to establish three separate accounts for a participant even though these regulations only require that a single separate rollover account be maintained for all amounts that are rolled into an eligible governmental plan: first, an account for all amounts deferred under that plan; second, an account for any rollover from another eligible governmental plan (disregarding any amounts that originated from an IRA, qualified plan, or section 403(b) contract); and third, an account for any rollover amount from an IRA, qualified plan, or section 403(b) contract (including any amounts rolled over from another eligible governmental plan that originated from an IRA, qualified plan, or section 403(b) contract). These regulations include an example illustrating that the early withdrawal income tax would not apply to a partial distribution from a plan with such accounts assuming that the plan debits either of the first two such other accounts to reflect the distribution.

6. Ineligible Plans: The proposed regulations included guidance regarding ineligible plans under section 457(f). Section 457(f) generally provides that, in the case of an agreement or arrangement for the deferral of compensation, the deferred compensation is included in gross income when deferred or, if later, when the rights to payment of the deferred compensation cease to be subject to a substantial risk of forfeiture. Section 457(f) was in section 457 when it was added to the Code in 1978 for governmental employees, and extended to employees of tax-exempt organizations (other than churches or certain church-controlled organizations) in 1986, because unfunded amounts held by a tax-exempt entity compound tax free like an eligible plan, a qualified plan, or a section 403(b) contract. Section 457(f) was viewed as essential in order to provide an incentive for employers that are not subject to income taxes to adopt an eligible plan, a qualified plan, or a section 403(b) contract. [See generally the *Report to the Congress on the Tax Treatment of Deferred Compensation under Section 457*, Department of the Treasury, January 1992 (available from the Office of Tax Policy, Room 5315, Treasury Department, 1500 Pennsylvania Avenue NW, Washington DC 20220).]

Section 457(f) does not apply to an eligible plan, a qualified plan, a section 403(b) contract, a section 403(c) contract, a transfer of property described in section 83, a trust to which section 402(b) applies, or a qualified governmental excess benefit arrangement described in section 415(m). The proposed regulations stated that section 457(f) applies if the date on which there is no substantial risk of forfeiture with respect to the compensation deferred precedes the date on which there is a transfer of property to which section 83 applies. The proposed regulations included several examples, including an example illustrating that section 457(f) does not fail to apply merely because benefits are subsequently paid by a transfer of property. Comments were requested on the coordination of sections 457(f) and 83 under the proposed regulations.

In response, a number of commentators objected to the proposed coordination of sections 457(f) and 83, including arguing that the proposed regulation would place tax-exempt organizations at a competitive disadvantage when it comes to attracting and retaining executive talent because it would effectively eliminate the use of discounted mutual fund options as a tax effective component of total compensation. Some commentators also asserted that the proposed regulations were ambiguous as to their applicability to steeply discounted mutual fund options, and recommended that, if the provision is not removed, at a minimum future guidance should be more specific.

The final regulations retain the interpretation of the coordination of sections 457(f) and 83 that was in the proposed regulations, and also clarify the application of the rule by adding an example involving an option grant. The regulations also include a clarification that, when benefits are paid or made available under an ineligible plan, the amount included in gross income is equal to the amount paid or made available, but only to the extent that the amount exceeds the amount the participant included in gross income when he or she obtained a vested right to the benefit.

7. Severance Pay and Other Exceptions: In 2000, the IRS issued Announcement 2000-1 (2000-1 C.B. 294), which provided interim guidance on certain broad-based, nonelective plans of a state or local government that were in existence before 1999. Comments were requested on arrangements, such as those maintained by certain state or local governmental educational institutions, under which supplemental compensation is payable as an incentive to terminate employment, or as an incentive to retain retirement-eligible employees, to ensure an appropriate workforce during periods in which a temporary surplus or deficit in workforce is anticipated. Treasury and the IRS continue to be interested in receiving comments on this issue, which should be sent to the following address: Internal Revenue Service, Attn: CC:DOM:CORP:R (Section 457 Plans), Room 5201, P.O. Box 7604, Ben Franklin Station, Washington, DC 20044. Written comments may be hand delivered Monday through Friday between 8 a.m. and 4 p.m. to: Internal Revenue Service, Courier's Desk, Attn: CC:PA:RU (Section 457 Plans), 1111 Constitution Avenue, NW, Washington, DC 20224. Alternatively, written comments may be submitted electronically via the Internet by selecting the "Tax Regs" option on the IRS Home Page, or by submitting them directly to the IRS Internet site at: http://www.irs.gov/tax_regs/reglist.html. Comments should be received by October 9, 2003.

8. Effective Date of the Regulations: The proposed regulations included a general effective date under which the regulations would have applied to taxable years beginning after December 31, 2001. This is the general effective date for the changes made in section 457 by EGTRRA. Commentators did not express concern about this effective date and some commentators also stated that eligible governmental plans have adopted plan amendments to address the changes that have been allowed by EGTRRA, so that it would be appropriate to have the final regulations effective date coincide with the effective date for EGTRRA.

These regulations are generally applicable to taxable years beginning after December 31, 2001, subject to certain specific transition rules. Under one of these transition rules, for taxable years beginning after December 31, 2001, and before January 1, 2004, a plan will not fail to be an eligible plan if it is operated in accordance with a reasonable, good faith interpretation of section 457(b). Whether a plan is operated in accordance with a reasonable, good faith interpretation of section 457(b) will generally be determined based on all of the relevant facts and circumstances, including the extent to which the employer has resolved unclear issues in its favor. The regulations state that a plan will be deemed to be operated in accordance with a reasonable, good faith interpretation of section 457(b) if it is operated in accordance with the terms of these regulations. The IRS will also deem a plan to be operated in accordance with a reasonable, good faith interpretation of section 457(b) if it is operated in accordance with the terms of the 1982 regulations as in effect for taxable years beginning before January 1, 2002 (to the extent those 1982 regulations are consistent with subsequent changes in law, including EGTRRA) or in accordance with the terms of the 2001 proposed regulations. However, a plan will be deemed not to be operated in accordance with a reasonable, good faith interpretation of section 457(b) if it is operated in a manner that is inconsistent with the terms of the 1982 regulations as in effect for taxable years beginning before January 1, 2002 (to the extent those 1982 regulations are consistent with subsequent changes in law, including EGTRRA) except to the extent permitted under either these final regulations or the 2001 proposed regulations.

Further, there is a special delayed effective date for the rule under which an eligible governmental plan cannot distribute rollover account benefits to a participant who is not yet eligible for a distribution. Thus, this rule is not applicable until years beginning after December 31, 2003, since this issue is expected to be resolved before that date.

The regulations also retain the rule in the proposed regulations under which the regulations do not apply with respect to an option that lacked a readily ascertainable fair market value (within the meaning of section 83(e)(3)) at grant that was granted on or before May 8, 2002. Thus, the status of such an option under section 457(f) would be determined without regard to these regulations.

Compensation Deferred Under Eligible Deferred Compensation Plans

Treasury Regulations Section 1.457

Section 1.457-1 General overviews of section 457

Section 457 provides rules for nonqualified deferred compensation plans established by eligible employers as defined under section 1.457-2(d). Eligible employers can establish either deferred compensation plans that are eligible plans and that meet the requirements of section 457(b) and section 1.457-3 through 1.457-10, or deferred compensation plans or arrangements that do not meet the requirements of section 457(b) and sections 1.457-3 through 1.457-10 and that are subject to tax treatment under section 457(f) and section 1.457-11.

Section 1.457-2 Definitions

This section sets forth the definitions that are used under sections 1.457-1 through 1.457-11.

(a) *Amount(s) deferred. Amount(s) deferred* means the total annual deferrals under an eligible plan in the current and prior years, adjusted for gain or loss. Except as provided at sections 1.457-4(c)(1)(iii) and 1.457-6(a), amount(s) deferred includes any rollover amount held by an eligible plan as provided under section 1.457-10(e).

(b) *Annual deferral(s)—*

(1) *Annual deferral(s)* means, with respect to a taxable year, the amount of compensation deferred under an eligible plan, whether by salary reduction or by nonelective employer contribution. The amount of compensation deferred under an eligible plan is taken into account as an annual deferral in the taxable year of the participant in which deferred, or, if later, the year in which the amount of compensation deferred is no longer subject to a substantial risk of forfeiture.

(2) If the amount of compensation deferred under the plan during a taxable year is not subject to a substantial risk of forfeiture, the amount taken into account as an annual deferral is not adjusted to reflect gain or loss allocable to the compensation deferred. If, however, the amount of compensation deferred under the plan during the taxable year is subject to a substantial risk of forfeiture, the amount of compensation deferred that is taken into account as an annual deferral in the taxable year in which the substantial risk of forfeiture lapses must be adjusted to reflect gain or loss allocable to the compensation deferred until the substantial risk of forfeiture lapses.

(3) If the eligible plan is a defined benefit plan within the meaning of section 414(j), the annual deferral for a taxable year is the present value of the increase during the taxable year of the participant's accrued benefit that is not subject to a substantial risk of forfeiture (disregarding any such increase attributable to prior annual deferrals). For this purpose, present value must be determined using actuarial assumptions and methods that are reasonable (both individually and in the aggregate), as determined by the Commissioner.

(4) For purposes solely of applying section 1.457-4 to determine the maximum amount of the annual deferral for a participant for a taxable year under an eligible plan, the maximum amount is reduced by the amount of any deferral for the participant under a plan described at paragraph (k)(4)(i) of this section (relating to certain plans in existence before January 1, 1987) as if that deferral were an annual deferral under another eligible plan of the employer.

(c) *Beneficiary. Beneficiary* means a person who is entitled to benefits in respect of a participant following the participant's death or an alternate payee as described in section 1.457-10(c).

(d) *Catch-up.* *Catch-up* amount or *catch-up* limitation for a participant for a taxable year means the annual deferral permitted under section 414(v) (as described in section 1.457-4(c)(2)) or section 457(b)(3) (as described in section 1.457-4(c)(3)) to the extent the amount of the annual deferral for the participant for the taxable year is permitted to exceed the plan ceiling applicable under section 457(b)(2) (as described in section 1.457-4(c)(1)).

(e) *Eligible employer.* *Eligible employer* means an entity that is a State that establishes a plan or a tax-exempt entity that establishes a plan. The performance of services as an independent contractor for a State or local government or a tax-exempt entity is treated as the performance of services for an eligible employer. The term *eligible employer* does not include a church as defined in section 3121(w)(3)(A), a qualified church-controlled organization as defined in section 3121(w)(3)(B), or the Federal government or any agency or instrumentality thereof. Thus, for example, a nursing home which is associated with a church, but which is not itself a church (as defined in section 3121(w)(3)(A)) or a qualified church-controlled organization as defined in section 3121(w)(3)(B)), would be an eligible employer if it is a tax-exempt entity as defined in paragraph (m) of this section.

(f) *Eligible plan.* An *eligible plan* is a plan that meets the requirements of sections 1.457-3 through 1.457-10 that is established and maintained by an eligible employer. An *eligible governmental plan* is an eligible plan that is established and maintained by an eligible employer as defined in paragraph (l) of this section. An arrangement does not fail to constitute a single eligible governmental plan merely because the arrangement is funded through more than one trustee, custodian, or insurance carrier. An *eligible plan of a tax-exempt entity* is an eligible plan that is established and maintained by an eligible employer as defined in paragraph (m) of this section.

(g) *Includible compensation.* *Includible compensation* of a participant means, with respect to a taxable year, the participant's compensation, as defined in section 415(c)(3), for services performed for the eligible employer. The amount of includible compensation is determined without regard to any community property laws.

(h) *Ineligible plan.* *Ineligible plan* means a plan established and maintained by an eligible employer that is not maintained in accordance with sections 1.457-3 through 1.457-10. A plan that is not established by an eligible employer as defined in paragraph (e) of this section is neither an eligible nor an ineligible plan.

(i) *Nonelective employer contribution.* A *nonelective employer contribution* is a contribution made by an eligible employer for the participant with respect to which the participant does not have the choice to receive the contribution in cash or property. Solely for purposes of section 457 and sections 1.457-2 through 1.457-11, the term *nonelective employer contribution* includes employer contributions that would be described in section 401(m) if they were contributions to a qualified plan.

(j) *Participant.* *Participant* in an eligible plan means an individual who is currently deferring compensation, or who has previously deferred compensation under the plan by salary reduction or by nonelective employer contribution and who has not received a distribution of his or her entire benefit under the eligible plan. Only individuals who perform services for the eligible employer, either as an employee or as an independent contractor, may defer compensation under the eligible plan.

(k) *Plan.* Plan includes any agreement or arrangement between an eligible employer and a participant or participants (including an individual employment agreement) under which the payment of compensation is deferred (whether by salary reduction or by nonelective employer contribution). The following types of plans are not treated as agreements or arrangements under which compensation is deferred: a bona fide vacation leave, sick leave, compensatory time, severance pay, disability pay, or death benefit plan described in section 457(e)(11)(A)(i) and any plan paying length of service awards to bona fide volunteers (and their beneficiaries) on account of qualified services performed by such volunteers as described in section 457(e)(11)(A)(ii). Further, the term *plan* does not include any of the following (and section 457 and sections 1.457-2 through 1.457-11 do not apply to any of the following)—

(1) Any nonelective deferred compensation under which all individuals (other than those who have not satisfied any applicable initial service requirement) with the same relationship with the eligible employer are covered under the same plan with no individual variations or options under the plan as described in section 457(e)(12), but only to the extent the compensation is attributable to services performed as an independent contractor;

(2) An agreement or arrangement described in section 1.457-11(b);

(3) Any plan satisfying the conditions in section 1107(c)(4) of the Tax Reform Act of 1986 (100 Stat. 2494) (TRA '86) (relating to certain plans for State judges); and

(4) Any of the following plans or arrangements (to which specific transitional statutory exclusions apply)—

(i) A plan or arrangement of a tax-exempt entity in existence prior to January 1, 1987, if the conditions of section 1107(c)(3)(B) of the TRA '86, as amended by section 1011(e)(6) of the Technical and Miscellaneous Revenue Act of 1988 (102 Stat. 3700) (TAMRA), are satisfied (see section 1.457-2(b)(4) for a special rule regarding such plan);

(ii) A collectively bargained nonelective deferred compensation plan in effect on December 31, 1987, if the conditions of section 6064(d)(2) of TAMRA are satisfied;

(iii) Amounts described in section 6064(d)(3) of TAMRA (relating to certain nonelective deferred compensation arrangements in effect before 1989); and

(iv) Any plan satisfying the conditions in section 1107(c)(4) or (5) of TRA '86 (relating to certain plans for certain individuals with respect to which the Service issued guidance before 1977).

(l) *State.* State means a State (treating the District of Columbia as a State as provided under section 7701(a)(10)), a political subdivision of a State, and any agency or instrumentality of a State.

(m) *Tax-exempt entity.* Tax-exempt entity includes any organization exempt from tax under subtitle A of the Internal Revenue Code, except that a governmental unit (including an international governmental organization) is not a tax-exempt entity.

(n) *Trust.* Trust means a trust described under section 457(g) and section 1.457-8. Custodial accounts and contracts described in section 401(f) are treated as trusts under the rules described in section 1.457-8(a)(2).

Section 1.457-3 General introduction to eligible plans

(a) *Compliance in form and operation.* An eligible plan is a written plan established and maintained by an eligible employer that is maintained, in both form and operation, in accordance with the requirements of sections 1.457-4 through 1.457-10. An eligible plan must contain all the material terms and conditions for benefits under the plan. An eligible plan may contain certain optional features not required for plan eligibility under section 457(b), such as distributions for unforeseeable emergencies, loans, plan-to-plan transfers, additional deferral elections, acceptance of rollovers to the plan, and distributions of smaller accounts to eligible participants. However, except as otherwise specifically provided in sections 1.457-4 through 1.457-10, if an eligible plan contains any optional provisions, the optional provisions must meet, in both form and operation, the relevant requirements under section 457 and sections 1.457-2 through 1.457-10.

(b) *Treatment as single plan.* In any case in which multiple plans are used to avoid or evade the requirements of sections 1.457-4 through 1.457-10, the Commissioner may apply the rules under sections 1.457-4 through 1.457-10 as if the plans were a single plan. See also section 1.457-4(c)(3)(v) (requiring an eligible employer to have no more than one normal retirement age for each participant under all of the eligible plans it sponsors), the second sentence of section 1.457-4(e)(2) (treating deferrals under all eligible plans under which an individual participates by virtue of his or her relationship with a single employer as a single plan for purposes of determining excess deferrals), and section 1.457-5 (combining annual deferrals under all eligible plans).

Section 1.457-4 Annual deferrals, deferral limitations, and deferral agreements under eligible plans

(a) *Taxation of annual deferrals.* Annual deferrals that satisfy the requirements of paragraphs (b) and (c) of this section are excluded from the gross income of a participant in the year deferred or contributed and are not includible in gross income until paid to the participant in the case of an eligible governmental plan, or until paid or otherwise made available to the participant in the case of an eligible plan of a tax-exempt entity. See section 1.457-7.

(b) *Agreement for deferral.* In order to be an eligible plan, the plan must provide that compensation may be deferred for any calendar month by salary reduction only if an agreement providing for the deferral has been entered into before the first day of the month in which the compensation is paid or made available. A new employee may defer compensation payable in the calendar month during which the participant first becomes an employee if an agreement providing for the deferral is entered into on or before the first day on which the participant performs services for the eligible employer. An eligible plan may provide that if a participant enters into an agreement providing for deferral by salary reduction under the plan, the agreement will remain in effect until the participant revokes or alters the terms of the agreement. Nonelective employer contributions are treated as being made under an agreement entered into before the first day of the calendar month.

(c) *Maximum deferral limitations—*

(1) *Basic annual limitation*

(i) Except as described in paragraphs (c)(2) and (3) of this section, in order to be an eligible plan, the plan must provide that the annual deferral amount for a taxable year (the plan ceiling) may not exceed the lesser of—

(A) The applicable annual dollar amount specified in section 457(e)(15): $11,000 for 2002; $12,000 for 2003; $13,000 for 2004; $14,000 for 2005; and $15,000 for 2006 and thereafter. After 2006, the $15,000 amount is adjusted for cost-of-living in the manner described in paragraph (c)(4) of this section; or

(B) 100 percent of the participant's includible compensation for the taxable year.

(ii) The amount of annual deferrals permitted by the 100 percent of includible compensation limitation under paragraph (c)(1)(i)(B) of this section is determined under section 457(e)(5) and section 1.457-2(g).

(iii) For purposes of determining the plan ceiling under this paragraph (c), the annual deferral amount does not include any rollover amounts received by the eligible plan under section 1.457-10(e).

(iv) The provisions of this paragraph (c)(1) are illustrated by the following examples:

Example 1. (i) *Facts.* Participant A, who earns $14,000 a year, enters into a salary reduction agreement in 2006 with A's eligible employer and elects to defer $13,000 of A's compensation for that year. A is not eligible for the catch-up described in paragraph (c)(2) or (3) of this section, participates in no other retirement plan, and has no other income exclusions taken into account in computing includible compensation.

(ii) *Conclusion.* The annual deferral limit for A in 2006 is the lesser of $15,000 or 100 percent of includible compensation, $14,000. A's annual deferral of $13,000 is permitted under the plan because it is not in excess of $14,000 and thus does not exceed 100 percent of A's includible compensation.

Example 2. (i) *Facts.* Assume the same facts as in *Example 1*, except that A's eligible employer provides an immediately vested, matching employer contribution under the plan for participants who make salary reduction deferrals under A's eligible plan. The matching contribution is equal to 100 percent of elective contributions, but not in excess of 10 percent of compensation (in A's case, $1,400).

(ii) *Conclusion.* Participant A's annual deferral exceeds the limitations of this paragraph (c)(1). A's maximum deferral limitation in 2006 is $14,000. A's salary reduction deferral of $13,000 combined with A's eligible employer's nonelective employer contribution of $1,400 exceeds the basic annual limitation of this paragraph (c)(1) because A's annual deferrals total $14,400. A has an excess deferral for the taxable year of $400, the amount exceeding A's permitted annual deferral limitation. The $400 excess deferral is treated as described in paragraph (e) of this section.

Example 3. (i) *Facts.* Beginning in year 2002, Eligible Employer X contributes $3,000 per year for five years to B's eligible plan account. B's interest in the account vests in 2006. B has annual compensation of $50,000 in each of the five years 2002 through 2006. B is 41 years old. B is not eligible for the catch-up described in paragraph (c)(2) or (3) of this section, participates in no other retirement plan, and has no other income exclusions taken into account in computing includible compensation. Adjusted for gain or loss, the value of B's benefit when B's interest in the account vests in 2006 is $17,000.

(ii) *Conclusion.* Under this vesting schedule, $17,000 is taken into account as an annual deferral in 2006. B's annual deferrals under the plan are limited to a maximum of $15,000 in 2006. Thus, the aggregate of the amounts deferred, $17,000, is in excess of B's maximum deferral limitation by $2,000. The $2,000 is treated as an excess deferral described in paragraph (e) of this section.

(2) *Age 50 catch-up—*

(i) *In general.* In accordance with section 414(v) and the regulations thereunder, an eligible governmental plan may provide for catch-up contributions for a participant who is age 50 by the end of the year, provided that such age 50 catch-up contributions do not exceed the catch-up limit under section 414(v)(2) for the taxable year. The maximum amount of age 50 catch-up contributions for a taxable year under section 414(v) is as follows: $1,000 for 2002; $2,000 for 2003; $3,000 for 2004; $4,000 for 2005; and $5,000 for 2006 and thereafter. After 2006, the $5,000 amount is adjusted for cost-of-living. For additional guidance, see regulations under section 414(v).

(ii) *Coordination with special section 457 catch-up.* In accordance with sections 414(v)(6)(C) and 457(e)(18), the age 50 catch-up described in this paragraph (c)(2) does not apply for any taxable year for which a higher limitation applies under the special section 457 catch-up under paragraph (c)(3) of this section. Thus, for purposes of this paragraph (c)(2)(ii) and paragraph (c)(3) of this section, the special section 457 catch-up under paragraph (c)(3) of this section applies for any taxable year if and only if the plan ceiling taking into account paragraph (c)(1) of this section and the special section 457 catch-up described in paragraph (c)(3) of this section (and disregarding the age 50 catch-up described in this paragraph (c)(2)) is larger than the plan ceiling taking into account paragraph (c)(1) of this section and the age 50 catch-up described in this paragraph (c)(2) (and disregarding the special section 457 catch-up described in paragraph (c)(3) of this section). Thus, if a plan so provides, a participant who is eligible for the age 50 catch-up for a year and for whom the year is also one of the participant's last three taxable years ending before the participant attains normal retirement age is eligible for the larger of—

(A) The plan ceiling under paragraph (c)(1) of this section and the age 50 catch-up described in this paragraph (c)(2) (and disregarding the special section 457 catch-up described in paragraph (c)(3) of this section) or

(B) The plan ceiling under paragraph (c)(1) of this section and the special section 457 catch-up described in paragraph (c)(3) of this section (and disregarding the age 50 catch-up described in this paragraph (c)(2)).

(iii) *Examples.* The provisions of this paragraph (c)(2) are illustrated by the following examples:

Example 1. (i) *Facts.* Participant C, who is 55, is eligible to participate in an eligible governmental plan in 2006. The plan provides a normal retirement age of 65. The plan provides limitations on annual deferrals up to the maximum permitted under paragraphs (c)(1) and (3) of this section and the age 50 catch-up described in this paragraph (c)(2). For 2006, C will receive compensation of $40,000 from the eligible employer. C desires to defer the maximum amount possible in 2006. The applicable basic dollar limit of paragraph (c)(1)(i)(A) of this section is $15,000 for 2006 and the additional dollar amount permitted under the age 50 catch-up is $5,000 for 2006.

(ii) *Conclusion.* C is eligible for the age 50 catch-up in 2006 because C is 55 in 2006. However, C is not eligible for the special section 457 catch-up under paragraph (c)(3) of this section in 2006 because 2006 is not one of the last three taxable years ending before C attains normal retirement age. Accordingly, the maximum that C may defer for 2006 is $20,000.

Example 2. (i) *Facts.* The facts are the same as in *Example 1*, except that, in 2006, C will attain age 62. The maximum amount that C can elect under the special section 457 catch-up under paragraph (c)(3) of this section is $2,000 for 2006.

(ii) *Conclusion.* The maximum that C may defer for 2006 is $20,000. This is the sum of the basic plan ceiling under paragraph (c)(1) of this section equal to $15,000 and the age 50 catch-up equal to $5,000. The special section 457 catch-up under paragraph (c)(3) of this section is not applicable since it provides a smaller plan ceiling.

Example 3. (i) *Facts.* The facts are the same as in *Example 2*, except that the maximum additional amount that C can elect under the special section 457 catch-up under paragraph (c)(3) of this section is $7,000 for 2006.

(ii) *Conclusion.* The maximum that C may defer for 2006 is $22,000. This is the sum of the basic plan ceiling under paragraph (c)(1) of this section equal to $15,000, plus the additional special section 457 catch-up under paragraph (c)(3) of this section equal to $7,000. The additional dollar amount permitted under the age 50 catch-up is not applicable to C for 2006 because it provides a smaller plan ceiling.

(3) *Special section 457 catch-up—*

(i) *In general.* Except as provided in paragraph (c)(2)(ii) of this section, an eligible plan may provide that, for one or more of the participant's last three taxable years ending before the participant attains normal retirement age, the plan ceiling is an amount not in excess of the lesser of—

(A) Twice the dollar amount in effect under paragraph (c)(1)(i)(A) of this section; or

(B) The underutilized limitation determined under paragraph (c)(3)(ii) of this section.

(ii) *Underutilized limitation.* The underutilized amount determined under this paragraph (c)(3)(ii) is the sum of—

(A) The plan ceiling established under paragraph (c)(1) of this section for the taxable year; plus (B) The plan ceiling established under paragraph (c)(1) of this section (or under section 457(b)(2) for any year before the applicability date of this section) for any prior taxable year or years, less the amount of annual deferrals under the plan for such prior taxable year or years (disregarding any annual deferrals under the plan permitted under the age 50 catch-up under paragraph (c)(2) of this section).

(iii) *Determining underutilized limitation under paragraph (c)(3)(ii)(B) of this section.* A prior taxable year is taken into account under paragraph (c)(3)(ii)(B) of this section only if it is a year beginning after December 31, 1978, in which the participant was eligible to participate in the plan, and in which compensation deferred (if any) under the plan during the year was subject to a plan ceiling established under paragraph (c)(1) of this section. This paragraph (c)(3)(iii) is subject to the special rules in paragraph (c)(3)(iv) of this section.

(iv) *Special rules concerning application of the coordination limit for years prior to 2002 for purposes of determining the underutilized limitation—(A) General rule.* For purposes of determining the underutilized limitation for years prior to 2002, participants remain subject to the rules in effect prior to the repeal of the coordination limitation under section 457(c)(2). Thus, the applicable basic annual limitation under paragraph (c)(1) of this section and the special section 457 catch-up under this paragraph (c)(3) for years in effect prior to 2002 are reduced, for purposes of determining a participant's underutilized amount under a plan, by amounts excluded from the participant's income for any prior taxable year by reason of a nonelective employer contribution, salary reduction or elective contribution under any other eligible section 457(b) plan, or a salary reduction or elective contribution under any 401(k) qualified cash or deferred arrangement, section 402(h)(1)(B) simplified employee pension (SARSEP), section 403(b) annuity contract, and section 408(p) simple retirement account, or under any plan for which a deduction is allowed because of a contribution to an organization described in section 501(c)(18) (pre-2002 coordination plans). Similarly, in applying the section 457(b)(2)(B) limitation for includible compensation for years prior to 2002, the limitation is 33⅓ percent of the participant's compensation includible in gross income.

(B) *Coordination limitation applied to participant.* For purposes of determining the underutilized limitation for years prior to 2002, the coordination limitation applies to pre-2002 coordination plans of all employers for whom a participant has performed services, whether or not those are plans of the participant's current eligible employer. Thus, for purposes of determining the amount excluded from a participant's gross income in any prior taxable year under paragraph (c)(3)(ii)(B) of this section, the participant's annual deferrals under an eligible plan, and salary reduction or elective deferrals under all other pre-2002 coordination plans, must be determined on an aggregate basis. To the extent that the combined deferrals for years prior to 2002 exceeded the maximum deferral limitations, the amount is treated as an excess deferral under paragraph (e) of this section for those prior years.

(C) *Special rule where no annual deferrals under the eligible plan.* A participant who, although eligible, did not defer any compensation under the eligible plan in any year before 2002 is not subject to the coordinated deferral limit, even though the participant may have deferred compensation under one of the other pre-2002 coordination plans. An individual is treated as not having deferred compensation under an eligible plan for a prior taxable year if all annual deferrals under the plan are distributed in accordance with paragraph (e) of this section. Thus, to the extent that a participant participated solely in one or more of the other pre-2002 coordination plans during a prior taxable year (and not the eligible plan), the participant is not subject to the coordinated limitation for that prior taxable year. However, the participant is treated as having deferred an amount in a prior taxable year, for purposes of determining the underutilized limitation for that prior taxable year under this paragraph (c)(3)(iv)(C), to the extent of the participant's aggregate salary reduction contributions and elective deferrals under all pre-2002 coordination plans up to the maximum deferral limitations in effect under section 457(b) for that prior taxable year. To the extent an employer did not offer an eligible plan to an individual in a prior given year, no underutilized limitation is available to the individual for that prior year, even if the employee subsequently becomes eligible to participate in an eligible plan of the employer.

(D) *Examples.* The provisions of this paragraph (c)(3)(iv) are illustrated by the following examples:

Example 1. (i) *Facts.* In 2001 and in years prior to 2001, Participant D earned $50,000 a year and was eligible to participate in both an eligible plan and a section 401(k) plan. However, D had always participated only in the section 401(k) plan and had always deferred the maximum amount possible. For each year before 2002, the maximum amount permitted under section 401(k) exceeded the limitation of paragraph (c)(3)(i) of this section. In 2002, D is in the 3-year period prior to D's attainment of the eligible plan's normal retirement age of 65, and D now wants to participate in the eligible plan and make annual deferrals of up to $30,000 under the plan's special section 457 catch-up provisions.

(ii) *Conclusion*. Participant D is treated as having no underutilized amount under paragraph (c)(3)(ii)(B) of this section for 2002 for purposes of the catch-up limitation under section 457(b)(3) and paragraph (c)(3) of this section because, in each of the years before 2002, D has deferred an amount equal to or in excess of the limitation of paragraph (c)(3)(i) of this section under all of D's coordinated plans.

Example 2. (i) *Facts*. Assume the same facts as in *Example 1*, except that D only deferred $2,500 per year under the section 401(k) plan for one year before 2002.

(ii) *Conclusion*. D is treated as having an underutilized amount under paragraph (c)(3)(ii)(B) of this section for 2002 for purposes of the special section 457 catch-up limitation. This is because D has deferred an amount for prior years that is less than the limitation of paragraph (c)(1)(i) of this section under all of D's coordinated plans.

Example 3. (i) *Facts*. Participant E, who earned $15,000 for 2000, entered into a salary reduction agreement in 2000 with E's eligible employer and elected to defer $3,000 for that year under E's eligible plan. For 2000, E's eligible employer provided an immediately vested, matching employer contribution under the plan for participants who make salary reduction deferrals under E's eligible plan. The matching contribution was equal to 67 percent of elective contributions, but not in excess of 10 percent of compensation before salary reduction deferrals (in E's case, $1,000). For 2000, E was not eligible for any catch-up contribution, participated in no other retirement plan, and had no other income exclusions taken into account in computing taxable compensation.

(ii) *Conclusion*. Participant E's annual deferral equaled the maximum limitation of section 457(b) for 2000. E's maximum deferral limitation in 2000 was $4,000 because E's includible compensation was $12,000 ($15,000 minus the deferral of $3,000) and the applicable limitation for 2000 was one-third of the individual's includible compensation (one-third of $12,000 equals $4,000). E's salary reduction deferral of $3,000 combined with E's eligible employer's matching contribution of $1,000 equals the limitation of section 457(b) for 2000 because E's annual deferrals totaled $4,000. E's underutilized amount for 2000 is zero.

(v) *Normal retirement age*—

(A) *General rule*. For purposes of the special section 457 catch-up in this paragraph (c)(3), a plan must specify the normal retirement age under the plan. A plan may define normal retirement age as any age that is on or after the earlier of age 65 or the age at which participants have the right to retire and receive, under the basic defined benefit pension plan of the State or tax-exempt entity (or a money purchase pension plan in which the participant also participates if the participant is not eligible to participate in a defined benefit plan), immediate retirement benefits without actuarial or similar reduction because of retirement before some later specified age, and that is not later than age 70½. Alternatively, a plan may provide that a participant is allowed to designate a normal retirement age within these ages. For purposes of the special section 457 catch-up in this paragraph (c)(3), an entity sponsoring more than one eligible plan may not permit a participant to have more than one normal retirement age under the eligible plans it sponsors.

(B) *Special rule for eligible plans of qualified police or firefighters*. An eligible plan with participants that include qualified police or firefighters as defined under section 415(b)(2)(H)(ii)(I) may designate a normal retirement age for such qualified police or firefighters that is earlier than the earliest normal retirement age designated under the general rule of paragraph (c)(3)(i)(A) of this section, but in no event may the normal retirement age be earlier than age 40. Alternatively, a plan may allow a qualified police or firefighter participant to designate a normal retirement age that is between age 40 and age 70½.

(vi) *Examples*. The provisions of this paragraph (c)(3) are illustrated by the following examples:

Example 1. (i) *Facts.* Participant F, who will turn 61 on April 1, 2006, becomes eligible to participate in an eligible plan on January 1, 2006. The plan provides a normal retirement age of 65. The plan provides limitations on annual deferrals up to the maximum permitted under paragraphs (c)(1) through (3) of this section. For 2006, F will receive compensation of $40,000 from the eligible employer. F desires to defer the maximum amount possible in 2006. The applicable basic dollar limit of paragraph (c)(1)(i)(A) of this section is $15,000 for 2006 and the additional dollar amount permitted under the age 50 catch-up in paragraph (c)(2) of this section for an individual who is at least age 50 is $5,000 for 2006.

(ii) *Conclusion.* F is not eligible for the special section 457 catch-up under paragraph (c)(3) of this section in 2006 because 2006 is not one of the last three taxable years ending before F attains normal retirement age. Accordingly, the maximum that F may defer for 2006 is $20,000. See also paragraph (c)(2)(iii) *Example 1* of this section.

Example 2. (i) *Facts.* The facts are the same as in *Example 1* except that, in 2006, F elects to defer only $2,000 under the plan (rather than the maximum permitted amount of $20,000). In addition, assume that the applicable basic dollar limit of paragraph (c)(1)(i)(A) of this section continues to be $15,000 for 2007 and the additional dollar amount permitted under the age 50 catch-up in paragraph (c)(2) of this section for an individual who is at least age 50 continues to be $5,000 for 2007. In F's taxable year 2007, which is one of the last three taxable years ending before F attains the plan's normal retirement age of 65, F again receives a salary of $40,000 and elects to defer the maximum amount permissible under the plan's catch-up provisions prescribed under paragraph (c) of this section.

(ii) *Conclusion.* For 2007, which is one of the last three taxable years ending before F attains the plan's normal retirement age of 65, the applicable limit on deferrals for F is the larger of the amount under the special section 457 catch-up or $20,000, which is the basic annual limitation ($15,000) and the age 50 catch-up limit of section 414(v) ($5,000). For 2007, F's special section 457 catch-up amount is the lesser of two times the basic annual limitation ($30,000) or the sum of the basic annual limitation ($15,000) plus the $13,000 underutilized limitation under paragraph (c)(3)(ii) of this section (the $15,000 plan ceiling in 2006, minus the $2,000 contributed for F in 2006), or $28,000. Thus, the maximum amount that F may defer in 2007 is $28,000.

Example 3. (i) *Facts.* The facts are the same as in *Examples 1* and *2*, except that F does not make any contributions to the plan before 2010. In addition, assume that the applicable basic dollar limitation of paragraph (c)(1)(i)(A) of this section continues to be $15,000 for 2010 and the additional dollar amount permitted under the age 50 catch-up in paragraph (c)(2) of this section for an individual who is at least age 50 continues to be $5,000 for 2010. In F's taxable year 2010, the year in which F attains age 65 (which is the normal retirement age under the plan), F desires to defer the maximum amount possible under the plan. F's compensation for 2010 is again $40,000.

(ii) *Conclusion.* For 2010, the maximum amount that F may defer is $20,000. The special section 457 catch-up provisions under paragraph (c)(3) of this section are not applicable because 2010 is not a taxable year ending before the year in which F attains normal retirement age.

(4) *Cost-of-living adjustment.* For years beginning after December 31, 2006, the $15,000 dollar limitation in paragraph (c)(1)(i)(A) of this section will be adjusted to take into account increases in the cost-of-living. The adjustment in the dollar limitation is made at the same time and in the same manner as under section 415(d) (relating to qualified plans under section 401(a)), except that the base period is the calendar quarter beginning July 1, 2005 and any increase which is not a multiple of $500 will be rounded to the next lowest multiple of $500.

(d) *Deferral of sick, vacation, and back pay under an eligible plan—*(1) *In general.* An eligible plan may provide that a participant may elect to defer accumulated sick pay, accumulated vacation pay, and back pay under an eligible plan if the requirements of section 457(b) are satisfied. For example, the plan must provide, in accordance with paragraph (b) of this section, that these amounts may be deferred for any calendar month only if an agreement providing for the deferral is entered into before the beginning of the month in which the amounts would otherwise be paid or made available and the participant is an employee in that month. In the case of accumulated sick pay, vacation pay, or back pay that is payable before the participant has a severance from employment, the requirements of the preceding sentence are deemed to be satisfied if the agreement providing for the deferral is entered into before the amount is currently available (as defined in regulations under section 401(k)).

(2) *Examples*. The provisions of this paragraph (d) are illustrated by the following examples:

Example 1. (i) *Facts*. Participant G, who is age 62 in 2003, is an employee who participates in an eligible plan providing a normal retirement age of 65. Under the terms of G's employer's eligible plan and G's sick leave plan, G may, during November of 2003 (which is one of the three years prior to normal retirement age), make a one-time election to contribute amounts representing accumulated sick pay to the eligible plan in December of 2003 (within the maximum deferral limitations). Alternatively, such amounts may remain in the "bank" under the sick leave plan. No cash out of the sick pay is available until the month in which a participant ceases to be employed by the employer. The total value of G's accumulated sick pay (determined, in accordance with the terms of the sick leave plan, by reference to G's current salary) is $4,000 in December of 2003.

(ii) *Conclusion*. Under the terms of the eligible plan and sick leave plan, G may elect before December of 2003 to defer the $4,000 value of accumulated sick pay under the eligible plan, provided that G's other annual deferrals to the eligible plan for 2003, when added to the $4,000, do not exceed G's maximum deferral limitation for the year.

Example 2. (i) *Facts*. Same facts as in *Example 1*, except that G will separate from service on January 17, 2004, and elects, on January 4, 2004, to defer G's accumulated sick and vacation pay (which totals $12,000) that is payable on January 15, 2004.

(ii) *Conclusion*. G may elect before January 15, 2004 to defer the accumulated sick and vacation pay under the eligible plan, even if the election is made after the beginning of January, because the agreement providing for the deferral is entered into before the amount is currently available and G does not cease to be an employee before the amount is currently available. G will have $12,000 of includible compensation in 2004 because the deferral is taken into account in the definition of includible compensation.

Example 3. (i) *Facts*. Employer X maintains an eligible plan and a vacation leave plan. Under the terms of the vacation leave plan, employees generally accrue three weeks of vacation per year. Up to one week's unused vacation may be carried over from one year to the next, so that in any single year an employee may have a maximum of four weeks vacation time. At the beginning of each calendar year, under the terms of the eligible plan (which constitutes an agreement providing for the deferral), the value of any unused vacation time from the prior year in excess of one week is automatically contributed to the eligible plan, to the extent of the employee's maximum deferral limitations. Amounts in excess of the maximum deferral limitations are forfeited.

(ii) *Conclusion*. The value of the unused vacation pay contributed to X's eligible plan pursuant to the terms of the plan and the terms of the vacation leave plan is treated as an annual deferral to the eligible plan in the calendar year the contribution is made. No amounts contributed to the eligible plan will be considered made available to a participant in X's eligible plan.

(e) *Excess deferrals under an eligible plan*—(1) *In general.* Any amount deferred under an eligible plan for the taxable year of a participant that exceeds the maximum deferral limitations set forth in paragraphs (c)(1) through (3) of this section, and any amount that exceeds the individual limitation under section 1.457-5, constitutes an excess deferral that is taxable in accordance with section 1.457-11 for that taxable year. Thus, an excess deferral is includible in gross income in the taxable year deferred or, if later, the first taxable year in which there is no substantial risk of forfeiture.

(2) *Excess deferrals under an eligible governmental plan other than as a result of the individual limitation.* In order to be an eligible governmental plan, the plan must provide that any excess deferral resulting from a failure of a plan to apply the limitations of paragraphs (c)(1) through (3) of this section to amounts deferred under the eligible plan (computed without regard to the individual limitation under section 1.457-5) will be distributed to the participant, with allocable net income, as soon as administratively practicable after the plan determines that the amount is an excess deferral. For purposes of determining whether there is an excess deferral resulting from a failure of a plan to apply the limitations of paragraphs (c)(1) through (3) of this section, all plans under which an individual participates by virtue of his or her relationship with a single employer are treated as a single plan (without regard to any differences in funding). An eligible governmental plan does not fail to satisfy the requirements of paragraphs (a) through (d) of this section or sections 1.457-6 through 1.457-10 (including the distribution rules under section 1.457-6 and the funding rules under section 1.457-8) solely by reason of a distribution made under this paragraph (e)(2). If such excess deferrals are not corrected by distribution under this paragraph (e)(2), the plan will be an ineligible plan under which benefits are taxable in accordance with section 1.457-11.

(3) *Excess deferrals under an eligible plan of a tax-exempt employer other than as a result of the individual limitation.* If a plan of a tax-exempt employer fails to comply with the limitations of paragraphs (c)(1) through (3) of this section, the plan will be an ineligible plan under which benefits are taxable in accordance with section 1.457-11. However, a plan may distribute to a participant any excess deferrals (and any income allocable to such amount) not later than the first April 15 following the close of the taxable year of the excess deferrals. In such a case, the plan will continue to be treated as an eligible plan. However, any excess deferral is included in the gross income of a participant for the taxable year of the excess deferral. If the excess deferrals are not corrected by distribution under this paragraph (e)(3), the plan is an ineligible plan under which benefits are taxable in accordance with section 1.457-11. For purposes of determining whether there is an excess deferral resulting from a failure of a plan to apply the limitations of paragraphs (c)(1) through (3) of this section, all eligible plans under which an individual participates by virtue of his or her relationship with a single employer are treated as a single plan.

(4) *Excess deferrals arising from application of the individual limitation.* An eligible plan may provide that an excess deferral that is a result solely of a failure to comply with the individual limitation under section 1.457-5 for

a taxable year may be distributed to the participant, with allocable net income, as soon as administratively practicable after the plan determines that the amount is an excess deferral. An eligible plan does not fail to satisfy the requirements of paragraphs (a) through (d) of this section or sections 1.457-6 through 1.457-10 (including the distribution rules under section 1.457-6 and the funding rules under section 1.457-8) solely by reason of a distribution made under this paragraph (e)(4). Although a plan will still maintain eligible status if excess deferrals are not distributed under this paragraph (e)(4), a participant must include the excess amounts in income as provided in paragraph (e)(1) of this section.

(5) *Examples.* The provisions of this paragraph (e) are illustrated by the following examples:

Example 1. (i) *Facts.* In 2006, the eligible plan of State Employer X in which Participant H participates permits a maximum deferral of the lesser of $15,000 or 100 percent of includible compensation. In 2006, H, who has compensation of $28,000, nevertheless defers $16,000 under the eligible plan. Participant H is age 45 and normal retirement age under the plan is age 65. For 2006, the applicable dollar limit under paragraph (c)(1)(i)(A) of this section is $15,000. Employer X discovers the error in January of 2007 when it completes H's 2006 Form W-2 and promptly distributes $1,022 to H (which is the sum of the $1,000 excess and $22 of allocable net income).

(ii) *Conclusion.* Participant H has deferred $1,000 in excess of the $15,000 limitation provided for under the plan for 2006. The $1,000 excess must be included by H in H's income for 2006. In order to correct the failure and still be an eligible plan, the plan must distribute the excess deferral, with allocable net income, as soon as administratively practicable after determining that the amount exceeds the plan deferral limitations. In this case, $22 of the distribution of $1,022 is included in H's gross income for 2007 (and is not an eligible rollover distribution). If the excess deferral were not distributed, the plan would be an ineligible plan with respect to which benefits are taxable in accordance with section 1.457-11.

Example 2. (i) *Facts.* The facts are the same as in *Example 1*, except that X uses a number of separate arrangements with different trustees and annuity insurers to permit employees to defer and H elects deferrals under several of the funding arrangements none of which exceeds $15,000 for any individual funding arrangement, but which total $16,000.

(ii) *Conclusion.* The conclusion is the same as in *Example 1*.

Example 3. (i) *Facts.* The facts are the same as in *Example 1*, except that H's deferral under the eligible plan is limited to $11,000 and H also makes a salary reduction contribution of $5,000 to an annuity contract under section 403(b) with the same Employer X.

(ii) *Conclusion.* H's deferrals are within the plan deferral limitations of Employer X. Because of the repeal of the application of the coordination limitation under former paragraph (2) of section 457(c), H's salary reduction deferrals under the annuity contract are no longer considered in determining

H's applicable deferral limits under paragraphs (c)(1) through (3) of this section.

Example 4. (i) *Facts.* The facts are the same as in *Example 1*, except that H's deferral under the eligible governmental plan is limited to $14,000 and H also makes a deferral of $4,000 to an eligible governmental plan of a different employer. Participant H is age 45 and normal retirement age under both eligible plans is age 65.

(ii) *Conclusion.* Because of the application of the individual limitation under section 1.457-5, H has an excess deferral of $3,000 (the sum of $14,000 plus $4,000 equals $18,000, which is $3,000 in excess of the dollar limitation of $15,000). The $3,000 excess deferral, with allocable net income, may be distributed from either plan as soon as administratively practicable after determining that the combined amount exceeds the deferral limitations. If the $3,000 excess deferral is not distributed to H, each plan will continue to be an eligible plan, but the $3,000 must be included by H in H's income for 2006.

Example 5. (i) *Facts.* Assume the same facts as in *Example 3*, except that H's deferral under the eligible governmental plan is limited to $14,000 and H also makes a deferral of $4,000 to an eligible plan of Employer Y, a tax-exempt entity.

(ii) *Conclusion.* The results are the same as in *Example 3*, namely, because of the application of the individual limitation under section 1.457-5, H has an excess deferral of $3,000. If the $3,000 excess deferral is not distributed to H, each plan will continue to be an eligible plan, but the $3,000 must be included by H in H's income for 2006.

Example 6. (i) *Facts.* Assume the same facts as in *Example 5*, except that X is a tax-exempt entity and thus its plan is an eligible plan of a tax-exempt entity.

(ii) *Conclusion.* The results are the same as in *Example 5*, namely, because of the application of the individual limitation under section 1.457-5, H has an excess deferral of $3,000. If the $3,000 excess deferral is not distributed to H, each plan will continue to be an eligible plan, but the $3,000 must be included by H in H's income for 2006.

Section 1.457-5 Individual limitation for combined annual deferrals under multiple eligible plans

(a) *General rule.* The individual limitation under section 457(c) and this section equals the basic annual deferral limitation under section 1.457-4(c)(1)(i)(A), plus either the age 50 catch-up amount under section 1.457-4(c)(2), or the special section 457 catch-up amount under section 1.457-4(c)(3), applied by taking into account the combined annual deferral for the participant for any taxable year under all eligible plans. While an eligible plan may include provisions under which it will limit deferrals to meet the individual limitation under section 457(c) and this section, annual deferrals by a participant that exceed the individual limit under section 457(c) and this section (but do not exceed the limits under section 1.457-4(c)) will not cause a plan to lose its eligible status. However, to the extent the combined annual deferrals for a participant for any taxable year exceed the individual limitation under section 457(c) and this section for that year, the amounts are treated as excess deferrals as described in section 1.457-4(e).

(b) *Limitation applied to participant.* The individual limitation in this section applies to eligible plans of all employers for whom a participant has performed services, including both eligible governmental plans and eligible plans of a tax-exempt entity and both eligible plans of the employer and eligible plans of other employers. Thus, for purposes of determining the amount excluded from a participant's gross income in any taxable year (including the underutilized limitation under section 1.457-4(c)(3)(ii)(B)), the participant's annual deferral under an eligible plan, and the participant's annual deferrals under all other eligible plans, must be determined on an aggregate basis. To the extent that the combined annual deferral amount exceeds the maximum deferral limitation applicable under section 1.457-4(c)(1)(i)(A), (c)(2), or (c)(3), the amount is treated as an excess deferral under section 1.457-4(e).

(c) *Special rules for catch-up amounts under multiple eligible plans.* For purposes of applying section 457(c) and this section, the special section 457 catch-up under section 1.457-4(c)(3) is taken into account only to the extent that an annual deferral is made for a participant under an eligible plan as a result of plan provisions permitted under section 1.457-4(c)(3). In addition, if a participant has annual deferrals under more than one eligible plan and the applicable catch-up amount under section 1.457-4(c)(2) or (3) is not the same for each such eligible plan for the taxable year, section 457(c) and this section are applied using the catch-up amount under whichever plan has the largest catch-up amount applicable to the participant.

(d) *Examples.* The provisions of this section are illustrated by the following examples:

Example 1. (i) *Facts.* Participant F is age 62 in 2006 and participates in two eligible plans during 2006, Plans J and K, which are each eligible plans of two different governmental entities. Each plan includes provisions allowing the maximum annual deferral permitted under section 1.457-4(c)(1) through (3). For 2006, the underutilized amount under section 1.457-4(c)(3)(ii)(B) is $20,000 under Plan J and is $40,000 under Plan K. Normal retirement age is age 65 under both plans. Participant F defers $15,000 under each plan. Participant F's includible compensation is in each case in excess of the deferral. Neither plan designates the $15,000 contribution as a catch-up permitted under each plan's special section 457 catch-up provisions.

(ii) *Conclusion.* For purposes of applying this section to Participant F for 2006, the maximum exclusion is $20,000. This is equal to the sum of $15,000 plus $5,000, which is the age 50 catch-up amount. Thus, F has an excess amount of $10,000 which is treated as an excess deferral for Participant F for 2006 under section 1.457-4(e).

Example 2. (i) *Facts.* Participant E, who will turn 63 on April 1, 2006, participates in four eligible plans during 2006: Plan W which is an eligible governmental plan; and Plans X, Y, and Z which are each eligible plans of three different tax-exempt entities. For 2006, the limitation that applies to Participant E under all four plans under section 1.457-4(c)(1)(i)(A) is $15,000. For 2006, the additional age 50 catch-up limitation that applies to Participant E under all four plans under section 1.457-4(c)(2) is $5,000. Further, for 2006, different limitations under section 1.457-4(c)(3) and (c)(3)(ii)(B) apply to Participant E under each of these plans, as follows: under Plan W, the underutilized limitation under section 1.457-4(c)(3)(ii)(B) is $7,000; under Plan X, the underutilized limitation under section 1.457-4(c)(3)(ii)(B) is $2,000; under Plan Y, the underutilized limitation under section 1.457-4(c)(3)(ii)(B) is $8,000; and under Plan Z, section 1.457-4(c)(3) is not applicable since normal retirement age is age 62 under Plan Z. Participant E's includible compensation is in each case in excess of any applicable deferral.

(ii) *Conclusion.* For purposes of applying this section to Participant E for 2006, Participant E could elect to defer $23,000 under Plan Y, which is the maximum deferral limitation under section 1.457-4(c)(1) through (3), and to defer no amount under Plans W, X, and Z. The $23,000 maximum amount is equal to the sum of $15,000 plus $8,000, which is the catch-up amount applicable to Participant E under Plan Y and which is the largest catch-up amount applicable to Participant E under any of the four plans for 2006. Alternatively, Participant E could instead elect to defer the following combination of amounts: an aggregate total of $20,000 to any of the four plans; or $22,000 to Plan W and none to any of the other three plans.

(iii) If the underutilized amount under Plans W, X, and Y for 2006 were in each case zero (because E had always contributed the maximum amount or E was a new participant) or an amount not in excess of $5,000, the maximum exclusion under this section would be $20,000 for Participant E for 2006 ($15,000 plus the $5,000 age 50 catch-up amount), which Participant E could contribute to any of the plans.

Section 1.457-6 Timing of distributions under eligible plans

(a) *In general.* Except as provided in paragraph (c) of this section (relating to distributions on account of an unforeseeable emergency), paragraph (e) of this section (relating to distributions of small accounts), section 1.457-10(a) (relating to plan terminations), or section 1.457-10(c) (relating to domestic relations orders), amounts deferred under an eligible governmental plan may not be paid to a participant or beneficiary before the participant has a severance from employment with the eligible employer or when the participant attains age 70½, if earlier. For rules relating to loans, see paragraph (f) of this section. This section does not apply to distributions of excess amounts under section 1.457-4(e). However, except to the extent set forth by the Commissioner in revenue rulings, notices, and other guidance published in the Internal Revenue Bulletin, this section applies to amounts held in a separate account for eligible rollover distributions maintained by an eligible governmental plan as described in section 1.457-10(e)(2).

(b) *Severance from employment*—(1) *Employees.* An employee has a severance from employment with the eligible employer if the employee dies, retires, or otherwise has a severance from employment with the eligible employer. See regulations under section 401(k) for additional guidance concerning severance from employment.

(2) *Independent contractors*—(i) *In general.* An independent contractor is considered to have a severance from employment with the eligible employer upon the expiration of the contract (or in the case of more than one contract, all contracts) under which services are performed for the eligible employer if the expiration constitutes a good-faith and complete termination of the contractual relationship. An expiration does not constitute a good faith and complete termination of the contractual relationship if the eligible employer anticipates a renewal of a contractual relationship or the independent contractor becoming an employee. For this purpose, an eligible employer is considered to anticipate the renewal of the contractual relationship with an independent contractor if it intends to contract again for the services provided under the expired contract, and neither the eligible employer nor the independent contractor has eliminated the independent contractor as a possible provider of services under any such new contract. Further, an eligible employer is considered to intend to contract again for the services provided under an expired contract if the eligible employer's doing so is conditioned only upon incurring a need for the services, the availability of funds, or both.

(ii) *Special rule.* Notwithstanding paragraph (b)(2)(i) of this section, the plan is considered to satisfy the requirement described in paragraph (a) of this section that no amounts deferred under the plan be paid or made available to the participant before the participant has a severance from employment with the eligible employer if, with respect to amounts payable to a participant who is an independent contractor, an eligible plan provides that—

(A) No amount will be paid to the participant before a date at least 12 months after the day on which the contract expires under which services are performed for the eligible employer (or, in the case of more than one contract, all such contracts expire); and

(B) No amount payable to the participant on that date will be paid to the participant if, after the expiration of the contract (or contracts) and before that date, the participant performs services for the eligible employer as an independent contractor or an employee.

(c) *Rules applicable to distributions for unforeseeable emergencies*—(1) *In general.* An eligible plan may permit a distribution to a participant or beneficiary faced with an unforeseeable emergency. The distribution must satisfy the requirements of paragraph (c)(2) of this section.

(2) *Requirements*—(i) *Unforeseeable emergency defined.* An unforeseeable emergency must be defined in the plan as a severe financial hardship of the

participant or beneficiary resulting from an illness or accident of the participant or beneficiary, the participant's or beneficiary's spouse, or the participant's or beneficiary's dependent (as defined in section 152(a)); loss of the participant's or beneficiary's property due to casualty (including the need to rebuild a home following damage to a home not otherwise covered by homeowner's insurance, e.g., as a result of a natural disaster); or other similar extraordinary and unforeseeable circumstances arising as a result of events beyond the control of the participant or the beneficiary. For example, the imminent foreclosure of or eviction from the participant's or beneficiary's primary residence may constitute an unforeseeable emergency. In addition, the need to pay for medical expenses, including non-refundable deductibles, as well as for the cost of prescription drug medication, may constitute an unforeseeable emergency. Finally, the need to pay for the funeral expenses of a spouse or a dependent (as defined in section 152(a)) may also constitute an unforeseeable emergency. Except as otherwise specifically provided in this paragraph (c)(2)(i), the purchase of a home and the payment of college tuition are not unforeseeable emergencies under this paragraph (c)(2)(i).

(ii) *Unforeseeable emergency distribution standard.* Whether a participant or beneficiary is faced with an unforeseeable emergency permitting a distribution under this paragraph (c) is to be determined based on the relevant facts and circumstances of each case, but, in any case, a distribution on account of unforeseeable emergency may not be made to the extent that such emergency is or may be relieved through reimbursement or compensation from insurance or otherwise, by liquidation of the participant's assets, to the extent the liquidation of such assets would not itself cause severe financial hardship, or by cessation of deferrals under the plan.

(iii) *Distribution necessary to satisfy emergency need.* Distributions because of an unforeseeable emergency must be limited to the amount reasonably necessary to satisfy the emergency need (which may include any amounts necessary to pay any federal, state, or local income taxes or penalties reasonably anticipated to result from the distribution).

(d) *Minimum required distributions for eligible plans.* In order to be an eligible plan, a plan must meet the distribution requirements of section 457(d)(1) and (2). Under section 457(d)(2), a plan must meet the minimum distribution requirements of section 401(a)(9). See section 401(a)(9) and the regulations thereunder for these requirements. Section 401(a)(9) requires that a plan begin lifetime distributions to a participant no later than April 1 of the calendar year following the later of the calendar year in which the participant attains age 70½ or the calendar year in which the participant retires.

(e) *Distributions of smaller accounts*—(1) *In general.* An eligible plan may provide for a distribution of all or a portion of a participant's benefit if this paragraph (e)(1) is satisfied. This paragraph (e)(1) is satisfied if the participant's total amount deferred (the participant's total account balance) which is not attributable to rollover contributions (as defined in section 411(a)(11)(D)) is not in excess of the dollar limit under section 411(a)(11)(A), no amount has been deferred under the plan by or for the participant during the two-year period ending on the date of the distribution, and there has been no prior distribution under the plan to the participant under this paragraph (e). An eligible plan is not required to permit distributions under this paragraph (e).

(2) *Alternative provisions possible.* Consistent with the provisions of paragraph (e)(1) of this section, a plan may provide that the total amount deferred for a participant or beneficiary will be distributed automatically to the participant or beneficiary if the requirements of paragraph (e)(1) of this section are met. Alternatively, if the requirements of paragraph (e)(1) of this section are met, the plan may provide for the total amount deferred for a participant or beneficiary to be distributed to the participant or beneficiary only if the participant or beneficiary so elects. The plan is permitted to substitute a specified dollar amount that is less than the total amount deferred. In addition, these two alternatives can be combined; for example, a plan could provide for automatic distributions for up to $500, but allow a participant or beneficiary to elect a distribution if the total account balance is above $500.

(f) *Loans from eligible plans*—(1) *Eligible plans of tax-exempt entities.* If a participant or beneficiary receives (directly or indirectly) any amount deferred as a loan from an eligible plan of a tax-exempt entity, that amount will be treated as having been paid or made available to the individual as a distribution under the plan, in violation of the distribution requirements of section 457(d).

(2) *Eligible governmental plans.* The determination of whether the availability of a loan, the making of a loan, or a failure to repay a loan made from a trustee (or a person treated as a trustee under section 457(g)) of an eligible governmental plan to a participant or beneficiary is treated as a distribution (directly or indirectly) for purposes of this section, and the determination of whether the availability of the loan, the making of the loan, or a failure to repay the loan is in any other respect a violation of the requirements of section 457(b) and the regulations, depends on the facts and circumstances. Among the facts and circumstances are whether the loan has a fixed repayment schedule and bears a reasonable rate of interest, and whether there are repayment safeguards to which a prudent lender would adhere. Thus, for example, a loan must bear a reasonable rate of interest in order to satisfy the exclusive benefit requirement of section 457(g)(1) and section 1.457-8(a)(1). See also section 1.457-7(b)(3) relating to the application of section 72(p) with respect to the taxation of a loan made under an eligible governmental plan, and section 1.72(p)-1 relating to section 72(p)(2).

(3) *Example.* The provisions of paragraph (f)(2) of this section are illustrated by the following example:

Example. (i) *Facts.* Eligible Plan X of State Y is funded through Trust Z. Plan X permits an employee's account balance under Plan X to be paid in a single sum at severance from employment with State Y. Plan X includes a loan program under which any active employee with a vested account balance may receive a loan from Trust Z. Loans are made pursuant to plan provisions regarding loans that are set forth in the plan under which loans bear a reasonable rate of interest and are secured by the employee's account balance. In order to avoid taxation under section 1.457-7(b)(3) and section 72(p)(1), the plan provisions limit the amount of loans and require loans to be repaid in level installments as required under section 72(p)(2). Participant J's vested account balance under Plan X is $50,000. J receives a loan from Trust Z in the amount of $5,000 on December 1, 2003, to be repaid in level installments made quarterly over the 5-year period ending on November 30, 2008. Participant J makes the required repayments until J has a severance from employment from State Y in 2005 and subsequently fails to repay the outstanding loan balance of $2,250. The $2,250 loan balance is offset against J's $80,000 account balance benefit under Plan X, and J elects to be paid the remaining $77,750 in 2005.

(ii) *Conclusion.* The making of the loan to J will not be treated as a violation of the requirements of section 457(b) or the regulations. The cancellation of the loan at severance from employment does not cause Plan X to fail to satisfy the requirements for plan eligibility under section 457. In addition, because the loan satisfies the maximum amount and repayment requirements of section 72(p)(2), J is not required to include any amount in income as a result of the loan until 2005, when J has income of $2,250 as a result of the offset (which is a permissible distribution under this section) and income of $77,750 as a result of the distribution made in 2005.

Section 1.457-7 Taxation of distributions under eligible plans

(a) *General rules for when amounts are included in gross income.* The rules for determining when an amount deferred under an eligible plan is includible in the gross income of a participant or beneficiary depend on whether the plan is an eligible governmental plan or an eligible plan of a tax-exempt entity. Paragraph (b) of this section sets forth the rules for an eligible governmental plan. Paragraph (c) of this section sets forth the rules for an eligible plan of a tax-exempt entity.

(b) *Amounts included in gross income under an eligible governmental plan—* (1) *Amounts included in gross income in year paid under an eligible governmental plan.* Except as provided in paragraphs (b)(2) and (3) of this section (or in section 1.457-10(c) relating to payments to a spouse or former spouse pursuant to a qualified domestic relations order), amounts deferred under an eligible governmental plan are includible in the gross income of a participant or beneficiary for the taxable year in which paid to the participant or beneficiary under the plan.

(2) *Rollovers to individual retirement arrangements and other eligible retirement plans.* A trustee-to-trustee transfer in accordance with section 401(a)(31) (generally referred to as a direct rollover) from an eligible government plan is not includible in gross income of a participant or beneficiary in the year transferred. In addition, any payment made from an eligible government plan in the form of an eligible rollover distribution (as defined in section 402(c)(4)) is not includible in gross income in the year paid to the extent the payment is transferred to an eligible retirement plan (as defined in section 402(c)(8)(B)) within 60 days, including the transfer to the eligible retirement plan of any property

distributed from the eligible governmental plan. For this purpose, the rules of section 402(c)(2) through (7) and (9) apply. Any trustee-to-trustee transfer under this paragraph (b)(2) from an eligible government plan is a distribution that is subject to the distribution requirements of section 1.457-6.

(3) *Amounts taxable under section 72(p)(1)*. In accordance with section 72(p), the amount of any loan from an eligible governmental plan to a participant or beneficiary (including any pledge or assignment treated as a loan under section 72(p)(1)(B)) is treated as having been received as a distribution from the plan under section 72(p)(1), except to the extent set forth in section 72(p)(2) (relating to loans that do not exceed a maximum amount and that are repayable in accordance with certain terms) and section 1.72(p)-1. Thus, except to the extent a loan satisfies section 72(p)(2), any amount loaned from an eligible governmental plan to a participant or beneficiary (including any pledge or assignment treated as a loan under section 72(p)(1)(B)) is includible in the gross income of the participant or beneficiary for the taxable year in which the loan is made. See generally section 1.72(p)-1.

(4) *Examples*. The provisions of this paragraph (b) are illustrated by the following examples:

Example 1. (i) *Facts*. Eligible Plan G of a governmental entity permits distribution of benefits in a single sum or in installments of up to 20 years, with such benefits to commence at any date that is after severance from employment (up to the later of severance from employment or the plan's normal retirement age of 65). Effective for participants who have a severance from employment after December 31, 2001, Plan X allows an election—as to both the date on which payments are to begin and the form in which payments are to be made—to be made by the participant at any time that is before the commencement date selected. However, Plan X chooses to require elections to be filed at least 30 days before the commencement date selected in order for Plan X to have enough time to be able to effectuate the election.

(ii) *Conclusion*. No amounts are included in gross income before actual payments begin. If installment payments begin (and the installment payments are payable over at least 10 years so as not to be eligible rollover distributions), the amount included in gross income for any year is equal to the amount of the installment payment paid during the year.

Example 2. (i) *Facts*. Same facts as in *Example 1*, except that the same rules are extended to participants who had a severance from employment before January 1, 2002.

(ii) *Conclusion*. For all participants (that is, both those who have a severance from employment after December 31, 2001, and those who have a severance from employment before January 1, 2002, including those whose benefit payments have commenced before January 1, 2002), no amounts are included in gross income before actual payments begin. If installment payments begin (and the installment payments are payable over at least 10 years so as not to be eligible rollover distributions), the amount included in gross income for any year is equal to the amount of the installment payment paid during the year.

(c) *Amounts included in gross income under an eligible plan of a tax-exempt entity*—(1) *Amounts included in gross income in year paid or made available under an eligible plan of a tax-exempt entity.* Amounts deferred under an eligible plan of a tax-exempt entity are includible in the gross income of a participant or beneficiary for the taxable year in which paid or otherwise made available to the participant or beneficiary under the plan. Thus, amounts deferred under an eligible plan of a tax-exempt entity are includible in the gross income of the participant or beneficiary in the year the amounts are first made available under the terms of the plan, even if the plan has not distributed the amounts deferred. Amounts deferred under an eligible plan of a tax-exempt entity are not considered made available to the participant or beneficiary solely because the participant or beneficiary is permitted to choose among various investments under the plan.

(2) *When amounts deferred are considered to be made available under an eligible plan of a tax-exempt entity*—(i) *General rule.* Except as provided in paragraphs (c)(2)(ii) through (iv) of this section, amounts deferred under an eligible plan of a tax-exempt entity are considered made available (and, thus, are includible in the gross income of the participant or beneficiary under this paragraph (c)) at the earliest date, on or after severance from employment, on which the plan allows distributions to commence, but in no event later than the date on which distributions must commence pursuant to section 401(a)(9). For example, in the case of a plan that permits distribution to commence on the date that is 60 days after the close of the plan year in which the participant has a severance from employment with the eligible employer, amounts deferred are considered to be made available on that date. However, distributions deferred in accordance with paragraphs (c)(2)(ii) through (iv) of this section are not considered made available prior to the applicable date under paragraphs (c)(2)(ii) through (iv) of this section. In addition, no portion of a participant or beneficiary's account is treated as made available (and thus currently includible in income) under an eligible plan of a tax-exempt entity merely because the participant or beneficiary under the plan may elect to receive a distribution in any of the following circumstances:

(A) A distribution in the event of an unforeseeable emergency to the extent the distribution is permitted under section 1.457-6(c).

(B) A distribution from an account for which the total amount deferred is not in excess of the dollar limit under section 411(a)(11)(A) to the extent the distribution is permitted under section 1.457-6(e).

(ii) *Initial election to defer commencement of distributions*—(A) *In general.* An eligible plan of a tax-exempt entity may provide a period for making an initial election during which the participant or beneficiary may elect, in accordance with the terms of the plan, to defer the payment of some or all of the amounts deferred to a fixed or determinable future time. The period for making this initial election must expire prior to the first time that any such amounts would be considered made available under the plan under paragraph (c)(2)(i) of this section.

(B) *Failure to make initial election to defer commencement of distributions.* Generally, if no initial election is made by a participant or beneficiary under this paragraph (c)(2)(ii), then the amounts deferred under an eligible plan of a tax-exempt entity are considered made available and taxable to the participant or beneficiary in accordance with paragraph (c)(2)(i) of this section at the earliest time, on or after severance from employment (but in no event later than the date on which distributions must commence pursuant to section 401(a)(9)), that distribution is permitted to commence under the terms of the plan. However, the plan may provide for a default payment schedule that applies if no election is made. If the plan provides for a default payment schedule, the amounts deferred are includible in the gross income of the participant or beneficiary in the year the amounts deferred are first made available under the terms of the default payment schedule.

(iii) *Additional election to defer commencement of distribution.* An eligible plan of a tax-exempt entity is permitted to provide that a participant or beneficiary who has made an initial election under paragraph (c)(2)(ii)(A) of this section may make one additional election to defer (but not accelerate) commencement of distributions under the plan before distributions have commenced in accordance with the initial deferral election under paragraph (c)(2)(ii)(A) of this section. Amounts payable to a participant or beneficiary under an eligible plan of a tax-exempt entity are not treated as made available merely because the plan allows the participant to make an additional election under this paragraph (c)(2)(iii). A participant or beneficiary is not precluded from making an additional election to defer commencement of distributions merely because the participant or beneficiary has previously received a distribution under section 1.457-6(c) because of an unforeseeable emergency, has received a distribution of smaller amounts under section 1.457-6(e), has made (and revoked) other deferral or method of payment elections within the initial election period, or is subject to a default payment schedule under which the commencement of benefits is deferred (for example, until a participant is age 65).

(iv) *Election as to method of payment.* An eligible plan of a tax-exempt entity may provide that an election as to the method of payment under the plan may be made at any time prior to the time the amounts are distributed in accordance with the participant or beneficiary's initial or additional election to defer commencement of distributions under paragraph (c)(2)(ii) or (iii) of this section. Where no method of payment is elected, the entire amount deferred will be includible in the gross income of the participant or beneficiary when the amounts first become made available in accordance with a participant's initial or additional elections to defer under paragraphs (c)(2)(ii) and (iii) of this section, unless the eligible plan provides for a default method of payment (in which case amounts are considered made available and taxable when paid under the terms of the default payment schedule). A method of payment means a distribution or a series of periodic distributions commencing on a date determined in accordance with paragraph (c)(2)(ii) or (iii) of this section.

(3) *Examples.* The provisions of this paragraph (c) are illustrated by the following examples:

Example 1. (i) *Facts.* Eligible Plan X of a tax-exempt entity provides that a participant's total account balance, representing all amounts deferred under the plan, is payable to a participant in a single sum 60 days after severance from employment throughout these examples, unless, during a 30-day period immediately following the severance, the participant elects to receive the single sum payment at a later date (that is not later than the plan's normal retirement age of 65) or elects to receive distribution in 10 annual installments to begin 60 days after severance from employment (or at a later date, if so elected, that is not later than the plan's normal retirement age of 65). On November 13, 2004, K, a calendar year taxpayer, has a severance from employment with the eligible employer. K does not, within the 30-day window period, elect to postpone distributions to a later date or to receive payment in 10 fixed annual installments.

(ii) *Conclusion.* The single sum payment is payable to K 60 days after the date K has a severance from employment (January 12, 2005), and is includible in the gross income of K in 2005 under section 457(a).

Example 2. (i) *Facts.* The terms of eligible Plan X are the same as described in *Example 1.* Participant L participates in eligible Plan X. On November 11, 2003, L has a severance from the employment of the eligible employer. On November 24, 2003, L makes an initial deferral election not to receive the single-sum payment payable 60 days after the severance, and instead elects to receive the amounts in 10 annual installments to begin 60 days after severance from employment.

(ii) *Conclusion.* No portion of L's account is considered made available in 2003 or 2004 before a payment is made and no amount is includible in the gross income of L until distributions commence. The annual installment payable in 2004 will be includible in L's gross income in 2004.

Example 3. (i) *Facts.* The facts are the same as in *Example 1*, except that eligible Plan X also provides that those participants who are receiving distributions in 10 annual installments may, at any time and without restriction, elect to receive a cash out of all remaining installments. Participant M elects to receive a distribution in 10 annual installments commencing in 2004.

(ii) *Conclusion.* M's total account balance, representing the total of the amounts deferred under the plan, is considered made available and is includible in M's gross income in 2004.

Example 4. (i) *Facts.* The facts are the same as in *Example 3*, except that, instead of providing for an unrestricted cash out of remaining payments, the plan provides that participants or beneficiaries who are receiving distributions in 10 annual installments may accelerate the payment of the amount remaining payable to the participant upon the occurrence of an unforeseeable emergency as described in section 1.457-6(c)(1) in an amount not exceeding that described in section 1.457-6(c)(2).

(ii) *Conclusion.* No amount is considered made available to participant M on account of M's right to accelerate payments upon the occurrence of an unforeseeable emergency.

Example 5. (i) *Facts.* Eligible Plan Y of a tax-exempt entity provides that distributions will commence 60 days after a participant's severance from employment unless the participant elects, within a 30-day window period following severance from employment, to defer distributions to a later date (but no later than the year following the calendar year the participant attains age 70½). The plan provides that a participant who has elected to defer distributions to a later date may make an election as to form of distribution at any time prior to the 30th day before distributions are to commence.

(ii) *Conclusion.* No amount is considered made available prior to the date distributions are to commence by reason of a participant's right to defer or make an election as to the form of distribution.

Example 6. (i) *Facts.* The facts are the same as in *Example 1*, except that the plan also permits participants who have made an initial election to defer distribution to make one additional deferral election at any time prior to the date distributions are scheduled to commence. Participant N has a severance from employment at age 50. The next day, during the 30-day period provided in the plan, N elects to receive distribution in the form of 10 annual installment payments beginning at age 55. Two weeks later, within the 30-day window period, N makes a new election permitted under the plan to receive 10 annual installment payments beginning at age 60 (instead of age 55). When N is age 59, N elects under the additional deferral election provisions, to defer distributions until age 65.

(ii) *Conclusion.* In this example, N's election to defer distributions until age 65 is a valid election. The two elections N makes during the 30-day window period are not additional deferral elections described in paragraph (c)(2)(iii) of this section because they are made before the first permissible payout date under the plan. Therefore, the plan is not precluded from allowing N to make the additional deferral election. However, N can make no further election to defer distributions beyond age 65 (or accelerate distribution before age 65) because this additional deferral election can only be made once.

Section 1.457-8 Funding rules for eligible plans

(a) *Eligible governmental plans*—(1) *In general.* In order to be an eligible governmental plan, all amounts deferred under the plan, all property and rights purchased with such amounts, and all income attributable to such amounts, property, or rights, must be held in trust for the exclusive benefit of participants and their beneficiaries. A trust described in this paragraph (a) that also meets the requirements of sections 1.457-3 through 1.457-10 is treated as an organization exempt from tax under section 501(a), and a participant's or beneficiary's interest in amounts in the trust is includible in the gross income of the participants and beneficiaries only to the extent, and at the time, provided for in section 457(a) and sections 1.457-4 through 1.457-10.

(2) *Trust requirement.* (i) A trust described in this paragraph (a) must be established pursuant to a written agreement that constitutes a valid trust under State law. The terms of the trust must make it impossible, prior to the satisfaction of all liabilities with respect to participants and their beneficiaries, for any part of the assets and income of the trust to be used for, or diverted to, purposes other than for the exclusive benefit of participants and their beneficiaries.

(ii) Amounts deferred under an eligible governmental plan must be transferred to a trust within a period that is not longer than is reasonable for the proper administration of the participant accounts (if any). For purposes of this requirement, the plan may provide for amounts deferred for a participant under the plan to be transferred to the trust within a specified period after the date the amounts would otherwise have been paid to the participant. For example, the plan could provide for amounts deferred under the plan at the election of the participant to be contributed to the trust within 15 business days following the month in which these amounts would otherwise have been paid to the participant.

(3) *Custodial accounts and annuity contracts treated as trusts—*(i) *In general.* For purposes of the trust requirement of this paragraph (a), custodial accounts and annuity contracts described in section 401(f) that satisfy the requirements of this paragraph (a)(3) are treated as trusts under rules similar to the rules of section 401(f). Therefore, the provisions of section 1.401(f)-1(b) will generally apply to determine whether a custodial account or an annuity contract is treated as a trust. The use of a custodial account or annuity contract as part of an eligible governmental plan does not preclude the use of a trust or another custodial account or annuity contract as part of the same plan, provided that all such vehicles satisfy the requirements of section 457(g)(1) and (3) and paragraphs (a)(1) and (2) of this section and that all assets and income of the plan are held in such vehicles.

(ii) *Custodial accounts—*(A) *In general.* A custodial account is treated as a trust, for purposes of section 457(g)(1) and paragraphs (a)(1) and (2) of this section, if the custodian is a bank, as described in section 408(n), or a person who meets the nonbank trustee requirements of paragraph (a)(3)(ii)(B) of this section, and the account meets the requirements of paragraphs (a)(1) and (2) of this section, other than the requirement that it be a trust.

(B) *Nonbank trustee status.* The custodian of a custodial account may be a person other than a bank only if the person demonstrates to the satisfaction of the Commissioner that the manner in which the person will administer the custodial account will be consistent with the requirements of section 457(g)(1) and (3). To do so, the person must demonstrate that the requirements of section 1.408-2(e)(2) through (6) (relating to nonbank trustees) are met. The written application must be sent to the address prescribed by the Commissioner in the same manner as prescribed under section 1.408-2(e). To the extent that a person has already demonstrated to the satisfaction of the Commissioner that the person satisfies the requirements of section 1.408-2(e) in connection with a qualified trust (or custodial account or annuity contract) under section 401(a), that person is deemed to satisfy the requirements of this paragraph (a)(3)(ii)(B).

(iii) *Annuity contracts.* An annuity contract is treated as a trust for purposes of section 457(g)(1) and paragraph (a)(1) of this section if the contract is an annuity contract, as defined in section 401(g), that has been issued by an insurance company qualified to do business in the State, and the contract meets the requirements of paragraphs (a)(1) and (2) of this section, other than the requirement that it be a trust. An annuity contract does not include a life, health or accident, property, casualty, or liability insurance contract.

(4) *Combining assets.* [Reserved]

(b) *Eligible plans maintained by tax-exempt entity*—(1) *General rule.* In order to be an eligible plan of a tax-exempt entity, the plan must be unfunded and plan assets must not be set aside for participants or their beneficiaries. Under section 457(b)(6) and this paragraph (b), an eligible plan of a tax-exempt entity must provide that all amounts deferred under the plan, all property and rights to property (including rights as a beneficiary of a contract providing life insurance protection) purchased with such amounts, and all income attributable to such amounts, property, or rights, must remain (until paid or made available to the participant or beneficiary) solely the property and rights of the eligible employer (without being restricted to the provision of benefits under the plan), subject only to the claims of the eligible employer's general creditors.

(2) *Additional requirements.* For purposes of paragraph (b)(1) of this section, the plan must be unfunded regardless of whether or not the amounts were deferred pursuant to a salary reduction agreement between the eligible employer and the participant. Any funding arrangement under an eligible plan of a tax-exempt entity that sets aside assets for the exclusive benefit of participants violates this requirement, and amounts deferred are generally immediately includible in the gross income of plan participants and beneficiaries. Nothing in this paragraph (b) prohibits an eligible plan from permitting participants and their beneficiaries to make an election among different investment options available under the plan, such as an election affecting the investment of the amounts described in paragraph (b)(1) of this section.

Section 1.457-9 Effect on eligible plans when not administered in accordance with eligibility requirements

(a) *Eligible governmental plans.* A plan of a State ceases to be an eligible governmental plan on the first day of the first plan year beginning more than 180 days after the date on which the Commissioner notifies the State in writing that the plan is being administered in a manner that is inconsistent with one or more of the requirements of sections 1.457-3 through 1.457-8, or section 1.457-10. However, the plan may correct the plan inconsistencies specified in the written notification before the first day of that plan year and continue to maintain plan eligibility. If a plan ceases to be an eligible governmental plan, amounts subsequently deferred by participants will be includible in income when deferred, or, if later, when the amounts deferred cease to be subject to a substantial risk of forfeiture, as provided at section 1.457-11. Amounts deferred before the date on which the plan ceases to be an eligible governmental plan, and any earnings thereon, will be treated as if the plan continues to be an eligible governmental plan and will not be includible in participant's or beneficiary's gross income until paid to the participant or beneficiary.

(b) *Eligible plans of tax-exempt entities.* A plan of a tax-exempt entity ceases to be an eligible plan on the first day that the plan fails to satisfy one or more of the requirements of sections 1.457-3 through 1.457-8, or section 1.457-10. See section 1.457-11 for rules regarding the treatment of an ineligible plan.

Section 1.457-10 Miscellaneous provisions

(a) *Plan terminations and frozen plans*—(1) *In general.* An eligible employer may amend its plan to eliminate future deferrals for existing participants or to limit participation to existing participants and employees. An eligible plan may also contain provisions that permit plan termination and permit amounts deferred to be distributed on termination. In order for a plan to be considered terminated, amounts deferred under an eligible plan must be distributed to all plan participants and beneficiaries as soon as administratively practicable after termination of the eligible plan. The mere provision for, and making of, distributions to participants or beneficiaries upon a plan termination will not cause an eligible plan to cease to satisfy the requirements of section 457(b) or the regulations.

(2) *Employers that cease to be eligible employers*—(i) *Plan not terminated.* An eligible employer that ceases to be an eligible employer may no longer maintain an eligible plan. If the employer was a tax-exempt entity and the plan is not terminated as permitted under paragraph (a)(2)(ii) of this section, the tax consequences to participants and beneficiaries in the previously eligible (unfunded) plan of an ineligible employer are determined in accordance with either section 451 if the employer becomes an entity other than a State or section 1.457-11 if the employer becomes a State. If the employer was a State and the plan is neither terminated as permitted under paragraph (a)(2)(ii) of this section nor transferred to another eligible plan of that State as permitted under paragraph (b) of this section, the tax consequences to participants in the previously eligible governmental plan of an ineligible employer, the assets of which are held in trust pursuant to section 1.457-8(a), are determined in accordance with section 402(b) (section 403(c) in the case of an annuity contract) and the trust is no longer to be treated as a trust that is exempt from tax under section 501(a).

(ii) *Plan termination.* As an alternative to determining the tax consequences to the plan and participants under paragraph (a)(2)(i) of this section, the employer may terminate the plan and distribute the amounts deferred (and all plan assets) to all plan participants as soon as administratively practicable in accordance with paragraph (a)(1) of this section. Such distribution may include eligible rollover distributions in the case of a plan that was an eligible governmental plan. In addition, if the employer is a State, another alternative to determining the tax consequences under paragraph (a)(2)(i) of this section is to transfer the assets of the eligible governmental plan to an eligible governmental plan of another eligible employer within the same State under the plan-to-plan transfer rules of paragraph (b) of this section.

(3) *Examples.* The provisions of this paragraph (a) are illustrated by the following examples:

Example 1. (i) *Facts.* Employer Y, a corporation that owns a State hospital, sponsors an eligible governmental plan funded through a trust. Employer Y is acquired by a for-profit hospital and Employer Y ceases to be an eligible employer under section 457(e)(1) or section 1.457-2(e). Employer Y terminates the plan and, during the next 6 months, distributes to participants and beneficiaries all amounts deferred that were under the plan.

(ii) *Conclusion.* The termination and distribution does not cause the plan to fail to be an eligible governmental plan. Amounts that are distributed as eligible rollover distributions may be rolled over to an eligible retirement plan described in section 402(c)(8)(B).

Example 2. (i) *Facts.* The facts are the same as in *Example 1*, except that Employer Y decides to continue to maintain the plan.

(ii) *Conclusion.* If Employer Y continues to maintains the plan, the tax consequences to participants and beneficiaries will be determined in accordance with either section 402(b) if the compensation deferred is funded through a trust, section 403(c) if the compensation deferred is funded through annuity contracts, or section 1.457-11 if the compensation deferred is not funded through a trust or annuity contract. In addition, if Employer Y continues to maintain the plan, the trust will no longer be treated as exempt from tax under section 501(a).

Example 3. (i) *Facts.* Employer Z, a corporation that owns a tax-exempt hospital, sponsors an unfunded eligible plan. Employer Z is acquired by a for-profit hospital and is no longer an eligible employer under section 457(e)(1) or section 1.457-2(e). Employer Z terminates the plan and distributes all amounts deferred under the eligible plan to participants and beneficiaries within a one-year period.

(ii) *Conclusion.* Distributions under the plan are treated as made under an eligible plan of a tax-exempt entity and the distributions of the amounts deferred are includible in the gross income of the participant or beneficiary in the year distributed.

Example 4. (i) *Facts.* The facts are the same as in *Example 3*, except that Employer Z decides to maintain instead of terminate the plan.

(ii) *Conclusion.* If Employer Z maintains the plan, the tax consequences to participants and beneficiaries in the plan will thereafter be determined in accordance with section 451.

(b) *Plan-to-plan transfers—(1) General rule.* An eligible governmental plan may provide for the transfer of amounts deferred by a participant or beneficiary to another eligible governmental plan if the conditions in paragraphs (b)(2), (3), or (4) of this section are met. An eligible plan of a tax-exempt entity may provide for transfers of amounts deferred by a participant to another eligible plan of a tax-exempt entity if the conditions in paragraph (b)(5) of this section are met. In addition, an eligible governmental plan may accept transfers from another eligible governmental plan as described in the first sentence of this paragraph (b)(1), and an eligible plan of a tax-exempt entity may accept transfers from another eligible plan of a tax-exempt entity as described in the preceding sentence. However, a State may not transfer the assets of its eligible governmental plan to a tax-exempt entity's eligible plan and the plan of a tax-exempt entity may not accept such a transfer. Similarly, a tax-exempt entity may not transfer the assets of its eligible plan to an eligible governmental plan and an eligible governmental plan may not accept such a transfer. In addition, if the conditions in paragraph (b)(4) of this section (relating to permissive past service credit and repayments under section 415) are met, an eligible governmental plan of a State may provide for the transfer of amounts deferred by a participant or beneficiary to a qualified plan (under section 401(a)) maintained by a State. However, a qualified plan may not transfer assets to an eligible governmental plan or to an eligible plan of a tax-exempt entity, and an eligible governmental plan or the plan of a tax-exempt entity may not accept such a transfer.

(2) *Requirements for post-severance plan-to-plan transfers among eligible governmental plans.* A transfer under paragraph (b)(1) of this section from an eligible governmental plan to another eligible governmental plan is permitted if the following conditions are met—

(i) The transferor plan provides for transfers;

(ii) The receiving plan provides for the receipt of transfers;

(iii) The participant or beneficiary whose amounts deferred are being transferred will have an amount deferred immediately after the transfer at least equal to the amount deferred with respect to that participant or beneficiary immediately before the transfer; and

(iv) In the case of a transfer for a participant, the participant has had a severance from employment with the transferring employer and is performing services for the entity maintaining the receiving plan.

(3) *Requirements for plan-to-plan transfers of all plan assets of eligible governmental plan.* A transfer under paragraph (b)(1) of this section from an eligible governmental plan to another eligible governmental plan is permitted if the following conditions are met—

(i) The transfer is from an eligible governmental plan to another eligible governmental plan within the same State;

(ii) All of the assets held by the transferor plan are transferred;

(iii) The transferor plan provides for transfers;

(iv) The receiving plan provides for the receipt of transfers;

(v) The participant or beneficiary whose amounts deferred are being transferred will have an amount deferred immediately after the transfer at least equal to the amount deferred with respect to that participant or beneficiary immediately before the transfer; and

(vi) The participants or beneficiaries whose deferred amounts are being transferred are not eligible for additional annual deferrals in the receiving plan unless they are performing services for the entity maintaining the receiving plan.

(4) *Requirements for plan-to-plan transfers among eligible governmental plans of the same employer.* A transfer under paragraph (b)(1) of this section from an eligible governmental plan to another eligible governmental plan is permitted if the following conditions are met—

(i) The transfer is from an eligible governmental plan to another eligible governmental plan of the same employer (and, for this purpose, the employer is not treated as the same employer if the participant's compensation is paid by a different entity);

(ii) The transferor plan provides for transfers;

(iii) The receiving plan provides for the receipt of transfers;

(iv) The participant or beneficiary whose amounts deferred are being transferred will have an amount deferred immediately after the transfer at least equal to the amount deferred with respect to that participant or beneficiary immediately before the transfer; and

(v) The participant or beneficiary whose deferred amounts are being transferred is not eligible for additional annual deferrals in the receiving plan unless the participant or beneficiary is performing services for the entity maintaining the receiving plan.

(5) *Requirements for post-severance plan-to-plan transfers among eligible plans of tax-exempt entities.* A transfer under paragraph (b)(1) of this section from an eligible plan of a tax-exempt employer to another eligible plan of a tax-exempt employer is permitted if the following conditions are met—

(i) The transferor plan provides for transfers;

(ii) The receiving plan provides for the receipt of transfers;

(iii) The participant or beneficiary whose amounts deferred are being transferred will have an amount deferred immediately after the transfer at least equal to the amount deferred with respect to that participant or beneficiary immediately before the transfer; and

(iv) In the case of a transfer for a participant, the participant has had a severance from employment with the transferring employer and is performing services for the entity maintaining the receiving plan.

(6) *Treatment of amount transferred following a plan-to-plan transfer between eligible plans.* Following a transfer of any amount between eligible plans under paragraphs (b)(1) through (b)(5) of this section—

(i) the transferred amount is subject to the restrictions of section 1.457-6 (relating to when distributions are permitted to be made to a participant under an eligible plan) in the receiving plan in the same manner as if the transferred amount had been [sic] originally been deferred under the receiving plan if the participant is performing services for the entity maintaining the receiving plan, and

(ii) in the case of a transfer between eligible plans of tax-exempt entities, except as otherwise determined by the Commissioner, the transferred amount is subject to section 1.457-7(c)(2) (relating to when amounts are considered to be made available under an eligible plan of a tax-exempt entity) in the same manner as if the elections made by the participant or beneficiary under the transferor plan had been made under the receiving plan.

(7) *Examples.* The provisions of paragraphs (b)(1) through (6) of this section are illustrated by the following examples:

Example 1. (i) *Facts.* Participant A, the president of City X's hospital, has accepted a position with another hospital which is a tax-exempt entity. A participates in the eligible governmental plan of City X. A would like to transfer the amounts deferred under City X's eligible governmental plan to the eligible plan of the tax-exempt hospital.

(ii) *Conclusion.* City X's plan may not transfer A's amounts deferred to the tax-exempt employer's eligible plan. In addition, because the amounts deferred would no longer be held in trust for the exclusive benefit of participants and their beneficiaries, the transfer would violate the exclusive benefit rule of section 457(g) and section 1.457-8(a).

Example 2. (i) *Facts.* County M, located in State S, operates several health clinics and maintains an eligible governmental plan for employees of those clinics. One of the clinics operated by County M is being acquired by a hospital operated by State S, and employees of that clinic will become employees of State S. County M permits those employees to transfer their balances under County M's eligible governmental plan to the eligible governmental plan of State S.

(ii) *Conclusion.* If the eligible governmental plans of County M and State S provide for the transfer and acceptance of the transfer (and the other requirements of paragraph (b)(1) of this section are satisfied), then the requirements of paragraph (b)(2) of this section are satisfied and, thus, the transfer will not cause either plan to violate the requirements of section 457 or these regulations.

Example 3. (i) *Facts.* City Employer Z, a hospital, sponsors an eligible governmental plan. City Employer Z is located in State B. All of the assets of City Employer Z are being acquired by a tax-exempt hospital. City Employer Z, in accordance with the plan-to-plan transfer rules of paragraph (b) of this section, would like to transfer the total amount of assets deferred under City Employer Z's eligible governmental plan to the acquiring tax-exempt entity's eligible plan.

(ii) *Conclusion.* City Employer Z may not permit participants to transfer the amounts to the eligible plan of the tax-exempt entity. In addition, because the amounts deferred would no longer be held in trust for the exclusive benefit of participants and their beneficiaries, the transfer would violate the exclusive benefit rule of section 457(g) and section 1.457-8(a).

Example 4. (i) *Facts.* The facts are the same as in *Example 3,* except that City Employer Z, instead of transferring all of its assets to the eligible plan of the tax-exempt entity, decides to transfer all of the amounts deferred under City Z's eligible governmental plan to the eligible governmental plan of County B in which City Z is located. County B's eligible plan does not cover employees of City Z, but is willing to allow the assets of City Z's plan to be transferred to County B's plan, a related state government entity, also located in State B.

(ii) *Conclusion.* If City Employer Z's (transferor) eligible governmental plan provides for such transfer and the eligible governmental plan of County B permits the acceptance of such a transfer (and the other requirements of paragraph (b)(1) of this section are satisfied), then the requirements of paragraph (b)(3) of this section are satisfied and, thus, City Employer Z may transfer the total amounts deferred under its eligible governmental plan, prior to termination of that plan, to the eligible governmental plan maintained by County B. However, the participants of City Employer Z whose deferred amounts are being transferred are not eligible to participate in the eligible governmental plan of County B, the receiving plan, unless they are performing services for County B.

Example 5. (i) *Facts.* State C has an eligible governmental plan. Employees of City U in State C are among the eligible employees for State C's plan and City U decides to adopt another eligible governmental plan only for its employees. State C decides to allow employees to elect to transfer all of the amounts deferred for an employee under State C's eligible governmental plan to City U's eligible governmental plan.

(ii) *Conclusion.* If State C's (transferor) eligible governmental plan provides for such transfer and the eligible governmental plan of City U permits the acceptance of such a transfer (and the other requirements of paragraph (b)(1) of this section are satisfied), then the requirements of paragraph (b)(4) of this section are satisfied and, thus, State C may transfer the total amounts deferred under its eligible governmental plan to the eligible governmental plan maintained by City U.

(8) *Purchase of permissive past service credit by plan-to-plan transfers from an eligible governmental plan to a qualified plan*—(i) *General rule.* An eligible governmental plan of a State may provide for the transfer of amounts deferred by a participant or beneficiary to a defined benefit governmental plan (as defined in section 414(d)), and no amount shall be includible in gross income by reason of the transfer, if the conditions in paragraph (b)(8)(ii) of this section are met. A transfer under this paragraph (b)(8) is not treated as a distribution for purposes of section 1.457-6. Therefore, such a transfer may be made before severance from employment.

(ii) *Conditions for plan-to-plan transfers from an eligible governmental plan to a qualified plan.* A transfer may be made under this paragraph (b)(8) only if the transfer is either—

(A) For the purchase of permissive past service credit (as defined in section 415(n)(3)(A)) under the receiving defined benefit governmental plan; or

(B) A repayment to which section 415 does not apply by reason of section 415(k)(3).

(iii) *Example.* The provisions of this paragraph (b)(8) are illustrated by the following example:

Example. (i) *Facts.* Plan X is an eligible governmental plan maintained by County Y for its employees. Plan X provides for distributions only in the event of death, an unforeseeable emergency, or severance from employment with County Y (including retirement from County Y). Plan S is a qualified defined benefit plan maintained by State T for its employees. County Y is within State T. Employee A is an employee of County Y and is a participant in Plan X. Employee A previously was an employee of State T and is still entitled to benefits under Plan S. Plan S includes provisions allowing participants in certain plans, including Plan X, to transfer assets to Plan S for the purchase of past service credit under Plan S and does not permit the amount transferred to exceed the amount necessary to fund the benefit resulting from the past service credit. Although not required to do so, Plan X allows Employee A to transfer assets to Plan S to provide a past service benefit under Plan S.

(ii) *Conclusion.* The transfer is permitted under this paragraph (b)(8).

(c) *Qualified domestic relations orders under eligible plans*—(1) *General rule.* An eligible plan does not become an ineligible plan described in section 457(f) solely because its administrator or sponsor complies with a qualified domestic relations order as defined in section 414(p), including an order requiring the distribution of the benefits of a participant to an alternate payee in advance of the general rules for eligible plan distributions under section 1.457-6. If a distribution or payment is made from an eligible plan to an alternate payee pursuant to a qualified domestic relations order, rules similar to the rules of section 402(e)(1)(A) shall apply to the distribution or payment.

(2) *Examples.* The provisions of this paragraph (c) are illustrated by the following examples:

Example 1. (i) *Facts.* Participant C and C's spouse D are divorcing. C is employed by State S and is a participant in an eligible plan maintained by State S. C has an account valued at $100,000 under the plan. Pursuant to the divorce, a court issues a qualified domestic relations order on September 1, 2003 that allocates 50 percent of C's $100,000 plan account to D and specifically provides for an immediate distribution to D of D's share within 6 months of the order. Payment is made to D in January of 2004.

(ii) *Conclusion.* State S's eligible plan does not become an ineligible plan described in section 457(f) and section 1.457-11 solely because its administrator or sponsor complies with the qualified domestic relations order requiring the immediate distribution to D in advance of the general rules for eligible plan distributions under section 1.457-6. In accordance with section 402(e)(1)(A), D (not C) must include the distribution in gross income. The distribution is includible in D's gross income in 2004. If the qualified domestic relations order were to provide for distribution to D at a future date, amounts deferred attributable to D's share will be includible in D's gross income when paid to D.

Example 2. (i) *Facts.* The facts are the same as in *Example 1,* except that S is a tax-exempt entity, instead of a State.

(ii) *Conclusion.* State S's eligible plan does not become an ineligible plan described in section 457(f) and section 1.457-11 solely because its administrator or sponsor complies with the qualified domestic relations order requiring the immediate distribution to D in advance of the general rules for eligible plan distributions under section 1.457-6. In accordance with section 402(e)(1)(A), D (not C) must include the distribution in gross income. The distribution is includible in D's gross income in 2004, assuming that the plan did not make the distribution available to D in 2003. If the qualified domestic relations order were to provide for distribution to D at a future date, amounts deferred attributable to D's share would be includible in D's gross income when paid or made available to D.

(d) *Death benefits and life insurance proceeds.* A death benefit plan under section 457(e)(11) is not an eligible plan. In addition, no amount paid or made available under an eligible plan as death benefits or life insurance proceeds is excludable from gross income under section 101.

(e) *Rollovers to eligible governmental plans*—(1) *General rule.* An eligible governmental plan may accept contributions that are eligible rollover distributions (as defined in section 402(c)(4)) made from another eligible retirement plan (as defined in section 402(c)(8)(B)) if the conditions in paragraph (e)(2) of this section are met. Amounts contributed to an eligible governmental plan as eligible rollover distributions are not taken into account for purposes of the limit on annual deferrals by a participant in section 1.457-4(c) or section 1.457-5, but are otherwise treated in the same manner as amounts deferred under section 457 for purposes of sections 1.457-3 through 1.457-9 and this section.

(2) *Conditions for rollovers to an eligible governmental plan.* An eligible governmental plan that permits eligible rollover distributions made from another eligible retirement plan to be paid into the eligible governmental plan is required under this paragraph (e)(2) to provide that it will separately account for any eligible rollover distributions it receives. A plan does not fail to satisfy this requirement if it separately accounts for particular types of eligible rollover distributions (for example, if it maintains a separate account for eligible rollover distributions attributable to annual deferrals that were made under other eligible governmental plans and a separate account for amounts attributable to other eligible rollover distributions), but this requirement is not satisfied if any such separate account includes any amount that is not attributable to an eligible rollover distribution.

(3) *Example*. The provisions of this paragraph (e) are illustrated by the following example:

Example. (i) *Facts*. Plan T is an eligible governmental plan that provides that employees who are eligible to participate in Plan T may make rollover contributions to Plan T from amounts distributed to an employee from an eligible retirement plan. An eligible retirement plan is defined in Plan T as another eligible governmental plan, a qualified section 401(a) or 403(a) plan, or a section 403(b) contract, or an individual retirement arrangement (IRA) that holds such amounts. Plan T requires rollover contributions to be paid by the eligible retirement plan directly to Plan T (a direct rollover) or to be paid by the participant within 60 days after the date on which the participant received the amount from the other eligible retirement plan. Plan T does not take rollover contributions into account for purposes of the plan's limits on amounts deferred that conform to section 1.457-4(c). Rollover contributions paid to Plan T are invested in the trust in the same manner as amounts deferred under Plan T and rollover contributions (and earnings thereon) are available for distribution to the participant at the same time and in the same manner as amounts deferred under Plan T. In addition, Plan T provides that, for each participant who makes a rollover contribution to Plan T, the Plan T record-keeper is to establish a separate account for the participant's rollover contributions. The record-keeper calculates earnings and losses for investments held in the rollover account separately from earnings and losses on other amounts held under the plan and calculates disbursements from and payments made to the rollover account separately from disbursements from and payments made to other amounts held under the plan.

(ii) *Conclusion*. Plan T does not lose its status as an eligible governmental plan as a result of the receipt of rollover contributions. The conclusion would not be different if the Plan T record-keeper were to establish two separate accounts, one of which is for the participant's rollover contributions attributable to annual deferrals that were made under an eligible governmental plan and the other of which is for other rollover contributions.

(f) *Deemed IRAs under eligible governmental plans*. See regulations under section 408(q) for guidance regarding the treatment of separate accounts or annuities as individual retirement plans (IRAs).

Section 1.457-11 Tax treatment of participants if plan is not an eligible plan

(a) *In general*. Under section 457(f), if an eligible employer provides for a deferral of compensation under any agreement or arrangement that is an ineligible plan—

(1) Compensation deferred under the agreement or arrangement is includible in the gross income of the participant or beneficiary for the first taxable year in which there is no substantial risk of forfeiture (within the meaning of section 457(f)(3)(B)) of the rights to such compensation;

(2) If the compensation deferred is subject to a substantial risk of forfeiture, the amount includible in gross income for the first taxable year in which there is no substantial risk of forfeiture includes earnings thereon to the date on which there is no substantial risk of forfeiture;

(3) Earnings credited on the compensation deferred under the agreement or arrangement that are not includible in gross income under paragraph (a)(2) of this section are includible in the gross income of the participant or beneficiary only when paid or made available to the participant or beneficiary, provided that the interest of the participant or beneficiary in any assets (including amounts deferred under the plan) of the entity sponsoring the agreement or arrangement is not senior to the entity's general creditors; and

(4) Amounts paid or made available to a participant or beneficiary under the agreement or arrangement are includible in the gross income of the participant or beneficiary under section 72, relating to annuities.

(b) *Exceptions.* Paragraph (a) of this section does not apply with respect to—

(1) A plan described in section 401(a) which includes a trust exempt from tax under section 501(a);

(2) An annuity plan or contract described in section 403;

(3) That portion of any plan which consists of a transfer of property described in section 83;

(4) That portion of any plan which consists of a trust to which section 402(b) applies; or

(5) A qualified governmental excess benefit arrangement described in section 415(m).

(c) *Amount included in income.* The amount included in gross income on the applicable date under paragraphs (a)(1) and (a)(2) of this section is equal to the present value of the compensation (including earnings to the extent provided in paragraph (a)(2) of this section) on that date. For purposes of applying section 72 on the applicable date under paragraphs (a)(3) and (4) of this section, the participant is treated as having paid investment in the contract (or basis) to the extent that the deferred compensation has been taken into account by the participant in accordance with paragraphs (a)(1) and (a)(2) of this section.

(d) *Coordination of section 457(f) with section 83*—(1) *General rules.* Under paragraph (b)(3) of this section, section 457(f) and paragraph (a) of this section do not apply to that portion of any plan which consists of a transfer of property described in section 83. For this purpose, a transfer of property described in section 83 means a transfer of property to which section 83 applies. Section 457(f) and paragraph (a) of this section do not apply if the date on which there is no substantial risk of forfeiture with respect to compensation deferred under an agreement or arrangement that is not an eligible plan is on or after the date on which there is a transfer of property to which section 83 applies. However, section 457(f) and paragraph (a) of this section apply if the date on which there is no substantial risk of forfeiture with respect to compensation deferred under an agreement or arrangement that is not an eligible plan precedes the date on which there is a transfer of property to which section 83 applies. If deferred compensation payable in property is includible in gross income under section 457(f), then, as provided in section 72, the amount includible in gross income when that property is later transferred or made available to the service provider is the excess of the value of the property at that time over the amount previously included in gross income under section 457(f).

(2) *Examples*. The provisions of this paragraph (d) are illustrated in the following examples:

Example 1. (i) *Facts*. As part of an arrangement for the deferral of compensation, an eligible employer agrees on December 1, 2002 to pay an individual rendering services for the eligible employer a specified dollar amount on January 15, 2005. The arrangement provides for the payment to be made in the form of property having a fair market value equal to the specified dollar amount. The individual's rights to the payment are not subject to a substantial risk of forfeiture (within the meaning of section 457(f)(3)(B)).

(ii) *Conclusion*. In this *Example 1*, because there is no substantial risk of forfeiture with respect to the agreement to transfer property in 2005, the present value (as of December 1, 2002) of the payment is includible in the individual's gross income for 2002. Under paragraph (a)(4) of this section, when the payment is made on January 15, 2005, the amount includible in the individual's gross income is equal to the excess of the fair market value of the property when paid, over the amount that was includible in gross income for 2002 (which is the basis allocable to that payment).

Example 2. (i) *Facts*. As part of an arrangement for the deferral of compensation, individuals A and B rendering services for a tax-exempt entity each receive in 2010 property that is subject to a substantial risk of forfeiture (within the meaning of section 457(f)(3)(B) and within the meaning of section 83(c)(1)). Individual A makes an election to include the fair market value of the property in gross income under section 83(b) and individual B does not make this election. The substantial risk of forfeiture for the property transferred to individual A lapses in 2012 and the substantial risk of forfeiture for the property transferred to individual B also lapses in 2012. Thus, the property transferred to individual A is included in A's gross income for 2010 when A makes a section 83(b) election and the property transferred to individual B is included in B's gross income for 2012 when the substantial risk of forfeiture for the property lapses.

(ii) *Conclusion*. In this *Example 2*, in each case, the compensation deferred is not subject to section 457(f) or this section because section 83 applies to the transfer of property on or before the date on which there is no substantial risk of forfeiture with respect to compensation deferred under the arrangement.

Example 3. (i) *Facts*. In 2004, Z, a tax-exempt entity, grants an option to acquire property to employee C. The option lacks a readily ascertainable fair market value, within the meaning of section 83(e)(3), has a value on the date of grant equal to $100,000, and is not subject to a substantial risk of forfeiture (within the meaning of section 457(f)(3)(B) and within the meaning of section 83(c)(1)). Z exercises the option in 2012 by paying an exercise price of $75,000 and receives property that has a fair market value (for purposes of section 83) equal to $300,000.

(ii) *Conclusion.* In this *Example 3*, under section 83(e)(3), section 83 does not apply to the grant of the option. Accordingly, C has income of $100,000 in 2004 under section 457(f). In 2012, C has income of $125,000, which is the value of the property transferred in 2012, minus the allocable portion of the basis that results from the $100,000 of income in 2004 and the $75,000 exercise price.

Example 4. (i) *Facts.* In 2010, X, a tax-exempt entity, agrees to pay deferred compensation to employee D. The amount payable is $100,000 to be paid 10 years later in 2020. The commitment to make the $100,000 payment is not subject to a substantial risk of forfeiture. In 2010, the present value of the $100,000 is $50,000. In 2018, X transfers to D property having a fair market value (for purposes of section 83) equal to $70,000. The transfer is in partial settlement of the commitment made in 2010 and, at the time of the transfer in 2018, the present value of the commitment is $80,000. In 2020, X pays D the $12,500 that remains due.

(ii) *Conclusion.* In this *Example 4*, D has income of $50,000 in 2010. In 2018, D has income of $30,000, which is the amount transferred in 2018, minus the allocable portion of the basis that results from the $50,000 of income in 2010. (Under section 72(e)(2)(B), income is allocated first. The income is equal to $30,000 ($80,000 minus the $50,000 basis), with the result that the allocable portion of the basis is equal to $40,000 ($70,000 minus the $30,000 of income).) In 2020, D has income of $2,500 ($12,500 minus $10,000, which is the excess of the original $50,000 basis over the $40,000 basis allocated to the transfer made in 2018).

Section 1.457-12 Effective dates

(a) *General effective date.* Except as otherwise provided in this section, sections 1.457-1 through 1.457-11 apply for taxable years beginning after December 31, 2001.

(b) *Transition period for eligible plans to comply with EGTRRA.* For taxable years beginning after December 31, 2001, and before January 1, 2004, a plan does not fail to be an eligible plan as a result of requirements imposed by the Economic Growth and Tax Relief Reconciliation Act of 2001 (115 Stat. 385) (EGTRRA) (Public Law 107-16) June 7, 2001, if it is operated in accordance with a reasonable, good faith interpretation of EGTRRA.

(c) *Special rule for distributions from rollover accounts.* The last sentence of section 1.457-6(a) (relating to distributions of amounts held in a separate account for eligible rollover distributions) applies for taxable years beginning after December 31, 2003.

(d) *Special rule for options.* Section 1.457-11(d) does not apply with respect to an option without a readily ascertainable fair market value (within the meaning of section 83(e)(3)) that was granted on or before May 8, 2002.

(e) *Special rule for qualified domestic relations orders.* Section 1.457-10(c) (relating to qualified domestic relations orders) applies for transfers, distributions, and payments made after December 31, 2001.

Excise Accumulations

Treasury Regulations Section 54.4974

Section 54.4974-2 Excise Tax on Accumulations in Qualified Retirement Plans

Q-1. Is any tax imposed on a payee under any qualified retirement plan or any eligible deferred compensation plan (as defined in section 457(b)) to whom an amount is required to be distributed for a taxable year if the amount distributed during the taxable year is less than the required minimum distribution?

A-1. Yes, if the amount distributed to a payee under any qualified retirement plan or any eligible deferred compensation plan (as defined in section 457(b)) for a calendar year is less than the required minimum distribution for such year, an excise tax is imposed on such payee under section 4974 for the taxable year beginning with or within the calendar year during which the amount is required to be distributed. The tax is equal to 50 percent of the amount by which such required minimum distribution exceeds the actual amount distributed during the calendar year. Section 4974 provides that this tax shall be paid by the payee. For purposes of section 4974, the term required minimum distribution means the minimum distribution amount required to be distributed pursuant to section 401(a)(9), 403(b)(10), 408(a)(6), 408(b)(3), or 457(d)(2), as the case may be, and the regulations thereunder. Except as otherwise provided in A-6 of this section, the required minimum distribution for a calendar year is the required minimum distribution amount required to be distributed during the calendar year. A-6 of this section provides a special rule for amounts required to be distributed by an employee's (or individual's) required beginning date.

Q-2. For purposes of section 4974, what is a qualified retirement plan?

A-2. For purposes of section 4974, each of the following is a qualified retirement plan—

(a) A plan described in section 401(a) which includes a trust exempt from tax under section 501(a);

(b) An annuity plan described in section 403(a);

(c) An annuity contract, custodial account, or retirement income account described in section 403(b);

(d) An individual retirement account described in section 408(a) (including a Roth IRA described in section 408A);

(e) An individual retirement annuity described in section 408(b) (including a Roth IRA described in section 408A); or

(f) Any other plan, contract, account, or annuity that, at any time, has been treated as a plan, account, or annuity described in paragraphs (a) through (e) of this A-2, whether or not such plan, contract, account, or annuity currently satisfies the applicable requirements for such treatment.

Q-3. If a payee's interest under a qualified retirement plan is in the form of an individual account, how is the required minimum distribution for a given calendar year determined for purposes of section 4974?

A-3. (a) **General rule.** If a payee's interest under a qualified retirement plan is in the form of an individual account and distribution of such account is not being made under an annuity contract purchased in accordance with A-4 of § 1.401(a)(9)-6T, the amount of the required minimum distribution for any calendar year for purposes of section 4974 is the required minimum distribution amount required to be distributed for such calendar year in order to satisfy the minimum distribution requirements in § 1.401(a)(9)-5 as provided in the following (whichever is applicable)—

(1) Section 401(a)(9) and §§ 1.401(a)(9)-1 through 1.401(a)(9)-5 and 1.401(a)(9)-7 through 1.401(a)(9)-9 in the case of a plan described in section 401(a) which includes a trust exempt under section 501(a) or an annuity plan described in section 403(a);

(2) Section 403(b)(10) and § 1.403(b)-3 (in the case of an annuity contract, custodial account, or retirement income account described in section 403(b));

(3) Section 408(a)(6) or (b)(3) and § 1.408-8 (in the case of an individual retirement account or annuity described in section 408(a) or (b)); or

(4) Section 457(d) in the case of an eligible deferred compensation plan (as defined in section 457(b)).

(b) **Default provisions.** Unless otherwise provided under the qualified retirement plan (or, if applicable, the governing instrument of the qualified retirement plan), the default provisions in A-4(a) of § 1.401(a)(9)-3 apply in determining the required minimum distribution for purposes of section 4974.

(c) **Five-year rule.** If the 5-year rule in section 401(a)(9)(B)(ii) applies to the distribution to a payee, no amount is required to be distributed for any calendar year to satisfy the applicable enumerated section in paragraph (a) of this A-3 until the calendar year which contains the date 5 years after the date of the employee's death. For the calendar year which contains the date 5 years after the employee's death, the required minimum distribution amount required to be distributed to satisfy the applicable enumerated section is the payee's entire remaining interest in the qualified retirement plan.

Q-4. If a payee's interest in a qualified retirement plan is being distributed in the form of an annuity, how is the amount of the required minimum distribution determined for purposes of section 4974?

A-4. If a payee's interest in a qualified retirement plan is being distributed in the form of an annuity (either directly from the plan, in the case of a defined benefit plan, or under an annuity contract purchased from an insurance company), the amount of the required minimum distribution for purposes of section 4974 will be determined as follows:

(a) **Permissible annuity distribution option.** A permissible annuity distribution option is an annuity contract (or, in the case of annuity distributions from a defined benefit plan, a distribution option) which specifically provides for distributions which, if made as provided, would for every calendar year equal or exceed the minimum distribution amount required to be distributed to satisfy the applicable section enumerated in paragraph (a) of A-2 of this section for every calendar year. If the annuity contract (or, in the case of annuity distributions from a defined benefit plan, a distribution option) under which distributions to the payee are being made is a permissible annuity distribution option, the required minimum distribution for a given calendar year will equal the amount which the annuity contract (or distribution option) provides is to be distributed for that calendar year.

(b) **Impermissible annuity distribution option.** An impermissible annuity distribution option is an annuity contract (or, in the case of annuity distributions from a defined benefit plan, a distribution option) under which distributions to the payee are being made that specifically provides for distributions which, if made as provided, would for any calendar year be less than the minimum distribution amount required to be distributed to satisfy the applicable section enumerated in paragraph (a) of A-3 of this section. If the annuity contract (or, in the case of annuity distributions from a defined benefit plan, the distribution option) under which distributions to the payee are being made is an impermissible annuity distribution option, the required minimum distribution for each calendar year will be determined as follows:

(1) If the qualified retirement plan under which distributions are being made is a defined benefit plan, the minimum distribution amount required to be distributed each year will be the amount which would have been distributed under the plan if the distribution option under which distributions to the payee were being made was the following permissible annuity distribution option:

(i) In the case of distributions commencing before the death of the employee, if there is a designated beneficiary under the impermissible annuity distribution option for purposes of section 401(a)(9), the permissible annuity distribution option is the joint and survivor annuity option under the plan for the lives of the employee and the designated beneficiary that provides for the greatest level amount payable to the employee determined on an annual basis. If the plan does not provide such an option or there is no designated beneficiary under the impermissible distribution option for purposes of section 401(a)(9), the permissible annuity distribution option is the life annuity option under the plan payable for the life of the employee in level amounts with no survivor benefit.

(ii) In the case of distributions commencing after the death of the employee, if there is a designated beneficiary under the impermissible annuity distribution option for purposes of section 401(a)(9), the permissible annuity distribution option is the life annuity option under the plan payable for the life of the designated beneficiary in level amounts. If there is no designated beneficiary, the 5-year rule in section 401(a)(9)(B)(ii) applies. See paragraph (b)(3) of this A-4. The determination of whether or not there is a designated beneficiary and the determination of which designated beneficiary's life is to be used in the case of multiple beneficiaries will be made in accordance with § 1.401(a)(9)-4 and A-7 of § 1.401(a)(9)-5. If the defined benefit plan does not provide for distribution in the form of the applicable permissible distribution option, the required minimum distribution for each calendar year will be an amount as determined by the Commissioner.

(2) If the qualified retirement plan under which distributions are being made is a defined contribution plan and the impermissible annuity distribution option is an annuity contract purchased from an insurance company, the minimum distribution amount required to be distributed each year will be the amount that would have been distributed in the form of an annuity contract under the permissible annuity distribution option under the plan determined in accordance with paragraph (b)(1) of this A-4 for defined benefit plans. If the defined contribution plan does not provide the applicable permissible annuity distribution option, the required minimum distribution for each calendar year will be the amount that would have been distributed under an annuity described in paragraph (b)(2)(i) or (ii) of this A-4 purchased with the employee's or individual's account used to purchase the annuity contract that is the impermissible annuity distribution option.

(i) In the case of distributions commencing before the death of the employee, if there is a designated beneficiary under the impermissible annuity distribution option for purposes of section 401(a)(9), the annuity is a joint and survivor annuity for the lives of the employee and the designated beneficiary which provides level annual payments and which would have been a permissible annuity distribution option. However, the amount of the periodic payment which would have been payable to the survivor will be the applicable percentage under the table in A-2(c) of § 1.401(a)(9)-6T of the amount of the periodic payment which would have been payable to the employee or individual. If there is no designated beneficiary under the impermissible distribution option for purposes of section 401(a)(9), the annuity is a life annuity for the life of the employee with no survivor benefit which provides level annual payments and which would have been a permissible annuity distribution option.

(ii) In the case of a distribution commencing after the death of the employee, if there is a designated beneficiary under the impermissible annuity distribution option for purposes of section 401(a)(9), the annuity option is a life annuity for the life of the designated beneficiary which provides level annual payments and which would have been a permissible annuity distribution option. If there is no designated beneficiary, the 5-year rule in section 401(a)(9)(B)(ii) applies. See paragraph (b)(3) of this A-4. The amount of the payments under the annuity contract will be determined using the interest rate and actuarial tables prescribed under section 7520 determined using the date determined under A-3 of § 1.401(a)(9)-3 when distributions are required to commence and using the age of the beneficiary as of the beneficiary's birthday in the calendar year that contains that date. The determination of whether or not there is a designated beneficiary and the determination of which designated beneficiary's life is to be used in the case of multiple beneficiaries will be made in accordance with § 1.401(a)(9)-4 and A-7 of § 1.401(a)(9)-5.

(3) If the 5-year rule in section 401(a)(9)(B)(ii) applies to the distribution to the payee under the contract (or distribution option), no amount is required to be distributed to satisfy the applicable enumerated section in paragraph (a) of this A-4 until the calendar year which contains the date 5 years after the date of the employee's death. For the calendar year which contains the date 5 years after the employee's death, the required minimum distribution amount required to be distributed to satisfy the applicable enumerated section is the payee's entire remaining interest in the annuity contract (or under the plan in the case of distributions from a defined benefit plan).

(4) If the plan provides that the required beginning date for purposes of section 401(a)(9) for all employees is April 1 of the calendar year following the calendar year in which the employee attained age 70½ in accordance with paragraph A-2(e) of § 1.401(a)(9)-2, the required minimum distribution for each calendar year for an employee who is not a 5-percent owner for purposes of this section will be the lesser of the amount determined based on the required beginning date as set forth in A-2(a) of § 1.401(a)(9)-2 or the required beginning date under the plan. Thus, for example, if an employee dies after attaining age 70½, but before April 1 of the calendar year following the calendar year in which the employee retired, and there is no designated beneficiary as of September 30 year of the year following the employee's year of death, required minimum distributions for calendar years after the calendar year containing the employee's date of death may be based on either the applicable distribution period provided under either the 5-year rule of A-1 of § 1.401(a)(9)-3 or the employee's remaining life expectancy as set forth in A-5(c)(3) of § 1.401(a)(9)-5.

Q-5. If there is any remaining benefit with respect to an employee (or IRA owner) after any calendar year in which the entire remaining benefit is required to be distributed under section 401(a)(9), what is the amount of the required minimum distribution for each calendar year subsequent to such calendar year?

A-5. If there is any remaining benefit with respect to an employee (or IRA owner) after the calendar year in which the entire remaining benefit is required to be distributed, the required minimum distribution for each calendar year subsequent to such calendar year is the entire remaining benefit.

Q-6. With respect to which calendar year is the excise tax under section 4974 imposed in the case in which the amount not distributed is an amount required to be distributed by April 1 of a calendar year (by the employee's or individual's required beginning date)?

A-6. In the case in which the amount not paid is an amount required to be paid by April 1 of a calendar year, such amount is a required minimum distribution for the previous calendar year, i.e., for the employee's or the individual's first distribution calendar year. However, the excise tax under section 4974 is imposed for the calendar year containing the last day by which the amount is required to be distributed, i.e., the calendar year containing the employee's or individual's required beginning date, even though the preceding calendar year is the calendar year for which the amount is required to be distributed. There is also a required minimum distribution for the calendar year which contains the employee's or individual's required beginning date. Such distribution is also required to be made during the calendar year which contains the employee's or individual's required beginning date.

Q-7. Are there any circumstances when the excise tax under section 4974 for a taxable year may be waived?

(a) **Reasonable cause.** The tax under section 4974(a) may be waived if the payee described in section 4974(a) establishes to the satisfaction of the Commissioner the following—

(1) The shortfall described in section 4974(a) in the amount distributed in any taxable year was due to reasonable error; and

(2) Reasonable steps are being taken to remedy the shortfall.

(b) **Automatic waiver.** The tax under section 4974 will be automatically waived, unless the Commissioner determines otherwise, if—

(1) The payee described in section 4974(a) is an individual who is the sole beneficiary and whose required minimum distribution amount for a calendar year is determined under the life expectancy rule described in § 1.401(a)(9)-3 A-3 in the case of an employee's or individual's death before the employee's or individual's required beginning date; and

(2) The employee's or individual's entire benefit to which that beneficiary is entitled is distributed by the end of the fifth calendar year following the calendar year that contains the employee's or individual's date of death.

Appendix C

SEC No-action Letters

March 3, 1998

Our Ref. No. 98-65-CC
Public Employees' Retirement
Board of the State of Oregon
File No. 132-3

RESPONSE OF THE OFFICE OF CHIEF COUNSEL

DIVISION OF INVESTMENT MANAGEMENT

By letter dated February 10, 1998, you request our assurance that we would not recommend enforcement action to the Commission if, as more fully described in your letter, plans of local governments within the State of Oregon (the "State") that meet the definition of "eligible deferred compensation plan" in Section 457 of the Internal Revenue Code of 1986, as amended ("Section 457 plans" and the "Code," respectively) were to participate in a program authorized by Oregon state law under which the assets of these Oregon local government plans would be commingled with the assets of the State deferred compensation plan in a fund (the "Fund"): (i) without registering the Fund with the Commission as an investment company in reliance upon Section 2(b) of the Investment Company Act of 1940 (the "Investment Company Act"); and (ii) without registering the interests in the Fund under the Securities Act of 1933 (the "Securities Act") in reliance on Section 3(a)(2) of the Securities Act, or under the Securities Exchange Act of 1934 (the "Exchange Act") in reliance on Section 3(a)(12) of the Exchange Act.

Background

You note that Congress amended Section 457 of the Code to require that Section 457 plans be fully funded and that assets of such plans "be held in trust for the exclusive benefit of participants and their beneficiaries."[1] You state that since 1991, legislation has authorized the Oregon Investment Council (the "Council") to allow local governments to invest monies in the investment program established by the Council for the State deferred compensation plan. Until recently, however, there had not been a structure in place to facilitate such investments. You represent that the State legislature enacted a bill that amended the law to, among other things, (i) place the assets of the State's Section 457 plan in a trust and create the Fund to hold and invest the trust's assets, and (ii) allow local government Section 457 plans to deposit assets in the Fund.

While the legislation does not expressly state that the Fund is an instrumentality of the State, you represent that State law provides for various investment funds that are in the custody and control of the State treasurer and under the investment oversight of the Council, and are segregated from the State general fund. You represent that the legislation adds the Fund as another such fund. You further represent that the Fund was created by State statute and is controlled by State officials acting in their official capacities.

Section 2(b) of the Investment Company Act

Section 2(b) of the Investment Company Act generally provides that, unless otherwise specified, the provisions of the Act shall not apply to a state, any political subdivision of a state, or any agency, authority, or instrumentality of a state, or any corporation which is wholly owned, directly or indirectly, by any of the foregoing, or officers, agents, or employees of any of the foregoing acting in the course of their official duties. You believe that the Fund may rely on the Section 2(b) exclusion from the Investment Company Act because it is an instrumentality of the State and local governments. You represent that the creation, authorization and control of the Fund will be entirely under the auspices of local and State governmental entities. You maintain that the recent amendment to Section 457 of the Code, which requires Section 457 plan assets to be held for the exclusive benefit of plan participants, should not alter the staff's analysis of Section 457 plans under Section 2(b).[2]

Whether an entity is a political subdivision, agency, authority or instrumentality of a state ("State Entity"), and whether an individual is an officer, agent or employee of a state or a State Entity, is determined by reference to state law. If, under state law, an issuer is a State Entity, then the issuer is excluded from regulation as an investment company under Section 2(b) of the Investment Company Act, regardless of how it is structured or operated.[3]

Based on the facts and representations in your letter, the staff of the Division of Investment Management would not recommend enforcement action to the Commission under Section 7 of the Investment Company Act if the Fund does not register with the Commission under the Investment Company Act in reliance on Section 2(b) of that Act.

Having stated its views on this subject, and because the crucial inquiries in this area concern questions of state law, the Division of Investment Management will not respond to letters regarding the status under Section 2(b) of the Investment Company Act of Section 457 plans or entities administering such plans, unless the letters raise a novel or unique issue of federal law.[4]

Section 3(a)(2) of the Securities Act and Section 3(a)(12) of the Exchange Act

The Division of Corporation Finance has asked us to inform you that it would not recommend enforcement action to the Commission if, in reliance on your opinion as counsel that the exemptions from registration provided by Section 3(a)(2) of the Securities Act and Section 3(a)(12) of the Exchange Act are available, interests in the Fund are offered in the manner and for the purposes described in your letter without compliance with the registration requirements of the respective Acts. The Division of Market Regulation has asked us to inform you that it concurs in this position with respect to the Exchange Act.

The Divisions of Corporation Finance and Market Regulation (the "Divisions") positions are based on the facts and representations in your letter. Any different facts or circumstances may require different conclusions. Further, this response expresses the positions of the Divisions on enforcement action only and does not express any legal conclusion on the questions presented.

Sarah A. Buescher
Senior Counsel

August 10, 1998
Our Ref. No. IP-1-98
Massachusetts Mutual Life Insurance Company

RESPONSE OF THE OFFICE OF INSURANCE PRODUCTS

DIVISION OF INVESTMENT MANAGEMENT

By letter dated July 17, 1998, Massachusetts Mutual Life Insurance Company ("MassMutual") requests our assurance that we would not recommend enforcement action to the Commission if, as more fully described in your letter, MassMutual offers and sells MassMutual group annuity contracts and interests in MassMutual separate investment accounts ("Separate Accounts") funding the group annuity contracts to State and local government deferred compensation plans qualifying under Section 457 of the Internal Revenue Code of 1986, as amended (the "Code"). MassMutual does not intend to register the group annuity contracts or the Separate Accounts under the federal securities laws in reliance on Section 3(a)(2) of the Securities Act of 1933 ("Securities Act"), and Section 3(c)(11) of the Investment Company Act of 1940 ("Investment Company Act").

Facts

MassMutual is a mutual life insurance company established under the laws of the Commonwealth of Massachusetts and operating in all fifty states, the District of Columbia, and the Commonwealth of Puerto Rico. Currently, MassMutual offers and sells group annuity contracts to pension or profit-sharing plans that qualify for favorable tax treatment under Code Section 401(a) or for the deduction for the employer's contributions under Code Section 404(a)(2) ("Qualified Plans"), and to governmental plans under Code Section 414(d) described in Section 3(a)(2) of the Securities Act ("Section 414(d) Plans").[5]

MassMutual proposes to issue group annuity contracts to deferred compensation plans established by State and local governments pursuant to Code Section 457 that satisfy the requirement of Code Section 457(g) that plan assets and income be held for the exclusive benefit of plan participants and beneficiaries ("New Section 457 Plans"). Each group annuity contract to be issued to a New Section 457 Plan will require that the assets and income of the New Section 457 Plan held under the group annuity contract be used for the exclusive benefit of the plan's participants and beneficiaries.

MassMutual group annuity contracts provide for plan contributions to be allocated to MassMutual's general investment account, to one or more Separate Accounts, or to both MassMutual's general investment account and to one or more Separate Accounts. Contributions to MassMutual's general investment account are credited with a stated, guaranteed rate of return. Obligations under group annuity contracts funded through the general investment account are backed by MassMutual's reserves and statutory surplus.

Investment returns of a Separate Account vary based upon the investment experience of the Separate Account.[6] The income, gains, and losses of a Separate Account are credited to or charged against the net assets held in the Separate Account without regard to the income, gains and losses arising out of any other Separate Account or business that MassMutual may conduct.

Assets of New Section 457 Plans that are held under group annuity contracts and invested in MassMutual Separate Accounts will be commingled with assets of Qualified Plans and Section 414(d) Plans that are held under group annuity contracts and invested in Mass-Mutual Separate Accounts. The Separate Accounts will be used for no purpose other than to fund Qualified Plans, Section 414(d) Plans, and New Section 457 Plans investing in the Separate Accounts through MassMutual group annuity contracts. No assets of individual retirement accounts or annuities established pursuant to Code Section 408 or tax-sheltered annuities or custodial accounts established pursuant to Code Section 403(b) are or may be invested in the Separate Accounts.

MassMutual states that prior to the enactment of the Small Business Job Protection Act of 1996 ("Job Protection Act"),[7] in order for a deferred compensation plan of a State or local government or instrumentality to be eligible under Code Section 457, the assets of the plan were required to remain the property and right of the sponsoring employer and to be subject to the employer's general creditors. In the Job Protection Act, however, Congress added Code Section 457(g) to require that the assets and income of an eligible deferred compensation plan maintained by a State, political subdivision of a State, and any agency or instrumentality of a State or political subdivision of a State be held in trust for the exclusive benefit of plan participants and their beneficiaries. Section 457(g)(3) treats a custodial account or contract described in Code Section 401(f), such as an insurance company group annuity contract, as a trust for this purpose.[8] This "exclusive benefit" requirement applies immediately to all State and local government plans created after August 20, 1996, and applies beginning January 1, 1999, to plans in existence on August 20, 1996.

Analysis

Section 3(a)(2) of the Securities Act and Section 3(a)(12) of the Exchange Act exempt from registration any security arising out of a contract issued by an insurance company, which security is issued in connection with a governmental plan as defined in Section 414(d) of the Code that has been "established by an employer for the exclusive benefit of its employees . . . if under such plan it is impossible . . . for any part of the corpus or income to be used for, or diverted to, purposes other than the exclusive benefit of such employees. . . ."[9] Section 3(c)(11) of the Investment Company Act excludes from the definition of "investment company" any separate account the assets of which are derived solely from such plans.

MassMutual notes that the staff has previously granted relief from registration under Section 3(a)(2) of the Securities Act to insurers and banks offering contracts and interests in collective trusts, respectively, to State and local government plans under Code Section 457 and has consistently treated these plans as "governmental plans" for purposes of the exemptions under the Securities Act, Exchange Act, and Investment Company Act.[10] MassMutual also notes that in the staff's most recent letter, State Street Bank and Trust Co. (pub. avail. Aug. 1, 1996), the staff indicated that its earlier letters no longer represented its position on the availability of the specified exemptions to State and local government plans that complied with Code Section 457 as it existed prior to amendment by the Job Protection Act ("Old Section 457 Plans").

In State Street, the staff noted that the positions taken in the earlier letters were based largely on the general representation that plan assets would not be used for any purpose other than the exclusive benefit of participants except to the extent that plan assets were required to remain subject to the claims of general creditors of the employer to preserve the plan's eligibility under Code Section 457. The staff also stated its belief that this general representation no longer provided an adequate basis for no-action relief without specific additional restrictions on the ability of an employer to withdraw assets similar to those described in State Street.

MassMutual notes that the State Street restrictions prevented the employer/sponsor of an Old Section 457 Plan from using plan assets for its own purposes and effectively enabled the assets to be held for the exclusive benefit of plan participants and beneficiaries. MassMutual asserts that the amendment of Code Section 457 by the Job Protection Act provides assurance that New Section 457 Plans provide protections to plan participants and beneficiaries similar to those provided by Qualified Plans and Section 414(d) Plans, as to which exemptions from registration are available under Section 3(a)(2) of the Securities Act.

MassMutual's counsel is of the opinion that New Section 457 Plans are substantially similar to Section 414(d) Plans in purpose and effect. This opinion is based on similarities between the plans, most importantly, that New Section 457 Plans and Section 414(d) Plans share the requirement that all assets and income be held for the exclusive benefit of the plan's participants and beneficiaries.

MassMutual argues that the staff's reasoning in State Street demonstrates the availability of the federal securities laws exemptions in connection with State and local government plans under Code Section 457 that satisfy the requirements of a Section 414(d) Plan as set forth under Section 3(a)(2) of the Securities Act. Specifically, the plan must be established for the exclusive benefit of its participants and their beneficiaries; and it must be impossible, prior to the satisfaction of all liabilities with respect to the participants and beneficiaries, for any part of the plan's corpus or income to be used for, or diverted to, purposes other than the exclusive benefit of the participants and beneficiaries. MassMutual asserts that the New Section 457 Plans to which MassMutual proposes to issue group annuity contracts will satisfy these requirements.

In light of the foregoing, we would not recommend enforcement action to the Commission under Section 7 of the Investment Company Act if Mass-Mutual offers and sells interests in the Separate Accounts to New Section 457 Plans without registering the Separate Accounts as investment companies in reliance on Section 3(c)(11) of the Investment Company Act.[11] The Division of Corporation Finance has asked us to inform you that it would not recommend enforcement action to the Commission under Section 5 of the Securities Act or Section 12 of the Exchange Act if MassMutual, in reliance upon your opinion as counsel that the exemptions under Section 3(a)(2) of the Securities Act and Section 3(a)(12) of the Exchange Act are available, offers group annuity contracts to New Section 457 Plans without registration under these Acts. The Division of Market Regulation has asked us to inform you that it concurs in this position with respect to the Exchange Act. The Divisions' positions are based on the facts and representations in your letter. You should note that any different facts or circumstances might require a different conclusion. Furthermore, this response represents only the Divisions' positions on enforcement action and does not express any legal conclusions on the questions presented.

Status of Prior Letters

New Section 457 Plans

In light of the amendment of Code Section 457 by the Job Protection Act, which extended an "exclusive benefit" requirement to Code Section 457 State and local government plans, the staff believes that specific additional restrictions on the ability of an employer to withdraw assets similar to those described in State Street are no longer necessary. Therefore, this letter, rather than State Street, represents the staff's position on enforcement action in cases where New Section 457 Plans, i.e., plans complying with the "exclusive benefit" requirement of Code Section 457(g), as amended by the Job Protection Act, are included in a bank collective trust or insurance company separate account.

Old Section 457 Plans

In State Street, the staff indicated that it would not recommend enforcement action to the Commission if, for Old Section 457 Plans, i.e., plans not complying with the "exclusive benefit" requirement of Code Section 457(g), banks and insurance companies continued to rely on the no-action letters issued prior to State Street until August 1, 1997. The staff also stated that, after that date, banks and insurance companies wishing to continue including Old Section 457 Plans in their collective trust funds or separate accounts should, for new contracts, enter into an agreement similar to that described in State Street with the sponsor of each Old Section 457 Plan, and, for existing contracts, use reasonable efforts to amend plan documents and/or supporting contracts to conform to the State Street requirements.

The Job Protection Act provided a transition rule for Old Section 457 Plans in existence on the date of enactment. Those Old Section 457 Plans are not required to comply with the "exclusive benefit" requirement until January 1, 1999.

Subsequent to issuing State Street, the staff has informally advised requestors that it would not recommend enforcement action to the Commission if banks and insurance companies including Old Section 457 Plans in their collective trust funds or separate accounts, respectively, during the period from August 1, 1997, through December 31, 1998, continue to rely on the staff's no-action letters issued prior to State Street. The staff was persuaded that the process of amending plan documents and contracts and securing state regulatory approvals of contract forms to comply with State Street during the interim period from August 1, 1997 (the State Street compliance date), to December 31, 1998 (the date after which Old Section 457 Plans must become New Section 457 Plans to comply with Code Section 457), could impose undue costs and burdens. This informal advice represents the staff's position on enforcement.

Laura A. Novack
Special Counsel

Notes

1. See Sections 1448(a) and (b) of the Small Business Job Protection Act of 1996, P.L. 104-188 (1996). You note that prior to the amendment, assets and income of Section 457 plans were the property of the public employer sponsoring the Section 457 plan and thus could be reached by creditors of the sponsor.

2. One of the many factors that the staff relied on in its response to ICMA Retirement Trust (pub. avail. Feb. 7, 1983) was that, in accordance with Section 457 of the Code, plan assets were the property of the employer. Upon further reflection, however, we have concluded that the issue of whether plan assets are the property of the sponsoring employer or the participant employees is not relevant to determining whether a fund is an instrumentality of a state. Cf. Colorado Prepaid Tuition Fund by the Colorado Student Obligation Bond Authority (pub. avail. Sept. 12, 1997) ("Colorado") (in a prepaid tuition program, the contributions made to the program could be transferred to another beneficiary or refunded under certain circumstances).

3. Colorado, supra note 2. You have not asked for our views concerning the status of the Council under Section 202(b) of the Investment Advisers Act of 1940 ("Advisers Act"), but we also note that the issue of whether the officers, agents and employees of a state or a State Entity may rely on the exclusion from the definition of "investment adviser" in Section 202(b) of the Advisers Act in connection with activities performed in the course of their official duties is determined by reference to state law.

4. The Division of Investment Management also will not respond to letters regarding the status under Section 202(b) of the Advisers Act of officers, agents and employees of Section 457 plans or entities administering such plans, unless the letters raise a novel or unique issue of federal law.

5. Plans for self-employed individuals within the meaning of Code Section 401(c)(1) may be considered Qualified Plans. Group annuity contracts are only offered without registration to these plans, and the assets of these plans will only be held in the Separate Accounts, if the conditions for exemption from registration pursuant to Rule 180 under the Securities Act are satisfied.

6. No New Section 457 Plan assets will be allocated to the purchase of securities issued by a New Section 457 Plan employer or any company directly or indirectly controlling, controlled by, or under common control with any New Section 457 Plan employer.

7. Pub. L. No. 104-188.

8. Code Section 401(f) treats an annuity contract as a qualified trust under Code Section 401(a) if, among other things, the requirements of Code Sections 401(a) and 401(a)(2) are met. Code Sections 401(a)(1) and 401(a)(2) generally provide that a trust constitutes a qualified trust if

(1) contributions are made to the trust for the purpose of distributing to employees or their beneficiaries the corpus and income of the trust; and (2) under the trust instrument, it is impossible, at any time prior to the satisfaction of all liabilities with respect to the employees and their beneficiaries, for any part of the corpus or income to be used for, or diverted to, purposes other than the exclusive benefit of the employees or their beneficiaries.

9. Section 414(d) of the Code provides that a "'governmental plan' means a plan established and maintained for its employees by the Government of the United States, by the government of any State or political subdivision thereof, or by any agency or instrumentality of any of the foregoing."

10. See, e.g., State Street Bank and Trust Co. (pub. avail. Aug. 1, 1996); The Lincoln National Life Insurance Co. (pub. avail. Oct. 26, 1992); Hartford Life Insurance Co. (pub. avail. June 24, 1992); Pan American Life Insurance Co. (pub. avail. Nov. 19, 1991); Standard Insurance Co. (pub. avail. Sept. 11, 1991); Aetna Life Insurance and Annuity Co. (pub. avail. Sept. 11, 1991); Principal Mutual Life Insurance Co. (pub. avail. June 27, 1991); Metropolitan Life Insurance Co. (pub. avail. June 6, 1991); Monarch Life Insurance Co. (pub. avail. Apr. 3, 1991); The Travelers Insurance Co. (pub. avail. Aug. 6, 1990); Great-West Life & Annuity Insurance Co. (pub. avail. Feb. 1, 1990); Fidelity Management Trust Co. (pub. avail. Nov. 2, 1989); Aetna Life Insurance Co. (pub. avail. Oct. 18, 1989); Nationwide Life Insurance Co. (pub. avail. May 12, 1989); North Shore Savings and Loan Ass'n. (pub. avail. Dec. 8, 1998); Wells Fargo Bank, N.A. (pub. avail. Sept. 7, 1998).

11. MassMutual does not seek, and we are not providing, any assurances as to the applicability of Securities Act Section 3(a)(8) to the offer or sale of group annuity contracts funded through MassMutual's general investment account.

Appendix D

Model Rabbi Trust Provisions (Rev. Proc. 92-64)

[Summary: The IRS has published a model grantor trust for use in executive compensation arrangements that are commonly referred to as "rabbi trusts." Revenue Procedure 92-64 also provides guidance for requesting rulings on nonqualified deferred compensation plans that use those trusts; see, for e.g., Letter Ruling 200321002, reproduced in Appendix E.

The model trust is intended to serve as a safe harbor for a taxpayer that adopts and maintains a grantor trust in connection with an unfunded deferred compensation arrangement. If the model trust is used in accordance with Revenue Procedure 92-64, an employee will not be in constructive receipt of income or incur an economic benefit solely on account of the adoption or maintenance of the trust. The desired tax effect will be achieved only if the nonqualified deferred compensation arrangement effectively defers compensation. Therefore, no inference may be drawn by reason of adoption of the model trust concerning constructive receipt or economic benefit issues that may be present in the underlying plan. The IRS noted that the use of the model trust does not change the rules generally applicable under Code Section 6321 regarding the attachment of a federal tax lien on a taxpayer's property and rights to property. It should be noted that the model trust does not allow for participant direction or control of investments made with trust assets.

The IRS states that it will continue to rule on unfunded deferred compensation plans that do not use a trust, on unfunded deferred compensation plans that use the model trust, and, when the model trust is used, generally, on the issue of whether a trust constitutes a grantor trust. "Except in rare and unusual circumstances," however, the IRS will not issue rulings on unfunded deferred compensation arrangements that use a trust other than the model trust.

Revenue Procedure 92-64

SECTION 1. PURPOSE

This revenue procedure contains a model grantor trust for use in executive compensation arrangements that are popularly referred to as "rabbi trust" arrangements. This revenue procedure also provides guidance for requesting rulings on nonqualified deferred compensation plans that use such trusts.

SECTION 2. BACKGROUND

The Internal Revenue Service receives and responds to many requests for rulings on the federal income tax consequences of trusts established in connection with unfunded deferred compensation arrangements. In many of these requests, the trust instruments are very similar. Consequently, in order to aid taxpayers and to expedite the processing of ruling requests on these arrangements, this revenue procedure provides a model trust instrument that plan sponsors may use.

SECTION 3. SCOPE AND OBJECTIVE

The model trust provided in this revenue procedure is intended to serve as a safe harbor for taxpayers that adopt and maintain grantor trusts in connection with unfunded deferred compensation arrangements. If the model trust is used in accordance with this revenue procedure, an employee will not be in constructive receipt of income or incur an economic benefit solely on account of the adoption or maintenance of the trust. However, the desired tax effect will be achieved only if the nonqualified deferred compensation arrangement effectively defers compensation. Thus, no inference may be drawn by reason of adoption of the model trust concerning constructive receipt or economic benefit issues that may be present in the underlying nonqualified deferred compensation plan. In addition, the use of the model trust does not change the rules generally applicable under section 6321 of the Code with respect to the attachment of a federal tax lien to a taxpayer's property and rights to property.

The Service will continue to rule on unfunded deferred compensation plans that do not use a trust, on unfunded deferred compensation plans that use the model trust, and, where the model trust is used, generally, on the issue of whether a trust constitutes a grantor trust within the meaning of subpart E, part I, subchapter J, chapter 1, subtitle A of the Internal Revenue Code of 1986. However, rulings will not be issued on unfunded deferred compensation arrangements that use a trust other than the model trust, except in rare and unusual circumstances.

Taxpayers that adopt the model trust and wish to obtain a ruling on the underlying nonqualified deferred compensation plan, must include a representation that the plan, as amended, is not inconsistent with the terms of the trust and must follow the guidelines outlined in Section 4 of this revenue procedure and Revenue Procedure 92-65 of this Bulletin. Rulings issued on such deferred compensation arrangements will continue to provide that the Service expresses no opinion as to the consequences of the arrangement under Title I of the Employee Retirement Income Security Act of 1974 ("ERISA"). The Department of Labor has advised that whether a "top hat" or excess benefit plan is funded or unfunded depends upon all of the facts and circumstances. However, it is the DOL's view that such plans will not fail to be "unfunded" for purposes of sections 4(b)(5), 201(2), 301(a)(3) and 401(a)(1) of ERISA solely because there is maintained in connection with such a plan a trust which conforms to the model trust described in Section 5 of this revenue procedure.

In addition, rulings issued on deferred compensation arrangements using the model trust will provide that the Service expresses no opinion on the consequences under subchapter C of chapter 1 of subtitle A of the Code or under sections 1501 through 1504 on the trust's acquisition, holding, sale or disposition of stock of the grantor.

SECTION 4. GUIDANCE REGARDING TRUSTS

A private letter ruling on a nonqualified deferred compensation arrangement using a grantor trust subject to the claims of the employer's creditors will be issued only if the trust conforms to the model language contained in Section 5 of this revenue procedure. The model language must be adopted verbatim, except where substitute language is expressly permitted.

The request for a ruling must be accompanied by a representation that the trust conforms to the model trust language contained in this revenue procedure, including the order in which sections of the model trust language appear, and that the trust adopted does not contain any inconsistent language, in substituted portions or elsewhere, that conflicts with the model trust language. Of course, provisions may be renumbered if appropriate, language in brackets may be omitted, and blanks may be completed. In addition, the taxpayer may add sections to the model language provided that such additions are not inconsistent with the model language. Finally, the submission must also include a copy of the trust on which all substituted or additional language is either underlined or otherwise clearly marked and on which the location of the required investment authority language is indicated.

The request for a ruling must contain a representation that the trust is a valid trust under state law and that all of the material terms and provisions of the trust, including the creditors' rights clause, are enforceable under the appropriate state laws.

The trustee of the trust must be an independent third party that may be granted corporate trustee powers under state law, such as a bank trust department or other similar party.

SECTION 5. MODEL PROVISIONS

The model trust language in this section contains all provisions necessary for operation of the trust except for provisions describing the trustee's investment powers. Provisions agreed to by the parties should be used to describe investment powers. The trustee must be given some investment discretion, such as the authority to invest within broad guidelines established by the parties (e.g., invest in government securities, bonds with specific ratings, or stocks of Fortune 500 companies).

The model trust language contains a number of optional provisions, which are printed in italics and marked as *"OPTIONAL."* The taxpayer may substitute language of its choice for any optional provision, provided that the substituted language is not inconsistent with the language of the model trust. The model trust language also contains several alternative provisions, which are printed in italics and marked as *"ALTERNATIVE."* The taxpayer must choose one of these alternatives. Items in brackets are explanatory.

The text of the model trust follows.

TRUST UNDER _____ PLAN

OPTIONAL

This Agreement made this _____ day of _____, by and between _____ (Company) and _____ (Trustee);

OPTIONAL

WHEREAS, Company has adopted the nonqualified deferred compensation Plan(s) as listed in Appendix _____.

OPTIONAL

WHEREAS, Company has incurred or expects to incur liability under the terms of such Plan(s) with respect to the individuals participating in such Plan(s);

WHEREAS, Company wishes to establish a trust (hereinafter called "Trust") and to contribute to the Trust assets that shall be held therein, subject to the claims of Company's creditors in the event of Company's Insolvency, as herein defined, until paid to Plan participants and their beneficiaries in such manner and at such times as specified in the Plan(s);

WHEREAS, it is the intention of the parties that this Trust shall constitute an unfunded arrangement and shall not affect the status of the Plan(s) as an unfunded plan maintained for the purpose of providing deferred compensation for a select group of management or highly compensated employees for purposes of Title I of the Employee Retirement Income Security Act of 1974;

WHEREAS, it is the intention of Company to make contributions to the Trust to provide itself with a source of funds to assist it in the meeting of its liabilities under the Plan(s);

NOW, THEREFORE, the parties do hereby establish the Trust and agree that the Trust shall be comprised, held and disposed of as follows:

Section 1. *Establishment Of Trust*

Company hereby deposits with Trustee in trust _____ *[insert amount deposited]*, which shall become the principal of the Trust to be held, administered and disposed of by Trustee as provided in this Trust Agreement.

ALTERNATIVES—Select one provision.

The Trust hereby established shall be revocable by Company.

The Trust hereby established shall be irrevocable.

The Trust hereby established is revocable by Company; it shall become irrevocable upon a Change of Control, as defined herein.

The Trust shall become irrevocable _____ [insert number] days following the issuance of a favorable private letter ruling regarding the Trust from the Internal Revenue Service.

The Trust shall become irrevocable upon approval by the Board of Directors.

The Trust is intended to be a grantor trust, of which Company is the grantor, within the meaning of subpart E, part I, subchapter J, chapter 1, subtitle A of the Internal Revenue Code of 1986, as amended, and shall be construed accordingly.

The principal of the Trust, and any earnings thereon shall be held separate and apart from other funds of Company and shall be used exclusively for the uses and purposes of Plan participants and general creditors as herein set forth. Plan participants and their beneficiaries shall have no preferred claim on, or any beneficial ownership interest in, any assets of the Trust. Any rights created under the Plan(s) and this Trust Agreement shall be mere unsecured contractual rights of Plan participants and their beneficiaries against Company. Any assets held by the Trust will be subject to the claims of Company's general creditors under federal and state law in the event of Insolvency, as defined in Section 3(a) herein.

ALTERNATIVES—Select one or more provisions, as appropriate.

Company, in its sole discretion, may at any time, or from time to time, make additional deposits of cash or other property in trust with Trustee to augment the principal to be held, administered and disposed of by Trustee as provided in this Trust Agreement. Neither Trustee nor any Plan participant or beneficiary shall have any right to compel such additional deposits.

Upon a Change of Control, Company shall, as soon as possible, but in no event longer than _____ [fill in blank] days following the Change of Control, as defined herein, make an irrevocable contribution to the Trust in an amount that is sufficient to pay each Plan participant or beneficiary the benefits to which Plan participants or their beneficiaries would be entitled pursuant to the terms of the Plan(s) as of the date on which the Change of Control occurred.

Within _____ [fill in blank] days following the end of the Plan year(s), ending after the Trust has become irrevocable pursuant to Section 1(b) hereof, Company shall be required to irrevocably deposit additional cash or other property to the Trust in an amount sufficient to pay each Plan participant or beneficiary the benefits payable pursuant to the terms of the Plan(s) as of the close of the Plan year(s).

Section 2. *Payments to Plan Participants and Their Beneficiaries.*

Company shall deliver to Trustee a schedule (the "Payment Schedule") that indicates the amounts payable in respect of each Plan participant (and his or her beneficiaries), that provides a formula or other instructions acceptable to

Trustee for determining the amounts so payable, the form in which such amount is to be paid (as provided for or available under the Plan(s)), and the time of commencement for payment of such amounts. Except as otherwise provided herein, Trustee shall make payments to the Plan participants and their beneficiaries in accordance with such Payment Schedule. The Trustee shall make provision for the reporting and withholding of any federal, state or local taxes that may be required to be withheld with respect to the payment of benefits pursuant to the terms of the Plan(s) and shall pay amounts withheld to the appropriate taxing authorities or determine that such amounts have been reported, withheld and paid by Company.

The entitlement of a Plan participant or his or her beneficiaries to benefits under the Plan(s) shall be determined by Company or such party as it shall designate under the Plan(s), and any claim for such benefits shall be considered and reviewed under the procedures set out in the Plan(s).

Company may make payment of benefits directly to Plan participants or their beneficiaries as they become due under the terms of the Plan(s). Company shall notify Trustee of its decision to make payment of benefits directly prior to the time amounts are payable to participants or their beneficiaries. In addition, if the principal of the Trust, and any earnings thereon, are not sufficient to make payments of benefits in accordance with the terms of the Plan(s), Company shall make the balance of each such payment as it falls due. Trustee shall notify Company where principal and earnings are not sufficient.

Section 3. *Trustee Responsibility Regarding Payments to Trust Beneficiary When Company Is Insolvent.*

Trustee shall cease payment of benefits to Plan participants and their beneficiaries if the Company is Insolvent. Company shall be considered "Insolvent" for purposes of this Trust Agreement if (i) Company is unable to pay its debts as they become due, or (ii) Company is subject to a pending proceeding as a debtor under the United States Bankruptcy Code.

OPTIONAL

, *or (iii) Company is determined to be insolvent by* _____ *[insert names of applicable federal and/or state regulatory agency].*

At all times during the continuance of this Trust, as provided in Section 1(d) hereof, the principal and income of the Trust shall be subject to claims of general creditors of Company under federal and state law as set forth below.

The Board of Directors and the Chief Executive Officer [or substitute the title of the highest ranking officer of the Company] of Company shall have the duty to inform Trustee in writing of Company's Insolvency. If a person claiming to be a creditor of Company alleges in writing to Trustee that Company has become Insolvent, Trustee shall determine whether Company is Insolvent and, pending such determination, Trustee shall discontinue payment of benefits to Plan participants or their beneficiaries.

Unless Trustee has actual knowledge of Company's Insolvency, or has received notice from Company or a person claiming to be a creditor alleging that Company is Insolvent, Trustee shall have no duty to inquire whether Company is Insolvent. Trustee may in all events rely on such evidence concerning Company's solvency as may be furnished to Trustee and that provides Trustee with a reasonable basis for making a determination concerning Company's solvency.

If at any time Trustee has determined that Company is Insolvent, Trustee shall discontinue payments to Plan participants or their beneficiaries and shall hold the assets of the Trust for the benefit of Company's general creditors. Nothing in this Trust Agreement shall in any way diminish any rights of Plan participants or their beneficiaries to pursue their rights as general creditors of Company with respect to benefits due under the Plan(s) or otherwise.

Trustee shall resume the payment of benefits to Plan participants or their beneficiaries in accordance with Section 2 of this Trust Agreement only after Trustee has determined that Company is not Insolvent (or is no longer Insolvent).

Provided that there are sufficient assets, if Trustee discontinues the payment of benefits from the Trust pursuant to Section 3(b) hereof and subsequently resumes such payments, the first payment following such discontinuance shall include the aggregate amount of all payments due to Plan participants or their beneficiaries under the terms of the Plan(s) for the period of such discontinuance, less the aggregate amount of any payments made to Plan participants or their beneficiaries by Company in lieu of the payments provided for hereunder during any such period of discontinuance.

Section 4. *Payments to Company.*

[The following need not be included if the first alternative under 1(b) is selected.]

Except as provided in Section 3 hereof, after the Trust has become irrevocable, Company shall have no right or power to direct Trustee to return to Company or to divert to others any of the Trust assets before all payment[s] of benefits have been made to Plan participants and their beneficiaries pursuant to the terms of the Plan(s).

Section 5. *Investment Authority.*

ALTERNATIVES—Select one provision, as appropriate

In no event may Trustee invest in securities (including stock or rights to acquire stock) or obligations issued by Company, other than a de minimis amount held in common investment vehicles in which Trustee invests. All rights associated with assets of the Trust shall be exercised by Trustee or the person designated by Trustee, and shall in no event be exercisable by or rest with Plan participants.

Trustee may invest in securities (including stock or rights to acquire stock) or obligations issued by Company. All rights associated with assets of the Trust shall be exercised by Trustee or the person designated by Trustee, and shall in no event be exercisable by or rest with Plan participants.

OPTIONAL

, except that voting rights with respect to Trust assets will be exercised by Company.

OPTIONAL

, except that dividend rights with respect to Trust assets will rest with Company.

Company shall have the right, at anytime, and from time to time in its sole discretion, to substitute assets of equal fair market value for any asset held by the Trust.

[If the second Alternative 5(a) is selected, the trust must provide either (1) that the trust is revocable under Alternative 1(b), or (2) the following provision must be included in the Trust]:

"Company shall have the right at anytime, and from time to time in its sole discretion, to substitute assets of equal fair market value for any asset held by the Trust. This right is exercisable by Company in a nonfiduciary capacity without the approval or consent of any person in a fiduciary capacity."

Section 6. *Disposition of Income.*

ALTERNATIVES—Select one provision.

During the term of this Trust, all income received by the Trust, net of expenses and taxes, shall be accumulated and reinvested.

During the term of this Trust, all, or _____ [insert amount] part of the income received by the Trust, net of expenses and taxes, shall be returned to Company.

Section 7. *Accounting by Trustee.*

OPTIONAL

Trustee shall keep accurate and detailed records of all investments, receipts, disbursements, and all other transactions required to be made, including such specific records as shall be agreed upon in writing between Company and Trustee. Within _____ [insert number] days following the close of each calendar year and within _____ [insert number] days after the removal or resignation of Trustee, Trustee shall deliver to Company a written account of its administration of the Trust during such year or during the period from the close of the last preceding year to the date of such removal or resignation, setting forth all investments, receipts, disbursements and other transactions effected by it, including a description of all securities and investments purchased and sold with the cost or net proceeds of such purchases or sales (accrued interest paid or receivable being shown separately), and showing all cash, securities and other property held in the Trust at the end of such year or as of the date of such removal or resignation, as the case may be.

Section 8. *Responsibility of Trustee.*

OPTIONAL

Trustee shall act with the care, skill, prudence and diligence under the circumstances then prevailing that a prudent person acting in like capacity and familiar with such matters would use in the conduct of an enterprise of a like character and with like aims, provided, however, that Trustee shall incur no liability to any person for any action taken pursuant to a direction, request or approval given by Company which is contemplated by, and in conformity with, the terms of the Plan(s) or this Trust and is given in writing by Company. In the event of a dispute between Company and a party, Trustee may apply to a court of competent jurisdiction to resolve the dispute.

OPTIONAL

If Trustee undertakes or defends any litigation arising in connection with this Trust, Company agrees to indemnify Trustee against Trustee's costs, expenses and liabilities (including, without limitation, attorneys' fees and expenses) relating thereto and to be primarily liable for such payments. If Company does not pay such costs, expenses and liabilities in a reasonably timely manner, Trustee may obtain payment from the Trust.

OPTIONAL

Trustee may consult with legal counsel (who may also be counsel for Company generally) with respect to any of its duties or obligations hereunder.

OPTIONAL

Trustee may hire agents, accountants, actuaries, investment advisors, financial consultants or other professionals to assist it in performing any of its duties or obligations hereunder.

Trustee shall have, without exclusion, all powers conferred on Trustees by applicable law, unless expressly provided otherwise herein, provided, however, that if an insurance policy is held as an asset of the Trust, Trustee shall have no power to name a beneficiary of the policy other than the Trust, to assign the policy (as distinct from conversion of the policy to a different form) other than to a successor Trustee, or to loan to any person the proceeds of any borrowing against such policy.

OPTIONAL

However, notwithstanding the provisions of Section 8(e) above, Trustee may loan to Company the proceeds of any borrowing against an insurance policy held as an asset of the Trust.

Notwithstanding any powers granted to Trustee pursuant to this Trust Agreement or to applicable law, Trustee shall not have any power that could give this Trust the objective of carrying on a business and dividing the gains therefrom, within the meaning of section 301.7701-2 of the Procedure and Administrative Regulations promulgated pursuant to the Internal Revenue Code.

Section 9. *Compensation and Expenses of Trustee.*

OPTIONAL

Company shall pay all administrative and Trustee's fees and expenses. If not so paid, the fees and expenses shall be paid from the Trust.

Section 10. *Resignation and Removal of Trustee.*

Trustee may resign at any time by written notice to Company, which shall be effective _____ [*insert number*] days after receipt of such notice unless Company and Trustee agree otherwise.

OPTIONAL

Trustee may be removed by Company on _____ [insert number] days notice or upon shorter notice accepted by Trustee.

OPTIONAL

Upon a Change of Control, as defined herein, Trustee may not be removed by Company for _____ [*insert number*] year(s).

OPTIONAL

If Trustee resigns within _____ [insert number] year(s) after a Change of Control, as defined herein, Company shall apply to a court of competent jurisdiction for the appointment of a successor Trustee or for instructions.

OPTIONAL

If Trustee resigns or is removed within _____ [insert number] year(s) of a Change of Control, as defined herein, Trustee shall select a successor Trustee in accordance with the provisions of Section 11(b) hereof prior to the effective date of Trustee's resignation or removal.

Upon resignation or removal of Trustee and appointment of a successor Trustee, all assets shall subsequently be transferred to the successor Trustee. The transfer shall be completed within _____ [*insert number*] days after receipt of notice of resignation, removal or transfer, unless Company extends the time limit.

If Trustee resigns or is removed, a successor shall be appointed, in accordance with Section 11 hereof, by the effective date of resignation or removal under paragraph(s) (a) [*or (b)*] of this section. If no such appointment has been made, Trustee may apply to a court of competent jurisdiction for appointment of a successor or for instructions. All expenses of Trustee in connection with the proceeding shall be allowed as administrative expenses of the Trust.

Section 11. *Appointment of Successor.*

OPTIONAL

If Trustee resigns [or is removed] in accordance with Section 10(a) [or (b)] hereof, Company may appoint any third party, such as a bank trust department or other party that may be granted corporate trustee powers under state law, as a successor to replace Trustee upon resignation or removal. The appointment shall be effective when accepted in writing by the new Trustee, who shall have all of the rights and powers of the former Trustee, including ownership rights in the Trust assets. The former Trustee shall execute any instrument necessary or reasonably requested by Company or the successor Trustee to evidence the transfer.

OPTIONAL

If Trustee resigns [or is removed] pursuant to the provisions of Section 10(e) hereof and selects a successor Trustee, Trustee may appoint any third party such as a bank trust department or other party that may be granted corporate trustee powers under state law. The appointment of a successor Trustee shall be effective when accepted in writing by the new Trustee. The new Trustee shall have all the rights and powers of the former Trustee, including ownership rights in Trust assets. The former Trustee shall execute any instrument necessary or reasonably requested by the successor Trustee to evidence the transfer.

OPTIONAL

The successor Trustee need not examine the records and acts of any prior Trustee and may retain or dispose of existing Trust assets, subject to Sections 7 and 8 hereof. The successor Trustee shall not be responsible for and Company shall indemnify and defend the successor Trustee from any claim or liability resulting from any action or inaction of any prior Trustee or from any other past event, or any condition existing at the time it becomes successor Trustee.

Section 12. *Amendment or Termination.*

This Trust Agreement may be amended by a written instrument executed by Trustee and Company. [Unless the first alternative under 1(b) is selected, the following sentence must be included.] Notwithstanding the foregoing, no such amendment shall conflict with the terms of the Plan(s) or shall make the Trust revocable after it has become irrevocable in accordance with Section 1(b) hereof.

The Trust shall not terminate until the date on which Plan participants and their beneficiaries are no longer entitled to benefits pursuant to the terms of the Plan(s) [unless the second alternative under 1(b) is selected, the following must be included:], "unless sooner revoked in accordance with Section 1(b) hereof." Upon termination of the Trust any assets remaining in the Trust shall be returned to Company.

OPTIONAL

Upon written approval of participants or beneficiaries entitled to payment of benefits pursuant to the terms of the Plan(s), Company may terminate this Trust prior to the time all benefit payments under the Plan(s) have been made. All assets in the Trust at termination shall be returned to Company.

Section(s) _____ [insert number(s)] of this Trust Agreement may not be amended by Company for _____ [insert number] year(s) following a Change of Control, as defined herein.

Section 13. *Miscellaneous.*

Any provision of this Trust Agreement prohibited by law shall be ineffective to the extent of any such prohibition, without invalidating the remaining provisions hereof.

Benefits payable to Plan participants and their beneficiaries under this Trust Agreement may not be anticipated, assigned (either at law or in equity), alienated, pledged, encumbered or subjected to attachment, garnishment, levy, execution or other legal or equitable process.

This Trust Agreement shall be governed by and construed in accordance with the laws of _____.

OPTIONAL

For purposes of this Trust, Change of Control shall mean: [insert objective definition such as: "the purchase or other acquisition by any person, entity or group of persons, within the meaning of section 13(d) or 14(d) of the Securities Exchange Act of 1934 ('Act'), or any comparable successor provisions, of beneficial ownership (within the meaning of Rule 13d-3 promulgated under the Act) of 30 percent or more of either the outstanding shares of common stock or the combined voting power of Company's then outstanding voting securities entitled to vote generally, or the approval by the stockholders of Company of a reorganization, merger, or consolidation, in each case, with respect to which persons who were stockholders of Company immediately prior to such reorganization, merger or consolidation do not, immediately thereafter, own more than 50 percent of the combined voting power entitled to vote generally in the election of directors of the reorganized, merged or consolidated Company's then outstanding securities, or a liquidation or dissolution of Company or of the sale of all or substantially all of Company's assets"].

Section 14. *Effective Date.*

The effective date of this Trust Agreement shall be _____, 19___.

SECTION 6. EFFECTIVE DATE

This revenue procedure is effective on July 28, 1992.

Ruling requests with respect to grantor trusts used in executive compensation arrangements and subject to the claims of the employer's creditors that are submitted to the Service subsequent to the effective date of this revenue procedure must comply with the terms of this revenue procedure.

This revenue procedure does not affect any private letter rulings that were issued prior to the effective date. If a plan or trust that was the subject of such a ruling is amended, and such amendments affect the rights of participants or other creditors, such ruling will generally not remain in effect.

SECTION 7. PUBLIC COMMENT

. . .

DRAFTING INFORMATION

. . .

[Rev Proc 92-64, 1992-2 CB 422]

Appendix E

Private Letter Rulings

Letter Ruling 9815039, Dated January 7, 1998

[Summary: The amounts of deferred compensation credited to a participant's account under an ineligible deferred compensation plan are includible in the gross income of the participant for the first tax year for which the participant's rights to the amounts are not subject to a substantial risk of forfeiture.]

This is in response to your request for a ruling submitted on behalf of X regarding the federal income tax consequences under sections 83, 451 and 457 of the Internal Revenue Code with respect to the [sic] X's nonqualified deferred compensation plan (the "Plan") and the Plan's related Trust. X is represented to be a nonprofit corporation that is exempt from federal income tax under section 501(c)(3) of the Code. The Plan will be administered by a committee ("the Committee").

X has represented that participation in the Plan is limited to certain employees who are within a "select group of management or highly compensated employees" of X within the meaning of sections 201(2), 301(a)(3) and 401(a)(1) of the Employee Retirement Income Security Act of 1974, as amended. No member of the Committee will be eligible to participate in the Plan.

Under the Plan, a participant may elect to defer a percentage of his or her compensation from X through a salary-reduction agreement (the "Election Form"). Except for the participant's initial year of eligibility (including the year the Plan is adopted), participation in the Plan will be effective as of the January 1 following the Committee's receipt of the participant's Election Form. All elections under the Plan must be made prior to the period of service in which the compensation relating to the election is earned. In addition, X will make a contribution in the amount of 3% of the participant's compensation each year.

In the Election Form, the participant must irrevocably elect a period (in whole years, not less than two and not greater than ten years) over which to defer the receipt of amounts deferred under that particular Election Form (the "Deferral Period"). If no Deferral Period is elected, the participant is deemed to have elected a Deferral Period of two years. The participant will become vested in amounts deferred under a particular Election Form if he or she is still employed by X as of the date the Deferral Period expires. Participants may not enter into an Election Form in the two-year period immediately preceding the participant's retirement age (age 65 or another age selected by the participant in the participant's first Election Form).

X will establish a deferred compensation account for each participant to reflect the amount of compensation deferred and company contributions, plus certain adjustments described below. The deferred compensation account is a bookkeeping account established solely for the purpose of crediting deferred compensation. Within the limits set by the Plan, each participant is permitted to select and to revise the investment(s) in which his/her account is deemed to be invested from among a variety of investments options; however, X is not required to accept the participant's selections. Pursuant to the terms of the Plan, each participant's account will be credited with the earnings, losses and changes in fair market value experienced by the investment option(s) in which the account is deemed to be invested.

The Plan provides for a risk of forfeiture by stating that a participant generally only vests in the deferred benefits (i.e., such amounts become nonforfeitable) if the participant remains in X's employ until the end of the Deferral Period. If a participant voluntarily terminates employment with X prior to the completion of the Deferral Period or the participant is terminated for cause prior to the completion of the Deferral Period, the participant forfeits amounts under the Plan which are not vested. The participant will not forfeit such amounts if the termination of employment is on account of one of the following events: (a) the participant's death, (b) the participant's disability, (c) the termination of the Plan, (d) the participant's attainment of the retirement age under the Plan, (e) the involuntary termination of the participant other than for cause.

A participant can select the benefit commencement date on the participant's Election Form. The benefit commencement date cannot be earlier than the end of the Deferral Period. If no benefit commencement date is elected, benefits shall be paid on the first day of the first month after the end of the Deferral Period. In all cases, benefit payments under the Plan will commence no later than 60 days after the end of the plan year during which the participant attains retirement age. The Plan provides that benefits will be paid in a lump sum, in annual installments over a period of 3 to 10 years, or in a single sum as of the benefit commencement date and annual installments of the balance over a 3 to 10 year period. The election of the payment form is made by the participant on the participant's Election Form. The selection of payment form is irrevocable.

In accordance with the provisions of Rev. Proc. 92-65, 1992-2 C.B. 428, the Plan states that it is intended to be unfunded for tax purposes and for purposes of Title I of ERISA. All amounts deferred remain the property of X and may be attached or otherwise reached by X's general creditors until such amounts are distributed to the participants. The Plan constitutes no more than a mere promise by X to make benefit payments in the future. Under the Plan, a participant's right to benefit payments may not be anticipated, alienated, sold, transferred, assigned, pledged, encumbered, attached, or garnished by creditors of the participant or the participant's beneficiary.

The Plan allows, but does not require, X to set aside assets in a trust to pay benefits under the Plan. By agreement with an unrelated third party (the "Trustee"), X has established a trust (the "Trust") in order to provide a source from which X may pay its obligations to participants. X has represented that the Trust conforms with the model provisions set forth in Rev. Proc. 92-64, 1992-2 C.B. 422. Additionally, X has represented that the arrangement does not contain any inconsistent language that conflicts with the model trust language. X further represents that the Trust is a valid trust under state law, and that all material terms and provisions of the Trust, including the creditors' rights clause, are enforceable under the appropriate state law.

Under the terms of the Trust, assets may be placed in trust to provide deferred compensation benefits to Plan participants and beneficiaries. However, in the event X becomes insolvent, the Trustee will have the obligation to hold the Trust assets for the benefit of X's general creditors. The Trust further provides that a participant has no beneficial ownership in or preferred claim on any Trust assets and has the status of a general, unsecured creditor. Therefore, contributed assets will be held in trust and in the event of the insolvency of X, those assets will be fully within the reach of X's creditors, as are its other assets.

Section 457 of the Code provides the rules governing the deferral of compensation by an individual participating in a deferred compensation plan of an eligible employer. Under section 457(e)(1)(B), a tax-exempt organization is an eligible employer covered by section 457. Since X is a tax-exempt organization under section 501(c)(3), X is an eligible employer within the meaning of section 457(e)(1).

Section 457(a) of the Code provides that in the case of a participant in an eligible deferred compensation plan, any amount of compensation deferred under the plan and any income attributable to the amounts so deferred is [sic] includible in gross income only for the taxable year in which the compensation or other income is paid or otherwise made available to the participant or beneficiary.

Section 457(b) of the Code and section 1.457-2 of the Income Tax Regulations define the term "eligible deferred compensation plan." The plan is not an eligible deferred compensation plan within the meaning of these provisions.

Under section 457(f)(1)(A) of the Code, if an eligible employer's plan deferring compensation is not an eligible deferred compensation plan, the compensation is included in gross income for the first year in which the participant's right to the compensation is not subject to a substantial risk of forfeiture. Section 457(f)(1)(B) provides that the tax treatment of any amount made available under the eligible plan to a participant is determined under section 72 of the Code (relating to annuities, etc.).

Section 457(f)(3)(B) provides that the rights of a person to compensation are subject to a substantial risk of forfeiture if the person's rights to the compensation are conditioned upon the future performance of substantial services by any individual.

Section 83(a) of the Code provides that the excess (if any) of the fair market value of property transferred in connection with the performance of services over the amount paid (if any) for the property is includible in the gross income of the person who performed the services in the first taxable year in which the property becomes transferable or is not subject to a substantial risk of forfeiture.

Section 1.83-3(e) of the Treasury Regulations (the "Regulations") provides that for purposes of section 83, the term "property" includes real and personal property other than either money or an unfunded and unsecured promise to pay money or property in the future. Property also includes a beneficial interest in assets (including money) transferred or set aside from claims of the transferor's creditors, for example, in a trust or escrow account.

Section 83(c)(1) provides that the rights of a person in property are subject to a substantial risk of forfeiture if such person's rights to full enjoyment of such property are conditioned upon the future performance of substantial services by any individual.

Section 404(a)(5) of the Code provides the general deduction timing rules applicable to any plan or arrangement for the deferral of compensation, regardless of the Code section under which the amounts might otherwise be deductible. Pursuant to section 404 (a)(5) of the Code and section 1.404(a)-12(b)(2) of the Regulations, contributions to or compensation deferred under a nonqualified plan or arrangement are [sic] deductible in the taxable year in which they are paid or made available to the employee, whichever is earlier, provided that they otherwise meet the requirements for deductibility.

Section 451(a) of the Code and section 1.451-1(a) of the Regulations provide that an item of gross income is includible in gross income in the taxable year in which it is actually or constructively received by the taxpayer using the cash receipts and disbursements method of accounting. Under section 1.451-2(a) of the Regulations, income is constructively received in the taxable year during which it is credited to a taxpayer's account, set apart or otherwise made available so that the taxpayer may draw on it at any time. However, income is not constructively received if the taxpayer's control of its receipt is subject to substantial limitations or restrictions.

Under the economic benefit doctrine, an employee has currently includible income from an economic or financial benefit received as compensation, even if the benefit is not in cash form. Economic benefit applies when assets are unconditionally and irrevocably paid into a fund or trust to be used for the employee's sole benefit. Sproull v. Commissioner, 16 T.C. 244 (1951), aff'd per curiam, 194 F.2d 541 (6th Cir. 1952), Rev. Rul. 60-31, Situation 4, 1960-1 C.B. 174.

Various revenue rulings have considered the tax consequences of nonqualified deferred compensation arrangements. Rev. Rul. 60-31, Situations 1-3, holds that a mere promise to pay, not represented by notes or secured in any way, does not constitute receipt of income within the meaning of the cash receipts and disbursements method of accounting. See also, Rev. Rul. 69-650, 1969-2 C.B. 106, and Rev. Rul. 69-649, 1969-2 C.B. 106. In Rev. Rul. 72-25, 1972-1 C.B. 127, and Rev. Rul. 68-99, 1968-1 C.B. 193, an employee does not receive income as a result of the employer's purchase of an insurance contract to provide a source of funds for deferred compensation because the insurance contract is the employer's asset, subject to claims of the employer's creditors.

Provided that (i) the creation of the Trust does not cause the Plan to be other than "unfunded" for purposes of Title I of ERISA, and (ii) the provision in the Trust requiring use of the Trust assets to satisfy the claims of general creditors in the event of insolvency is enforceable by the general creditors of X under federal as well as state law, and based on the information submitted and representations made, we conclude that:

The Plan constitutes an ineligible deferred compensation plan within the meaning of section 457(f) of the Code.

Pursuant to section 457(f), the amounts of deferred compensation credited to a participant's account under the Plan are includible in the gross income of the participant (or, in the case of the participant's death, the gross income of his or her beneficiary) for the first taxable year for which the participant's or the beneficiary's rights to these amounts are not subject to a substantial risk of forfeiture. This will be the taxable year of the participant or beneficiary in which the participant becomes vested in the amounts of deferred compensation. The entire amount of deferred compensation is includible in gross income for that taxable year even if the participant elected a later benefit commencement date or if the participant elected to receive installment distributions.

Amount[s] made available to a participant or beneficiary under the Plan are includible in the gross income of the participant or beneficiary in accordance with the rules of section 72 of the Code. Amounts are made available when the participant or beneficiary becomes entitled to receive them under the Plan. Therefore, no portion of the deemed earnings credited to a participant's account under the Plan will be included in gross income until the taxable year in which the participant or beneficiary becomes entitled to receive them. The portion of any installment distribution includible in gross income will be determined under section 72.

None of the following events will constitute a transfer of property for purposes of section 83 of the Code or section 1.83-3(e) of the Regulations: (a) the adoption of the Plan, (b) the creation of the trust, (c) the contribution of assets to the Trust, or (d) the realization of earnings by the Trust.

Under the economic benefit and constructive receipt doctrines of sections 61 and 451 of the Code, neither the creation of the Plan or the Trust, nor the contribution of assets to the Trust will create taxable income for the participants or their beneficiaries under the cash receipts and disbursements method of accounting.

A participant's right to designate the investment of amounts deferred by such participant under the Plan and the right to change such designation will not cause these amounts to be includible in the participant's gross income until the taxable year in which such amounts are not subject to a substantial risk of forfeiture, are actually distributed or otherwise made available, whichever is earliest.

None of the following events will constitute a contribution to a non-exempt trust under section 402(b) of the Code: (a) the adoption of the Plan, (b) the creation of the trust, (c) the contribution of assets to the Trust, or (d) the realization of earnings by the Trust.

This ruling applies to the copies of the Plan and Trust submitted with your letter dated June 17, 1997, and the proposed amendments to the Plan and the Trust submitted on December 5, 1997 and January 5, 1998. This ruling is contingent on the adoption of the Plan and the Trust, and the proposed amendments to the Plan and the Trust. If the Plan or the Trust are otherwise modified, this ruling may no longer apply.

This ruling is directed only to the taxpayer who requested it. Section 6110(j)(3) of the Code provides that this ruling may not be used or cited as precedent. Except as specifically ruled on above, no opinion is expressed as to the federal tax consequences of the above transaction under any other provision of the Code.

Letter Ruling 9809038, Dated November 25, 1997

[Summary: The IRS ruled that a tax-exempt association's deferred compensation program for independent contractors will not result in income until the beneficiary receives payments from the plan. Neither the allocation of amounts to the participant's account, nor the amount in the account becoming nonforfeitable, nor the amount of the beneficiary's installment payment being determined will result in constructive receipt of income to the beneficiary.]

This is in response to your request for a private letter ruling on behalf of X dated August 12, 1997, concerning the federal income tax consequences to X, who is on the cash receipts and disbursements method of accounting, of participation in the Association Deferred Compensation Program for Independent Contractors ("Plan"). The Association is an organization exempt from tax under section 501(c)(6) of the Internal Revenue Code. The Plan, which was established this year, is intended to meet the requirements of section 457(e)(12) of the Internal Revenue Code.

The Plan provides that contestants participating in certain Association sanctioned events will participate in the Plan. The Board of Directors determines the amount of the annual contribution that the Association makes to the Plan and a bookkeeping account is maintained for each participant. Amounts are allocated annually to a participant's bookkeeping account according to a formula set forth in the Plan which is based on prize money, points earned in contests, years as a contestant and account earnings.

Benefits under the Plan are subject to a vesting schedule set forth in the Plan and are payable, once vested, at the later of 30 days after the end of the plan year in which active participation ceases, as defined in the Plan, or within 30 days of the end of the plan year in which the participant attains the age of 55. In addition, benefits are also payable within 30 days of the determination that the participant has incurred a total and permanent disability, and within 30 days after the end of the plan year in which the participant dies. Benefit payments are made in installments over a number of years as set forth in the Plan and are based on the size of the account balance. The Plan does not provide for any individual variations or elections.

The Plan states that assets of the Plan are subject to the claims of the Association's general creditors and a participant or other beneficiary has no ownership interest or rights in assets of the Plan prior to distribution. The terms of the Plan provide that participants may not assign, alienate, pledge, or encumber any rights under the Plan and that it is not subject to garnishment, levy, execution or other legal or equitable process. In addition, it provides that the Plan represents merely a contractual right to pay benefits.

Section 457 provides for the treatment of compensation deferred under a nonqualified deferred compensation plan of an eligible employer. The term eligible employer includes an organization exempt from tax. If a plan of an eligible employer is not an eligible deferred compensation plan, as defined in section 457(b), then under section 457(f)(1), the compensation deferred under the plan is included in the gross income of a participant or beneficiary in the first taxable year in which there is no substantial risk of forfeiture of the rights to the compensation.

Section 1.457-2(b) of the Income Tax Regulations provides that a plan includes any agreement or arrangement maintained by an eligible employer, under which the payment of compensation is deferred. Question and Answer 26 of IRS Notice 87-13 clarifies that section 457 applies to both elective and nonelective deferred compensation plans. The Notice states that section 457 applies regardless of whether the plan is in the nature of an individual account plan or a defined benefit plan.

Section 457(e)(12), however, provides that section 457 does not apply to nonelective deferred compensation attributable to services not performed as an employee. Under section 457(e)(12)(B), deferred compensation is nonelective only if all individuals (other than those who have not satisfied any applicable initial service requirement) with the same relationship to the payor are covered under the same plan with no individual variations or options under the plan.

The Association is an eligible employer and the deferred compensation under the Plan is not attributable to services performed as an employee. The Plan covers all similarly situated participants, without any variations or options. Accordingly, section 457(e)(12)(A) exempts the Plan from section 457 and its tax consequences must be determined without regard to section 457.

Section 451(a) of the Code and section 1.451-1(a) of the regulations provide that an item of gross income is includible in gross income for the taxable year in which actually or constructively received by a taxpayer using the cash receipts and disbursements method of accounting. Under section 1.451-2(a) of the regulations, income is constructively received in the taxable year during which it is credited to a taxpayer's account or set apart or otherwise made available so that the taxpayer may draw on it at any time. However, income is not constructively received if the taxpayer's control of its receipt is subject to substantial limitations or restrictions.

Various revenue rulings have considered the tax consequences of nonqualified deferred compensation arrangements. Rev. Rul. 60-31, Situations 1-3, 1960-1 C.B. 174, holds that a mere promise to pay, not represented by notes or secured in any way, does not constitute receipt of income within the meaning of the cash receipts and disbursements method of accounting. See also Rev. Rul. 69-650, 1969-2 C.B. 106, and Rev. Rul. 69-649, 1969-2 C.B. 106.

Based on the information submitted and the representations made, we conclude that X's participation in the Plan will not result in constructive receipt of income at the time that (1) amounts are allocated to X's account, (2) the amount in X's account becomes nonforfeitable, or (3) the amount of X's installment payment is determined. Rather, X will realize taxable income when X actually receives payments under the Plan.

Except as specifically ruled on above, no opinion is expressed as to the federal tax consequences of the above transaction under any other provision of the Code.

This ruling is directed only to the taxpayer who requested it and applies only to the Plan as of the date of this ruling, if the Plan is amended, this ruling may not remain in effect.

Temporary or final regulations pertaining to one or more of the issues addressed in this ruling have not yet been adopted, particularly section 457 and the scope of section 457(e)(12). Therefore, this ruling may be modified or revoked by adoption of temporary or final regulations that are inconsistent with the conclusions of this ruling. In addition, section 6110(j)(3) of the Code provides that this ruling may not be used or cited as precedent.

Letter Ruling 9805030, Dated November 3, 1997

[Summary: The IRS ruled that neither an exempt organization's adoption of a supplemental executive retirement plan, nor a participant's right to designate the deemed investment of the deferred compensation amounts credited to his plan bookkeeping account, will cause any amount to be included in the gross income of the participant or his beneficiary under either the constructive receipt doctrine of Code Section 451 or the economic benefit doctrine of Code Section 457(f). The IRS also ruled that the adoption of the plan will not be a transfer of property to the participant or his beneficiaries for purposes of Code Section 83.]

This responds to your request for a ruling submitted in your letter of June 30, 1997 on behalf of Entity E regarding the proper income tax treatment of the nonqualified supplemental retirement benefits provided to Participant P pursuant to its supplemental executive retirement plan (the "Plan") under sections 83 and 457(f) of the Internal Revenue Code of 1986 ("Code"). Entity E is represented to be a nonprofit organization that is exempt from federal income tax under section 501(c)(3) of the Code.

The Plan provides supplemental deferred compensation benefits to Participant P, a key management employee. The Plan provides for "deemed" investments selected by P; the value of P's bookkeeping account under the Plan would be increased or decreased by the net amount of investment earnings or losses that would have occurred if such account value had been invested in such deemed investments. The benefits payable to the participant or his beneficiary are determined in accordance with the Plan. The Plan provides for a risk of forfeiture by stating that P generally vests in the deferred benefits (i.e., such amounts become nonforfeitable and taxable) only upon his remaining in E's employ until reaching the normal retirement age set by the Plan; he will not reach that age for a period of time substantially longer than two years.

Generally, if P's employment with E is terminated prior to his attaining the normal retirement age set by the Plan, all of his rights and benefits thereunder are forfeited and E has no further obligation to him under the Plan. However, his accrued benefit also vests and becomes nonforfeitable if he dies while employed by E or if he separates from service due to disability as set forth in the Plan. The Plan also provides that within a short time following the date when an Employee's accrued benefit becomes nonforfeitable (and taxable) Entity E will pay his accrued benefit under the Plan to him (or to his beneficiary after his death) in a lump-sum. In addition, the Plan does not include provisions that limit the amounts deferrable under the Plan to the lesser of $7,500 or 33⅓ percent of the participant's includible compensation.

The Plan provides that all amounts in the deferred compensation account under the Plan will remain (until vested under the Plan in the participant or beneficiary) solely the property and rights of E, subject only to the claims of E's general creditors. Participant P and his beneficiaries have only the status of general unsecured creditors of Entity E. The rights of the participant or beneficiaries to payment pursuant to the Plan are nonassignable, and their interests in benefits under the Plan are not subject to alienation, transfer, pledge, encumbrance or other legal process.

Section 457(a) of the Code provides that in the case of a participant in an eligible deferred compensation plan, any amount of compensation deferred under the plan and any income attributable to the amounts so deferred shall be includible in gross income only for the taxable year in which such compensation or other income is paid or otherwise made available to the participant or beneficiary.

Section 457(b) of the Code, and section 1.457-2 of the Income Tax Regulations define the term "eligible deferred compensation plan." Those provisions contain the various requirements for an eligible plan, including rules for participation, deferral of compensation, and payment of benefits.

Section 457(f)(1) of the Code governs the tax treatment of a participant in a plan of an eligible employer, if the plan provides for a deferral of compensation, but is not an eligible deferred compensation plan. The term "eligible employer" is defined in section 457(e)(1), and includes a state or any political subdivision or any agency or instrumentality of a state, and any other tax-exempt organization. Section 457(f)(2) states that section 457(f)(1) does not apply to a plan described in section 401(a) which includes a trust exempt from tax under section 501(a), to an annuity plan or contract described in section 403, to that portion of any plan which consists of a transfer of property described in section 83, or to that portion of any plan which consists of a trust to which section 402(b) applies.

In general, section 457(f)(1)(A) of the Code provides that the amount of compensation which is deferred under a plan subject to section 457(f)(1) is included in the participant's or beneficiary's gross income for the first taxable year in which there is no substantial risk of forfeiture of the rights to the compensation. Section 457(f)(3)(B) provides that, for purposes of section 457(f), the rights of a person to compensation are subject to a substantial risk of forfeiture if such person's rights to such compensation are conditioned upon the future performance of substantial services by any individual.

Section 1.83-3(c) of the Income Tax Regulations provides that for purposes of section 83 and the regulations thereunder, whether a risk of forfeiture is substantial depends upon the facts and circumstances. A substantial risk of forfeiture exists where rights in property that are transferred are conditioned, directly or indirectly, upon the future performance of substantial services by any person, or the occurrence of a condition related to a purpose of the transfer, and the possibility of forfeiture is substantial if such condition is not satisfied. The regularity of the performance of services and the time spent in performing such services tend to indicate whether services required by a condition are substantial. See section 1.83-3(c)(2).

Section 1.83-3(c)(4), Example (1) of the regulations provides, by way of example, that where a corporation transfers to an employee 100 shares of stock in the corporation, at $90 per share, and the employee is obligated to sell the stock to the Corporation at $90 per share if he terminates his employment with the Corporation for any reason prior to the expiration of a two year period of employment, the employee's rights to the stock are subject to a substantial risk of forfeiture during such two year period. If the conditions on transfer are not satisfied, it is assumed that the forfeiture provision will be enforced.

Participant P will be entitled to receive benefits under the Plan only if he continues in full-time employment with the sponsoring employer E until he has attained normal retirement age, dies, or terminates service due to disability. Eased [Based] on these facts, P's benefits under the Plan are subject to a substantial risk of forfeiture until they vest. Accordingly, under section 457(f) of the Internal Revenue Code, no contributions or benefits are taxable to a participant or his beneficiary until the benefits vest under the terms of the Plan.

Section 83(a) of the Internal Revenue Code provides that the excess (if any) of the fair market value of property transferred in connection with the performance of services over the amount paid (if any) for the property is includible in the gross income of the person who performed the services for the first taxable year in which the property becomes transferable or is not subject to a substantial risk of forfeiture.

Section 1.83-3(e) of the Income Tax Regulations provides that for purposes of section 83 the term "property" includes real and personal property other than money or an unfunded and unsecured promise to pay money or property in the future. Property also includes a beneficial interest in assets (including money) transferred or set aside from claims of the transferor's creditors, for example, in a trust or escrow account.

Section 451(a) of the Code and section 1.451-1(a) of the regulations provide that an item of gross income is includible in gross income for the taxable year in which actually or constructively received by a taxpayer using the cash receipts and disbursements method of accounting. Under section 1.451-2(a) of the regulations, income is constructively received in the taxable year during which it is credited to a taxpayer's account or set apart or otherwise made available so that the taxpayer may draw on it at any time. However, income is not constructively received if the taxpayer's control of its receipt is subject to substantial limitations or restrictions.

Under the economic benefit doctrine, an employee has currently includible income from an economic or financial benefit received as compensation, though not in cash form. Economic benefit applies when assets are unconditionally and irrevocably paid into a fund or trust to be used for the employee's sole benefit. Sproull v. Commissioner, 16 T.C. 244 (1951), aff'd per curiam, 195 F.2d 541 (6th Cir. 1952), Rev. Rul. 60-31, Situation 4. In Rev. Rul. 72-25, 1972-1 C.B. 127, and Rev. Rul. 68-99, 1968-1 C.B. 193, an employee does not receive income as a result of the employer's purchase of an insurance contract to provide a source of funds for deferred compensation because the insurance contract is the employer's asset, subject to claims of the employer's creditors.

Based on the information submitted and representations made, we conclude that:

Neither the adoption of the Plan, nor Participant P's right to designate the deemed investment of the deferred compensation amounts credited to his Plan bookkeeping account will cause any amount to be included in the gross income of P or his beneficiary under the cash receipts and disbursements method of accounting, pursuant to either the constructive receipt doctrine of section 451, the economic benefit doctrine or section 457(f).

The adoption of the Plan will not constitute the transfer of property to Participant P or his beneficiaries for purposes of section 83 of the Internal Revenue Code or section 1.83-3(e) of the regulations.

Benefits under the Plan are subject to a substantial risk of forfeiture until Participant P attains normal retirement age under the Plan after continuous employment with E, dies as E's employee, or terminates employment with E due to disability. Accordingly, under section 457(f)(1)(A), amounts credited by the participant's employer under the Plan are included in the gross income of P or his beneficiary in the first taxable year in which he attains normal retirement age under the Plan, dies or separates from service due to disability, assuming P has remained continuously employed by E until any such date.

This ruling is contingent upon the adoption of the Plan submitted on June 30, 1997 and is directed only to P and to E, the entity which requested it. Section 6110(j)(3) of the Internal Revenue Code provides that this ruling may not be used or cited as precedent. No opinion is expressed concerning the timing of the inclusion in income of amounts deferred under any deferred compensation plan other than the Plan. If the Plan is substantially amended, this ruling letter may not necessarily remain in effect.

Temporary or final regulations pertaining to one or more of the issues addressed in this ruling have not yet been adopted. Therefore, this ruling may be modified or revoked if the adopted temporary or final regulations are inconsistent with any conclusion in the ruling. See section 12.04 of Rev. Proc. 97-1, 1997-1 I.R.B. 43. However, when the criteria in section 12.05 of Rev. Proc. 97-1 are satisfied, a ruling is not revoked or modified retroactively except in rare or unusual circumstances.

Letter Ruling 9631034, Dated February 2, 1996

[Summary: The IRS approved amendments to a governmental entity's eligible deferred compensation plan which would provide participants with more flexible distribution options. One amendment would allow participants and beneficiaries to elect certain forms of payment that include an automatic annual cost-of-living adjustment based on an identified and nationally recognized cost-of-living index. The other amendment would permit participants to split the method for payout among the various distribution options offered under the plan, so long as the minimum distribution requirements of Code Section 457(d)(2) are not violated.]

This replies to your request for a ruling submitted on behalf of X, an eligible employer within the meaning of section 457(e)(1)(A), with respect to proposed amendments to X's deferred compensation plan that covers its employees and individuals who contract independently with X.

X has previously received favorable letter rulings concluding that the Plan is an eligible plan for purposes of section 457 of the Internal Revenue Code ("Code"). X now proposes to amend the Plan to provide participants with more flexible distribution options. One such amendment will provide participants or beneficiaries with the option of electing certain forms of payment that include an automatic annual cost-of-living adjustment based on an identified and nationally recognized cost-of-living index. A second amendment will permit participants to split the method for payout among the various distribution options offered under the plan, so long as the minimum distribution requirements of section 457(d)(2) are not violated. The effect of the amendments will allow participants to elect inter alia to have amounts paid to them first as a large lump sum followed by periodic payments of a lesser annual amount and then to have those periodic payments reduced to reflect the commencement of social security payments or increased to reflect an increase in the cost-of-living.

Section 457(a) of the Internal Revenue Code provides that in the case of a participant in an eligible deferred compensation plan, any amount of compensation deferred under the plan and any income attributable to the amounts so deferred shall be includible in gross income only for the taxable year in which such compensation or other income is paid or otherwise made available to the participant or beneficiary.

Section 457(b) of the Code and section 1.457-2 of the Income Tax Regulations define the term "eligible deferred compensation plan." Those provisions contain the various requirements for an eligible plan, including rules for participation, deferral of compensation, and payment of benefits.

Section 457(d) of the Code provides explicit distribution requirements for an eligible plan and section 457(d)(2) of the Code sets out the minimum distribution requirements. Section 457(d)(2)(C) requires that, with respect to an eligible plan, any distribution payable over a period of more than 1 year can only be made in substantially nonincreasing amounts (paid not less frequently than annually).

No regulations define the term "substantially non-increasing amounts." Under the plain meaning of that term, amounts distributed need not be equal but they also should not be radically or unexplainably dissimilar. A specified and generally recognized cost-of-living index used to provide an inflation adjustment to payments that would not otherwise be made in substantially increasing amounts will not create radically or unexplainably dissimilar increasing payments. Additionally, we note that the economic reality of a reasonable adjustment for inflation does not provide participants with increased purchasing power that could cause the new payout amounts to be construed as substantially increasing a participant's prior purchasing power. Thus, the Plan's provision to permit cost-of-living indexing of payout amounts will not cause the indexed payments to violate the "substantially nonincreasing" requirement of section 457(d)(2)(C).

Section 457 does not prohibit a plan from making distributions in decreasing amounts. For example, a participant may be allowed to elect payment of a lump sum upon separation from service with the remainder of the benefit to be paid out in substantially nonincreasing periodic payments of a lesser amount (calculated on an annual basis). Similarly, prior to the time any amounts become payable, a participant may be allowed to elect a payment option that provides for a reduction in the amount of substantially nonincreasing periodic payments, where the reduction is scheduled to take effect once the participant attains social security retirement age.

With respect to a split distribution from an eligible plan, however, section 457 does not permit a lapse of time between the time of commencement of payment of various payout options that may be available to participants. For purposes of section 457(d)(2), a split distribution is a single distribution system made up of several different payment options. There can be only one benefit payout commencement date. Accordingly, to avoid violating the requirement of section 457(d)(2)(C) that any distribution payable over a period of more than 1 year can only be made in amounts paid not less frequently than annually, there can be no time lapse between payments that equals or exceeds two years. Thus, if a participant elects to have a series of periodic payments follow the distribution of a partial lump sum payment, the first payment of the series must be made no later than within the first year after the year in which the initial lump sum was paid.

Because the proposed amended Plan limits the flexibility in distribution options provided so as not to violate the requirements of section 457(d)(2) of the Code and because the cost-of-living adjustment option does not violate the substantially nonincreasing rule of section 457(d)(2)(C), we conclude that the amendments to the Plan will not cause the Plan to become other than an eligible plan for purposes of section 457.

This ruling is contingent on the adoption of the proposed amended Plan in the form submitted with your letter dated January 23, 1996. It is directed only to X, to X's employees, and to individuals who contract independently with X. Section 6110(j)(3) of the Code provides that it may not be used or cited as precedent. If the Plan is subsequently modified, this ruling will not necessarily remain applicable.

Temporary or final regulations pertaining to one or more of the issues addressed in this ruling have not yet been adopted. Therefore, this ruling may be modified or revoked if the adopted temporary or final regulations are inconsistent with any conclusion in the ruling. See section 11.04 of Rev. Proc. 96-1, 1996-1 I.R.B. 39. However, when the criteria in section 11.05 of Rev. Proc. 96-1, 1996-1 I.R.B. 40, are satisfied, a ruling is not revoked or modified retroactively except in rare or unusual circumstances.

Letter Ruling 9629022, Dated April 23, 1996

[1] This responds to your letter of January 19, 1996, and subsequent correspondence requesting a ruling concerning the federal income tax status of a nonqualified supplemental retirement arrangement (the "Arrangement") established by Entity E, a tax-exempt entity described in section 501(c)(6) of the Internal Revenue Code. E's executive committee established the Arrangement in December, 1987 and set forth its purpose and provisions in executive committee minutes dated December 15, 1987. The purpose of the Arrangement is

to supplement the retirement benefits that Participant P, a key executive of E, would receive under E's qualified retirement plan.

[2] The Arrangement establishes a goal for P's total post-retirement income relating to his services for E, including distributions, from E's qualified plan and under the Arrangement. Using this goal, an actuary determined the amount that E would have to credit and accumulate under the Arrangement to provide the total retirement income level described in the minutes of the December, 1987 executive committee meeting. This amount was set forth in the minutes of the December 15, 1987, executive committee meeting.

[3] Section 457 of the Code provides rules for the deferral of compensation by an individual participating in an eligible deferred compensation plan (as defined in section 457(b)).

[4] Section 457(a) of the Code provides that in the case of a participant in an eligible deferred compensation plan, any amount of compensation deferred under the plan and any income attributable to the amounts so deferred shall be includible in gross income only for the taxable year in which such compensation or other income is paid or otherwise made available to the participant or beneficiary.

[5] Section 457(e)(1)(B) defines the term "eligible employer" as any organization (other than a governmental unit) that is exempt from tax under subtitle A of the Code, which includes organizations described in section 501(c)(6) of the Code.

[6] Section 1107 of the Tax Reform Act of 1986 (the "Act") amended section 457 of the Code to apply its restrictions and limitations to the unfunded deferred compensation plans maintained by nongovernmental tax-exempt organizations, effective for taxable years beginning after December 31, 1986, except as provided under section 1107(c) of the Act. Section 1107(c)(3)(B) of the Act states that section 457 does not apply to amounts deferred under a deferred compensation plan of a tax-exempt organization that:

were deferred from taxable years beginning before January 1, 1987, or

were deferred from taxable years beginning after December 31, 1986, pursuant to an agreement that (I) was in writing on August 16, 1986, and (II) on such date, provides for a deferral for each taxable year covered by the agreement of a fixed amount or of an amount determined pursuant to a fixed formula. If there is any modification of the fixed amount or fixed formula, however, section 457 applies to any taxable year ending after the date on which the modification is effective.

[7] Section 6064(d)(3) of the Technical and Miscellaneous Revenue Act of 1988 ("TAMRA") modifies this transition rule enacted in the Tax Reform Act of 1986. Section 6064(d)(3) of TAMRA states that section 457 shall not apply to amounts deferred under a nonelective deferred compensation plan maintained by an eligible employer described in section 457(e)(1)(A) of the Code (A) if such amounts were deferred from periods before July 14, 1988, or (B) if such amounts are deferred from periods on or after such date pursuant to an

agreement which was in writing on such date, and which on such date pro-vides for a deferral for each taxable year covered by the agreement of a fixed amount or of an amount determined pursuant to a fixed formula, and the individual for whom the deferral is made was covered under such agreement on such date. Notice 88-8, 1988-1 C.B. 477, states that the IRS has determined that a nonelective deferred compensation plan maintained by a state or local government or tax-exempt organization, will not be subject to the provisions of section 457 for taxable years of employees beginning before January 1, 1988.

[8] Section 6064(d)(3) of TAMRA also provides that this grandfather rule for nonqualified deferred compensation plans under section 457 maintained by tax-exempt organizations does not cease to apply merely because of a modifi-cation to the deferred compensation agreement prior to January 1, 1989, that does not increase benefits for participants in the plan. The legislative history of TAMRA indicates that Congress wanted to provide relief only to a post-August 16, 1986 "modification which does not increase benefits for participants in the plan" that would otherwise be covered under section 457. H.R. Rep. No. 1104 100th Cong., 2nd. Sess. 154 (1988).

[9] Based upon the information and documents submitted, and the provi-sions of the Arrangement summarized above, we conclude as follows:

Section 457 of the Internal Revenue Code, as amended by section 1107(c)(3)(B) of the Act and section 6064(d)(3)(B) of TAMRA, does not apply to the Arrangement.

[10] This ruling concerns only the application of section 457 to the Arrangement. No opinion is expressed regarding whether the Arrangement effectively defers the taxation of compensation deferred thereunder. Also, if the Arrangement is amended to increase, directly or indirectly, the formula set on December 15, 1987, this ruling will no longer apply.

[11] This ruling is directed only to Participant P and Entity E, and applies only to the Arrangement established on December 15, 1987. Section 6110(j)(3) of the Code provides that it may not be used or cited as precedent. Except as specifically stated above, no opinion is expressed on the federal tax conse-quences of the Arrangement under any other provision of the Code.

Letter Ruling 9628020, Dated April 15, 1996

[1] This is in response to your request for a ruling on behalf of X, concern-ing the federal income tax consequences of the establishment of a trust to assist X, in providing nonqualified deferred compensation benefits under the Plan for certain management or highly compensated employees (the "Partici-pants") designated by X. The Plan states that it is intended to comply with the provisions of section 457(f) of the Internal Revenue Code and in accordance with Rev. Proc. 92-65, 1992-2 C.B. 428, it states that it is intended to be an

unfunded arrangement for tax purposes and for purposes of Title I of the Employee Retirement Income Security Act of 1974 (ERISA).

[2] X is a section 501(c)(3) tax-exempt entity. The Plan provides that Participants may execute deferral agreements pursuant to which they elect to defer a portion of their compensation to be allocated as a bookkeeping account among X's other general assets. The Plan states that the account and all amounts, property or rights in property and all income, if any, attributable to the amounts, accounts or property or right to property, remain (until paid to a Participant or beneficiary) solely the assets, property and rights of X, subject to the claims of X's general creditors. Subject to the forfeiture provisions stated in the Plan, at the time the deferral agreement is entered into, a Participant also irrevocably selects the manner in which payment of benefits is to be made (e.g. lump sum, installments, etc.) and date upon which distribution of benefits is to commence.

[3] The Plan states that the deferred compensation amounts are a contingent benefit and that a Participant has no vested, secured or preferred position with respect to an account. Furthermore, the Plan states that no Participant shall have any right to payment under the Plan and benefit amounts will be forfeited unless payment is deferred to a distribution date which occurs no sooner than two years from the effective date of the deferral agreement. In addition, a Participant has no right to receive any benefits under the Plan and any benefits are forfeited under the Plan if the Participant terminates employment with X or if the Participant is discharged by X prior to the distribution date. A Participant's right to any benefit payments may not be anticipated, alienated, sold, transferred, assigned, pledged, encumbered, attached, or garnished.

[4] By agreement with an unrelated third party (the "Trustee"), X has established an irrevocable trust (the "Trust") in order to pay its obligations to Participants. X has represented that the Trust conforms with the model provisions set forth in Revenue Procedure 92-64 1992-2, C.B. 422, that the arrangement does not contain any inconsistent language that conflicts with the model trust language, and that the Trust is a valid trust under state law.

[5] Section 457(a) of the Code provides that in the case of a participant in an eligible deferred compensation plan, any amount of compensation deferred under the plan and any income attributable to the amounts so deferred shall be includible in gross income only for the taxable year in which such compensation or other income is paid or otherwise made available to the participant or beneficiary.

[6] Section 457(b) of the Code, and section 1.457-2 of the Income Tax Regulations define the term "eligible deferred compensation plan." Those provisions contain the requirements for an eligible plan, including rules for participation, limits on the amount that may be deferred, and payment of benefits.

[7] Section 457(f)(1) of the Code governs the tax treatment of a participant in a plan of an eligible employer, if the plan is not an eligible deferred compensation plan. There [sic] term "eligible employer" is defined in section 457(e)(1),

and includes a state or any political subdivision or any agency or instrumentality of a state, and any other tax-exempt organization. Section 457(f)(2) provides that section 457(f)(1) does not apply to a plan described in section 401(a) which includes a trust exempt from tax under section 501(a), to an annuity plan or contract described in section 403, [or] to that portion of any plan which consists of a trust to which section 402(b) applies.

[8] In general, section 457(f)(1)(A) of the Code provides that the amount of compensation that is deferred under a plan subject to section 457(f)(1) is included in a participant's or beneficiary's gross income for the first taxable year in which there is no substantial risk of forfeiture of the rights to the compensation. Section 457(f)(3)(B) provides that for purposes of section 457(f), the rights of a person to compensation are subject to a substantial risk of forfeiture if such person's rights to such compensation are conditioned upon the future performance of substantial services by any individual.

[9] Section 83(a) of the Code provides that the excess (if any) of the fair market value of property transferred in connection with the performance of services over the amount paid (if any) for the property is includible in the gross income of the person who performed the services for the first taxable year in which the property becomes transferable or is not subject to a substantial risk of forfeiture.

[10] Section 1.83-3(c) of the Regulations provides that for purposes of section 83 and the regulations thereunder, whether a risk of forfeiture is substantial depends upon the facts and circumstances. A substantial risk of forfeiture exists where rights in property that are transferred are conditioned, directly or indirectly, upon the future performance of substantial services by any person, or the occurrence of a condition related to the purposes of the transfer, and the possibility of forfeiture is substantial if such condition is not satisfied. The regularity of the performance of services and the time spent in performing such services tend to indicate whether the services required by a condition are substantial or not.

[11] Section 1.83-3(c)(4), Example (1) of the Regulations provides an illustration of a substantial risk of forfeiture. In the Example a corporation transfers to an employee 100 shares of stock in the corporation, at $90 per share. Because the employee is obligated to sell the stock to the corporation at $90 per share if he terminates his employment with the corporation for any reason prior to the expiration of a two year period of employment, the employee's rights to the stock are subject to a substantial risk of forfeiture during this two year period. If the conditions on transfer are not satisfied, it is assumed that the forfeiture provision will be enforced.

[12] Section 1.83-3(e) of the Regulations provides that for purposes of section 83 the term "property" includes real and personal property other than money or an unfunded and unsecured promise to pay money or property in the future. Property also includes a beneficial interest in assets (including money) transferred or set aside from claims of the transferor's creditors, for example, in a trust or escrow account.

[13] Section 402(b) of the Code provides that contributions made by an employer to an employees' trust that is not exempt from tax under section 501(a) are included in the employee's gross income in accordance with section 83, except that the value of the employees' interest in the trust will be substituted for the fair market value of the property in applying section 83. Under section 1.402(b)-1(a)(1) of the Regulations, employer contributions to a nonexempt employee's trust are included as compensation in the employee's gross income for the taxable year in which the contribution is made, but only to the extent that the employee's interest in such contribution is substantially vested, as defined in the Regulations under section 83.

[14] Section 451(a) of the Code and section 1.451-1(a) of the Regulations provide that an item of gross income is includible in gross income for the taxable year in which actually or constructively received by a taxpayer using the cash receipts and disbursements method of accounting. Under section 1.451-2(a) of the regulations, income is constructively received in the taxable year during which it is credited to a taxpayer's account or set apart or otherwise made available so that the taxpayer may draw on it at any time. However, income is not constructively received if the taxpayer's control of its receipt is subject to substantial limitations or restrictions.

[15] Various revenue rulings have considered the tax consequences of nonqualified deferred compensation arrangements. Rev. Rul. 60-31, Situations 1-3, 1960-1 C.B. 174, holds that a mere promise to pay, not represented by notes or secured in any way, does not constitute receipt of income within the meaning of the cash receipts and reimbursements method of accounting. See also Rev. Rul. 69-650, 1969-2 C.B. 106, and Rev. Rul. 69-649, 1969-2 C.B. 106.

[16] Under the economic benefit doctrine, an employee has currently includible income from an economic or financial benefit received as compensation, though not in cash form. Economic benefit applies when assets are unconditionally and irrevocably paid into a fund or trust to be used for the employee's sole benefit. Sproull v. Commissioner, 16 T.C. 244 (1951), aff'd per curiam, 194 F.2d 541 (6th Cir. 1952), Rev. Rul. 60-31, Situation 4. In Rev. Rul. 72-25, 1972-1 C.B. 127, and Rev. Rul. 68-99, 1968-1 C.B. 193, an employee does not receive income as a result of the employer's purchase of an insurance contract to provide a source of funds for deferred compensation because the insurance contract is the employer's asset, subject to claims of the employer's creditors.

[17] Section 301.7701-4(a) of the Procedure and Administration Regulations provides that, generally, an arrangement will be treated as a trust if it can be shown that the purpose of the arrangement is to vest in trustees the responsibility for the protection and conservation of property for beneficiaries who cannot share in the discharge of this responsibility and, therefore, are not associates in a joint enterprise for the conduct of business for profit.

[18] Section 671 of the Code provides that where a grantor shall be treated as the owner of any portion of a trust under subpart E, part I, subchapter J, chapter 1 of the Code, there shall then be included in computing the taxable income and credits of the grantor those items of income, deductions, and cred-

its against tax of the trust which are attributable to that portion of the trust to the extent that such items would be taken into account under chapter 1 in computing taxable income or credits against tax of an individual.

[19] Section 677(a)(2) of the Code provides that the grantor shall be treated as the owner of any portion of a trust whose income without the approval or consent of any adverse party, is, or, in the discretion of the grantor or a nonadverse party, or both, may be held or accumulated for the future distribution to the grantor.

[20] Section 1.677(a)-1(d) of the Regulations provides that under section 677 of the Code, a grantor is, in general, treated as the owner of a portion of a trust whose income, or in the discretion of the grantor or a nonadverse party, or both, may be applied in discharge of a legal obligation of the grantor.

[21] Under the terms of the Trust, amounts have been placed in trust to provide deferred compensation benefits to Participants. However, the Trustee has the obligation to hold the Trust assets and income for the benefit of X's general creditors in the event of X's insolvency. The Trust agreement further provides that a Participant receives no beneficial ownership in or preferred claim on the trust assets. Therefore, although amounts are held in trust in the event of X's insolvency, they are fully within reach of X's general creditors, as are any other assets of X.

[22] Provided: (i) that creation of the Plan does not cause it to be other than "unfunded" for purposes of Title I of the Employee Retirement Income Security Act of 1974, (ii) that the provision of the Plan requiring use of Plan assets to satisfy claims of the [sic] X's general creditors in the event of X's insolvency is enforceable by such creditors under federal and state law, and, (iii) that the amendments proposed are adopted by X as part of the Plan, and based on the information submitted and representations made, we conclude that effective with the date of this ruling:

The Plan is neither an eligible deferred compensation [plan] within the meaning of section 457(b) of the Code nor exempt from the application of section 457(f)(1) of the Code by any of the exceptions set forth in section 457(f)(2).

Benefits under the Plan are subject to a substantial risk of forfeiture with respect to a Participant until that Participant's distribution date has been reached.

Benefit amounts under the Plan will be includible in a Participant's or beneficiary's gross income on the distribution date.

Earnings, if any, that accumulate on benefit amounts after the expiration of the substantial risk of forfeiture are includible in a Participant's or beneficiary's gross income when paid or made available in accordance with the rules of section 72 of the Code. See section 1.457-3(a)(2) and (3).

A Participant that irrevocably elects installment payments of all or a part of the deferral amount will nevertheless include the entire deferral account balance in gross income on the distribution date because such amount is no longer subject to a substantial risk of forfeiture.

The Trust is classified as a trust within the meaning of section 301.7701-4(a) of the Regulations. Because the Trust's assets may be used to discharge X's obligations to Participants, X shall be treated as the owner of the Trust under section 677 of the Code. Accordingly, under section 671, there shall be included in computing the taxable income and credits of X all items of income, deductions, and credits against tax of the Trust.

The adoption of the Plan and the establishment and settlement of the Trust and the contribution of assets, including the crediting of earnings to the Trust, will not constitute a transfer of property within the meaning of section 83 of the Code and section 1.83-3(e) of the Regulations, and will not result in current realization of income by Participants under section 402(b) of the Code.

[23] Except as specifically ruled on above, no opinion is expressed as to the federal tax consequences of the above transaction under any other provision of the Code.

[24] This ruling is directed only to the taxpayer who requested it and applies only to the Plan if it is amended as proposed as of the date of this ruling. Section 6110(j)(3) of the Code provides that this ruling may not be used or cited as precedent.

Letter Ruling 9627007, Dated April 2, 1996

[Summary: The IRS ruled that the imposition of a five-year service condition under an ineligible deferred compensation plan is a substantial risk of forfeiture that defers the taxation of benefits.

The employer, a public agency in a state, adopted the plan to provide retirement benefits above the limits set by Code Sections 401(k), 415, and 457. The plan is not an eligible deferred compensation plan within the meaning of Code Section 457(b) and Treasury Regulations Section 1.457-2. Under the plan, the employer will contribute a stated monthly sum to a book account for the benefit of the participant. The participant or his beneficiary will be entitled to the full amount standing to the credit in the book account upon termination. However, the participant will forfeit the entire amount if he does not complete five continuous years of service, except in the case of his death or disability. Any rights created under the plan will be unsecured contractual rights. Benefits may not be alienated or anticipated.

The IRS concluded that benefits under the ineligible deferred compensation plan will not be income to the participant until the participant completes five continuous years of service with the employer, dies, or becomes disabled.]

Letter Ruling 9623027, Dated March 7, 1996

[Summary: The IRS ruled that an employer's creation of a non-qualified deferred compensation plan and trust and the employer's contribution of assets to the trust will not trigger income to a participant or a beneficiary under the constructive receipt doctrine or the economic benefit doctrine.

The employer, which is exempt under Code Section 501(c)(3), established the deferred compensation plan and trust to benefit a select group of management or highly compensated employees. A participant vests in the plan's deferred benefits if the participant reaches retirement age, dies, or becomes disabled while employed with the employer. The employer established the trust to assist in providing assets from which to pay its obligations to the participants. The plan and trust both provide that all amounts deferred are solely the property and rights of the employer and are subject to the claims of the employer's creditors. The participant's interests are no greater than the interests of any of the employer's general unsecured creditors.

The IRS concluded that benefits under the nonqualified deferred compensation plan and trust will not be income to a recipient until the participant reaches retirement age, dies, or becomes disabled.]

[1] This responds to your request for a ruling submitted in your letter of November 3, 1995 and subsequent correspondence on behalf of Entity E regarding the proper income tax treatment of the nonqualified supplemental retirement benefits provided pursuant to its supplemental executive retirement plan (the "Plan") and the associated grantor trust under sections 83, 402(b), and 457(f) of the Internal Revenue Code of 1986 ("Code"). Entity E is represented to be a nonprofit corporation that is exempt from federal income tax under section 501(c)(3) of the Code.

[2] The Plan provides supplemental retirement benefits to certain employees in a "select group of management or highly compensated employees" designated by E's board of directors. The benefits payable to the participant or his beneficiary are determined in accordance with the Plan. The Plan provides for a risk of forfeiture by stating that a participant generally only vests in the deferred benefits (i.e., such amounts become nonforfeitable and taxable) upon his remaining in E's employ until his normal retirement age. The Plan also states that no employee will be designated as a participant later than two years before he attains normal retirement age.

[3] Generally, if the participant's employment with E is terminated prior to his attaining the normal retirement age set by the Plan, all his rights and benefits thereunder are forfeited and E has no further obligation to him under the Plan. However, a participant's accrued benefit also vests and becomes nonforfeitable if the employee dies while employed by E or if he separates from service due to disability as set forth in the Plan. The Plan also provides that at the beginning of the month following the month when an Employee's accrued benefit becomes nonforfeitable (and taxable), Entity E will pay his accrued benefit under the Plan to him (or to his beneficiary after his death) in a lump-sum. In addition, the Plan does not include provisions that limit the amounts deferrable under the Plan to the lesser of $7,500 or 33⅓ percent of the participant's includible compensation.

[4] To assist it in providing assets from which to pay the benefit obligations to the participants, Entity E has established by a trust agreement, drafted to

conform to the requirements of Rev. Proc. 92-64, 1992-2 C.B. 422, with an independent third party ("Trustee"), a trust to which E intends to contribute funds or other property from which accrued supplemental retirement benefits may be paid. The Trustee has the duty to invest the trust assets in accordance with the terms of the trust agreement. At all times, the trust assets will be subject to the claims of E's general creditors if E becomes insolvent, as defined in the trust agreement. E's Chief Executive Officer and its Board of Trustees have the duty to inform the Trustee of E's insolvency. Upon receipt of such notice or other written allegations of E's insolvency, the Trustee will suspend the payment of benefits with respect to participants in E's Plan. If the Trustee determines in good faith that E is not insolvent or is no longer insolvent, the Trustee will resume the payment of benefits. If E is insolvent, the Trustee shall hold the trust corpus for the benefit of E's general creditors.

[5] The Plan and trust agreement both provide that all amounts deferred under the Plan, all property and rights purchased with such amounts, and all income attributable to such amounts, property, or rights will remain (until made available to the participant or beneficiary) solely the property and rights of the employer, subject only to the claims of E's general creditors. Participants have only the status of general unsecured creditors of their employer E. The rights of any participant or beneficiary to payments pursuant to the Plan and trust agreement are nonassignable, and their interests in benefits under the Plan and the trust agreement are not subject to attachment, garnishment, pledge, encumbrance or other legal process.

[6] Section 457(a) of the Code provides that in the case of a participant in an eligible deferred compensation plan, any amount of compensation deferred under the plan and any income attributable to the amounts so deferred shall be includible in gross income only for the taxable year in which such compensation or other income is paid or otherwise made available to the participant or beneficiary.

[7] Section 457(b) of the Code, and section 1.457-2 of the Income Tax Regulations define the term "eligible deferred compensation plan." Those provisions contain the various requirements for an eligible plan, including rules for participation, deferral of compensation, and payment of benefits.

[8] Section 457(f)(1) of the Code governs the tax treatment of a participant in a plan of an eligible employer, if the plan provides for a deferral of compensation, but is not an eligible deferred compensation plan. The term "eligible employer" is defined in section 457(e)(1), and includes a state or any political subdivision or any agency or instrumentality of a state, and any other tax-exempt organization. Section 457(f)(2) states that section 457(f)(1) does not apply to a plan described in section 401(a) which includes a trust exempt from tax under section 501(a), to an annuity plan or contract described in section 403, to that portion of any plan which consists of a transfer of property described in section 83, or to that portion of any plan which consists of a trust to which section 402(b) applies.

[9] In general, section 457(f)(1)(A) of the Code provides that the amount of compensation which is deferred under a plan subject to section 457(f)(1) is

included in the participant's or beneficiary's gross income for the first taxable year in which there is no substantial risk of forfeiture of the rights to the compensation. Section 457(f)(3)(B) provides that, for purposes of section 457(f), the rights of a person to compensation are subject to a substantial risk of forfeiture if such person's rights to such compensation are conditioned upon the future performance of substantial services by any individual.

[10] Section 1.83-3(c) of the Income Tax Regulations provides that for purposes of section 83 and the regulations thereunder, whether a risk of forfeiture is substantial depends upon the facts and circumstances. A substantial risk of forfeiture exists where rights in property that are transferred are conditioned, directly or indirectly, upon the future performance of substantial services by any person, or the occurrence of a condition related to a purpose of the transfer, and the possibility of forfeiture is substantial if such condition is not satisfied. The regularity of the performance of services and the time spent in performing such services tend to indicate whether services required by a condition are substantial. See section 1.83-3(c)(2).

[11] Section 1.83-3(c)(4), Example (1) of the regulations provides, by way of example, that where a corporation transfers to an employee 100 shares of stock in the corporation, at $90 per share, and the employee is obligated to sell the stock to the Corporation at $90 per share if he terminates his employment with the Corporation for any reason prior to the expiration of a two year period of employment, the employee's rights to the stock are subject to a substantial risk of forfeiture during such two year period. If the conditions on transfer are not satisfied, it is assumed that the forfeiture provision will be enforced.

[12] A participant will be entitled to receive benefits under the Plan only if he continues in full-time employment with the sponsoring employer E until he has attained normal retirement age, dies, or terminates service due to disability. Based on these facts, a participant's benefits under the Plan are subject to a substantial risk of forfeiture until they vest. Accordingly, under section 457(f) of the Internal Revenue Code, no contributions or benefits are taxable to a participant or his beneficiary until the benefits vest under the terms of the Plan.

[13] Section 83(a) of the Internal Revenue Code provides that the excess (if any) of the fair market value of property transferred in connection with the performance of services over the amount paid (if any) for the property is includible in the gross income of the person who performed the services for the first taxable year in which the property becomes transferable or is not subject to a substantial risk of forfeiture.

[14] Section 1.83-3(e) of the Income Tax Regulations provides that for purposes of section 83 the term "property" includes real and personal property other than money or an unfunded and unsecured promise to pay money or property in the future. Property also includes a beneficial interest in assets (including money) transferred or set aside from claims of the transferor's creditors, for example, in a trust or escrow account.

[15] Section 402(b) of the Code provides that contributions made by an employer to an employee's trust that is not exempt from tax under section 501(a)

are included in the employee's gross income in accordance with section 83, except that the value of the employee's interest in the trust will be substituted for the fair market value of the property in applying section 83. Under section 1.402(b)-1(a)(1) of the regulations, an employer's contributions to a nonexempt employees' trust are included as compensation in an employee's gross income for the taxable year in which the contribution is made, but only to the extent that the employee's interest in such contribution is substantially vested, as defined in the regulations under section 83.

[16] Section 451(a) of the Code and section 1.451-1(a) of the regulations provide that an item of gross income is includible in gross income for the taxable year in which actually or constructively received by a taxpayer using the cash receipts and disbursements method of accounting. Under section 1.451-2(a) of the regulations, income is constructively received in the taxable year during which it is credited to a taxpayer's account or set apart or otherwise made available so that the taxpayer may draw on it at any time. However, income is not constructively received if the taxpayer's control of its receipt is subject to substantial limitations or restrictions.

[17] Under the economic benefit doctrine, an employee has currently includible income from an economic or financial benefit received as compensation, though not in cash form. Economic benefit applies when assets are unconditionally and irrevocably paid into a fund or trust to be used for the employee's sole benefit. Sproull v. Commissioner, 16 T.C. 244 (1951), aff'd per curiam, 195 F.2d 541 (6th. Cir. 1952), Rev. Rul. 60-31, Situation 4. In Rev. Rul. 72-25, 1972-1 C.B. 127, and Rev. Rul. 68-99, 1968-1 C.B. 193, an employee does not receive income as a result of the employer's purchase of an insurance contract to provide a source of funds for deferred compensation because the insurance contract is the employer's asset, subject to claims of the employer's creditors.

[18] Section 301.7701-4(a) of the Procedure and Administration Regulations provides that, generally, an arrangement will be treated as a trust if it can be shown that the purposes of the arrangement is to vest in trustees the responsibility for the protection and conservation of property for beneficiaries who cannot share in the discharge of this responsibility and, therefore, are not associates in a joint enterprise for the conduct of a business for profit.

[19] Section 671 of the Code provides that where a grantor shall be treated as the owner of any portion of a trust under Subpart E, part I, subchapter J, chapter 1 of the Code, there shall then be included in computing the taxable income and credits of the grantor those items of income, deductions, and credits against tax of the trust which are attributable to that portion of the trust to the extent that such items would be taken into account under chapter 1 in computing taxable income or credits against tax of an individual.

[20] Section 677(a)(2) of the Code provides that the grantor shall be treated as the owner of any portion of a trust whose income without the approval or consent of any adverse party is, or, in the discretion of the grantor or a nonadverse party, or both, may be held or accumulated for future distribution to the grantor.

[21] Section 1.677(a)-1(d) of the regulations provides that under section 677 of the Code, a grantor is, in general, treated as the owner of a portion of a trust whose income is, or, in the discretion of the grantor or a nonadverse party, or both, may be applied in discharge of a legal obligation of the grantor.

[22] Under the terms of the trust, assets may be placed in trust to provide deferred supplemental benefits to the Plan's participants. However, the Trustee has the obligation to hold the trust assets and income for the benefit of E's general creditors in the event of E's insolvency. The trust agreement further provides that a participant receives no beneficial ownership in or preferred claim on the trust assets. Therefore, assets are held in trust and, in the event of E's insolvency, they are fully within reach of its creditors, as are any other assets of E.

[23] Provided (i) that the creation of the trust does not cause the Plan to be other than "unfunded" for purposes of Title I of the Employee Retirement Income Security Act of 1974, and (ii) that the provisions of the trust requiring use of the trust assets to satisfy the claims of general creditors in the event of E's insolvency is [sic] enforceable by E's creditors under federal and state law, and based on the information submitted and representations made, we conclude that:

Neither the adoption of the Plan, nor the designation of Plan participants, nor the creation of the trust, nor E's contributions of assets to the trust will cause any amount to be included in the gross income of a participant or his beneficiary under the cash receipts and disbursements method of accounting, pursuant to either the constructive receipt doctrine of section 451, the economic benefit doctrine, or section 457(f).

Benefits under the Plan are subject to a substantial risk of forfeiture until the participant attains normal retirement age under the Plan, dies or terminates employment due to disability. Accordingly, under section 457(f)(1)(A), amounts credited by the participant's employer under the Plan are included in the gross income of the participant or his beneficiary in the first taxable year in which participant attains normal retirement age under the Plan, dies or separates from service due to disability.

The Trust will be classified as a trust within the meaning of section 301.7701-4(a) of the Procedure and Administration Regulations. Because the principal and income of the Trust may be applied in discharge of legal obligations of the grantor, under section 677 of the Code Entity E shall be treated as the owner of the trust. Accordingly, under section 671, there shall be included in computing E's taxable income and credits, those items of income, deductions, and credits against tax of the trust, subject to the provisions of the Internal Revenue Code applicable to section 501(c)(3) organizations.

Neither the adoption of the Plan, nor the designation of Plan participants, nor the creation of the trust, nor the contributions of assets to the trust, nor the crediting of earnings on those assets will constitute the transfer of property to participating employees for purposes of section 83 of the Internal Revenue Code or section 1.83-3(e) of the regulations or an employer's contribution to an employees' trust under section 402(b) of the Internal Revenue Code.

[24] This ruling is contingent upon the adoption of the amendment to the Plan submitted on December 21, 1995 and is directed only to E, the entity which requested it. Section 6110(j)(3) of the Internal Revenue Code provides that this ruling may not be used or cited as precedent. No opinion is expressed concerning the timing of the inclusion in income of amounts deferred under any deferred compensation plan other than the Plan as revised by the December 21, 1995 amendment. If the Plan or trust is substantially amended, this ruling letter may not necessarily remain in effect.

[25] Temporary or final regulations pertaining to one or more of the issues addressed in this ruling have not yet been adopted. Therefore, this ruling may be modified or revoked if the adopted temporary or final regulations are inconsistent with any conclusion in the ruling. See section 11.04 of Rev. Proc. 96-1, 1996-1 I.R.B. 39. However, when the criteria in section 11.05 of Rev. Proc. 96-1 are satisfied, a ruling is not revoked or modified retroactively except in rare or unusual circumstances.

Letter Ruling 9619029, Dated February 2, 1996

[1] This is in response to your letter of June 29, 1995, requesting a ruling on behalf of the Board, concerning the State Plan and the Model Plan (collectively, the "Plans"). State X intends the Plans to be eligible deferred compensation plans under section 457 of the Internal Revenue Code of 1986 (the "Code"). Each Plan has been or will be adopted only by employers that are state or local governmental entities described in Code section 457(e)(1)(A). Pursuant to the laws of State X, the Board established the State Plan for the benefit of eligible employees of State X and of other public jurisdictions in State X that adopt the State Plan. The Board also promulgated the Model Plan, which may be adopted by local public employers in State X for the benefit of their employees.

[2] In 1991 the Internal Revenue Service (the "Service") ruled that the Plans as amended and restated at that time were eligible state deferred compensation plans as defined in Code section 457. The Plans have been amended and restated again to include several amendments effective in 1996 (the "Amendments"). The Amendments allow segregation of accounts on behalf of and payments to an alternate payee pursuant to a Plan Certified Domestic Relations Order (a "PCDRO"). A PCDRO is defined in the Plans as a domestic relations order determined by a specified agency to meet the requirements of a qualified domestic relations order within the meaning of Code section 414(p).

[3] The Plans as amended provide that no distribution may be made to an alternate payee before the amount distributed would otherwise be available to the participant, that the rights of an alternate payee may never be greater than those of the participant, and that an alternate payee may not receive a distribution for an unforeseeable emergency. An alternate payee may direct the investment of amounts segregated on his or her behalf.

[4] Several unrelated Amendments have also been made. Any local employer that adopted the Model Plan before the Amendments become effective may adopt any, all, or none of the Amendments. Any local employer adopting the Model Plan thereafter must adopt the Model Plan including all of the Amendments.

[5] Under the Plans an employee may elect to defer compensation he or she would have received for services rendered to an employer in any taxable year. The deferral extends until the employee reaches age 70½, separates from service, or has an unforeseeable emergency. The election to defer compensation must be made by the 10th of the calendar month before the month for which the compensation is earned (in some cases earlier). The Plans provide for a maximum amount that may be deferred by a participant in any taxable year and for a catch-up computation for amounts deferred for one or more of the participant's last three taxable years ending before normal retirement age under the Plans. The amounts that may be deferred under the annual maximum limitation and the catch-up provision are within the limitations set out in section 457 of the Code.

[6] With certain limitations, a participant or beneficiary (or an alternate payee as described above) may elect the manner in which his or her deferred amounts will be distributed. The election must be made before the date that payments must commence. If the participant or beneficiary fails to make a timely election concerning distribution of the deferred amounts, distributions are made at the time and in the manner prescribed by the Plan. Regardless of who makes the election, the manner and time of benefits must meet the distribution requirements of sections 401(a)(9) and 457(d)(2) of the Code.

[7] The Plans also provide that all amounts deferred under the Plans, all property and rights purchased with such amounts, and all income attributable to such amounts, property, or rights will remain (until paid or made available to the participant or beneficiary) solely the property and rights of the employer, subject only to the claims of the employer's general creditors. The rights of any participant or beneficiary to payments under either Plan are generally nonassignable.

[8] Section 457 of the Code provides rules for the deferral of compensation by an individual participating in an eligible deferred compensation plan (as defined in section 457(b)). Section 457(a) provides that any amount of compensation deferred under the plan or any income attributable to that amount is includable in gross income only for the taxable year in which such compensation or other income is paid or otherwise made available to the participant or beneficiary.

[9] Section 457(b)(6) requires, inter alia, that an eligible deferred compensation plan provide that all amounts of compensation deferred under the plan, all rights purchased with such amounts, and all income attributable to such amounts, property, or rights remain (until properly made available to the participant or other beneficiary) solely the property and rights of the employer (not restricted to providing benefits under the plan). They must be subject only to the claims of the employer's general creditors.

[10] Section 457(b)(5) provides that an eligible deferred compensation plan must meet the distribution requirements of section 457(d). Section 457(d)(1)(A) requires an eligible plan to provide that amounts will not be made available to participants or beneficiaries earlier than (i) the calendar year in which the participant attains age 70½, (ii) when the participant is separated from service with the employer, or (iii) when the participant is faced with an unforeseeable emergency as determined under Treasury regulations. Section 1.457-2(h)(4) of the Income Tax Regulations defines an unforeseeable emergency as a severe financial hardship to the participant resulting from a sudden and unexpected illness or accident of the participant or a dependent, loss of the participant's property due to casualty, or other similar extraordinary and unforeseeable circumstances arising as a result of events beyond the control of the participant. Since a divorce or separation does not itself create an unforeseeable emergency, a participant who is still employed by the employer and who is under age 70½ cannot demand payment. Therefore an alternate payee may not receive payment until the participant separates from service or reaches age 70½.

[11] Section 457(f) provides that if a state governmental plan is or becomes an ineligible plan then the deferred compensation is included in the gross income of the participant or beneficiary for the first taxable year in which there is no substantial risk of forfeiture of the rights to the compensation. The tax treatment of any amount made available under [sic] to a participant or beneficiary is determined under section 72.

[12] In essence, an eligible section 457 state governmental plan is an unfunded, nonqualified deferred compensation plan in which the employee has only the employer's contractual promise that benefits will be paid, as provided in section 457(b)(6). Under that paragraph and section 1.457-2(j) of the regulations, the employee cannot have any interest in employer assets, and any benefits must be paid from funds available to the employer's general creditors. In other words a section 457 plan is not treated as a qualified exempt trust described in section 401(a). In addition an eligible plan must meet the section 457(d) distribution requirements described above. A section 457 plan would violate these provisions if the participant or anyone else received an interest in employer assets earlier than the earliest date established in section 457(d)(1)(A).

[13] Based upon the provisions of the plan summarized above, and the documents presented, we conclude as follows:

The State Plan as amended and restated is an eligible deferred compensation plan as defined in section 457 of the Code. Amounts of compensation deferred under the State Plan, including any income attributable to the deferred compensation, will not be includable in gross income until the taxable year or years in which amounts are paid or otherwise made available to an employee, beneficiary, or alternate payee under the terms of the State Plan.

The Model Plan as amended and restated (or including some but not all of the Amendments) is an eligible deferred compensation plan as defined in section 457 of the Code. A local employer that is an eligible employer under

Code section 457(e)(1)(A) and that adopts the Model Plan as amended and restated (without change other than adopting some but not all of the Amendments) in accordance with the Board's Rules and Regulations may rely on this ruling that its plan is an eligible plan. Amounts of compensation deferred under the Model Plan as adopted by a local employer, including any income attributable to the deferred compensation, will not be includable in gross income until the taxable year or years in which amounts are paid or otherwise made available to an employee, beneficiary, or alternate payee under the terms of the Model Plan.

[14] No opinion is expressed concerning the time of inclusion in income of amounts deferred under any deferred compensation plan other than the Plans. If a Plan is modified, this ruling will not necessarily remain applicable. Also, no opinion is expressed concerning which taxpayer includes any distribution to an alternate payee in gross income. This ruling is directed only to State X. Section 6110(j)(3) of the Code provides that it may not be used or cited as precedent.

[15] Temporary or final regulations pertaining to one or more of the issues addressed in this ruling have not yet been adopted. Therefore this ruling may be modified or revoked if the adopted temporary or final regulations are inconsistent with any conclusion in the ruling. See section 11.04 of Rev. Proc. 95-1, 1995-1 I.R.B. 9, 41. When the criteria in section 11.05 of Rev. Proc. 95-1 are satisfied, however, a ruling is not revoked or modified retroactively except in rare or unusual circumstances.

Letter Ruling 9549003, Dated August 30, 1995

This replies to your request for a ruling submitted on behalf of X, an eligible employer within the meaning of section 457(e)(1)(B) of the Internal Revenue Code ("Code"). X maintains a qualified plan for its staff and an unfunded, nonqualified plan for its executive officers. X proposes to amend its qualified plan to include participation of its executive officers and to contribute amounts to the qualified plan for the benefit of those executives. X, then, intends to reduce or offset X's unfunded promises to its officers by the benefit these officers will receive through the qualified plan. You request a ruling that this transaction will not adversely effect the application of the grandfather rule of section 457 of the Code with respect to any remaining unfunded portion of the nonqualified benefit and that the funding of any portion of that benefit through a qualified plan will not cause Individuals A and B to recognize income with respect to the funded portion until the date such benefit is actually received.

X's Constitution mandates that, upon leaving office, its elected President and Secretary-Treasurer ("Executive Officers") will receive certain defined retirement and survivor benefits if such elected official has served 5 years as an Executive Officer and has either attained age 65 or provided 20 years of service to X. This is referred to as the "Constitutional Promise." The Constitution is silent as to how X should prepare to fulfill this obligation. You represent that X has never adopted a more formal deferred compensation plan with respect to this obligation and that for more than 50 years, X has treated this obligation as a nonqualified, unfunded deferred compensation plan pursuant to which amounts were paid from X's general assets and no amounts were set aside from X's general creditors.

For its other employees, X provides retirement and survivor benefits through a defined benefit plan and trust agreement ("Plan Q"). Plan Q specifically excludes X's President and Secretary-Treasurer from participating in it. You represent that Plan Q satisfies the qualified plan requirements under section 401(a) of the Code and constitutes a qualified trust within the meaning of section 501(a) of the Code.

You have made the following additional representations. The fixed formula in the Constitutional Promise has remained the same since before 1985. Individual A (who has been an elected official since 1969, who has credit under Plan Q for pre-officer service, and who is over age 65) has announced he will retire on Date a. Individual B (who has been an elected official since 1979, who has credit under Plan Q for pre-officer service, and who is also over age 65) will become X's President after Individual A retires. Thereafter, it is anticipated a new Secretary-Treasurer will be elected at X's forthcoming convention.

X proposes to amend Plan Q to provide that, for persons employed on or after Date b, a Participant shall also include X's President and Secretary-Treasurer. The proposed amendment also provides that Covered Employment, as defined in Plan Q, shall include all periods of compensation earned by these Executive Officers for services provided to X both before and after the date these Executive Officers are elected to their positions.

You represent that X intends to contribute amounts to Plan Q for the benefit of Individuals A and B to the extent possible and consistent with the defined benefit formula of Plan Q. You further represent that X does not intend to amend the fixed formula of the Constitutional Promise with respect to Individuals A and B, but will offset the amounts due under the Constitutional Promise by the benefits provided these individuals under Plan Q. To the extent the Constitutional Promise exceeds the benefit paid from Plan Q, X will pay any remaining amounts due under the Constitutional Promise on an unfunded basis only.

With respect to the amendment to Plan Q, you represent that because both Individuals A and B have a sufficient number of years as participants in Plan Q, the limitations imposed by section 415(b)(5) will not be violated. You also represent that any benefit paid from Plan Q to any of X's highly compensated Executive Officers is the same benefit non-highly compensated employees will receive and that the proposed amendment to Plan Q will not cause the plan to fail to satisfy the discrimination rules of section 401(a)(4) of the Code.

Section 1107 of the Tax Reform Act of 1986 ("TRA '86") amended section 457 of the Code to apply its restrictions and limitations to unfunded deferred compensation plans maintained by non-governmental, tax-exempt organizations, effective for taxable years beginning after December 31, 1986, except as provided under section 1107(c) of the Act. Section 1107(c)(3)(B) addresses non-governmental, tax-exempt organizations only and provides that section 457 of the Code does not apply to amounts deferred under a nonqualified deferred compensation plan of such organization that:

were deferred from taxable years beginning before January 1, 1987, or

are deferred from taxable years beginning after December 31, 1986, pursuant to an agreement that

was in writing on August 16, 1986, and

on such date, provides for a deferral for each taxable year covered by the agreement of a fixed amount or of an amount determined pursuant to a fixed formula.

Section 1107(c)(3)(B) also provides that if there is any modification of the fixed amount or fixed formula, section 457 will apply to any taxable year ending after the date on which the modification is effective. As amended by section 6064(d)(3) of the Technical and Miscellaneous Revenue Act of 1988, section 1107(c)(3)(B) further provides that the grandfather provision shall only apply to individuals who were covered under the nonqualified plan on August 16, 1986.

Notice 87-13, 1987-1 C.B. 432, gives guidance, in the form of questions and answers, with respect to certain provisions of TRA '86, including section 1107. A-28 of Notice 87-13 provides that section 457 of the Code shall not apply to deferrals of compensation that would have been paid or made available (but for the deferred compensation plan) in taxable years of an individual beginning after December 31, 1986, under a deferred compensation plan of a tax-exempt organization to the extent that such deferrals were fixed pursuant to a written plan on August 16, 1986. For purposes of this grandfather rule, in the case of a deferred compensation plan that is in the nature of a defined benefit plan, deferrals of amounts that are allocable to taxable years of the individual are to be treated as deferrals of compensation that would have been paid or made available in such taxable years (but for the deferred compensation plan).

A deferral with respect to an individual is treated as fixed on August 16, 1986, to the extent that a written plan on such date provided for such deferral for each taxable year of the plan and such deferral was determinable on such date under written terms of the plan as a fixed dollar amount, a fixed percentage of a fixed base amount (i.e., regular salary, commissions, bonus, or total compensation) or an amount to be determined by a fixed formula.

A-28 of Notice 87-13 further provides that an amount of deferral pursuant to a written plan on August 16, 1986, will cease to be treated as fixed on such date, and thus will be subject to section 457, as of the effective date of any modification to the written plan that directly or indirectly alters the fixed dollar amount, the fixed percentage, the fixed base amount to which the percentage is applied, or the fixed formula. An example of a fixed formula is a deferred compensation plan that is in the nature of a defined benefit plan under which the deferred compensation to be paid to an employee in the future (i.e., on or after separation from service) is in the form of an annual benefit equal to 1 percent of each of the employee's years of service with the employer times the employee's final average salary.

The legislative history of TRA '86 explains that Congress recognized that the tension between an employee's desire to defer tax on compensation and the employer's desire to obtain a current deduction for compensation paid is not present in the case of a tax-exempt organization. Accordingly, Congress sought to limit the amount of compensation that could be deferred on a non-qualified basis by an employee of a tax-exempt organization. At the same time, Congress enacted more restrictive distribution rules for eligible section 457 plans so that the distribution rules would be similar to those of Congressionally favored qualified plans. See, H.R. Rep. No. 99-426, 99th Cong., 2d Sess. pt. 2, at 700 (1986).

Section 457 of the Code has never limited the amounts that may be deferred through a qualified plan and Congress has never barred tax-exempt organizations from adopting qualified plans or prohibited their executive officers from participation in such plans. Section 457(f)(2) specifically excepts from the limitations of section 457 amounts contributed to qualified plans, described in section 401(a) of the Code, and tax-favored, funded section 403(b) annuities. Additionally, section 457(f)(2) excepts from the limitations of section 457 amounts deferred under nonqualified, funded arrangements that are taxed under sections 83, 402(b), and 403(c). Like section 457, sections 83, 402(b), and 403(c) specifically exclude amounts contributed to qualified plans from their application.

The legislative history of TRA '86 clarifies that Congress anticipated that the limitations imposed on nonqualified plans of tax-exempt organizations would apply to plans providing benefits that supplement the limited benefits paid under tax-favored qualified plans. Consistent with this rationale, section 1107 of TRA '86 contains no prohibition against the use of offsetting a mere promise to pay through the use of a qualified plan. Rather, the grandfather provision of section 1107 looks to whether the fixed amount or the amount determined by a fixed formula under a grandfathered plan has been modified, either directly or indirectly. See, H.R. Rep. No. 99-426.

X's Constitution contains a fixed defined benefit formula that was in writing on August 16, 1986 and that has not been modified since that date. The benefit under this formula has been paid on a nonqualified, unfunded basis and, as such, qualifies for exclusion from section 457 with respect to all individuals covered by the Constitutional Promise on or before August 16, 1986. Nothing in X's Constitution prohibits the fulfilling of X's Constitutional Promise through a qualified plan. Also, the participation of X's Executive Officials in the qualified plan does not serve to increase or reduce the total amount due those officials with respect to X's Constitutional Promise. Thus, the contribution of amounts to a qualified plan for the benefit of Individuals A and B and the use of those qualified plan benefits to offset X's obligations under the

Constitutional Promise will not serve to modify, either directly or indirectly, the defined benefit formula set out in X's Constitution.

Accordingly, based on the documents submitted and the representations made, we conclude that:

The use of benefits received through a qualified plan to off-set X's Constitutional Promise to its Executive Officials will not adversely affect the application of the grandfather rule of section 457 to the portion of the Constitutional Promise that will remain to be paid on an unfunded basis.

For purposes of the grandfather rules of section 457 of the Code only, the use of funded and tax-favored qualified plan benefits to offset any part of X's unfunded Constitutional Promise to Individual A and Individual B will not cause Individual A or Individual B to be taxed on any part of the Constitutional Promise until amounts pursuant to that promise are paid or made available to that individual.

This ruling only concerns the effect of the proposed qualified plan amendment on the grandfather status of the Constitutional Promise with respect to Individuals A and B. No opinion is expressed with regard to the status of the qualified plan or the tax consequences of the proposed transaction with respect to the qualified plan. Additionally, if the fixed formula for the Constitutional Promise with respect to Individuals A and B is later modified, this ruling will not apply to amounts deferred after the modification.

This ruling is directed only to X. It applies to no individuals other than Individuals A and B. Section 6110(j)(3) of the Code provides that it may not be used or cited as precedent.

Temporary or final regulations pertaining to one or more of the issues addressed in this ruling have not yet been adopted. Therefore, this ruling may be modified or revoked if the adopted temporary or final regulations are inconsistent with any conclusion in the ruling. See section 11.04 of Rev. Proc. 95-1, 1995-1 I.R.B. 41. However, when the criteria in section 11.05 of Rev. Proc. 95-1 are satisfied, a ruling is not revoked or modified retroactively except in rare or unusual circumstances.

Letter Ruling 9543010, Dated July 24, 1995

This responds to your letter of February 3, 1995 and subsequent correspondence, on behalf of Entity E, requesting a ruling concerning the proposed amended Deferred Compensation Plan (the "Plan") which E intends to be an eligible deferred compensation plan under section 457 of the Internal Revenue Code of 1986. You have represented that Entity E is a state or local governmental entity described in section 457(e)(1)(A). Under the Plan an employee may elect to defer compensation he would have received for services rendered to E in any taxable year until attainment of age 70½, death, separation from service with E, or until the occurrence of an unforeseeable emergency. The election to defer compensation must be filed no later than the 15th of the month prior to the beginning of the month for which the compensation is earned. The Plan provides for a maximum amount that may be deferred by a participant in any taxable year and also provides for a catch-up computation for amounts deferred for one or more of the participant's last three taxable years ending before he attains normal retirement age under the plan. The amounts that may be deferred under the annual maximum limitation and the catch-up provision are within the limitations set out in section 457.

With certain limitations, a participant or his beneficiary (including an alternate payee as described below) may elect the manner in which his deferred amounts will be distributed. The election must be made prior to the date any such payment must commence to the participant or the beneficiary. Regardless of who makes the election, the manner and time of benefit payout must meet the distribution requirements of sections 401(a)(9) and 457(d)(2) of the Code.

The Plan further provides that all amounts deferred under the plan, all property and rights purchased with such amounts, and all income attributable to such amounts, property, or rights will remain (until made available to the participant or beneficiary) solely the property and rights of E, subject only to the claims of E's general creditors. The rights of any participant or beneficiary to payments pursuant to the Plan are generally nonassignable.

The plan provides that distribution to a former spouse (an "alternate payee") pursuant to a domestic relations order may occur or commence only when the participant himself becomes eligible to receive distributions under the Plan and under section 457(d). If an alternate payee receives rights to amounts in a participant's account under a domestic relations order and makes certain elections, the Plan may maintain a bookkeeping account for the participant's alternate payee. In certain cases, the Plan permits an alternate payee to make certain elections concerning distribution from his or her account established pursuant to a domestic relations order.

Section 457 of the Code provides rules for the deferral of compensation by an individual participating in an eligible deferred compensation plan (as defined in section 457(b)).

Section 457(a) of the Code provides that in the case of a participant in an eligible deferred compensation plan, any amount of compensation deferred under the plan and any income attributable to the amounts so deferred shall be includible in gross income only for the taxable year in which such compensation or other income is paid or otherwise made available to the participant or beneficiary.

Section 457(b)(5) prescribes that an eligible deferred compensation plan must meet the distribution requirements of section 457(d).

Section 457(b)(6) prescribes that, among other things that a section 457 plan must do to be an eligible deferred compensation plan, it must provide that all amounts of compensation deferred under the plan, all rights purchased with such amounts, and all income attributable to such amounts, property, or rights shall remain (until properly made available to the participant or other beneficiary) solely the property and rights of the employer (without being restricted to providing benefits under the plan) subject only to the claims of the employer's general creditors.

Section 457(d)(1)(A) provides that for a section 457 plan to be an eligible plan, the plan must have distribution requirements providing that under the plan amounts will not be made available to participants or beneficiaries earlier than i) the calendar year in which the participant attains age 70½, ii) when the participant is separated from service with the employer, or iii) when the participant is faced with an unforeseeable emergency as determined under Treasury regulations. Section 1.457-2(h)(4) of the Income Tax Regulations defines an unforeseeable emergency as severe financial hardship to the participant resulting from a sudden and unexpected illness or accident of the participant or of a dependent, loss of the participant's property due to casualty, or other similar extraordinary and unforeseeable circumstances arising as a result of events beyond the control of the participant. Since a divorce or separation generally does not give rise to an unforeseeable emergency within the meaning of these regulations, a participant who is still employed by the state and who is under 70½ cannot demand payment. The spouse or other alternate payee likewise could not request payment before the participant himself separates from service or attains age 70½.

Section 457(f) provides that if a state governmental plan is or becomes an ineligible plan then the deferred compensation shall be included in the gross income of the participant or beneficiary for the first taxable year in which there is no substantial risk of forfeiture of the rights to such compensation, and the tax treatment of any amount made available under such plan to a participant or beneficiary shall be determined under section 72 relating to annuities.

In essence, an eligible section 457 state or local government plan is an unfunded, non-qualified deferred compensation plan in which the employee-participant has only the employer's contractual promise that benefits will be paid, as provided in section 457(b)(6). Under that paragraph and section 1.457-2(j) of the regulations, the employee cannot have any interest in employer assets, and any payments of benefits must be made from funds that are available to the employer's general creditors. In other words, a section 457 plan is not treated as a qualified exempt trust described in section 401(a). In addition, an eligible section 457 plan must meet the section 457(d) distribution requirements described above. A section 457 plan would violate these provisions of section 457 and the regulations thereunder if the participant or anyone else received an interest in employer assets earlier than the earliest date established in section 457(d)(1)(A).

Based upon the provisions of the amended plan summarized above, and the documents presented, we conclude as follows:

The Deferred Compensation Plan of Entity E is an eligible deferred compensation plan as defined in section 457 of the Internal Revenue Code of 1986.

Amounts of compensation deferred in accordance with the plan, including any income attributable to the deferred compensation, will be includible in gross income for the taxable year or years in which amounts are paid or otherwise made available to an employee (including a participant who is involved in Plan administration) or beneficiary (including an alternate payee) in accordance with the terms of the Plan.

Entity E's Plan will not become an ineligible plan described in section 457(f) solely because its administrator complies with a domestic relations order requiring the distribution of the benefits of a participant in pay status (currently eligible to receive distributions) under section 457(d)(1)(A) to the participant's spouse or ex-spouse to meet the participant's obligations with respect to alimony, support, or division of marital rights.

No opinion is expressed concerning the timing of the inclusion in income of amounts deferred under any deferred compensation plan other than E's Plan described above. In addition, this ruling applies only to deferrals made after the date this ruling was issued. If the Plan is modified, this ruling will not necessarily remain applicable. Also, no opinion is expressed concerning to whom the distributions made pursuant to a domestic relations order are taxed. This ruling is directed only to Entity E and its employees, and applies only to the amended Plan as submitted on July 21, 1995. Section 6110(j)(3) of the Code provides that it may not be used or cited as precedent.

Temporary or final regulations pertaining to one or more of the issues addressed in this ruling have not yet been adopted. Therefore, this ruling may be modified or revoked if the adopted temporary or final regulations are inconsistent with any conclusion in the ruling. See section 11.04 of Rev. Proc. 95-1, 1995-1 I.R.B. 9, 41. However, when the criteria in section 11.05 of Rev. Proc. 95-1 are satisfied, a ruling is not revoked or modified retroactively except in rare or unusual circumstances.

Letter Ruling 9538021, Dated June 23, 1995

This responds to your letter of May 2, 1995, and subsequent correspondence requesting a ruling concerning the federal income tax consequences of a proposed amendment (the "Amendment") to the compensation deferral plan (the "Plan") established by Entity E, a tax-exempt entity described in sections 457(e)(1)(B) and 501(c)(3). The original Plan was established in 1975. Although this nonqualified deferred compensation plan was generally available to any eligible employee, officer, and independent contractor performing services for E, only one person, Participant P, has ever elected to defer compensation pursuant to this plan.

The Plan generally permits its participants to defer a portion of their compensation for the next year. The participants must file their deferral election with E before December 31 specifying the portion of compensation to be earned in the succeeding year that is to be deferred. Under the Plan, the participant, his beneficiary, or his estate would receive benefits for services performed to be paid commencing upon his separation from service, retirement, or death, or upon the occurrence of an unforeseeable emergency. Within certain limits, the Plan also provides for the participant's election of the manner of payment of benefits under such Plan.

The proposed Amendment would prevent the Plan from accepting any additional deferrals of compensation in the future, and require the Plan's benefits to be paid in accordance with the provisions established under the Amendment. The Amendment also states that the amount of the benefit will be determined by the investment results of the deemed investment of the deferred compensation amounts credited to the participant's bookkeeping account under the Plan.

Section 457 of the Code provides rules for the deferral of compensation by an individual participating in an eligible deferred compensation plan (as defined in section 457(b)).

Section 457(a) of the Code provides that in the case of a participant in an eligible deferred compensation plan, any amount of compensation deferred under the plan and any income attributable to the amounts so deferred shall be includible in gross income only for the taxable year in which such compensation or other income is paid or otherwise made available to the participant or beneficiary.

Section 1107 of the Tax Reform Act of 1986 (the "Act") amended section 457 of the Code to apply its restrictions and limitations to the unfunded deferred compensation plans maintained by non-governmental tax-exempt organizations, effective for taxable years beginning after December 31, 1986, except as provided under section 1107(c) of the Act. Section 1107(c)(3)(B) states that section 457 does not apply to amounts deferred under a deferred compensation plan of a tax-exempt organization that:

were deferred from taxable years beginning before January 1, 1987, or

were deferred from taxable years beginning after December 31, 1986, pursuant to an agreement that (I) was in writing on August 16, 1986, and (II) on such date, provides for a deferral for each taxable year covered by the agreement of a fixed amount or of an amount determined pursuant to a fixed formula. If there is any modification of the fixed amount or fixed formula, however, section 457 applies to any taxable year ending after the date on which the modification is effective.

Section 6064(d)(3) of the Technical and Miscellaneous Revenue Act of 1988 (the "TAMRA") provides that this grandfathering rule for nonqualified deferred compensation plans under section 457 maintained by tax-exempt organizations does not cease to apply merely because of a modification to the deferred compensation agreement prior to January 1, 1989, that does not increase benefits for participants in the plan. The legislative history of TAMRA indicates that Congress wanted to provide relief only to a post-August 16, 1986 "modification which does not increase benefits for participants in the plan" that would otherwise be covered under section 457. H.R. Rep. No. 1104, 100th Cong., 2d. Sess. 154 (1988).

Section 6064(d)(3) of TAMRA is silent regarding the legal effect of a post-1988 modification that does not increase benefits for participants in a pre-1987 plan that would otherwise be covered under section 457. However, the legislative history of section 6064 shows that Congress intended this rule to endure. The reports of both the House Committee and the Conference Committee explain that the grandfather rule for nonelective deferred compensation under governmental plans for amounts deferred under agreements in effect on July 14, 1988 is meant to apply to all section 457 plans.

The proposed Amendment would significantly reduce (to zero) the amount and value of the participant's future deferrals under E's Plan. It should be noted that such reduced amount remains within the level of the amounts deferred as of July 14, 1988, under the Plan, and that Congress had enacted no provision penalizing those who made post 1986 and 1988 modifications significantly reducing the amount of deferred benefits under a prior plan that would otherwise be covered under section 457.

Based upon the provisions of the proposed Amendment summarized above, we conclude as follows:

The Plan, as revised by the Amendment, continues to be exempt from section 457 of the Internal Revenue Code under section 1107(c)(3)(B) of the Tax Reform Act of 1986 as modified by section 6064 of TAMRA, and the amounts already deferred thereunder will not be subject to the provisions of section 457 of the Code.

The Amendment, if adopted, will not constitute a modification to the "fixed amount" or "fixed formula" subjecting the Plan and the amounts previously deferred thereunder to the section 457 limitations.

This ruling concerns only the effect of the proposed Amendment. No opinion is expressed concerning the timing of the inclusion in income of amounts previously deferred under the Plan. Moreover, if the Plan, as revised by the Amendment, is further amended in the future to increase, directly or indirectly, the amount of the deferrals under the Plan, this ruling will no longer apply to amounts deferred under this Plan as revised by the Amendment. This ruling is directed only to Participant P and Entity E, and applies only to the Plan and Amendment submitted on May 2, 1995. Section 6110(j)(3) of the Code provides that it may not be used or cited as precedent. Except as specifically stated above, no opinion is expressed on the federal tax consequences of the Plan and Amendment under any other provision of the Code.

Letter Ruling 9521038 (Date not available)

LEGEND:	Church = ***	Corporation A = ***
	Official B = ***	Plan = ***
	Conference C = ***	Corporation D = ***
	Association E = ***	School F = ***
	State G = ***	City H = ***
	City I = ***	Clergy = ***

This is in response to a letter dated September 15, 1994, in which your authorized representative requested a letter ruling on your behalf as to whether your pension plan is a church plan under section 414(e) of the Internal Revenue Code.

In support of your letter ruling request your authorized representative has submitted the following facts and representations:

Corporation A is the "corporate sole" of Official B and represents the Church in western State G. Corporation A is a State G nonprofit corporation and is an entity as described in section 501(c)(3) of the Internal Revenue Code. As such, it is exempt from tax under section 501(a) of the Code.

In 1988, Corporation A established the Plan, a money purchase pension plan, for the benefit of its lay employees. These employees are engaged in, among other activities, the administration of Corporation A, the education of the Church's young people, the administration of Corporation A's schools, and other activities related to Corporation A's religious purposes. Corporation A is the Plan's administrator and sponsor and has so acted since the Plan's establishment. Presently, approximately 1,997 employees of Corporation A participate in the Plan.

In 1988, Conference C became a participating employer in the Plan. Conference C is a Code section 501(c)(3) organization and is exempt from tax under section 501(a) by virtue of a group exemption letter issued by the Internal Revenue Service to all agencies and instrumentalities operated, supervised, or controlled by or in connection with the Church in the United States.

The Articles of Incorporation for Conference C provide that it is a civil entity of Church officials of State G. Conference C assists these Church officials in their service to the Church by developing, coordinating, and implementing interdiocesan and interfaith programs and services for the Church in State G. Conference C officials are guided by and report directly to Official B and Church officials in Cities H and I. Approximately two Conference C employees participate in the Plan. Conference C is listed in the official Church directory.

Also in 1988, Corporation D became a participating employer in the Plan. Corporation D is a Code section 501(c)(3) nonprofit corporation organized under the laws of State G. Corporation D's Articles of Incorporation state that its main function is to provide mental health, therapy, and counseling services that are Christian in their vision. All of Corporation D's officers and its director have taken religious vows and have pledged their lives and careers to the Church. Corporation D operates a psychotherapy and consultation center whose patient base is drawn mainly from Church clergy and career lay ministers. Corporation D's employees utilize the teachings of the Church to provide primarily Church employees and volunteers with psychotherapy to resolve issues arising out of their employment or other relationship with the Church. Corporation D was established in 1985 at the request of the then current Official B. Approximately three Corporation D employees participate in the Plan. Corporation D is listed in the official Church directory.

Effective as of July 1, 1993, Association E and School F became participating employers in the Plan. Both Association E and School F are State G nonprofit corporations and exempt from tax under Code section 501(a) by virtue of their status as section 501(c)(3) organizations. These institutions operate private religious schools. School F's Articles of Incorporation stipulate that its main purpose is to operate a private school for pre-school and elementary school children which provides opportunity for suitable religious instruction. Likewise, Association E's Articles of Incorporation state that it is organized to operate a four-year co-educational Church high school.

Association E and School F both teach the tenets of the Church at every level of their students' education. Their teachers are also integrated into Corporation A's schools by their participation in joint training sessions and annual education conferences. Several teachers in Association E and School F have taken religious vows and have pledged their lives and careers to the Church. In addition, School F is listed in the official Church directory. Association E has applied to be listed in the official Church directory and expects to receive approval shortly. There are a total of approximately sixty-one Association E and school F employees participating in the Plan.

The Plan was established and will be maintained by Corporation A, which is the "corporate sole" of Official B. Official B has appointed seven members to the Plan's Investment Board. These members include four employees of Corporation A, two parishioners, and one investment advisor who is not affiliated with the Church. Official B has the sole authority to appoint and remove the Investment Board members. The principal purpose of the Investment Board is to make recommendations to the Plan trustee concerning the funding policy of the Plan and to make decisions regarding Plan investments.

Based on the foregoing statements and representations, you request a ruling that the Plan is a church plan within the meaning of section 414(e) of the Internal Revenue Code.

To qualify under section 401(a) of the Code, an employees' plan generally must meet the minimum participation standards of section 410 and the minimum vesting standards of section 411. Qualified pension plans also must meet the minimum funding standards of section 412. Each of these sections, however, contains an exception for a church plan as defined in section 414(e), unless an election has been made in accordance with section 410(d). See sections 410(c)(1)(B), 411(e)(1)(B) and 412(h)(4).

Section 414(e)(1) of the Code generally defines a church plan as a plan established and maintained for its employees (or their beneficiaries) by a church or by a convention or association of churches which is exempt from taxation under section 501 of the Code.

Section 414(e)(3)(A) of the Code provides that a plan, which otherwise meets the requirements of section 414(e), will be treated as a church plan if it is maintained by an organization, whether a civil law corporation or otherwise, the principal purpose or function of which is the administration or funding of a plan or program for the provision of retirement benefits or welfare benefits, or both, for the employees of a church or a convention or association of churches, if such organization is controlled by or associated with a church or a convention or association of churches.

In pertinent part, section 414(e)(3)(B) of the Code provides that an "employee" of a church or convention or association of churches includes an employee of an organization, whether a civil law corporation or otherwise, which is exempt from tax under section 501, and which is controlled by or associated with a church or a convention or association of churches.

Section 414(e)(3)(C) of the Code provides that a church or a convention or association of churches which is exempt from tax under section 501 shall be deemed the employer of any individual included as an employee under subparagraph (B).

Section 414(e)(3)(D) of the Code provides that an organization, whether a civil law corporation or otherwise, is "associated" with a church or a convention or association of churches if the organization shares common religious bonds and convictions with that church or convention or association of churches.

In order for an organization to have a church plan, it must establish that its employees are employees or deemed employees of a church or a convention or association of churches under section 414(e)(3)(B) of the Code. In addition, in the case of a plan established by an organization that is not itself a church or a convention or association of churches but is associated with a church or a convention or association of churches as described in section 414(e)(3)(D), the plan must be maintained by an organization described in section 414(e)(3)(A) of the Code.

In this case, Corporation A is the "corporate sole" of Official B and represents the Church in State G. Corporation A employees are engaged in the education of the Church's young people, the administration of Corporation A's schools, and other activities related to the religious purposes of Corporation A. Conference C assists the officials of the Church by developing, coordinating and implementing religious programs and services for the Church in State G. Conference C officials are guided by and report directly to Church officials. Corporation D was established by Church officials and utilizes the Church's teachings to provide mental health and counseling services to Church clergy and career ministers of the Church. Association E and School F operate private Church schools which provide the opportunity for suitable religious instruction, and teach the tenets of the Church at every level of their students' education.

In addition, Conference C, Corporation D and School F are listed in the official directory of the Church for the United States of America. Association E has applied to be listed in the official Church directory and expects to receive approval. The IRS has determined that any organization listed or appearing in the Church's official directory is an organization described in section 501(c)(3) of the Code, and exempt from tax under section 501(a). Also, the IRS has determined that any organization that is listed in the official directory of the

Church shares common religious bonds with that Church and is associated with a church or a convention or association of churches within the meaning of section 414(e)(3)(D) of the Code.

If an organization is associated with the Church and shares common religious bonds and convictions with the Church, that organization's employees are deemed to be Church employees. In view of the common religious bonds and convictions between the Church, Corporation A, Conference C, Corporation D, Association E, and School F, their recognition as nonprofit organizations under State G law, and the association of all of these organizations with the Church, it is concluded that the employees of Corporation A, Conference C, Corporation D, Association E, and School F meet the definition of employee under section 414(e)(3)(B) of the Code. Accordingly, these employees are deemed to be employees of the Church for purposes of the church plan rules.

Having established that the above organizations' employees are Church employees, the remaining issue is whether the Board which administers the Plan is an organization controlled by or associated with a church or a convention or association of churches and has as its principal purpose or function the administration or funding of a plan within the meaning of section 414(e)(3)(A) of the Code.

In this case, the Plan was established and is maintained by Corporation A, which is the "corporate sole" of Official B. Official B has appointed seven members to the Plan's Investment Board, including four employees of Corporation A, two parishioners, and an investment advisor who is not affiliated with the Church and has the sole authority to appoint and remove the Investment Board members. The majority of board members are affiliated with the Church by religious beliefs as well as by employment. The principal purpose of the Investment Board is to make recommendations to the Plan trustee concerning the funding policy of the Plan and to make decisions concerning Plan investments. Thus, the Investment Board is an organization that is controlled by or associated with a church or a convention or association of churches and that has as its principal purpose or function the administration or funding of a plan for the provision of retirement benefits for individuals (and their beneficiaries) who are deemed to be employees of a church or a convention or association of churches. It is concluded, therefore, that the Plan, as administered by the Investment Board, is a plan administered by an organization described in section 414(e)(3)(A) of the Code.

Accordingly, it is ruled that the Plan is a church plan within the meaning of section 414(e) of the Internal Revenue Code.

This letter expresses no opinion as to whether the Plan continues to be a qualified plan under section 401(a) of the Code. The determination as to whether a plan remains qualified under section 401(a) is within the jurisdiction of the appropriate Key District Director's office of the Internal Revenue Service.

In accordance with a power of attorney on file with this office, this letter is being sent to your authorized representative.

Letter Ruling 9443041, Dated August 4, 1994

[Summary: An insurance company has a contractual arrangement with entities that sell its insurance products. Under the contract, the insurer provides clerical support for the entities through the insurer's employees. These clerical employees are common law employees of the insurer, and participate in a profit sharing plan with a cash or deferred arrangement maintained by the insurer. The employees work for the entities at their facilities. The insurer has the right to discipline and terminate the employees.

The insurer proposes to terminate the contractual arrangement with the entities and discharge the clerical employees, with the expectation that they may be rehired by the entities to perform identical clerical services. There will be no liquidation, merger, transfer of corporate assets, or any other corporate transaction associated with the discharge of any employee, nor will there be a directed transfer of assets and liabilities from the insurer's plan to any plan maintained by an entity. The insurer will continue to maintain a business relationship with the entities.

The IRS ruled that a distribution from the plan to a discharged clerical employee under age 59½ who is rehired by an entity will not be considered as made upon separation from service within the meaning of Code Section 401(k)(2)(B)(i)(I) and regulation Code[sic] Section 1.401(k)-1(d)(1)(i). Although there is neither a corporate transaction nor a transfer of plan assets associated with the discharge of any employee, the insurer and the entities will continue to maintain a business relationship, and the clerical workers will continue to perform the same work at the same location.]

Letter Ruling 9344038, Dated August 2, 1993

[Summary: A company maintains a supplemental executive retirement plan under which participants have only an unsecured promise to receive deferred compensation. Independently of the sponsoring company, a participant negotiated with an insurance company for a policy to further protect the deferred compensation benefits payable to the participant under the plan.

The insurance company issued the policy without entering any collateral agreements with the sponsoring company, and without obtaining information about the sponsoring company other than publicly available information. The sponsoring company may increase the participant's compensation in the amount of the premium payment, and the participant will include that increase in gross income.

The IRS ruled that the issuance of the policy will not cause the deferred compensation to be included in the participant's income until paid or made available.]

Letter Ruling 9226058, Dated March 31, 1992

[Summary: In 1983, an individual established an individual retirement account (IRA) with a bank, designating his wife as the primary beneficiary and his two children as contingent beneficiaries. The individual died on February 21, 1991, survived by his wife and children. On November 15, 1991, the wife filed a disclaimer with the applicable state court. The disclaimer stated that she irrevocably and without qualification disclaimed and refused to accept her interest in the IRA. The bank has made no distributions of the IRA benefits.

The IRS ruled that the wife's disclaimer is a qualified disclaimer under Code Section 2518. The IRS concluded that, as a result of the disclaimer, the wife's interest in the IRA will pass under the husband's beneficiary designation form as if she had predeceased him; that is, it will go to the contingent beneficiaries, the two children, in equal shares.]

Letter Ruling 9204010, Dated October 10, 1991

[Summary: On August 16, 1982, a trustee and other entities set up a trust. It had one beneficiary. On April 4, 1991, the trust purchased a deferred variable annuity contract with an annuity starting date of April 4, 2060, from a life insurance company. The provisions of the trust provide that the trustee may pay income or corpus, or both, to the beneficiary, until the beneficiary reaches age 40. At that time, the trustee must deliver the entire corpus of the trust, including the annuity contract, to the beneficiary. The trustee will not receive any consideration from the beneficiary in exchange for the distribution of the annuity contract.

The IRS ruled that the annuity contract is considered owned by a natural person under Code Section 72(u)(1), and the distribution of the annuity contract by the trust to the beneficiary will not be treated as an assignment of an annuity contract without full and adequate consideration under Code Section 72(e)(4)(C).]

Letter Ruling 9152026, Dated September 27, 1991

[Summary: A local government entity maintains two Code Section 457 plans. It also maintains two Code Section 401(k) plans (under a transition rule in the Tax Reform Act of 1986 that exempts certain governmental plans from the general rule that state and local governments may not maintain a 401(k) plan). The employer asked the IRS to interpret Code Section 457(c)(2) to permit the greater of the Code Section 457(c)(2) limitation or Code Section 402(a)(8) limitation (relating to Code Section 401(k) plans) to apply to the aggregate of deferrals made under both plans.

The IRS ruled that the aggregate amount that may be deferred and excluded from income under the plans will be limited by the lower Code Section 457(c)(2) limitation. The IRS noted that Code Section 457(c)(2) treats amounts excluded from gross income under a Code Section 401(k) plan as an amount deferred under an eligible 457(f) plan subject to the maximum $7,500 limitation applicable to Code Section 457 plans. Even though an employee may otherwise defer under a 401(k) plan a greater amount of gross income under the Code Section 402(a)(8) limitation for years 1990 and beyond, if the same employee also participates in a 457 plan in 1990 and later years, that employee would be limited to the $7,500 limit.]

Letter Ruling 9145010, Dated July 31, 1991

[Summary: An individual separated from her spouse, who is a participant in a Code Section 457 plan. A state court issued an order, which is represented to be a qualified domestic relations order (QDRO), that states that the spouse's employer, a state, is authorized to pay the individual her portion of the Code Section 457 plan immediately, in a lump sum.

The IRS ruled that the Code Section 457 plan cannot make the distribution to the individual and remain an eligible plan under Code Section 457(b) unless the distribution is made at or after the time permitted under Code Section 457(d)(1)(A). Under that section, payments from the plan cannot begin until after the participant has separated from service, has reached age 70½, or has suffered an unforeseeable emergency. The IRS stated that a divorce or separation is not an unforeseeable emergency under the regulations.

The IRS also ruled that if the participant is in pay status, the 457 plan will not become an ineligible plan solely because its administrator complies with a court order requiring distribution of the benefits to a participant's spouse to meet the participant's alimony or support obligations.

The IRS further ruled that the provision permitting tax-deferred rollovers of QDRO-mandated distributions to an individual retirement account does not apply to distributions from a Code Section 457 plan because those plans are not exempt trusts nor are they treated as exempt trusts under Code Section 402(a)(6)(F).]

Letter Ruling 9008043, Dated November 28, 1989

[Summary: A local government entity adopted a plan under which a participant may elect to defer compensation. Participants may select investment vehicles for their deferred compensation. These selections may be used to determine the value of the deferred accounts. Participants may select the commencement time of their distributions and the mode of payments. No payment option available to the participant will provide benefits to beneficiaries over a third of the maximum benefit that would have been payable to the participant if no provision would have been made for payment to a beneficiary. The employer may purchase life insurance contracts as one vehicle of investment; these contracts will be registered in the name of the employer as beneficiary and owner.

The IRS ruled that the plan is an eligible deferred compensation plan under Code Section 457. The IRS ruled that amounts deferred under the plan will not be treated as made available under the plan by reason of being invested in a universal life insurance contract, or other life insurance contract, at the participant's election and at the discretion of the employer. The IRS ruled that amounts paid to a beneficiary under any life insurance contract are not excludable from the beneficiary's income under Code Sections 101(a) or 101(b). The IRS held that if a distribution to the participant is made in the form of delivering a life insurance contract, the value of the contract at the time of receipt will be treated as made available to the participant and will be includable in the participant's income.]

Letter Ruling 8824049, Dated March 22, 1988

[Summary: This ruling involves a religious congregation of women that operates health care facilities. The congregation of women formed a controlled organization, which established one or more employee plans for the employees of the health care facilities. The religious order controls the board of directors of the organization that maintains the plan.

The IRS held that the plans are administered by an organization described in Code Section 414(e)(3)(A) and that the plans qualify as church plans under Code Section 414(e).]

Letter Ruling 8824019, Dated March 17, 1988

[Summary: A tax-exempt organization entered into a collective bargaining agreement on July 1, 1984. Under the agreement, the company agreed to contribute amounts into supplemental pension plans for covered employees. Each plan was to be an "individual account-type plan." In 1987, the company adopted a simplified employee pensionindividual retirement account contribution agreement (SEP-IRA agreement). The agreement was designed to provide the type of plan provided for in the collective bargaining agreement. The SEP-IRA agreement was adopted using the IRS Form 5305-SEP. IRAs were established for the employees with another company, which accepted the employer contributions that were set aside under the agreement. Company contributions to the IRAs are determined at a stated rate per hour, regardless of compensation level. The employees are salaried and are not compensated for overtime. All the employees are credited with 80 hours every two-week period.]

Letter Ruling 8752029, Dated September 28, 1987

[Summary: A city adopted an amended version of the state's model deferred compensation plan. In a prior unidentified ruling, the IRS held that the plan was an eligible state deferred compensation plan. The city will now amend the plan to allow another method of payment and to allow in-service withdrawals.

The IRS ruled that the plan continues to be an eligible state deferred compensation plan under Code Section 457. The IRS also ruled that the amendments to the plan do not alter the earlier ruling. The IRS also held that the transfer of amounts held by a custodian for an eligible Code Section 457 plan to the custodian of the city's plan will not cause an employee for whom the transfer is made to be in constructive receipt of the transferred amount.]

Letter Ruling 8629012, Dated April 14, 1986

[Summary: A state agency established a deferred compensation plan for its employees. The state established a deferred compensation plan in which the agency's employees were eligible to participate. The agency asked the state to permit transfers from its original plan to the state's plan so that it need not administer two plans. The IRS held that the proposed transfer of all the accounts of the first plan to the second plan will not adversely affect the qualification of the first plan under Code Section 457. The IRS also held that the second plan's receipt of the transferred funds will not adversely affect the qualification of the second plan under Code Section 457.]

Letter Ruling 200308032, Dated November 8, 2002

[Summary: IRS allows proposed investment in nonpublic funds. The IRS has ruled that an insurance company's proposed investment arrangement calling for beneficial interests in nonpublic funds to be held by an eligible deferred compensation plan satisfies the lookthrough rule of Treasury Regulations Section 1.817-5(f)(2)(i). The company proposes an arrangement offering participant-directed investments in a variety of mutual funds. The trustee of a rabbi trust, who will be the registered owner of the mutual fund shares, will make the investments. Currently, the funds offered under the arrangement are available to the public. The company proposes to allow investments in nonpublic, institutional mutual funds, including certain of the nonpublic investment funds already available through the company's existing options. The IRS explained that the proposed trust arrangement is part of a Code Section 457(b) eligible deferred compensation plan.]

[1] This is in response to your submission dated July 12, 2002, and subsequent submissions, requesting rulings on behalf of the Company concerning

the treatment under section 817(h) of the Internal Revenue Code of direct investments in certain institutional mutual funds (the "Non-Public Funds") that are proposed to be made in connection with Section 457(b) eligible deferred compensation plans sponsored by tax-exempt entities.

FACTS

A. The Company: [2] The Company is a life insurance company organized under the laws of State X. Until Date 1, it was named Y Company. The Company is licensed to conduct an insurance business in Jurisdictions. The Company is a wholly-owned subsidiary of Parent. The Company is also registered as an investment adviser under the Investment Adviser Act of 1940 and is registered as such with the Securities and Exchange Commission. In this capacity, the Company acts as the investment adviser for certain of the Non-Public Funds discussed herein.

[3] The Company represents that it is a life insurance company within the definition of section 816(a). It joins with its subsidiary, Sub, in the filing of a "life/life" consolidated Federal income tax return. The Company uses the accrual method of accounting for Federal income tax purposes and files its returns on a calendar year basis.

B. The Contracts: [4] The Company issues nonparticipating life insurance and annuity contracts (the "Contracts"), which offer both fixed and variable investment options (the "Variable Contracts"), as well as contracts offering solely fixed investment options (the "Fixed Contracts"). Some of the Contracts (the "Qualified Contracts") are issued in connection with qualified retirement plans, including: group annuity contracts issued to trustees of pension or profit sharing plans and trusts which qualify under section 401(a) ("Section 401 Contracts"); group annuity contracts issued to trustees of qualified plans established by self-employed individuals under section 401(a) and (c) ("H.R. 10 Contracts"); group annuity contracts issued to state and local governments and to tax-exempt organizations in connection with deferred compensation plans under section 457 ("Section 457 Contracts"); group and individual annuity contracts which qualify as "individual retirement annuities" within the meaning of section 408(b) ("IRA Contracts"); and group and individual annuity contracts which satisfy the requirements of section 403(b) ("TSA Contracts").

[5] The Company represents that the Qualified Contracts constitute "annuity contracts" for Federal income tax purposes, except to the extent that section 72(u) requires otherwise, and are "pension plan contracts" within the meaning of sections 817(h)(1) and 818(a).

[6] Certain of the Contracts are not issued in connection with a qualified plan, but rather are purchased with "after-tax" monies (the "Non-Qualified Contracts"). The Company represents that the Non-Qualified Contracts are either (1) annuity contracts for Federal income tax purposes, except to the extent that section 72(u) requires otherwise, or (2) life insurance contracts within the meaning of section 7702(a).

[7] The Contracts are purchased with the payment of one or more premiums ("Purchase Payments"). For the Fixed Contracts, each Purchase Payment is allocated to the Fixed Account maintained as part of the Company's general account. For Variable Contracts, each Purchase Payment is allocated as directed by the policyholder among the contract's investment options. The investment options available differ somewhat amongst the Variable Contracts, but all offer as investment options a Fixed Account option, and one or more variable options. The "Current Value" of a Variable Contract at any time generally equals the sum of the amounts in the various investment options. At any time before an annuity option is elected (for those Contracts that are annuity contracts), or before the death of an insured under a life insurance contract, all or part of the Current Value may be transferred among the investment options, subject to certain limitations on the timing, amount, and frequency of such transfers.

[8] The Contracts that are annuity contracts provide for payments under the applicable annuity options. Some of the Variable Contracts provide annuity payments which are fixed, variable, or a combination of fixed and variable, as the policyholder specifies, and some of the Contracts, including all Fixed Contracts, provide only fixed annuity payments. The Contracts that are annuities may also provide a death benefit payable to the beneficiary upon the death of the Annuitant.

C. The Separate Accounts: [9] Amounts allocated to the variable options under the Variable Contracts currently are invested in one of the following separate accounts of the Company:

1. amounts allocated to the variable options under some TSA Contracts, some IRA Contracts, certain Section 457 Contracts, and under the Non-Qualified Contracts that are annuities, are held in Annuity Separate Account 2.

2. amounts allocated to the variable options under some TSA Contracts, some Section 401 Contracts, some IRA Contracts and most Section 457 Contracts are held in Annuity Separate Account 3;

3. amounts allocated to the variable options under most Section 401 Contracts, and certain Section 457 Contracts, are held in Annuity Separate Account 4;

4. amounts allocated to the variable options under most of the Company's Non-Qualified Contracts that are life insurance contracts are held in Life Separate Account 2;

5. amounts allocated to the variable options under one of the Company's Non-Qualified Contracts that is a life insurance contract issued to a state retirement system are held in Life Separate Account 3;

6. amounts allocated to the variable options under certain Section 401 Contracts and Section 457(b) Contracts that invest in shares of certain publicly available mutual funds are held in Annuity Separate Account 6; and

7. amounts allocated to the variable options under a closed block of Qualified Contracts and Non-Qualified Contracts that are annuities and that were assumed by the Company pursuant to an assumption reinsurance agreement are held in Annuity Separate Account 7.

The aforementioned separate accounts were established pursuant to the insurance laws of State X for the purpose of segregating assets attributable to the variable portions of the Contracts from other assets of the Company. Annuity Separate Account 2, Annuity Separate Account 3, Annuity Separate Account 7, Life Separate Account 2 and Life Separate Account 3 are registered under the Investment Company Act of 1940 (the "1940 Act") with the Securities and Exchange Commission as unit investment trusts. Pursuant to section 3(a)2 of the Securities Act of 1933 and section 3(c)11 of the 1940 Act, Annuity Separate Account 4 and Annuity Separate Account 6 are not registered with the Securities and Exchange Commission.

D. The Funds: [10] The assets of Annuity Separate Accounts 2, 3, 4 and 7, and Life Separate Accounts 2 and 3, currently may be invested in shares of several investment companies that are not available to the general public (the "Non-Public Funds"). Each of the Non-Public Funds is registered under the 1940 Act with the Securities and Exchange Commission as an open-end investment company, i.e., each is a mutual fund. Certain of the Non-Public funds are managed by the Company or one of its affiliates, while others are managed by unaffiliated entities. The Company represents that each of the Non-Public Funds managed by the Company or one of its affiliates qualifies as a regulated investment company within the meaning of section 851 and is considered a "segregated asset account" within the meaning of Treas. Reg. § 1.817-5(e). The Company further represents, to the best of its knowledge and belief, that each of the Non-Public Funds not managed by the Company or one of its affiliates qualifies as a regulated investment company within the meaning of section 851 and is considered a "segregated asset account" within the meaning of Treas. Reg. 1.817-5(e). Pursuant to Treas. Reg. 1.817-5(f)(2), all of the shares of the Non-Public Funds are held either by segregated asset accounts of insurance companies or by interests otherwise allowed by Treas. Reg. 1.817-5(f)(3). With the exception of those interests permitted under Treas. Reg. 1.817-5(f)(3), public access to the Non-Public Funds is available exclusively through the purchase of a variable contract within the meaning of sections 817(d) and (e). Also, the Company represents that the investments of the Non-Public Funds managed by the Company or one of its affiliates in which the Non-Qualified Contracts can invest satisfy, and will continue to satisfy, the diversification requirements of section 817(h) and the regulations thereunder. Further, the Company represents, to the best of its knowledge and belief, the investments in the Non-Public Funds not managed by the Company or one of its affiliates in which the Non-Qualified Contracts can invest satisfy, and will continue to satisfy, the diversification requirements of section 817(h) and the regulations thereunder.

[11] Assets held in Annuity Separate Accounts 3 and 4 on behalf of certain Section 401 Contracts, TSA Contracts and Section 457 Contracts, as well as the assets of Annuity Separate Account 6, may be invested in shares of investment companies that are available to the general public. Each of these funds is registered under the 1940 Act with the Securities and Exchange Commission as open-ended investment companies, each qualifies as a regulated investment company, and each is considered a "segregated asset account" under Treas. Reg. 1.817-5(e).

E. Proposed Arrangement for Section 457(b) Non-governmental Plans: [12] As a result of expanded deferral limits allowed by provisions of the Economic Growth and Tax Relief Reconciliation Act of 2001, there has been increased interest in top hat deferred compensation plans for tax-exempt organizations described in section 457(e)(1)(B). In response to this interest, the Company has developed an arrangement (the "Arrangement") that combines administrative services in connection with such top hat plans, along with a facility providing a variety of participant-directed investment options.

[13] The Arrangement consists of several agreements. Initially, there is a Plan Services Agreement. Under this agreement between the Company and the plan sponsor, the Company agrees to provide required participant record keeping and related services in connection with the administration of the Section 457(b) plan. As outlined in the Plan Services Agreement, these services may include plan installation services, maintenance of individual account records for each participant, balancing and allocation of plan contributions to individual participant accounts, monitoring contribution limits, provision of quarterly statements for the plan sponsor and participants, processing of distributions and in-service withdrawals, tax withholding and reporting, providing toll-free phone and internet access to plan participants, minimum required distribution processing, and the calculating, processing and distribution of lump sum and installment payments to participants.

[14] Consistent with the rules of section 457, a variety of participant-directed fixed and variable investment options are offered under the Arrangement. A guaranteed, fixed income investment option is offered to plan participants through a fixed deferred annuity contract (the "Annuity Contract"). The Annuity Contract is a group contract issued by the Company to the plan sponsor or to the trustee of a Rabbi trust, discussed below. Separate record keeping accounts are maintained by the Company with respect to amounts directed to the contract on behalf of each plan participant. Contributions to, and distributions from, the Annuity Contract will be made at the direction of the plan sponsor on behalf of plan participants.

[15] In addition to the guaranteed investment option offered through the Annuity Contract, the Arrangement offers direct investments in a variety of mutual funds. Administrative costs to plan sponsors may be lower through the direct investment in these funds rather than through indirect investment by the purchase of a variable annuity contract. Investments on behalf of plan participants to these mutual fund options will be made, at the direction of the plan sponsor, by the trustee of a Rabbi Trust, established pursuant to a trust agreement entered into between the plan sponsor and a trust institution (the "Trustee"). The Trustee will be the registered owner of the shares of the mutual funds. Generally, Affiliate, an affiliate of the Company, will be the trustee under the Arrangement, although in some instances an unrelated trust institution may be utilized by the plan sponsor. Where an alternate trustee is involved, Affiliate's role will be that of a custodian to the trustee. The Trust has

been established in order to provide a centralized facility for making direct mutual fund investments with respect to the Section 457(b) plan, and to offer additional security for plan participants. The Company represents to the best of its knowledge and belief that Trust is a grantor trust, subject to the provisions of sections 671-679 of the Code, and the trust assets will remain subject to the claims of the plan sponsor's general creditors in the event of insolvency.

[16] Currently, all of the funds offered under the Arrangement are available for purchase by the general public. However, subject to the receipt of a favorable ruling, the Arrangement would also allow plan investments in institutional mutual funds that are not publicly available. These options would include certain of the Non-Public Funds that presently are available solely through the purchase of a Variable Contract or through direct purchase by qualified pension or retirement plans described in Treas. Reg. 1.817-5(f)(3)(iii) and Rev. Rul. 94-62, 1994-2 C.B. 164. It is the proposed investment in the Non-Public Funds under the Arrangement that is the subject of this ruling request.

[17] Subject to certain limitations, participants will be able to transfer investments between the fixed options under the Annuity Contract and the mutual fund investments made through the Trust, as well as among the various mutual fund options. At the time a participant retires, or otherwise reaches a distributable event under the Section 457(b) plan, amounts invested on behalf of the individual under the Arrangement will be payable to the participant in a lump sum, in installments, or in the form of an annuity.

LAW AND ANALYSIS

[18] For purposes of section 457 of the Code, the term "eligible deferred compensation plan" is defined in section 457(b) as a plan established and maintained by an eligible employer meeting certain requirements.

[19] For purposes of section 457, the term "eligible employer" is defined in section 457(e)(1) as:

(A) a State, political subdivision of a State, and any agency or instrumentality of a State or political subdivision of a State, and

(B) any other organization (other than a governmental unit) exempt from tax under this subtitle.

Section 817(h)(1) of the Code provides that, for purposes of subchapter L, section 72 (relating to annuities), and section 7702(a) (relating to the definition of life insurance contract), a variable contract (other than a pension plan contract), which is otherwise described in section 817 and which is based on a segregated asset account, shall not be treated as an annuity, endowment, or life insurance contract for any period (and any subsequent period) for which the investments made by such account are not, in accordance with regulations prescribed by the Secretary, adequately diversified.

[20] Treas. Reg. 1.817-5 contains the diversification requirements for variable contracts based on segregated asset accounts. Treas. Reg. 1.817-5(f) provides a

look-through rule for the application of the diversification requirements of 1.817-5. Treas. Reg. 1.817-5(f)(1) provides that, if the look-through rule applies, a beneficial interest in a regulated investment company will not be treated as a single investment of a segregated asset account; instead, a pro rata portion of each asset of the investment company will be treated, for purposes of 1.817-5, as an asset of the segregated asset account.

[21] Treas. Reg. 1.817-5(f)(2)(i) provides that the look-through rule of 1.817-5(f) shall apply to an investment company if:

(A) all the beneficial interests in the investment company (other than those described in 1.817-5(f)(3)) are held by one or more segregated asset accounts of one or more insurance companies; and

(B) public access to such investment company is available exclusively (except as otherwise permitted under 1.817-5(f)(3)) through the purchase of a variable contract. Solely for this purpose, the status of the contract as a variable contract will be determined without regard to section 817(h) of the Code and 1.817-5 of the regulations.

Treas. Reg. 1.817-5(f)(3) provides that satisfaction of the requirements of Treas. Reg. 1.817-5(f)(2)(i) shall not be prevented by reason of beneficial interests in the investment company that are "(iii) Held by the trustee of a qualified pension or retirement plan."

[22] Rev. Rul. 94-62, 1994-2 C.B. 164, lists nine arrangements that qualify as a "qualified pension or retirement plan" for purposes of Treas. Reg. 1.817-5(f)(3)(iii). Specifically, the list under Rev. Rul. 94-62, includes: "6. A governmental plan within the meaning of 414(d) or an eligible deferred compensation plan within the meaning of Section 457(b) . . ."

[23] The Company has represented that the retirement plans underlying the Arrangement are nongovernmental "eligible deferred compensation plans" within the meaning of section 457(b).

CONCLUSION

[24] Based on the facts presented and the representations made we hold:

[25] Satisfaction of the look-through rule of Treas. Reg. 1.817-5(f)(2)(i) by Taxpayer shall not be prevented by reason of beneficial interests in the Non-Public Funds being held by an eligible deferred compensation plan within the meaning of section 457(b) under the Arrangement offered by Taxpayer.

[26] Except as expressly provided herein, no opinion is expressed or implied concerning the tax consequences of any aspect of any transaction or item discussed or referenced in this letter.

[27] This ruling is directed only to the taxpayer(s) requesting it. Section 6110(k)(3) of the Code provides that it may not be used or cited as precedent.

[28] A copy of this letter must be attached to any income tax return to which it is relevant.

[29] In accordance with the Power of Attorney on file with this office, a copy of this letter is being sent to the taxpayer.

[30] The rulings contained in this letter are based upon information and representations submitted by the taxpayer and accompanied by a penalty of perjury statement executed by an appropriate party. While this office has not verified any of the material submitted in support of the request for rulings, it is subject to verification on examination.

Letter Ruling 200303041, Dated October 4, 2002

[Summary. A pooling of assets won't jeopardize exemption. The IRS ruled that the pooling of assets of three retirement plans will not cause the plans or their trusts to lose their tax- exempt status or fail to meet the definition of a group trust. The assets of the three plans will be held for the exclusive benefit of their respective participants and beneficiaries. The IRS ruled that the pooling of assets associated with the three plans will not cause the trust into which the assets are pooled nor any subcomponent plan or trust to lose its tax-exempt status or fail to meet the definition of a group trust under Code Section 401(a)(24). Also, the pooling arrangements will not make the 457(b) plan fail to satisfy the requirements of Code Section 457(b) and will not cause the 403(b) plan to fail to satisfy the requirements of Code Section 403(b), the IRS ruled. The IRS also ruled that the elective contributions made on behalf of an employee under the defined contribution plan will not constitute wages subject to income tax withholding under Code Section 3402.]

[1] This is in reply to your request for a ruling on whether State X can properly sponsor a section 403(b) plan, as well as other rulings concerning the status of Trust D as a group trust under section 401(a)(24) of the Code and the proper treatment under section 3402 of the Code of elective contributions made on behalf of participants of Plan A.

[2] Employer, State X, is an eligible employer within the meaning of section 457(e)(1)(A) of the Code.

[3] State X's Merit System of Personnel Administration ("Merit System") is responsible for administering plans sponsored by State X and its political subdivisions. Responsibility for administering the retirement plans has been delegated to the Merit System by the Employee Benefit Plan Council ("Council") and the State Personnel Board ("Board'). The Council is a statutory body responsible for the establishment of qualified retirement plans enacted by State X's legislature. The Board is a statutory body in State X responsible for the establishment of nonqualified plans, such as section 457 deferred compensation plans.

[4] The Council established Plan A effective on December 18, 1985. It is represented that Plan A is a defined contribution plan with a cash or deferred arrangement and meets the requirements of sections 401(a) and 401(k) of the

Code. A favorable determination letter was issued regarding Plan A by the Internal Revenue Service on June 26, 1987. Plan A was subsequently amended and received its most recent favorable determination letter on September 4, 1998. Plan A allows certain employees of State X to make pre-tax contributions of up to fifteen percent of their compensation. In addition, Plan A provides for discretionary matching contributions and other employer contributions if appropriated by the legislature. Although state and local governments may not currently adopt section 401(k) plans, it is represented that Plan A was adopted prior to May 6, 1986, and that State X may therefore continue to maintain Plan A.

[5] The Council and the trustees of Plan A established Trust A to hold the assets of Plan A for the exclusive benefit of Plan A participants and beneficiaries. It is represented that Trust A meets the requirements of section 401(a) of the Code and is exempt from tax under section 501(a) of the Code.

[6] Effective July 25, 1979, the Board established Plan B. Plan B is meant to be an eligible deferred compensation plan under section 457(b) of the Code. A ruling was issued by the Internal Revenue Service on September 30, 1999, that determined that State X's 457 Plan is an eligible deferred compensation plan as defined under section 457(b) of the Code.

[7] In order to comply with the trust requirements for section 457 plans under section 457(g), the Board and the trustees of Plan B established the State X Deferred Compensation Plan Trust Agreement, Trust B, effective January 1, 1999, to hold the assets of Plan B for the exclusive benefit of Plan B participants and beneficiaries.

[8] Effective January 1, 1999, Trust D was established by appropriate governmental authorities to pool the assets of Trust A and the assets of Trust B to improve the overall investment return. On September 30, 1999, the Service approved the pooling of assets, ruling that Trust D met the definition of a group trust as stated in section 401(a)(24) of the Code and was exempt from tax under section 501(a) of the Code. The assets associated with Plan A and Plan B each have separate accounting and the assets are pooled in Trust D for investment purposes only.

[9] The Merit System, as an instrumentality of State X, has the authority to administer various defined contribution retirement plans for the benefit of state employees. State X wants to sponsor a new, unified section 403(b) tax deferred annuity plan, Plan C, for the employees of the various State X technical schools that currently maintain separate section 403(b) plans. Only those employees of the various state technical schools currently eligible to participate in a Code section 403(b) plan or other state employees who otherwise meet the eligibility requirements specified in Code section 403(b)(1)(A) will be allowed to participate in Plan C. Upon creation of Plan C, the Merit System will combine all assets currently held by the various, separate 403(b) plans established by the various technical schools whose employees will be covered by the unified Plan C and hold all such assets in a unified 403(b) trust, Trust C. Subsequent contributions by these employees pursuant to the unified Plan C will also be held by Trust C.

[10] The Merit System proposes to hold the assets associated with Plan C in Trust D and pool such assets with the assets associated with Plan A and Plan B in Trust D. The assets associated with Plan C will remain invested exclusively in group annuities or the stock of registered investment companies held within Trust C, as required by Code sections 403(b)(1) and 403(b)(7). The assets associated with Plan C, along with the assets from Plan A and Plan B will each have a separate accounting and the assets will be pooled in Trust D for investment purposes only. The assets of Plan C, along with Plan A and Plan B, will be held for the exclusive benefit of their respective participants and beneficiaries.

[11] Based on the foregoing, you have asked us to respond to the following rulings, as they relate to section 403(b) of the code:

1. Assuming that (i) Plan A otherwise satisfies the requirements of sections 401(a) and 401(k) of the Code (ii) Plan B otherwise satisfies the requirements of section 457(b) of the Code; and (iii) Plan C otherwise satisfies the requirements of section 403(b) of the Code, the pooling of assets associated with each of these plans in Trust D will not cause Trust D nor any individual subcomponent plan or trust to lose its exemption from taxation under section 501(a) of the Code or Trust D to fail to meet the definition of a group trust under section 401(a)(24) of the Code.

2. Assuming that Plan B otherwise satisfies the requirements of section 457(b) of the Code and that the pooling of assets associated with Plan A, Plan B and Plan C in Trust D will not cause the 457 Trust B to lose its exemption from taxation under section 501(a) of the Code, the pooling of assets associated with Plan B with the assets associated with Plan A and Plan C in Trust D will not result in Plan B failing to satisfy the requirements of section 457(b) of the Code.

3. Assuming that Plan C otherwise satisfies the requirements of section 403(b) of the Code and that the pooling of assets associated with the Plan A, Plan B and Plan C in Trust D will not cause the 403(b) Trust C to lose its exemption from taxation under section 501(a) of the Code, the pooling of assets associated with Plan C with the assets associated with Plan A and Plan B in Trust D will not result in Plan C failing to satisfy the requirements of section 403(b) of the Code.

[12] Section 401(k)(2) of the Code states, in part, that a qualified cash or deferred arrangement is any arrangement which is part of a profit-sharing or stock bonus plan, a pre-ERISA money purchase plan, or a rural cooperative plan which meets the requirements of section 401(a) under which a covered employee may elect to have the employer make payments as contributions to a trust under the plan on behalf of the employee, or to the employee directly in cash. Such arrangements must meet special standards governing withdrawals, forfeitures, and discrimination in order to qualify for tax benefits.

[13] The Tax Reform Act of 1986 (Public Law 99-514) added Section 401(k)(4)(B)(ii) which provides that a cash or deferred arrangement shall not be treated as a qualified cash or deferred arrangement if it is part of a plan maintained by a State or local government or political subdivision thereof, or any

agency or instrumentality thereof. However, a transition rule included in section 1116(f)(2)(B) of the Tax Reform Act of 1986 states that Section 401(k)(4)(B)(ii) added above shall not apply to any cash or deferred arrangement adopted by a state or local government or political subdivision before May 6, 1986.

[14] Section 402(e)(3) provides that contributions made by an employer on behalf of an employee to a trust which is a part of a qualified cash or deferred arrangement (as defined in section 401(k)(2)) shall not be treated as distributed or made available to the employee nor as contributions made to the trust by the employee merely because the arrangement includes provisions under which the employee has an election whether the contribution will be made to the trust or received by the employee in cash.

[15] Section 1.401(k)-1(a)(2) of the Income Tax Regulations provides that generally, a cash or deferred arrangement is an arrangement under which an eligible employee may make a cash or deferred election with respect to contributions to, or accruals or other benefits under, a plan that is intended to satisfy the requirements of section 401(a) of the Code.

[16] Section 1.401(k)-1(a)(3)(i) of the regulations provides that a cash or deferred election is any election (or modification of an earlier election) by an employee to have the employer either (A) provide an amount to the employee in the form of cash or some other taxable benefit that is not currently available, or (B) contribute an amount to a trust, or provide an accrual or other benefit, under a plan deferring the receipt of compensation. A cash or deferred election includes a salary reduction agreement between an employee and employer under which a contribution is made under a plan only if the employee elects to reduce cash compensation or to forgo an increase in cash compensation.

[17] Section 1.401(k)-1(a)(3)(ii) of the regulations provides that a cash or deferred election can only be made with respect to an amount that is not currently available to the employee on the date of the election. Further, a cash or deferred election can only be made with respect to an amount that would (but for the cash or deferred election) become currently available after the later of the date on which the employer adopts the cash or deferred arrangement or the date on which the arrangement first becomes effective.

[18] Section 1.401(k)-1(a)(3)(iii) of the regulations provides that cash or another taxable amount is currently available to the employee if it has been paid to the employee or if the employee is able currently to receive the cash or other taxable amount at the employee's discretion. An amount is not currently available to an employee if there is a significant restriction or limitation on the employee's right to receive the amount before a particular time in the future. The determination of whether an amount is currently available to an employee does not depend on whether it has been constructively received by the employee for purposes of section 451.

[19] Section 1.401(k)-1(a)(4)(i) of the regulations provides that a qualified cash or deferred arrangement is a cash or deferred arrangement that satisfies the requirements of paragraphs (b), (c), (d), and (e) of section 1.401(k)-1 and that is part of a plan that otherwise satisfies the requirements of section 401(a).

[20] Section 1.401(k)-1(a)(4)(ii) of the regulations provides that, except as provided in section 1.401(k) of the Code, elective contributions under a qualified cash or deferred arrangement are treated as employer contributions.

[21] Section 1.401(k)-1(a)(4)(iii) of the regulations provides that except as provided in section 402(g) of the Code, and in section 1.401(k)-1(f), elective contributions under a quailed cash or deferred arrangement are neither includible in an employee's gross income at the time the cash or other taxable amounts would have been includible in the employee's gross income (but for the cash or deferred election), nor at the time the elective contributions are contributed to the plan.

[22] Section 403(b)(1) of the Code provides, for years beginning after December 31, 2001, that certain amounts contributed by an employer to purchase an annuity contract for an employee shall be excluded from the gross income of the employee for the taxable year, to the extent the aggregate of such amount does not exceed the applicable limit under section 415 provided (1) the employee performs services for an employer which is exempt from tax under section 501(a) of the Code as an organization described in section 501(c)(3), or the employee performs services for an educational institution (as defined in section 170(b)(1)(A)(ii) of the Code) which is a state, a political subdivision of a state, or an agency or instrumentality of any one or more of the foregoing; (2) the annuity contract is not subject to section 403(a) of the Code; (3) the employee's rights under the contract are nonforfeitable, except for failure to pay future premiums; (4) such contract is purchased under a plan which meets the nondiscrimination requirements of paragraph (12), except in the case of a contract purchased by a church; and, (5) in the case of a contract purchased under a plan which provides a salary reduction agreement, the plan meets the requirements of section 401(a)(30). Section 403(b)(1) of the Code provides further that the employee shall include in his gross income the amounts actually distributed under such contract in the year distributed as provided in section 72 of the Code.

[23] Revenue Ruling 81-100, 1981-1 C.B. 326 holds that trusts which are parts of qualified retirement plans and individual retirement accounts may pool their assets in a group trust without affecting the exempt status of the separate trusts.

[24] Section 401(a)(24) of the Code provides that any group trust which otherwise meets the requirements of section 401(a) shall not be treated as not meeting such requirements on account of the participation or inclusion in such trust of the moneys of any plan or governmental unit described in section 818(a)(6)[.]

[25] Section 818(a)(6) of the Code states that the term "pension plan" includes (A) a governmental plan (within the meaning of section 414(d), or an eligible deferred compensation plan (within the meaning of section 457(b)); or (B) the Government of the United States, the government of any state or political subdivision thereof, or by any agency or instrumentality of the foregoing, or any organization (other than a governmental unit) exempt from tax under this subtitle, for use in satisfying an obligation of such government, political subdivision, agency or instrumentality, or organization to provide a benefit under a plan described in section 818(a)(6)(A)[.]

[26] The Committee Report pertaining to section 401(a)(24) of the Code contained in Rep. No. 760, 97th Cong., 2d Sess. 639 (1982), states that under the conference agreement, the tax-exempt status of a group trust will not be adversely affected merely because the trust accepts monies from (a) a retirement plan of a State or local government, whether or not the plan is a qualified plan and whether or not the assets are held in trust, (b) any state or local government monies intended for use in satisfying an obligation of such State or local government to provide a retirement benefit under a government plan.

[27] Nothing in the Internal Revenue Code nor the Income Tax Regulations thereunder would prevent an arrangement such as described herein to result in an arrangement being one other than as described under section 403(b) or section 401(k) of the Code. The arrangement described herein is analogous to the facts presented in Rev. Rul. 81-100, wherein individual trusts were combined into a group trust.

[28] Accordingly, with respect to your ruling requests, we conclude:

1. Assuming that (i) Plan A satisfies the requirements of sections 401(a) and 401(k) of the Code; (ii) Plan B otherwise satisfies the requirements of section 457(b) of the Code; and (iii) Plan C otherwise satisfies the requirements of section 403(b) of the Code, the pooling of assets associated with each of these plans in Trust D will not cause Trust D nor any individual subcomponent plan or trust to lose its exemption from taxation under section 501(a) of the Code or Trust D to fail to meet the definition of a group trust under section 401(a)(24) of the Code.

2. Assuming that Plan B otherwise satisfies the requirements of section 457(b) of the Code and that the pooling of assets associated with Plan A, Plan B and Plan C in Trust D will not cause the Trust B to lose its exemption from taxation under section 501(a) of the Code, the pooling of assets associated with Plan B, the 457 Plan, with the assets associated with Plan A and Plan C in Trust D will not result in Plan B failing to satisfy the requirements of section 457(b) of the Code.

3. Assuming that Plan C otherwise satisfies the requirements of section 403(b) of the Code and that the pooling of assets associated with Plan A and Plan B with Plan C in Trust D will not cause the 403(b) Trust C to lose its exemption from taxation under section 501(a) of the Code, the pooling of assets associated with Plan C with the assets associated with Plan A and Plan B in Trust D will not result in Plan C failing to satisfy the requirements of section 403(b) of the Code.

[29] The final ruling requested is, assuming that Plan A otherwise satisfies the requirements of sections 401(a) and 401(k), that the elective contributions made by its participants in the manner represented will not constitute "wages" subject to income tax withholding under section 3402 of the Code.

[30] Federal income tax withholding under section 3402(a) is imposed on "wages" as defined in section 3401(a). The term "wages" is defined generally

as including all remuneration for services performed by an employee for his or her employer, with certain specified exceptions.

[31] Section 3401(a)(12)(A) provides an exception from wages for income tax withholding purposes for remuneration paid to, or behalf of, an employee or the employee's beneficiary, from or to a trust described in section 401(a) which is exempt from tax under section 501(a) at the time of such payment unless such payment is made to an employee of the trust as remuneration for services rendered as such employee and not as a beneficiary of the trust.

[32] Section 31.3401(a)(12)-1(a) of the regulations provides that the term "wages" does not include any payment made (1) by an employer, on behalf of an employee or his beneficiary, into a trust, or (2) to, or on behalf of, an employee or his beneficiary from a trust, if at the time of such payment the trust is exempt from tax under section 501(a) as an organization described in section 401(a).

[33] The exception provided by section 3401(a)(12)(A) does not apply to amounts that are treated as employee contributions under the Code and are includible in the income of the employee prior to contribution to the qualified trust. Here the elective contributions to Plan a are treated as employer contributions and are not includible in the income of the employee at the time the contributions would have been includible but for the cash or deferred election under section 401(k), or at the time contributed to the fund.

[34] Based on the information provided and the representations made, we conclude as follows:

4. The elective contributions made on behalf of an employee under Plan A will not constitute wages subject to income tax withholding under section 3402. This ruling is based on the assumption that Plan A will otherwise be qualified under sections 401(a) and 401(k).

[35] The Federal Insurance Contributions Act (FICA) tax consists of (1) the old-age, survivors and disability insurance tax imposed by sections 3101(a) and 3111(a), which is referred to as "social security tax" in IRS publications and forms; and (2) the hospital insurance tax imposed by sections 3101(b) and 3111(b), which is referred to as Medicare tax.

[36] FICA tax is imposed on wages, as that term is defined in section 3121(a). Section 3121(a) defines the term "wages" for FICA purposes as all remuneration for employment unless specifically excepted. The term "employment" is defined in section 3121(b).

[37] Section 3121(b)(7) contains various rules that apply in determining whether services for state or local governmental entities are considered "employment" for purposes of the social security tax portion of the FICA. Section 3121(b)(7)(E) provides that if services are covered under an agreement between the State and the Social Security Administration under section 218 of the Social Security Act ("section 218 agreement"), the services are included in employment for purposes of the social security tax. If the services are not covered under a section 218 agreement, the services may nevertheless be employment for purposes of the social security tax depending upon the applicability of the various

subparagraphs of section 3121(b)(7). If the services for the state or local governmental entity are included in employment for purposes of the social security tax, the services are also included in employment for purposes of the Medicare tax. If the services are excepted from employment by section 3121(b)(7) for social security tax purposes, section 3121(u) generally provides that such services are nevertheless employment for Medicare tax purposes unless the "continuing employment exception" applies.

[38] Section 3121(v)(1)(A) of the Code provides that nothing in any paragraph of subsection (a) (other than paragraph (1)) shall exclude from the term "wages" any employer contribution under a qualified cash or deferred arrangement (as defined in section 401(k)) to the extent not included in gross income by reason of section 402(e)(3).

[39] Based on the above, we also conclude as follows:

5. The elective contributions made on behalf of an employee to Plan A are subject to social security taxes unless the services of the employee are excepted from employment by section 3121(b)(7) or unless remuneration equal to the contribution and benefit base has been paid to the employee during the calendar year by that employer. The elective contributions to Plan B are subject to Medicare taxes unless the continuing employment exception provided under section 3121(u) is applicable to the services of the employee. If the services of the employee are covered under a section 218 agreement, the elective contributions to Plan B are subject to social security tax (unless wages equal to the contribution and benefit base have been paid to the employee during the calendar year) and Medicare tax.

[40] This ruling letter is directed only to State X and the participants of State X's Plan and applies only to the Plans and Trusts originally submitted and revised, including the amended plans submitted. Section 6110(k)(3) of the Internal Revenue Code provides that it may not be used or cited as precedent.

[41] Temporary or final regulations pertaining to one or more of the issues addressed in this ruling have not yet been adopted. Therefore, this ruling may be modified or revoked if the adopted temporary or final regulations are inconsistent with any conclusion in the ruling. See section 12.04 of Rev. Proc. 2002-1, 2002-1 I.R.B.1, 50. However, when the criteria in section 12.05 of Rev. Proc. 2002-1 are satisfied, a ruling is not revoked or modified retroactively except in rare or unusual circumstances.

Letter Ruling 200303058, Dated October 18, 2002

[Summary: The IRS has ruled that a city's plan is an eligible deferred compensation plan as defined in Code Section 457. The IRS also ruled that amounts of compensation deferred under the plan, including any income attributable to the deferred compensation, will be includable in gross income for the tax year or years in which amounts are paid or otherwise made available to a participant or a participant's beneficiary under the terms of the plan. Also, the trust established for the plan under Code Section 457(b) will be treated as a tax-exempt organization under Code Section 501(a).]

[1] This responds to your letter of April 15, 2002 and subsequent correspondence, on behalf of City C, requesting a ruling concerning the proposed amended and restated deferred compensation plan (the "Plan") which C intends to be an eligible deferred compensation plan under section 457(b) of the Internal Revenue Code of 1986, as amended under the Economic Growth and Tax Relief Reconciliation Act of 2001 (EGTRRA). C is represented to be a political subdivision of a state described in section 457(e)(1)(A) of the Code.

[2] Under the Plan an employee may elect to defer compensation that would have been received for services rendered to C in any taxable year until death, severance from employment with C, attainment of age 70½, or until the occurrence of an unforeseeable emergency. The Plan also includes a provision providing an automatic in-service distribution of $5,000.00 or less to be paid to a participant from his or her account in certain limited circumstances set forth thereunder and in section 457(e)(9)(A). The Plan does not provide that a loan may be made from assets held by the Plan to any participant or beneficiary under the Plan.

[3] The participant's election to defer compensation not yet earned under the Plan must be filed prior to the beginning of the month in which his or her salary reduction agreement becomes effective. The Plan provides for a maximum amount that may be deferred by a participant in any taxable year and also provides for a catch-up computation for amounts deferred for one or more of the participant's last three taxable years ending before he attains normal retirement age under the plan. In addition, the Plan also provides for the age 50 plus catch-up contributions described in section 414(v). However, the Plan provides that a participant can only utilize one of these two catch-up contribution provisions during a single year. The amounts that may be deferred under the annual maximum limitation and the catch-up provisions are within the limitations of section 457 including the section 457(c) coordinated deferral provision.

[4] With certain limitations, a participant may elect the manner in which his deferred amounts will be distributed. If the participant fails to make a timely election by the required minimum distribution date, distribution will commence at the time and in the manner set forth in the Plan. The Plan provides that the manner and time of benefit payout must meet the distribution requirements of sections 401(a)(9) and 457(d) of the Code.

[5] The Plan provides that amounts of compensation deferred thereunder are to be transferred to and invested in a trust described in section 457(g)(1) and/or in an annuity contract described in section 457(g)(3) for the exclusive benefit of the participants and their beneficiaries. All amounts deferred under the Plan must be transferred to the trust and/or annuity contract within an administratively reasonable time period. The annuity contract is represented to meet the requirements of section 401(f) and thus will be treated as a trust

pursuant to section 457(g)(3). The rights of any participant or beneficiary to payments pursuant to the Plan are generally nonassignable and not subject to pledge, transfer or encumbrance.

[6] Section 457 of the Code provides rules for the deferral of compensation by an individual participating in an eligible deferred compensation plan as defined in section 457(b).

[7] Section 457(a)(1)(A) of the Code provides that in the case of a participant in an eligible governmental deferred compensation plan, any amount of compensation deferred under the plan and any income attributable to the amounts so deferred shall be includible in gross income only for the taxable year in which such compensation or other income is paid to the participant or beneficiary.

[8] Section 457(b)(5) prescribes that an eligible deferred compensation plan must meet the distribution requirements of section 457(d).

[9] Section 457(d)(1)(A) provides that for a section 457 plan to be an eligible plan, the plan must have distribution requirements providing that under the plan amounts will not be made available to participants or beneficiaries earlier than i) the calendar year in which the participant attains age 70½, ii) when the participant has a severance from employment with the employer, or iii) when the participant is faced with an unforeseeable emergency as determined under Treasury regulations.

[10] Section 457(g) provides that a plan maintained by an eligible governmental employer shall not be treated as an eligible deferred compensation plan unless all assets and rights purchased with such deferred compensation amounts and all income attributable to such amounts, property, or rights of the plan are held in trust for the exclusive benefit of participants and their beneficiaries. Section 457(g)(2)(A) provides that a trust described in section 457(g)(1) shall be treated as an organization exempt from tax under section 501(a). Section 457(g)(3) states that custodial accounts and contracts described in section 401(f) shall be treated as trusts under rules similar to the rules under section 401(f).

[11] Based upon the provisions of the Plan summarized above, and the documents presented, we conclude as follows:

1. The amended and restated Deferred Compensation Plan established by City C is an eligible deferred compensation plan as defined in section 457(b) of the Internal Revenue Code of 1986 as amended under the EGTRRA.

2. Amounts of compensation deferred in accordance with the Plan, including any income attributable to the deferred compensation, will be includible under section 457(a)(1)(A) in the recipient's gross income for the taxable year or years in which amounts are paid to a participant or beneficiary in accordance with the terms of the Plan.

3. The annuity contract and the trust associated with C's section 457(b) Plan are each treated under section 457(g) as a trust which is treated as an organization exempt from taxation under section 501(a).

[12] No opinion is expressed concerning the timing of the inclusion in income of amounts deferred under any deferred compensation plan other than C's amended and restated Plan described above. In addition, this ruling applies only to deferrals made after the date this ruling was issued. If the Plan is significantly modified, this ruling will not necessarily remain applicable. This ruling is directed only to City C and applies only to the amended and restated Plan submitted on April 15, 2002 as revised by the September 9, amendments and to the annuity contract submitted on May 17, 2002, as revised by the amendments submitted on September 9, 2002. Section 6110(k)(3) of the Internal Revenue Code provides that this ruling may not be used or cited as precedent.

[13] Temporary or final regulations pertaining to one or more of the issues addressed in this ruling have not yet been adopted. Therefore, this ruling may be modified or revoked if the adopted temporary or final regulations are inconsistent with any conclusion in the ruling. See section 12.04 of Rev. Proc. 2002-1, 2002-1 I.R.B. 1, 50. However, when the criteria in section 12.05 of Rev. Proc. 2002-1 are satisfied, a ruling is not revoked or modified retroactively except in rare or unusual circumstances.

Letter Ruling 200302015, Dated September 30, 2002

[Summary: The IRS has ruled that an organization's nonqualified deferred compensation (NQDC) plans will not be an eligible deferred compensation plan as defined under section 457 after it converts into a tax-exempt entity. Citing the legislative history of section 457, the IRS concluded that the NQDC plans would not be subject to section 457, provided that the organization adopted the resolution barring additional deferrals into the plans.]

[1] This responds to the submission of November 5, 2001 and subsequent correspondence, on behalf of Entity E and its Plan, requesting a ruling concerning the possible application of section 457 of the Internal Revenue Code of 1986 to a number of different nonqualified deferred compensation (NQDC) plans maintained by Entity E. Although E is currently a taxable entity, E represents that it expects soon to receive a favorable determination letter from the Internal Revenue Service concerning its tax-exempt status under section 501(c)(3) of the Code.

[2] E, as a taxable entity, has in recent years established for its directors and a select group of highly compensated or key employees a number of different NQDC plans such as 1) a supplemental executive pension plan, 2) an excess benefit plan similar to a number of corporate NQDC arrangements providing deferred compensation benefits in excess of the section 401(a)(17) and section 415 limitations respectively upon qualified plan benefits, 3) an incentive compensation plan similar to other corporate deferred bonus plans, 4) a trustees' deferred compensation plan resembling other corporate directors' NQDC arrangements, and 5) Plan P, a stock appreciation right/restricted equity plan discussed below. All these NQDC plans specify that the amounts in the participants' accounts are nonassignable and nontransferable. In addition, the

supplemental executive pension plan, excess benefit plans, incentive compensation plan and trustees' deferred compensation plan all provide that the amounts in their participants' bookkeeping accounts are unfunded and unsecured promises to pay in the future the NQDC provided pursuant to the plans. These NQDC plans were all established after July 14, 1988.

[3] Entity E has requested this ruling to resolve whether section 457 (which imposes a number of additional requirements upon NQDC arrangements of tax-exempt entities and state and local governmental entities) would, upon E's becoming a tax-exempt entity, apply to E's NQDC plans which hitherto have been subject to the more liberal NQDC provisions of section 451 and the regulations thereunder. E represents that its board intends to adopt a corporate resolution that freezes and bars future deferrals to its five existing NQDC plans described above upon E's receiving a favorable determination letter establishing its status as a tax-exempt organization described in section 501(c)(3). The amounts in the frozen plans (and the deemed earning thereon) would be held and distributed in accordance with these plans' provisions.

[4] Under Plan P, E can grant key employees either restricted stock or stock appreciation rights (SAR) in spun-off or outside corporate entities relating to E's operations.

[5] Section 83(a) of the Internal Revenue Code provides that the excess (if any) of the fair market value of property transferred in connection with the performance of services over the amount paid (if any) for the property is includible in the gross income of the person who performed the services for the first taxable year in which the property becomes transferable or is not subject to a substantial risk of forfeiture.

[6] Section 451(a) of the Code and section 1.451-1(a) of the regulations provide that an item of gross income is includible in gross income for the taxable year in which actually or constructively received by a taxpayer using the cash receipts and disbursements method of accounting. Under section 1.451-2(a) of the regulations, income is constructively received in the taxable year during which it is credited to the taxpayer's account, set apart, or otherwise made available so that the taxpayer may draw on it at any time. However, income is not constructively received if the taxpayer's control of its receipt is subject to substantial limitations or restrictions.

[7] Various revenue rulings have considered the tax consequences of non-qualified deferred compensation arrangements. Rev. Rul. 60-31, Situations 1-3, 1960-1 C.B. 174, holds that a mere promise to pay, not represented by notes or secured in any way, does not constitute receipt of income within the meaning of the cash receipts and disbursements method of accounting. See also, Rev. Rul. 69-650, 1969-2 C.B. 106, and Rev. Rul. 69-649, 1969-2 C.B. 106.

[8] Section 457 of the Internal Revenue Code of 1986 governs the taxation of eligible deferred compensation plans of eligible employers. The term "eligible employer" is defined in section 457(e)(1) as a state, political subdivision of a state, and any agency or instrumentality of a state or political subdivision of a state, and any other organization (other that a governmental unit) exempt

from tax under subtitle A of the Code. An "eligible deferred compensation plan" as defined in section 457(b) must, among other things, provide that the maximum amount which may be deferred under the plan for a taxable year shall not exceed the lesser of the applicable dollar amount (as determined under sections 457(b)(2) and (e)(15), $11,000 in 2002) or 100 percent of the participant's includible compensation. None of E's NQDC plans currently conforms to this or other limitations of section 457.

[9] Section 457(f)(1)(A) provides that if a plan of an eligible employer providing for a deferral of compensation is not an eligible deferred compensation plan, compensation deferred under such plan shall be included in the participant's gross income for the first taxable year in which there is no substantial risk of forfeiture of the rights to such compensation. Section 457(f)(3)(B) states that a person's rights to compensation are subject to a substantial risk of forfeiture if such person's rights are conditioned upon the future performance of substantial services by any individual.

[10] The legislative history of section 457 must be examined to determine the appropriate tax impact upon E's NQDC plans, originally established during E's period as a taxable entity, of E's becoming a tax-exempt organization. The House Ways and Means Committee Report concerning the 1978 enactment of section 457 states, "The committee believes that limitations should be imposed on the amounts of compensation that can be deferred under these arrangements and allowed to accumulate on a tax-deferred basis. The committee realizes that the denial of a compensation deduction to a nontaxable entity until an amount is includible in the income of the person providing services does not act as a restraint on the amounts that nontaxable entities are willing to let employees defer as it does when a taxable entity is involved. Accordingly, the committee believes that a percentage-of-compensation limit on amounts that can be deferred, as well as an absolute dollar limitation to prevent excessive deferrals by highly-compensated employees, is necessary . . . [T]he denial of a compensation deduction until there is a corresponding income inclusion by a [corporate] plan participant places some natural restraints on the amounts of compensation that can be deferred under private plans." (H.R. Report No. 95-1445 at 53 and 59, 1978-3 CB 227 and 233).

[11] This indicates that a significant Congressional concern when it enacted section 457 was limiting the revenue loss that occurs when an employee defers compensation that his tax-exempt employer is unable to deduct since it pays no income tax, whereas in a corporate NQDC arrangement, the revenue loss attributable to executive NQDC deferrals is offset to a significant degree by the corporate employer's inability to currently deduct such amounts against its taxable corporate income.

[12] In E's case, when unrestricted amounts were deferred into its NQDC arrangements due to its taxable status, E was subject to corporate income taxation upon the amounts deferred. However allowing E to continue unlimited deferrals in these plans under section 451 after its conversion into a tax-exempt entity would produce the type of revenue loss that Congress intended to limit when it enacted section 457 in 1978. Thus, to comply with this Congressional

intent that E's plan not produce revenue losses in excess of those permitted under section 457, E would have to freeze deferrals under its existing NQDC plans upon its becoming a tax-exempt organization.

[13] To comply with the above-discussed Congressional intent, E, after it becomes a tax-exempt organization, would be able to allow its employees to make income tax deferrals under a NQDC arrangement only in a plan that meets the requirements of section 457(b). E's board of directors will adopt a resolution freezing these five plans as of the date when E receives a favorable determination letter from the IRS approving its status as an exempt organization described in section 501(c)(3). Amounts credited to the NQDC plan accounts of its employees (and the earnings thereon) due to deferrals made after E becomes a tax exempt organization would be subject to section 457 and would have to comply with the requirements of section 457(b) and the regulations thereunder for such amounts to remain tax-deferred under section 457(a) until they are paid or made available.

[14] In light of the documents presented and the representations made, we conclude as follows: Provided that E adopts and implements its corporate resolution freezing and barring any additional deferrals to its five NQDC plans described in this letter after E receives a favorable determination letter establishing its status as a tax-exempt organization, its five above-described NQDC plans will remain subject to the nonqualified deferred compensation rules under section 451 and the regulations thereunder, and these five NQDC plans will not be subject to section 457.

[15] No opinion is expressed concerning the timing of the inclusion in income of amounts deferred under any deferred compensation plan other than the five NQDC plans discussed above and mentioned in the corporate resolution submitted on July 25. If the plans are significantly modified other than as provided in the July 25 corporate resolution, this ruling will not necessarily remain applicable. In addition, no opinion is expressed concerning whether any of E's five pre-existing NQDC plans constitutes a non-qualified deferred compensation plan that complies with the NQDC provisions under section 451 and the regulations thereunder. This ruling is directed only to the taxpayer requesting it. Section 6110(k)(3) of the Code provides that it may not be used or cited as precedent.

[16] Temporary or final regulations pertaining to one or more of the issues addressed in this ruling have not yet been adopted. Therefore, this ruling may be modified or revoked if the adopted temporary or final regulations are inconsistent with any conclusion in the ruling. See section 12.04 of Rev. Proc. 2002-1, 2002-1 I.R.B. 1, 50. However, when the criteria in section 12.05 of Rev. Proc. 2002-1 are satisfied, a ruling is not revoked or modified retroactively except in rare or unusual circumstances.

Letter Ruling 200302032, Dated September 30, 2002

[Summary: The IRS has ruled that a governmental employer's contributions from sick leave and emergency leave programs to eligible retirees' deferred compensation arrangements under a sick leave conversion plan won't be included in the employees' taxable income. The IRS ruled that the employer's contributions from a sick leave and an emergency leave programs under a conversion plan to the retirees' accounts in the employer's Code Section 401(a) or 403(b) arrangements won't be included in an employee's income under Code Section 457 or under the constructive receipt or economic benefit doctrine for the year in which the contribution is made. The IRS also ruled that the provision of the conversion plan that gives the employer the option of contributing amounts to either the retiree's supplemental health benefits or retirement plan accounts doesn't make the value of the medical benefit taxable to the retiring employee under the anticipatory assignment-of-income doctrine.]

[1] This responds to your letter of October 2, 2001 and subsequent correspondence, on behalf of Entity E, requesting a ruling concerning the application of sections 403(b), 451(a) and 457 of the Internal Revenue Code (the "Code") to E's Unused Sick Leave Conversion Plan (the "Plan") which E intends to implement for its eligible employees in the near future. E is represented to be a school district which is an eligible governmental employer described in section 457(e)(1)(A) of the Code.

[2] Under two programs, one for its rank-and-file employees and another for its administrators, E provides sick leave benefits to its employees. E's employees are permitted a set number of paid days of sick leave annually and, subject to limits set by the plans, can accumulate any unused sick days in their sick leave account from year to year. You have represented that E intends to adopt the Sick Leave Conversion Plan (the "Plan") that will provide eligible employees of E who retire in accordance with E's retirement policy either with supplemental health benefits or with a contribution to their accounts in E's section 401(a) and section 403(b) plans. The conversion of leave would be calculated under a formula E establishes which will assign a dollar value to the sick days. The Plan does not provide E's employees with any election of the form of benefits to be provided.

[3] Under the Plan, E will make contributions, measured by the value of the retiring employee's accumulated unused sick leave to one of the following supplemental benefits prior to an employee's retirement: (1) additional medical coverage which will commence after the lapse of the retiree health insurance provided by E and which will continue until the retiree's converted sick leave is exhausted or (2) contributions to a section 401(a) plan or section 403(b) account in the employee's name which will begin on the date of the employee's retirement. E's contribution to either the supplemental medical benefit or the retirement plan will be based on several factors including the retiring employee's access to other health insurance coverage, the value of the retiring employee's unused accumulated sick leave, and the willingness of E's insurance carrier to cover retired employees. At no time does the retiring employee have a choice of contributions to the supplemental medical benefit or the deferred compensation plan.

[4] E represents that it understands that the section 401(a) plan is a qualified plan described in section 401(a) and that its section 403(b) arrangement is

an arrangement described in section 403(b). E also represents that it will make contributions to the employee's account in the section 401(a) plan or section 403(b) arrangement only up to the appropriate statutory limitations.

[5] E has previously received a ruling from the Internal Revenue Service that its contributions to the Plan to provide supplemental medical benefits to retiring employees are excludable from a retiring employee's gross income under section 106 of the Code. We have been asked to determine whether section 457 of the Code applies to any of the benefits provided under E's sick leave conversion plan.

[6] Section 403(b)(1) of the Code states, in part, that amounts contributed by an eligible employer to a tax sheltered annuity arrangement which meets the requirements of section 403(b) on or after such rights become non-forfeitable shall be excluded from the gross income of the employee for the taxable year to the extent that the aggregate of such amounts does not exceed the applicable limit under section 415.

[7] Section 457 of the Code provides rules regarding the taxation of deferred compensation plans of eligible employers. For this purpose, the term "eligible employer" is defined in section 457(e)(1)(A) as a state, political subdivision of a state, and any agency or instrumentality of a state or political subdivision of a state. E is an eligible employer within the meaning of section 457(e)(1)(A).

[8] Section 457(b) of the Code and section 1.457-2 of the regulations define the term "eligible deferred compensation plan." Those provisions contain the various requirements for an eligible plan, including rules for participation, deferral of compensation, and payment of benefits. Pursuant to section 457(b)(2), an eligible plan must provide that the maximum amount that may be deferred under an eligible plan shall not exceed the lesser of the applicable dollar amount ($11,000 in 2002) or 100 percent of the participant's includible compensation.

[9] Under section 457(e)(11)(A)(i), a bona fide sick or vacation leave plan is treated as not providing for the deferral of compensation for purposes of section 457. In the present case, the primary function of E's plans for the crediting and use of sick and emergency leave is to provide employees with paid time off from work when appropriate because of sickness or for other personal reasons. Thus, the sick leave and emergency leave programs are part of a bona fide sick or vacation leave plan within the meaning of section 457(e)(11), notwithstanding that the contributions made under the Plan to E's tax sheltered annuity arrangement and qualified retirement plans pursuant to the Plan will result in a deferral of compensation. Accordingly, the rules of section 457 are not applicable to E's sick leave programs.

[10] Section 457(f) of the Code governs the tax treatment of a participant in a plan of an eligible employer, if the plan provides for a deferral of compensation, but is not an eligible deferred compensation plan. The term "eligible employer" is defined in section 457(e)(1) and includes a state or any political subdivision or any agency or instrumentality of a state, and any other tax-exempt organization. Section 457(f)(2) states that section 457(f)(1) does not

apply to a plan described in section 401(a) which includes a trust exempt from tax under section 501(a), to an annuity plan or contract described in section 403, to that portion of any plan which consists of a transfer of property described in section 83, or to that portion of any plan which consists of a trust to which section 402(b) applies.

[11] In general, section 457(f)(1)(A) of the Code provides that the amount of compensation which is deferred under a plan subject to section 457(f)(1) is included in the participant's or beneficiary's gross income for the first taxable year in which there is no substantial risk of forfeiture of the rights to the compensation. [Section 457(f)(3)(B) provides that, for purposes of section 457(f), the rights of a person to compensation are subject to a substantial risk of forfeiture if such person's rights to such compensation are conditioned upon the future performance of substantial services by any individual. This language is substantially similar to language contained in section 83 of the Code.]

[12] Section 451(a) of the Code and section 1.451-1(a) of the regulations provide that an item of gross income is includible in gross income for the taxable year in which actually or constructively received by a taxpayer using the cash receipts and disbursements method of accounting. Under section 1.451-2(a) of the regulations, income is constructively received in the taxable year during which it is credited to the taxpayer's account, set apart, or otherwise made available so that the taxpayer may draw on it at any time. However, income is not constructively received if the taxpayer's control of its receipt is subject to substantial limitations or restrictions.

[13] Various revenue rulings have considered the tax consequences of nonqualified deferred compensation arrangements. Rev. Rul. 60-31, Situations 1-3, 1960-1 C.B. 174, holds that a mere promise to pay, not represented by notes or secured in any way, does not constitute receipt of income within the meaning of the cash receipts and disbursements method of accounting. See also, Rev. Rul. 69-650, 1969-2 C.B. 106, and Rev. Rul. 69-649, 1969-2 C.B. 106.

[14] Section 457(f) does not apply in this case to the amounts contributed to the employee's account in the supplemental health benefit or retirement plan. The amounts credited to the retiring employee's health benefits account are excluded from his income under section 106, as noted in the ruling you previously received, and do not constitute deferred compensation subject to section 457(f). Although the amounts properly contributed to the employee's section 401(a) and section 403(b) plan accounts constitute deferred compensation, they are excluded from the application of section 457(f) under sections 457(f)(2).

[15] Based upon the provisions of the Plan summarized above, the documents presented and the representations made, and provided that E's sick leave and emergency leave programs are modified to incorporate the Plan's provisions, that E's section 401(a) plan constitutes a qualified retirement plan described in section 401(a) and that E's section 403(b) plan constitutes an arrangement described in section 403(b), and that E's contributions to the employees'

accounts in their retirement plan accounts comply with the appropriate statutory limitations, we conclude as follows:

1. E's contribution of amounts from the sick leave and emergency leave programs pursuant to the Plan to the eligible retiree's account in E's section 401(a) plan or section 403(b) arrangement will not cause inclusion of such amounts in his/her taxable income under section 457 of the Code or under the constructive receipt or economic benefit doctrine for the year in which the contribution is made.

2. The Plan's provision that provides E the option to contribute the amounts available to the retiree under the sick leave programs for either the retiree's supplemental health benefits or retirement plan account does not make the value of the medical benefit taxable to the retiring employee under the anticipatory assignment of income doctrine.

[16] No opinion is expressed concerning the timing of the inclusion in income of amounts deferred or payable under any plan other than E's Plan described above. If the Plan is significantly modified, this ruling will not necessarily remain applicable. This ruling is directed only to Entity E and applies only to the sick leave conversion plan described in the taxpayer's submission. Section 6110(k)(3) of the Internal Revenue Code provides that this ruling may not be used or cited as precedent.

[17] Temporary or final regulations pertaining to one or more of the issues addressed in this ruling have not yet been adopted. Therefore, this ruling may be modified or revoked if the adopted temporary or final regulations are inconsistent with any conclusion in the ruling. See section 12.04 of Rev. Proc. 2002-1, 2002-1 I.R.B. 1, 50. However, when the criteria in section 12.05 of Rev. Proc. 2002-1 are satisfied, a ruling is not revoked or modified retroactively except in rare or unusual circumstances.

Letter Ruling 200301032, Dated September 30, 2002

[Summary: The IRS has ruled on the tax treatment of various early retirement benefits provided under a school district's proposed plan. Under the plan, individuals who retire before age 65 receive benefits that depend partly on accumulated unused sick and personal leave amounts on the date they retire and partly on the number of years between their early retirement date and the year in which they turn 65. The district will determine benefits equal to the value of all unused sick pay and special leave pay on the early retirement date. The district will then use the benefits to provide a series of pension and/or welfare benefits predetermined by the plan, with no election allowed to the employee. The IRS concluded that health insurance premiums paid by the district for retired employees are excludable from the retirees' gross income under Code Section 106. The district's contribution of amounts from the sick and special leave accounts to the retiree's account in either a 457(b) or 403(b) plan won't be includable in the retiree's income under Code Sections 451 or

457 or under the constructive receipt or economic benefit or anticipatory assignment of income doctrine for the year in which the contribution is made. The IRS also ruled that any excess benefits remaining in the retiree's sick and personal leave accounts will be subject to income taxes under Code Section 457(f) in the year in which the employee retires, regardless of whether the excess payments are made in the year of retirement or over two or more years. Finally, the excess benefits will be treated as wages and will be subject to FICA and FUTA taxes when actually or constructively paid.]

[1] This responds to your letter of December 6, 2001 and subsequent correspondence, on behalf of Entity E, requesting a ruling concerning the application of sections 106, 403(b), (451(a)) and 457 of the Internal Revenue Code (the "Code") to E's Unused Sick Leave Conversion and Early Retirement Benefits Plan (the "Plan") which E intends to implement for its eligible employees in the near future. E is represented to be a school district which is an eligible governmental employer described in section 457(e)(1)(A) of the Code.

[2] E intends to revise its pre-existing sick leave and personal leave programs providing qualified members of its staff with paid time off for sick days and personal days. Within limits these programs allow employees to accumulate unused sick and personal leave from year to year. E's proposed Early Retirement Benefits Plan (the "Plan") provides eligible employees of E who retire before the normal age 65 retirement date in accordance with the Plan's terms with a variety of benefits depending partly on the accumulated unused amounts in their sick and personal leave accounts on the date they retire and partly on the number of years between their early retirement date and the year when they attain age 65. The Plan does not provide E's employees with any election of the form of benefits to be provided to qualifying early retirees. You have represented that E's Plan will become effective only after E has received this ruling.

[3] To become a participant in E's Plan, an eligible employee seeking to retire before age 65 at the end of a school year must timely file an early retirement application with E, which then, in its absolute discretion, accepts or rejects the employee's application. Approved applicants are then entitled to receive certain benefits described below as of the date they retire early.

[4] Under the Plan, E will determine an amount (the "Benefits") equal to the value of all unused sick pay and special leave pay when an employee retires pursuant to the Early Retirement Plan. E will then use the Benefits to provide a series of pension and/or welfare benefits predetermined by the Plan with no election allowed to the employee. We have been asked to determine whether section 457(f) of the Code applies to any of the benefits provided under the Plan.

[5] First, the Benefits are used to provide post retirement health coverage. An amount will be determined to provide health insurance coverage for the retiring employee from retirement until age 65 based on E's computed cost of coverage. Whenever a premium is due, until the retiree reaches age 65, E pays the required premium for health insurance coverage for the retiree and reduces

the pre-determined cost of coverage by an amount equal to the paid premium. When the retired employee reaches age 65 and the actual cost of health insurance coverage from retirement to age 65 is less than the pre-determined cost of coverage computed when the employee retired, the difference will be paid to the retiree in a lump sum. Should the retired employee die before reaching age 65, the unused portion of the computed cost of health insurance coverage will be paid in a lump sum to the retiree's beneficiaries.

[6] Where Benefits remain in the employee's sick and special leave accounts after payment for health coverage, the Employer makes nonelective contributions up to the section 403(b) and section 415(c) limitations pursuant to the Plan to the retiring employee's tax-sheltered annuity benefit qualified under Code section 403(b). If an employee's leave accounts still have Benefits remaining after the section 403(b) contributions, the Employer makes a contribution up to the annual statutory limit to an account in E's section 457(b) eligible deferred compensation plan for the retiring employee. If Benefits for the retiree are still available in his leave accounts after this contribution, the remaining amount (the "excess benefits") is paid in a lump sum, within a week after the employee retirees pursuant to E's Plan. We have also been asked to determine whether such excess benefits will be taxable as wages under section 3121 of the Code.

[7] Section 106 of the Code provides that the gross income of an employee does not include employer-provided coverage under an accident or health plan.

[8] Section 1.106-1 of the regulations states that the gross income of an employee does not include contributions which his employer makes to an accident or health plan for compensation (through insurance or otherwise) to the employee for personal injuries or sickness incurred by the employee, the employee's spouse, or the employee's dependents, as defined in section 152 of the Code. The employer may contribute to an accident or health plan either by paying the premium on a policy of accident or health insurance covering one or more of the employees, or by contributing to a separate trust or fund which provides accident or health benefits directly or through insurance to one or more of the employees. However, if the insurance policy, trust, or fund provides other benefits in addition to accident or health section 106 applies only to the portion of the contributions allocable to the accident or health benefits.

[9] In Rev. Rul. 62-199, 1962-2 CB 38, the Service concluded that section 106 applies to retired employees as well as active employees.

[10] Section 403(b)(1) of the Code states, in part, that amounts contributed by an eligible employer to a tax sheltered annuity arrangement which meets the requirements of section 403(b) on or after such rights become nonforfeitable shall be excluded from the gross income of the employee for the taxable year to the extent that the aggregate of such amounts does not exceed the applicable limit under section 415.

[11] Section 403(b)(3) of the Code, as amended by the Job Creation and Worker Assistance Act of 2002, provides that, for purposes of section 403(b), the term "includible compensation" means, in the case of any employee, the

amount of compensation which is received from the eligible employer described in section 403(b)(1)(A), and which is includible in gross income for the most recent period (ending not later than the close of the taxable year) which under section 403(b)(4) may be counted as one year of service, and which precedes the taxable year by no more than five years. The term "includible compensation" does not include any amount contributed by the employer for any annuity contract to which section 403(b) applies.

[12] Section 403(b)(4) of the Code provides that, in determining the number of years of service for purposes of section 403(b), there shall be included — (A) one year for each full year during which the individual was a full-time employee of the organization purchasing the annuity for him, and (B) a fraction of a year (determined in accordance with regulations) for each full year during which such individual was a part-time employee of such organization and for each part of a year during which such individual was a full-time or part-time employee of such organization. In no case shall the number of years of service be less than one.

[13] Section 415(a)(2) generally requires that for a section 403(b) arrangement to qualify for favorable tax treatment under section 403(b), it must comply with the section 415(b) limitation upon annual benefits from defined benefit plans or with the section 415(c) limitation upon annual contributions to defined contribution plans, whichever is applicable, and it must not have been disqualified under the section 415(g) aggregation of plans provision.

[14] Section 415(c)(1) of the Code states that the limit on the amounts of annual additions (as defined in section 415(c)(2)) which may be contributed to an individual's account in all defined contribution plans (including tax-sheltered annuities described in section 403(b)) maintained by the employer in any one year is the lesser of (A) $40,000, or (B) 100 percent of the participant's compensation.

[15] Section 415(c)(3)(E) provides that in the case of an annuity contract described in section 403(b), the term "participant's compensation" means the participant's includible compensation determined under section 403(b)(3).

[16] As a result of these above-described section 403(b) and section 415 provisions, an eligible employer may make non-elective contributions to an employee's account in a section 403(b) plan up to the section 415(c) limit for each of the five years following the employee's most recent year of service, using compensation for that year in determining the applicable section 415(c) limit for each of those five years. Assuming contributions to E's tax-sheltered annuity satisfy such limits and that E's tax-sheltered annuity otherwise satisfies the requirements of section 403(b), such contributions would not be includible in gross income, provided they do not constitute contributions made pursuant to a salary reduction agreement.

[17] Section 457 of the Code provides rules regarding the taxation of deferred compensation plans of eligible employers. For this purpose, the term "eligible employer" is defined in section 457(e)(1)(A) as a state, political subdivision of a state, and any agency or instrumentality of a state or political subdivision of a state. E is an eligible employer within the meaning of section 457(e)(1)(A).

[18] Section 457(b) of the Code and section 1.457-2 of the regulations define the term "eligible deferred compensation plan." Those provisions contain the various requirements for an eligible plan, including rules for participation, deferral of compensation, and payment of benefits. Pursuant to section 457(b)(2), an eligible plan must provide that the maximum amount that may be deferred under an eligible plan shall not exceed the lesser of the applicable dollar amount ($11,000 in 2002) or 100 percent of the participant's includible compensation.

[19] Under section 457(e)(11)(A)(i), a bona fide sick or vacation leave plan is treated as not providing for the deferral of compensation for purposes of section 457. In the present case, the primary function of E's program for the crediting and use of sick and special leave (including the proposed Plan) is to provide employees with paid time off from work when appropriate because of sickness or for other personal reasons. Thus, the sick and special leave programs are part of a bona fide sick or vacation leave plan within the meaning of section 457(e)(11), notwithstanding that the permitted contributions to E's tax sheltered annuity arrangement and eligible deferred compensation plans pursuant to the Plan will result in a deferral of compensation. Accordingly, the rules of section 457(f) are not applicable to the leave programs before the employee qualifies for early retirement pursuant to the Plan. However, the extent to which section 457(f) applies to the Benefits under the Plan is discussed below.

[20] Section 457(f) of the Code governs the tax treatment of a participant in a plan of an eligible employer, if the plan provides for a deferral of compensation, but is not an eligible deferred compensation plan. The term "eligible employer" is defined in section 457(e)(1), and includes a state or any political subdivision or any agency or instrumentality of a state, and any other tax-exempt organization. Section 457(f)(2) states that section 457(f)(1) does not apply to a plan described in section 401(a) which includes a trust exempt from tax under section 501(a), to an annuity plan or contract described in section 403, to that portion of any plan which consists of a transfer of property described in section 83, or to that portion of any plan which consists of a trust to which section 402(b) applies.

[21] In general, section 457(f)(1)(A) of the Code provides that the amount of compensation which is deferred under a plan subject to section 457(f)(1) is included in the participant's or beneficiary's gross income for the first taxable year in which there is no substantial risk of forfeiture of the rights to the compensation. Section 457(f)(3)(B) provides that, for purposes of section 457(f), the rights of a person to compensation are subject to a substantial risk of forfeiture if such person's rights to such compensation are conditioned upon the future performance of substantial services by any individual. This language is substantially similar to language contained in section 83 of the Code.

[22] Section 451(a) of the Code and section 1.451-1(a) of the regulations provide that an item of gross income is includible in gross income for the taxable year in which actually or constructively received by a taxpayer using the cash receipts and disbursements method of accounting. Under section 1.451-2(a) of the regulations, income is constructively received in the taxable year

during which it is credited to the taxpayer's account, set apart, or otherwise made available so that the taxpayer may draw on it at any time. However, income is not constructively received if the taxpayer's control of its receipt is subject to substantial limitations or restrictions.

[23] Various revenue rulings have considered the tax consequences of non-qualified deferred compensation arrangements. Rev. Rul. 60-31, Situations 1-3, 1960-1 C.B. 174, holds that a mere promise to pay, not represented by notes or secured in any way, does not constitute receipt of income within the meaning of the cash receipts and disbursements method of accounting. See also, Rev. Rul. 69-650, 1969-2 C.B. 106, and Rev. Rul. 69-649, 1969-2 C.B. 106.

[24] Section 457(f) applies in this case to the excess benefit amounts remaining in an eligible employee's sick and special leave accounts after the employer has contributed the appropriate amounts for the employee's health insurance benefit and to the employee's accounts in E's section 403(b) and section 457(b) plans. The amounts credited to the retiring employee's health insurance account are excluded from his income under section 106 and do not constitute deferred compensation subject to section 457(f). Although the amounts properly contributed to the employee's section 403(b) and section 457(b) plan accounts constitute deferred compensation, they are excluded from the application of section 457(f) under sections 457(f)(2) and 457(b).

[25] The employee is not subject to a substantial risk of forfeiture with respect to the excess benefit amounts remaining after E has contributed the appropriate amount to the eligible retiring employee's health insurance benefits and section 403(b) and section 457(b) plan accounts. Thus, the amount subject to immediate taxation under section 457(f) is the excess benefit amount still available in the eligible retiring employee's sick and special leave accounts after E has credited or contributed the appropriate amounts to such employee's health insurance benefits and section 403(b) and section 457(b) plan accounts.

[26] Section 3101(a) imposes FICA tax "on the income of every individual" in an amount equal to a percentage "of the wages received by him with respect to employment." Section 3111(a) provides that the employer portion of FICA tax is imposed directly upon the employer as "an excise tax, with respect to having individuals in his employ." Similarly, section 3301 provides that FUTA tax is imposed on every employer as an excise tax with respect to individuals in his employ equal to a percentage of wages paid by the employer with respect to employment.

[27] Section 3121(a) provides for FICA purposes and section 3306(b) provides for FUTA purposes, with certain exceptions, that the term "wages" means "all remuneration for employment." Section 3121(a)(5) for FICA purposes and section 3306(b)(5) for FUTA purposes, excludes from the definition of wages certain qualified retirement plans and tax favored annuities.

[28] Wages are generally subject to FICA tax when they are actually or constructively paid. Employment Tax Regulations section 31.3121(a)-2(a). However, in 1983, Congress enacted section 3121(v)(2) which created a special timing rule for amounts paid from a "nonqualified deferred compensation plan."

[29] Section 3121(v)(2) provides that any amount deferred under a non-qualified deferred compensation plan (including a section 457(b) plan) shall be taken into account for FICA purposes as of the later of when the services are performed, or when there is no substantial risk of forfeiture of the rights to such amounts. Section 3121(v)(2)(C) provides that the term "nonqualified deferred compensation plan" means any plan or other arrangement for the deferral of compensation other than a plan described in section 3121(a)(5). Any amount taken into account as wages by reason of section 3121(v)(2)(A) (and the income attributable thereto) shall not thereafter be treated as wages for FICA tax purposes. Section 3121(v)(2)(B).

[30] Employment Tax Regulations section 31.3121(v)(2)-1(b)(1) defines the term "nonqualified deferred compensation plan" as any plan or other arrangement, other than a plan described in section 3121(a)(5), that is established by an employer for one or more of its employees, and that provides for the deferral of compensation. A plan provides for the "deferral of compensation" with respect to an employee only if, under the terms of the plan and the relevant facts and circumstances, the employee has a legally binding right during a calendar year to compensation that has not been actually or constructively received and that, pursuant to the terms of the plan, is payable in a later year. Regulation section 31.3121(v)(2)-1(b)(3). A nonqualified deferred compensation plan is established on the latest of the date on which it is adopted, the date on which it is effective, and the date on which the material terms of the plan are set forth in writing. Regulations section 31.3121(v)(2)-1(b)(2)(i).

[31] Section 31.3121(v)(2)-1(b)(4) describes plans, arrangements and benefits that do not provide for the deferral of compensation. Specifically, section 31.3121(v)(2)-1(b)(4)(v) provides that benefits provided in connection with impending termination of employment under paragraph (b)(4)(v)(B) or (C) of this section do not result from the deferral of compensation within the meaning of section 3121(v)(2). Section 31.3121(v)(2)-1(b)(4)(v)(C) provides the following:

> Termination within 12 months of establishment of a benefit or plan. For purposes of this paragraph (b)(4)(v), a benefit is provided in connection with impending termination of employment, without regard to whether it constitutes a window benefit, if—

> (1) An employee's termination of employment occurs within 12 months of the establishment of the plan (or amendment) providing the benefit; and

> (2) The facts and circumstances indicate that the plan (or amendment) is established in contemplation of the employee's impending termination of employment.

Since the excess benefit amounts, which are amounts other than amounts paid under the Plan excluded from the definition of wages under sections 3121(a)(5) and 3306(b)(5), are wages as defined in sections 3121(a) and 3306(b), such amounts are subject to FICA and FUTA taxes.

Participation in the Plan is conditioned on the participant's termination of services. Under the terms of the Plan, employment for the affected participants will terminate within 12 months of establishment of the Plan. The other relevant facts are: (1) the Plan is not yet effective, (2) in order to participate in the Plan and receive excess benefit payments, an employee must agree to retire, or for these purposes "terminate employment," and (3) the date of termination is June 30, 2003, which is less than 12 months away.

Under section 31.3121(v)(2)-1(b)(4)(v), the Plan provides benefits in connection with impending termination, and therefore, the benefits do not result from deferral of compensation. Accordingly, the excess benefit amounts made under the Plan are not made under a nonqualified deferred compensation plan, and the special timing rule of section 3121(v)(2) does not apply. Based upon the provisions of the Plan summarized above, the documents presented and the representations made, and provided that E's section 457(b) plan constitutes an eligible deferred compensation plan described in section 457(b) and that E's section 403(b) plan constitutes an arrangement described in section 403(b), we conclude as follows:

1. Amounts paid by Employer E under the Plan for the cost of health insurance premiums for retired employees are excludable from the gross income of the retirees pursuant to section 106 of the Code.

2. E's contribution of amounts from the sick and special leave accounts pursuant to the Plan to the eligible retiree's account in E's section 457(b) plan will not cause inclusion of such amounts in his/her taxable income under section 457 of the Code or under the constructive receipt or economic benefit or anticipatory assignment of income doctrine for the year in which the contribution is made.

3. E's contribution of amounts from the sick and special leave accounts pursuant to the Plan to the eligible retiree's account in E's section 403(b) arrangement, which contribution will not cause the employer's yearly contribution on behalf of individuals to exceed the limits of sections 415(c) and 403(b) of the Code, will not cause inclusion of such amounts in his/her taxable income under sections 451 or 457 of the Code or under the constructive receipt or economic benefit [or anticipatory assignment of income doctrine] or for the year(s) in which this contribution is made.

4. Any excess benefits remaining in the eligible retiree's sick and personal leave accounts, after E has made or set aside the appropriate contributions under the Plan to the retiree's health insurance and section 403(b) and section 457(b) plan accounts, will be subject to current income tax taxation under section 457(f) in the year when the employee retires regardless of whether such excess benefit payments are made in the year when the employee retires or over two or more years.

5. The excess benefit amounts provided to employees under the Plan are wages under sections 3121(a) and 3306(b) and will be subject to FICA and FUTA taxes when actually or constructively paid.

No opinion is expressed concerning the timing of the inclusion in income of amounts deferred or payable under any plan other than E's Plan described above. If the Plan is significantly modified, this ruling will not necessarily remain applicable. This ruling is directed only to Entity E and applies only to the Plan submitted on December 6, 2001, as modified by the revisions submitted on June 21,2002. Section 6110(k)(3) of the Internal Revenue Code provides that this ruling may not be used or cited as precedent.

Temporary or final regulations pertaining to one or more of the issues addressed in this ruling have not yet been adopted. Therefore, this ruling may be modified or revoked if the adopted temporary or final regulations are inconsistent with any conclusion in the ruling. See section 12.04 of Rev. Proc. 2002-1, 2002-1 I.R.B. 1, 50. However, when the criteria in section 12.05 of Rev. Proc. 2002-1 are satisfied, a ruling is not revoked or modified retroactively except in rare or unusual circumstances.

Letter Ruling 200321002, Dated February 11, 2003

[Summary: The IRS ruled that a tax-exempt organization's two plans are an eligible deferred compensation plan under Code Section 457(b) and an ineligible deferred compensation plan under Code Section 457(f). A Code Section 501(c)(3) organization that is also a supporting organization under section 509(a) established two deferred compensation agreements as a retirement plan for a participant. The first agreement establishing a plan is designed to be an eligible deferred compensation plan. The second plan is designed to be an ineligible deferred compensation plan. Both plans have different features and requirements and are supervised by a trust. The IRS ruled that the first plan will be an eligible deferred compensation plan under Code Section 457(b) and that the second plan is an ineligible deferred compensation plan under Code Section 457(f).]

This responds to your letter of January 25, 2002, and subsequent correspondence on behalf of Employer, requesting a ruling concerning the proposed deferred compensation plan under which Employer intends to provide benefits under sections 457(b) and 457(f) of the Internal Revenue Code of 1986 and a related trust.

Employer is exempt from federal income tax under section 501(c)(3) and is a supporting organization within the meaning of section 509(a). Employer has recently established a retirement plan comprised of two deferred compensation agreements that Employer has entered into with Participant, a key employee of Employer. The first of the agreements (Plan A) is designed to be an eligible deferred compensation plan within the meaning of section 457(b). The second of these agreements (Plan B) is designed to be an ineligible deferred compensation plan within the meaning of section 457(f). Both Plan A and Plan B are designed solely to benefit Participant.

Under Plan A, Participant may elect to defer compensation he would have received for services rendered to Employer until attainment of age 70½, disability, death, separation from service with Employer or until the occurrence of an unforeseeable emergency. Participant may participate in Plan A only by signing a participation agreement.

Participant's election to defer compensation under Plan A must be filed prior to the beginning of the month in which his salary reduction agreement becomes effective. Plan A provides for a maximum amount that may be deferred by Participant in any taxable year and also provides for a catch up contribution for amounts deferred for one or more of Participant's last three taxable years ending before he attains normal retirement age under Plan A.

With certain limitations, participant may elect the manner in which the deferred amounts will be distributed. Subsequent to the Participant's sever-ance from employment, and prior to the date benefits would commence under Plan A, the Participant may make one election, which shall be irrevocable, to determine when benefits will be distributed or to change a previous election made prior to separation from service. If Participant fails to make a timely elec-tion, distribution will commence at the time and in the manner set forth in the Plan. The manner and time of benefit payout must meet the distribution requirements of sections 401(a)(9) and 457(d)(2).

Under Plan B, Employer will credit certain amounts to Participant's account in the Plan. Plan B does not include provisions limiting the amount deferred to the lesser of $12,000 or 100 percent of Participant's includible compensation.

Participant will receive all amounts credited to the section 457(f) account (including all earnings and gains and losses allocable thereto) only if the Participant's employment ends due to (a) full completion of the employment term under Plan B on or after reaching Retirement Date (the first day of the month that occurs after Participant attains age 58), (b) death, (c) disability, or (d) termination of employment by Employer other than for cause.

If the Participant voluntarily terminates employment with Employer, or if he is terminated by Employer for good cause, prior to his retirement date, all amounts credited to the section 457(f) account shall be irrevocably forfeited and no further amounts shall be paid to him. Any such forfeited amounts shall be paid by the Trustee to Employer pursuant to the terms of the Trust.

Upon the termination of the Participant's employment with the Employer prior to his retirement date by reason of disability, all amounts credited to the section 457(f) account shall be paid to him in a lump sum sixty days after such termination.

Upon the death of the participant prior to his retirement date, all amounts credited to the section 457(f) account shall be paid to a beneficiary designated by the Participant in a lump sum sixty days after the Participant's death, provided that if the Participant fails to designate a beneficiary, or if such desig-nation is for any reason illegal or ineffective, or if no designated beneficiary survives the Participant, the amounts credited to the section 457(f) account shall be paid to the duly appointed legal representative of his estate.

To assist it in providing assets from which to pay the benefit obligations to the Participant under Plan A and Plan B, Employer has adopted a trust (the

Trust) with an unrelated third party as trustee (Trustee). The Trust, as amended, conforms to the model language contained in section 5 of Rev. Proc. 92-64, 1992-2 C.B. 422, that serves as a safe harbor against the constructive receipt of income and the realization of economic benefit. The Trust is a valid trust under state M's law. Under the plans and the Trust, the interests of Participant and his beneficiaries in the trust are no greater than those of any other general unsecured creditor of the Employer.

Under the plans, Participant has the right to request that Employer designate deferred amounts credited to his plan accounts as invested among the available investment options established by Employer. Employer may choose whether it invests according to such requests in its sole discretion. By contrast, the Trustee has complete discretion regarding his investment of amounts contributed to the Trust.

The Trustee has the duty to invest the trust assets in accordance with the terms of the trust agreement. At all times, the trust assets will be subject to the claims of Employer's general creditors if Employer becomes insolvent, as defined in the trust agreement. Employer's Chief Executive Officer and its Board of Directors have the duty to inform the Trustee of Employer's insolvency. Upon receipt of such notice or other written allegations of Employer's insolvency, the Trustee will suspend the payment of benefits with respect to Participant and any beneficiaries in the Plan. If the Trustee determines in good faith that Employer is not insolvent or is no longer insolvent, the Trustee will resume the payment of benefits. If Employer is insolvent, the Trustee shall hold the trust corpus for the benefit of Employer's general creditors.

The plans and Trust provide that all amounts deferred under the plans, all property and rights purchased with such amounts, and all income attributable to such amounts, property, or rights will remain (until made available to the Participant or other beneficiary) solely the property and rights of Employer, subject only to the claims of Employer's general creditors. Participant has only Employer's unsecured promise to pay deferred compensation pursuant to the plans. The rights of the Participant or his beneficiaries to payments pursuant to the plans and trust agreement are nonassignable, and the interests in benefits under the plans and the trust agreement are not subject to attachment, pledge, garnishment, encumbrance or other legal process.

Section 83(a) of the Internal Revenue Code provides that the excess (if any) of the fair market value of property transferred in connection with the performance of services over the amount paid (if any) for the property is includible in gross income of the person who performed the services for the first taxable year in which the property becomes transferable or is not subject to a substantial risk of forfeiture.

Section 1.83-3(e) of the Income Tax Regulations provides that for purposes of section 83 the term property includes real and personal property other than money or an unfunded and unsecured promise to pay money or property in the future. Property also includes a beneficial interest in assets (including money) transferred or set aside from claims of the transferor's creditor, for example, in a trust or escrow account.

Section 451(a) of the Code and section 1.451-1(a) of the regulations provide that an item of gross income is includible in gross income for the taxable year in which actually or constructively received by a taxpayer using the cash receipts and disbursements method of accounting. Under section 1.451-2(a) of the regulations, income is constructively received in the taxable year during which it is credited to a taxpayer's account or set apart or otherwise made available so that the taxpayer may draw upon it at any time. However, income is not constructively received if the taxpayer's control of its receipt is subject to substantial limitations or restrictions.

Under the economic benefit doctrine, an employee has currently includible income from an economic or financial benefit received as compensation, though not in cash form. Economic benefit applies when assets are unconditionally and irrevocably paid into a fund or trust to be used for the employee's sole benefit. Sproull v. Commissioner, 16 T.C. 244 (1951), aff'd per curiam, 194 F.2d 541 (6th Cir. 1952); Rev. Rul. 60-31, Situation 4. In Rev. Rul. 72-25, 1972-1 C.B. 127, and Rev. Rul. 68-99, 1968-1 C.B. 193, an employee does not receive income as a result of the employer's purchase of an insurance contract to provide a source of funds for deferred compensation because the insurance contract is the employer's asset, subject to claims of the employer's creditors.

Section 457 of the Code provides rules for the deferral of compensation by an individual participant in an eligible deferred compensation plan (as defined in section 457(b)).

Section 457(a) of the Code provides that in the case of a participant in an eligible deferred compensation plan, any amount of compensation deferred under the plan and any income attributable to the amounts so deferred shall be includible in gross income only for the taxable year in which such compensation or other income is paid or otherwise made available to the participant or beneficiary.

Section 457(b)(5) prescribes that an eligible deferred compensation plan must meet the distribution requirements of section 457(d).

Section 457(d)(1)(A) provides that for a section 457 plan to be a eligible plan, the plan must have distribution requirements providing that under the plan amounts will not be made available to participants or beneficiaries earlier than (i) the calendar year in which the participant attains age 70½, (ii) when the participant is separated from service with the employer, or (iii) when the participant is faced with an unforeseeable emergency as determined under Treasury regulations. However, section 401(a)(9)(C)(i) generally allows plans to postpone the required beginning date until April 1 of the calendar year following the later of the calendar year in which the employee retires or in which he attains 70½.

Section 457(f) provides that if a section 457 plan is or becomes an ineligible plan, then the deferred compensation shall be included in the gross income of the participant or beneficiary for the first taxable year in which there is no substantial risk of forfeiture of the rights to such compensation, and the tax treatment of any amount made available under such plan to a participant or beneficiary shall be determined under section 72 relating to annuities.

Section 457(f)(1) of the Code governs the tax treatment of a participant in a plan of an eligible employer, if the plan provides for a deferral of compensation, but is not an eligible deferred compensation plan. Section 457(f)(2) states that section 457(f)(1) does not apply to a plan described in section 401(a) which includes a trust exempt from tax under section 501(a), to an annuity plan or contract described in section 403, to that portion of any plan which consists of a transfer of property described in section 83, or to that portion of any plan which consists of a trust to which section 402(b) applies.

In general, section 457(f)(1)(A) of the Code provides that the amount of compensation which is deferred under a plan subject to section 457(f)(1) is included in the participant's or beneficiary's gross income for the first taxable year in which there is no substantial risk of forfeiture of the rights to the compensation. Section 457(f)(3)(B) provides that, for purposes of section 457(f), the rights of a person to compensation are subject to a substantial risk of forfeiture if such person's rights to such compensation are conditioned upon the future performance of substantial services by any individual.

Section 1.83-3(c) of the Income Tax Regulations provides that for purposes of section 83 and the regulations thereunder, whether a risk of forfeiture is substantial depends upon the facts and circumstances. A substantial risk of forfeiture exists where rights in property that are transferred are conditioned, directly or indirectly, upon the future performance of substantial services by a person, or the occurrence of a condition related to a purpose of the transfer, and the possibility of forfeiture is substantial if such condition is not satisfied. The regularity of the performance of services and the time spent in performing such services tend to indicate whether services required by a condition are substantial. See section 1.83-3(c)(2).

Section 1.83-3(c)(4), Example (1) of the regulations provides, by way of example, that where a corporation transfers to an employee 100 shares of stock in the corporation, at $90 per share, and the employee is obligated to sell the stock to the corporation at $90 per share if he terminates his employment with the corporation for any reason prior to the expiration of a two year period of employment, the employee's rights to the stock are subject to a substantial risk of forfeiture during such two year period. If the conditions on transfer are not satisfied, it is assumed that the forfeiture provision will be enforced.

Section 301.7701-4(a) of the Procedure and Administration Regulations provides that, generally, an arrangement will be treated as a trust if it can be shown that the purpose of the arrangement is to vest in trustees responsibility for the protection and conservation of property for beneficiaries who cannot share in the discharge of this responsibility and therefore, are not associates in a joint enterprise for the conduct of business for profit.

Section 671 of the Code provides that where a grantor shall be treated as the owner of any portion of a trust under subpart E, part I, subchapter J, chapter 1 of the Code, there shall then be included in computing the taxable income and credits of the grantor those items of income, deductions, and credits against tax of the trust which are attributable to that portion of the trust to the extent that such items would be taken into account under chapter 1 in computing taxable income or credits against tax of an individual.

Section 677(a)(2) of the Code provides that the grantor shall be treated as the owner of any portion of a trust whose income without the approval or consent of any adverse party is, or, in the discretion of the grantor or a nonadverse party is or both may be held or accumulated for future distribution to the grantor.

Section 1.677(a)-1(d) of the regulations provides that under section 677 of the Code, a grantor is, in general, treated as the owner of a portion of a trust whose income is, or in the discretion of the grantor or a nonadverse party, or both, may be applied in discharge of a legal obligation of the grantor.

Under the terms of the Trust, assets may be placed in trust to be used to provide deferred compensation benefits to Participant. However, the trustee has the obligation to hold the Trust assets and income for the benefit of Employer's general creditors in the event of insolvency. The trust agreement further provides that an employee receives no beneficial ownership in or preferred claim on the Trust assets. Therefore, although the assets are held in trust, in the event of Employer's insolvency they are fully within reach of Employer's general creditors, as are any other general assets of Employer.

Provided, (i) that the creation of the Trust does not cause either Plan A or Plan B to be other than unfunded for purposes of Title I of the Employee Retirement Income Security Act of 1974, and (ii) that the provision of the Trust requiring use of the trust assets to satisfy the claims of Employer's general creditors in the event of Employer's insolvency is enforceable by the general creditors of Employer under federal and state law, and based on the information submitted and representations made, we conclude as follows:

1. Plan A established by Employer constitutes an eligible deferred compensation plan as defined in section 457(b).

2. Plan B established by Employer constitutes an ineligible deferred compensation plan as defined in section 457(f).

3. Amounts of compensation deferred in accordance with Plan A, including any income attributable to the deferred compensation, will be includible in gross income for the taxable year or years in which amounts are paid or otherwise made available to Participant or a beneficiary in accordance with the terms of Plan A.

4. Benefits under Plan B are subject to a substantial risk of forfeiture until the earliest of the date Participant dies, terminates service due to disability, or attains age 58. Accordingly, under section 457(f)(1)(A), amounts credited by Employer under Plan B are included in the gross income of Participant or his beneficiaries when they vest in the earliest of the taxable year in which Participant dies, terminates service due to disability, or attains age 58, if Participant is in Employer's employ on attaining age 58.

5. The Trust will be classified as a trust within the meaning of Treasury Regulations section 301.7701-4(a). Because the principal and income of the Trust may be applied in discharge of legal obligations of Employer, under section 677, Employer shall be treated as the owner of the Trust. Accordingly, under section 677, there shall be included in computing Employer's taxable income and credits, those items of income, deductions, and credits against tax of Trust, subject to the provisions of the Code applicable to section 501(c)(3) organizations.

6. Neither the adoption of Plan A or Plan B, nor the creation of the Trust, nor Employer's contributions of assets to the Trust will result in a transfer of property to Participant or beneficiary for purposes of section 83 or Treasury Regulations section 1.83-3(e).

7. Neither the adoption of Plan B, nor the creation of the Trust, nor Employer's contributions of assets to the Trust will cause any amount to be included in the gross income of Participant or his beneficiaries under the cash receipts and disbursements method of accounting, pursuant to either the constructive receipt doctrine of section 451, the economic benefit doctrine, or section 457(f).

No opinion is expressed concerning the timing of the inclusion in income of amounts deferred or payable under any plan other than Employer's Plans described above. If the Plans are significantly modified, this ruling will not necessarily remain applicable. This ruling is directed only to Employer and applies only to the Plans submitted on January 25, 2002, as modified by the revisions submitted on November 19, 2002. Section 6110(k)(3) of the Internal Revenue Code provides that it may not be used or cited as precedent.

Temporary or final regulations pertaining to one or more of the issues addressed in this ruling have not yet been adopted. Therefore, this ruling may be modified or revoked if the adopted temporary or final regulations are inconsistent with any conclusion in the ruling. See section 12.04 of Rev. Proc. 2003-1, 2003-1 I.R.B. 1. However, when the criteria in section 12.05 of Rev. Proc. 2003-1 are satisfied, a ruling is not revoked or modified retroactively except in rare or unusual circumstances.

Letter Ruling 200317022, Dated September 24, 2002

[Summary: The IRS ruled that retirement plans maintained by a retirement home and day care center are church plans within the meaning of Section 414. A retirement home and day care center employer is organized under Code Section 501(c)(3). It is sponsored by and affiliated with a church. The church provides oversight and control over the employer through its board of directors. The employer's tax-exempt status is dependent on its relationship to the church. The IRS concluded that the plans meet the requirements regarding church plan administration under Code Section 414(e)(4). In addition, the IRS ruled that the plans are relieved from the Code Section 6058 reporting requirements, and the employer's transfer or rollover of all plan assets from one plan to another will not cause the participants' assets to be includible in income as a taxable distribution.]

This is in response to correspondence dated December 12, 2001, as supplemented by correspondence dated April 26 and July 29, 2002, submitted on your behalf by your authorized representative in which you request a private letter ruling.

The following facts and representations support your ruling request.

Employer M is a retirement home for the elderly that employs 280 individuals. Employer M provides various levels of care for residents, depending on a particular resident's need. Employer M also operates a day care center with a capacity for 36 children. All employees perform services exclusively for Employer M. Employer M is not engaged in any other business or work activities. Employer M is an organization described in section 501(c)(3) of the Internal Revenue Code and is tax exempt under section 501(a).

Employer M is an organization sponsored by and affiliated with Church A. The relationship between Employer M and Church A is multi-faceted and essential to Employer M's identity. Employer M is a Social Ministry Organization of Church A, which means that Church A provides both oversight to and control over Employer M through its Board of Directors. Employer M's Board of Directors is comprised of members from seven local Church A congregations, which adds another layer of relationship between Church A and Employer M. In addition, the Employer M Home Auxiliary and the Employer M Endowment held by Church A provide additional ties between Employer M and Church A. Employer M receives financial support from Church A. Finally, Employer M's tax-exempt status is dependent upon its relationship to Church A.

Since January 1, 1992, Employer M has maintained Plan X, a defined contribution pension plan that operates in conjunction with Plan Y, a tax-deferred annuity plan. The effective date of Plan Y is also January 1, 1992; Plan Y was amended and restated on January 1, 1998. On April 15, 2002 Employer M also adopted Plan Z, a profit-sharing plan with a cash or deferred arrangement. All of the participants in Plans X, Y and Z are employees of Employer M. Employer M has not made the election under section 410(d) of the Code with regard to these Plans.

Through its Board of Directors, Employer M is the sponsor of Plan X, Plan Y and Plan Z. The Plans are administered by Committee N, which was established on April 15, 2002, by the Board of Directors of Employer M. Committee N was created to be a permanent, standing committee of the Board. The Board of Directors of Employer M appoints the members of Committee N. Committee N shall at all times be comprised of five members, one of whom will be the President of the Board of Directors of Employer M. Committee N regularly reports to the full Board of Directors of Employer M concerning the status of the administration and funding of Plan X, Plan Y and Plan Z. The sole purpose and function of Committee N is to supervise the administration and funding of Plan X, Plan Y and Plan Z. The Employer M Director of Personnel and Payroll is the staff member who reports to the Board of Directors on retirement plan matters.

Employer M wishes to consolidate the assets of its retirement plan participants into one unified investment and reporting system. Currently, the Plans' assets are divided among several companies in various annuity contracts; three separate companies manage funds and provide reports on five separate contracts. Even though there are legitimate historical reasons for such a scattering of plan assets, it is difficult for the employees, administrators and local financial advisor to make asset reports manageable and understandable. This situation is further complicated by contract demands of large surrender charges due under annuity contracts. In order to make investment reporting easier for the employees to understand and to simplify plan administration, Employer M desires to consolidate all of its assets into one, unified investment system. Rather than freeze the current assets and continue reporting on the status of those investments to participants, Employer M wants to roll over or transfer all plan assets from Plan Y to Plan Z.

Based on the above, you request the following rulings:

1. Plan X, Plan Y and Plan Z qualify as church plans within the meaning of section 414(e) of the Code, and have so qualified since their dates of adoption.

2. Plan X, Plan Y and Plan Z are exempt from the filing requirements of section 6058 of the Code.

3. Employer M's transfer or rollover of all plan assets from Plan Y to Plan Z will not cause participants' assets to be includible in income until the assets are distributed.

Section 414(e)(1) of the Code generally defines a church plan as a plan established and maintained for its employees (or their beneficiaries) by a church or a convention or association of churches which is exempt from taxation under section 501 of the Code.

Section 414(e) was added to the Code by section 1015 of the Employee Retirement Income Security Act of 1974 (ERISA), Public Law 93-406, 1974-3 C.B. 1, enacted September 2, 1974. Section 1017(e) of ERISA provides that section 414(e) applied as of the date of ERISA's enactment. However, section 414(e) was amended by section 407(b) of the Multiemployer Pension Plan Amendments Act of 1980, Public Law 96-364, to provide that section 414(e) was effective as of January 1, 1974.

Section 414(e)(3)(A) of the Code provides that a plan established and maintained for its employees (or their beneficiaries) by a church or a convention or association of churches includes a plan maintained by an organization, whether a civil law corporation or otherwise, the principal purpose or function of which is the administration or funding of a plan or program for the provision of retirement benefits or welfare benefits, or both, for the employees of a church or a convention or association of churches, if such organization is controlled by or associated with a church or a convention or association of churches.

Section 414(e)(3)(B) of the Code defines "employee" to include a duly ordained, commissioned, or licensed minister of a church in the exercise of his or her ministry, regardless of the source of his or her compensation, and an employee of an organization, whether a civil law corporation or otherwise, which is exempt from tax under section 501, and which is controlled by or associated with a church or a convention or association of churches.

Section 414(e)(3)(C) of the Code provides that a church or a convention or association of churches which is exempt from tax under section 501 shall be deemed the employer of any individual included as an employee under subparagraph (B).

Section 414(e)(3)(D) of the Code provides that an organization, whether a civil law corporation or otherwise, is associated with a church or a convention or association of churches if it shares common religious bonds and convictions with that church or convention or association of churches.

Section 414(e)(4)(A) of the Code provides that if a plan, intended to be a church plan, fails to meet one or more of the church plan requirements and corrects its failure within the correction period, then that plan shall be deemed to meet the requirements of this subsection for the year in which the correction was made and for all prior years. Section 414(e)(4)(C)(i) provides, in pertinent part, that the term "correction period" means the period ending 270 days after the date of mailing by the Secretary of a notice of default with respect to the plan's failure to meet one or more of the church plan requirements.

In order for an organization to have a qualified church plan, it must establish that its employees are employees or deemed employees of the church or convention or association of churches under section 414(e)(3)(B) of the Code by virtue of the organization's affiliation with the church or convention or association of churches and that the plan will be administered by an organization of the type described in section 414(e)(3)(A).

Employer M is an organization sponsored by and affiliated with Church A. Employer M is tax exempt under section 501(a) of the Code through its association with Church A. Employer M is a Social Ministry Organization of Church A, receives financial support from Church A, and receives oversight from Church A through its Board of Directors, which is comprised of members from seven local Church A congregations.

In view of the stated purpose of Employer M, its organization and structure, its actual activities and its recognized status within Church A, Employer M employees meet the definition of section 414(e)(3)(B) of the Code and are deemed to be employees of an organization, whether a civil law corporation or otherwise, which is exempt from tax under section 501 and which is controlled by or associated with a church or convention or association of churches.

However, an organization must also establish that its plan is established and maintained by a church or a convention or association of churches or by an organization described in section 414(e)(3)(A) of the Code. To be described in section 414(e)(3)(A) of the Code, an organization must have as its principal purpose the administration of the plan and must also be controlled by or associated with a church or a convention or association of churches.

In this regard, Plan X, Plan Y and Plan Z are maintained by Employer M and have been administered by Committee N since April 15, 2002. Committee N was established by the Board of Directors of Employer M to be a permanent, standing committee of the Board. The members of Committee N are appointed by the Board of Directors of Employer M. At all times, one of the members of Committee N will be the President of the Board of Directors of Employer M. Committee N regularly reports to the full Board of Directors of Employer M concerning the status of the administration and controlled by and associated with Church A through its relationship with Employer M. The sole purpose and function of Committee N is the supervision and administration of Plans X, Y and Z.

Also, as provided under section 414(e)(4) of the Code, where a plan fails to meet one or more of the church plan requirements and corrects its failure within the correction period, then that plan shall be deemed to meet the requirements of section 414(e) for the year in which the correction is made and for all prior years. Committee N was established to administer Plan X, Plan Y and Plan Z on April 15, 2002.

Therefore, the administration of Plan X, Plan Y and Plan Z satisfies the requirements regarding church plan administration under section 414(e)(3)(A) of the Code. Accordingly, Plans X, Y and Z are maintained by an organization that is controlled by or associated with a church or convention or association of churches, and the principal purpose or function of which is the administration of the Plans for the provision of retirement benefits for the employees of Employer M.

Accordingly, with respect to your first ruling request, we conclude that Plan X, Plan Y and Plan Z qualify as church plans within the meaning of section 414(e) of the Code and have so qualified since their dates of adoption.

Regarding your second ruling request, section 6058(a) of the Code provides that every employer who maintains a pension, annuity, stock bonus, profit-sharing or other funded plan of deferred compensation described in Part I of Subchapter D of Chapter 1, or the plan administrator (within the meaning of section 414(g)) of the plan, shall file an annual return stating such information as the Secretary may by regulations prescribe with respect to the qualification, financial condition, and operations of the plan; except that, in the discretion of the Secretary, the employer may be relieved from stating in its return any information which is reported in other returns.

Announcement 82-146, 1982-47 I.R.B. 53 provides that church pension benefit plans that do not elect coverage under section 410(d) of the Code are not required to file annual information returns for pension benefit plans.

Therefore, with respect to your second ruling request, since Plan X, Plan Y and Plan Z are church plans within the meaning of section 414(e) of the Code and have not elected coverage under section 410(d), we conclude that Plan X, Plan Y and Plan Z are relieved from the reporting requirements of section 6058 of the Code.

Regarding your third ruling request, section 401(a) of the Code provides the general requirements for qualification for a stock bonus, pension or profit-sharing plan of an employer.

Section 403(b) of the Code provides the requirements for tax-sheltered arrangements. In pertinent part, section 403(b)(1) provides that amounts contributed by the employer shall be excluded from the gross income of the employee for the taxable year to the extent that the aggregate of such amounts does not exceed the applicable limit under section 415, provided the employee performs services for an employer which is exempt from tax under section 501(a) of the Code as an organization described in section 501(c)(3).

Section 403(b)(10) of the Code requires that arrangements pursuant to section 403(b) of the Code must satisfy requirements similar to the requirements of section 401(a)(9) and similar to the incidental death benefit requirements of section 401(a) with respect to benefits accruing after December 31, 1986, in taxable years ending after such date. In addition, this section requires that, for distributions made after December 31, 1992, the requirements of section 401(a)(311), regarding direct rollovers, are met.

Section 403(b)(11) of the Code provides, in general, that section 403(b) annuity contract distributions attributable to contributions made pursuant to a salary reduction agreement (within the meaning of section 402(g)(3)(C)) may be paid only when the employee attains age 59½, has a severance of employment, dies, becomes disabled (within the meaning of section 72(m)(7)), or in the case of hardship.

Section 403(b)(7) of the Code provides, in general, that the amounts paid by a qualifying employer to a custodial account which satisfies the requirements of section 401(f)(2) shall be treated as amounts contributed by the employer for an annuity contract for his employee if the amounts are to be invested in regulated investment company stock to be held in that custodial account, and under the custodial account no such amounts may be paid or made available to any distributee before the employee dies, attains age 59½, separates from service, becomes disabled (within the meaning of section 72(m)(7)), or, in the case of contributions made pursuant to a salary reduction agreement, encounters financial hardship.

Revenue Procedure 90-24, 1990-1 C.B. 97 discusses whether the transfer of all or part of the holder's interest in a Code section 403(b) arrangement to another Code section 403(b) arrangement constitutes an actual distribution to the holder within the meaning of section 403(b)(1). Rev. Rul. 90-24 concludes that a direct transfer between Code section 403(b) investment vehicles does not constitute an actual distribution under section 403(b)(1) of the Code.

The premise underlying Revenue Procedure 90-24 involves transfers between arrangements described in section 403(b) of the Code. Nontaxability of such transfers, as discussed in the revenue ruling, does not encompass transfers from arrangements described in section 403(b) to arrangements not described in section 403(b), such as section 401(a).

In addition, since a rollover is in the nature of a distribution, a distributable event which meets the requirements of section 403(b)(11) and section 403(b)(7) of the Code must occur in order for an individual participant to take advantage of such action.

Therefore, with respect to your third ruling request, we conclude that Employer M's transfer or rollover of all plan assets from Plan Y to Plan Z will cause participants' assets to be includible in income as a taxable distribution.

No opinion is expressed as to the tax treatment of the transaction described herein under the provisions of any other section of either the Code or regulations which may be applicable thereto.

This ruling expresses no opinion with respect to whether Plan X and Plan Z satisfy the requirements for qualification under section 401(a) of the Code, or whether Plan Y is considered an arrangement as described in section 403(b) of the Code.

This letter is directed only to the taxpayer who requested it. Section 6110(k)(3) of the Code provides that it may not be used or cited as precedent.

Pursuant to a power of attorney on file with this office, the original of this ruling letter is being sent to your authorized representative. . . .

Appendix F

Tax Court Decisions

The following Tax Court decisions primarily concern the exemption for certain types of state judicial plans that was included in the Revenue Act of 1978. Today, unless grandfathered, such plans would be subject to Code Section 457. Qualified state judicial plans and the grandfather provisions are more fully discussed in Q 2:17.

The legislative history of the grandfather exception clearly indicated that there was no intention to allow a plan to reap the benefits of Code Section 457(a) if the plan qualified under Code Section 457(b) but to escape the sanction of Code Section 457(f)(1) if the plan failed to so qualify. In general, a cash basis taxpayer must report gross income for the year in which it is received. [IRC § 451(a)] Usually, this is the year in which it is actually received; however, if gross income is constructively received before it is actually received, then the income is taxable for the earlier year of constructive receipt.

Stewart, James W., et ux. v. Commissioner, T.C. Memo. 1989-365 (July 25, 1989)

SUMMARY. The Tax Court held that contributions made by a state municipal judge to the state's retirement system are not excludable from gross income, citing Foil v. Commissioner, 92 TC 376 (1989), Sims v. Commissioner, 72 TC 996 (1979), and Yegan v. Commissioner, TC Memo 1989-291. The court ruled that the contributions are excluded from Code Section 457 and are not excludable from Stewart's gross income. The tax treatment of contributions under a qualified state judicial plan is not determined under Code Section 457 or any other part of Section 131 of the Revenue Act of 1978, as amended by TEFRA Section 252.

Yegan, Kenneth R., et ux. v. Commissioner, T.C. Memo. 1989-291 (June 15, 1989)

SUMMARY. The Tax Court has ruled that a state municipal judge may not exclude from income contributions he made to the state's judicial retirement system. The taxpayer asserted that his contributions were excludable under Code Section 457, as modified by Section 252 of TEFRA. The IRS asserted that TEFRA Section 252 amended Section 131(c) of the Revenue Act of 1978 to *exclude* deferred compensation plans for state judges. Yegan petitioned the Tax Court. The parties agreed that the retirement system was a "qualified state judicial plan." They did not agree, however, on the effect of TEFRA Section 252 on Code Section 457. The taxpayers contended that the effect of TEFRA Section 252 is to exclude specifically qualified state judicial plans from the general rule for ineligible plans set forth in Code Section 457(e)(1), now Section 457(f)(1), that compensation deferred under an ineligible Code Section 457 plan is to be included currently in gross income. The IRS argued, however, that TEFRA Section 252 clearly and unambiguously excludes from the coverage of Code Section 457 all qualified state judicial plans and that the tax treatment for contributions to these plans is governed by other provisions of the Code. [Section 252 of TEFRA added a new paragraph to the effective date provisions of Section 131 of the Revenue Act of 1978. The reference in the new paragraph (3)(A) to "the amendments made by this section" is a reference to the amendments made by Section 131 of the Revenue Act of 1978; the major such amendment is the one made by Section 131(a) of the Revenue Act of 1978, adding Code Section 457 to the Code. Thus, the direct effect of the new paragraph (3)(A) is to provide that Code Section 457 does not apply to "any qualified state judicial plan." The Tax Court agreed with the IRS that the tax treatment of contributions under a qualified state judicial plan is not determined under Code Section 457. Thus, Judge Yegan's mandatory employee contributions are excluded by TEFRA Section 252 from coverage under Code Section 457.

Foil, Frank F., et ux. v. Commissioner, 92 T.C. 376 (Feb. 22, 1989)

SUMMARY. The court rejected the Foils' argument that the exclusion under Code Section 457 was intended to exclude the plan only from the Section 457(e)(1) penalties (now Code Section 457(f)(1)). Rather, the court ruled that a qualified judicial plan is also denied the benefits of an eligible state deferred compensation plan. The Tax Court came to its conclusion based on a detailed investigation of the legislative history of the Tax Equity and Fiscal Responsibility Act, as amended (TEFRA). The court held that the judges' plan was not an eligible state deferred compensation plan. The court held that since the retirement system did not resolve to pick up employee contributions until 1984, Foil's 1981 contributions were not picked up and are not excludable from income under Code Section 414(h)(2).

The taxpayers argued that contributions made under the judicial plan in 1981 are excludable from gross income for one of the following reasons:

The judicial plan is an "eligible State deferred compensation plan" as that term is defined in Code Section 457; alternatively,

The judicial plan is a "qualified State judicial plan" as defined by Section 131(c)(3) of the Revenue Act of 1978, as amended by Section 252 of TEFRA, and so all contributions Foil made under the judicial plan are excludable from his gross income until made available to him; alternatively,

The contributions Foil made under the judicial plan in 1981 are excludable from his gross income under the pick-up provisions of Code Section 414(h).

The IRS argued that for 1981:

The plan is a qualified plan under Code Section 401(a) and includes a trust exempt under Code Section 501(a);

The exclusion petitioners seek is governed by Section 131(c)(2) of the Revenue Act of 1978;

Section 131(c)(2) does not provide benefits to such tax-qualified plans; and

Therefore, taxpayers are not entitled to the claimed exclusion.

The Tax Court agreed with the IRS that Foil's 1981 employee contributions to the plan are not excludable from petitioners' gross income for that year. The court concluded as follows:

The judicial plan [with a full discussion] is a qualified state judicial plan.

As a result of Section 131(c)(3)(A) of the Revenue Act of 1978, as added by Section 252 of TEFRA, Code Section 457 does not apply to any qualified state judicial plan and so Code Section 457 does not apply to the judicial plan.

The taxpayers are not entitled to the deferral provided by Code Section 457(a), or by Section 131(c)(2) of the Revenue Act of 1978.

The judicial plan is not a "pick-up" plan under Code Section 414(h)(2).

As a result of the foregoing, taxpayers are not entitled to exclude from their 1981 gross income the amounts that Foil contributed in 1981 to the judicial plan.

Foil, Frank F., et ux. v. Commissioner, Memorandum Sur Order (May 13, 1987)

SUMMARY. The Foils contended that they were entitled to exclude from their income amounts contributed by Frank under a judicial retirement plan maintained by the state that was a qualified state judicial plan. At trial, the IRS attorney cited the wrong provision of law. The court denied the IRS's motion to be relieved of earlier concessions made in reliance on the error and ruled that the IRS "is not permitted to contend that the Judicial Plan fails to be a 'qualified State judicial plan' for 1981 for any reason other than the asserted failure to meet the requirements of section 131(c)(3)(B)(iii) of RA '78, as amended by section 252 of TEFRA '82."

Appendix G

Ineligible Church Hospital Plan

Illustrative Specimen Form for Attorney's Use Only

Model 457(f) Plan for a Church Hospital

Church plan status avoids ERISA top-hat participant limitations, but, as a plan of a nonqualified church-controlled organization, the plan still has to meet the requirements of Code Section 457 (see Qs 6:6–6:21). The plan uses a clear substantial risk of forfeiture (continued employment until age 62) to defer taxation, but, in practice, more subjective risks that are more likely to be challenged by the IRS, such as noncompetition agreements, are used by some employees.

Because of these limitations, this plan will principally be useful only where participants have already made maximum deferrals to 403(b) and 457(b) plans.

The plan, including the related salary reduction agreement and beneficiary designation form, was prepared by and reprinted with the permission of the Groom Law Group, Chartered, Washington, D.C.

CHURCH HOSPITAL, INC.
NONQUALIFIED DEFERRED COMPENSATION PLAN
FOR
PHYSICIANS

ARTICLE I

GENERAL

Section 1.1 *Name of Plan.* The name of this plan is the "Church Hospital, Inc. Nonqualified Deferred Compensation Plan for Physicians" (referred to hereinafter as the "Plan").

Section 1.2 *Purpose.* The Plan has been established to provide additional future compensation to certain physician employees so that such employees may be retained and their productive efforts encouraged.

Section 1.3 *Effective Date.* The "Effective Date" of the Plan, the date as of which the Plan was established, is _____.

Section 1.4 *Employer.* The "Employer" is Church Hospital, Inc., a [name of State] non-profit corporation, and any Successor Employer thereto.

Section 1.5 *Construction and Applicable Law.* The Plan is intended to be an unfunded plan providing deferred compensation for certain physician employees. The Employer is a 501(c)(3) corporation controlled by or associated with [name of religious denomination]. The Plan is a church plan within the meaning of section 414(e) of the Internal Revenue Code of 1986, as amended (the "Code"), and section 3(33) of the Employee Retirement Income Security Act of 1974, as amended ("ERISA"). The Plan shall be administered and construed consistent with such intent. This Plan also shall be governed and construed in accordance with the laws of the State of _____ as applied to contracts executed and to be wholly performed within said State to the extent that such laws are not preempted by the laws of the United States of America.

ARTICLE II

DEFINITIONS

Section 2.1 *Account.* An "Account" shall be established for each eligible Participant reflecting the deferred compensation owed to the Participant or the Participant's Beneficiary under the terms of this Plan.

Section 2.2 *Beneficiary.* "Beneficiary" means the person or persons designated as such by a Participant on a form provided for that purpose by the Plan Administrator and filed with the Plan Administrator. If no such Beneficiary exists, the Participant's Beneficiary for purposes of this Plan shall mean the Participant's estate.

Section 2.3 *Board of Directors.* "Board of Directors" means the Board of Directors of the Employer.

Section 2.4 *Election Form.* The "Election Form" is the written agreement provided by the Plan Administrator and completed by a Participant regarding the Participant's contributions and benefits under this Plan. The form of the Election Form may be changed from time to time at the discretion of the Plan Administrator.

Section 2.5 *Entry Date.* "Entry Date" for any Participant shall be the date on which the Participant became a Participant under Section 3.1.

Section 2.6 *Participant.* A "Participant" is an individual described as such in Article III.

Section 2.7 *Plan Administrator.* The "Plan Administrator" is the Benefits Committee, consisting of not more than five persons appointed (and who may be removed) by the Board of Directors of the Employer for the purpose of operating and administering the Plan. The actions of the Plan Administrator may be taken by majority vote of the members of the Benefits Committee or by a member of the Benefits Committee who has been designated to take such actions by the Benefits Committee.

Section 2.8 *Plan Year.* A "Plan Year" is the 12-consecutive-month period commencing on each January 1 and ending December 31. However, the initial Plan Year shall begin on the Effective Date and end on December 31, ____.

Section 2.9 *Qualified Employee.* "Qualified Employee" means any physician employed by the Employer.

Section 2.10 *Successor Employer.* A "Successor Employer" is any entity that succeeds to the business of the Employer through merger, consolidation, acquisition of all or substantially all of its assets, or any other means and which elects before or within a reasonable time after such succession, by appropriate action evidenced in writing, to continue the Plan.

Section 2.11 *Termination of Employment.* The "Termination of Employment" of an employee for purposes of the Plan shall be deemed to occur upon the employee's resignation, discharge, retirement, death, failure to return to active work at the end of an authorized leave of absence or the authorized extension or extensions thereof, failure to return to work when duly called following a temporary layoff, or upon the happening of any other event or circumstance which, under the policy of the Employer as in effect from time to time, results in the termination of the employer-employee relationship.

ARTICLE III

PARTICIPATION

Section 3.1 *Eligibility for Participation.* An employee of the Employer shall become a Participant in the Plan on the earliest date (on or after the Effective Date) on which the employee is a Qualified Employee, is designated by the

Plan Administrator as eligible to participate, and files a duly completed Election Form to participate with the Plan Administrator.

Section 3.2 *Duration of Participation.* A Participant shall continue to be such until his or her Termination of Employment, provided, however, that for purposes of the credit of income or loss to an Account, a Participant shall continue to be such until forfeiture or distribution of all of his or her account under Article V.

Section 3.3 *No Guarantee of Employment.* Participation in the Plan does not constitute a guarantee or contract of employment with the Employer. Such participation shall in no way interfere with any rights the Employer would have in the absence of such participation to determine the duration of the employee's employment with the Employer.

ARTICLE IV

DEFERRED COMPENSATION AND ACCOUNTS

Section 4.1 *Amount of Deferred Compensation.* For each Plan Year ending on or after the Effective Date, the Employer shall credit to the Account of each Participant the amount elected by the Participant pursuant to the Election Form for such year in accordance with Section 4.2. The Plan Administrator may impose limitations on the amount of compensation which may be elected for a Plan Year pursuant to this section.

Section 4.2 *Election of Deferred Compensation.* For each Plan Year in which a Participant is eligible to participate in this Plan, he or she may elect, using an Election Form, to defer an amount of such Participant's compensation which would otherwise be earned by the Participant and paid to the Participant by the Employer during such Plan Year. Such election shall be made on or immediately following each new Participant's Entry Date, and prior to the beginning of each subsequent Plan Year, at a time designated by the Plan Administrator. Neither the Employer nor any other party guarantees the tax consequences of a deferral of compensation under this Plan.

Section 4.3 *Allocated to Accounts.* An Account shall be established under the Plan for each Participant. The deferred compensation credited under the Plan by the Employer on behalf of a Participant for a Plan Year shall be allocated to the Account of the Participant as soon as administratively practical following the date on which such compensation would otherwise have been received by the Participant.

Section 4.4 *Valuation of Accounts.* As of any date as of which an Account is to be valued, the value of the Account shall be adjusted to reflect the effect of additional credits under Section 4.2 and any credit for income (or loss) with respect to that Account, since the last date the value of the Account was determined. Income (or loss) shall be credited to the Account based on the Investment Return described in Sections 4.5 and 4.6.

Section 4.5 *Investment Return.* The Investment Return shall be the amount necessary to increase or decrease the Participant's Account to what it would have been had the Account balance during the Plan Year been invested in the Investment Options selected for the Account under Section 4.6, including adjustment for any surrender or other charges that would have been incurred if the Account balance had actually been invested in the Investment Options and withdrawn to pay benefits.

Section 4.6 *Investment Options.* The available Investment Options, and the rules for allocating an Account among such options, shall be determined by the Plan Administrator. The Plan Administrator may in its sole discretion change the Plan's Investment Options from time to time with respect to future periods. The Employer may, but is not required to, permit a Participant to elect among the available Investment Options with respect to his or her Account prior to the beginning of each Plan Year (or on or before a Participant's Entry Date in the Participant's first year of participation) or more frequently as permitted in the sole discretion of the Plan Administrator. If the Employer in its sole discretion does not permit Participants to elect any Investment Options, or if the Employer permits such Participant elections and a Participant fails to make such an election, the applicable Investment Options shall be determined by the Plan Administrator in its sole discretion. Neither the Employer, any affiliates of the Employer, their boards of directors, agents, employees or advisers, or the Plan Administrator or members of the Benefits Committee shall be liable for any decrease in a Participant's Account as a result of the preference or lack thereof of any Investment Option, by whomever chosen, or for any tax obligations on the part of a Participant with respect to the deferral of compensation under this Plan.

Section 4.7 *Unsecured Obligations.* The benefits under this Plan represent the mere unfunded promise of the Employer to pay such benefits. The Employer may, but is not required to, invest a portion of its general assets in the Investment Options selected pursuant to Section 4.6, but such investment shall be solely as a device for the measurement of the benefits payable to a Participant under this Plan, and shall not constitute or be treated as a fund or trust fund of any kind. A Participant's credits in his or her Account shall be an unsecured obligation of the Employer to pay the Participant (or the Participant's Beneficiary, in the event of the Participant's death) the amount of the credits at the time provided in Article V. Accounts are maintained for record-keeping purposes only.

ARTICLE V

DISTRIBUTION OF ACCOUNTS

Section 5.1 *Forfeiture Upon Premature Termination of Employment.* Except as provided in Section 5.2, 5.3, or 5.4, if a Participant has a Termination of Employment prior to the date the Participant is eligible for a distribution in accordance with said Sections, the Participant shall forfeit any right to benefits under this Plan.

Section 5.2 *Distribution at Age 62.* Upon attainment of age 62 by a Participant, the Employer shall pay to the Participant an amount equal to the entire balance of the Participant's Account as of the date of payment. Such payments shall be made in a single sum payment to the Participant as soon as administratively feasible after the Participant is eligible for a distribution.

Section 5.3 *Distribution Upon Disability.* Upon the Termination of Employment of a Participant on account of the Participant's total and permanent disability, the Employer shall pay to the Participant an amount equal to the entire balance of the Participant's Account as of the date of the payment. Such payment shall be made in a lump sum payment to the Participant as soon as administratively feasible after the Participant's Termination of Employment on account of total and permanent disability. A Participant shall be deemed to be totally and permanently disabled if the Participant is eligible for disability benefits under the Employer's long term disability insurance plan.

Section 5.4 *Distribution on Death.* Upon the Termination of Employment of a Participant due to the death of the Participant, the Employer shall pay to the Participant's Beneficiary an amount equal to the entire balance of the Participant's Account as of the date of payment. Such payment shall be made in a single sum payment to the Participant's Beneficiary as soon as administratively feasible after the Participant's death.

Section 5.5 *Withholding of Taxes.* The benefits payable under this Plan shall be subject to the deduction of any federal, state, or local income taxes, employment taxes or other taxes which are required to be withheld from such payments by applicable laws and regulations. If any employment taxes are payable at a time earlier than the time for distribution of such benefits, the Employer may withhold such taxes from other compensation of the Participant.

ARTICLE VI

ADMINISTRATION

Section 6.1 *Administration by Plan Administrator.* The Plan Administrator shall administer the Plan, establish, adopt, or revise such rules and regulations as it may deem necessary or advisable for the administration of the Plan and shall have discretionary authority to interpret the provisions of the Plan. The interpretations of the Plan Administrator shall be conclusive and afforded the maximum deference permitted by law.

ARTICLE VII

AMENDMENT AND TERMINATION

Section 7.1 *Amendment.* The Board of Directors of the Employer may at any time amend the Plan in whole or in part for any reason; provided, however, that no amendment shall decrease the benefits under the Plan which have accrued prior to the date of such amendment.

Section 7.2 *Termination of Plan.* The Employer, by action of its Board of Directors, may at any time terminate the Plan. After such termination, no employee of the Employer shall become a Participant, and no further amounts shall be credited pursuant to Section 4.2 to Accounts of Participants. At the discretion of the Employer, the amounts credited to the Accounts of such Participants may be either (i) distributed to such Participants as soon as reasonably possible after the date of termination or (ii) distributed in accordance with Article V.

ARTICLE VIII

MISCELLANEOUS

Section 8.1 *Benefits May Not Be Assigned or Alienated.* Neither a Participant nor any Beneficiary thereof shall have the right to sell, assign, transfer, encumber or otherwise convey any right to receive any payment hereunder. No part of the amounts payable hereunder shall be subject to seizure or sequestration for the payment of any debts or judgments owed by a Participant or any other person.

Section 8.2 *Headings.* Headings at the beginning of articles and sections hereof are for convenience of reference, shall not be considered a part of the text of the Plan, and shall not influence its construction.

Section 8.3 *Capitalized Definitions.* Capitalized terms used in the Plan shall have their meaning as defined in the Plan unless the context clearly indicates to the contrary.

Section 8.4 *Gender.* Any references to the masculine gender include the feminine and vice versa.

Section 8.5 *Construed as a Whole.* The provisions of the Plan shall be construed as a whole in such manner as to carry out the provisions hereof and shall not be construed separately without relation to the context.

Salary Reduction Agreement and Beneficiary Designation Form for the Church Hospital, Inc. Nonqualified Deferred Compensation Plan for Physicians

CHURCH HOSPITAL, INC.
NONQUALIFIED DEFERRED COMPENSATION PLAN
FOR PHYSICIANS

Salary Reduction Agreement
and
Beneficiary Designation Form

[For salary reduction purposes, except in the initial year of participation, this form must be received by Human Resources before the year to which it applies. For beneficiary designation purposes, this form is effective upon receipt by Human Resources.]

Name of
Employee: _____

I understand that I have been designated by the Benefits Committee of the Church Hospital, Inc. Nonqualified Deferred Compensation Plan for Physicians (the "Plan") as eligible to participate in the Plan. I have received a copy of the Plan and agree to all of the provisions of the Plan.

1. Deferral of Compensation:

   A. [Check One]

   ☐ Initial election to become a participant (for compensation earned during the remainder of this year)

   ☐ Annual election (for compensation earned next year, 200_)

   B. I elect to have the following amount of my compensation which is earned this year, if this is an initial election to participate, or next year, if this is an annual election, credited to my Account under the Plan:

   i. $_____ per biweekly pay period, for a total of $_____;
   or

   ii. _____ percent (but not more than 30 percent, except in the year in which the Participant's Entry Date occurs) of each payment of my base compensation (before all taxes, withholding and other applicable deductions, *i.e.,* based on my "gross" compensation);
   or

   iii. ☐ I elect NOT to defer any compensation for 200_.

2. *Designation of Beneficiary*

   My Beneficiary(s) for benefits under the Plan, if any, payable in the event of my death, is (are):

   _____

   _____

   _____

   [Include name, address and relationship, and, if more than one, the percentage of benefits payable to each or whether a successor beneficiary.]

   If you do not complete this section 2, the most recent prior Beneficiary designation will remain in effect. If you complete this section 2, it will supersede prior designations for ALL benefits under the Plan, not merely for deferrals for this Plan Year.

   I understand that amounts I defer will reduce the amount of my compensation for purposes of determining benefits under other retirement plans for employees of Church Hospital, Inc. I further understand that neither

Church Hospital, Inc. nor any other person guarantees the tax consequences of this election or of the Plan, and that I have been advised to consult with my tax adviser with respect to the tax consequences of this election and the risks of forfeiture of my deferrals.

_____   _____

Signature   Date

_____

_____

Address

For Church Hospital, Inc. Human Resources Uses Only

_____

Received on _____, 200___, by _____

Appendix H

Model State Statute

Many state statutes that provide authority for state and local government employers to maintain an eligible deferred compensation plan require that plan assets be the sole property of the employer. In response to the enactment of Code Section 457(g) and recent developments that change the structure of eligible deferred compensation plans, many state legislatures are considering revisions of their statutes governing state and local government employer deferred compensation plans.

The model act that follows was prepared by Peter J. Gulia of Citi- Street Retirement Services for the convenience of selected government officials in considering changes in their state laws.

Be it enacted {appropriate legislative clauses}:

Section 1—Title

This Act or the statutes created or amended by this Act and the statutes codified from {citation} to {citation} may be referred to and cited as the Deferred Compensation Act.

Section 2—Findings

The Legislature finds that a revision of the statutes providing for state and local government employer eligible deferred compensation plans is appropriate.

Further, the Legislature finds as follows:

The provisions made by Section 5 are desirable to ensure that plans can provide a broad range of investment choices. The provisions made by Section 6 are desirable to ensure that participants' plan benefits will remain available for pension or retirement income.

The provisions made by Section 7 are necessary to ensure that every plan will meet the requirements of 26 U.S.C. § 457(b) and 26 U.S.C. § 457(g).

The provisions made by Section 8 are desirable to ensure that a plan account or plan benefits will be excluded from a participant's or beneficiary's bankruptcy estate.

The provisions made by Section 9 are desirable to clarify a participant's or beneficiary's means of enforcing his/her rights with respect to a plan.

The provisions made by Section 10 and Section 11 are desirable to induce government officials to be willing to assume positions of responsibility with respect to a plan or a plan's trust.

Section 3—Authority to adopt an eligible deferred-compensation plan

In addition to any other statute that grants authority to adopt a deferred compensation plan, any agency or instrumentality of the State, or any county, city, township, town, village, borough, or other political subdivision or agency or instrumentality thereof, or other State or local government employer that is described in 26 U.S.C. § 457(e)(1)(A) shall have authority and power to adopt and maintain an eligible deferred compensation plan.

Section 4—Plan provisions

Any statute that provides an employer authority to adopt or maintain an eligible deferred compensation plan shall be construed to provide the employer authority and complete discretion to include in its plan any provision that does not cause the plan to fail to be an eligible deferred compensation plan within the meaning of 26 U.S.C. § 457(b).

Any statute that provides an employer authority to adopt or maintain an eligible deferred compensation plan shall be construed to require the employer to include in its plan such provisions as are necessary to cause the plan to be an eligible deferred compensation plan within the meaning of 26 U.S.C. § 457(b).

Section 5—Plan investments

In addition to any other law, any investment or contract that is not prohibited by applicable banking, insurance, or securities law shall be a proper investment for any eligible deferred compensation plan if selected by the employer or the person appointed to select investments for the purposes of the plan.

Section 6—Benefits not to be alienated

In addition to (and not by limitation upon) any other law, any benefit or interest available under a plan, or any right to receive or instruct payments under a plan, or any distribution or payment made under a plan shall not, except as expressly specified by the plan, be subject to assignment, alienation, garnishment, attachment, transfer, anticipation, sale, mortgage, pledge, hypothecation, commutation, execution, or levy, whether by the voluntary or involuntary act of any interested person.

Section 7—Exclusive benefit

Every eligible deferred compensation plan established or maintained by any employer described in Section 3 shall be established and maintained for the exclusive benefit of the plan's participants and their beneficiaries; and all assets and income of a plan shall be held for the exclusive benefit of the plan's participants and their beneficiaries.

Section 8—Spendthrift trust

Any trust, custodial account, annuity contract, or life insurance contract made or held consistent with Section 6 and Section 7 is expressly declared to be a spendthrift trust, and any construction of a participant's plan account as self-settled shall not cause the plan account to be treated as other than a spendthrift trust.

Section 9—Civil enforcement

A civil action may be brought by a participant or beneficiary

To recover a benefit due to him/her under the plan;

To enforce his/her rights under the plan;

To enforce the terms of any plan trust or custodial account or annuity contract;

To clarify his/her right to future benefits under the terms of the plan;

To enjoin any act or practice which violates any provision of the plan or any plan's trust; or

To enjoin any act which violates any provision of the Deferred Compensation Act.

A civil action may be brought by the Attorney General;

To enjoin any act or practice which violates any provision of the plan or any plan's trust;

To enjoin any act which violates any provision of the Deferred Compensation Act; or

To obtain other appropriate equitable relief.

A civil action cannot obtain money damages against the State or political subdivision or any agency or instrumentality thereof.

Section 10—Relief from liability

Any natural person who at the relevant time was or is an official, officer, or employee (including, without limitation, an attorney-at-law) of the State or of any state or local government employer described in Section 3 shall be absolutely immune from any action (other than an action brought by the Attorney General) relating to any deferred compensation plan.

The preceding sentence shall not apply to the extent that any action states a claim that is authorized by Section 9 and such claim is stated against a person solely in his/her representative capacity. In addition to (and not by limitation upon) the provisions of Section 9, the Attorney General shall have the right to be a party to or to file any motion or brief in any action or proceeding if any party to the action or proceeding is an indemnified person described in Section 11.

Section 11—Indemnification

If any natural person who at the relevant time was or is an official, officer, or employee (including, without limitation, an attorney-at-law) of the State or of any state or local government employer described in Section 3 [hereafter in this Section referred to as an indemnified person] was or is a party or is threatened to be made a party to or was or is a witness or is threatened to be made a witness with respect to or was or is required to respond to any subpoena or similar process with respect to any threatened, pending, or completed claim (including a claim under a Plan), demand, action, suit, or proceeding of any kind, whether administrative, arbitrative, civil, criminal, investigative, or otherwise and whether formal or informal [proceeding], brought by any person other than the Attorney General, by reason of or arising from the fact that he/she is or was acting or serving with respect to any deferred compensation plan or any such plan's trust or custodial account, or by reason of or arising from any breach of a fiduciary responsibility regarding any plan or any plan's trust or custodial account, the State shall indemnify (including, without inquiry or examination or consideration of any kind, without limitation advancing reasonably paid or incurred actual expenses of defense and actual expenses relating to any counterclaim against any person other than the State, including but not limited to actual fees of lawyers, legal assistants, experts, and investigators, subject to an obligation to repay as provided below) the indemnified person against his/her reasonably paid or incurred expenses (including but not limited to actual fees of lawyers, legal assistants, experts, and investigators), liabilities, losses, damages, judgments, fines, penalties, taxes (including excise taxes), amounts paid or incurred to correct a fiduciary breach, and amounts paid in settlement of any kind, actually and reasonably paid or incurred by him/her, in connection with the defense or/and settlement of the proceeding [all in this Section referred to as expenses].

An indemnified person shall be entitled to indemnification, including advances for reasonably anticipated expenses, until a final and non-appealable court order determines that the otherwise indemnified person's act (or failure to act) was willful misconduct or resulted in an improper personal benefit, or with respect to a criminal proceeding a final and non-appealable court order in a proceeding other than the criminal proceeding determines that the indemnified person knew or reasonably should have believed that his/her conduct was a crime. The indemnified person shall promptly repay any amounts advanced if a final and non-appealable court order determines that he/she is not entitled to indemnification under this Section. The termination of any proceeding upon a plea of nolo contendere or no-contest or its equivalent or the settlement of any proceeding shall not, of itself, create any presumption or inference concerning the indemnified person's conduct.

The obligation of the State to indemnify an indemnified person under this Section, including the duty to advance expenses, shall be considered a contract between the State and the indemnified person, and no repeal or modification of any law shall affect, to the detriment of the indemnified person, the obligations of the State in connection with any proceeding based on any act or failure to act occurring before such modification or repeal. This Section shall inure to the benefit of the successors, assigns, executors, administrators, trustees, and heirs of the indemnified person. This Section is in addition to and shall not be deemed exclusive of, and shall not be construed to impair, any other right to which either the indemnified person or the State may be entitled under any other applicable law.

Section 12—Sovereign immunity maintained

Nothing in this Act shall be construed or interpreted as any kind of waiver of any sovereign immunity, governmental immunity, official immunity, or similar immunity. Further, this Act creates, establishes, and provides sovereign immunity, governmental immunity, and official immunity to the fullest extent not prohibited by the State Constitution.

Appendix I

Specimen Top-Hat Statement

XYZ COMPANY

E.I.N. _____

TOP-HAT PLAN DECLARATION

BY PLAN ADMINISTRATOR

_____, being the plan administrator for the _____ (Plan), does hereby declare that the Plan is maintained primarily for the purpose of providing deferred compensation for a select group of management or highly compensated employees. In addition, _____, the employer, maintains only _____ plan described in Department of Labor Regulations Section 2520.104-23(d). Furthermore, _____ employees will be covered under the Plan. _____

Date? _____

On behalf of Plan Administrator _____

Appendix J

Indexing of Employee Benefit Limits

Marjorie Martin
Aon Consulting

Many of the dollar thresholds used in limiting the level of benefits available through tax-advantaged programs are adjusted to reflect changes in the consumer price index (CPI) relative to the base period used for each limit. The limit for a particular year is adjusted based on the cumulative increase through the third quarter of the preceding calendar year. The adjusted limits are then rounded down to the nearest multiplier specified for the particular limit. The limits for 2005, for example, are based on the CPI factors through the third quarter of 2004. Estimated changes for 2005 based on the CPI through January 2004 are shown in the following table.

A change of about 1.3 percent through September 2004 would be required before any of the limits move up further (defined contribution annual addition to $42,000, Highly Compensated Employee threshold to $95,000, and the compensation limit to $210,000).

The Economic Growth and Tax Relief Reconciliation Act of 2001 (EGTRRA) overrides many of the pre-EGTRRA CPI adjustments with specific increases over a five-year period before CPI increases restart for items with fixed increments. The following table shows what the fixed limits will be through 2006 for the limits modified by EGTRRA.

Prepared: February 26, 2004

Indexing of Employee Benefit Limits

Purpose	Calendar Year			
	2003	2004	2005	2006
Base 402(g) deferral limit	$12,000	$13,000	$14,000	$15,000
457 limit	$12,000	$13,000	$14,000	$15,000
401(k)/403(b)/457/SARSEP,[1] catch-up deferrals	$2,000	$3,000	$4,000	$5,000
SIMPLE limit	$8,000	$9,000	$10,000	
SIMPLE catch-up deferrals	$1,000	$1,500	$2,000	$2,500
IRA/Roth-IRA limit	$3,000	$3,000	$4,000	$4,000
IRA/Roth-IRA catch-up contributions	$500	$500	$500	$1,000
DB[2] maximum benefit	$160,000	$165,000	$165,000*	
DC[3] maximum addition	$40,000	$41,000	$41,000*	
HCE compensation[4]	$90,000	$90,000	$90,000*	
Key employee:				
Officer[5]	$130,000	$130,000	$135,000*	
1% Owners	$150,000	$150,000	$150,000	
Compensation[6]	$200,000	$205,000	$205,000*	
SEP threshold	$450	$450	$450*	
ESOP (5-year distribution factor)	$160,000	$165,000	$165,000*	
ESOP (account balance)	$810,000	$830,000	$830,000*	
Taxable wage base[7]	$87,000	$87,900	90,300*	
SECA tax for self-employed individuals, combined rate	15.3%	15.3%	15.3%	15.3%
Old-age, survivors, and disability insurance tax rate	12.4%	12.4%	12.4%	12.4%
Hospital insurance (Medicare)	2.9%	2.9%	2.9%	2.9%
Social Security tax for employees and employers, combined rate	7.65%	7.65%	7.65%	7.65%
Old-age, survivors, and disability insurance tax rate	6.20%	6.20%	6.20%	6.20%
Hospital insurance (Medicare)	1.45%	1.45%	1.45%	1.45%

---

*Estimated limits.

Note. If not replaced by the OBRA '93 $150,000 maximum compensation cap and then by the EGTRRA $200,000 compensation cap for 2002, using the January 2004 CPI, the pre-1994 $200,000 limit on plan compensation would have reached $300,000 by 2005 (with $10,000 rounding). Certain grandfathered governmental plans use the pre-1994 limit with $5,000 rounding, resulting in a projected $305,000 limit for 2005.

Source: Marjorie Martin, AON Consulting, Inc., Somerset, NJ. Prepared February 26, 2004.

---

[1]This number represents the catch-up limit available under Code Section 414(v). Code Sections 457(b)(3) and 402(g)(8) provide separate catch-up rules that must also be considered in an appropriate situation.

[2]Defined Benefit limit applies to limitation years ending in indicated year.

[3]Defined Contribution limit applies to limitation years ending in indicated year.

[4]Compensation during the plan year beginning in the indicated year identifies Highly Compensated Employees for the following plan year.

[5]Generally, compensation during the determination year ending in the indicated year identifies Key Employees for the following plan year.

[6]Compensation limit applies to plan years beginning in indicated year.

[7]Calculation differs from CPI description provided above. Estimate reflects projection from the 2003 OASDI Trustees Report using High Cost assumptions.

Internal Revenue Code

[References are to question numbers.]

I.R.C. §

Treasury Regulations

[References are to question numbers.]

Letter Rulings, Revenue Procedures, and Revenue Rulings

[References are to question numbers.]

Notices and Announcements

[References are to question numbers.]

Notice

87-13. . . . . 2:12, 2:17, 2:20,
2:35, 11:3, 11:7
87-13, § G 1:10
88-8. . . . . 2:12, 2:13, 11:3, 11:6
88-68. . . . . 1:11, 2:12, 11:6
88-98. . . . . 2:17, 11:7
89-23. 7:8
89-25. . . . . 13:45, 13:46, 13:48
89-25, Q&A-3 . . . . 13:53
89-25, Q&A-4 . . . . 13:53
93-26. . . . . 13:47
94-96. . . . . 12:99
97-6, Q&A B-4 . . . . 2:15
97-26. 12:7
98-8. . . . . 1:15, 3:4, 6:2
98-8, § IV 2:72
98-8, § VI 2:44, 2:49
98-8, § VII 2:44
2000-38 . . . . 2:136, 2:138, 2:150,
12:39, 13:57
2000-38 § VIII 2:137
2001-10 . . . . 2:179
2001-46 . . . . 14:27
2002-3. . . . . 2:244, 7:15, 12:83
2002-4. . . . . 7:6, 7:13
2002-8. . . . . 2:13
2002-59 . . . . 2:13, 2:179
2002-62 . . . . 12:7

Notice

2003-20. . . . . 2:136–2:139, 2:173,
12:17, 12:29, 12:39,
12:87, 12:98, 12:100,
12:101, 12:132, 12:133
2003-20 § IV.A 2:140, 2:141
2003-20 § IV.B. 2:142
2003-20 § IV.C. 2:143
2003-20 § IV.D 2:144
2003-20 § VI.B 2:147
2003-20 § VI.C 2:147
2003-20 § VI.D 2:148
2003-20 § VII.A. 2:149
2003-20 § VII.B. 2:150
2003-38 § IV.E. 2:145
2003-38 § V.A. 2:146

Ann.

82-146 . . . . 6:21, 14:12
84-40 . . . . 2:145
94-101 . . . . 7:9
96-24 . . . . 2:10
98-73 . . . . 12:84
2000-1 . . . . 1:15
2001-1 . . . . 11:6
2001-120. . . . . 2:248
2001-160. . . . . 2:248

Employee Retirement Income Security Act

[References are to question numbers.]

Department of Labor Regulations and Advisory Opinions

[References are to question numbers.]

Miscellaneous United States Code and Code of Federal Regulations Provisions

[References are to question numbers.]

Table of Cases

[References are to question numbers.]

Index

[References are to question numbers.]